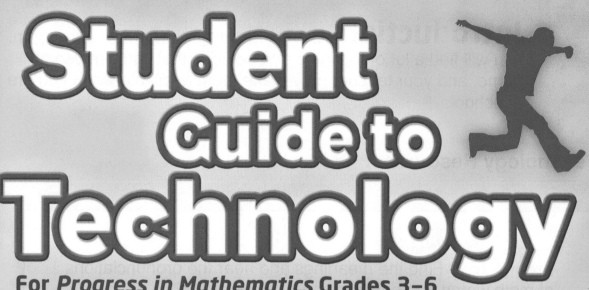

Student Guide to Technology

For *Progress in Mathematics* Grades 3–6

www.progressinmathematics.com

AUDIO LEARNING
HEAR THE MATH!

VISUAL LEARNING
SEE THE MATH!

INTERACTIVE LEARNING
DO THE MATH!

SHARED LEARNING
SHARE THE MATH!

Sadlier-Oxford

SGT 1

Introduction

At <u>www.progressinmathematics.com</u>, you will find a lot of technology resources that you can use at home, and your teacher may make them available when you are at school.

Technology Resources:

www.progressinmathematics.com

↗ AUDIO GLOSSARY

<u>From A to Z</u> Find the meanings and hear the pronunciations of math words and phrases.

↗ ALTERNATIVE TEACHING MODELS

<u>Tutorials</u> Watch and listen to these animated math lessons.

↗ VIRTUAL MANIPULATIVES

<u>Manipulatives</u> Practice and model math concepts with virtual manipulatives.

↗ PRACTICE

<u>Problem of the Day</u> Tackle a new problem every day!

<u>Skills Update</u> Review your skills with Lesson and Practice pages.

<u>Math Minutes</u> Race against the clock with timed activities!

<u>Practice Activities</u> Practice makes perfect with these fun activities!

<u>Vocabulary Activities</u> Review your math vocabulary while playing Hangman or Word Scramble.

↗ ENRICHMENT

<u>Activities</u> Challenge yourself with these interactive activities.

↗ MATH ALIVE AT HOME

<u>Take-Home Activities</u> Share your math experience at home!

Hear the Math!

⚲ AUDIO GLOSSARY

Click **From A to Z**.

If you are not sure what a certain word means or how to pronounce it, use your online Audio Glossary. The glossary is easy to use. Just choose your grade level and the first letter of the term you want to review.

INTERACTIVE *Whiteboard* COMPATIBLE

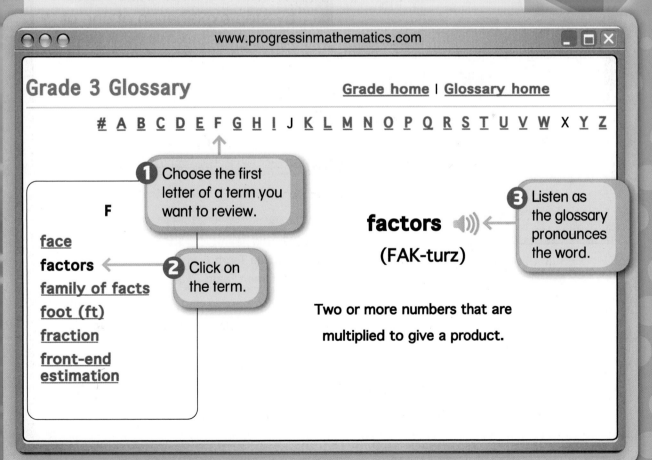

www.progressinmathematics.com

Grade 3 Glossary

Grade home | Glossary home

\# A B C D E F G H I J K L M N O P Q R S T U V W X Y Z

1 Choose the first letter of a term you want to review.

F

face
factors
family of facts
foot (ft)
fraction
front-end estimation

2 Click on the term.

factors ◀))

(FAK-turz)

3 Listen as the glossary pronounces the word.

Two or more numbers that are multiplied to give a product.

GRADE 3

VISUAL LEARNING

See the Math!

ALTERNATIVE TEACHING MODELS

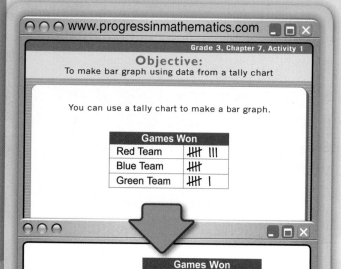

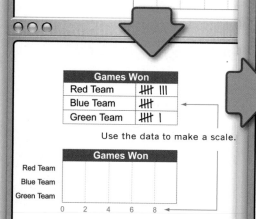

Click **Tutorials**.
If there is a skill or concept that you need help with or do not understand, review the animated Alternative Teaching Models (there are 2 for each chapter). Each Alternative Teaching Model gives a step-by-step explanation of one of the skills or concepts in the chapter.

GRADE 3

⚡ VIRTUAL MANIPULATIVES

Click **Manipulatives.**
Virtual Manipulatives are visual models that you can actually move or manipulate to show what is happening. You can use these tools to build numbers, rotate shapes, and even jump on a number line.

Select your grade and the chapter you are working on. The manipulatives that are listed will be ones that you can use to visualize the concepts of the chapter.

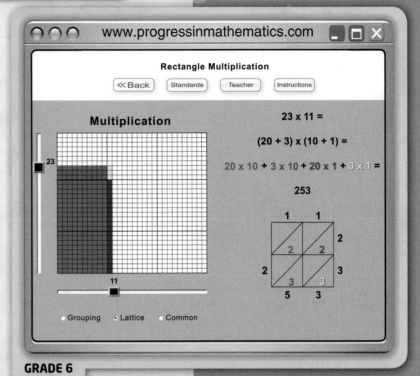

GRADE 6

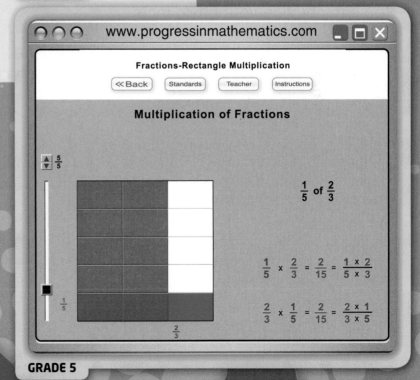

GRADE 5

INTERACTIVE LEARNING

Do the Math!

⬈ PRACTICE

Click **Practice Activities**.
There is an interactive activity for each chapter in your textbook. The activity practices the most important skills of the chapter. Use the activity while you are learning the skills, or come back to it later to review.

Click **Math Minutes**.
You can practice your basic facts as well as compute with larger numbers to see how accurately you can compute if you are given a time limit.

Click **Vocabulary Activities**.
In each chapter, you will be learning new math terms that you will need to know. A good way to review these terms is to play either the Hangman game or Word Scramble in your online vocabulary activities.

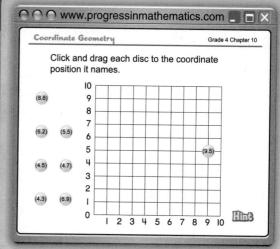

GRADE 4

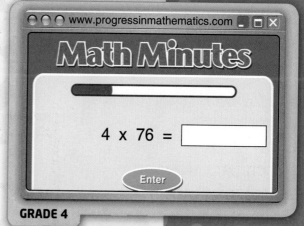

GRADE 4

GRADE 5

Click **Problem of the Day**.*
Sharpen your problem-solving skills every day. Print and solve one problem each day!

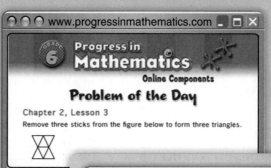

GRADE 6

Click **Skills Update**.*
Print Skills Update lessons and practice pages to review previously taught math skills and concepts.

Skills Update

Name _____ Date _____

Count by 2s, 5s, 10s

Count by 2s.

1. 12, _____, _____, _____ 20, _____, _____, _____, _____

2. 15, _____, _____, _____ 23, _____, _____, _____, _____

Count by 5s.

3. 15, _____, 25, _____, _____, _____, _____, _____

4. 30, _____, 40, _____, _____, _____, _____, _____

Count by 10s.

5. 10, _____, _____, _____, _____, _____, _____, _____

6. 20, _____, _____, _____, _____, _____, _____, _____

Write the missing numbers.

7. 10, 12, 14, _____, _____ 20   8. 22, 24, 26, _____, 30, _____

GRADE 3

ENRICHMENT

Click **Activities**.
The Enrichment activities online are topics that go beyond what you are learning in class.

Each activity starts with a page that explains the concept and then gives you time to practice the concept.

Enrichment

Use Clustering to Estimate

You can use clustering to estimate numbers.
Example

324 + 299 + 315 + 287

Round each number to the same number.

324 + 299 + 315 + 287

300 + 300 + 300 + 300 = 1200

4 x 300 = 1200

Next

GRADE 3

*Whiteboard projectable only.

SHARED LEARNING

Share the Math

MATH ALIVE AT HOME

Click **Take-Home Activities**. Keep your family involved in what you are learning. For each chapter, there are two letters to your family. Use the first letter at the beginning of the chapter, to review previously learned skills with a family activity, and read about the new skills you will learn. The second letter tells your family about the skills you learned in the chapter and has another fun activity that you and your family members can do together.

Both letters are in English and in Spanish.

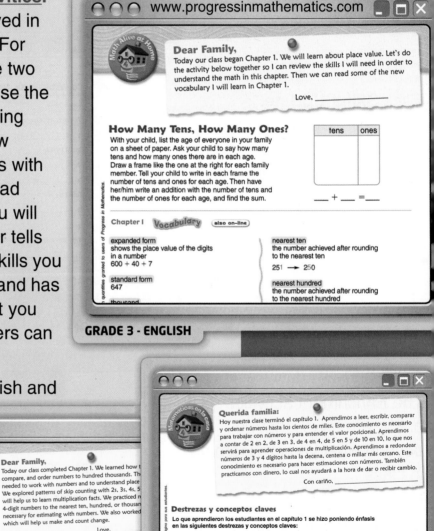

GRADE 3 - ENGLISH

GRADE 3 - SPANISH

GRADE 3 - ENGLISH

SADLIER-OXFORD

Progress in Mathematics

Authors

Catherine D. LeTourneau

Alfred S. Posamentier

with
Elinor R. Ford

Program Consultants

Madelaine Gallin
Former Math Coordinator
Community School District #6
New York, NY

Frank Lucido
Associate Professor in
Bilingual/Multicultural Education
Texas A&M University
Corpus Christi, TX

Lucy Lugones
Math Coordinator
St. Luke's School
Whitestone, NY

Tim Mason
Title 1 Specialist
Palm Beach County School District
West Palm Beach, FL

Regina Panasuk
Professor of Mathematics Education
University of Massachusetts
Lowell, MA

Rosalie Pedalino Porter
Consultant Bilingual/ESL Programs
Amherst, MA

Sadlier-Oxford
A Division of William H. Sadlier, Inc.
www.sadlier-oxford.com

The publisher gratefully acknowledges Rose Anita McDonnell (1905–2003) and her colleagues for the important role they played in the development of *Progress in Mathematics* for more than sixty years.

Reviewers

The publisher wishes to thank the following teachers and administrators, who read portions of the series prior to publication, for their valuable contributions.

Grades 3-6 Reviewers

Madonna Atwood
Teacher
St. Louis, MO

John Palladino
Professor at Eastern Michigan University
Ypsilanti, MI

Debra Wright
Principal
Winter Haven, FL

Judith A. Devine
Educational Consultant
Springfield, PA

Stephanie D. Garland
Educational Consultant
St. Louis, MO

Grade-Level Reviewers

Marie Bicsak
Math Coordinator
Mt. Clemens, MI

Sara Kobylarz
Grade 3 Teacher
Bronx, NY

Br. Ralph Darmento, F.S.C.
Deputy Superintendent of Schools
Newark, NJ

Suzanne Ryan
Grade 4 Teacher
Orono, MN

Candace Govin
Grades 4–8 Math Teacher/Coordinator
Plantation, FL

Sr. Adriana Cernoch
Grade 6 Teacher
Dallas, TX

Brandy Roth
Grade 3 Teacher
Kissimmee, FL

Elizabeth M. Johnson
Grade 5 Teacher
Bettendorf, IA

Linda Hamby
Grade 5 Teacher
DesPeres, MO

Barbara Murphy
Grade 4 Teacher
Chesterfield, MO

Sr. Martha Carmody, O.P.
Grade 4 Teacher
Springfield, IL

Jacqueline A. Byrd
Grade 5 Teacher
Chesterfield, MO

Sr. Maristella Dunlavy, O.P.
Principal
Springfield, IL

Jeannine Frey
Grade 3 Teacher
Chesterfield, MO

Mary E. Stokes
Grade 5 Teacher
Oak Forest, IL

Dear Family

Progress in Mathematics, now in its sixth decade of user-proven success, is a complete basal mathematics program. Written by experienced teacher-authors, it integrates a traditional course of study and today's academic Standards with the most up-to-date methods of teaching.

Progress in Mathematics is designed to meet the individual needs of all learners. Teachers who use *Progress* come to understand that students may progress as quickly as they can or as slowly as they must.

In Grade 6, the concepts of integers and rational numbers will be further developed as well as ratios, percents, and coordinate geometry. There will be an increased emphasis on algebraic thinking. Other topics that are studied include: data and statistics, probability, geometry, measurement, and proportions. Special attention is given to critical thinking, problem solving, mental math, and journalizing.

But overall success in achieving the goals of this program depends on ongoing teacher-family-student interaction. It is important for you to encourage your sixth grader to achieve success in mathematics and enjoy it as well. You can help your student see math as useful and practical by relating it to everyday situations. It is also helpful to provide a quiet space and time for homework, and to reinforce the idea that by practicing math concepts and skills in your home environment, your student can have fun while learning mathematics.

Throughout the school year, you and your student can access *Math Alive At Home* pages at www.sadlier-oxford.com. These pages include the math vocabulary of each chapter plus fun-filled activities that will help you relate the math your student is learning in school to the real world.

We know that by using **Progress in Mathematics** your sixth grader will not only learn to value math, but become a confident problem solver and learn to reason and communicate mathematically as well.

The Authors

Contents

Skills Update

A handbook for reviewing essential and previously taught skills

Introduction to Problem Solving

Algebra Lesson promotes algebraic reasoning.

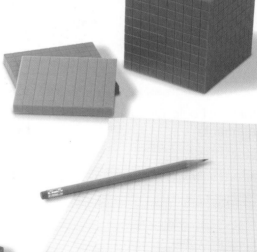

Algebra Lesson promotes algebraic reasoning.

Algebra Lesson promotes algebraic reasoning.

Algebra Lesson promotes algebraic reasoning.

Algebra Lesson promotes algebraic reasoning.

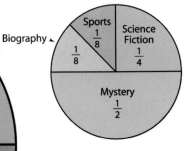

Algebra Lesson promotes algebraic reasoning.

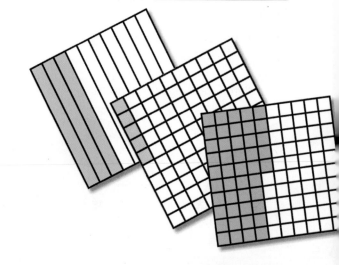

★ Develops concept or skill with manipulatives.   *Algebra* Lesson promotes algebraic reasoning.

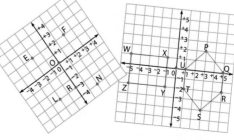

Algebra Lesson promotes algebraic reasoning.

Skills Update

A Review of Mathematical Skills from Grade 5

Progress in Mathematics includes a "handbook" of essential skills, Skills Update, at the beginning of the text. These one-page lessons review skills you learned in previous years. It is important for you to know this content so that you can succeed in math this year.

If you need to review a concept in Skills Update, your teacher can work with you, using manipulatives, which will help you understand the concept better.

The Skills Update handbook can be used throughout the year to review skills you may already know. Since many lessons in your textbook refer to pages in the Skills Update, you can use a particular lesson at the beginning of class as a warm-up activity. Or your class may choose to do the Skills Update lessons at the beginning of the year so that you and your teacher can assess your understanding of these previously learned skills.

You may even want to practice specific skills at home. If you need more practice than what is provided on the Skills Update page, you can use the practice pages available online at www.sadlier-oxford.com. These practice pages have an abundance of exercises for each one-page lesson.

Algebra
Whole Numbers: Place Value, Compare, and Order

The value of each digit in a number depends on its place in the number. Each place is 10 times the value of the next place to its right.

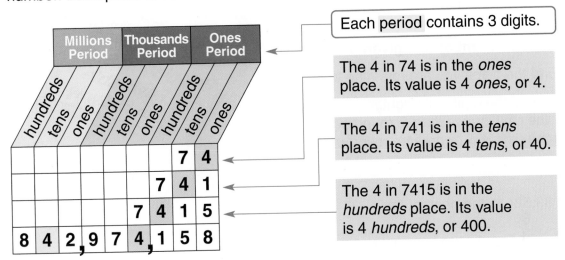

Each period contains 3 digits.

The 4 in 74 is in the *ones* place. Its value is 4 *ones*, or 4.

The 4 in 741 is in the *tens* place. Its value is 4 *tens*, or 40.

The 4 in 7415 is in the *hundreds* place. Its value is 4 *hundreds*, or 400.

▶ **To compare and order whole numbers:**

- Align the digits by place value.

- Compare the digits in each place, starting with the greatest place.

39,630	There are no hundred
19,578	thousands in the other
130,434	numbers. 130,434 is
36,415	greatest.

39,630	3 = 3 and 1 < 3
19,578	19,578 is least.
130,434	6 < 9
36,415	36,415 < 39,630

In order from greatest to least, the numbers are:
130,434; 39,630; 36,415; 19,578.

Name the period of the underlined digits.

1. 943,862

2. 802,400,253

3. 603,411,218

4. 9,527,000

Write the place of the underlined digit. Then write its value.

5. 73

6. 6,423,728

7. 36,250

8. 24,983,402

Write in order from greatest to least.

9. 9996; 999; 10,000; 9997

10. 32,423; 38,972; 36,401; 31,276

Round Whole Numbers

The population of Midway is 83,524. Since populations change frequently, a rounded number may be used instead of the exact number.

▶ **To round a number to a given place:**

- Find the place you are rounding to.

- Look at the digit to its right.
  If the digit is *less than 5*, round *down*.
  If the digit is *5 or greater*, round *up*.

Round 83,524 to the nearest ten.

83,524
↓
83,520

| The digit to the right is 4. |
| 4 < 5 |
| Round down to 83,520. |

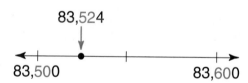

Round 83,524 to the nearest hundred.

83,524
↓
83,500

| The digit to the right is 2. |
| 2 < 5 |
| Round down to 83,500. |

Round 83,524 to the nearest thousand.

83,524
↓
84,000

| The digit to the right is 5. |
| 5 = 5 |
| Round up to 84,000. |

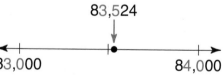

Round each to the nearest ten, hundred, and thousand.
Use a number line to help you.

1. 6709　　　**2.** 1256　　　**3.** 7893　　　**4.** 5649　　　**5.** 42,314

6. 11,987　　　**7.** 49,678　　　**8.** 76,432　　　**9.** 148,786　　　**10.** 940,067

Numeration II

Factors, Multiples, and Divisibility

▶ Factors are numbers that are multiplied to find a product.

$8 \times 3 = 24$ $4 \times 2 \times 3 = 24$

factors   factors

To find all the factors of a number, use multiplication sentences. Find all the factors of 20.

$5 \times 4 = 20$
$10 \times 2 = 20$
$20 \times 1 = 20$

Factors of 20:

1, 2, 4, 5, 10, 20

▶ The multiples of a number are the products of that number and any whole number.

$3 \times 0 = 0$ $3 \times 4 = 12$ $3 \times 8 = 24$

Multiples of 3:   0,   3,   6,   9,   12,   15,   18,   21,   24,   . . .

Multiples of 6:   0,   6,   12,   18,   24,   30,   36,   42,   48,   . . .

Multiples of 8:   0,   8,   16,   24,   32,   40,   48,   56,   64,   . . .

A number is divisible by another number when you divide and the remainder is zero.

Divisibility by 2
A number is divisible by 2 if its ones digit is divisible by 2.

80, 32, 294, 856, and 1908 are divisible by 2.

Divisibility by 5
A number is divisible by 5 if its ones digit is 0 or 5.

60, 225, 400, 1240, and 125,605 are divisible by 5.

Divisibility by 10
A number is divisible by 10 if its ones digit is 0.

40, 280, 500, 2070, and 46,790 are divisible by 10.

All even numbers are divisible by 2.

List all the factors of each number.

1. 12   2. 18   3. 22   4. 35   5. 7   6. 108

List the first ten nonzero multiples of each number.

7. 4   8. 5   9. 6   10. 7   11. 10   12. 12

Which numbers are divisible by 2? by 5? by 10?

13. 300   14. 7875   15. 22,892   16. 360,000

Numeration III

Decimals to Hundredths

The value of a digit in a decimal depends on its position, or place, in the decimal. Each place is 10 times the value of the next place to its right.

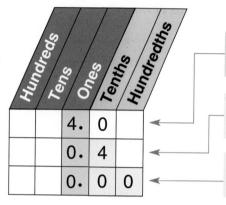

The 4 is in the *ones* place. Its value is 4 *ones*, or 4.

The 4 in 0.4 is in the *tenths* place. Its value is 4 *tenths*, or 0.4.

The 4 in 0.04 is in the *hundredths* place. Its value is 4 *hundredths*, or 0.04.

▶ **To read a decimal less than 1:**

- Start at the decimal point.

- Read the number as a whole number. Then say the name of the place.

0.92 — hundredths

Read: ninety-two hundredths

Study this example.

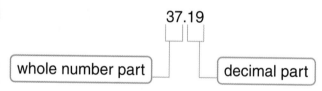

37.19

whole number part — decimal part

Read: thirty-seven *and* nineteen hundredths

Read each decimal. Then write the place of the underlined digit and its value.

1. 0.<u>8</u>   **2.** 0.0<u>2</u>   **3.** 0.1<u>3</u>   **4.** <u>5</u>.6

5. 7.<u>1</u>   **6.** 0.<u>4</u>5   **7.** 9.6<u>3</u>   **8.** 1<u>0</u>.1

9. 42.7<u>8</u>   **10.** <u>2</u>6.9   **11.** <u>3</u>00.09   **12.** 1<u>5</u>6.8

Numeration IV

Add Whole Numbers and Decimals

Add: 8164 + 4676 = __?__.

First estimate by rounding: 8000 + 5000 = 13,000. Then add.

▶ **To add whole numbers:**

Add the ones. Regroup.	Add the tens. Regroup.	Add the hundreds.	Add the thousands. Regroup.
$\begin{array}{r} {\scriptstyle 1} \\ 8\,1\,6\,4 \\ +\,4\,6\,7\,6 \\ \hline 0 \end{array}$	$\begin{array}{r} {\scriptstyle 1\ 1} \\ 8\,1\,6\,4 \\ +\,4\,6\,7\,6 \\ \hline 4\,0 \end{array}$	$\begin{array}{r} {\scriptstyle 1\ 1} \\ 8\,1\,6\,4 \\ +\,4\,6\,7\,6 \\ \hline 8\,4\,0 \end{array}$	$\begin{array}{r} {\scriptstyle 1\ 1} \\ 8\,1\,6\,4 \\ +\ \ 4\,6\,7\,6 \\ \hline 1\,2{,}8\,4\,0 \end{array}$

The sum is 12,840.

Think.......... 12,840 is close to the estimate of 13,000.

Add: 0.44 + 0.3 + 0.85 = __?__.

First estimate by rounding to the nearest tenth: 0.4 + 0.3 + 0.9 = 1.6. Then add.

▶ **To add decimals:**

Line up the decimal points.	Add. Regroup if necessary.	Write the decimal point.
$\begin{array}{r} 0.4\ 4 \\ 0.3\ 0 \\ +\,0.8\ 5 \\ \hline \end{array}$	$\begin{array}{r} {\scriptstyle 1} \\ 0.4\ 4 \\ 0.3\ 0 \\ +\,0.8\ 5 \\ \hline 1\ 5\ 9 \end{array}$	$\begin{array}{r} {\scriptstyle 1} \\ 0.4\ 4 \\ 0.3\ 0 \\ +\,0.8\ 5 \\ \hline 1.5\ 9 \end{array}$

The sum is 1.59.

Think.......... 1.59 is close to the estimate of 1.6.

Estimate by rounding. Then add.

1.	2.	3.	4.	5.
$\begin{array}{r} 536 \\ +\,143 \\ \hline \end{array}$	$\begin{array}{r} 1578 \\ +\,6421 \\ \hline \end{array}$	$\begin{array}{r} 1768 \\ +\ \ \ 63 \\ \hline \end{array}$	$\begin{array}{r} 17{,}243 \\ +\,13{,}963 \\ \hline \end{array}$	$\begin{array}{r} 567{,}892 \\ +\,132{,}104 \\ \hline \end{array}$

Align and estimate by rounding. Then add.

6. 5751 + 756   7. 0.56 + 0.41   8. 0.8 + 0.47   9. $9.78 + $43.85 + $5

Subtract Whole Numbers and Decimals

Subtract: 4816 − 1932 = __?__ .

First estimate by rounding: 5000 − 2000 = 3000. Then subtract.

▶ **To subtract whole numbers:**

Subtract the ones.	More tens needed. Regroup. Subtract.	More hundreds needed. Regroup. Subtract.	Subtract the thousands.

$$
\begin{array}{r}
4\,8\,1\,6 \\
-\,1\,9\,3\,2 \\
\hline
4
\end{array}
$$

$$
\begin{array}{r}
{}^{7}\;{}^{11} \\
4\,\cancel{8}\,\cancel{1}\,6 \\
-\,1\,9\,3\,2 \\
\hline
8\,4
\end{array}
$$

$$
\begin{array}{r}
{}^{17} \\
3\;\cancel{7}\;{}^{11} \\
\cancel{4}\,\cancel{8}\,\cancel{1}\,6 \\
-\,1\,9\,3\,2 \\
\hline
8\,8\,4
\end{array}
$$

$$
\begin{array}{r}
{}^{17} \\
3\;\cancel{7}\;{}^{11} \\
\cancel{4}\,\cancel{8}\,\cancel{1}\,6 \\
-\,1\,9\,3\,2 \\
\hline
2\,8\,8\,4
\end{array}
$$

The difference is 2884.

.Think............
2884 is close to the estimate of 3000.

Subtract: 0.7 − 0.46 = __?__ .

First estimate by rounding to the nearest tenth: 0.7 − 0.5 = 0.2. Then subtract.

▶ **To subtract decimals:**

Line up the decimal points.	Subtract. Regroup if necessary.	Write the decimal point.

$$
\begin{array}{r}
0.7\,0 \\
-\,0.4\,6 \\
\end{array}
$$

$$
\begin{array}{r}
6\;\;10 \\
0.\cancel{7}\,\cancel{0} \\
-\,0.4\,6 \\
\hline
2\,4
\end{array}
$$

$$
\begin{array}{r}
6\;\;10 \\
0.\cancel{7}\,\cancel{0} \\
-\,0.4\,6 \\
\hline
0.2\,4
\end{array}
$$

The difference is 0.24.

.Think............
0.24 is close to the estimate of 0.2.

Estimate by rounding. Then subtract.

	1.	2.	3.	4.	5.
	489 − 366	6244 − 29	36,243 − 13,963	456,781 − 179,660	587,893 − 498,721

	6.	7.	8.	9.	10.
	0.74 − 0.39	0.81 − 0.6	$.95 − .59	$14.97 − 10.49	0.8 − 0.29

Operations II

Inverse Operations: Addition and Subtraction

Inverse operations are mathematical operations that *undo* each other.

▶ Addition and subtraction are inverse operations.

> Let a, b, and c be any numbers.
>
> If $a + b = c$, then $c - b = a$.
> Subtraction "undoes" addition.
>
> If $c - b = a$, then $a + b = c$.
> Addition "undoes" subtraction.

Find the missing number.

$x + 5 = 12$
$x = 12 - 5$
$x = 7$

.Think.........................
7 + 5 = 12 and
12 − 5 = 7 are
related sentences.

Find the missing number.

$x - 9 = 15$
$x = 15 + 9$
$x = 24$

.Think.........................
24 − 9 = 15 and
15 + 9 = 24 are
related sentences.

▶ Multiplication and division are also inverse operations.

> Let a, b, and c be any numbers.
>
> If $a \times b = c$, then $c \div b = a$.
> Division "undoes" multiplication.
>
> If $c \div b = a$, then $a \times b = c$.
> Multiplication "undoes" division.

Find the missing number.

$y \times 4 = 12$
$y = 12 \div 4$
$y = 3$

.Think.........................
3 × 4 = 12 and
12 ÷ 4 = 3 are
related sentences.

Find the missing number.

$y \div 6 = 18$
$y = 18 \times 6$
$y = 108$

.Think.........................
108 ÷ 6 = 18 and
18 × 6 = 108 are
related sentences.

Find the missing number using inverse operations.

1. $8 + a = 12$

2. $36 - b = 9$

3. $r + \$2.96 = \$10.00$

4. $n - 40 = 56$

5. $19 \times d = 418$

6. $y \div 3 = 233$

7. $45a = 675$

8. $23 \times c = \$115.00$

9. $e + 468 = 9921$

10. $99{,}999 - f = 9898$

11. $g \div 321 = 123$

12. $\$101.00 = 2h$

Properties of Addition and Multiplication

The following properties of addition and multiplication are true for any numbers *a, b,* and *c.*

- **Commutative Property of Addition**
  Changing the *order* of the addends does not change the sum.

  $a + b = b + a$

  $5 + 9 = 9 + 5$
  $14 = 14$

  > Think...
  > "order"

- **Commutative Property of Multiplication**
  Changing the *order* of the factors does not change the product.

  $a \times b = b \times a$

  $3 \times 8 = 8 \times 3$
  $24 = 24$

- **Associative Property of Addition**
  Changing the *grouping* of the addends does not change the sum.

  $(a + b) + c = a + (b + c)$

  $(1 + 4) + 7 = 1 + (4 + 7)$
  $\quad 5 \quad + 7 = 1 + \quad 11$
  $\qquad 12 = 12$

  > Think...
  > "grouping"

- **Associative Property of Multiplication**
  Changing the *grouping* of the factors does not change the product.

  $(a \times b) \times c = a \times (b \times c)$

  $(6 \times 5) \times 2 = 6 \times (5 \times 2)$
  $\quad 30 \quad \times 2 = 6 \times \quad 10$
  $\qquad 60 = 60$

- **Identity Property of Addition**
  The sum of zero and a number is that number.

  $a + 0 = a \qquad 0 + a = a$

  $89 + 0 = 89 \quad 0 + 89 = 89$

  > Think...
  > "same"

- **Identity Property of Multiplication**
  The product of one and a number is that number.

  $1 \times a = a \qquad a \times 1 = a$

  $1 \times 8 = 8 \qquad 8 \times 1 = 8$

- **Zero Property of Multiplication**
  The product of zero and a number is zero.

  $0 \times a = 0 \qquad a \times 0 = 0$

  $0 \times 33 = 0 \qquad 33 \times 0 = 0$

  > Think...
  > "0 product"

Name the property of addition or multiplication used.

1. $18 + 53 = 53 + 18$

2. $(7 + 8) + 2 = 7 + (8 + 2)$

3. $90 + 0 = 90$

4. $11 \times 12 = 12 \times 11$

5. $2 \times (30 \times 8) = (2 \times 30) \times 8$

6. $1 \times 25 = 25$

Operations IV

Multiply 1- and 2-Digit Numbers

Multiply: $7 \times 27 =$ __?__ .

First estimate by rounding: $7 \times 30 = 210$.
Then multiply.

▶ **To multiply by a one-digit number:**

Multiply the ones. Then regroup.	Multiply the tens. Then regroup.
⁴ 2 7 × 7 ―――― 9	⁴ 2 7 × 7 ―――― 1 8 9

The product is 189.

.Think...........
189 is close to the
estimate of 210.

Multiply: $32 \times 46 =$ __?__ .

First estimate by rounding: $30 \times 50 = 1500$.
Then multiply.

▶ **To multiply by a two-digit number:**

Multiply the ones.	Multiply the tens.	Add the partial products.
4 6 ×3 2 ―――― 9 2 ← 2 × 46	4 6 ×3 2 ―――― 9 2 1 3 8 0 ← 30 × 46	4 6 ×3 2 ―――― 9 2 ← partial +1 3 8 0 ← products ―――――― 1 4 7 2

.Think...........
1472 is close to the
estimate of 1500.

The product is 1472.

Estimate by rounding. Then find the poduct.

1.   55
   × 6

2.   613
   ×   9

3. $7 \times \$8.64$

4.   67
   ×34

5.   329
   × 43

6. $92 \times \$7.68$

Trial Quotients

Divide: $2183 \div 46 = \underline{\ ?\ }$.

Follow these steps to divide:

- *Decide* where to begin the quotient.

$$4\ 6\overline{)2\ 1\ 8\ 3}$$

$46 < 218$

The quotient begins in the tens place.

- *Estimate.*

Think: $\textcircled{4}\ 6\overline{)\ \textcircled{2}\ \textcircled{1}\ 8\ 3} \longrightarrow 4 \times \underline{\ ?\ } = 21 \longrightarrow$ Try 5.

- *Divide.*

- *Multiply:* $5 \times 46 = 230$

$$\begin{array}{r} 5 \\ 4\ 6\overline{)2\ 1\ 8\ 3} \\ -\,2\ 3\ 0 \end{array}$$

The digit used in the quotient is too large.

- *Subtract* and *compare* remainder with divisor.

$$\begin{array}{r} 4 \\ 4\ 6\overline{)2\ 1\ 8\ 3} \\ -\,1\ 8\ 4 \\ \hline 3\ 4 \end{array}$$

Try 4.

$34 < 46$

- *Bring down* the next digit from the dividend and repeat the steps.

$$\begin{array}{r} 4\ 7 = 47 \ \ \text{R21} \\ 4\ 6\overline{)2\ 1\ 8\ 3} \\ -\,1\ 8\ 4\ \downarrow \\ \hline 3\ 4\ 3 \\ -\,3\ 2\ 2 \\ \hline 2\ 1 \end{array}$$

$21 < 46$

- *Check.*

$46 \times 47 = 2162$ $2162 + 21 = 2183$

Estimate to find the missing digit in the quotient.
Complete the division.

$$\begin{array}{r} 8? \\ \textbf{1.}\ 49\overline{)4018} \\ -\,392 \\ \hline 98 \end{array}$$

$$\begin{array}{r} 7? \\ \textbf{2.}\ 67\overline{)5226} \\ -\,469 \\ \hline 536 \end{array}$$

$$\begin{array}{r} 3? \\ \textbf{3.}\ 65\overline{)2573} \\ -\,195 \\ \hline 623 \end{array}$$

$$\begin{array}{r} 4? \\ \textbf{4.}\ 27\overline{)1234} \\ -\,108 \\ \hline 154 \end{array}$$

Operations VI

Divide Whole Numbers

Divide: 4782 ÷ 83 = __?__ .

Estimate by using compatible numbers: 4800 ÷ 80 = 60.

Decide where to begin the quotient.

    8 3)4 7 8 2   83 > 47

    8 3)4 7 8 2   83 < 478

The quotient begins in the tens place.

Divide the tens.	Divide the ones.	Check.

Divide the tens.

```
        5
8 3)4 7 8 2
  - 4 1 5
      6 3
```

Divide the ones.

```
          5 7 R 5 1
8 3)4 7 8 2
  - 4 1 5↓
      6 3 2
    - 5 8 1
        5 1
```

Check.

```
        5 7
      × 8 3
      1 7 1
    4 5 6
    4 7 3 1
  +     5 1
    4 7 8 2
```

The quotient is 57 R51.

Think
57 R51 is close to the estimate of 60.

Study these examples.

```
   $.2 8
3)$.8 4
  - 6
    2 4
  - 2 4
```

Think
Estimate:
$.90 ÷ 3 = $.30

```
      $.1 7
23)$ 3.9 1
  - 2 3
    1 6 1
  - 1 6 1
```

Think
Estimate:
$4.00 ÷ 20 = $.20

Estimate by using compatible numbers. Then find the quotient.

1. 24)522   **2.** 45)3268   **3.** 79)5576   **4.** 65)$9.10

5. 38)1589   **6.** 17)1634   **7.** 59)4267   **8.** 19)$18.24

Add and Subtract Fractions: Like Denominators

▶ **To add fractions with *like* denominators:**

- Add the numerators.

$$\frac{2}{8} + \frac{4}{8} = \frac{2+4}{8}$$

- Write the result over the common denominator.

$$= \frac{6}{8}$$

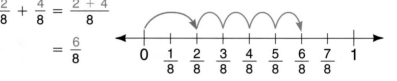

- Express the sum in simplest form.

$$\frac{6}{8} = \frac{6 \div 2}{8 \div 2} = \frac{3}{4}$$ ◄ GCF of 6 and 8: 2

▶ **To subtract fractions with *like* denominators:**

- Subtract the numerators.

$$\begin{array}{r} \frac{4}{8} \\ -\frac{2}{8} \\ \hline \frac{2}{8} \end{array}$$

- Write the result over the common denominator.

- Express the difference in simplest form.

$$\frac{2}{8} = \frac{2 \div 2}{8 \div 2} = \frac{1}{4}$$ ◄ GCF of 2 and 8: 2

Study these examples.

$$\begin{array}{r} \frac{1}{12} \\ +\frac{7}{12} \\ \hline \frac{8}{12} \end{array} = \frac{8 \div 4}{12 \div 4} = \frac{2}{3}$$

$$\begin{array}{r} \frac{4}{9} \\ -\frac{1}{9} \\ \hline \frac{3}{9} \end{array} = \frac{3 \div 3}{9 \div 3} = \frac{1}{3}$$

Add or subtract the fractions. Write each answer in simplest form.

1. $\begin{array}{r} \frac{3}{5} \\ +\frac{1}{5} \\ \hline \end{array}$

2. $\begin{array}{r} \frac{2}{3} \\ -\frac{1}{3} \\ \hline \end{array}$

3. $\begin{array}{r} \frac{5}{9} \\ +\frac{1}{9} \\ \hline \end{array}$

4. $\begin{array}{r} \frac{7}{12} \\ -\frac{5}{12} \\ \hline \end{array}$

5. $\begin{array}{r} \frac{3}{4} \\ +\frac{3}{4} \\ \hline \end{array}$

6. $\frac{8}{9} + \frac{1}{9}$

7. $\frac{8}{10} + \frac{7}{10}$

8. $\frac{11}{24} - \frac{2}{24}$

9. $\frac{12}{12} - \frac{12}{12}$

Fractions I

Make Pictographs

You can make a pictograph to display the data in the table.

▶ **To make a pictograph:**

- List each category of music.

- Choose a symbol or picture to use to represent a number of CDs sold. Examine your data. Select a convenient value for the symbol.

  Let ◉ = 50 CDs.

- Draw the symbols to represent the data. Round data to help you do this. For example:

  391 ➝ 400   247 ➝ 250

- Write a key to show the value of the symbol used.

- Give your graph a title.

CDs Sold at Al's Audio Outlet	
Category	**Number Sold**
Rock	391
Classical	151
Folk	77
R&B	247
Jazz	126
World Music	169

CDs Sold at Al's Audio Outlet	
Rock	◉ ◉ ◉ ◉ ◉ ◉ ◉ ◉
Classical	◉ ◉ ◉
Folk	◉ ◖
R&B	◉ ◉ ◉ ◉ ◉
Jazz	◉ ◉ ◖
World Music	◉ ◉ ◉ ◖
Key: Each ◉ = 50 CDs.	

Solve. Use the pictograph above.

1. What does ◖ represent? How many symbols were used for R&B? for Jazz?

2. About how many more CDs are needed so that Jazz and R&B would have the same number?

3. About how many CDs were sold in all? How can you use multiplication to help you answer?

4. Which categories had between 100 CDs and 200 CDs?

5. Make a pictograph using the same data from Al's Audio Outlet. Change the key so that each symbol represents 10 CDs. How does this change the pictograph? What would it look like if each represented 100 CDs?

Make Bar Graphs

Henry displayed the data at the right in a horizontal bar graph.

▶ **To make a horizontal bar graph:**

- Draw horizontal and vertical axes on grid paper.

- Use the data from the table to choose an appropriate scale. (The data range from 26 to 82. Choose intervals of 10.)

- Draw and label the scale along the horizontal axis. Start at 0 and label equal intervals.

- Label the vertical axis. List the name of each dinosaur.

- Draw horizontal bars to represent each length. Make the bars of equal width.

- Write a title for your graph.

Lengths of Some Dinosaurs	
Name	**Length**
Albertosaurus	26 ft
Allosaurus	36 ft
Brachiosaurus	52 ft
Tyrannosaurus	39 ft
Ultrasaurus	82 ft

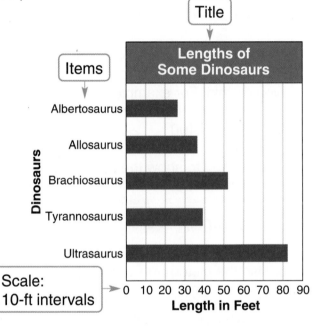

▶ To make a **vertical bar graph**, place the scale along the vertical axis and the items along the horizontal axis.

Solve. Use the bar graph above.

1. What data are along the vertical axis? the horizontal axis?

2. Which dinosaurs have lengths between 30 and 40 feet?

3. Make a horizontal or vertical bar graph using the data on lengths of dinosaurs. Change the scale to represent 20-ft intervals.

Statistics and Graphs II

Equally/Not Equally Likely Outcomes

For each of the spinners, there are 5 possible results, or outcomes: 1, 3, 5, 7, 9.

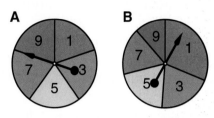

A   **B**

▶ With Spinner *A*, each number has the same chance of occurring. The outcomes are equally likely.

▶ With Spinner *B*, the outcomes are not equally likely. The spinner is more likely to land on 1 than on 9.

The spinner has 8 *equal* sections. Of the equal sections, 3 are red, 3 are green, and 2 are blue.

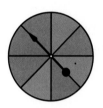

▶ The probability of the spinner landing on
  • red is 3 out of 8.
  • green is 3 out of 8.
  • blue is 2 out of 8.

For each experiment, list the possible outcomes. Then write whether the outcomes are *equally likely* or *not equally likely*.

1. Toss a marker on the board.

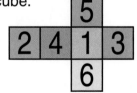

| 1 | 2 |
| 3 | 4 |

2. Spin the spinner.

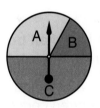

3. Roll the number cube.

4. A jar contains 4 balls: 1 red, 1 white, 1 yellow, and 1 blue. Choose a ball without looking.

Use the spinner on the right to find the probability of landing on:

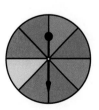

5. red   **6.** blue   **7.** green   **8.** yellow

List Outcomes

▶ You can make an organized list to show all possible
outcomes of an experiment.

In an experiment, Sandra spins the two given
spinners. Find all possible outcomes. How many
possible outcomes are there?

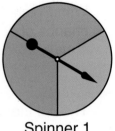

Spinner 1

• Look at the spinners to find the possible outcomes.

Spinner 1: Blue (B), Red (R), or Green (G)

Spinner 2: 1, 2, or 3

• Make an organized list of the possible pairs of
outcomes. Then count the number of outcomes.

Blue (B) - 1	Red (R) - 1	Green (G) - 1
Blue (B) - 2	Red (R) - 2	Green (G) - 2
Blue (B) - 3	Red (R) - 3	Green (G) - 3

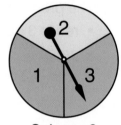

Spinner 2

So there are 9 possible outcomes.

Make a list of all possible outcomes for each experiment.
Then write the total number of outcomes.

1. toss a coin and toss a
green/red counter

2. toss a coin and spin the spinner

3. pick a card without looking
and roll a number cube

 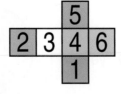

4. spin the spinner and pick a cube
without looking

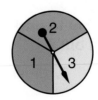 

Geometric Figures

Some simple geometric figures:

G and H are points.

- **point**—an exact location in space, usually represented by a dot

- **line**—a set of points in a plane that forms a straight path and extends indefinitely in opposite directions

$\overleftrightarrow{GH}$ is a line.

- **line segment**—part of a line with two endpoints

$\overline{GH}$ is a line segment.

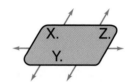

- **plane**—a flat surface that extends indefinitely in all directions

Plane *XYZ* contains the points *X*, *Y*, and *Z*.

- **ray**—part of a line that starts at an endpoint and extends indefinitely in one direction.

Ray *EC* ($\overrightarrow{EC}$) has endpoint *E*.

- **angle**—formed by two rays with a common endpoint. The common endpoint is called the **vertex** of the angle. The letter naming the vertex is always in the middle.

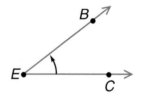

> **Think**
> Point *E* is the vertex of ∠*E*.

Angle *CEB* (∠*CEB*) is formed by $\overrightarrow{EC}$ and $\overrightarrow{EB}$.

Identify each figure. Then name it using symbols.

1. • *A*   **2.**   **3.**   **4.**   **5.** • *Q*

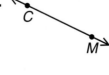

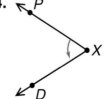

Lines: Intersecting and Parallel

Lines in the same plane either intersect (meet at a point)
or are parallel (never meet).

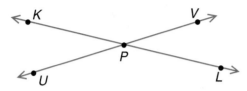

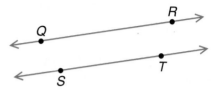

$\overleftrightarrow{KL}$ and $\overleftrightarrow{UV}$ are intersecting lines.
They meet at point *P*.

$\overleftrightarrow{QR}$ and $\overleftrightarrow{ST}$ are parallel lines.
$\overleftrightarrow{QR} \parallel \overleftrightarrow{ST}$

‖ means "is parallel to."

▶ Line segments and rays may also intersect or be parallel.

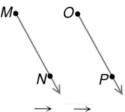

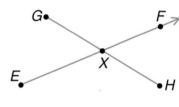

$\overline{AB} \parallel \overline{CD}$

$\overrightarrow{MN} \parallel \overrightarrow{OP}$

$\overrightarrow{EF}$ intersects $\overline{GH}$
at point *X*.

Identify each pair of geometric figures as *intersecting* or *parallel*.

1.   **2.**   **3.**   **4.**

Draw each. You may use dot paper.

5. two intersecting lines

6. two parallel rays

7. $\overline{UV} \parallel \overline{WX}$

8. $\overrightarrow{FG} \parallel \overleftrightarrow{HY}$

9. $\overline{AC}$ intersecting $\overrightarrow{DE}$ at point *M*

10. 3 lines intersecting at point *B*

11. $\overline{MX}$ and $\overline{CR}$ that do not intersect

12. $\overleftrightarrow{NP}$ and $\overleftrightarrow{QL}$ that are not parallel

Geometry II

Polygons

A polygon is a closed plane figure formed by line segments that intersect only at their endpoints. The line segments are the sides of the polygon.

The point where any two sides of a polygon meet is called a vertex (plural: vertices) of the polygon.

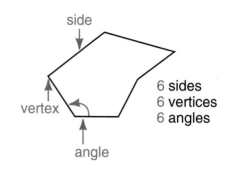

side

vertex

angle

6 sides
6 vertices
6 angles

The sides of a polygon do not cross each other.

Polygon	Number of Sides	Number of Vertices	Examples
Triangle *tri* means 3	3	3	
Quadrilateral *quad* means 4	4	4	
Pentagon *penta* means 5	5	5	
Hexagon *hexa* means 6	6	6	
Octagon *octa* means 8	8	8	

Decide if each figure is a polygon. Write *Yes* or *No*. Then name the polygon.

1.

2.

3.

4.

Metric Units of Length

The most commonly used units of length in the metric system of measurement are given below.

meter (m)—standard unit of length in the metric system

The height of a net on an actual tennis court is about 1 m.

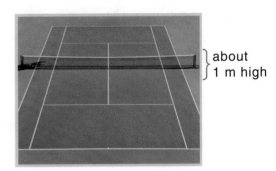

about 1 m high

millimeter (mm)

An actual dime is about 1 mm thick.

centimeter (cm)

A paper clip is about 1 cm wide.

decimeter (dm)

A photo frame is about 1 dm long.

kilometer (km)

It takes about 15 minutes to walk 1 km.

Use mm, cm, dm, m, or km to complete each sentence.

1. The length of a pair of scissors is about 20 _?_ .

2. The width of your hand is about 85 _?_ .

3. The swimming freestyle distance is 1500 _?_ .

4. The width of an electric wire is about 1 _?_ .

Measurement I

Metric Units of Capacity and Mass

▶ The metric units of liquid capacity are the milliliter (mL) and liter (L).

20 drops of water
is about 1 mL.

| 1000 milliliters (mL) = 1 liter (L) |

about 1 L

▶ The metric units of mass are the gram (g) and kilogram (kg).

A paper clip has
a mass of about 1 g.

| 1000 grams (g) = 1 kilogram (kg) |

A hardcover dictionary
has a mass of about 1 kg.

▶ Multiply or divide to rename units of measurement.

| Multiply to rename larger units as smaller units. |

25 L = __?__ mL
25 L = (25 × 1000) mL
     = (25 000 mL

| Divide to rename smaller units as larger units. |

72 000 g = __?__ kg
72 000 = (72 000 ÷ 1000) kg
       = 72 kg

Which metric unit of capacity is better to measure each? Write mL or L.

1. milk jug

2. bottle of eyedrops

3. glass of juice

Which metric unit of mass is better to measure each? Write g or kg.

4. a dozen bananas

5. personal computer

6. pencil

Multiply or divide to rename each unit.

7. 9 L = __?__ mL

8. 10 000 mL = __?__ L

9. 72 L = __?__ mL

10. 50 000 g = __?__ kg

11. 50 kg = __?__ g

12. 12 000 g = __?__ kg

Customary Units of Length

▶ The customary units of length are the inch, foot, yard, and mile.

1 foot (ft) = 12 inches (in.)
1 yard (yd) = 36 in. = 3 ft
1 mile (mi) = 5280 ft = 1760 yd

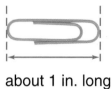

about 1 in. long

The length of an actual shoe box is about 1 ft.

The width of a door is about 1 yd.

A person walks a distance of about 1 mile in 20 minutes.

▶ Multiply or divide to rename units of measurement.

Multiply to rename larger units as smaller units.	Divide to rename smaller units as larger units.

5 mi = __?__ yd

5 mi = (5 × 1760) yd

    = 8800 yd

Think
1 mi = 1760 yd

816 in. = __?__ ft

816 in. = (816 ÷ 12) ft

    = 68 ft

Think
12 in. = 1 ft

Write the letter of the most reasonable estimate.

1. length of a pen   **a.** 6 ft   **b.** 6 in.   **c.** 6 yd

2. height of a table   **a.** $2\frac{1}{2}$ ft   **b.** $2\frac{1}{2}$ mi   **c.** $2\frac{1}{2}$ in.

3. distance between two cities   **a.** 225 mi   **b.** 225 yd   **c.** 225 ft

Multiply or divide to rename each unit.

4. 8 ft = __?__ in.   5. 25 yd = __?__ ft   6. 252 in. = __?__ yd

7. $2\frac{1}{2}$ mi = __?__ yd   8. 126 in. = __?__ yd   9. 26,400 ft = __?__ mi

Measurement III

Customary Units of Capacity and Weight

▶ The customary units of capacity are the fluid ounce, cup, pint, quart, and gallon.

1 cup (c) = 8 fluid ounces (fl oz)
1 pint (pt) = 2 c = 16 fl oz
1 quart (qt) = 2 pt = 4 c
1 gallon (gal) = 4 qt = 8 pt

 1 c

 1 pt

 1 qt

1 half gal

1 gal

▶ The customary units of weight are the ounce, pound, and ton.

1 pound (lb) = 16 ounces (oz)
1 ton (T) = 2000 lb

about 1 oz

about 1 lb

about 2 T

▶ **Multiply** or **divide** to rename units of measurement.

18 gal = __?__ qt

18 gal = (18 × 4) qt

     = 72 qt

Think
1 gal = 4 qt

56 oz = __?__ lb

56 oz = (56 ÷ 16) lb

     = $3\frac{1}{2}$ lb

Think
16 oz = 1 lb

Write the letter of the most reasonable estimate.

1. capacity of a can of soup   **a.** 2 pt   **b.** 2 c   **c.** 2 gal

2. weight of a tennis ball   **a.** 2 lb   **b.** 2 T   **c.** 2 oz

3. capacity of a large bowl   **a.** 4 qt   **b.** 4 fl oz   **c.** 4 c

Multiply or divide to rename each unit.

4. 6 pt = __?__ qt   **5.** 22 gal = __?__ pt   **6.** 144 oz = __?__ lb

7. $10\frac{1}{2}$ c = __?__ fl oz   **8.** 5000 lb = __?__ T   **9.** 5000 T = __?__ lb

Read an Inch Ruler

The tick marks on the scale of a ruler represent fractional parts of an inch.

The length of the tick mark indicates the particular part of an inch: half, fourth, eighth, or sixteenth. This helps you read and record measures in lowest terms.

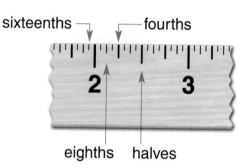

sixteenths — fourths

eighths   halves

inches

.Think....................................
On this ruler, the distance between
one tick mark and the next is $\frac{1}{16}$ in.
....

Read: $1 + \frac{3}{4}$

Record: $1\frac{3}{4}$ in. or $1\frac{6}{8}$ in. or $1\frac{12}{16}$ in.

.Think....................................
$1\frac{3}{4}$ in. is in lowest terms.
....

**Read each length and record it in lowest terms.
Then give the length in as many ways as you can.**

1.

2.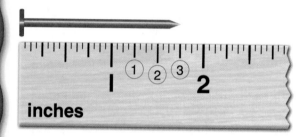

3.

4.

5.

6.

Measurement V

Perimeter and Area of Rectangles

Formulas can be used to find the perimeter and area of rectangles.

Perimeter of Rectangle
$P = (2 \times \ell) + (2 \times w)$
ℓ = length, w = width

Area of Rectangle
$A = (\ell \times w)$
ℓ = length, w = width

14 in.

3 in.

$P = (2 \times \ell) + (2 \times w)$

$P = (2 \times 14 \text{ in.}) + (2 \times 3 \text{ in.})$

$P = 28 \text{ in.} + 6 \text{ in.}$

$P = 34 \text{ in.}$

The distance around the rectangle is 34 in.

$A = \ell \times w$

$A = 14 \text{ in.} \times 3 \text{ in.}$

$A = 42 \text{ sq in.}$

(square inches)

The surface covered is 42 sq in.

Find the perimeter of each rectangle. Use the perimeter formula.

1.   13 in.

6 in.

2.   12 cm

20 cm

3.

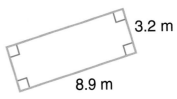

3.2 m

8.9 m

Find the area of each rectangle. Use the area formula.

4.   7 m

2.5 m

5.

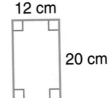

13 cm

13 cm

6.

2 yd

$6\frac{1}{2}$ yd

Dear Student,

Problem solvers are super sleuths. We invite you to become a super sleuth by using these *four steps* when solving problems.

1 Read   **2 Plan**   **3 Solve**   **4 Check**

Sleuths use clues to find a solution to a problem. When working together to solve a problem, you may choose to use one or more of these *strategies* as clues:

Strategy File

Use These Strategies
Guess and Test
Interpret the Remainder
Use a Graph
Write a Number Sentence
Use Simpler Numbers

Strategy File

Use These Strategies
More Than One Solution
Logical Reasoning
Use a Diagram
Find a Pattern
Use More Than One Step

Strategy File

Use These Strategies
Work Backward
Make an Organized List
Use Drawings/Models
Combine Strategies
Write an Equation
Make a Table

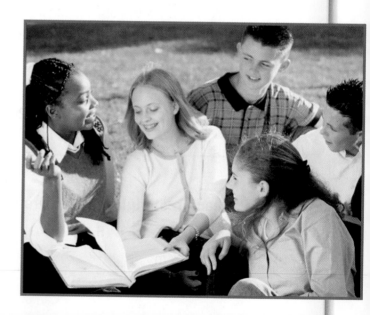

Create a mental picture.
List the facts and the questions.

As you read a problem, create a picture in your mind.
Make believe you are there in the problem.
This will help you think about:
- what facts you will need;
- what the problem is asking;
- how you will solve the problem.

After reading the problem, it might be helpful to sketch the picture you imagined so that you can refer to it.

Name or list all the facts given in the problem. Be aware of *extra* information not needed to solve the problem. Look for *hidden* information to help solve the problem. Identify the question or questions the problem is asking.

Plan

Choose and outline a plan.

Plan how to solve the problem by:
- looking at the picture you drew;
- thinking about what you did when you solved similar problems;
- choosing a strategy or strategies for solving the problem.

Solve

Work the plan.

Work with the listed facts and the strategy to find the solution. Sometimes a problem will require you to add, subtract, multiply, or divide. Multistep problems require more than one choice of operation or strategy. It is good to *estimate* the answer before you compute.

Check

Test that the solution is reasonable.

Ask yourself:
- "Have I answered the question?"
- "Is the answer reasonable?"

Check the answer by comparing it to the estimate. If the answer is not reasonable, check your computation.

Strategy: Guess and Test

Last summer Jane earned $75.50 mowing lawns. From these earnings, she saved $2.50 more than she spent. How much money did Jane save?

Read

Visualize yourself in the problem as you reread it. List the facts and the question.

Facts: Jane saved $2.50 more than she spent.
Jane earned $75.50.

Question: How much money did she save?

Plan

Since Jane made $75.50, choose a reasonable guess for the amount of money spent, such as $30.00. Make a table and compute the amount saved. Find the total to test your guess.

Solve

Spent	$30.00	$33.00	$36.00	$39.00
Saved	$32.50	$35.50	$38.50	$41.50
Total	$62.50	$68.50	$74.50	$80.50
Test	too low	too low	too low	too high

So the amount spent is between $36.00 and $39.00.
Try $37.00.

Spent	$37.00	$36.50
Saved	$39.50	$39.00
Total	$76.50	$75.50
Check	too high	correct

Jane saved $39.00.

Check

Subtract the amount saved from the amount earned to see if $36.50 was spent.

$75.50 − $39.00 = $36.50

The answer checks.

Strategy: Use More Than One Step

In a typical week, a chicken farmer collects about 1164 eggs each day. If all of the eggs are sent to the market, how many dozen eggs are sent each week?

Read ▶ **Visualize yourself in the problem as you reread it. List the facts and the question.**

Fact: Each day, 1164 eggs are collected.

Question: How many dozen eggs are collected in 1 week?

Plan ▶ Is there *hidden information* in the problem? Yes, there are two hidden facts.

$$7 \text{ days} = 1 \text{ week}$$
$$12 \text{ eggs} = \text{one dozen}$$

Step 1: First, to find how many eggs are collected in one week, multiply:

$$\underset{\text{days}}{7} \times \underset{\text{eggs per day}}{1164} = \underset{\text{eggs in one week}}{\underline{?}}$$

Step 2: Then, to find how many dozen eggs are sent to the market each week, divide:

$$\underset{\substack{\text{eggs collected} \\ \text{in one week}}}{} \div \underset{\text{eggs}}{12} = \underset{\substack{\text{number of dozens} \\ \text{sent to the market}}}{}$$

Solve ▶

```
  1 4 2
  1 1 6 4
×       7
  8 1 4 8
```
eggs collected each week

```
           6 7 9  ◀── dozen eggs sent
  1 2) 8 1 4 8         to the market
      -7 2
        9 4
       -8 4
        1 0 8
       -1 0 8
```

Each week 679 dozen eggs are sent to the market.

Check ▶ Check your computations by using inverse operations.

$8148 \div 7 \overset{?}{=} 1164$ Yes. $12 \times 679 \overset{?}{=} 8148$ Yes.

Strategy: Use a Graph

The science class plants 40 seeds. The students can display the number of seeds that sprout each day on a graph. How many seeds have not sprouted by May 10?

Seed Data — Number of Seeds Sprouted vs. Date in May

Read ▸ **Visualize yourself in the problem above as you reread it. List the facts and the question.**

> **Facts:** total number of seeds—40
> number of seeds sprouted each day—
> data given on the line graph
>
> **Question:** How many seeds have not sprouted by May 10?

Plan ▸ This problem has a *hidden question.*
How many seeds have already sprouted?

$$\text{total number of seeds planted} - \text{number of seeds sprouted} = \text{number of seeds not sprouted}$$

$$40 \quad - \quad \underline{?} \quad = \quad \underline{?}$$

So to find the number of seeds that have not sprouted by May 10, you must:

- First, use the data from the graph and add to find the number of seeds sprouted up to May 10.

- Then subtract your answer in Step 1 from 40.

Solve ▸ First add. (*Hint:* Look for tens.)

$$2 + 0 + 2 + 3 + 5 + 7 + 8 + 6 = 33$$

Then subtract: $40 - 33 = 7$ seeds not sprouted.

Seven seeds have not sprouted by May 10.

Check ▸ Does $2 + 0 + 2 + 3 + 5 + 7 + 8 + 6 + 7 = 40$? Yes.

Algebra
Strategy: Write an Equation

Stephanie and Alexandria made a survey about pet ownership. Their survey shows that a group of sixth graders owns 56 pets: 12 dogs, 13 cats, and the rest birds. How many of the pets are birds?

Pet Survey		
Animal	**Tally**	**Total**
Dog	~~HHT~~ ~~HHT~~ II	12
Cat	~~HHT~~ ~~HHT~~ III	13
Bird	?	?
		56

Read ▶ **Visualize yourself in the problem above as you reread it. List the facts and the question.**

Facts: 56 pets
12 dogs
13 cats
The rest are birds.

Question: How many pets are birds?

Plan ▶ Use the information to *write an equation.* Write words first.

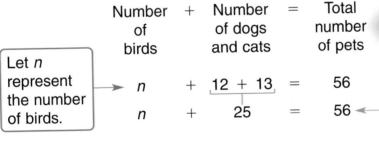

Number of birds	+	Number of dogs and cats	=	Total number of pets

Let *n* represent the number of birds.

$$n + \underbrace{12 + 13} = 56$$
$$n + 25 = 56$$

addition equation or addition sentence

You can solve the equation by the Guess and Test strategy or by using a related subtraction sentence.

Solve ▶

$$n + 25 = 56$$

Try 30. $30 + 25 = 55$

Try 31. $31 + 25 = 56$

There are 31 birds.

$n + 25 = 56$ and

$n = 56 - 25$

$n = 31$

Check ▶ Substitute 31 for *n* in the equation to test whether the equation is true.

$$n + 25 = 56$$
$$31 + 25 = 56 \quad \text{The answer checks.}$$

Applications: Mixed Review

Read ▸ Plan ▸ Solve ▸ Check ▸

Choose a strategy from the list or use another strategy you know to solve each problem.

1. Blanca has collected 59 boxes of paper clips. The paper clips in each box make a chain about 312 in. long. Does Blanca have enough clips to make a mile-long chain? (*Hint:* 1 mi = 63,360 in.)

2. Newgate School makes a chain with 12,250 paper clips and rubber bands. The chain uses four times more paper clips than rubber bands. How many paper clips does the chain use? how many rubber bands?

3. Each rubber band in the Newgate chain is 5 cm long. How many rubber bands are in a length of chain that measures 1695 cm?

4. A team of 18 students collects paper clips. The team collects an average of 375 paper clips per student. How many paper clips did the entire team collect?

5. Cathy and Bill spent $8.89 on rubber bands. Each box cost $1.27, and Cathy bought 3 more boxes than Bill. How many boxes of rubber bands did each student buy?

Strategy File

Use These Strategies
Write an Equation
Guess and Test
Use a Graph
Use More Than One Step

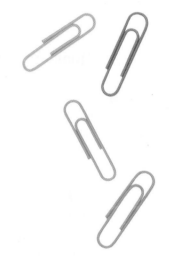

Use the graph for problems 6–8.

6. Sue bought 27 boxes of medium paper clips and 10 boxes of super paper clips. How many paper clips in all did she buy?

7. Would 40 boxes of large paper clips and 12 boxes of small paper clips be more than 15,000 paper clips?

8. Which is the greater quantity: 35 boxes of large paper clips or 25 boxes of medium paper clips?

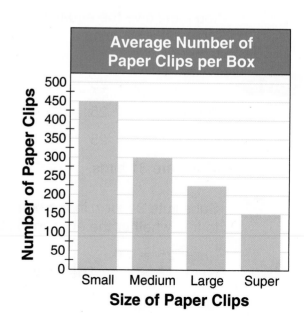

Average Number of Paper Clips per Box

Number of Paper Clips (vertical axis: 0, 50, 100, 150, 200, 250, 300, 350, 400, 450, 500)

Size of Paper Clips (horizontal axis: Small, Medium, Large, Super)

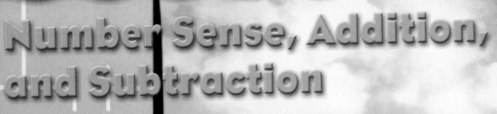

Number Sense, Addition, and Subtraction

TO BUILD A HOUSE

Here on this plot
Our house will rise
Against the hill
Beneath blue skies

Ruler and tape
Measure the size
Of windows and cupboards
The floors inside

We add, subtract,
Multiply, divide
To build closets and stairs
The porch outside

Without numbers and measure
Would our house ever rise
Against the hill
Beneath blue skies?

Lillian M. Fisher

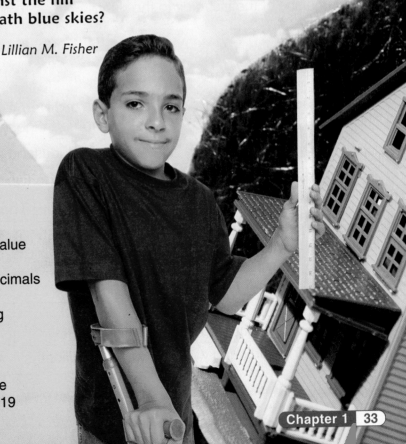

In this chapter you will:

Explore one trillion
Use exponents to understand place value
Compare and order decimals
Compute with whole numbers and decimals
Write and evaluate expressions
Solve problems by writing and solving
  an equation

Critical Thinking/Finding Together

Find Robert's house number if it is the
seventh number in this sequence: 4119
4008 4037 3926

Place Value

The digits and the position of each digit in a number determine the value of a number.

▶ To read the number 7,800,000,000,000, you need to know the place of each digit. The place-value chart below will help you.

A set of three digits separated by a comma is called a period.

The 7 is in the trillions place. Its value is 7 trillions, or 7,000,000,000,000.

The 8 is in the hundred billions place. Its value is 8 hundred billions, or 800,000,000,000.

Trillions Period			Billions Period			Millions Period			Thousands Period			Ones Period		
hundreds	tens	ones	hundreds	tens	ones	hundreds	tens	ones	hundreds	tens	ones	hundreds	tens	ones
	7	8	0	0	0	0	0	0	0	0	0	0	0	0

Place

Standard Form: 7,800,000,000,000
Word Name: seven trillion, eight hundred billion
Short Word Name: 7 trillion, 800 billion

▶ To read a decimal, read the numbers and say the place of the last digit to the right.

hundreds	tens	ones	tenths	hundredths	thousandths	ten thousandths	hundred thousandths	millionths
		0.	0	0	0	4		
		0.	0	6	0	5	4	
	4	0.	0	0	0	2	0	1

Word Name
← four ten thousandths
← six thousand fifty-four hundred thousandths
← forty and two hundred one millionths

The decimal point is read as "and."

Standard Form	Word Name	Short Word Name
0.0004	four ten thousandths	4 ten thousandths
0.06054	six thousand fifty-four hundred thousandths	6054 hundred thousandths
40.000201	forty and two hundred one millionths	40 and 201 millionths

Write the place of the underlined digit. Then write its value.

1. 131,24<u>1</u>,920,057

2. <u>6</u>70,901,230,001,400

3. <u>8</u>0,270,310,000

4. 0.42<u>9</u>7

5. 0.8152<u>3</u>

6. 7.01432<u>5</u>

7. 1<u>6</u>.1876

8. 17.927<u>4</u>3

9. 0.1976<u>0</u>8

Use the number 64,310,420,069,346.789125. Name the digit in the given place.

10. millions

11. ten trillions

12. hundred billions

13. trillions

14. millionths

15. hundredths

16. tenths

17. ten thousandths

18. hundred thousandths

Write the word name for each number.

19. 201,000,006,400

20. 20,030,010,000

21. 6,000,121,000,015

22. 0.004

23. 8.0408

24. 0.00062

25. 0.000079

26. 5.042019

27. 1.568970

Write each number in standard form.

28. thirteen million, five thousand

29. three hundred eight billion

30. one hundred twelve trillion

31. ninety-one billion, fifty

32. eleven millionths

33. two thousand ten hundred thousandths

34. 750 trillion

35. 42 ten thousandths

Problem Solving

Ellen wrote three statements about the decimals in the box. Tell whether each of her statements is true for (a) all of the numbers, (b) some of the numbers, or (c) none of the numbers. Explain your thinking.

16.07965
123.00938
3.789340

36. My millionth digit is 5.

37. My thousandths digit is 9.

38. My ten thousandths digit is 3 more than my millionths digit and the same as my ones digit.

CRITICAL THINKING

39. What is another name for a thousand million? For a million million?

Expanded Form

A number expressed in **expanded form** shows the sum of the products of each digit and its place value.

▶ To express a number in expanded form, multiply each digit by its value. Then express the products as a sum.

Trillions Period			Billions Period			Millions Period			Thousands Period			Ones Period		
hundreds	tens	ones	hundreds	tens	ones	hundreds	tens	ones	hundreds	tens	ones	hundreds	tens	ones
		3	0	0	7	0	0	0	0	9	1	8	0	6

> 3 has a value of three trillion or ($3 \times 1,000,000,000,000$).

Standard Form → 3,007,000,091,806

Expanded Form

You can write expanded form in two ways. Places that hold a zero may be omitted in expanded form.

→ ($3 \times 1,000,000,000,000$) + ($7 \times 1,000,000,000$) + ($9 \times 10,000$) + ($1 \times 1000$) + ($8 \times 100$) + ($6 \times 1$)

or

→ $3,000,000,000,000 + 7,000,000,000 + 90,000 + 1,000 + 800 + 6$

▶ Decimal numbers can also be written in expanded form. For decimals, the digits are multiplied by 0.1, 0.01, 0.001, and so on.

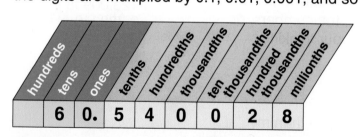

hundreds	tens	ones	tenths	hundredths	thousandths	ten thousandths	hundred thousandths	millionths
	6	0.	5	4	0	0	2	8

Standard Form	Expanded Form
60.540028	(6×10) + (5×0.1) + (4×0.01) + (2×0.00001) + (8×0.000001) or $60 + 0.5 + 0.04 + 0.00002 + 0.000008$

Complete each expanded form.

1. 38,500,000,700,000 (3 × _?_) + (8 × _?_) + (5 × _?_) + (7 × _?_)

2. 4.0008 (_?_ × 1) + (_?_ × 0.0001)   3. 0.000009 (_?_ × 0.000001)

Write each expanded form in two ways.

4. 5,042,102

5. 201,407,090,000

6. 15,000,087,000

7. 0.045678

8. 3.050904

9. 78.5009

Write each expanded form in standard form.

10. (9 × 10,000,000,000,000) + (3 × 100,000) + (4 × 100)

11. (4 × 1,000,000,000,000) + (5 × 10,000) + (2 × 1000) + (9 × 1)

12. 4 + 0.1 + 0.07 + 0.000009   13. 20 + 0.008 + 0.0001 + 0.00005

Write each number in standard form and in expanded form.

14. 95 trillion, 700 million

15. 8 trillion, twelve million, five

16. 13 billion, 7 hundred

17. 14 hundred thousandths

18. 80 and 13 ten thousandths

19. 907 millionths

Solve each problem.

20. In 2005, the population of the United States was approximately 294,000,000. How is this number written in expanded form?

21. In 2005, the population of the world was approximately six billion, four hundred forty million. How is this number written in standard form?

TEST PREPARATION

Choose the letter corresponding to the correct answer.

22. Which is 5.035 written in expanded form?

   A 5 + 0 + 3 + 5
   B (5 × 1) + (3 × 0.1) + (5 × 0.01)
   C (5 × 1) + (3 × 0.1) + (5 × 0.001)
   D (5 × 1) + (3 × 0.01) + (5 × 0.001)

23. What is (4 × 0.01) + (9 × 0.0001) in standard form?

   F 0.0409
   G 0.4009
   H 0.490
   J 4.0009

Place Value and Exponents

Another way to write 100 is 10 × 10, or 10^2.

10^2 ← **exponent**
← **base**

▶ An exponent tells how many times to use the base as a factor.

> $10^2 = 10 \times 10$
> Read 10^2 as "ten to the second power" or "ten squared."

> $10^3 = 10 \times 10 \times 10$
> Read 10^3 as "ten to the third power" or "ten cubed."

▶ Positive powers of 10 are used to show whole number place value.

$10^5 = 10 \times 10 \times 10 \times 10 \times 10 = 100{,}000$
$10^4 = 10 \times 10 \times 10 \times 10 = 10{,}000$
$10^3 = 10 \times 10 \times 10 = 1{,}000$
$10^2 = 10 \times 10 = 100$

> In positive powers of ten, the exponent indicates the number of zeros in the product.

$10^1 = 10 \times 1 = 10$ ← Any number raised to the first power equals that number.
$10^0 = 1$ ← Any nonzero number raised to the zero power is equal to 1.

▶ Negative powers of 10 are used to show decimal place value.

> In negative powers of ten, the exponent indicates the number of decimal places.

$10^{-1} = 0.1$
$10^{-2} = 0.01$
$10^{-3} = 0.001$

> Read 10^{-1} as "ten to the negative first power."

▶ You can write numbers in standard form in expanded form using exponents.

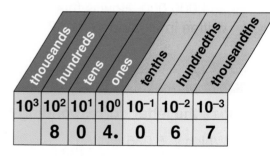

thousands	hundreds	tens	ones	tenths	hundredths	thousandths
10^3	10^2	10^1	10^0	10^{-1}	10^{-2}	10^{-3}
	8	0	4.	0	6	7

Standard Form   **Expanded Form**

804.067 ⟶ $(8 \times 10^2) + (4 \times 10^0) + (6 \times 10^{-2}) + (7 \times 10^{-3})$

or

$(8 \times 100) + (4 \times 1) + (6 \times 0.01) + (7 \times 0.001)$

Write each power of ten in standard form.

1. 10^8 2. 10^2 3. 10^{-2} 4. 10^{-4}

5. 10^{-1} 6. 10^{-3} 7. 10^0 8. 10^7

Write each as a power of ten.

9. $10 \times 10 \times 10$ 10. $10 \times 10 \times 10 \times 10 \times 10$ 11. 10

12. 0.0001   13. 0.1   14. 0.001

Write each number in expanded form using exponents.

15. 1005   16. 218   17. 52,905   18. 840,500
$(1 \times 10^3) + (5 \times 10^0)$

19. 2.0006   20. 9.107   21. 77.04   22. 7.0034

Write each in standard form.

23. $(5 \times 10^7) + (8 \times 10^3) + (3 \times 10^1)$ 24. $(1 \times 10^6) + (6 \times 10^3) + (2 \times 10^0)$

25. $(6 \times 10^2) + (8 \times 10^{-2}) + (2 \times 10^{-4})$ 26. $(9 \times 10^2) + (9 \times 10^0) + (9 \times 10^{-2})$

Problem Solving

27. Evaluate 10^1, 10^2, 10^3, and 10^4. Find the pattern in the products and predict what 10^9 would be. Explain how you found your answer.

28. The distance around Earth's equator is approximately 24,900 miles. How is this number written in expanded form using powers of 10?

29. Erica has 10^3 stamps in her collection and Jacob has $10^4 - 9000$ stamps in his collection. Who has more? Explain.

30. The distance from the planet Pluto to the sun is approximately 3,660,000,000 miles. How is this number written in expanded form?

CHALLENGE

Use the place-value chart at the right.

31. Copy and complete the place-value chart to the right. Explain the pattern you find as you fill in the bases and the exponents from left to right.

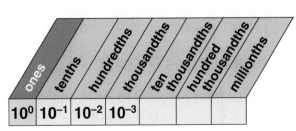

32. Write each in expanded form using exponents.

   a. 3 millionths   **b.** 6 hundredths

   c. 9 thousandths   **d.** 4 hundred thousandths

Compare and Order Decimals

You can compare decimals the same way you compare whole numbers. Start at the left and compare the digits in the same places.

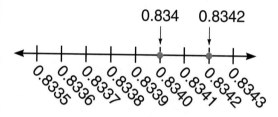

Remember: You can add a zero to the right of a decimal without changing its value. 0.834 = 0.8340

0.834 < 0.8342

Check using a number line.

0.834   0.8342

Since 0.834 is to the *left* of 0.8342 on the number line, 0.834 < 0.8342.

Order these decimals from greatest to least:
0.1285, 1.6993, 0.0668, 0.0914.

▶ **Use place value to compare and order decimals.**

- Line up the decimal points.

- Compare the digits in each place, starting with the greatest place.

0.1285
1.6993
0.0668
0.0914

1 > 0
1.6993 is greatest.

0.1285
0.0668
0.0914

0 = 0 and 1 > 0
0.1285 is next greatest.

0.0668
0.0914

6 < 9
0.0668 is least.

1.6993 > 0.1285 > 0.0914 > 0.0668

In order from greatest to least, the decimals are:
1.6993, 0.1285, 0.0914, 0.0668.

From least to greatest, the decimals are:
0.0668, 0.0914, 0.1285, 1.6993.

Compare. Write <, =, or >.

1. 0.46 ? 0.39

2. 0.709 ? 0.921

3. 0.06 ? 0.60

4. 9.8 ? 9.80

5. 0.509 ? 0.510

6. 0.623 ? 0.627

7. 0.4286 ? 0.4190

8. 0.5691 ? 0.5690

9. 0.53 ? 0.536

10. 0.8 ? 0.78

11. 7.610 ? 7.61

12. 7.3 ? 7.301

13. 2.34 ? 2.3513

14. 91.42 ? 90.425

15. 0.059 ? 0.59

Write in order from greatest to least.

16. 0.75, 0.39, 0.2, 0.35

17. 0.484, 0.495, 0.523, 0.54

18. 8.63, 8.6, 8.65, 7.99

19. 9.21, 9.0, 9.2, 9.06

20. 0.5478, 0.546, 0.5462, 0.5593

21. 8.134, 8.215, 8.2152, 8.2052

Write in order from least to greatest.

22. 2.7054, 0.9832, 1.2396, 0.9276

23. 2.7993, 0.0803, 0.0779, 0.2396

24. 0.1211, 0.12, 0.121, 0.0911

25. 0.052387, 0.52386, 0.05023, 0.0523

Order the decimals in each table from greatest to least.

26.

Batting Averages	
Ira	0.278
Henry	0.302
Sam	0.099
Steve	1.000
Mario	0.525

27.

Masses of Five Objects (kilograms)	
A	0.206
B	2.7564
C	0.2
D	0.8384
E	2.76

CHALLENGE

Solve. Use mental math or paper and pencil.

28. I am a decimal. I am more than 2 tenths greater than 0.029. I am between 0.2 and 0.3. What number am I?

1-5 Round Whole Numbers and Decimals

The rules for rounding are the same for whole numbers and decimals:

- Find the place you are rounding to.

- Look at the digit to its right. If the digit *is less than 5*, round *down.* If the digit *is 5 or greater*, round *up.*

> **Remember:** Nearest cent means the hundredths place.
> 1 cent = $0.01

▶ **Round $0.2274 to the nearest cent.**

$0.2274   7 > 5

$0.23   Round up to $0.23. For decimals, drop all digits to the right of the place you are rounding to.

$0.2274 rounded to the nearest cent is $0.23.

▶ **Round 0.362834 to the nearest ten thousandths place.**

0.362834   3 < 5

0.3638   Round down to 0.3638. Drop all the digits to the right.

▶ **Round 3,181,914,536,112 to its greatest place.**

> .Think....................
> The greatest place is the trillions.

3,181,914,536,112   1 < 5

3,000,000,000,000   Round down to 3,000,000,000,000. For whole numbers, replace each digit to the right of the place you are rounding to with a zero.

▶ **Round 0.96771 to its greatest place.**

> .Think....................
> The greatest place is the tenths.

0.96771   6 > 5

1.0   Round up to 1.0.

> When you round a 9 up, it becomes a 10. You must regroup.

Round to the nearest cent.

1. $4.368
2. $5.472
3. $35.476
4. $12.525

5. $.463
6. $.085
7. $1.5971
8. $99.9943

Round each number to the underlined place.

9. 94,329
10. 17,721
11. 0.19716
12. 3.14159

13. 2.71828
14. 100.5003
15. 99.59
16. 0.66666

Round each number in the table to its greatest place.

17.

Ocean	Average Depth (feet)
Pacific	12,925
Atlantic	11,730
Indian	12,598
Arctic	3,407

18.

Continent	Area in Square Miles
Europe	3,800,000
Asia	17,200,000
Africa	11,700,000
Australia	3,071,000

Round each number to the greatest nonzero place.

19. 2.814
20. 0.69
21. 0.073
22. 0.0394

23. 68.347
24. 44.8243
25. 0.008432
26. 0.00473

Place a decimal point in each numeral so that the sentence seems reasonable. Then round the decimal to the nearest tenth.

27. Conrad rode his racing bicycle 1575 miles in an hour.

28. Maria's science test grades averaged 8945 for the month.

Problem Solving

29. A meter is approximately 39.37 inches long. To the nearest inch, how long is one meter?

30. Gasoline is priced at $2.499 per gallon. What is the price per gallon rounded to the nearest cent?

31. The weight of a bag of marshmallows is labeled 6.5 ounces. This weight is rounded to the nearest tenth of an ounce. What is the least that the actual weight could be?

32. The average distance from the sun to Earth rounded to the nearest million is about 93,000,000 miles. What is the greatest whole number that the actual distance could be?

Estimate Decimal Sums and Differences

You can use front-end estimation or rounding to estimate decimal sums.

Estimate: 1.82 + 0.29 + 0.36

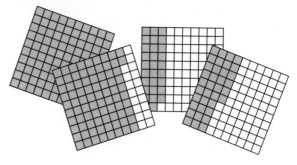

▶ **To use** front-end estimation:

- Add the front digits.

- Adjust the estimate by using the remaining digits to make 1.

  The estimated sum is 2.

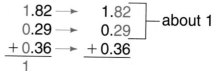

$$\begin{array}{r} 1.82 \longrightarrow \quad 1.82 \\ 0.29 \longrightarrow \quad 0.29 \\ +\,0.36 \longrightarrow +\,0.36 \\ \hline 1 \end{array} \bigg] \text{about } 1$$

Adjusted estimate: 1 + 1 = 2

▶ **To use** rounding **to estimate:**

- Round each decimal to the greatest *nonzero* place of the least number.

- Add the rounded numbers.

$$\begin{array}{r} \overset{1}{} \\ 1.82 \longrightarrow 1.8 \\ 0.29 \longrightarrow 0.3 \\ +\,0.36 \longrightarrow +\,0.4 \\ \hline 2.5 \end{array}$$

Both 2 and 2.5 are reasonable estimates of the actual sum of 2.47.

Use the same two methods to estimate differences of decimals.

▶ **Front-end Estimation**

- Subtract the front digits.

- Write zeros for the other digits in the whole-number part of the number.

$$\begin{array}{r} 93.36 \\ -\,45.09 \\ \hline \text{about } 50 \end{array}$$

▶ **Rounding**

- Round to the greatest *nonzero* place of the lesser number.

- Subtract the rounded numbers.

$$\begin{array}{r} 93.36 \longrightarrow \quad 90 \\ -\,45.09 \longrightarrow -\,50 \\ \hline \text{about } 40 \end{array}$$

Both 50 and 40 are reasonable estimates of the actual difference of 48.27.

Estimate the sum or difference. Use front-end estimation with adjustments.

1.	**2.**	**3.**	**4.**	**5.**
31.6 + 18.1	68.7 − 63.9	7.5 − 2.9	9.1 − 3.6	0.87 − 0.54

6.	**7.**	**8.**	**9.**	**10.**
0.74 − 0.15	76.67 23.89 + 69.47	16.34 44.59 + 39.07	0.66 0.7 + 0.19	0.84 0.59 + 0.8

Estimate the sum or difference by rounding.

11.	**12.**	**13.**	**14.**
18.1534 + 7.0901	4.8359 − 0.7473	0.45601 + 0.06428	4371.5902 − 127.3246

15.	**16.**	**17.**	**18.**
386,002,444 − 49,624,973	2.361912 − 0.19008	952.0667 232.608 + 351.03991	7.30267 45.37 + 0.84652

Estimate by rounding each amount to the nearest dollar.

19.	**20.**	**21.**	**22.**
$78.34 − 25.29	$156.39 45.48 + 9.87	$89.96 26.35 + 12.59	$702.66 − 55.45

Problem Solving

23. Kathleen has covered 46.75 m in the special race. About how much farther must she go to complete the 50 m race?

24. During a tour of Europe, Alfredo flew 112.5 km, 41.8 km, and 109.5 km. Estimate the total distance that Alfredo traveled.

25. Juan earned $15.63, $8.95, and $19.82 over a 3-day period. About how much did he earn?

26. About how much greater is the difference of 325.87 − 42.76 than the sum of 109.53 + 59.87? Explain how you could use estimation to get your answer.

Update your skills. See page 5.

Addition of Whole Numbers and Decimals

Mr. Kopald's class researched electric power usage in kilowatts. Three students collected the data in the table. Each calculated the total number of kilowatts used by the three appliances in a different way.

Study their computations below and decide which student has the correct answer.

Electric Power Usage	
Appliance	**Kilowatts (kW)**
Microwave oven	1.45067
Clothes dryer	4
Clock	0.00328

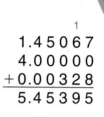

Charles

```
     1
  1.45067
  4
+  .00328
  1.85395
```

Answer: 1.85395 kW

Anetta

```
   1   1 1
  1.45067
   .00328
+        4
  1.48351
```

Answer: 1.48351 kW

Liz

```
     1
  1.45067
  4.00000
+ 0.00328
  5.45395
```

Answer: 5.45395 kW

Liz has the correct answer because she remembered to:

- Align decimal points in the addends, one underneath the other.

- Place the decimal point in a whole number to the right of the ones place and write zeros as placeholders as needed.

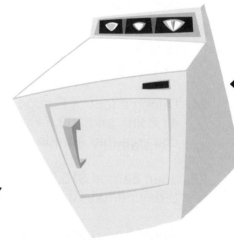

Study these examples.

Add: 53,301,089 + 1,962,752

```
    1    1 1
   53,301,089
 +  1,962,752
   55,263,841
```

Add: 5.0953 + 3.0107

```
   1 1
  5.0953
+ 3.0107
  8.106  ← You may drop the final zero.
```

Estimate using rounding. Then find the sum.

1. 7
    + 8.56

2. 6.4922
    + 15.58

3. $11,873.52
    +   4,906.09

4. 2,527,004,609
    +   38,211,073

5. 3,465,892
    + 2,396,087

6. 1.6902333
    + 0.7197807

7. 526,381,485
    + 574,626,009

8. 3,245,840,900
    +   80,059,275

9. 3.905 + 4.96

10. 0.4791 + 1.085

11. 0.10907 + 0.092

12. 0.2613 + 0.45 + 0.852

13. 0.5441 + 9.3 + 0.4637

14. 567,074 + 96,132 + 8650

15. 9,732,785 + 13,820,465

Choose the correct addends for each sum. Use estimation to help you.
Explain in your Math Journal the method you used for each exercise.

	Sum	Addends			
16.	6.0108	0.6	4.321	2.1408	3.27
17.	1.4868	0.814	0.143	0.6293	0.7145
18.	1.3861	1.2314	0.005	0.1497	1.147
19.	0.011	0.0009	0.009	0.0201	0.0011

Problem Solving

20. A businesswoman has $1123.56 in her checking account. She makes the following deposits: $23.82, $507.88, $595, $678.20. How much is in her account now?

21. The odometer on Anna's car showed | 2 2 4 5 6 . 8 |. She drove 234.7 mi. What did the odometer show then?

MENTAL MATH

Add. Explain any shortcuts that you use.

22. 186 + 324 $\overset{+14}{\longrightarrow}$ 200 + 324 = 524 $\longrightarrow$ $\overset{-14}{\longrightarrow}$ 524 − 14 = 510

23. $1.94 + $7.86 $\overset{+\$.06}{\longrightarrow}$ $2.00 + $7.86 = $9.86 $\longrightarrow$ $\overset{-\$.06}{\longrightarrow}$ $9.86 − $.06 = $9.80

24. 295 + 25

25. 1289 + 1514

26. $3.84 + $1.98 + $5.02

1-8 Subtraction of Whole Numbers and Decimals

The Panama Canal is 81.6 km long and the Suez Canal is 175.5 km long. How much longer than the Panama Canal is the Suez Canal?

First estimate by rounding.

180 − 80 = 100

Then to find how much longer, subtract: 175.5 − 81.6 = __?__

Line up the decimal points.	Subtract. Regroup if necessary.	Write the decimal point.

1 7 5.5
−   8 1.6
	0 17 4 15
	X̶ 7̶ 5̶.5̶
	− 8 1.6
	    9 3 9
		0 17 4 15
		X̶ 7̶ 5̶.5̶
		− 8 1.6
		    9 3.9

"is approximately equal to"

So the Suez Canal is 93.9 km longer than the Panama Canal.

93.9 ≈ 100
The answer is reasonable.

Study these examples.

8,309,000 − 777,625 = __?__

```
          12        9 9
     7  2  10  8  10 10 10
   8, 3  0  9 , 0  0  0
 −    7  7  7 , 6  2  5
   7, 5  3  1 , 3  7  5
```

Add to check:
7,531,375 + 777,625 = 8,309,000

The answer is reasonable.

3 − 0.7185 = __?__

```
            9  9  9
      2  10 10 10 10
   3 . 0  0  0  0      [ 3 = 3.0000 ]
 − 0 . 7  1  8  5
   2 . 2  8  1  5
```

Add to check:
2.2815 + 0.7185 = 3.0

The answer is reasonable.

Estimate by rounding. Then find the difference.

1.	0.586 − 0.492	2.	2.3004 − 0.1544	3.	$856,079 − 622,003	4.	5,034,012 − 316,948

5.	23,594,550 − 7,008,142	6.	12.80765 − 9.6153	7.	596,081,009 − 574,116,025	8.	403.0078 − 86.25

Align and estimate by rounding. Then find the difference.

9. 0.91 − 0.745

10. 0.9158 − 0.7444

11. 8 − 2.04735

12. 7,106,009 − 248,310

13. 20,700.675 − 700.775

14. 1 − 0.3856

15. $1,012,481.37 − 926,399.76

16. 5,391,602,140 − 4,387,899,000

Problem Solving

The table shows online sales totals for 2004 and 2005.
Use the table to answer exercises 17–19.

17. What is the difference in sporting goods sales from 2004 to 2005?

18. Which type of merchandise had a greater sales difference between 2004 and 2005?

19. Which year had greater total sales, 2004 or 2005? Explain how you know.

Total Online Sales: 2004 vs. 2005		
Merchandise	**2004**	**2005**
Books and Magazines	$1,961,000	$2,143,000
Music and Videos	$1,598,000	$1,733,000
Sporting Goods	$1,031,000	$1,155,000
Toys and Games	$1,321,000	$1,638,000

MENTAL MATH

Compute mentally.

20. 1286 − 1000

21. 0.98 − 0.08

22. 0.98 − 0.9

23. 14,500 − 1500

24. 7 − 0.5

25. 15.75 − 4.25

26. 0.525 − 0.5

27. 262,000 − 42,000

28. 242 − 0.75

Addition and Subtraction of Decimals

A recent survey shows the amount of liquid that the average person consumes per year: 43.7 gal of juice, 37.3 gal of water, 27.3 gal of coffee, 21.1 gal of milk, and 8.1 gal of soda. How many more gallons of juice, water, and milk were consumed than coffee and soda?

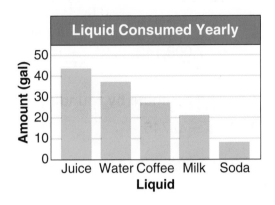

Liquid Consumed Yearly

To find how many more gallons, first add, then subtract.

First, find the amount of juice, water, and milk. Add: 43.7 + 37.3 + 21.1 = _?_

$$\begin{array}{r} {\scriptstyle 1\ 1} \\ 43.7 \\ 37.3 \\ +21.1 \\ \hline 102.1 \end{array}$$

Next, find the amount of coffee and soda. Add: 27.3 + 8.1 = _?_

$$\begin{array}{r} {\scriptstyle 1} \\ 27.3 \\ +\ \ 8.1 \\ \hline 35.4 \end{array}$$

Then find how many more gallons of juice, water, and milk were consumed than coffee and soda. Subtract: 102.1 − 35.4 = _?_

So 66.7 more gallons of juice, water, and milk were consumed than coffee and soda.

$$\begin{array}{r} {\scriptstyle 9\ \ 11} \\ {\scriptstyle 0\ \ 10\ \ 1\ \ 11} \\ \cancel{1}\ \cancel{0}\ 2.\cancel{1} \\ -\ \ 3\ 5.4 \\ \hline 6\ 6.7 \end{array}$$

Study these examples.

52.9045 + 63 + 0.7386 + 5.92 = _?_

$$\begin{array}{r} {\scriptstyle 1\,2\ \ \ 1\,1} \\ 52.9045 \\ 63.0000 \\ 0.7386 \\ +\ \ \ 5.9200 \\ \hline 122.5631 \end{array}$$

0.067 − 0.0095 = _?_

$$\begin{array}{r} {\scriptstyle 16} \\ {\scriptstyle 5\ \ 6\ \ 10} \\ 0.0\ 6\ 7\ 0 \\ -0.0\ 0\ 9\ 5 \\ \hline 0.0\ 5\ 7\ 5 \end{array}$$

Check. Change the order of the addends.

Add: 5.92 + 0.7386 + 63 + 52.9045 = 122.5631

Find the sum.

1. 3.12
      + 9.94

2. 0.51
      0.0029
      + 0.0018

3. 0.008
      0.11
      0.5
      + 0.993

4. 497.386
      + 556.22

5. 390.809
      905.5
      8.87064
      + 330.008

Find the difference.

6. $100
      − $55.99

7. 0.1
      − 0.0001

8. 412.009
      − 228.4

9. 1.2
      − 0.772

10. $50
      − 23.75

Align and add.

11. 0.67 + 39 + 7.5 + 58.22

12. 4,509.88 + 430.618 + 777.1

13. 0.49 + 0.006 + 0.213 + 0.1

14. 8.02029 + 28.98 + 617.7

15. 629.55 + 401.39201

16. 4,040 + 3,049.89 + 2057.52

Align and subtract.

17. 30 − 28.735

18. 9,002 − 4,887.56

19. 30.801 − 17.91

20. 497.1 − 437.805

21. 3,108.77 − 2,974.557

22. 1,001.1 − 802.22

Compare. Write <, =, or >.

23. 12 − 0.0009 _?_ 12 − 0.00009

24. 412.089 + 34.71 _?_ 498 − 52.075

25. 0.501 + 0.3 + 0.44993 _?_ 1.2593

26. 55.01 − 5.501 _?_ 50.001 − 0.99

Problem Solving

27. Dean bought a birthday card for $2.95. There was an additional $0.18 tax. Dean paid for his purchase using a $10 bill. How much change should Dean receive?

28. Wendy bought shoes for $39.99 and sneakers for $29.99. The tax on her purchase was $4.90. If Wendy paid using a $100 bill, what was her change?

29. Hans wants to buy 10 lb of hamburger meat for a barbecue. He picks out three packages at the supermarket. Their weights are labeled 2.73 lb, 3.2 lb, and 2.29 lb. How much more meat does Hans need?

30. Ellie gets her car's oil changed every 4,500 miles. Her last oil change was done at 33,798.7 miles. What will the odometer read when Ellie needs to get her next oil change?

Addition and Subtraction Expressions

Andie works 4.5 hours on Thursdays and 5.25 hours on Fridays. To represent the total hours she works on Thursdays and Fridays, Andie writes a numerical expression:

$4.5 + 5.25$ ← numerical expression

▶ A numerical expression is a mathematical phrase that has only numbers and operation symbols. Each of the following is a numerical expression:

$60.75 - 4$ $\quad$ $\dfrac{1}{2} + \dfrac{1}{4}$ $\quad$ $(14 - 7) + 10$ $\quad$ $3^2 + 8$

Suppose Andie decides to work on Saturdays as well, but does not know how many hours she will work. She could use a variable to represent the unknown number of hours worked on Saturdays. A variable is a symbol used to represent an unknown quantity.

To represent the total hours worked on Thursdays, Fridays, and Saturdays, Andie writes an algebraic expression:

$4.5 + 5.25 + x$ ← algebraic expression

▶ An expression that includes a variable is called an algebraic expression. Here are some examples:

$20 - a$ $\quad$ $x + 5.2$ $\quad$ $z + 10 - w$ $\qquad$ Any letter can be used as a variable.

Study these examples.

Word Phrase	Expression
sum of 1.2 and 2	$1.2 + 2$
sum of a number and 7	$n + 7$
5 *increased by* 20	$5 + 20$
x increased by 5	$x + 5$
9 *more than* 12	$12 + 9$
10 *more than* a number	$c + 10$
8 *added to* 6.5	$6.5 + 8$
a *number added* to 4	$4 + e$
3.2 *plus* a number	$3.2 + b$

Word Phrase	Expression
difference of 8 and 0.9	$8 - 0.9$
difference of *m* and 88	$m - 88$
0.5 *decreased by* 0.1	$0.5 - 0.1$
75 *decreased by* d	$75 - d$
18 *less than* 30	$30 - 18$
2 *less than* a number	$s - 2$
5.5 *subtracted from* 10	$10 - 5.5$
7 *subtracted from* t	$t - 7$
7.2 *minus* a number	$7.2 - w$

Write each word expression as a numerical expression.

1. the sum of two and seven

2. 14 less than 100

3. ten decreased by 0.5

4. 70 more than 350

Write each word expression as an algebraic expression. Use *x* as your variable.

5. the sum of a number and 45

6. 12 more than a number

7. the difference of 1 and a number

8. 13 subtracted from a number

9. a number decreased by five

10. eleven less than a number

11. a number added to sixteen

12. a number increased by fifty

13. eight more than a number

14. 45 decreased by a number

Write each mathematical expression as a word expression.

15. $100 - 5$

16. $10 - x$

17. $u + 7.99$

18. $95 + y$

19. $m - 65$

20. $35 - 18.3$

21. $7 + 8$

22. $a + 1$

23. $\$16.02 - c$

Problem Solving

Write a numerical expression or an algebraic expression to show how you would solve the problem.

24. A baby gained 0.8 pounds since its last visit to the doctor. The baby weighed 24.5 pounds at its last visit. How much does the baby weigh now, in pounds?

25. A tree grew 3.75 feet since its height was last measured. At the last measurement, the height of the tree was *h* feet. How many feet tall is the tree now?

26. A man weighs *m* pounds. The two packages he is carrying weigh 10 pounds and *d* pounds. What is the total weight, in pounds, of the two packages?

27. William earns $8.25 per hour, Suzyn earns $9.00 per hour, and Davy earns $7.50 per hour. How much more does William earn than Davy?

CRITICAL THINKING

28. A student makes a mistake and adds 140,235.97 instead of subtracting it. The incorrect answer is 3,629,817.4. What is the correct answer? Explain how you got your answer.

Evaluate Addition and Subtraction Expressions

Taylor is bowling. He knocks down some of the 10 pins.
How many pins are left standing?

10 − x ← | This algebraic expression represents the number of pins left standing.

What if Taylor knocks down 8 pins?

To determine how many pins are left standing,
evaluate the expression.

▶ To **evaluate** an algebraic expression:

- Replace the variable with a given number.
- Compute to find the value of the expression.

Evaluate 10 − x, when x = 8.

$\quad$ 10 − x ← Replace x with 8.

$\quad$ 10 − 8 ← Subtract.

$\quad\quad\downarrow$

$\quad$ 2 ← | value of expression

So the value of the expression 10 − x, when x = 8, is 2.
When 8 pins are knocked down, there are 2 pins left standing.

Study these examples.
Evaluate each expression for the given number.

w − $3.50, when w = $100

$\quad$ w $\quad$ − $\quad$ $3.50 ← Replace w with $100.

$100 − $3.50 ← Subtract.

$\quad\quad\downarrow$

$\quad$ $96.50 ← | value of expression

8 + m + p, when m = 3.54 and p = 18

8 + m + p ← Replace m with 3.54
$\quad\quad\quad\quad\quad\quad\quad\quad$ and p with 18.

8 + 3.54 + 18 ← Add.

$\quad\quad\downarrow$

$\quad\quad$ 29.54 ← | value of expression

Evaluate each expression.

1. 30.6 − 8.7

2. 18,204 − 3619

3. 16.8 + 7.5 + 30.04

4. j − 42, when j = 98

5. 300 − f, when f = 250

6. r + 9.3, when r = 1.5

Find the value of each algebraic expression when $c = 0.75$ and $d = 2.06$. Remember to work from left to right.

7. $8 + c + d$

8. $c + d + 5.5$

9. $35 - c - d$

10. $10 - c - d$

11. $c + 5.37 + d$

12. $d + 12.8 + c$

13. $5 + c - d$

14. $14.9 - c + d$

15. $d + 0.02 - c$

16. $34.09 - c - d$

Write and evaluate an expression for each situation.

17. Miguel had x dollars. He spent $16.25 of that amount. What expression represents the amount of money he has left? Evaluate the expression when $x = \$34.10$.

18. Alex scored 5 points fewer than Devon. Devon scored 14 points. What expression shows the number of points Alex scored? Evaluate the expression.

19. Let y represent the number of home runs Maddy hit last season. Brianna hit 6 more home runs than Maddy. What expression shows how many home runs Brianna hit? How many did she hit when y equals 8?

20. Elizabeth collected 38 more cans to be recycled than Evan. If Evan collected m cans, what expression shows how many cans Elizabeth collected? Evaluate the expression when m equals 87.

DO YOU REMEMBER?

Complete the sentences. Use the terms in the box.

21. An _?_ tells how many times you use the base as a factor.

22. $(3 \times 1000) + (8 \times 100) + (2 \times 1)$ is the _?_ of 3802.

23. A symbol used to represent an unknown number is a _?_ .

24. To find the nearest value of a number based on a given place, you _?_ .

25. In 10^3, 10 is called the _?_ .

26. The number 7.023 is expressed in _?_ form.

base
expanded form
exponent
round
standard
variable

Problem-Solving Strategy:
Write an Equation

On Friday, 52,200 tickets were sold for a baseball game. On Saturday, 58,400 tickets were sold. If 165,100 tickets were sold on Friday, Saturday, and Sunday in total, how many tickets were sold on Sunday?

Read

Visualize yourself in the problem above as you reread it. List the facts and the question.

Facts: tickets sold on Friday ⟶ 52,200
tickets sold on Saturday ⟶ 58,400
total tickets sold all 3 days ⟶ 165,100

Question: How many tickets were sold on Sunday?

Plan

Use the information to write an equation.

Tickets sold Friday	+	Tickets sold Saturday	+	Tickets sold Sunday	=	Total number sold all 3 days
52,200	+	58,400	+	n	=	165,100
	110,600		+	n	=	165,100 ← equation

You can solve the equation using the Guess and Test strategy or by using a related equation.

Solve

$110,600 + n = 165,100$

Try 55,000. $110,600 + 55,000 \neq 165,600$
Try 54,000. $110,600 + 54,000 \neq 164,600$
Try 54,500. $110,600 + 54,500 = 165,100$

There were 54,500 tickets sold on Sunday.

$110,600 + n = 165,100$
$n = 165,100 - 110,600$
$n = 54,500$

Check

Substitute 54,500 for the n in the equation to test whether the equation is true.

$110,600 + n = 165,100$
$110,600 + 54,500 = 154,100$ The answer checks.

Write an equation to solve each problem.

1. Burrows farm uses 450.75 acres for corn. The remaining acres are used for potatoes. If the farm has 825 acres, how many acres are used for potatoes?

Burrows Farm

 Read Visualize yourself in the problem above as you reread it. List the facts and the question.

| Corn 450.75 acres | Potatoes ? |

825 acres

Facts: 450.75 acres for corn
remaining acres for potatoes

Question: How many acres are used for potatoes?

Plan Use the information to write a number sentence.

Acres used + Acres used = total acres on
for corn   for potatoes   the farm

450.74   + p =   825

To find how many acres are used for potatoes, subtract:
825 − 450.75 = p ← number of acres for potatoes

 Solve **Check**

2. Bernice has a collection of 90 stamps from Europe and Africa. Sixty stamps are from Europe. How many stamps does she have from Africa?

3. On Monday, Ginger packed 426 boxes, Tuesday 573, and Wednesday 685. How many boxes did she pack in 3 days?

4. Frank paid $40 for a pair of shoes, $78 for a jacket, and $6.75 for a pair of socks. He chose not to buy a $32.95 shirt. After purchasing these articles he had $20.50 left. How much money did Frank have at first?

5. Carol read 120 pages of a book on Saturday. She read 45 pages on Sunday. On Monday she read the same number of pages that she read on Sunday and finished the book. How many pages does the book contain?

6. Marco earned $240 baby-sitting and put the money into his savings account. He now has $1041.17 in his account. How much was in his account to begin with?

Read ▶ Plan ▶ Solve ▶ Check

Solve each problem and explain the method you used.

1. Moki and Meg set up a model railroad. The engine of the train is 10.205 cm long. Write 10.205 in expanded form.

2. The caboose is 9.826 cm long. How long is it to the nearest hundredth of a centimeter? to the nearest tenth of a centimeter?

3. Fred connects three freight cars. The red car is 12.64 cm long, the blue car is 12.4 cm long, and the steel-colored car is 12.6 cm long. Write the lengths in order from longest to shortest.

4. Marva puts together three sections of railroad track that are 20.5 cm, 22 cm, and 9.75 cm long. How long is the section of track that Marva creates?

5. A coal car is 3.87 cm tall. A refrigerator car is 5.02 cm tall. Which car is taller? by how much?

6. Bud buys two miniature buildings for his train set. A railroad station costs $15.95 and a gas station costs $1.19 less. How much does the gas station cost?

7. Loretta buys a set of miniature trees that costs $8.59. How much change does she receive from a $20 bill?

Use the table for problems 8–10.

8. Jackson bought a freight car and a coal car at the sale. How much money did he save?

9. On which type of car do buyers save the most money during this sale?

10. Lea buys a caboose, a passenger car, and an engine on sale. Does she spend more than $26.00?

Item	Original Price	Sale Price
Engine	$11.95	$9.50
Freight Car	$ 8.95	$7.69
Passenger Car	$ 9.50	$8.55
Coal Car	$ 7.75	$6.99
Caboose	$10.29	$8.09

Use a strategy from the list or another strategy you know to solve each problem.

11. A train set has 40 six-inch-long pieces of track and 8 nine-inch-long pieces. What is the longest track you can build with this set?

12. Pam's train can travel one fourth of the track in 25.48 seconds. If the train continues at the same rate of speed, how long will it take to travel the entire track?

13. Daryll spends $6.08 for three signs for the train set. None of the signs costs the same amount, but each sign costs more than $2. What is the price of each sign?

14. Train A travels 1387.5 cm uphill at a rate of 55.5 cm per second. Train B travels 1372.5 cm downhill at a rate of 54.9 cm per second. Which train arrives at its destination first?

15. Mai builds a mountain for her train set. She uses 2.4 yd of green cloth as grass, 1.75 yd of white cloth as snow, and 0.8 yd of brown cloth as dirt roads. Does Mai use more than 4.5 yd of cloth?

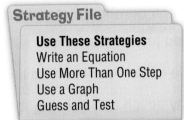

Strategy File

Use These Strategies
Write an Equation
Use More Than One Step
Use a Graph
Guess and Test

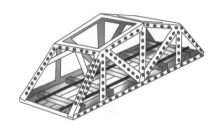

Use the graph for problems 16–19.

16. About how many minutes of travel time is the State Capital Tour?

17. About how many minutes of travel time should Kim allow if she is taking the Rush Hour Express and then going on the Park Nature Tour?

18. About how many more minutes of travel time will Theresa spend on the River Valley Tour than Bob will spend on the Beach Getaway?

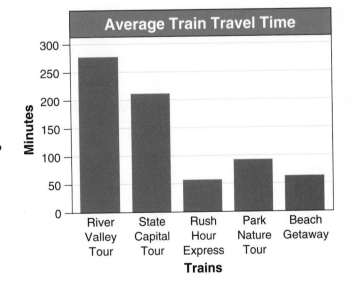

Average Train Travel Time

19. Make up a problem using the bar graph data. Have a classmate solve it.

Write each number in standard form. *(See pp. 34–35)*

1. three ten thousandths

2. nine trillion, four hundred thousand, twenty

3. sixty-seven and sixty-eight millionths

Write each number in expanded form using exponents. *(See pp. 36–39)*

4. four and eighty-three thousandths

5. 200,070,040,333

6. 734

7. 329,050

8. 24,082,006

Write in order from greatest to least. *(See pp. 40–41)*

9. 0.3014; 3.014; 0.0314; 0.314

10. 0.031289; 3.001289; 33.1289

Round each number to its underlined place. *(See pp. 42–43)*

11. 6,7<u>4</u>5,199

12. 399.<u>9</u>7022

13. 11,<u>5</u>42,391.956

Estimate. Use front-end estimation with adjustments. Then use rounding. *(See pp. 44–45)*

14. $3.45 + 6 + 1.02$

15. $39.28 + 46.91 + 12.24$

16. $98 - 44.01$

Add or subtract. *(See pp. 46–51)*

17. $0.97 - 0.426$

18. $\$500.58 - \$3.79$

19. $99.0152 + 400 + 3.9848$

Write each as an algebraic expression. Use n as your variable. *(See pp. 52–53)*

20. 8 more than a number

21. a number decreased by 200

Evaluate each expression. *(See pp. 54–55)*

22. $y - 52$, for $y = 96$

23. $17.96 + m$, for $m = 50.42$

Problem Solving

(See pp. 56–59)

24. Dana worked for 7 hours on Thursday, 8 hours on Friday, and 4 hours on Saturday. She is scheduled to work 20 hours next week. How many hours did she work this week?

25. Yousif paid $38.55 for cable and $62.37 for electricity. He also wrote a check to the phone company. If he paid a total of $157.41, how much did he pay to the phone company?

(See *Still More Practice*, p. 521.)

Roman Numerals

The ancient Romans used the symbols given below to represent numerals.

Symbol	I	V	X	L	C	D	M
Value	1	5	10	50	100	500	1000

All other numerals are represented through combinations of these seven different symbols.

▶ **Rules for Forming Roman Numerals**

- No symbol, except for M, is repeated more than three times in a row.

- When a symbol is followed by a symbol with an equal or lesser value, **add** the values of the symbols.

  XX = 10 + 10 = 20   **CCC** = 100 + 100 + 100 = 300
  DC = 500 + 100 = 600   **MD** = 1000 + 500 = 1500

- When a symbol is followed by a symbol with a greater value, **subtract** the lesser value from the greater value.

  IX = 10 − 1 = 9   **XL** = 50 − 10 = 40
  XC = 100 − 10 = 90   **CM** = 1000 − 100 = 900

- Only subtract powers of ten (I, X, or C, but not V or L). For the numeral 95, do NOT write VC (100 − 5). Do write XCV (XC + V or 90 + 5).

- Sometimes you must add *and* subtract.

  MCMIV = 1000 + (1000 − 100) + (5 − 1) = 1904
  CMLX = (1000 − 100) + (50 + 10) = 960

> .Think...
> Roman numerals I, X, and C are powers of ten.
> $I = 10^0$ $X = 10^1$
> $C = 10^2$

Write each as a standard numeral.

1. CL

2. XXXIX

3. MM

4. CDIX

5. CMXC

6. LXVI

7. MCMXCV

8. MCLV

Write the Roman numeral for each.

9. 127

10. 1914

11. 4300

12. 6320

Chapter I Test

Write each number in expanded form two ways.

1. 46,000,000

2. eight thousand, eighty and eighty-three millionths

Write each number in standard form.

3. 10^5

4. $(2 \times 10^3) + (5 \times 10^2) + (4 \times 10^0) + (9 \times 10^{-2})$

Write in order from least to greatest.

5. 0.7968; 0.7000; 0.7909

6. 1.058; 1.0058; 10.0058

Round each number to its greatest place.

7. 3,429,099

8. 0.96153301

9. 954,313.8701

**Estimate using front-end estimation with adjustments.
Then find the sum or difference.**

10. 1229.13 + 756 + 3890.88

11. 1,007,291 − 2,364.065

Write each as an algebraic expression. Use _y_ as your variable.

12. 24 more than a number

13. a number decreased by 7000

Evaluate each expression.

14. $y - 14$, when $y = 32$

15. 3851.26 + m, when $m = 5257.74$

Problem Solving

*Use a strategy or strategies you
have learned.*

16. Abbey scores 9.985, 8.895, 9.110, and
9.65 in four gymnastics events. A perfect
score is 40.00. How many more points
would Abbey have needed to receive a
perfect score?

Tell About It

17. On Thursday, 30,861 people attended
the baseball game. On Friday, 60,192
people attended. On Saturday 30,100
more people attended the game than
on Thursday. On which day did more
people attend the baseball game:
Friday or Saturday? Explain.

Performance Assessment

**Tell which estimation strategy produces an estimate
closer to the actual answer. Explain why.**

18. 9.585 + 36.42 + 7.75

19. 6,207,198 − 4,582,311

Choose the best answer.

1. In 136,299,426.10758 which digit is in the ten thousandths place?

    a. 1   **b.** 5
    c. 7   **d.** 8

2. Which is ordered from least to greatest?

    a. 2.47280; 0.204728; 0.024728
    b. 0.024728; 0.204728; 2.47280
    c. 0.024728; 2.47280; 0.204728
    d. none of these

3. Estimate. Round to the greatest place.

    492,488
    241,630
  + 352,701

    a. 900,000
    b. 1,000,000
    c. 1,100,000
    d. 1,200,000

4. Choose the algebraic expression.

A number plus 4

    a. $m - 4$ **b.** $4 - m$
    c. $m + 4$ **d.** none of these

5. Choose the standard form.

thirty-two billion, seven million, forty-five thousand, six

    a. 32,007,045,006
    b. 320,007,045,006
    c. 32,000,007,045,006
    d. 32,007,000,045,006

6. Subtract.

7,204,819 − 834,605

    a. 6,360,214   **b.** 6,370,214
    c. 7,470,214   **d.** 8,039,424

7. Add.

13,492,488.068 + 306 + 247.00195

    a. 6,879,268.3068
    b. 13,491,935.05
    c. 13,493,041.06995
    d. 13,517,188.569

8. Choose the standard form.

10^5

    a. 10,000
    b. 100,000
    c. 1,000,000
    d. 10,000,000

9. Name the place of the underlined digit.

3,821.00304̲6

    a. hundred thousandths
    b. ten thousandths
    c. ten thousands
    d. hundred thousands

10. Choose the standard form.

$(3 \times 10^4) + (7 \times 10^1) + (5 \times 10^0)$

    a. 370   **b.** 375
    c. 30,705   **d.** 30,075

11. Choose the correct value for the evaluated expression.

$10 - p$, when $p = 4.9$

    a. 4.9
    b. 5
    c. 5.1
    d. 14.9

12. Choose the standard form.

$(8 \times 10^8) + (4 \times 10^5) + (7 \times 10^4) + (2 \times 10^2) + (9 \times 10^1) + (8 \times 10^{-2})$

    a. 800,470,290.8   **b.** 800,470,290.08
    c. 80,470,290.8   **d.** 80,470,290.08

13. Which is ordered from greatest to least?

    a. 3.068; 0.3068; 36.068; 0.0368
    b. 0.0368; 36.068; 0.3068; 3.068
    c. 36.068; 0.0368; 0.3068; 3.068
    d. 36.068; 3.068; 0.3068; 0.0368

14. Choose correct value for the evaluated expression.

$482 + r$, when $r = 64$

    a. 418   **b.** 546
    c. 560   **d.** none of these

15. Choose the standard form.

$(5 \times 10^5) + (4 \times 10^0)$

    a. 5004   **b.** 50,004
    c. 50,040   **d.** 500,004

16. Which is the correct expanded form?

300.7005

    a. $(3 \times 10) + (7 \times 1) + (5 \times 1000)$
    b. $(3 \times 10) + (7 \times 0.1) + (5 \times 0.001)$
    c. $(3 \times 100) + (7 \times 10) + (5 \times 0.005)$
    d. $(3 \times 100) + (7 \times 0.1) + (5 \times 0.0001)$

17. Add.

$3.35 + $0.86 + 7.00

    a. $4.28   **b.** $10.11
    c. $11.20   **d.** $11.21

18. Which statement is true?

    a. $1.025 > 10.25$ **b.** $10.205 < 10.025$
    c. $10.25 = 10.250$ **d.** $10.205 = 10.025$

19. Choose the algebraic expression.

15 less than a number

    a. $15 + m$ **b.** $15 - m$
    c. $m - 15$ **d.** none of these

20. Estimate. Use front-end estimation with adjustments.

    8.035
    2.862
    + 4.311

    a. 13   **b.** 14
    c. 15   **d.** 16

21. Round 0.874 to its greatest place.

    a. 1.0   **b.** 0.9
    c. 0.8   **d.** 0.7

22. Name the place of the underlined digit.

9,0<u>2</u>1,488,107,035

    a. hundred billions
    b. hundred millions
    c. ten billions
    d. ten millions

23. Choose the word form.

40.044

    a. forty and forty-four millionths
    b. forty and forty-four hundredths
    c. forty and forty-four thousandths
    d. four hundred forty-four

24. What is the value of 9 in 2,192,435,471?

    a. 9,000,000,000   **b.** 900,000,000
    c. 90,000,000   **d.** 9,000,000

Explain how you solved each problem. Show all of your work.

25. Argentina has an area of 1,068,296 square miles. Brazil has an area of 8,511,965 square kilometers. India has an area of 1,296,338 square miles. How much greater is the area of India than the area of Argentina?

26. Hillside Golf Club used 37,628 golf balls last summer. Indian Springs Golf Club only used 13,629 golf balls. About how many did both clubs use?

Multiplication: Whole Numbers and Decimals

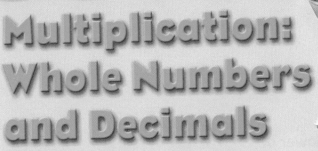

The Old Math. One.

If a train leaves Union Station, in Chicago, at eight in the morning carrying three thousand dozen gross of dark almond bark and travels the average speed of fifty-seven miles per hour for one day, then c o l l i d e s with a train that left San Francisco one day earlier full of fifteen hundred dozen bite-sized chocolate puppies, how many days will the residents of Left Foothills, Colorado, have to spend in the high school gym while the National Guard, the Environmental Protection Agency, and the local sheriff's department remove the worst bite-sized bark bits (or the worst bark-sized bite bits) and return the area to its former habitable condition?

Arnold Adoff

In this chapter you will:

Discover patterns in multiplication
Estimate products
Learn about exponents,
   scientific notation, and square roots
Solve problems by using simpler numbers

Critical Thinking/Finding Together

Our product is less than 1125 and our sum is 64. What two 2-digit numbers are we?

Multiplication Patterns

You can use patterns to multiply by powers and multiples of 10.

▶ **To multiply a whole number by a power or multiple of 10:**

- Multiply the nonzero digits in the factors.

- Write one zero to the right of the product for each zero in the factor or factors.

| nonzero digits |

$1 \times 34 = 34$
$10 \times 34 = 340$
$100 \times 34 = 3400$
$1000 \times 34 = 34{,}000$

$35 \times 2 = 70$
$35 \times 20 = 700$
$35 \times 200 = 7000$
$35 \times 2000 = 70{,}000$

Power of 10:
$10^1 = 10$
$10^2 = 100$
$10^3 = 1000$, and so on.

Multiple of 10:
$10 \times 1 = 10$
$10 \times 2 = 20$
$10 \times 3 = 30$, and so on.

$6 \times 5 = 30$
$60 \times 50 = 3000$
$600 \times 500 = 300{,}000$
$6000 \times 5000 = 30{,}000{,}000$

▶ **To multiply a decimal by 10, 100, or 1000:**

- Count the number of zeros in the multiplier.

- Move the decimal point in the multiplicand to the *right* one place for each zero.

- Write as many zeros in the product as needed to place the decimal point correctly.

0.07 ← multiplicand
$\times\ 1000$ ← multiplier with 3 zeros
0.070. ← 3 places to the right
Write 1 zero.

Study these examples.

$10 \times 0.56 = 5.6$ — 1 zero: Move 1 place to the right.

$100 \times 0.004 = 0.4$ — 2 zeros: Move 2 places to the right.

$1000 \times 2.003 = 2003$ — 3 zeros: Move 3 places to the right.

$100 \times 0.80 = 80$ — 2 zeros: Move 2 places to the right. Write 1 zero as a placeholder.

$1000 \times 15.800 = 15{,}800$ — 3 zeros: Move 3 places to the right. Write 2 zeros as placeholders.

Multiply.

1. 10×77 **2.** 30×40 **3.** 10×0.5 **4.** 10×0.0049

5. 100×13 **6.** 400×125 **7.** 100×0.7 **8.** 100×0.1003

9. 20×51 **10.** 5000×30 **11.** $10,000 \times 0.02$ **12.** $20,000 \times 0.02$

13. 3000×50.123 **14.** 4000×22 **15.** 100×19.41 **16.** 1000×12.0006

Find the products. Then write them in order from least to greatest.

17. a. 10×94 **b.** 100×930 **c.** 1000×92

18. a. 100×0.05 **b.** 10×0.7 **c.** 1000×0.94

19. a. 1000×0.0062 **b.** 100×0.005 **c.** 10×0.042

20. a. 100×0.61 **b.** 100×0.70 **c.** 1000×0.0010

Find the missing factor.

21. $b \times 45 = 900$ **22.** $y \times 96 = 9600$ **23.** $300 \times a = 5100$

24. $n \times 2.06 = 206$ **25.** $1000 \times y = 8.77$ **26.** $10 \times m = 0.02$

27. $48.21 \times t = 48,210$ **28.** $200 \times p = 70,000$ **29.** $g \times 40 = 20,000$

Problem Solving

30. Hesperoyucca whipplei is a plant that can grow 0.857 ft in one day. At that rate, how much taller is it after 100 days than after 10 days?

31. The largest tomato ever grown had a mass of 1.9 kg. The largest cabbage had a mass of 51.8 kg. Which mass is greater: 100 of those tomatoes or 10 of those cabbages?

Write Your Own

32. Explain in your Math Journal.

    a. What happens to a whole number such as 2300 when it is multiplied by 10, 100, and 1000?

    b. What happens to a decimal such as 0.42 when it is multiplied by 10, 100, and 1000?

Estimate Products

A long time ago, the land an ox could plow in a day was called an "acre." Today, an acre is defined as 4840 square yards. Andy says that an ox could plow 1,766,600 square yards in a year. Is Andy's statement reasonable?

Use estimation to find an approximate answer or to determine if an exact answer is reasonable.

▶ **To estimate a product by rounding:**

- Round each factor to its greatest place.
- Multiply the rounded factors.

Estimate: 365×4840

$400 \times 5000 = 2,000,000$ square yards

2,000,000 is close to 1,766,600. Andy's statement is reasonable.

Study these examples.

Estimate: 47×18

$50 \times 20 = 1000$

$47 \times 18 \approx 1000$

Both factors are rounded up. The actual product *is less than* 1000.

Estimate: 3.42×53

$3 \times 50 = 150$

$3.42 \times 53 \approx 150$

Both factors are rounded down. The actual product *is greater than* 150.

Estimate: 10.25×0.87

$10 \times 0.9 = 9$

$10.25 \times 0.87 \approx 9$

One factor is rounded down and the other is rounded up. The actual product *is close to* 10.

Estimate each product by rounding. Tell whether the actual product
is greater than, *is less than*, or *is close to* the estimated product.

1. $\begin{array}{r} 95 \\ \times\ 67 \\ \hline \end{array}$

2. $\begin{array}{r} 491 \\ \times\ 52 \\ \hline \end{array}$

3. $\begin{array}{r} 4.45 \\ \times\ 62 \\ \hline \end{array}$

4. $\begin{array}{r} 9.42 \\ \times\ 74 \\ \hline \end{array}$

Practice

Estimate the product.

5. 335
   × 129

6. 824
   × 617

7. 925
   × 376

8. 5847
   × 219

9. 7932
   × 324

10. $44.25
    × 142

11. $53.38
    × 319

12. $847.69
    × 293

13. $795.20
    × 498

14. 10.6 × 23

15. 5.52 × 1.78

16. 0.9 × 13.6

17. 137 × 2.85

18. 6235 × 3.7

19. 2.8 × 31.89

20. 3.2 × 14.79

21. 0.7 × 103.95

22. 10.7 × 2.9 × 28.04

23. 1.5 × 2.8 × 12.1

24. 4.3 × 18.07 × 1.79

25. 3.54 × 13.9 × 428

26. 19.45 × 24 × 2.3

27. 7.81 × 67.19 × 112

Estimate to compare. Write <, =, or >.

28. 679 × 325 _?_ 679 × 425

29. 7976 × 853 _?_ 7976 × 753

30. 225 × 1125 _?_ 425 × 1300

31. 9651 × 438 _?_ 438 × 9651

32. 31 × 239 _?_ 327 × 24

33. 3618 × 2431 _?_ 3299 × 2514

Problem Solving

34. Volunteers set up two sections of seating for a concert. The first section has 44 rows of 16 seats. The second section has 25 rows of 14 seats. About how many seats are set up altogether?

35. Two numbers, each rounded to the nearest ten, have a product of 800. What are two possible numbers?

MENTAL MATH

Estimate by rounding *one* factor to the nearest 10, 100, or 1000.

36. 9.7 × 0.672

37. 10.2 × 5.6

38. 100.8 × 0.8

39. 96 × 1.235

40. 122 × 4.125

41. 10.3 × 17.7

42. 96 × 0.837

43. 997 × 14.5

Multiply Whole Numbers

When multiplying by a number with a zero, you may save a step by omitting a partial product.

Multiply: $620 \times 372 = n$

First estimate by rounding: $600 \times 400 = 240,000$

Then multiply 620×372.

Long Way

```
      3 7 2
    × 6 2 0
      0 0 0  ←—— 0 × 372      Omit this
    7 4 4 0  ←—— 20 × 372     partial
+ 2 2 3 2 0 0 ←— 600 × 372    product.
  2 3 0,6 4 0
```

Short Way

```
      3 7 2
    × 6 2 0
    7 4 4 0  ←— Align partial
+ 2 2 3 2        products by
  2 3 0,6 4 0    place value.
```

The product is 230,640.

Think
230,640 is close to the estimate of 240,000.

Change the order of the factors to check your answer.

```
      6 2 0
    × 3 7 2
    1 2 4 0
    4 3 4 0 0
+ 1 8 6 0 0 0
  2 3 0,6 4 0
```

► You may use the Distributive Property to help find products of larger numbers.

$902 \times 41,736 = (900 + 2) \times 41,736$

$= (900 \times 41,736) + (2 \times 41,736)$

$= 37,562,400 + 83,472$

$= 37,645,872$

Remember: You do not need to multiply by 0 tens.

Practice

Estimate the product by rounding. Then multiply.

1. 237 × 380	**2.** 593 × 506	**3.** 817 × 609	**4.** 385 × 806	**5.** 2365 × 580	**6.** 6549 × 302

Estimate by rounding. Then find each product.

7. 403 × 585

8. 209 × 791

9. 601 × 482

10. 830 × 793

11. 740 × 5565

12. 310 × 1893

13. 240 × 3548

14. 902 × 6071

15. 4003 × 4203

Use the Distributive Property to compute.

16. 506 × 831

17. 780 × 311

18. 470 × 1211

19. 209 × 4921

20. 640 × 39,215

21. 640 × 390,215

22. In exercise 17, were you able to multiply 780 by 311 mentally? Explain how you can use the Distributive Property and mental math to find the product.

Problem Solving

23. There are 375 audience tickets available for each taping of the Win It All game show. If 204 shows are taped each year, how many tickets are there in all?

24. The producers of Win It All hand out 150 contestant applications for 204 shows. Did the producers hand out more or less than 30,000 applications?

TEST PREPARATION

25. Lydia has displayed her entire stamp collection in two 100-page books. She has filled each page of the books with 25 stamps. How many stamps does she have in her collection?

A 250   **B** 500   **C** 2500   **D** 5000

Multiply with Decimals

Mariko exchanged American dollars for British pounds. If she had $48, and the exchange rate was 0.68 pounds for each dollar, how many pounds did she receive?

To find the number of pounds, *n*, multiply: $48 \times 0.68 = n$.

First estimate by rounding: 48 × 0.68.

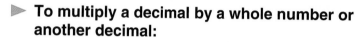

$$50 \times 0.7 = 35$$

Then multiply.

▶ **To multiply a decimal by a whole number or another decimal:**

- Multiply as you would with whole numbers.

- Count the number of decimal places in both factors.

- Mark off the *same number* of decimal places in the product.

Multiply as with whole numbers.

```
    0.6 8
  ×   4 8
    5 4 4
  + 2 7 2
    3 2 6 4
```

Write the decimal point in the product.

```
    0.6 8 ◄
  ×   4 8
    5 4 4        2 decimal places
  + 2 7 2
    3 2.6 4 ◄
```

Mariko received 32.64 pounds.

.....Think.....
32.64 is close to the estimate of 35.

Study these examples.

```
    0.3 2 9   ◄ 3 decimal places
  ×     0.0 2 ◄ 2 decimal places
  0.0 0 6 5 8   5 decimal places
                Write 2 zeros.
```

```
    $ 7 2.2 5  ◄ 2 decimal places
  ×       0.7 5 ◄ 2 decimal places
      3 6 1 2 5
  +   5 0 5 7 5
    $ 5 4.1 8 7 5 ◄ 4 decimal places
```

$54.1875 rounded to the nearest cent is $54.19.

Write the decimal point in each product.

1.
$$\begin{array}{r} 5.9 \\ \times 3 \\ \hline 1\ 7\ 7 \end{array}$$

2.
$$\begin{array}{r} 0.2\ 3\ 5 \\ \times 7 \\ \hline 1\ 6\ 4\ 5 \end{array}$$

3.
$$\begin{array}{r} 9.2\ 7 \\ \times 1.5 \\ \hline 1\ 3\ 9\ 0\ 5 \end{array}$$

4.
$$\begin{array}{r} 0.4\ 6\ 3 \\ \times 0.2\ 2\ 6 \\ \hline 0\ 1\ 0\ 4\ 6\ 3\ 8 \end{array}$$

5.
$$\begin{array}{r} 1\ 2.9\ 2 \\ \times 0.7 \\ \hline 9\ 0\ 4\ 4 \end{array}$$

Multiply. Round to the nearest cent when necessary.

6.
$$\begin{array}{r} 0.9 \\ \times 22 \end{array}$$

7.
$$\begin{array}{r} 0.7 \\ \times 79 \end{array}$$

8.
$$\begin{array}{r} 0.59 \\ \times 43 \end{array}$$

9.
$$\begin{array}{r} 0.47 \\ \times 21 \end{array}$$

10.
$$\begin{array}{r} 0.32 \\ \times 73 \end{array}$$

11.
$$\begin{array}{r} 0.43 \\ \times 0.19 \end{array}$$

12.
$$\begin{array}{r} 0.61 \\ \times 0.93 \end{array}$$

13.
$$\begin{array}{r} 0.163 \\ \times 0.03 \end{array}$$

14.
$$\begin{array}{r} 0.911 \\ \times 9.11 \end{array}$$

15.
$$\begin{array}{r} 0.414 \\ \times 0.72 \end{array}$$

16.
$$\begin{array}{r} 13.5 \\ \times 9.2 \end{array}$$

17.
$$\begin{array}{r} 0.20 \\ \times 9.1 \end{array}$$

18.
$$\begin{array}{r} \$8.05 \\ \times 1.9 \end{array}$$

19.
$$\begin{array}{r} \$9.20 \\ \times 4.5 \end{array}$$

20.
$$\begin{array}{r} \$10.50 \\ \times 8 \end{array}$$

21. $59.50 \times 2.4

22. 8.5×0.6

23. 4.12×1.8

24. 8.74×3.15

25. $9 \times \$56.95$

26. 1.5×8.00

27. 6.2×9.5

28. $4.75 \times \$85$

29. $2.3 \times 0.2 \times 5.1$

30. $12.3 \times 0.9 \times 0.8$

31. $2.7 \times 19.5 \times 0.5$

Use estimation to check the products. Correct unreasonable products.

32. $0.8 \times 0.817 \stackrel{?}{=} 65.36$

33. $4.7 \times 2.6 \stackrel{?}{=} 12.22$

34. $6.4 \times 0.8 \stackrel{?}{=} 51.2$

35. $4.8 \times 15.94 \stackrel{?}{=} 7.6512$

36. $6.6 \times 48.3 \stackrel{?}{=} 31.878$

37. $0.94 \times 5.8 \stackrel{?}{=} 5.452$

Problem Solving

38. Which costs more, 7 lb of beef at $3.25 per pound or 12 lb of chicken at $1.79 per pound? How much more?

39. Sadie hiked 37.6 km. Sam hiked 0.4 as far. How much farther than Sam did Sadie hike?

MENTAL MATH — Algebra

Find the missing factor.

40. $500 \times n = 50{,}000$

41. $9000 \times s = 900{,}000$

42. $10 \times r = 30{,}000$

43. $w \times 0.004 = 0.4$

44. $t \times 0.21 = 210$

45. $100 \times h = 5$

Exponents

An exponent is used to express a number that is a product of factors that are the same.

Remember: An *exponent* tells how many times to use the *base* as a factor.

$2^0 = 1$

$2^1 = 2$

$2^2 = 2 \times 2 = 4$

$2^3 = 2 \times 2 \times 2 = 8$

$2^4 = 2 \times 2 \times 2 \times 2 = 16$

$2^5 = 2 \times 2 \times 2 \times 2 \times 2 = 32$

$2^6 = 2 \times 2 \times 2 \times 2 \times 2 \times 2 = 64$

$2^7 = 2 \times 2 \times 2 \times 2 \times 2 \times 2 \times 2 = 128$

$2^8 = 2 \times 2 \times 2 \times 2 \times 2 \times 2 \times 2 \times 2 = 256$

exponent

$2^6 = 2 \times 2 \times 2 \times 2 \times 2 \times 2$

base

Read 2^6 as:
"two to the sixth power," or
"the sixth power of two."

Study these examples.

$$4^2 = 4 \times 4$$

$$4^2 = 16$$

exponential form   standard form

Read 4^2 as:
"four squared,"
"four to the second power," or
"the second power of four."

$$5^3 = 5 \times 5 \times 5$$

$$5^3 = 125$$

exponential form   standard form

Read 5^3 as:
"five cubed,"
"five to the third power," or
"the third power of five."

Write each product in exponential form.

1. $7 \times 7 \times 7 \times 7$

2. $3 \times 3 \times 3 \times 3 \times 3$

3. $9 \times 9 \times 9$

4. 11×11

5. $15 \times 15 \times 15 \times 15$

6. $100 \times 100 \times 100$

7. $8 \times 8 \times 8 \times 8 \times 8 \times 8$

8. $6 \times 6 \times 6 \times 6 \times 6 \times 6 \times 6 \times 6$

9. $2 \times 2 \times 2 \times 2 \times 2 \times 2 \times 2$

10. $5 \times 5 \times 5 \times 5 \times 5$

Write the standard form for each.

11. 3^1 **12.** 2^7 **13.** 7^3 **14.** 6^5 **15.** 9^4

16. 8^2 **17.** 10^5 **18.** 4^4 **19.** 5^0 **20.** 13^2

21. 6^2 **22.** 4^3 **23.** 1^7 **24.** 25^1 **25.** 7^0

26. 3^5 **27.** 5^4 **28.** 12^2 **29.** 1^5 **30.** 9^3

31. 2 to the 6th power   **32.** the square of 21   **33.** 19 cubed   **34.** the 5th power of 3

Write the missing exponents.

35. $7^n = 49$ **36.** $3^x = 27$ **37.** $9^d = 81$ **38.** $11^w = 121$ **39.** $5^t = 125$

40. $2^y = 32$ **41.** $10^n = 1000$ **42.** $4^n = 64$ **43.** $6^a = 36$ **44.** $8^x = 1$

Compare. Write <, =, or >.

45. 6^3 _?_ 3^4 **46.** 9^1 _?_ 3^2 **47.** 10^3 _?_ 5^5 **48.** 2^4 _?_ 4^2

49. 4^4 _?_ 10^2 **50.** 8^2 _?_ 4^3 **51.** 8^3 _?_ 16^2 **52.** 17^0 _?_ 2^1

53. 1^4 _?_ $1 + 1 + 1 + 1$ **54.** 5^2 _?_ $5 + 5 + 5 + 5 + 5$

Problem Solving

55. Cole puts pennies in a jar for 9 days. He puts in 2^1 pennies the first day, 2^2 pennies the second day, 2^3 pennies the third day, and so on. If he continues this pattern, how many more pennies would Cole put in on the ninth day than on the fifth day?

56. The librarian puts away 6^3 books on shelves. He divides the books evenly among 2^3 shelves. How many books does the librarian put away? On to how many shelves does he put them?

CRITICAL THINKING — Algebra

Find the missing exponent.

57. $9^2 = 3^z$ **58.** $16^1 = 4^m$ **59.** $1^3 = 256^t$ **60.** $5^c = 25^2$

61. $3^0 = 27^r$ **62.** $3^a = 9^1$ **63.** $9^x = 3^8$ **64.** $2^k = 4^4$

Scientific Notation

Scientists use scientific notation as a more compact and useful way to write very large or very small numbers.

The Sun is about 93,000,000 miles from Earth.

▶ To write a number in scientific notation, express it as a *product* of two factors:

- One factor is a number greater than or equal to 1, but less than 10.

- The other factor is a power of 10, such as 10^2, 10^3, and so on.

Write 93,000,000 in scientific notation.

- Move the decimal point to the *left* to get a number greater than or equal to 1, but less than 10.

$9.3000000.$

- Count the number of places the decimal point is moved. This is the power of ten.

7 places moved.
The power of 10 is 10^7.

- Drop the zeros to the right of the decimal. Express the number as a product of the factors.

9.3×10^7 ◀— power of 10

number ≥ 1, but < 10

In scientific notation, $93,000,000 = 9.3 \times 10^7$.

"greater than or equal to"

Study these examples.

$185,000 = 1.85000. = 1.85 \times 10^5$

number ≥ 1, but < 10

power of 10

$4,064,000 = 4.064000. = 4.064 \times 10^6$

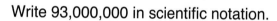

Write in scientific notation.

1. 350,000   **2.** 475,000   **3.** 2,500,000   **4.** 1,360,000

5. 87,000   **6.** 82,000,000   **7.** 25,500,000   **8.** 477,000,000

9. 205,000   **10.** 7,050,000   **11.** 100,000,000   **12.** 9,000,000,000

Practice

Scientific Notation to Standard Form

Scientific Notation	*Standard Form*	

$3.6 \times 10^3 = 3.600 = 3600$ — To multiply by 10^3, move the decimal point 3 places to the right.

$9.07 \times 10^4 = 9.0700 = 90{,}700$ — To multiply by 10^4, move the decimal point 4 places to the right.

Write in standard form.

13. 3×10^2 **14.** 8×10^3 **15.** 3.5×10^3 **16.** 3.8×10^4

17. 4.04×10^5 **18.** 1.77×10^6 **19.** 4.015×10^5 **20.** 6×10^8

21. 2.65×10^4 **22.** 2.165×10^6 **23.** 4.323×10^5 **24.** 8.743×10^8

DO YOU REMEMBER?

Complete each sentence. Use the terms in the box.

25. In 4^6, 4 is called the __?__ .

26. The $\approx$ symbol means __?__ .

27. To __?__ an algebraic expression, replace the variable with a given number, then compute.

28. An expression that includes a variable is called a(n) __?__ .

> algebraic expression
> approximately equal to
> base
> evaluate
> exponent
> numerical expression

Problem-Solving Strategy: Use Simpler Numbers

A scientist conducted a series of experiments with a liter of polluted water. At the beginning of the experiment, the pollutants reached a volume of 13.17 cubic centimeters (cm^3). Over the next two weeks there was a decrease of 2.08 cm^3 and then an increase of 1.19 cm^3. What was the volume of pollutants after two weeks?

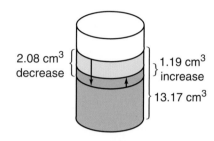

2.08 cm^3 decrease
1.19 cm^3 increase
13.17 cm^3

Read ▶ Visualize yourself in the problem above as you reread it. List the facts and the question.

Facts: 13.17 cm^3 at the beginning
2.08 cm^3 decrease
1.19 cm^3 increase

Question: What was the volume of pollutants after two weeks?

Plan ▶ Substitute simpler numbers to help you choose the operation(s) to use.

13.17 cm^3 ⟶ 13   2.08 cm^3 ⟶ 2   1.19 cm^3 ⟶ 1

Start with 13. Subtract the amount of the decrease, 2.
Then add the amount of the increase, 1.

$13 - 2 = 11$ cm^3 $11 + 1 = 12$ cm^3

Solve ▶ Now solve the problem using the actual numbers.

$$13.17 \text{ cm}^3 - 2.08 \text{ cm}^3 = 11.09 \text{ cm}^3$$
$$11.09 \text{ cm}^3 + 1.19 \text{ cm}^3 = 12.28 \text{ cm}^3$$

After two weeks the volume of pollutants was 12.28 cm^3.

Check ▶ Work backward to check the answer.

amount increased   original amount

$(12.28 \text{ cm}^3 - 1.19 \text{ cm}) + 2.08 \text{ cm}^3 = 13.17 \text{ cm}^3$

amount after 2 weeks   amount decreased

The answer checks.

Solve. Use simpler numbers to help you decide what to do.

1. Eva had $164.37 in her bank account on September 1. She has since made four withdrawals of $18.50 and two withdrawals of $14.25. She has also deposited a check for $76.18. How much is in her account now?

 Read Visualize yourself in the problem above as you reread it. List the facts and the question.

Facts: in her account — $164.37
withdrawals — 4 × $18.50; 2 × $14.25
deposits — $76.18

Question: How much is in her account now?

 Plan Substitute simpler numbers.

$164.37 ⟶ $160 $18.50 ⟶ $20
$14.25 ⟶ $10 $76.18 ⟶ $80

(4 × $20) + (2 × $10) ⟶ $80 + $20 = $100 *amount withdrawn*
$160 − $100 = $60 *balance after withdrawals*
$60 + $80 = $140 *balance plus the deposit*

So there is about $140 in Eva's account now.

Now solve the problem using the actual numbers.

 Solve **Check**

2. A manufacturer makes a certain machine part that measures 26.4 cm in length. A part will pass inspection if it is no more than 0.04 cm shorter than 26.4 cm or no more than 0.04 cm longer than 26.4 cm. What is the shortest measure that can pass inspection?

3. Andy owed Lynn $35.50. He paid back $20.75 but borrowed $5 more. Then he borrowed $8.50. When he was paid, he gave her $25. How much money does Andy still owe Lynn?

4. Ryan earned $122.75 baby-sitting. Vinnie earned $37.15 more than that. Sharon earned $70.95 less than Vinnie. How much money did Sharon earn?

5. Craig is on the school track team. He practices seven days a week. On each of the first five days he runs 4.7 km. On the next day he runs 6.1 km, and on the last day he runs 3.4 km. How far does Craig run in one week?

Townville Savings

DATE	WITHDRAWAL	DEPOSIT	BAL
			164.37
01 Sept	18.50		
06 Sept	18.50		
09 Sept		76.18	
12 Sept	18.50		
18 Sept	14.25		
22 Sept	18.50		
24 Sept	18.50		
28 Sept	14.25		

Practice

Solve each problem and explain the method you used.

1. A pound of apples costs $.79. How much would ten pounds cost? a hundred pounds? a thousand pounds?

2. Marco plans to return empty soda cans to the market and collect the deposit money. If he receives $0.10 for each can he returns, how much money will he get for 136 cans?

3. Cashews cost $3.98 a pound. Jake's bag weighed 2.7 pounds. Use estimation to find the cost of the cashews.

4. Ming earned $2 working at the grocery store on Monday, $4 on Tuesday, and $8 on Wednesday. If this pattern continues, how much would he earn on Sunday? How can you use exponents to solve the problem?

5. Dried apricots cost $.29 per ounce. Mr. Carlson's bag of dried apricots weighs 18.8 ounces. How much will his bag of apricots cost?

6. Ted buys 100 packages of artificial sweetener. Each pack holds 0.035 oz of sweetener. How many ounces of sweetener does Ted buy?

7. How many ounces of cereal are in a package that includes this information on the nutrition label?
   serving size............................1.25 oz (1 cup)
   servings per package 8.2

8. Andy found that he could buy individual teabags for $0.30 each or a package of 20 teabags for $4.79. If he plans to buy 20 teabags, which is the better buy: individual bags or the package?

9. The grocery store sold about 9.6×10^6 lb of coffee this year and 1.1×10^7 lb last year. Which year did the grocery store sell more coffee? How much more was sold?

10. Ms. Lee plans to buy 1.8 lb of pasta at $2.95 per pound; 2 lb of ground beef at $4.29 per pound; and 2.5 lb of tomatoes at $3.98 per pound. She has a $20 bill. Is this enough for the purchase?

Choose a strategy from the list or use another strategy you know to solve each problem.

Strategy File

Use These Strategies
Use More Than One Step
Use Simpler Numbers
Write an Equation
Guess and Test

11. Fine Foods sells a 2-lb wheel of cheese for $9.28. Stacey's Snacks sells the same cheese for $0.27 per ounce. Which store has the better price?

12. Raphael bought 3 pounds of red apples at $2.39 per pound. Kim bought 2.5 pounds of green apples at $2.99 per pound. The green apples are larger than the red apples. Who paid more?

13. A box of macaroni and cheese contains 2.4 servings. Each serving is 3.5 oz. How many ounces does the container hold?

14. Fine Foods sells raisins in bulk for $0.32 per ounce. A 7-oz box of raisins sells for $2.39. If Shannon wants to purchase 14 oz of raisins, which would be a better option: buying the raisins in bulk or buying 2 boxes of raisins?

15. A shop began the day with $437 in the cash register. Three purchases were made for $7.12, five for $5.68, and two for $11.35. The shop owner took $300 from the register at noon. How much was left in the register?

16. Lily uses the $25.00 she earns each week from her part-time job to pay for lunches and snacks. She spends $30.00 more each week on lunches than she does on snacks. How much does Lily spend on lunches each week?

Use the table for problems 17–20.

17. What is the price of the larger bottle of oregano?

18. How many more ounces does the large bag of wild rice contain than the small bag?

19. A restaurant needs 9 pounds of white rice. Will it be less expensive to buy one 5-lb bag and four 1-lb bags or two 5-lb bags?

20. Cindy buys 3 small boxes of raisins. How much less would she have had to spend to buy one large box instead?

Product	Size	Unit Price
Oregano	0.25 oz	$.48/oz
	0.5 oz	$.42/oz
White Rice	1 lb	$.09/oz
	5 lb	$.07/oz
Wild Rice	0.5 lb	$.37/oz
	3.25 lb	$.25/oz
Raisins	500 g	$5.48/kg
	1.2 kg	$5.20/kg

Write Your Own

21. Use the table to write a problem modeled on problem 19 above. Have a classmate solve it.

Multiply. Look for patterns. *(See pp. 66–67.)*

1. 10×45
   100×45
   1000×45

2. 25×2
   25×20
   25×200
   25×2000

3. 10×0.3
   100×0.3
   1000×0.3
   $10{,}000 \times 0.3$

Use rounding to estimate the product. *(See pp. 68–69.)*

4. 62×19

5. 874×26

6. 54.2×1.78

7. 431×156

8. 5.49×62.83

9. 177.08×2684

Round to estimate. Then find each product. *(See pp. 68–73.)*

10. 709×333

11. 0.26×9.3

12. 382×1101

13. $\$58.79 \times 209$

14. 8009×3206

15. $\$13.50 \times 42$

Write the standard form for each. *(See pp. 74–75.)*

16. 2^4

17. 3^4

18. 9^1

19. 5^3

20. 30^2

Write in scientific notation. *(See pp. 76–77.)*

21. $46{,}000$

22. $309{,}000$

23. $85{,}000{,}000$

24. $9{,}020{,}000{,}000$

Write the standard form for each.

25. 9×10^2

26. 6.1×10^4

27. 3.88×10^5

28. 5.167×10^6

Problem Solving
(See pp. 78–81.)

29. Tim had $672 in his bank account on October 1. He has since made three withdrawals of $44.50 each, and one of $128.95. He has also made two deposits of $83.20. How much does he have in his account now?

30. Anna plans to buy 2.75 lb of cheese at $2.96 per pound. She also wants 3 lb of potato salad that sells for $3.45 per pound. She has $25 in her wallet. Is this enough for the cheese and the potato salad?

(See Still More Practice, pp. 521–522.)

Square Roots

A square is the product of a number and itself.

$$4 \times 4 = 16$$

two equal factors | square

Remember: You can also express 4×4 as 4^2.

A square root is *one* of two equal factors of a given number. For the number 16, 4 is a square root because $4 \times 4 = 16$.

The symbol for a positive square root is $\sqrt{}$.

$$\sqrt{16} = 4$$

You can read $\sqrt{16}$ as "the square root of 16."

▶ For some numbers you can use multiplication facts to determine the square root of a number. The $\sqrt{49}$ is 7 since 7×7, or $7^2 = 49$.

$2^2 = 4 \rightarrow \sqrt{4} = 2$ $4^2 = 16 \rightarrow \sqrt{16} = 4$

$3^2 = 9 \rightarrow \sqrt{9} = 3$ $5^2 = 25 \rightarrow \sqrt{25} = 5$

▶ You can also use a calculator to find square roots.

To find the square root of 361, or $\sqrt{361}$:

Press these keys

   *19.* ← Display

So, the $\sqrt{361} = 19$.

Find the square root of each number using multiplication facts or a calculator.

1. $\sqrt{64}$ 2. $\sqrt{36}$ 3. $\sqrt{100}$ 4. $\sqrt{81}$ 5. $\sqrt{49}$

6. $\sqrt{121}$ 7. $\sqrt{144}$ 8. $\sqrt{900}$ 9. $\sqrt{256}$ 10. $\sqrt{400}$

Multiply. Look for patterns.

1. 18 × 10
   18 × 100
   18 × 1000
   18 × 10,000

2. 40 × 5
   40 × 50
   40 × 500
   40 × 5000

3. 10 × 3.46
   100 × 3.46
   1000 × 3.46
   10,000 × 3.46

Use rounding to estimate the product.

4. 37 × 88

5. 521 × 64

6. 23.2 × 9.18

Round to estimate. Then find each product.

7. 88 × 567

8. 3.05 × 2.3

9. 513 × 1901

10. $45.19 × 140

11. 6070 × 2820

12. 97.45 × 220

Write the standard form for each.

13. 5^2

14. 4^3

15. 6^0

16. 1^6

17. 2^5

Write in scientific notation.

18. 17,000

19. 421,000

20. 20,800,000

21. 503,300,000

Write the standard form for each.

22. $2 × 10^2$

23. $3.6 × 10^4$

24. $9.01 × 10^5$

25. $3.026 × 10^6$

Problem Solving

Use a strategy or strategies you have learned.

26. Leah had $312 in her bank account on August 1. She has made two withdrawals of $29.75 each, and one of $165.95. She also made two deposits of $94.20. How much does Leah have in her account now?

Tell About It

27. Jack plans to buy 2.25 lb of coleslaw at $2.80 per pound. He also wants 2 lb of macaroni salad that sells for $3.15 per pound. Jack has a $10 bill in his wallet. Is this enough for the coleslaw and the macaroni salad? Explain.

Performance Assessment

How many zeros will be in the product? Explain your answer.

28. 300 × 300

29. 10,000 × 1000

30. 200 × 35,000

Choose the best answer.

1. Estimate by rounding.

43.09×361

- **a.** 1200
- **b.** 1600
- **c.** 12,000
- **d.** 16,000

2. Which is ordered from least to greatest?

- **a.** 3.47260; 0.304726; 0.034726
- **b.** 0.015708; 0.105708; 1.572
- **c.** 0.094768; 9.47680; 0.904768
- **d.** none of these

3. Estimate. Use front-end estimation.

$$34,929$$
$$16,815$$
$$+ \ 49,320$$

- **a.** 60,000
- **b.** 70,000
- **c.** 90,000
- **d.** 100,000

4. Choose the standard form.

4^3

- **a.** 12
- **b.** 16
- **c.** 32
- **d.** 64

5. Choose the correct value for the evaluated expression.

$29.8 - p$, when $p = 3.6$

- **a.** 26
- **b.** 26.2
- **c.** 26.4
- **d.** 33.4

6. Subtract.

$5,003,208 - 611,019$

- **a.** 5,614,227
- **b.** 5,492,299
- **c.** 4,492,289
- **d.** 4,392,189

7. Multiply.

4302×145

- **a.** 43,120
- **b.** 236,610
- **c.** 623,790
- **d.** 645,000

8. Choose the standard form.

10^4

- **a.** 10,000
- **b.** 100,000
- **c.** 1,000,000
- **d.** 10,000,000

9. Name the place of the underlined digit.

$3,821.003\underline{0}46$

- **a.** thousandths
- **b.** ten thousandths
- **c.** hundred thousandths
- **d.** millionths

10. Choose the standard form.

$$(5 \times 10^2) + (2 \times 10^1) + (3 \times 10^{-2})$$

- **a.** 502.03
- **b.** 502.3
- **c.** 520.03
- **d.** 520.3

11. Choose the correct standard form.

6.24×10^5

- **a.** 6240
- **b.** 62,400
- **c.** 624,000
- **d.** none of these

12. Choose the standard form.

$$(4 \times 10^7) + (9 \times 10^5) + (7 \times 10^2)$$

- **a.** 4,900,700
- **b.** 40,900,700
- **c.** 400,900,700
- **d.** none of these

13. Add.

$16.25 + $220.86 + $3

    a. $236.04
    b. $237.14
    c. $239.01
    d. $240.11

14. Choose the related algebraic expression.

67 less than a number

    a. $67 + m$
    b. $67 - m$
    c. $m - 67$
    d. none of these

15. Choose the correct standard form.

two trillion, fifty million, three hundred one

    a. 2,000,050,000,301
    b. 2,050,000,301
    c. 2,000,050,301
    d. none of these

16. Multiply.

500×8000

    a. 40,000
    b. 400,000
    c. 4,000,000
    d. 40,000,000

17. Which has an estimated product of 36,000?

    a. 87×42
    b. 856×399
    c. 917×481
    d. 873×39

18. Which statement is true?

    a. $100 \times 48 > 10 \times 480$
    b. $315 \times 10 = 3.15 \times 1000$
    c. $56 \times 10 > 560 \times 100$
    d. $800 \times 40 = 8 \times 400$

19. Round 9.602 to its greatest place.

    a. 9.0
    b. 9.6
    c. 10.0
    d. 10.6

20. Choose the correct value for the evaluated expression.

$8.06 - c$, when $c = 0.052$

    a. 0.754
    b. 0.854
    c. 8.008
    d. 8.112

21. Estimate. Use front-end estimation with adjustments.

$$\begin{array}{r} 2.111 \\ 2.652 \\ + 9.370 \\ \hline \end{array}$$

    a. 13
    b. 14
    c. 15
    d. 16

22. Which correctly expresses the number below in scientific notation?

4,070,000

    a. 4.7×10^7
    b. 4.07×10^6
    c. 4.07×10^5
    d. 4.07×10^4

Tell About It

Explain how you solved each problem. Show all of your work.

23. José purchased a shirt for $37.85, a coat for $84.99, and a pair of pants for $39.75. He also bought two packages of socks for $3.87 each. How much did he spend in all?

24. Mary Ann borrowed $62.45 from Karen. She paid back $40.00, but borrowed $16.00 more. When she was paid, she gave Karen $35.00. How much does Mary Ann still owe?

Division: Whole Numbers and Decimals

In this chapter you will:

Learn about short division
Discover patterns in division
Estimate and find quotients
Evaluate multiplication and division expressions
Solve problems by interpreting the remainder

Critical Thinking/Finding Together

The tenth term in a sequence is 1004.58. If the pattern rule is × 100, ÷ 10, ..., what is the first term?

A Dividend Opinion

Said the Aliquant to the Aliquot,
"You're all used up, and I am not."
"Used up?" said the Aliquot. "Not a bit.
I happen to be a perfect fit.
You're a raveled thread. A wrong number.
You're about as useful as scrap lumber.
I slip into place like a mitered joint.
You hang out over your **decimal point**
Like a monkey asquat in a cuckoo's nest
With your tail adangle, self-impressed
By the way you twitch the thing about.
Stuck up about nothing but sticking out,
If I'm used up, you will discover
You're no fresh start. You're just left over
From nothing anyone would want,"
Said the Aliquot to the Aliquant.

John Ciardi

3-1

Short Division

Leilani's sister saved the same amount of money each month for 9 months for a vacation. The vacation cost $1908. How much did she save each month?

To find the amount she saved each month, *n*, divide: $1908 ÷ 9 = *n*.

▶ You can use short division to divide mentally by a one-digit divisor.

$$\begin{array}{r} \$\ \ \ 2 \\ 9\overline{)\$\ 1\ 9\ ^1 0\ 8} \end{array}$$

$$\boxed{\begin{array}{l} 2 \times 9 = 18 \\ 19 - 18 = 1 \end{array}}$$

$$\begin{array}{r} \$\ \ \ 2\ 1 \\ 9\overline{)\$\ 1\ 9\ ^1 0\ ^1 8} \end{array}$$

$$\boxed{\begin{array}{l} 1 \times 9 = 9 \\ 10 - 9 = 1 \end{array}}$$

$$\begin{array}{r} \$\ \ \ 2\ 1\ 2 \\ 9\overline{)\$\ 1\ 9\ ^1 0\ ^1 8} \end{array}$$

$$\boxed{\begin{array}{l} 2 \times 9 = 18 \\ 18 - 18 = 0 \end{array}}$$

Division Steps
1. Estimate.
2. Divide.
3. Multiply.
4. Subtract and compare.
5. Bring down and repeat.

Leilani's sister saved $212 each month.

▶ To predict if a quotient has a remainder, you can use divisibility rules.

Remember:
A number is divisible by:
• 2 if it is an even number.
• 3 if the sum of its digits is divisible by 3.
• 5 if its last digit is a 0 or a 5.

153,278 ÷ 2

$$\boxed{\begin{array}{l} \text{153,278 is an} \\ \text{even number.} \\ \text{no remainder} \end{array}}$$

59,679 ÷ 5

$$\boxed{\begin{array}{l} \text{59,679 does not} \\ \text{have 0 or 5 as} \\ \text{its last digit.} \\ \text{has a remainder} \end{array}}$$

69,123 ÷ 3

$$\boxed{\begin{array}{l} 69,123 \longrightarrow \\ 6 + 9 + 1 + 2 + 3 = 21; \\ 21 \div 3 = 7 \\ \text{no remainder} \end{array}}$$

$$\begin{array}{r} 7\ 6,6\ 3\ 9 \\ 2\overline{)1\ 5\ ^1 3,^1 2\ 7\ ^1 8} \end{array}$$

$$\begin{array}{r} 1\ 1,9\ 3\ 5\ \text{R4} \\ 5\overline{)5\ 9,^4 6\ ^1 7\ ^2 9} \end{array}$$

$$\begin{array}{r} 2\ 3,0\ 4\ 1 \\ 3\overline{)6\ 9,1\ ^1 2\ 3} \end{array}$$

Divide using short division.

1. $3\overline{)81{,}993}$ 2. $6\overline{)84{,}174}$ 3. $5\overline{)490{,}135}$ 4. $7\overline{)315{,}714}$

5. $688{,}932 \div 4$ 6. $912{,}848 \div 8$ 7. $2{,}496{,}598 \div 2$ 8. $6{,}975{,}687 \div 3$

Predict if the quotient has a remainder. Explain why or why not. Then divide to check your prediction.

9. $5\overline{)509{,}845}$ 10. $3\overline{)68{,}734}$ 11. $2\overline{)149{,}568}$ 12. $3\overline{)710{,}625}$

Find each quotient by short division. Use R to write remainders.
Check by multiplying the divisor and the quotient
and then adding the remainder.

13. $4\overline{)137{,}973}$ 14. $9\overline{)836{,}138}$ 15. $5\overline{)139{,}864}$ 16. $7\overline{)180{,}523}$

17. $\$8157.75 \div 5$ 18. $\$644.68 \div 4$ 19. $36{,}570 \div 7$ 20. $19{,}580 \div 6$

Write the divisor. Use divisibility rules to help you.

21. $\overset{2891}{?\overline{)5782}}$ 22. $\overset{1966}{?\overline{)5898}}$ 23. $\overset{7{,}489 \ \text{R3}}{?\overline{)67{,}404}}$ 24. $\overset{7{,}915 \ \text{R7}}{?\overline{)63{,}327}}$

Problem Solving

25. A manufacturer has 368,536 bottles to pack into 8-bottle cartons. Will 46,065 cartons be enough to pack all the bottles? Explain.

26. Air Ways shipped 20,799 radios. The radios were packed 9 to a box. Will 2311 boxes be enough to pack all the radios? Explain.

Write About It

You can divide by powers and by multiples of 10 mentally.

27. Copy and complete the division patterns below. Write a rule that tells how to divide by a power of 10 and a rule that tells how to divide by a multiple of 10.

$34{,}000 \div 1 = 34{,}000$ $40{,}000 \div 5 = 8{,}000$

$34{,}000 \div 10 = \underline{\ ?\ }$ $40{,}000 \div 50 = 800$

$34{,}000 \div 100 = \underline{\ ?\ }$ $40{,}000 \div 500 = \underline{\ ?\ }$

$34{,}000 \div 1000 = 34$ $40{,}000 \div 5000 = \underline{\ ?\ }$

3-2

Estimate Quotients

There are 1895 students and teachers in the district going by bus to the science fair. The district is renting buses that hold 48 people each. About how many buses are needed?

To find about how many buses are needed, estimate: 1895 ÷ 48.

▶ **One way to estimate the quotient of two numbers is to use compatible numbers.**

- Write the nearest compatible whole numbers for the dividend and the divisor.

- Divide.

$$\underbrace{1895}_{\text{about } 2000} \div \underbrace{48}_{\text{about } 50} \longrightarrow 2000 \div 50 = 40$$

> Two numbers are **compatible numbers** when one number divides the other evenly.

> 2000 and 50 are compatible numbers. They are easy to divide mentally.

About 40 buses are needed.

Study these examples.

> To make compatible numbers, you can change both the dividend and the divisor.

> To make compatible numbers, you can change just the dividend (or just the divisor).

$$893\overline{)27{,}056} \longrightarrow \overset{30}{900\overline{)27{,}000}}$$

$$420\overline{)\$415{,}786} \longrightarrow \overset{\$\ 1{,}000}{420\overline{)\$420{,}000}}$$

$$893\overline{)27{,}056} \approx 30$$

$$420\overline{)\$415{,}786} \approx \$1000$$

"is approximately equal to"

Estimate the quotient. Use compatible numbers.

1. 2164 ÷ 43

2. 5838 ÷ 28

3. 7842 ÷ 37

4. 3984 ÷ 19

5. 82,461 ÷ 41

6. $51,206 ÷ 53

7. 13,642 ÷ 206

8. 85,136 ÷ 409

9. $485,725 ÷ 520

10. 672,385 ÷ 710

11. 879,500 ÷ 425

12. $972,360 ÷ 325

Choose the best estimate.

13. $32\overline{)2940}$ ≈ ___

    a. 1   **b.** 10   **c.** 100   **d.** 1000

14. $19\overline{)6248}$ ≈ ___

    a. 3   **b.** 30   **c.** 300   **d.** 3000

15. $210\overline{)380,493}$ ≈ ___

    a. 2   **b.** 20   **c.** 200   **d.** 2000

16. $389\overline{)792,432}$ ≈ ___

    a. 2   **b.** 20   **c.** 200   **d.** 2000

Problem Solving

17. A truck driver drove 5845 miles in 19 days. Did he average more than 250 miles a day? How do you know?

18. Sheila's company mails 3580 advertising flyers in 25 days. Do the mailings average more than 200 flyers per day? How do you know?

19. The mileage on Michael's new car is 686 miles. The mileage on his sister's car is 45,650. About how many times greater is the mileage on her car?

DO YOU REMEMBER?

Estimate by rounding. Then find the product.

20. 54 × 426

21. 76 × 549

22. 65 × 5305

23. 48 × 4017

24. 630 × 4454

25. 801 × 7182

26. 420 × $17.82

27. 350 × $24.37

3-3

Divide Whole Numbers

Alaska has 33,904 miles of shoreline.
Connecticut has 618 miles of shoreline.
How many times the length of Connecticut's
shoreline is Alaska's?

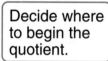

▶ To find how many times the length, *n*,
divide: 33,904 ÷ 618 = *n*.

First estimate by using compatible numbers:
30,000 ÷ 600 = 50.
Then divide.

Decide where to begin the quotient.	618)‾33,904‾	**Think** 618 > 339 **Not enough hundreds**
	618)‾33,904‾	618 < 3390 **Enough tens**
		The quotient begins in the tens place.

Divide the tens.

```
           5
6 1 8)3 3,9 0 4
     -3 0 9 0
       3 0 0
```

Divide the ones.

```
          5 4  R532
6 1 8)3 3,9 0 4
     -3 0 9 0
       3 0 0 4
      -2 4 7 2
         5 3 2
```

Check.

```
        6 1 8
    ×     5 4
      2 4 7 2
   +3 0 9 0
    3 3,3 7 2
   +      5 3 2
    3 3,9 0 4
```

Alaska's shoreline is about 55 times
the length of Connecticut's shoreline.

Think
54 R532 is close to
the estimate of 50.

▶ Sometimes you need to write one or more zeros in the quotient.

```
        2 0  R13
5 3)1 0 7 3
   -1 0 6 ↓
       1 3
```
53 > 13

Write zero in
the quotient.

```
        3 0 0 1  R5
3 3)9 9,0 3 8
   -9 9 ↓ ↓ ↓
    0 0 3 8
       -3 3
          5
```

Write two zeros
in the quotient.

Estimate by using compatible numbers. Then find each quotient.

1. $52\overline{)6638}$

2. $34\overline{)5777}$

3. $15\overline{)1634}$

4. $40\overline{)2060}$

5. $36,389 \div 82$

6. $30,139 \div 93$

7. $25,297 \div 84$

8. $72,072 \div 72$

9. $86,129 \div 43$

10. $36,408 \div 912$

11. $2710 \div 759$

12. $88,408 \div 514$

Find the value of the variable.

13. $n = 28,671 \div 57$

14. $d = 14,558 \div 29$

15. $504,144 \div 36 = m$

16. $696,024 \div 24 = a$

17. $c = 400,458 \div 186$

18. $b = 681,042 \div 223$

Use the table to find the number of carats in each gem. (1 carat = 20 centigrams)

19. Cut diamond

20. Ruby

21. Emerald

22. Sapphire

23. Opal

Gem	Mass (in centigrams)
Cut diamond	10 600
Ruby	170 000
Emerald (single crystal)	140 500
Sapphire (carved)	46 040
Opal	527 000

Problem Solving

24. Arizona's land area is 113,642 square miles and its water area is 364 square miles. How many times greater is the land area than the water area?

25. Kansas's land area is 81,823 square miles and its water area is 459 square miles. How many times greater is the land area than the water area?

26. On planet NO-LEAP, each year has exactly 365 days. EU-2's father is 14,977 days old. How many days ago was his birthday? (Hint: $14,977 \div 365 = $? years ? days)

CRITICAL THINKING

Use each statement and the numbers in the box to write number sentences. Tell whether the statement is *always*, *sometimes*, or *never* true for *all* the given numbers.

133, 1, 0, 133, 4056

27. The sum is zero.

28. The quotient is zero.

29. The difference is zero.

30. The sum is greater than or equal to 0.

Divide Decimals by 10, 100, and 1000

Eddie divided six decimals by 10, 100, and 1000 and discovered some patterns.

637.4 ÷ 10 = 63.74	53.8 ÷ 10 = 5.38	8.7 ÷ 10 = 0.87
637.4 ÷ 100 = 6.374	53.8 ÷ 100 = 0.538	8.7 ÷ 100 = 0.087
637.4 ÷ 1000 = 0.6374	53.8 ÷ 1000 = 0.0538	8.7 ÷ 1000 = 0.0087
21.76 ÷ 10 = 2.176	6.15 ÷ 10 = 0.615	0.47 ÷ 10 = 0.047
21.76 ÷ 100 = 0.2176	6.15 ÷ 100 = 0.0615	0.47 ÷ 100 = 0.0047
21.76 ÷ 1000 = 0.02176	6.15 ÷ 1000 = 0.00615	0.47 ÷ 1000 = 0.00047

He used these patterns to help him divide by 10, 100, and 1000.

▶ **To divide a decimal by 10, 100, or 1000:**

- Count the number of zeros in the divisor.

- Move the decimal point to the *left* one place in the dividend for each zero in the divisor.

- Write zeros in the quotient as needed.

Study these examples.

6 8.4 ÷ 1 0 = 6.8 4 ⟵ | 1 zero: Move 1 place to the left.

2 6 8.7 ÷ 1 0 0 = 2.6 8 7 ⟵ | 2 zeros: Move 2 places to the left.

0 3 2.5 ÷ 1 0 0 0 = 0.0 3 2 5 ⟵ | 3 zeros: Move 3 places to the left. Write 1 zero as a placeholder.

0 0 1.8 2 ÷ 1 0 0 0 = 0.0 0 1 8 2 ⟵ | 3 zeros: Move 3 places to the left. Write 2 zeros as placeholders.

Find the quotients. Use the patterns.

1. 8329 ÷ 10
8329 ÷ 100
8329 ÷ 1000

2. 724.8 ÷ 10
724.8 ÷ 100
724.8 ÷ 1000

3. 56.39 ÷ 10
56.39 ÷ 100
56.39 ÷ 1000

4. 2.8 ÷ 10
2.8 ÷ 100
2.8 ÷ 1000

5. 4.27 ÷ 10
4.27 ÷ 100
4.27 ÷ 1000

6. 8.1 ÷ 10
8.1 ÷ 100
8.1 ÷ 1000

7. 0.6 ÷ 10
0.6 ÷ 100
0.6 ÷ 1000

8. 0.18 ÷ 10
0.18 ÷ 100
0.18 ÷ 1000

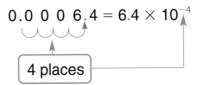

Divide.

9. $0.02 \div 100$ **10.** $0.105 \div 10$ **11.** $30.8 \div 100$ **12.** $9.9 \div 10$

13. $849 \div 1000$ **14.** $3.9 \div 100$ **15.** $0.63 \div 10$ **16.** $0.17 \div 100$

17. $0.245 \div 100$ **18.** $5.628 \div 1000$ **19.** $9 \div 1000$ **20.** $19.95 \div 10$

Find the value of the variable.

21. $4.07 \div n = 0.0407$ **22.** $0.18 \div m = 0.018$ **23.** $22.8 \div x = 0.0228$

24. $a \div 100 = 56.7$ **25.** $d \div 10 = 0.07$ **26.** $y \div 1000 = 0.05$

Scientific Notation of Decimals Between 0 and 1

Scientific notation can be used to rename decimals that are between 0 and 1. Negative exponents are used for the powers of 10.

$$0.00064 = \frac{6.4}{10{,}000} = 6.4 \times \frac{1}{10{,}000} = 6.4 \times 10^{-4}$$

4 zeros

The **scientific notation** of a number is a product of two factors:
- One factor is greater than or equal to 1, but less than 10.
- The other factor is a power of 10 in exponent form.

Write 0.00064 in scientific notation.

▶ To write a decimal between 0 and 1 in scientific notation:

- Write the first factor by placing the decimal point to the right of the first nonzero digit.

  $0.00064 \longrightarrow 6.4$

- Count the number of places the decimal point was moved to the right and use this number as the negative exponent of the power of 10.

  $0.0\,0\,0\,6.4 = 6.4 \times 10^{-4}$

  4 places

In scientific notation, $0.00064 = 6.4 \times 10^{-4}$.

Write in scientific notation.

27. 0.015 **28.** 0.0000086 **29.** 0.00000079 **30.** 0.000124

31. 0.0069 **32.** 0.0000000147 **33.** 0.000000009 **34.** 0.0000716

Problem Solving

35. Mike divided 815.6 m of fencing into 100 equal sections. How long is each section?

36. A wasp has a mass of 0.005 mg. Rename this mass in kilograms using scientific notation.

Divide Decimals by Whole Numbers

Elena and five of her friends went out for pizza. The total bill was $18.66. They shared the bill equally. How much did each person pay?

To find the amount each person paid, *n*, divide: $18.66 ÷ 6 = *n*.

First estimate by using compatible numbers, $18 ÷ 6 = $3. Then divide.

▶ **To divide a decimal by a whole number:**

Write the decimal point in the quotient directly above the decimal point in the dividend.

Divide as you would with whole numbers.

Check.

```
         .
6)$ 1 8.6 6
```

```
$   3.1 1
6)$ 1 8.6 6
  − 1 8 ↓
        6
      − 6 ↓
        0 6
        − 6
          0
```

Write the dollar sign in the quotient.

```
   $ 3.1 1
  ×       6
  $ 1 8.6 6
```

Each person paid $3.11.

Think
$3.11 is close to the estimate of $3.

Study these examples.

```
    2.1 9
4)8.7 6
 − 8 ↓
  0 7
  − 4 ↓
    3 6
  − 3 6
      0
```

```
     0.3 7
2 6)9.6 2
  − 7 8 ↓
    1 8 2
  − 1 8 2
        0
```

Short Division

```
     0.4 8
3)1.4 ²4
```

Divide and check.

1. $67.2 \div 6$ **2.** $7.5 \div 3$ **3.** $49.32 \div 9$ **4.** $0.95 \div 5$

5. $21.60 \div 15$ **6.** $13.2 \div 22$ **7.** $0.784 \div 7$ **8.** $8.792 \div 4$

9. $62.1 \div 3$ **10.** $9.520 \div 7$ **11.** $\$77.20 \div 8$ **12.** $0.732 \div 6$

13. $5\overline{)99.5}$ **14.** $6\overline{)135.6}$ **15.** $7\overline{)\$17.85}$ **16.** $8\overline{)41.52}$

17. $12\overline{)\$34.80}$ **18.** $42\overline{)349.44}$ **19.** $4\overline{)0.8644}$ **20.** $5\overline{)0.8325}$

21. $2\overline{)0.9314}$ **22.** $5\overline{)\$50.25}$ **23.** $3\overline{)0.732}$ **24.** $4\overline{)\$24.12}$

25. $6\overline{)14.10}$ **26.** $3\overline{)0.1077}$ **27.** $8\overline{)0.016}$ **28.** $6\overline{)7.836}$

Compare. Write <, =, or >.

29. $0.57 \div 30$ _?_ $0.57 \div 3$ **30.** $92.4 \div 6$ _?_ $9.24 \div 6$

31. $4\overline{)48}$ _?_ $4\overline{)4.8}$ **32.** $5\overline{)0.015}$ _?_ $5\overline{)0.15}$

Problem Solving

33. If 6 packages weigh 0.936 lb, what does 1 package weigh? What do 12 packages weigh?

34. Mary spent $.96 for 8 m of ribbon. What does 1 m of ribbon cost?

35. Irma wants to divide a bill of $48.24 equally among 8 people. How much should each person pay?

36. Mr. Clark traveled 456.4 km in 14 days. If he traveled the same distance each day, how far did he travel each day?

37. Ray has 1.92 m of copper tubing that he cuts into 4 equal pieces. How long is each piece?

38. A large carton of books weighs 34.5 lb and is three times the weight of a smaller carton. How much does the smaller carton weigh?

CHALLENGE

Find the mean (average) of each set of numbers.

39. 6.8, 4.9, 5.5, 7.2

40. $35.92, $37.16, $39, $33.95, $40.02

41. 0.099, 0.2, 0.089, 0.12, 0.092, 0.108

42. 4.8, 5, 4.5, 5.1, 4.75, 4.6, 5.25, 4.2, 4.1

Patterns with Tenths, Hundredths, Thousandths

Mario used these patterns for dividing numbers by 0.1, 0.01, and 0.001 to find the number of tenths, hundredths, and thousandths in a whole number or decimal.

$34 \div 0.1 = 340$
$34 \div 0.01 = 3400$
$34 \div 0.001 = 34{,}000$

$631.8 \div 0.1 = 6318$
$631.8 \div 0.01 = 63{,}180$
$631.8 \div 0.001 = 631{,}800$

▶ **To divide by 0.1, 0.01, or 0.001:**

- Count the number of decimal places in the divisor.
- Move the decimal point to the *right* one place in the dividend for each decimal place in the divisor.
- Write zeros in the quotient as needed.

Study these examples.

$4.3\,6 \div 0.1 = 4\,3.6$ ◀ — 1 decimal place in the divisor. Move 1 place to the right.

$4.3\,6 \div 0.0\,1 = 4\,3\,6$ ◀ — 2 decimal places in the divisor. Move 2 places to the right.

$4.3\,6\,0 \div 0.0\,0\,1 = 4\,3\,6\,0$ ◀ — 3 decimal places in the divisor. Move 3 places to the right. Write 1 zero.

When you divide by 0.1, 0.01, or 0.001, the quotient increases as the divisor decreases.

Find the quotients. Use the patterns.

1. $16 \div 0.1$
$16 \div 0.01$
$16 \div 0.001$

2. $329 \div 0.1$
$329 \div 0.01$
$329 \div 0.001$

3. $5.8 \div 0.1$
$5.8 \div 0.01$
$5.8 \div 0.001$

4. $27.6 \div 0.1$
$27.6 \div 0.01$
$27.6 \div 0.001$

Divide.

5. 237 ÷ 0.1

6. 157.5 ÷ 0.1

7. 42.23 ÷ 0.1

8. 27.16 ÷ 0.01

9. 82.06 ÷ 0.01

10. 784.19 ÷ 0.01

11. 2.5 ÷ 0.001

12. 0.8 ÷ 0.001

13. 0.72 ÷ 0.1

14. 0.9 ÷ 0.01

15. 188 ÷ 0.001

16. 427.01 ÷ 0.01

17. 56.56 ÷ 0.01

18. 0.88 ÷ 0.1

19. 1.56 ÷ 0.01

20. 1 ÷ 0.001

Compare. Write <, =, or >.

21. 12.9 ÷ 0.01 __?__ 12.9 ÷ 0.001

22. 15.4 ÷ 0.01 __?__ 15.4 ÷ 0.1

23. 5.9 ÷ 0.01 __?__ 59 ÷ 0.01

24. 6.2 ÷ 0.01 __?__ 62 ÷ 0.1

Problem Solving

25. How many dimes are in $18.60?

26. How many pennies are in $56?

CRITICAL THINKING · Algebra

27. Compare the patterns in the first two columns below. Then compare the patterns in the last two columns. Summarize your findings in your Math Journal.

0.63 × 1000 = 630	0.63 ÷ 1000 = 0.00063	0.63 ÷ 3000 = 0.00021
0.63 × 100 = 63	0.63 ÷ 100 = 0.0063	0.63 ÷ 300 = 0.0021
0.63 × 10 = 6.3	0.63 ÷ 10 = 0.063	0.63 ÷ 30 = 0.021
0.63 × 1 = 0.63	0.63 ÷ 1 = 0.63	0.63 ÷ 3 = 0.21
0.63 × 0.1 = 0.063	0.63 ÷ 0.1 = 6.3	0.63 ÷ 0.3 = 2.1
0.63 × 0.01 = 0.0063	0.63 ÷ 0.01 = 63	0.63 ÷ 0.03 = 21
0.63 × 0.001 = 0.00063	0.63 ÷ 0.001 = 630	0.63 ÷ 0.003 = 210

28. Find the value of each variable. Use the patterns in exercise 27 to help you.

a. $0.6 \times a = 0.006$

b. $44 \div m = 4400$

c. $7.6 \div c = 3800$

d. $5.42 \times t = 542$

e. $3.16 \div n = 0.316$

f. $2.05 \div w = 41$

g. $1.14 \times b = 0.00114$

h. $0.216 \times r = 0.00216$

i. $10.2 \div s = 0.34$

Estimate Decimal Quotients

The fabric Hannah needs costs $4.65 per yard. She has $23.50. About how many yards of fabric can she buy?

To find about how many yards Hannah can buy, estimate: $23.50 ÷ $4.65.

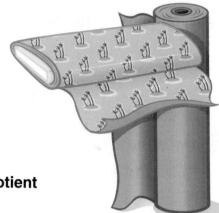

▶ **Use compatible numbers to estimate the quotient of two decimals (or two money amounts):**

- Write the nearest compatible whole $23.50 ⟶ $24
  numbers for the dividend and the divisor. $4.65 ⟶ $4

- Divide. $24 ÷ $4 = 6

She can buy about 6 yards of fabric.

▶ Compare the dividend and the divisor to help estimate a quotient if it is greater than or less than 1.

| Dividend > Divisor | ⟶ | Quotient > 1 |

Think
$8 ÷ 0.16$ $8 > 0.16$ $8 ÷ 0.16 > 1$

| Dividend < Divisor | ⟶ | Quotient < 1 |

Think
$0.16 ÷ 8$ $0.16 < 8$ $0.16 ÷ 8 < 1$

Estimate to place the decimal point in the quotient.

1. $29.52 ÷ 7.2 = 41$

2. $18.7 ÷ 5.5 = 34$

3. $49.6 ÷ 8 = 62$

4. $38.13 ÷ 15.5 = 246$

5. $40.18 ÷ 19.6 = 205$

6. $225.15 ÷ 7.5 = 3002$

7. $396.5 ÷ 12.2 = 325$

8. $9.21 ÷ 7.5 = 1228$

9. $37.75 ÷ 5 = 755

Practice

Estimate each quotient. Use compatible numbers.

10. $41.9 \div 8.6$

11. $54.3 \div 9.3$

12. $47.17 \div 6.88$

13. $358.8 \div 5.99$

14. $225.741 \div 6.8$

15. $182.827 \div 3.5$

16. $505.905 \div 52.7$

17. $798.238 \div 68.4$

18. $328 \div 15.9$

19. $885 \div 30.9$

20. $\$63.28 \div 4.4$

21. $\$596.78 \div \$9.50$

Compare. Write <, =, or > .

22. $8 \div 9$? 1

23. $27.6 \div 7.4$? 1

24. $14.9 \div 8.7$? 1

25. $6.8 \div 18.9$? 1

26. 1 ? $0.7 \div 5.88$

27. 1 ? $41.1 \div 0.999$

28. 1 ? $1.28 \div 3.01$

29. 1 ? $12.1 \div 0.894$

30. $1 \div 0.1$? 1

Three Ways to Estimate Quotients		
Front End	*Compatible Numbers*	*Rounding*
$35.5 \div 3.6$	$35.5 \div 3.6$	$35.5 \div 3.6$
$30 \div 3 = 10$	$40 \div 4 = 10$	$36 \div 4 = 9$

Estimate each quotient to complete the table.

		Front End	Compatible Numbers	Rounding
31.	$\$225.50 \div 15.8$	?	?	?
32.	$152.8 \div 6.7$	?	?	?
33.	$60 \div 5.8$	?	?	?

34. Which method seems to give the most accurate estimate in each of exercises 31–33?

35. The closest estimate of $36.142 \div 8.95$ is ? .

    A 4 **B** 0.4 **C** 0.04 **D** 0.004

36. The closest estimate of $\$464.36 \div \$9.25$ is ? .

    A 0.5 **B** 5 **C** 50 **D** 500

Decimal Divisors

Mrs. Martinez is shingling the roof of her house. Each shingle is 0.2 m wide. If the roof is 8.46 m wide, how many shingles can she put in each row?

To find the number of shingles, *n*, divide: $8.46 \div 0.2 = n$.

First estimate by using front-end estimation: $8 \div 0.2 = 40$.
Then divide.

▶ **To divide by a decimal:**

- Move the decimal point in the *divisor* to form a whole-number divisor. Then move the decimal point in the *dividend* to the right the *same number* of places.

$$0.2\overline{)8.4\,6}$$

- Place the decimal point in the quotient and then divide.

$$\begin{array}{r} 4\,2.3 \\ 2\overline{)8\,4.6} \end{array}$$

- Check by multiplying.

$$\begin{array}{r} 4\,2.3 \\ \times\ \ 0.2 \\ \hline 8.4\,6 \end{array}$$

Each row will have 42.3 shingles.

.Think
42.3 is close to the estimate of 40.

Study these examples.

Remember: The *divisor* must always be a whole number.

$$2.4\overline{)1.2\,7\,2}$$

Move the decimal points one place to the right.

$$\begin{array}{r} 0.5\,3 \\ 2\,4\overline{)1\,2.7\,2} \\ -1\,2\,0 \\ \hline 7\,2 \\ -\,7\,2 \\ \hline 0 \end{array}$$

$$0.0\,2\,7\overline{)0.1\,6\,2}$$

Move the decimal points three places to the right.

$$\begin{array}{r} 6 \\ 2\,7\overline{)1\,6\,2} \\ -1\,6\,2 \\ \hline 0 \end{array}$$

Move the decimal points in the divisor and in the dividend.
Then write the decimal point in the quotient.

1. $2.3\overline{)6.4\ 6\ 3}$ quotient: 2 8 1

2. $0.1\ 9\overline{)0.1\ 7\ 4\ 8}$ quotient: 0 9 2

3. $0.9\ 2\overline{)2.8\ 6\ 1\ 2}$ quotient: 3 1 1

4. $0.8\overline{)4.8\ 2\ 4}$ quotient: 6 0 3

5. $0.0\ 1\ 1\overline{)0.0\ 9\ 3\ 5}$ quotient: 8 5

6. $0.0\ 1\ 2\overline{)0.0\ 0\ 1\ 4\ 4}$ quotient: 0 1 2

7. $1.5\overline{)0.0\ 0\ 4\ 5}$ quotient: 0 0 0 3

8. $0.1\ 8\overline{)0.0\ 3\ 6}$ quotient: 0 2

9. $0.0\ 2\ 4\overline{)0.0\ 0\ 1\ 4\ 4}$ quotient: 0 0 6

Divide and check.

10. $0.5\overline{)7.55}$

11. $0.6\overline{)9.66}$

12. $0.4\overline{)0.76}$

13. $0.7\overline{)8.61}$

14. $92.4 \div 0.4$

15. $6.3 \div 0.3$

16. $257.2 \div 0.4$

17. $0.96 \div 0.8$

18. $2.214 \div 0.9$

19. $0.084 \div 0.3$

20. $555.6 \div 0.6$

21. $391.2 \div 0.4$

22. $0.28\overline{)4.396}$

23. $0.75\overline{)0.7725}$

24. $0.07\overline{)3.5028}$

25. $0.08\overline{)1.9216}$

26. $6.9 \div 2.3$

27. $8.93 \div 4.7$

28. $0.78 \div 0.26$

29. $0.014 \div 0.07$

Problem Solving

30. Mike is tiling a floor. If each tile is 0.3 m wide and the floor is 5.4 m wide, how many tiles will fit in each row?

31. Carlos cut a 25.8-ft length of rope into 0.6-ft segments. How many segments did he cut?

32. The perimeter of a square floor is 48.8 ft. How long is each side?

33. Yvette grew 13.68 in. in 12 months. On the average, how many inches did she grow per month?

CRITICAL THINKING — Algebra

Complete the pattern to find each quotient.

Think...........
$24 \div 3 = 8$

34. $24 \div 0.3 = \underline{\ ?\ }$ $24 \div 0.03 = \underline{\ ?\ }$ $24 \div 0.003 = \underline{\ ?\ }$

Think...........
$42 \div 6 = 7$

35. $42 \div 0.6 = \underline{\ ?\ }$ $42 \div 0.06 = \underline{\ ?\ }$ $42 \div 0.006 = \underline{\ ?\ }$

Zeros in Division

Erin used 8.75 gal of gasoline to drive her car 210 mi. How many miles per gallon of gasoline did her car get?

To find the miles per gallon, *n*, divide: $210 \div 8.75 = n$.

First estimate by using front-end estimation, $200 \div 8 = 25$. Then divide.

▶ It is sometimes necessary to write one or more zeros as placeholders *in the dividend* to complete the division.

$$8.7\,5\overline{)2\ 1\ 0.}\quad \longrightarrow \quad 8.7\,5\overline{)2\ 1\ 0.0\ 0}\quad \longrightarrow$$

$$
\begin{array}{r}
2\ 4 \\
8\ 7\ 5\overline{)2\ 1\ 0\ 0\ 0} \\
-1\ 7\ 5\ 0\downarrow \\
\hline
3\ 5\ 0\ 0 \\
-3\ 5\ 0\ 0 \\
\hline
0
\end{array}
$$

| Place a decimal point after 210. |
| Move decimal points 2 places to the right. Write 2 zeros as placeholders. |

Erin's car got 24 miles per gallon.

Think
24 is close to the estimate of 25.

▶ If needed, write one or more zeros *in the quotient* to show the correct place value.

$$
\begin{array}{r}
0.0\ 3 \\
4.7\overline{)0.1\,4\ 1} \\
-1\ 4\ 1 \\
\hline
0
\end{array}
$$

Write 1 zero in the quotient.

$$
\begin{array}{r}
0.0\ 0\ 3 \\
5\ 9\overline{)0.1\ 7\ 7} \\
-1\ 7\ 7 \\
\hline
0
\end{array}
$$

Write 2 zeros in the quotient.

Study this example.

$$
0.5\overline{)0.0\,2\ 4}
$$

$$
\begin{array}{r}
0.0\ 4\ 8 \\
5\overline{)0.2\ 4\ 0} \\
-2\ 0\downarrow \\
\hline
4\ 0 \\
-4\ 0 \\
\hline
0
\end{array}
$$

Write a zero.

Write a zero.

Check.

Multiply:
$0.5 \times 0.048 = 0.024$

Divide. When needed, write zeros as placeholders in the dividend.

1. $0.4\overline{)0.2}$ 2. $0.5\overline{)0.7}$ 3. $0.8\overline{)0.5}$ 4. $1.5\overline{)0.3}$

5. $0.8\overline{)1}$ 6. $0.4\overline{)9}$ 7. $2.5\overline{)6}$ 8. $1.2\overline{)3}$

9. $0.05\overline{)0.7}$ 10. $0.32\overline{)0.4}$ 11. $0.08\overline{)0.7}$ 12. $0.08\overline{)16}$

13. $6\overline{)3}$ 14. $8\overline{)4}$ 15. $0.2\overline{)0.03}$ 16. $2.4\overline{)0.6}$

17. $0.7 \div 1.4$ 18. $0.3 \div 2$ 19. $0.03 \div 0.025$ 20. $0.8 \div 0.032$

Divide. Write zeros in the quotient as needed.

21. $5\overline{)0.15}$ 22. $4\overline{)0.36}$ 23. $8\overline{)0.168}$ 24. $80\overline{)0.8}$

25. $2.1\overline{)0.861}$ 26. $6.2\overline{)0.372}$ 27. $2.1\overline{)0.063}$ 28. $0.6\overline{)0.036}$

29. $7\overline{)0.035}$ 30. $9\overline{)0.414}$ 31. $2\overline{)1.802}$ 32. $9\overline{)0.099}$

33. $9.8\overline{)0.0196}$ 34. $0.8\overline{)0.0328}$ 35. $3.1\overline{)0.0279}$ 36. $0.71\overline{)0.0142}$

37. $0.405 \div 0.5$ 38. $0.352 \div 0.4$ 39. $0.00092 \div 0.4$ 40. $0.00042 \div 0.4$

41. $0.702 \div 9$ 42. $0.0096 \div 3$ 43. $4.32 \div 6$ 44. $2.62 \div 8$

Problem Solving

45. Forty laps around a track equal 2.5 km. How far is 1 lap around the track?

46. A wheel makes 1 turn in 0.7 second. What part of a turn can it make in 0.35 second?

47. Melons cost $.56 per pound. How many pounds can be bought with $5.60?

48. A can of juice costs $.48. How many cans can be bought with $12?

49. A greyhound runs at a speed of 39.35 miles per hour. How far will the greyhound run in 0.25 hour?

50. A baseball card is 0.65 mm thick. What is the thickness of 20 baseball cards? of 100 baseball cards?

51. Melinda bought 3.2 lb of cherries for $2.88. Cody paid $3.78 for 4.5 lb of cherries. Who paid more per pound? How much more?

Multiplication and Division Expressions

Linda washes dogs to earn extra money on weekends. She spends 30 minutes on each dog. If she washes 5 dogs on Saturday, write an expression for the total number of minutes she spends washing the dogs.

$$30 \times 5 \qquad 30 \cdot 5 \qquad 30(5)$$

multiplication expression

Write an expression for the total number of minutes Linda spends washing d dogs on Sunday.

$$30 \times d \qquad 30 \cdot d \qquad 30(d) \qquad 30d$$

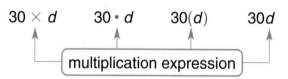

multiplication expression

Algebraic expressions involving multiplication commonly omit the multiplication sign.

$$30 \times d \longrightarrow 30d$$

Each of the expressions above can be read as:

30 times d d multiplied by 30

the product of 30 and d

▶ Linda will spend 280 minutes washing dogs next weekend. If she spends 20 minutes per dog, write an expression for the number of dogs she will wash.

$$280 \div 20 \qquad \frac{280}{20}$$

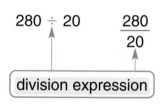

division expression

Write an expression for the number of dogs Linda will wash if she spends m minutes per dog.

$$280 \div m \qquad \frac{280}{m}$$

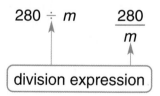

division expression

Each of the expressions above can be read as:

280 divided by m the quotient of 280 and m

the result of dividing 280 by m

Write each word phrase as a numerical expression.

1. eight times four

2. the product of two and 15

3. 27 divided by three

4. the quotient of 81 and nine

Write each word phrase as an algebraic expression. Use _x_ as a variable.

5. the product of 37 and a number

6. a number divided by 12

7. six times a number

8. a number multiplied by 29

9. a number divided by ten

10. 30.5 divided by a number

11. the quotient of 621 and a number

12. a number times 45

Write each mathematical expression as a word phrase.

13. 98×45

14. $62.5 \div 25$

15. $45 \cdot h$

16. $\frac{35}{7}$

17. $m - 65$

18. $35 - 18.3$

19. $81f$

20. $\frac{69}{s}$

21. $8.92(y)$

Write an expression for each situation.

22. Steve has 8 CD cases. He puts 12 CDs in each case. How many CDs in all does Steve have?

23. Jane buys packages of 8 hot dogs for a cookout. She buys _p_ packages in all. How many hot dogs does she buy?

24. Eric buys 20 pounds of dog food. He places an equal amount of food into each of 5 containers. How many pounds of dog food are in each container?

25. Sela ran 13.5 miles in _d_ days. She ran the same distance each day. How far did she run each day?

Write About It

The table shows the number of rows of strawberries that Osvaldo can pick per hour.

26. Let _t_ stand for the number of hours worked. Write an expression for the number of rows picked.

27. Let _r_ stand for the number of rows picked. Write an expression for the number of hours worked.

Number of Hours	Rows Picked
1	2
2	4
3	6
4	8

28. Explain in your Math Journal how the expressions you wrote are related.

Evaluate Multiplication and Division Expressions

A train travels at an average rate of 130 miles per hour. After a number of hours, the train reaches its destination. How many miles does the train travel in 2.5 hours?

To find how many miles, write the expression:

$130h$ ◄ Let h represent the number of hours traveled.

Then evaluate $130h$, when $h = 2.5$ hours. **Evaluate** means find the value.

▶ To evaluate an algebraic expression:

- Substitute the given number for the variable. $130h = 130 \cdot 2.5$

- Simplify to find the value of the expression. $= 325$ ◄ value of the expression

The train travels 325 miles in 2.5 hours at 130 miles per hour.

Study these examples.

Evaluate each expression for the value given.

$w \div 20$, when $w = \$500$

$\begin{array}{l} w \quad \div\ 20 \\ \$500 \div 20 \end{array}$ ◄ Replace w with $\$500$.
◄ Divide.

↓

$\$25$

$8a \times n$, when $a = 1.5$ and $n = 4$

$\begin{array}{l} 8a \times n \\ 8 \times 1.5 \times 4 \end{array}$ ◄ Replace a with 1.5 and n with 4.
◄ Multiply.

↓

48

Evaluate each expression.

1. $26 \cdot 2010$

2. $0.25 \times 8 \times 30.4$

3. $4.2n$, for $n = 20$

4. $33t$, for $t = 1.3$

5. $0.5r$, for $r = 6000$

6. $345 \div f$, for $f = 15$

7. $\dfrac{7568}{16}$

8. $\dfrac{8.4}{q}$, for $q = 1.2$

9. $\dfrac{x}{0.07}$, for $x = 2.94$

10. $n \div 160$, for $n = 2992$

11. $2 \cdot y \cdot 6$, for $y = 0.1$

12. $a(2.1 \cdot 0.02)$, for $a = 40$

Evaluate each algebraic expression for $c = 0.4$ and $d = 200$.
Remember to work from left to right.

13. $d \div 6 \times 30$

14. $d \div c \times 200$

15. $36 \div c \times d$

16. $35 \times c \times 500$

17. $10 \div c \times d$

18. $d \times 1500 \div c$

19. $d \div 20 \times c$

20. $cd \times 12$

21. $cd \div 8$

22. $(d + 4) \div c$

23. $8d + 100c$

24. $300c \div d$

Problem Solving

Write and evaluate an expression for each situation.

25. Lois spent x dollars on 12 books. Each book cost the same amount. How much did Lois spend on each book, if she spent a total of $143.88?

26. Leah spent three times the amount Damean spent on CDs. Damean spent $33.87. How much did Leah spend on CDs?

27. Let y represent the number of miles Mandi jogged each week. Brittany jogged double the amount Mandi jogged. How many miles did Brittany jog, if Mandi jogged 6.8 miles?

28. Kristy found the total weight of some packages to be 1.926 kilograms. Each package weighed the same amount. If there were 6 packages, what did each weigh?

29. Nina meets her friends for lunch. The bill was $40.24 and they left an $8 tip. How much did each of the eight friends pay if they shared the bill equally?

MENTAL MATH

Evaluate each algebraic expression for
$c = 1000$, $d = 2000$, $g = 0.001$, and $h = 0.009$.

30. c times d

31. d divided by c

32. h divided by g

33. the product of d and g

34. d minus c

35. h added to g

36. h multiplied by d

37. h divided by c

38. g times h

39. d more than c

40. g less than h

41. the quotient of d and g

Update your skills. See page 2.

3-12

Round Quotients

Mei bought 6 containers of apple juice for $1.90. To the nearest cent, what is the cost of each container of juice?

To find the cost of each container, *n*, divide: $1.90 ÷ 6 = *n*.

First estimate by using compatible numbers: $1.80 ÷ 6 = $.30. Then divide.

Sometimes the division results in a remainder, no matter how many zeros are written in the dividend. You can round these quotients. In this case, the quotient is rounded to the nearest cent (hundredths place).

Rules for Rounding:

- Look at the digit to the right of the place to which you are rounding.
- If the digit *is less than* 5, round *down*. If the digit is *5 or greater*, round *up*.

```
      $ . 3  1  6
6) $ 1 . 9  0  0
   - 1 8
        1  0
   -    6
        4  0
     - 3  6
        4
```

Divide to the thousandths place. Write 1 zero.

.....Think.....
$ .316666...
6)$1.900000

$.316
↓
$.32

6 > 5
Round up to $.32

To the nearest cent, each container of juice costs $.32.

Study these examples.

Round to the nearest tenth:
7 ÷ 3.

```
   2 . 3  3
3) 7 . 0  0
```

Divide to hundredths. Write 2 zeros.

3 < 5 Round down. | 7 ÷ 3 ≈ 2.3

Round to the nearest thousandth:
0.42 ÷ 0.19.

```
              2 . 2  1  0  5
0.1 9) 0.4 2 . 0  0  0  0
```

Divide to ten thousandths. Write 4 zeros.

5 = 5 Round up. | 0.42 ÷ 0.19 ≈ 2.211

Divide. Round to the nearest tenth.

1. $6\overline{)8}$

2. $17\overline{)6}$

3. $9.2\overline{)20}$

4. $6.5\overline{)15}$

5. $2.3\overline{)0.4}$

6. $0.9\overline{)2.1}$

7. $3.1\overline{)6.5}$

8. $0.3\overline{)0.8}$

9. $0.4\overline{)0.85}$

10. $0.4\overline{)1.23}$

11. $0.03\overline{)0.11}$

12. $0.09\overline{)0.61}$

Divide. Round to the nearest hundredth or nearest cent.

13. $6\overline{)5}$

14. $3\overline{)22}$

15. $7\overline{)9.2}$

16. $4\overline{)1.5}$

17. $1.1\overline{)4.5}$

18. $1.5\overline{)0.4}$

19. $3.3\overline{)8.1}$

20. $0.7\overline{)4.5}$

21. $0.06\overline{)7.1}$

22. $0.07\overline{)9.3}$

23. $0.7\overline{)0.58}$

24. $0.3\overline{)0.71}$

25. $8\overline{)\$1.24}$

26. $6\overline{)\$8.23}$

27. $2\overline{)\$1.11}$

28. $3\overline{)\$5.19}$

Divide. Round to the nearest thousandth.

29. $6\overline{)0.4}$

30. $8\overline{)2.73}$

31. $3\overline{)7.055}$

32. $27\overline{)0.578}$

33. $0.3\overline{)0.61}$

34. $9.5\overline{)1808}$

35. $2.3\overline{)237}$

36. $0.07\overline{)0.4}$

Problem Solving

37. A 32-oz box of cereal sells for $1.89. To the nearest cent, what is the price per ounce?

38. Juan can climb 3.7 km in 4 hours. To the nearest hundredth of a kilometer, how far can he climb in an hour?

39. Edna can run 5.5 km in 26 minutes. To the nearest tenth of a kilometer, what is her speed in kilometers per minute?

40. Mr. Shapiro used 14.7 gallons of gasoline to drive 392.7 miles. To the nearest tenth, what was his average number of miles per gallon?

Write About It

41.  Explain in your Math Journal how to find the *price per ounce* as in problem 37.

Problem-Solving Strategy:
Interpret the Remainder

To celebrate Somerville's 200th anniversary, 2000 people are invited to a formal dinner. If 12 people are seated at each table, how many tables will be needed?

Read ▶ **Visualize yourself in the problem above as you reread it. List the facts and the question.**

Facts: 2000 people invited to a dinner
each table seats 12 people

Question: How many tables will be needed?

Plan ▶ Since each table seats 12 people, divide 2000 by 12 to find how many tables, *n*, will be needed.

2000 ÷ 12 = *n*.

Solve ▶

```
        1 6 6  R8
 1 2)2 0 0 0
    −1 2 ↓
        8 0
      −7 2 ↓
          8 0
        −7 2
            8
```

> There is a remainder of 8 people, so 1 more table will be needed.

Somerville will need 167 tables to seat 2000 people.

Check ▶ Multiply and add to check your answer.

```
        1 6 6
      ×   1 2
        3 3 2
    +1 6 6
      1 9 9 2
    +       8
      2 0 0 0
```

> Remember: Check by multiplying the quotient and the divisor. Then add the remainder.

The answer checks.

Solve. Interpret the remainder.

1. A radio station is planning a 12.5 km walk for a fundraiser. The goal is to raise $98,003. If the pledge is $1.50 per km, how many people will need to walk 12.5 km to reach or surpass the goal?

 Read Visualize yourself in the problem above as you reread it. List the facts and the question.

        Facts: fundraiser walk—12.5 km
                     pledge per km—$1.50
                     goal—$98,003

        Question: How many people will need to walk 12.5 km to reach or go beyond the goal?

 Plan First, find how much a person will raise, a, if he or she walks 12.5 km. Multiply: $\$1.50 \times 12.5 = a$.

Then, to find the number of people needed to raise $98,003, n, divide: $\$98,003.00 \div a = n$.

.Think....................
What will a
remainder mean?

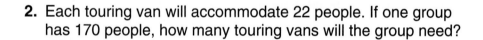

2. Each touring van will accommodate 22 people. If one group has 170 people, how many touring vans will the group need?

3. Two hundred twenty-five dignitaries are invited to a parade. There are three reviewing stands that each seat 70 people. How many extra chairs will be needed to seat all the dignitaries?

4. There are 17 floats in the parade. Each float is decorated with 1026 carnations. If 500 carnations cost $189.50, how much will it cost to decorate all 17 floats?

5. Festival organizers plan to have 170 fireworks set off at night. The show will last $\frac{1}{2}$ hour. If the same number of firecrackers are to go off each minute, how many should that be?

6. Local vendors plan to sell hot dogs during the festival. Their goal is to sell 5000 hot dogs. If hot dogs are packed 48 to a box, how many boxes should the vendors order?

Solve each problem and explain the method you used.

1. Rachel's craft group is building a collection of model ships. Rachel cuts 9 masts out of a 75-in. balsa wood dowel. How long is each mast?

2. A local lumber supplier sells 1000 balsa wood dowels for $990.00. How much would a hundred dowels cost? a dozen dowels? 1 dowel?

3. Ramon needs 50 wooden planks to build decks for 11 ships. If 50 planks cost $99.50, how much is Ramon spending per ship?

4. Jared uses twine for the ropes on a model ship. A 35-yd ball of twine costs $2.99. What is the cost per yard?

5. Miniature brass ship decorations sell for $.29 per ounce. If Talia pays $7.50 for a bag of decorations, how many ounces does the bag weigh? Round to the nearest ounce.

6. Ted sends Rachel 100 model sails that he has made. The total weight of the package is 13.75 oz. If the packaging weighs 0.25 oz, how much does one sail weigh?

7. The content weight of a box of models is 81 lb. If there are 9 each of 5 different models in the box, what is the average weight of an individual model?

8. A collection of model ships has a mass of 8064 g. The mass of each ship is 448 g. How many ships are in the collection?

9. Models built by four craft groups will be exhibited together. Each display case will hold 6 model ships. There will be 117 model ships in the exhibit. How many display cases will be needed?

Solve. Use a strategy from the list or another strategy you know to do each problem.

10. The History Museum displays a variety of models. A model fort is built entirely from miniature bricks. Each brick has a mass of 115 g. The model fort has a mass of 143 175 g. How many bricks are used in this model?

Strategy File

Use These Strategies
Interpret the Remainder
Write an Equation
Guess and Test
Use Simpler Numbers
Use More Than One Step
Use a Graph

11. Another historical model shows a Civil War battlefield. There are twice as many Confederate soldiers as Union soldiers in the model. There are 639 soldiers in the display. How many Confederate soldiers are there?

12. A model of the *Monitor* requires 2350 bolts. The bolts are produced in sets of 15. How many sets of bolts must be ordered to make this model?

13. Joe's handmade wooden toy train car weighs 4.923 oz. A 15-car wooden train set at a local toy store weighs 65.64 oz. How much lighter or heavier is Joe's train car than the average for the store's train cars?

14. A craft club wants to buy model paint kits to raffle off at their next meeting. The kits come in three sizes: small, 24 oz of paint for $5.19; medium, 32 oz of paint for $6.19; and large, 48 oz of paint for $7.19. Which is the best buy?

15. The model builder of the *Spirit of St. Louis* took 45 seconds to place each toothpick. If 4781 toothpicks were used, how many minutes did it take her to build the entire model?

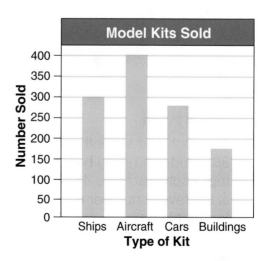

Use the bar graph for problems 16 and 17.

16. How many more kits for model aircraft were sold than for model buildings?

17. Model car kits cost $8.95 each. How much money was spent on model car kits?

18. Write a problem modeled on problem 12 above. Have a classmate solve it.

Model Kits Sold

Number Sold (y-axis): 0, 50, 100, 150, 200, 250, 300, 350, 400

Type of Kit (x-axis): Ships, Aircraft, Cars, Buildings

Divide using short division. *(See pp: 88–89.)*

1. $6\overline{)689,347}$
2. $9\overline{)365,431}$
3. $5\overline{)705,830}$
4. $2\overline{)8,431,096}$

Estimate by using compatible numbers. Then find each quotient. *(See pp. 90–93.)*

5. $43\overline{)769}$
6. $35\overline{)3579}$
7. $432\overline{)9510}$
8. $389\overline{)\$2789.13}$

Write in scientific notation. *(See pp. 94–95.)*

9. 0.000021
10. 0.00543
11. 0.00065
12. 0.00000175

Divide. *(See pp. 94–105.)*

13. $0.79 \div 100$
14. $0.01\overline{)12.9}$
15. $26\overline{)250.9}$
16. $35\overline{)\$262.15}$

17. $0.084 \div 0.4$
18. $0.6\overline{)1.08}$
19. $4.8\overline{)2.544}$
20. $0.5\overline{)125}$

Write each word expression as an algebraic expression. Use *x* as the variable. *(See pp. 106–107.)*

21. the product of 95 and a number
22. a number divided by 25

23. eight times a number
24. the quotient of a number and 49

Evaluate each expression. *(See pp. 108–109.)*

25. $7.8n$, for $n = 30$
26. $45t$, for $t = 1.5$
27. $0.7r$, for $r = 9000$

28. $275 \div f$, for $f = 25$
29. $\frac{8.4}{q}$, for $q = 2.4$
30. $n \div 120$, for $n = 578.4$

Divide. Round to the nearest hundredth or nearest cent. *(See pp. 110–111.)*

31. $16 \div 6$
32. $0.11\overline{)5.9}$
33. $8\overline{)\$1.77}$
34. $9\overline{)\$57.59}$

Problem Solving
(See pp. 112–116.)

35. The sixth and seventh grades have 362 students taking buses for a field trip. Each bus holds 46 people. What is the fewest number of buses needed for the trip?

36. Rhode Island has an area of 1545 square miles and Texas has an area of 268,601 square miles. How many times greater is the area of Texas than that of Rhode Island?

(See Still More Practice, p. 522.)

Logic: Open and Closed Statements

In logic, a statement is a sentence that states a fact. A statement is true or false, but not both.

▶ A closed statement can be judged true or false.

All animals have wings.	False
A triangle has exactly 3 sides.	True
Ten is an odd number.	False

▶ An open statement contains an unknown. If you replace the unknown, the statement becomes closed. It can then be judged true or false.

All squares have exactly n sides.    n is an unknown.

All squares have exactly 3 sides.   False

$10 - x = 5$
$10 - 5 = 5$ True

Tell whether each statement is closed or open. If the statement is closed, write *True* or *False*.

1. Alabama is a continent.

2. A horse has 4 legs.

3. $7 - a = 5$

4. $15 \times 5 = 155$

5. Twenty-one is an even number.

6. Six ten thousandths = 0.006

7. $0.45 + \underline{\ ?\ } > 9$

8. $16 - 0.75 = 15.25$

Find a number or numbers that make each open statement true.

9. A pentagon has exactly n sides.

10. 0.456 rounded to nearest tenth is n.

11. $30 \times f = 270$

12. $48 \div m = 12$

13. $2 \times n \times 2 = 16$

14. $0.52 + 0.6 + 3 = n$

15. $0.24 + 0.34 > n$

Chapter 3 Test

Estimate each quotient. Use compatible numbers.

1. 3041 ÷ 82

2. 300,864 ÷ 66

3. 736 ÷ 4.2

4. 37.26 ÷ 7.1

Write in scientific notation.

5. 0.000056

6. 0.00158

7. 0.00012

8. 0.00000235

Find the quotient.

9. 0.83 ÷ 1000

10. $9\overline{)189{,}567}$

11. $4\overline{)\$14.24}$

12. $0.7\overline{)7.91}$

13. 0.558 ÷ 6.2

14. $0.032\overline{)0.288}$

15. $4.26\overline{)17{,}615.1}$

16. $0.25\overline{)7.625}$

Write each mathematical expression as a word phrase.

17. 98m

18. 62.5 ÷ q

19. 45 • 25

Find the value of each algebraic expression for c = 0.3 and d = 2340.

20. d ÷ 6 × 30

21. c × d ÷ 1000

22. 36 ÷ c × d

Problem Solving

Use a strategy you have learned.

23. If art paper comes in packs of 48 sheets, how many packs will Sam need to get 889 sheets?

Tell About It

24. Fred spent $10.69 on 9 used books. Fran spent $8.29 on 7 used books. Who spent less per book? Explain.

Performance Assessment

Tell how many digits could be in the quotient. Give an example to support your answer.

25. 5-digit number ÷ 2-digit number

26. 6-digit number ÷ 3-digit number

Find each quotient to complete each table. Describe any patterns you see.

27.

n	n ÷ 0.5
2.5	?
3.0	?
3.5	?

28.

x	x ÷ 0.2
0.08	?
0.06	?
0.04	?

Test Preparation

Choose the best answer.

1. Choose the standard form of 65 billion, 18 thousand and 7 ten thousandths.

   a. 65,000,018.0007
   b. 65,018.0007
   c. 65,000,018,000.0007
   d. not given

2. Choose the short word name for the number $(9 \times 10^6) + (7 \times 10^4) + (6 \times 10^2) + (8 \times 1)$.

   a. 9768
   b. 9 million, 70 thousand, 608
   c. 9 million, 7 thousand, 610
   d. not given

3. Which numbers are in order from greatest to least?

   a. 5.4534; 5.0435; 5.3403
   b. 5.4304; 5.4122; 5.041
   c. 5.4305; 5.42; 5.433
   d. 5.0415; 5.42; 5.4305

4. Subtract 2,665,050 from 30,880,200.

   a. 28,215,150
   b. 28,225,150
   c. 33,542,250
   d. not given

5. Which numbers are divisible by 3?

   A. 369,720   **B.** 307,111   **C.** 34,563

   a. A and B only
   b. A and C only
   c. B and C only
   d. A, B, and C

6. Choose the standard form.

   5.76×10^5

   a. 5,670,000
   b. 576,000
   c. 0.00576
   d. not given

7. Choose the scientific notation for 294 billion.

   a. 29.4×10^{11}
   b. 2.94×10^{11}
   c. 294.10^{10}
   d. 2.94×10^9

8. Round 97,491,608,123 to the nearest hundred million.

   a. 97,490,000,000
   b. 97,000,000,000
   c. 97,492,000,000
   d. 97,500,000,000

9. Estimate the quotient.

   $402,252 \div 218$

   a. 20
   b. 200
   c. 2000
   d. 20,000

10. Choose the product.

    $3 \times 0.4 \times 0.8$

    a. 0.096
    b. 0.96
    c. 9.6
    d. not given

11. $8.932 + 89.32 + 809.2 + 3.924$

    a. 65.780
    b. 908.4344
    c. 947.276
    d. not given

12. Choose the product.

    0.703×0.04

    a. 0.002802
    b. 0.02812
    c. 0.2812
    d. not given

13. Name the place of the underlined digit.

72,951.009846

a. hundred thousandths
b. ten thousandths
c. ten thousands
d. hundred thousands

14. Find the value of *n*.

$n = 13{,}024 \div 32$

a. 40 R7
b. 407
c. 407 R25
d. not given

15. 9.21×10^{-4} in standard form is:

a. 0.000921
b. 0.00921
c. 0.0921
d. not given

16. Which expression has a value of 10 when $n = 10$?

a. $20n$
b. $20 + n$
c. $20 - n$
d. $\dfrac{20}{n}$

17. The water in a tank weighs 728.45 lb. One cubic foot of water weighs 62.5 lb. About how many cubic feet of water does the tank hold?

a. 42,000 cu ft
b. 1200 cu ft
c. 100 cu ft
d. 12 cu ft

18. Estimate. Use front-end estimation with adjustments.

$3.681 + 9.54 + 0.87$

a. 12
b. 14
c. 16
d. not given

19. Find the quotient to the nearest hundredth.

$0.4\overline{)2.4508}$

a. 6.12
b. 6.13
c. 6.127
d. not given

20. Which number is divisible by both 2 and 4?

a. 903,612
b. 142,214
c. 46,106
d. 40,182

21. Choose the product.

9.009×0.9

a. 810.81
b. 81.081
c. 8.1081
d. 0.81901

22. Which number is 10^5 more than $(4 \times 10^4) + (3 \times 10^3) + (2 \times 10^2) + (1 \times 10)$?

a. 43,260
b. 53,210
c. 143,210
d. 1,432,100

Explain how you solved each problem. Show all your work.

23. Each letter in the statements below represents one number in the box. What is the value of each letter?

| 5 | 4.58 | 0.1764 | 4.7564 | 0.42 |

$C + A = D \qquad A^2 = E \qquad B - A < C$

Expressions and Equations

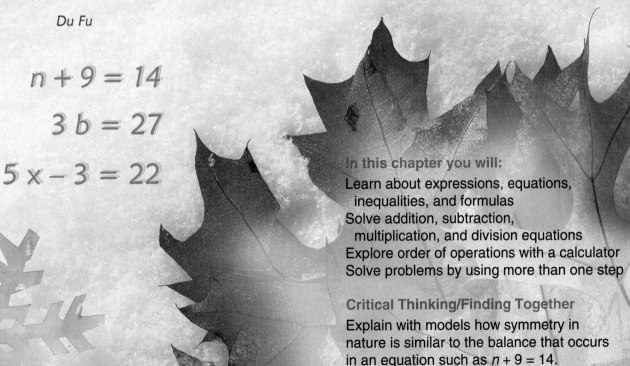

Symmetry

A pair of golden orioles sings in the green willows,
A line of white egrets flies across the blue sky.
Through my west window, snows of a thousand autumns cap the mountains.
Beyond my east door, boats from ten thousand miles away dot the river.

Du Fu

$$n + 9 = 14$$

$$3b = 27$$

$$5x - 3 = 22$$

In this chapter you will:

Learn about expressions, equations, inequalities, and formulas
Solve addition, subtraction, multiplication, and division equations
Explore order of operations with a calculator
Solve problems by using more than one step

Critical Thinking/Finding Together

Explain with models how symmetry in nature is similar to the balance that occurs in an equation such as $n + 9 = 14$.

Order of Operations

Frances has 215 apples in each of two crates. Three other crates have 150 apples each. How many apples does Frances have in all?

To find how many in all, compute:
$2 \times 215 + 3 \times 150$.

Frances computes as follows:

Number of apples $= 2 \times 215 + 3 \times 150$
$= 430 + 450$
$= 880$

Frances has 880 apples in all.

▶ Compute: $(42 \div 7) \times 3 - 4 \div 2 + 10^2$

When a mathematical expression contains more than one operation, mathematicians have agreed to follow these order of operations rules:

Grouping symbols include:
• parentheses $\longrightarrow 12 - (6 + 2) = 4$
• brackets $\longrightarrow [7 + 2] \div 3 = 3$
• fraction bars $\longrightarrow \dfrac{16 - 4 + 2}{2} = \dfrac{14}{2} = 7$

• First compute operations within *grouping symbols.*

$\underline{(42 \div 7)} \times 3 - 4 \div 2 + 10^2$

• Next simplify numbers with *exponents.*

$6 \times 3 - 4 \div 2 + \underline{10^2}$

• Then *multiply* or *divide* from left to right.

$6 \times 3 - 4 \div 2 + 100$

• Last *add* or *subtract* from left to right.

$18 - 2 + 100$

$16 + 100$

116

Study these examples.

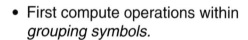

0.4×10^3

0.4×1000

400

$48 - (3 - 1)^3$

$48 - 2^3$

$48 - 8$

40

$\dfrac{5^2 - 1.4}{4}$

$\dfrac{25 - 1.4}{4}$

$\dfrac{23.6}{4} = 5.9$

Tell which operation is to be done first. Then compute.

1. $3 \times 9 + 8$

2. $16 \div 4 + 2$

3. $15 - 6 \div 3$

4. $\frac{7 + 11}{9} \times 3$

5. $21 - \frac{9 + 11}{10}$

6. $27 \div \frac{9 \times 3}{5 + 4}$

7. $(14 \div 2) + 6^2$

8. $2^2 \times [15 - 3]$

9. $64 \div (8 \times 8)$

Use the order of operations to compute. Justify each step in the process.

10. $4 \times 8 \times 3 - 2$

11. $18 \div 6 \div 3 - 1$

12. $9 + 3 \times 2 + 4^2$

13. $12 - 3 \times 1 + 2^3$

14. $(40 \div 4) + 5 - 3 + [0.6 \times 40]$

15. $5 + (34 - 2) \div 8 + (1.7 + 2)$

16. $10 \times 3 + (48 \div 6)^2 \times 0.4$

17. $(50 \div 10)^3 \times 2 + 6 \times 0.6$

18. $\frac{7 + 3}{2^2 + 1} - [5 \div 5 \times 2]$

19. $(24 + \frac{1 \times 7}{3^2 - 2^3} - 6) \div 5^2$

Insert parentheses to make each number sentence true.

20. $48 \div 3^2 - 1 + 7 = 13$

21. $5 \times 10^2 \div 41 - 4^2 = 20$

22. $6^2 - 8 - 2 \times 2 \div 2^2 = 35$

23. $3.2 + 4.3 \div 1.5 \times 2^3 = 40$

24. $8 + 0.5 + 6.7 \div 1.2 = 14$

25. $18 - 5^2 \div 10 + 4.5 = 20$

Problem Solving

Write the mathematical expression to solve each problem. Then evaluate.

26. Catherine works after school at a job for which she is paid $25 a day. She makes tips of $15 a day. How much money does she receive in 5 days?

27. Leon packs 30 business envelopes in each of 25 boxes and 30 regular envelopes in each of 20 boxes. How many envelopes does he pack?

TEST PREPARATION

28. $(42 \div 7) \times 3 - 4 \div 2 + 1$

A 0   **B** 2
C 8   **D** 17

29. $5^2 \div [3^3 - 2] + \frac{9 + 4}{7 - 6}$

F 14   **G** 589
H 638   **J** 51

Translate Expressions

Kari orders 5 CDs to give as gifts. Each CD costs $15. Shipping and handling is $5 per order. What is the total cost of her CD order?

▶ To find the total cost of her CD order, write a numerical expression and then compute.

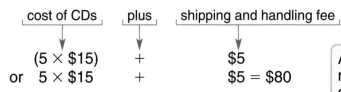

cost of CDs   plus   shipping and handling fee

$$(5 \times \$15) \quad + \quad \$5$$
or $\quad 5 \times \$15 \quad + \quad \$5 = \$80$

> A mathematical expression may contain more than one operation.

The total cost of Kari's order is $80.

Kari orders some books for the library. Each book costs $9. Shipping and handling is $8 per order. How much is the total cost of her order?

▶ The number of books Kari orders is unknown. To find the total cost of her book order, write an algebraic expression.

$$\$9b + \$8 \longleftarrow \boxed{\text{Let } b \text{ represent the number of books.}}$$

▶ Word phrases can be written as numerical or algebraic expressions.

Word Phrase	Expression
two plus 3, times 4	$(2 + 3) \times 4$
7 plus 5, divided by the sum of 3 and 1	$(7 + 5) \div (3 + 1)$
a number tripled, plus 2	$3n + 2$
one half of y squared, minus 14	$\frac{1}{2}y^2 - 14$
twice the difference of a number minus 10	$2 \times (m - 10)$

Practice

Write as a numerical expression. Then compute.

1. eight divided by four, plus 11

2. nine minus six, multiplied by seven

3. 27 times 11, minus 35

4. 20 subtracted from 68, divided by 12

5. 19 added to 21, times the sum of 7 and 2

6. 27 times the sum of 3.5 and 0.11

Write as an algebraic expression. Use *n* as the variable.

7. six times the cost of a card, decreased by $.05

8. one fourth of a number, increased by 17

9. 100 less than a number tripled

10. 8 added to a number, multiplied by 2

11. 98 times the sum of a number and 1.3

12. the quotient of a number squared and the difference of 5.9 and 7

Write as a word phrase.

13. $56 + 4.1 \times 2.5$

14. $3n - 8$

15. $\frac{y}{6} + 10$

16. $a^2 - (b + c)$

17. $6.5ab$

18. $98 \div 4.5x$

Problem Solving

Write an expression for each. Then compute if possible.

19. Aaron buys 8 videotapes. The tapes cost $7 each. He buys a carrying case for $12. How much does Aaron pay in all?

20. Laura orders 9 balls of yarn. Each ball of yarn costs $3. She pays $6 for shipping. How much does Laura spend in all?

21. Ed has 30 toy trucks. He puts an equal number of trucks on 6 shelves. He does the same with his 42 toy cars. How many toys are on each shelf?

22. Mac collects 135 golf balls. He throws away 10 of them. He divides the rest of the golf balls equally among some buckets in his cart. What is the number of golf balls Mac puts in each bucket?

23. Dee buys 12 cans of cat food at $1.50 each. She gets a discount. What is the total amount Dee pays?

24. Sue pays for herself and 4 friends to go to the fair. Admission is $6 per person plus a group fee. How much does Sue pay in all?

DO YOU REMEMBER?

Multiply. Round to the nearest cent when necessary.

25.	26.	27.	28.	29.
4.3	0.45	5.02	$7.49	$49.95
$\times\ 0.9$	$\times\ 0.14$	$\times\ 7.3$	$\times\ \ \ \ 6$	$\times\ \ \ \ 9$

30.	31.	32.	33.	34.
6.21	0.127	95.6	$7.46	$8.93
$\times\ 6.7$	$\times\ 0.33$	$\times\ 8.05$	$\times\ 3.25$	$\times\ 1.7$

Evaluate Algebraic Expressions

Some students are visiting a science museum. They pay $7 per student and a group fee of $25. Write an algebraic expression for the total cost of the trip.

Let s represent the number of students.

total students' cost	plus	group fee
↓	↓	↓
$7s	+	$25

If there are 124 students going on the trip, what is the total cost they will pay for the trip?

To find the total cost, evaluate the expression $7s + $25, when $s = 124$.

$$\$7s + \$25$$
$\$7 \cdot 124 + \$25$ ← Replace s with 124.
$\quad \$868 \ \ + \$25$ ← Simplify using the order of operations.
$\qquad \$893$

The students will pay a total cost of $893.

> Remember:
> To evaluate an expression is to find its value.

Study these examples. Evaluate each expression for the values given.

$7 + 3x^3 - y$, when $x = 2$
and $y = 4$

$7 + 3 \cdot 2^3 - 4$ ← Replace x with 2 and y with 4.
$7 + 3 \cdot 8 - 4$ ← Simplify using the order
$7 + 24 - 4$ of operations.
$31 - 4$

$\downarrow$

27

$\dfrac{12 + a^2}{b - c}$, when $a = 4$, $b = 0.3$,
and $c = 0.2$

$\dfrac{12 + 4^2}{0.3 - 0.2}$ ← Replace a with 4, b with 0.3, and c with 0.2.

$\dfrac{28}{0.1}$ ← Simplify using the order of operations.

$\downarrow$

280

Evaluate each expression.

1. $56 - p(q + r)$, when $p = 3$, $q = 4.2$, and $r = 5.1$

2. $(x + 1)^2 + y \div z$, when $x = 3$, $y = 8.8$, and $z = 4$

3. $15 + cj^3$, when $c = 6$ and $j = 5$

4. $(d + e \div 9)^2 - 14f$, when $d = 8$, $e = 45$, and $f = 2$

Combine Like Terms

Before evaluating some algebraic expressions, you can simplify them by combining like terms.

The parts of an algebraic expression that are separated by an addition or subtraction sign are called terms. Terms that have exactly the same variable parts are called like terms.

$$7a + 10a - 19 \qquad \frac{1}{2}x^2 + 15x - 4x^2$$

like terms   like terms

▶ Simplify by combining like terms. Then evaluate the expression for the given value of the variable.

$12w - 5w + 30$, when $w = 1.5$	$8c^2 - 6c + 3c^2$, when $c = 4$
$(12w - 5w) + 30$ ← Associative Property	$8c^2 + 3c^2 - 6c$ ← Commutative Property
$(12 - 5)w + 30$ ← Distributive Property	$(8 + 3)c^2 - 6c$ ← Distributive Property
$7w + 30$ ← Simplify.	$11c^2 - 6c$ ← Simplify.
$7 \cdot 1.5 + 30$ ← Replace w with 1.5.	$11 \cdot 4^2 - 6 \cdot 4$ ← Replace c with 4.
40.5 ← value of the expression	152 ← value of the expression

Simplify by combining like terms. Then evaluate the expression for the given value of the variable.

5. $20n - 6n - 3$, when $n = 2.5$

6. $6x + 7x + 14$, when $x = 0.34$

7. $378 + 15y - 2y$, when $y = 3.1$

8. $7m^2 + 3m^2 + 2$, when $m = 3$

9. $9z^2 - 5z + 3z^2$, when $z = 10$

10. $13b + 6b - 19 + 14c$, when $b = 15$ and $c = 0.4$

Problem Solving

Write and evaluate an algebraic expression.

11. Juan buys some T-shirts for $12.95 each and pays a sales tax of $2.33. If he buys 3 T-shirts, how much does Juan pay in all?

12. Lucy orders books from an online bookstore. She pays $12 per book and $8.95 for shipping and handling. How much does she pay in all for 13 books?

13. Stanley packs some paperback books in each of 5 boxes and some hardcover books in each of 4 boxes. If he packs 15 paperback books in each box and 11 hardcover books in each box, how many books in all does he pack?

Practice

Equations and Inequalities

Leslie and Clark each write a word sentence as an equation.
An equation is a statement that shows that two mathematical expressions are equal.

Leslie's equation is:

Twice nine decreased by three is fifteen.

$2 \cdot 9 \quad - \quad 3 \quad = \quad 15$

Leslie's equation is a closed sentence because it contains no variables. A closed sentence is either true or false.

▶ To determine whether an equation is true or false:

- Simplify each side of the equation using the order of operations.
- Compare the sides to determine if they make a true statement.

$$2 \cdot 9 - 3 = 15$$
$$18 - 3 \stackrel{?}{=} 15$$
$$15 = 15 \text{ true}$$

The equation, $2 \times 9 - 3 = 15$, is a true statement.

Clark's equation is:

Five times a number n, minus two equals eight.

$5n \quad - \quad 2 \quad = \quad 8$

Clark's equation is an open sentence because it contains a variable. An open sentence is neither true nor false.

▶ To determine whether a value is a solution of an equation:

- Replace the variable with the given value.
- Simplify using the order of operations and determine the value of the variable that makes a true statement.

$5n - 2 = 8$, when $n = 3$ and $n = 2$

$5(3) - 2 = 8$	and	$5(2) - 2 = 8$
$15 - 2 \stackrel{?}{=} 8$	and	$10 - 2 \stackrel{?}{=} 8$
$13 = 8$ false	and	$8 = 8$ true

2 is the solution of the equation. It makes a true statement.

Practice

Write as an equation. Then label each equation as *open* or *closed*. If the equation is closed, write whether it is *true* or *false*.

1. A number divided by 3.85 is equal to one.

2. Six less than three times ten is equal to twenty.

3. Two more than twice a number is three.

4. Half of eight is three less than seven.

Determine if the given value of the variable is the solution of the equation. Write *yes* or *no*.

5. $9x + 8 = 35$, when $x = 3$

6. $19 - 2p = 6$, when $p = 7$

7. $\frac{k}{3} + 4.9 = 8.5$, when $k = 12.3$

8. $18 - (8 - m) = 17$, when $m = 7$

Inequalities

A word sentence can also represent an inequality. An inequality is a statement that uses any of the symbols in the table at the right.

Symbol	Read As
<	is less than
>	is greater than
≤	is less than or equal to
≥	is greater than or equal to
≠	is not equal to

Eight plus twice two $\;$ is greater than $\;$ ten.

$$8 \;+\; 2(2) \qquad > \qquad 10 \quad \text{closed sentence}$$
$$12 \qquad\qquad\quad > \qquad 10 \quad \text{true}$$

Five less than a number $\;$ is less than $\;$ twenty-five.

$$n - 5 \qquad\qquad < \qquad 25 \quad \text{open sentence}$$
$$20 - 5 \qquad\quad\; < \qquad 25 \quad \text{for } n = 20$$
$$15 \qquad\qquad\;\; < \qquad 25 \quad \text{true}$$

$n = 15$ is one solution of the inequality.

An inequality that includes a variable, or is open, can have more than one solution. For $n - 5 < 25$, n can be any number less than 30.

**Write as an inequality. Then label each inequality *open* or *closed*.
If the inequality is closed, write whether it is *true* or *false*.**

9. One more than twice a number is greater than three.

10. Forty-seven is less than or equal to five times three, added to nine.

11. Nineteen is not equal to the sum of one and one tenth of one hundred.

12. One sixth of thirty-six hundredths is less than two-tenths less than four.

13. The quotient of a number divided by seven is greater than or equal to ten.

14. Eight is not equal to three times a number.

**Determine if the given value of the variable is a solution
of the inequality. Write *yes* or *no*.**

15. $50x + 12.5 < 55$, when $x = 0.5$

16. $7n - 6 \geq n + 12$, when $n = 2.1$

17. $\frac{q}{4} + 2.4 \neq 6.5$, when $q = 16.4$

18. $25 - (5 - r) > 19$, when $m = 2.3$

CRITICAL THINKING — Algebra

**Equations and inequalities can have more than one variable.
Find a value for each variable that will make each statement true.**

19. $5.5x - 1.5y = 3.5x$

20. $8.4x > 2.4x + 3.6y$

21. $\frac{12.6x}{6} - 2y \leq 0.4y$

Update your skills. See page 7.

Addition Equations

The seating capacity for football games at a sports stadium is 4117 more than the seating capacity for baseball games. If the seating capacity is 63,000 for football games, what is the seating capacity for baseball games?

To find the seating capacity for baseball games, write and solve an equation.

Let *x* represent the seating capacity for baseball games.

seating capacity for baseball   plus 4117   equals   seating capacity for football

$$x \quad + \quad 4117 \quad = \quad 63{,}000 \quad \longleftarrow \boxed{\text{addition equation}}$$

▶ To solve an **addition equation,** use the Subtraction Property of Equality.

$$x + 4117 = 63{,}000$$
$$x + 4117 - 4117 = 63{,}000 - 4117 \longleftarrow$$
$$x = 58{,}883$$

Subtract 4117 from both sides to isolate the variable.

> **Subtraction Property of Equality**
> When you subtract the same number from both sides of an equation, you get a true statement.

> Remember: Addition and subtraction are inverse operations.

Check:
$$x + 4117 \overset{?}{=} 63{,}000$$
$$58{,}883 + 4117 \overset{?}{=} 63{,}000$$
$$63{,}000 = 63{,}000 \text{ True}$$

The seating capacity for baseball games is 58,883.

Study this example.

Solve: $27.5 = y + 3.3 + 1.7$

$27.5 = y + 3.3 + 1.7$ ◀—Simplify by adding the numbers on one side.
$27.5 = y + 5.0$
$27.5 - 5.0 = y + 5.0 - 5.0$ ◀—Subtract 5.0 from both sides to isolate the variable.
$22.5 = y$

Check:
$$27.5 \overset{?}{=} 22.5 + 3.3 + 1.7$$
$$27.5 \overset{?}{=} 22.5 + 5.0$$
$$27.5 = 27.5 \text{ True}$$

Solve and check.

1. $x + 2597 = 6233$

2. $y + 13.84 = 20.29$

3. $0.793 = n + 0.65$

4. $119 + 246 + f = 893$

5. $1.1 + 1.83 + g = 6.25$

6. $0 + m = 2.3$

7. $4.263 = 4.263 + k$

8. $0.52 = 0.13 + 0.15 + r$

9. $3.415 = 1.626 + s$

10. $z + \$3.95 = \$9.20$

11. $\$8.31 = \$3.22 + w$

12. $\$75.40 = \$25.40 + b$

13. $p + 1.93 + 1.17 = 9$

14. $5 + r + 1.435 = 8.435$

15. $4 = s + 0.367 + 2.033$

16. $9.25 + x + 1.5 = 12$

17. $a + 286 = 123 + 459$

18. $798 + m = 89.5 + 943$

Write and solve an equation.

19. A number y increased by 3.7 is equal to 9.372.

20. The sum of a number w and 85 is equal to one hundred eight.

21. Twenty-three hundredths more than a number x is equal to six tenths.

22. When 245 is added to the sum of 130 and a number y, the result is 506.

Problem Solving

Write an addition equation for each. Then solve.

23. Some cats and 29 dogs are in the kennels at the vet. There are 45 animals altogether. How many cats are in the kennels?

24. There are 28 bicycles and some tricycles on sale at Bert's. There are a total of 50 bicycles and tricycles on sale. How many tricycles are on sale?

25. There are 35 students in Mr. Wohl's class. Some students are girls and 19 students are boys. How many girls are in Mr. Wohl's class?

26. Chen has 57 tropical fish. This is 15 more than Tad has. How many tropical fish does Tad have?

27. A total of 762 people, consisting of parents, students, and teachers, attended the Community Fair. If 212 parents and 386 students were at the event, how many teachers attended?

Write About It

28. Explain the steps you would use to compare the values of g and h, when $35 = 17 + g$ and $h + 24 = 42$.

Update your skills. See page 7.

Subtraction Equations

John caught a 5.2-lb fish. This was 3.9 lb less than the fish Sarah caught. How much did Sarah's fish weigh?

To find how much Sarah's fish weighed, write and solve an equation.

Let f represent the weight of Sarah's fish.

weight of Sarah's fish minus 3.9 equals weight of John's fish

$$f - 3.9 = 5.2 \quad \leftarrow \text{subtraction equation}$$

▶ To solve a **subtraction equation**, use the Addition Property of Equality.

Addition Property of Equality
When you add the same number to both sides of an equation, you get a true statement.

$$f - 3.9 = 5.2$$
$$f - 3.9 + 3.9 = 5.2 + 3.9 \quad \leftarrow \text{Add 3.9 to } both \text{ sides to isolate the variable.}$$
$$f = 9.1$$

Check:
$$f - 3.9 = 5.2$$
$$9.1 - 3.9 \stackrel{?}{=} 5.2$$
$$5.2 = 5.2 \text{ True}$$

Sarah's fish weighed 9.1 lb.

Study these examples.

Solve: $3125 - y = 1527$

When the subtrahend is the unknown, use a related fact to find its value.

Related Subtraction Facts:
$a - b = c$ and $a - c = b$

$$3125 - y = 1527$$
$$3125 - 1527 = y \quad \leftarrow \text{Write the related fact.}$$
$$1598 = y \quad \leftarrow \text{Simplify.}$$
Check:
$$3125 - y = 1527$$
$$3125 - 1598 \stackrel{?}{=} 1527$$
$$1527 = 1527 \text{ True}$$

Solve: $a - (29 + 3.1) = 5.3$

$$a - (29 + 3.1) = 5.3$$
$$a - 32.1 = 5.3$$
$$a - 32.1 + 32.1 = 5.3 + 32.1$$
$$a = 37.4$$
Check:
$$a - (29 + 3.1) = 5.3$$
$$37.4 - (29 + 3.1) = 5.3$$
$$37.4 - 32.1 \stackrel{?}{=} 5.3$$
$$5.3 = 5.3 \text{ True}$$

Solve and check.

1. $x - 1456 = 234$

2. $t - 13.27 = 6.041$

3. $c - \$3.48 = \$0.23$

4. $\$57.69 - z = \$28.35$

5. $17.82 - b = 17.82$

6. $3317 = f - 52{,}000$

7. $n - (451 + 513) = 630$

8. $p - (183 + 8462) = 135$

9. $s - (9.2 + 9.8) = 2.5$

10. $8.7 = e - (107 + 14.3)$

11. $446 = q - (235 + 925)$

12. $27.2 = d - (6.5 + 4.15)$

Write and solve an equation.

13. If Kerry decreases a number y by 9.2, the result is 7.239.

14. The difference between a number w and 87 is equal to three hundred one.

15. Thirty-four hundredths less than a number x is equal to nine tenths.

16. If Li subtracts the sum of 279 and 38 from a number y, the result is 126.

Problem Solving

Write a subtraction equation for each. Then solve.

17. At the first stop, 17 people got off the bus. Now there are 35 people on the bus. How many were on the bus to begin with?

18. Mrs. Lee has a balance of $125.37 in her checking account. What was her balance before she wrote checks for $43.06 and $27.25?

19. A sports club needs to raise $250 for supplies. If it already has $65.55, how much more money is needed?

20. Bill weighs 127 lb. His weight is 12 lb less than Sam. What is the weight of Sam?

21. If the Washington Monument were 250 ft shorter, it would be as tall as the Statue of Liberty. The Statue of Liberty is 305 ft tall. How tall is the Washington Monument?

DO YOU REMEMBER?

Match each definition with a term in the box.

22. one of two or more numbers that are multiplied to form a product

23. a symbol used to represent a number

24. a number that tells how many times another number is to be used as a factor

exponent
factor
variable
multiple

Multiplication and Division Equations

An object on Jupiter weighs about 2.6 times its weight on Earth. If a spacecraft weighs 4914 lb on Jupiter, what is its weight on Earth?

To find its weight on Earth, write and solve an equation.

Let y represent the spacecraft's weight on Earth.

2.6 times object's weight on Earth is object's weight on Jupiter

$$2.6y \qquad = \qquad 4914 \leftarrow \text{multiplication equation}$$

▶ To solve a **multiplication equation**, use the Division Property of Equality.

$$2.6y = 4914$$
$$2.6y \div 2.6 = 4914 \div 2.6 \leftarrow$$
$$y = 1890$$

Divide *both* sides by 2.6 to isolate the variable.

Division Property of Equality
When you divide both sides of an equation by the same number, you get a true statement.

Check: $\quad 2.6y = 4914$
$$2.6 \cdot 1890 \overset{?}{=} 4914$$
$$4914 = 4914 \quad \text{True}$$

Remember:
Multiplication and division are inverse operations.

The spacecraft weighs 1890 lb on Earth.

▶ To solve a **division equation**, use the Multiplication Property of Equality.

Solve: $\frac{x}{14} = 192 \leftarrow \boxed{\text{division equation}}$

$$\frac{x}{14} \cdot 14 = 192 \cdot 14 \leftarrow$$
$$x = 2688$$

Multiply *both* sides by 14 to isolate the variable.

Multiplication Property of Equality
When you multiply both sides of an equation by the same number, you get a true statement.

Check: $\frac{x}{14} = 192$

$$\frac{2688}{14} \overset{?}{=} 192$$
$$192 = 192 \quad \text{True}$$

Solve and check.

1. $38x = 760$

2. $1.7c = 25.5$

3. $8b = 0.2416$

4. $z \div 13 = 650$

5. $d \div 7.5 = 18.4$

6. $f \div 22.3 = 6.6$

7. $200 = 80n$

8. $1.13 = \dfrac{p}{0.09}$

9. $1.8769 = 1.37w$

10. $10.5 = e \div 4.3$

11. $44{,}664 = 16q$

12. $274.2 = \dfrac{d}{0.6}$

13. $\dfrac{b}{15} = \$120$

14. $\dfrac{\$128}{n} = \$8$

15. $n \cdot \$100 = \$25$

Write and solve an equation.

16. A number y divided by 5.5 is equal to 86.

17. The product of a number w and 3.6 is equal to one hundred twenty-six.

18. Three tenths multiplied by a number x is equal to one and eight tenths.

19. The quotient of a number y and 49 is three hundred two.

20. Divide a number c by fourteen. The quotient is six.

21. The factors are five and x. The product is fifty-six and one tenth.

Problem Solving

Write an equation for each. Then solve.

22. A piece of wood was cut into 15 equal pieces. The wood was originally 165 cm long. How long was each piece of wood?

23. A pair of designer jeans cost 7.2 times as much as an ordinary pair of jeans. If the designer jeans cost $93.24, what is the price of the ordinary pair of jeans?

24. Ms. Kelley divided the workbooks into 7 equal stacks. Each stack had 32 workbooks. How many workbooks were there in all?

25. Tim's horses eat 1000 lb of hay a week. This is one third of what Ben's horses eat. How much hay do Ben's horses eat?

MENTAL MATH — Algebra

Solve and check each equation.

26. $9n = 63$

27. $n \div 5 = 8$

28. $\dfrac{n}{3} = 7$

29. $8n = 24$

30. $\dfrac{n}{11} = 2$

31. $6n = 12$

32. $4n = 48$

33. $n \div 7 = 6$

Algebra

4-8

Use Formulas

A **formula** is a rule that describes a mathematical relationship involving two or more quantities. It gives a simplified way of solving a particular problem. Each variable in the formula represents a part of the problem.

A car travels 55 miles per hour. If the distance between two cities is 330 miles, how long does it take the car to travel this distance?

To find how long the car travels, use the Distance formula.

To solve a problem *using a formula*:

- Write the formula that will solve the problem.

- Substitute the numbers given in the problem.

- Solve for the unknown variable.

It takes the car 6 hours to travel 330 miles.

Distance formula:

distance = rate × time

d = r × t

$d = r \times t$

330 mi = 55 mph × t

$\dfrac{330}{55} = \dfrac{55t}{55}$

6 = t

t = 6 h

Study these examples.

Volume formula:

Volume = length × width × height

V = ℓ × w × h

Solve for height, h, when $V = 12$ m³, $\ell = 4$ m, and $w = 1.5$ m.

$V = \ell \times w \times h$

$12 = 4 \times 1.5 \times h$

$12 = 6h$

$2 = h \longrightarrow h = 2$ m

Perimeter formula:

Perimeter = twice the sum of length and width

$P = 2(\ell + w)$

Solve for Perimeter, P, when $\ell = 8$ in. and $w = 6$ in.

$P = 2(\ell + w)$

$P = 2(8 + 6)$

$P = 2(14)$

$P = 28 \longrightarrow P = 28$ in.

Use the Distance formula, $d = rt$, to complete.

1. $d = \underline{\ ?\ }$ mi
$r = 55$ mph
$t = 5$ h

2. $d = 11.7$ mi
$r = 3.9$ mph
$t = \underline{\ ?\ }$ h

3. $d = 227.5$ km
$r = \underline{\ ?\ }$ kph
$t = 3.5$ h

Practice

Use the Volume formula, $V = \ell \times w \times h$, to find each missing dimension.

4. $V = 75\ m^3$, $\ell = 5\ m$,
   $w = 5\ m$, $h = \underline{\ ?\ }\ m$

5. $V = 1504\ ft^3$, $\ell = \underline{\ ?\ }\ ft$,
   $w = 4\ ft$, $h = 8\ ft$

6. $V = 2304\ cm^3$, $\ell = 32\ cm$,
   $w = \underline{\ ?\ }\ cm$, $h = 8\ cm$

7. $V = 2912\ in.^3$, $\ell = 32\ in.$,
   $w = 13\ in.$, $h = \underline{\ ?\ }\ in.$

Describe the formula and solve for the missing dimension.
Use the table on page 547.

8. $A = \frac{1}{2}\ bh$, when $A = 200\ ft^2$
   and $h = 10\ ft$

9. $P = 2(\ell + w)$, when $\ell = 7\ yd$
   and $w = 4\ yd$

10. $P = 4s$, when $P = 36\ cm$

11. $V = e^3$, when $e = 6\ in.$

12. $A = bh$, when $A = 150\ m^2$
    and $h = 25\ m$

13. $a + b + c = 180°$, when $a = 57°$
    and $c = 39°$

Problem Solving

Write the formula that you would use to solve the problem. Then solve it.

14. A triangle has an area of 20 cm² and a height of 5 cm. How long is the base?

15. The perimeter of a square tile is 28 m. What is its area?

16. The length and width of a rectangle are doubled. Write a formula for the new area. How is the area changed?

17. A plane travels 2750 miles. If it flies at a rate of 500 miles per hour, how many hours does the plane fly?

18. Write a formula that expresses the following relationship: Savings (*s*) are what is left after subtracting taxes (*t*) and expenses (*e*) from wages (*w*).

19. Compare your formula in exercise 18 with that of a classmate. Then find *s* when *w* = $950.50, *t* = $266.14, and *e* = $499.

CHALLENGE — Algebra

Write a new formula for finding the indicated variable.
(*Hint:* Write a related sentence.)

20. Selling Price = Cost + Profit, or
    $S = C + P$. Find C.

21. Circumference = π × length of diameter, or $C = \pi d$. Find d.

22. Interest = principal × rate × time, or
    $I = prt$. Find r.

23. Area = $\frac{1}{2}$ × base × height, or $A = \frac{1}{2}bh$.
    Find h.

Explore Order of Operations with a Calculator

You can use a calculator to check your computation when using the order of operations.

Evaluate the expression:
$n^3 - (5 + 2) \times 4$, when $n = 6$

▶ Compute using paper and pencil:

- Substitute the value of the variable.

$$n^3 - (5 + 2) \times 4$$
$$6^3 - (5 + 2) \times 4$$

- Compute using the order of operations.

$$6^3 - (5 + 2) \times 4 \quad \longleftarrow \quad \text{1st – parentheses}$$
$$6^3 - 7 \times 4 \quad \longleftarrow \quad \text{2nd – exponents}$$
$$216 - 7 \times 4 \quad \longleftarrow \quad \text{3rd – multiply}$$
$$216 - 28 = 188 \quad \longleftarrow \quad \text{4th – subtract}$$

▶ Check your computation using a calculator. Most scientific calculators automatically follow the correct order of operations.

Input from left to right by pressing these keys:

display

`188.`

▶ For calculators that do not follow the correct order of operations, check your calculations for each step.

1st – Add the numbers in parentheses.

[5] [+] [2] [=] `7.`

2nd – Compute the exponent.

[6] [^] [3] [=] `216.`

3rd – Multiply.

[7] [×] [4] [=] `28.`

4th – Subtract.

[2] [1] [6] [–] [2] [8] [=] `188.`

The value of $n^3 - (5 + 2) \times 4$, when $n = 6$, is 188.

List the calculator keys you would press to evaluate each expression.

1. $12 + 7 \times 9^2$

2. $6 \times (7 - 4)^2 + 13$

3. $14 \times (6 + 79) \div 7$

4. $19^4 - 100 + (85 - 4 \times 2)$

5. $156 \div 3 \times 7^3 + 19$

6. $(19 \times 6)^4 + 214 \div 2$

Evaluate. Use a calculator to check your work.

7. $12 + 7 \times 9^2$

8. $6 \times (7 - 4)^3 + 13$

9. $10^4 \times (6 + 78) \div 7$

10. $19^2 - 100 + (85 - 4 \times 2)$

11. $156 \div 3 \times 7^2 + 19$

12. $(20 \times 6)^2 + 214 \div 2$

13. $(4 \times 7 + 5)^2 \div 11 + 1$

14. $87 - 54 + 12 \times 5^3$

15. $3^3 \times (15 + 19 - 10) \div 9$

16. $(9^2 - 19) + 42 \div 6 \times 2^3$

17. $51 + 5^2 \times 31 + 18^2 - 9 \times 7$

Compare. Write <, =, or >.

18. $16^2 \times 5 - 90$ ___?___ $90 \times 5 - 16^2$

19. $(64 + 192) \div 8^2$ ___?___ $64 + 192 \div 8^2$

20. $195 \div 5 \cdot 9^2$ ___?___ $195 \div (5 \cdot 9)^2$

21. $17(3)^2 \cdot (18 - 3)$ ___?___ $17 \cdot 3^2 \cdot (18 - 3)$

Problem Solving

Choose the correct expression to solve each problem. Then evaluate.

22. Jill drove 8 miles to her mother's house, and then drove home again. Then she drove 5 miles to school, 2 miles to the library, and 7 miles home. How far did Jill drive?

   a. $8 \times (2 + 5) + 2 + 7$
   b. $8 \times 2 + 5 + 2 + 7$
   c. $8 \times (2 + 5 + 2 + 7)$

23. Hunter had a $50 bill. He bought 3 notebooks at $7 each, 2 packs of pens at $3 each, and 3 folders at $0.79 each. How much change should Hunter get back?

   a. $\$50 - (3 \times \$7 + 2 \times \$3 + 3 \times \$0.79)$
   b. $\$(50 - 3) \times \$7 + 2 \times \$3 + 3 \times \$0.79$
   c. $\$50 - 3 \times \$7 + 2 \times \$3 + 3 \times \$0.79$

24. Ann buys one piece of fabric that is 6^2 sq ft and 2 pieces that are each 24 sq ft. She uses 4 sq ft to make a pillow. How many sq ft of fabric does Ann have left?

   a. $6^2 + 2 \times 24 - 4$
   b. $(6^2 + 2) \times 24 - 4$
   c. $6^2 + 2 \times (24 - 4)$

Problem–Solving Strategy:
Use More Than One Step

Eva has read 300 pages of a 652-page book.
If she reads 22 pages each day from now on,
in how many days will she finish the book?

Read

Visualize yourself in the problem above as you reread it. List the facts and the question.

Facts: 652-page book
　　　　　She has read 300 pages.
　　　　　She now reads 22 pages each day.

Question: How many days will it take her to finish?

Plan

To find how long it will take to finish the book, you must use more than one step. For each step, write an equation.

Step 1: To find the number of pages remaining, p,
　　　　to be read, subtract:
　　　　$652 - 300 = p$

Step 2: To find the number of days, n, it will take
　　　　to complete the book, divide:
　　　　$p \div 22 = n$

Solve

$652 - 300 = 352$

$$\begin{array}{r} 16 \\ 22{\overline{)352}} \\ -22 \\ \hline 132 \\ -132 \\ \hline \end{array}$$

Number of Days

Pages Remaining

It will take her 16 days to finish the book.

Check

Use inverse operations to check each step.

$$\begin{array}{r} 16 \\ \times\,22 \\ \hline 32 \\ +32 \\ \hline 352 \end{array}$$

$$\begin{array}{r} 352 \\ +300 \\ \hline 652 \end{array}$$

The answers check.

Solve each problem by using more than one step.
Use variables to represent the unknown.

1. Mrs. Lopez bought 2 lb of apples at $1.09 a pound,
   3 lb of oranges at $.89 a pound, and 3 lb of bananas
   at $.39 a pound. How much did the fruit cost her?

 Read ▸ Visualize yourself in the problem above as you
reread it. List the facts and the question.

> **Facts:** 2 lb apples at $1.09 a pound
> 3 lb oranges at $.89 a pound
> 3 lb bananas at $.39 a pound
>
> **Question:** How much did the fruit cost
> Mrs. Lopez?

 Plan ▸ To find the total cost you must use more than one step.

> **Step 1:** To find the total cost for each fruit, multiply:
> $2 \times \$1.09 = a$
> $3 \times \$.89 = b$
> $3 \times \$.39 = c$
>
> **Step 2:** To find the total cost of all the fruit, add the products.

···▸ **Solve** ···········▸ **Check** ▸

2. Dry cat food comes in regular and jumbo sizes.
   The 8-oz regular size costs $.96. The 12-oz
   jumbo size costs $1.35. Which is the better buy?

3. Judy's school has a 0.5-km track. One day at practice
   she ran around the track 9 times and then ran
   another 1 km in sprints. How far did she run that day?

4. An airplane travels 2044 mi in 3.5 h. Another
   travels 3146 mi in 5.2 h. Which airplane is faster?
   by how much?

5. Natural Apple Sauce comes in 8-oz, 10-oz, and 16-oz jars.
   The 8-oz jar sells for $.54, the 10-oz jar for $.62, and the
   16-oz jar for $1.00. Which size jar is most expensive
   per ounce?

6. Kim's mother is 3.5 times her age. Her father is 5 years
   older than her mother. Kim is 7 years older than her
   brother, who is 3. How old is Kim's father?

Problem-Solving Applications: Mixed Review

Read ▶ **Plan** ▶ **Solve** ▶ **Check**

Solve each problem and explain the method you used.

1. Regina buys a bag of oranges for $2.88. The average cost of an orange is $0.12. If *n* represents the number of oranges in the bag, write and solve an equation that can be used to find *n*.

2. Sarah bought 3 tacos for $0.59 each and 4 burritos for $0.89 each. Write and evaluate an expression that tells how much change Sarah would receive from a $10 bill.

3. A dozen plums cost $2.40, which is $0.60 less than a dozen peaches cost. If *p* represents the cost of a dozen peaches, write and solve an equation that can be used to find *p*.

4. Figs cost $2.96 a pound. Kathy bought 3.2 pounds. Write an expression to estimate the cost of the figs.

5. Ms. Lake buys some bags of pretzels for the sixth-grade class picnic. Each bag holds 10.5 oz of pretzels and all the bags hold about 787.5 oz. of pretzels. If *m* represents the total number of bags of pretzels Ms. Lake buys, write and solve an equation that can be used to find *m*.

6. The sale price (*SP*) is what you pay after deducting the discount (*d*) from the regular price (*RP*). Write and evaluate a formula to find the sale price of a jar of peanuts with a $\frac{1}{3}$ off discount from the regular price of $3.75

7. Anna shows this series of equations:
   $$\frac{a}{8} = 0.5 \rightarrow ax = 7.2 \rightarrow x + y = 5 \rightarrow z - y = 1.3.$$
   Solve for the value of *z*.

Use a strategy from the list or another strategy you know to solve each problem.

8. There are 19 boxes of cherries in the stockroom. This is 5 less than twice the number of boxes of kiwis. How many boxes of kiwis are in the stockroom?

Strategy File

Use These Strategies
Use More Than One Step
Interpret the Remainder
Make a Table
Use Simpler Numbers
Write an Equation
Guess and Test

9. At Sandwiches to Go, you can buy 1 sandwich at half price for every 1 you buy at regular price. Sandwiches are regularly $3.98 each. If Lisa and her friends buy 8 sandwiches, how much do they spend?

10. One box of apples weighs 3 lb less than twice another. If the heavier box weighs 29 lb, how much does the lighter box weigh?

11. Each day the price of a cookbook will be reduced by $\frac{1}{10}$ of the sale price until all the cookbooks have been sold. The original price of each cookbook is $10. What is the price on the 5th day of the sale?

12. On Monday, Martin packed 927 pieces of fruit for shipping. If he packed 250 apples and 302 oranges, how many pears did he pack?

Use the table for problems 13–16.

13. Tara has $7.50. Can she buy two 20-oz blocks of Monterey Jack cheese?

14. How much will Lindsey pay per ounce for sliced Swiss cheese? Round to the nearest cent.

15. A quiche recipe calls for 10 oz of cheese. Which block cheese would be the least expensive to use in the quiche: American, cheddar, or Monterey Jack?

Cheese	Quantity	Price
American	1 lb, sliced	$3.59
	$\frac{1}{2}$ lb, block	$1.89
Cheddar	8 oz, sliced	$2.29
	24 oz, block	$4.19
Swiss	$1\frac{1}{2}$ lb, sliced	$7.29
	16 oz, block	$5.39
Monterey Jack	$\frac{1}{2}$ lb, sliced	$2.49
	20 oz, block	$3.99

16. Use the table to write a problem modeled on exercise 15 above. Have a classmate solve it.

Check Your Progress
Lessons 1–11

Compute. Use a calculator to check your work. *(See pp. 121–122, 138–139.)*

1. $63 \div (2^2 + 3) - 7$
2. $21 + (0.8 + 6.4) \div 1.2$
3. $(3.2 + 4.3) \div 2.5 \times 3^3$

Write as an expression, equation, or inequality. Use a variable when necessary. *(See pp. 124–125, 128–129.)*

4. Six less than a number is 3.

5. 25 more than 7 times a number

6. the sum of a number and 41.5

7. A number doubled is greater than 484.

8. Half of ten is three less than eight.

9. Forty is the product of x and five.

10. $5z$ decreased by 3

11. The sum of z and 35 is less than 98.

Evaluate each expression. *(See pp. 126–127.)*

12. $(x + 2)^2 + y \div z$, when $x = 1$, $y = 1.2$, and $z = 4$

13. $r(q - 24) + w \div 2$, when $r = 3$, $q = 30$, and $w = 9$

Solve and check. *(See pp. 130–135.)*

14. $a - 12.5 = 35.93$
15. $2495 = n + 209$
16. $13.5c = 202.5$

17. $d \div 1.9 = 2.05$
18. $378 = 75 + x$
19. $r + 2.5 + 1.3 = 7.9$

20. $h - (3.01 + 2.3) = 5$
21. $185 = y + 123.9$
22. $6953 = 17m$

Solve for the missing dimension in each formula. *(See pp. 136–137.)*

23. $A = \frac{1}{2}bh$, when $A = 350 \text{ ft}^2$ and $h = 20 \text{ ft}$

24. $P = 2(\ell + w)$, when $\ell = 12 \text{ yd}$ and $w = 5 \text{ yd}$

25. $P = 4s$, when $P = 48.12 \text{ cm}$

26. $V = e^2$, when $e = 5 \text{ in.}$

Problem Solving
(See pp. 140–143.)

Write an equation for each. Then solve.

27. Sally is permitted 1000 calories a day on her diet. At lunch she consumed 279 and at breakfast 344. How many calories may she consume at dinner?

28. Two hundred twenty students competed in basketball. Teams of 5 players each were formed. How many teams were formed?

(See *Still More Practice*, p. 523.)

Patterns: Sequences

A sequence is a set of numbers in a certain order, usually by a pattern.
Each number is called a term. A term can be found by using a pattern rule.

▶ What is the rule for the sequence?
What is the next term in the sequence?

1,   5,   9,   13,   17, . . .
  $+4$ $+4$ $+4$ $+4$

> This is an arithmetic sequence because each new term is found by adding or subtracting a fixed number to the previous term.

Rule: Start with 1 and add 4 repeatedly.
Next term: $17 + 4$, or 21

▶ What is the rule for the sequence?
What is the next term in the sequence?

2.1,   4.2,   8.4,   16.8, . . .
   $\times 2$ $\times 2$ $\times 2$

> This is a geometric sequence because each new term is found by multiplying or dividing by a fixed number.

Rule: Start with 2.1 and multiply by 2 repeatedly.
Next term: 16.8×2, or 33.6

Find the rule.
Then use it to find the next term.
Label the sequence *arithmetic* or *geometric*.

1. 10, 18, 26, 34, 42, . . .

2. 5, 20, 80, 320, 1280, . . .

3. 106, 81, 56, 31, . . .

4. 2.5, 5, 7.5, 10, . . .

5. 0.4, 1.2, 3.6, 10.8, . . .

6. 176.5, 17.65, 1.765, 0.1765, . . .

7. 0.125, 0.25, 0.5, 1, . . .

8. 2, 0.4, 0.08, 0.016, . . .

Problem Solving

Use the sequence 1, 3, 5, 7, . . . for problems 9 and 10.

9. What is the sum of the first 2 terms? the first 3 terms? the first 4 terms? the first 5 terms?

10. Look at the sums you found. What pattern do you see? Use the pattern to predict the sum of the first 8 terms in the sequence. Check your prediction.

Chapter 4 Test

Evaluate each expression. Watch for the order of operations. Use a calculator to check your work.

1. $(d + e \div 8)^2 - 10f$, when $d = 18$, $e = 56$, and $f = 2$

2. $(2 + 4)^3 \times 66 \div 33$

3. $\dfrac{98 - w^2}{mt}$, when $w = 2$, $m = 10$, and $t = 2$

4. $35 + 4^2 \times 25 + 7^2 - 9 \times 7$

Write as an expression, equation, or inequality. Use a variable when necessary.

5. 7 multiplied by the sum of a number and 3

6. A number decreased by the product of 5 and 7 is not equal to 10.

7. Three times a number is greater than 30.

8. Half of a number increased by 10

Solve for the missing dimension in each formula.

9. $A = bh$, when $A = 105$ ft^2 and $h = 15$ ft

10. $P = 2(\ell + w)$, when $\ell = 14$ ft and $w = 9$ ft

11. $P = 4s$, when $P = 22$ in.

12. $d = rt$, when $d = 210$ mi and $t = 7$ h

Problem Solving

Use a strategy you have learned.

13. Ty works at a nursery. He plants lilies in 12 rows of 8 and ivy in 15 rows of 14. How many does he plant in all?

Tell About It

14. Evaluate the expressions $5x + 2$ and $5(x + 2)$, when $x = 2$. Are the values of the expressions the same or different? Explain your answer.

Performance Assessment

Match each sentence to an equation and each equation to its solution.

15. A number added to 2 is 64.
A number doubled is 64.
A number squared is 64.
2 subtracted from a number is 64.
64 subtracted from a number is 0.

$n - 2 = 64$	8
$n^2 = 64$	32
$2n = 64$	62
$n - 64 = 0$	64
$2 + n = 64$	66

16. Explain how you solved each equation in exercise 15.

Test Preparation

Choose the best answer.

1. Choose the standard form of 65 billion, 18 thousand and 7 hundredths.

   a. 65,000,018.07
   b. 65,018.6
   c. 65,000,018,000.07
   d. not given

2. Choose the short word name for the number $(9 \times 10^6) + (7 \times 10^4) + (6 \times 10^2) + (8 \times 1)$

   a. 9768
   b. 9 million, 70 thousand, 608
   c. 9 million, 7 thousand, 610
   d. not given

3. Which numbers are in order from least to greatest?

   a. 5.4032; 5.0432; 5.3402
   b. 5.4302; 5.4032; 5.0432
   c. 5.4302; 5.4032; 5.4332
   d. 5.0423; 5.4023; 5.4302

4. What is the missing number in the equation $4.7 + 19.3 = n \times 3$?

   a. 72
   b. 24
   c. 8
   d. 6

5. Find the quotient.

   $0.18\overline{)4212}$

   a. 2.34
   b. 23.4
   c. 234
   d. 23,400

6. Multiply.

   322×265

   a. 85,930
   b. 85,330
   c. 8533
   d. not given

7. Choose the scientific notation for 294 billion.

   a. 29.4×10^{11}
   b. 2.94×10^{11}
   c. 294.10^{10}
   d. 2.94×10^9

8. Round 597,491,608 to the nearest hundred thousand.

   a. 600,000,000
   b. 597,000,000
   c. 597,492,000
   d. 597,500,000

9. Use compatible numbers to estimate the quotient.

   $542,252 \div 258$

   a. 20
   b. 200
   c. 2000
   d. 20,000

10. Choose the value of $3^2 \times 4^3$.

    a. 60
    b. 72
    c. 576
    d. 648

11. Evaluate.

    $4^2 \times (15 - 6) - 18$

    a. 126
    b. 54
    c. 26
    d. not given

12. Solve for x.

    $x + 7.9 = 18.65$

    a. $x = 2.36$
    b. $x = 10.75$
    c. $x = 11.56$
    d. $x = 26.55$

13. Add.

$56.935 + 47.09 + 153.0818$

    a. 257.1068
    b. 257.1078
    c. 257.1168
    d. 257.1178

14. Solve for n.

$16n = 432$

    a. $n = 0.037$
    b. $n = 27$
    c. $n = 416$
    d. $n = 6912$

15. What number is five trillion, four billion, eight?

    a. 5,004,000,008
    b. 5,000,400,000,008
    c. 5,400,000,000,008
    d. not given

16. Find the value of n.

$106.09 \times 1000 = n$

    a. 0.10609
    b. 10,609
    c. 106,090
    d. not given

17. Amy drove 297 miles in 5.4 hours. At what rate did she drive?

    a. 50 miles per hour
    b. 55 miles per hour
    c. 60 miles per hour
    d. not given

18. Which inequality expresses the following statement?

length ℓ is less than 35 ft

    a. $\ell < 35$
    b. $35 > \ell$
    c. $35 < \ell$
    d. $\ell \leq 35$

19. Which is the algebraic expression for the phrase "six times as old as Mark (m)"?

    a. $6 + m$
    b. $6 - m$
    c. $6m$
    d. $\dfrac{6}{m}$

20. Choose the difference.

$\$6006.93 - \$17.89$

    a. $5098.04
    b. $5989.04
    c. $5999.14
    d. not given

21. Divide.

$47\overline{)28{,}567}$

    a. 678 R38
    b. 670 R38
    c. 607 R38
    d. 67 R38

22. A baseball was pitched at a speed of 88.5 miles per hour. A tennis ball was hit at a speed of 1.5 times faster. What was the speed of the tennis ball?

    a. 53.55 miles per hour
    b. 40 miles per hour
    c. 25.66 miles per hour
    d. not given

Explain how you solved each problem. Show all your work.

23. Kay can run 6 km in 26 min. Beth can run 4 km in 15.5 min. To the nearest tenth of a minute, how much faster does Beth run 1 km?

24. Naomi added 0.25 to the difference she obtained from subtracting 1.19 from 3.23. What number did Naomi end up with?

Integers

Some Opposites

What is the opposite of *riot*?
It's *lots of people keeping quiet.*

The opposite of *doughnut*? Wait
A minute while I meditate.
This isn't easy. Ah, I've found it!
A *cookie with a hole around it.*

What is the opposite of *two*?
A *lonely me, a lonely you.*

The opposite of a *cloud* could be
A *white reflection in the sea,*
Or *a huge blueness in the air,*
Caused by a cloud's not being there.

The opposite of *opposite*?
That's much too difficult. I quit.

Richard Wilbur

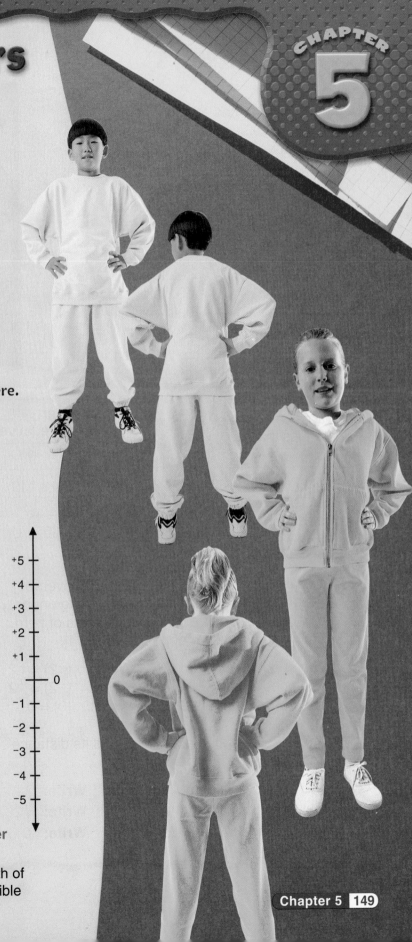

In this chapter you will:

Learn about opposites and
  absolute value of integers
Compare, order, and compute
  with integers
Evaluate expressions and solve
  equations with integers
Solve problems by making a table

Critical Thinking/Finding Together

House A: 5 mi east, 3 mi south of a
point; House B: 5 mi west, 3 mi north of
the point. What is the greatest possible
distance between the houses?

Integers

A mountain peak has an altitude of 11,560 ft above sea level. A desert location has an altitude of 185 ft below sea level.

You can write these numbers as integers. Integers are the whole numbers and their opposites. They are either positive, negative, or zero.

0 ft   ⟶ sea level
$^{+}$11,560 ft ⟶ above sea level
$^{-}$185 ft   ⟶ below sea level

▶ A number line can help you see the relationship between integers.

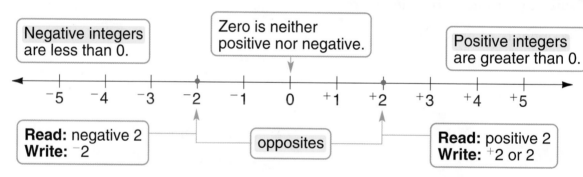

| Negative integers are less than 0. | Zero is neither positive nor negative. | Positive integers are greater than 0. |

$$\xleftarrow{\hspace{1cm}} \quad ^{-}5 \quad ^{-}4 \quad ^{-}3 \quad ^{-}2 \quad ^{-}1 \quad 0 \quad ^{+}1 \quad ^{+}2 \quad ^{+}3 \quad ^{+}4 \quad ^{+}5 \xrightarrow{\hspace{1cm}}$$

Read: negative 2   opposites   **Read:** positive 2
Write: $^{-}$2   **Write:** $^{+}$2 or 2

- Two integers are opposites (additive inverses) if they are the same distance from zero on the number line, but are on opposite sides of zero. Each integer has an opposite.

> Positive integers are commonly written without the positive sign.

The opposite of $^{+}$2 is $^{-}$2.   **Write:** $^{-}(^{+}2) = {^{-}}2$
The opposite of $^{-}$2 is $^{+}$2.   **Write:** $^{-}(^{-}2) = {^{+}}2$
The opposite of 0 is 0.   **Write:** $^{-}(0) = 0$

- The absolute value of an integer is its distance from zero on a number line.

The absolute value of $^{-}$2 is 2.   **Write:** $|^{-}2| = 2$
The absolute value of $^{+}$2 is 2.   **Write:** $|^{+}2| = 2$
The absolute value of 0 is 0.   **Write:** $|0| = 0$

Write the integer to represent the situation. Then describe the opposite situation and write the integer to represent it.

1. gain of 8 dollars
2. loss of 15 yards
3. 22 degrees warmer
4. 5 seconds before liftoff
5. withdrawal of $50
6. down 21 floors

Identify the point that corresponds to the integer on the number line.

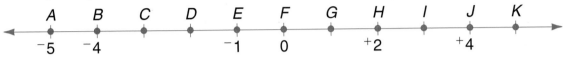

7. ⁻5
8. ⁺4
9. ⁻1
10. C
11. I
12. K

Write the integer that is just before and just after each given number on a number line.

13. ⁺7
14. ⁻2
15. ⁺1
16. ⁻10
17. ⁻99
18. ⁻14

Write the opposite of each integer.

19. ⁻9
20. ⁺20
21. ⁺16
22. ⁻15
23. ⁺13
24. ⁻10

Write the absolute value of the integer.

25. $|{-8}|$
26. $|{+17}|$
27. $|{-56}|$
28. $|293|$
29. $-|{-701}|$

Name each integer on a horizontal number line.

30. five to the right of negative five
31. seven to the right of negative eight
32. four to the left of positive five
33. three to the left of positive three

Problem Solving

34. In a game the card for ⁺10 says "Go ahead 10 steps." What would the card for ⁻10 say?

35. Describe your position on a number line, if you begin at 0, move right 5 steps, and then move left 5 steps.

CHALLENGE

Use the number line.

36. If integer *B* is the opposite of integer *E*, what integer is *D*?

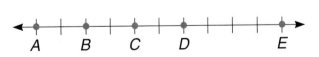

37. If integer *A* is the opposite of integer *E*, is integer *C* positive or negative? Why?

38. If integer *C* is the opposite of integer *E*, which of the labeled points has the greatest absolute value? Why?

Compare and Order Integers

You can use a number line to compare and to order integers.
Any positive number is greater than any negative number.

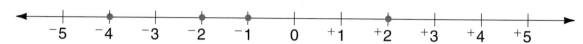

$-5 \quad -4 \quad -3 \quad -2 \quad -1 \quad 0 \quad +1 \quad +2 \quad +3 \quad +4 \quad +5$

▶ To **compare** integers you can use a number line.

On a *horizontal* number line:

- Any number is less than a number to its right.

  Compare: $-1 \underline{\ ?\ } +2$

  $+2$ is to the right of -1
  $-1 < +2$

- Any number is greater than a number to its left.

  Compare: $-2 \underline{\ ?\ } -4$

  -4 is to the left of -2
  $-2 > -4$

On a *vertical* number line:

- Any number is less than a number above it.

  Compare: $-2 \underline{\ ?\ } 0$

  0 is above -2
  $-2 < 0$

- Any number is greater than a number below it.

  Compare: $+1 \underline{\ ?\ } -3$

  -3 is below $+1$
  $+1 > -3$

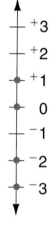

▶ To **order** integers using a horizontal number line:
- Least to greatest—Begin with the integer farthest to the *left*.
- Greatest to least—Begin with the integer farthest to the *right*.

Order $+2$, -5, and 0 from least to greatest.

The order from least to greatest is: -5, 0, $+2$.

The order from greatest to least is: $+2$, 0, -5.

> **Think**
> -5 is farthest to the left;
> $+2$ is farthest to the right;
> 0 is between -5 and $+2$.

Study these examples.

Compare: $|-4| \underline{\ ?\ } |-2|$

$4 > 2$

So $|-4| > |-2|$

> **Think**
> $|-4| = 4$
> $|-2| = 2$

Compare: $-|-7| \underline{\ ?\ } -(-3)$

$-7 < +3$

So $-|-7| < -(-3)$

> **Think**
> $-|-7| = -7$
> $-(-3) = +3$

Choose the greater integer. Use a number line to help.

1. $^+7, ^+10$

2. $^-9, ^-3$

3. $^+3, ^-5$

4. $^-7, ^+6$

5. $0, ^-9$

6. $^+8, 0$

7. $^-12, ^-25$

8. $^+20, ^-20$

Compare. Write <, =, or >.

9. $^-10 \underline{\ ?\ } ^+6$

10. $^+4 \underline{\ ?\ } ^+8$

11. $3 \underline{\ ?\ } ^-6$

12. $^-3 \underline{\ ?\ } ^+4$

13. $^+7 \underline{\ ?\ } 0$

14. $^-4 \underline{\ ?\ } ^+4$

15. $0 \underline{\ ?\ } ^-3$

16. $^-2 \underline{\ ?\ } ^-5$

17. $|^-8| \underline{\ ?\ } |^+7|$

18. $0 \underline{\ ?\ } ^-|8|$

19. $|^-6| \underline{\ ?\ } ^-(6)$

20. $^-(^-7) \underline{\ ?\ } ^-(^+4)$

21. $^-|11| \underline{\ ?\ } ^-13$

22. $^-(^+13) \underline{\ ?\ } 0$

23. $|^+12| \underline{\ ?\ } |^-12|$

24. $^-(^-10) \underline{\ ?\ } ^-|^-20|$

Arrange in order from least to greatest.

25. $^+6, ^+8, ^+7$

26. $^-10, ^-8, ^-6$

27. $^-6, 0, ^-3$

28. $^+9, 0, ^+3$

29. $^-5, ^-6, ^-3, ^-7$

30. $^+4, ^-2, ^+5, ^-4$

Arrange in order from greatest to least.

31. $^-6, ^+3, ^-4$

32. $^-2, ^-10, ^+5$

33. $0, ^-7, ^-12$

34. $^-4, ^+5, ^-3$

35. $^+8, ^+12, ^-15, ^-30$

36. $^+20, 0, ^-2, ^-1$

Write _always_, _sometimes_, or _never_ to make a true statement.

37. A negative integer is $\underline{\ ?\ }$ less than a positive integer.

38. A negative integer is $\underline{\ ?\ }$ less than another negative integer.

39. A negative integer is $\underline{\ ?\ }$ greater than 0.

40. The absolute value of an integer is $\underline{\ ?\ }$ positive.

Problem Solving

41. The temperature on Monday was $^-2°C$. On Tuesday the temperature was $^-7°C$. Which temperature was colder?

42. The average daily temperature in Toronto for each of five days was $^-2°C, ^+5°C, ^-3°C, ^+1°C,$ and $^+2°C$. What was the median temperature?

CRITICAL THINKING

43. Is there a least positive integer? a greatest positive integer? a least negative integer? a greatest negative integer? Explain.

Add Integers

On an oceanographic expedition, the crew took the first sonar reading at 2 km above sea level. The next reading was 3 km below the first reading. What was the depth of the second reading?

To find the depth of the second reading, n, add: $^+2 + ^-3 = n$.

▶ You can use a number line to model the addition of integers.

- Start at 0.
- Move *right* for positive integers.
- Move *left* for negative integers.

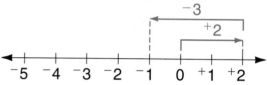

The depth of the second reading was at 1 km below sea level.

$$^+2 + ^-3 = ^-1$$

▶ You can also use absolute value to add integers.

To add integers with *like* signs:

- Add the absolute values of the addends.
- Use the sign of the addends for the sum.

$^-2 + ^-4 = m$	$^+5 + ^+3 = n$
$\|^-2\| + \|^-4\|$	$\|^+5\| + \|^+3\|$
$2 + 4 = 6$	$5 + 3 = 8$
$^-2 + ^-4 = ^-6$	$^+5 + ^+3 = ^+8$
$m = ^-6$	$n = ^+8$

To add integers with *unlike* signs:

- Subtract the addend with the lesser absolute value from the addend with the greater absolute value.
- Use the sign of the addend with the greater absolute value for the sum.

$^+5 + ^-8 = d$	$^+9 + ^-7 = s$
$\|^-8\| - \|^+5\|$	$\|^+9\| - \|^-7\|$
$8 - 5 = 3$	$9 - 7 = 2$
$5 + ^-8 = ^-3$	$^+9 + ^-7 = ^+2$
$d = ^-3$	$s = ^+2$

Study these examples.

$^+2 + ^+5 = a$

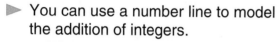

$$^+2 + ^+5 = ^+7 \rightarrow a = ^+7$$

$^-3 + x = ^-5$

$$^-3 + ^-2 = ^-5 \rightarrow x = ^-2$$

Write an addition sentence that is modeled by each number line.

1.

```
 ⟵──────┐
    ⟵──────┐
◄──┼──┼──┼──┼──┼──┼──┼──►
  ⁻6 ⁻5 ⁻4 ⁻3 ⁻2 ⁻1  0
```

2.

```
        ┌──────────────────►
    ⟵──────────┐
◄──┼──┼──┼──┼──┼──┼──┼──►
  ⁻4 ⁻3 ⁻2 ⁻1  0 ⁺1 ⁺2
```

Add. Use a number line to help.

3. $^+2 + {^+1}$

4. $^-4 + {^-3}$

5. $^-1 + {^-4}$

6. $^+6 + {^+1}$

7. $^-6 + {^+4}$

8. $^+7 + {^-5}$

9. $^-5 + {^-6}$

10. $^+4 + {^+4}$

11. $^-4 + {^+8}$

12. $^-8 + {^+5}$

13. $^+6 + 0$

14. $0 + {^-8}$

15. $^+4 + {^-5} + {^-6}$

16. $^-6 + {^-2} + {^+4}$

17. $^-3 + {^-3} + {^-3}$

18. $^-2 + {^-2} + {^-2}$

19. $^+7 + {^-5} + {^-2}$

20. $^-8 + {^+6} + {^+9}$

Find the value of the variable.

21. $^+7 + a = {^+16}$

22. $^-5 + b = {^+3}$

23. $^+11 + c = {^+9}$

24. $d + {^+7} = {^-7}$

25. $e + {^-8} = {^-13}$

26. $f + {^-15} = {^-12}$

27. $^+9 + k = 0$

28. $h + 7 = {^-6}$

29. $^-13 + i = {^-15}$

Problem Solving

30. On Monday Sally deposited $60 in her savings account. On Tuesday she withdrew $45. What was the net change in savings for the two days?

31. In January Raul lost 5 pounds. He gained back 3 pounds in February. What was his total weight gain or loss for the two months?

32. Rita started a checking account with $500. She later wrote a check for $50, made a deposit of $250, and wrote another check for $100. How much money was left in Rita's account?

33. An elevator starts at the 23rd floor, goes down 5 floors and then up 8 floors. At what floor is it then? Draw a vertical number line to illustrate.

Write About It

34. Explain in your Math Journal how you can use the rules on page 154 for adding with zeros (such as $0 + {^-7}$) or with opposites (such as $^+7 + {^-7}$).

Subtract Integers

Catherine wants to know how to complete this subtraction:

$4 - 5 = n$

To study the relationship between adding and subtracting integers, she makes the table at the right.

x	x + $^-$5	x − 5
7	7 + $^-$5 = 2	7 − 5 = 2
6	6 + $^-$5 = 1	6 − 5 = 1
5	5 + $^-$5 = 0	5 − 5 = 0
4	4 + $^-$5 = $^-$1	4 − 5 = ?

Look for a pattern in the table. The sequence of numbers in the last column is 2, 1, 0, ... Catherine determines that $4 - 5 = {}^-1$ or $^+4 - {}^+5 = {}^-1$. She also makes the following general conclusion.

Subtracting an integer is the same as *adding the opposite* of that integer.
$a - b = a + ({}^-b)$, for integers a and b.

▶ **To subtract integers:**

- Add the opposite of the subtrahend.
- Rewrite as an addition sentence.
- Then use the rules for adding integers.

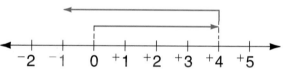

$$^+4 - {}^+5 = {}^-1$$

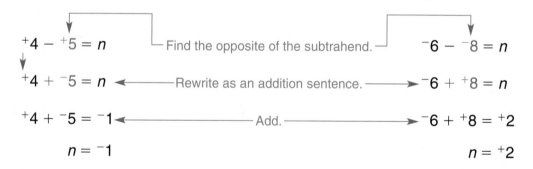

$^+4 - {}^+5 = n$ ⟶ Find the opposite of the subtrahend. ⟶ $^-6 - {}^-8 = n$

$^+4 + {}^-5 = n$ ⟵ Rewrite as an addition sentence. ⟶ $^-6 + {}^+8 = n$

$^+4 + {}^-5 = {}^-1$ ⟵ Add. ⟶ $^-6 + {}^+8 = {}^+2$

$n = {}^-1$ $\qquad\qquad$ $n = {}^+2$

Study these examples.

$^+7 - n = {}^+17$

$^+7 - n = {}^+7 + {}^+10$ $\qquad$ $^-9 - {}^+6 = n$ $\qquad$ $^-5 - 0 = n$

$^+7 - {}^-10 = {}^+7 + {}^+10$ $\qquad$ $^-9 + {}^-6 = {}^-15$ $\qquad$ $^-5 + 0 = {}^-5$

$n = {}^-10$ $\qquad\qquad$ $n = {}^-15$ $\qquad\qquad$ $n = {}^-5$

> **Think**
> 0 is its own opposite.

Write a subtraction sentence that is modeled by each number line.

1.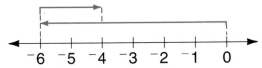

2.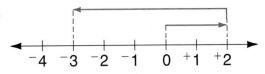

Subtract. Use a number line to help.

3. $^+8 - {}^+4$ **4.** $^+5 - {}^+8$ **5.** $^-4 - {}^+5$ **6.** $^-6 - {}^+2$

7. $^-3 - {}^-7$ **8.** $^+9 - {}^+7$ **9.** $^+7 - {}^-4$ **10.** $^-5 - {}^+8$

11. $^+8 - {}^+10$ **12.** $^+3 - {}^-2$ **13.** $^-8 - {}^-10$ **14.** $^-3 - {}^+5$

15. $^-7 - {}^+2$ **16.** $^+9 - {}^+11$ **17.** $^-5 - {}^-3$ **18.** $^+7 - {}^-9$

19. $^+5 - {}^-10$ **20.** $^-6 - {}^-7$ **21.** $^+6 - 0$ **22.** $^-12 - 0$

23. $^+9 - {}^+4$ **24.** $^+2 - {}^-3$ **25.** $0 - {}^-8$ **26.** $0 - {}^+4$

Find the value of the variable.

27. $^-9 - a = {}^-15$ **28.** $^+14 - b = {}^-13$ **29.** $^-8 - c = {}^+4$

30. $d - {}^-11 = {}^-6$ **31.** $e - {}^+15 = {}^+16$ **32.** $f - {}^-25 = {}^-3$

Problem Solving

33. The high temperature in Chicago was 67°F and that same day the low was ⁻24°F in Minneapolis. What was the difference between the high and the low temperatures?

34. Ben asked his mother to hold his savings. At the start of June, his savings was ⁺$16. That month he borrowed $20 to spend. What is the amount remaining or owed?

MENTAL MATH — Algebra

Add. Look for opposites.

$^+11 + {}^-2 + {}^-8 + {}^+4 + {}^-11 + {}^+2 = n \longrightarrow n = {}^-4$

.Think.........
$^-8 + {}^+4 = {}^-4$

35. $^+23 + {}^-17 + {}^-23 = n$ **36.** $^-12 + {}^+15 + {}^+12 + {}^-6 + {}^-15 + {}^-4 = n$

37. $^+35 + {}^+65 + {}^-65 = n$ **38.** $^+22 + {}^+14 + {}^-10 + {}^+10 + {}^-22 + {}^+14 = n$

Multiply Integers

▶ You can use repeated addition to multiply integers.
Multiply: $3 \times {}^-2 = n$

> **Think**
> $3 \times {}^-2$ means three groups of $^-2$.

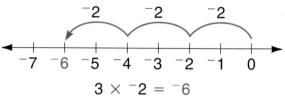

$$^-2 + {}^-2 + {}^-2 = {}^-6$$
$$3 \times {}^-2 = {}^-6$$

$$3 \times {}^-2 = {}^-6$$

▶ Patterns can also help you to understand how to multiply integers.

- When you multiply two positive ($^+$) integers, the product is positive ($^+$).

$^+2 \times {}^+3 = {}^+6$
$^+2 \times {}^+2 = {}^+4$
$^+2 \times {}^+1 = {}^+2$

- When you multiply two negative ($^-$) integers, the product is positive ($^+$).

$^-1 \times {}^-3 = {}^+3$
$^-2 \times {}^-3 = {}^+6$
$^-3 \times {}^-3 = {}^+9$

- When you multiply a positive ($^+$) integer, and a negative ($^-$) integer, the product is negative.

$^+3 \times {}^-3 = {}^-9$
$^+2 \times {}^-3 = {}^-6$
$^+1 \times {}^-3 = {}^-3$

▶ You can also use rules for multiplying integers.

To **multiply two integers,** multiply their absolute values.

- The product is positive when the factors have like signs.
  $$(^+)(^+) = {}^+ \qquad (^-)(^-) = {}^+$$

- The product is negative when the factors have unlike signs.
  $$(^+)(^-) = {}^- \qquad (^-)(^+) = {}^-$$

Study these examples.

$$^-12 \times {}^+3 = s \qquad\qquad\qquad {}^+7 \times {}^-7 = h$$

$$|{}^-12| \times |{}^+3| = s \qquad\qquad\qquad |{}^+7| \times |{}^-7| = h$$

$$12 \times 3 = 36 \quad \longleftarrow \text{Multiply the factors.} \longrightarrow \quad 7 \times 7 = 49$$
$$^-12 \times {}^+3 = {}^-36 \quad \longleftarrow \begin{array}{l}\text{Use the rules to determine} \\ \text{the sign of the product.}\end{array} \longrightarrow \quad {}^+7 \times {}^-7 = {}^-49$$
$$s = {}^-36 \qquad\qquad\qquad\qquad\qquad\qquad\qquad h = {}^-49$$

Write each repeated addition as a multiplication sentence.

1. $^+9 + {}^+9 + {}^+9 + {}^+9 + {}^+9 + {}^+9$

2. $^-6 + {}^-6 + {}^-6 + {}^-6 + {}^-6 + {}^-6$

3. $^+12 + {}^+12 + {}^+12 + {}^+12 + {}^+12$

4. $^-15 + {}^-15 + {}^-15 + {}^-15$

Write the sign of the underlined factor for the given product.

5. $^-5 \times \underline{9} = {}^+45$

6. $^+8 \times \underline{12} = {}^-96$

7. $^-9 \times \underline{15} = {}^-135$

8. $\underline{11} \times {}^+12 = {}^+132$

9. $\underline{7} \times {}^-26 = {}^+182$

10. $\underline{17} \times {}^-22 = {}^-374$

Find the product.

11. $^-75 \times 0$

12. $25 \times {}^-13$

13. $0 \times {}^+21$

14. $^-15 \times {}^-12$

15. $^-7 \times {}^-9 \times {}^-4$

16. $5 \times {}^-8 \times {}^-12$

17. $(4 + {}^-2) \times 6$

18. $8 \times |{}^-9 + {}^-2|$

Problem Solving

19. Climbing down from the mountain, Abe descends 12 m each minute. What is the total change in altitude for a 6-minute descent?

20. The change in the price of ABC stock was reported as $^-\$2$ per share. If Rita owns 8 shares of ABC stock, what is the total change in value of her shares of stock?

21. The table below shows Earl's weekly bank account transactions. Explain how the signs of the integers relate to the transactions.

Transaction	Representation	Result
3 deposits of $50	$^+3 \times {}^+50 = {}^+150$	increase of $150
2 withdrawals of $20	$^+2 \times {}^-20 = {}^-40$	decrease of $40
take away 4 deposits of $10	$^-4 \times {}^+10 = {}^-40$	decrease of $40
take away 5 withdrawals of $40	$^-5 \times {}^-40 = {}^+200$	increase of $200

CRITICAL THINKING

Write *positive* or *negative* to make a true statement. Give examples to support your answer.

22. When an even number of negative integers are multiplied, the product is _?_ .

23. When an odd number of negative integers are multiplied, the product is _?_ .

5-6

Divide Integers

A diver went 15 meters below the surface of the water in 3 minutes. What integer expresses the diver's average change in depth per minute?

To find the integer, n, divide: $^-15 \div 3 = n$.

Division and multiplication are inverse operations. You can use this relationship to find the quotient of a division with integers.

Multiplication	Division
$^+5 \times {}^+3 = {}^+15$ ⟶	$^+15 \div {}^+3 = {}^+5$
$^+5 \times {}^-3 = {}^-15$ ⟶	$^-15 \div {}^-3 = {}^+5$
$^-5 \times {}^-3 = {}^+15$ ⟶	$^+15 \div {}^-3 = {}^-5$
$^-5 \times {}^+3 = {}^-15$ ⟶	$^-15 \div {}^+3 = {}^-5$

$^-15 \div 3 = {}^-5$ or $^-15 \div {}^+3 = {}^-5$

The diver's average change in depth per minute is $^-5$ meters.

▶ You can use rules for dividing integers.

To divide two integers, divide their absolute values.

- the quotient is positive if the integers have like signs.

  $(^+) \div (^+) = {}^+$ $(^-) \div (^-) = {}^+$

- the quotient is negative if the integers have unlike signs.

  $(^+) \div (^-) = {}^-$ $(^-) \div (^+) = {}^-$

- the quotient is zero if the dividend is zero.

> **Think**
> You cannot divide an integer by zero.

Study these examples.

$^+18 \div {}^+6 = {}^+3$ | $^-18 \div {}^+6 = {}^-3$ | $0 \div {}^+6 = 0$ | $^-6 \div 0$ is impossible.

$\dfrac{^-18}{^-6} = {}^+3$ | $\dfrac{^+18}{^-6} = {}^-3$ | $0 \div {}^-6 = 0$

Find each quotient.

1. $^+54 \div ^-6$ 2. $^-25 \div ^+5$ 3. $^-80 \div ^+10$ 4. $0 \div ^+9$

5. $^-10 \div 0$ 6. $^+11 \div ^-1$ 7. $^-20 \div ^+1$ 8. $^-4 \div ^-4$

9. $\dfrac{^-36}{^-6}$ 10. $\dfrac{^-1}{^+1}$ 11. $\dfrac{50}{^-10}$ 12. $\dfrac{^-80}{5}$

Divide to complete each chart. Then write the rule.

13.

IN	OUT
$^+8$	$^-4$
$^+10$	$^-5$
$^+12$	$^-6$
$^+14$	?
$^+16$	?
?	$^-9$

Rule: **IN** $\div$ n = **OUT**

14.

IN	OUT
$^-30$	$^+5$
$^-24$	$^+4$
$^-18$	$^+3$
$^-12$	?
$^-6$	?
?	0

Rule: **IN** $\div$ n = **OUT**

15.

IN	OUT
$^-24$	$^-3$
$^-16$	$^-2$
$^-8$	?
0	?
?	$^+1$
$^+16$	$^+2$

Rule: **IN** $\div$ n = **OUT**

Compare. Write <, =, or >.

16. $^-5 \div ^-1$ __?__ $^-12 \div 4$ 17. $^-36 \div 6$ __?__ $20 \div ^-4$ 18. $^-18 \div ^-2$ __?__ $30 \div ^-6$

19. $^-12 \times 3$ __?__ $24 \div ^-3$ 20. $^-25 \div ^-5$ __?__ $^-4 \times 5$ 21. $^-48 \div ^-4$ __?__ 3×4

Problem Solving

22. Lisa's stock fund changed by $^-81¢$ during a 3-day period. If it changed at the same rate each day, what is the rate?

23. A submarine is at a depth of 250 meters. If it ascends at a rate of 15 meters per minute, can it reach the surface in a half hour?

CHALLENGE — **Algebra**

Write the pattern rule and the next three numbers in each sequence.

24. $^+3, ^-6, ^+12, ^-24,$ __?__ , __?__ , __?__

25. $^-128, ^+64, ^-32, ^+16,$ __?__ , __?__ , __?__

26. $^+1, ^-5, ^+25, ^-125,$ __?__ , __?__ , __?__

27. $^+6561, ^-2187, ^+729, ^-243,$ __?__ , __?__ , __?__

Integers and Order of Operations

A whale descends 5 feet from the surface of the ocean. Then it descends 13 more feet. It repeats this dive two more times. After the three dives, the whale ascends 20 feet. How many feet below the surface is the whale then?

To find how many feet, write and evaluate the expression: $^-5 + 3 \times {}^-13 + {}^+20$.

$$^-5 + \underline{3 \times {}^-13} + {}^+20$$
$$\underline{^-5 + \quad {}^-39} \quad + {}^+20$$
$$\underline{{}^-44 \qquad + {}^+20}$$
$$^-24$$

> Remember the *order of operations*:
> 1. Grouping Symbols
> 2. Exponents
> 3. Multiply or divide from left to right
> 4. Add or subtract from left to right

The whale is 24 feet below the surface.

Study these examples.

Evaluate each expression. Check using a calculator.

> Use $(-)$ to enter a negative number.

$$^-100 + \underline{{}^-175 \div {}^-25} + {}^+9 \times {}^-11$$
$$^-100 + \quad {}^+7 \quad + \underline{{}^+9 \times {}^-11}$$
$$\underline{^-100 + \quad {}^+7} \quad + \quad {}^-99 \qquad \text{Check.}$$
$$\underline{^-93 \qquad\qquad + \quad {}^-99}$$
$$^-192$$

> A scientific calculator follows the order of operations.

$(-)$ 100 $+$ $(-)$ 175 $\div$ $(-)$ 25

$+$ 9 $\times$ $(-)$ 11 Enter/= $\boxed{^-192}$ ← Display

$$^+150 \div {}^-75 - \underline{({}^-41 + {}^+111)} \times ({}^-3)^2$$
$$^+150 \div {}^-75 - \quad {}^+70 \quad \times ({}^-3)^2$$
$$\underline{^+150 \div {}^-75} - \quad {}^+70 \quad \times \quad {}^+9$$
$$^-2 \quad - \quad \underline{{}^+70 \quad \times \quad {}^+9} \qquad \text{Check.}$$
$$\underline{^-2 \quad - \qquad {}^+630}$$
$$^-632$$

> **Think**
>
> $({}^-3)^2$ means "negative 3, squared" or $^-3 \times {}^-3$.
> $^-(3)^2$ means "the opposite of 3 squared" or $^-(3 \times 3) = {}^-(9) = {}^-9$

$+$ 150 $\div$ $(-)$ 75 $-$ $($ $(-)$ 41 $+$ 111 $)$

$\times$ $($ $(-)$ 3 $)$ $\wedge$ 2 Enter/= $\boxed{^-632}$

Name the first step to simplify. Then evaluate the expression.

1. $^-62 - {^+84} \div {^-4} + {^+33}$

2. $^-92 \times ({^-91} + {^+93}) \div {^-23}$

3. $^+71 + {^-175} - {^+56} \div {^-8}$

4. $^+3 \times {^-16} - ({^+36})^2 \div {^-12}$

5. $^-4[6 + (8 - 5)^2]$

6. $^+4 \times [({^+6} - {^-4})^2 \times 15] + {^-5}$

Compute. Watch the order of operations.

7. $^+16 - {^-279} \div {^+31}$

8. $^-226 - {^+190} \div {^+10} + {^-28}$

9. $^+80 \div ({^+93} + {^-77}) + {^-304}$

10. $^+67 + ({^+68} - {^+80})^2 \times {^-30}$

11. $7 - ({^-9} - 5) \times 2^2$

12. $^-16 - {^+4} \div ({^+1} + {^+1})^2$

13. $^-87 - {^+60} \div {^+15} + ({^-40} + {^+36})^2$

14. $^+24({^+45} + {^-36}) - {^-21} - {^+38} \times {^+3}$

15. $({^-24} \div {^-3})({^-20} \div {^+4}) \div {^+2}$

16. $^-16 - {^-14} + {^-14} - {^-16} + {^-8} + {^+3}$

Problem Solving

Write an expression to solve each. Then compute.

17. A dolphin descends 12 feet from the surface of the ocean and then ascends 7 feet. Then it descends 15 feet and repeats this descent three more times. How many feet below the surface is the dolphin then?

18. A spider crawls up 12 inches on Bo's deck to go to its web. Next it drops down 15 inches to go to another web. Then it crawls up 9^2 inches to get out of the rain. How far above or below Bo's deck is the spider then?

TEST PREPARATION

Compute. Choose the best answer.

19. $^-91 + {^+116} \div {^-29} \times ({^+7} + {^+7}) \div {^-7}$

    A $^-120$ **B** $^-83$
    C $^+83$ **D** $^+120$

20. $^+173 - {^+143} + {^-79} \times {^-108} \div ({^+3})^2$

    F $^-8622$ **G** $^-978$
    H $^+978$ **J** $^+8622$

Expressions and Equations with Integers

▶ Greg has $80 in his bank account. He withdraws
$50. If the bank charges a monthly fee, f, of $12,
what is the balance of Greg's bank account?

To find the balance, write and
evaluate the algebraic expression:

$^+\$80 + {}^-\$50 + f$, when $f = {}^-\$12$
$^+\$80 + {}^-\$50 + {}^-\$12$ ◀— Replace f with $^-\$12$.
$^+\$30 \quad + {}^-\$12$
$\$18$ ◀— Simplify.

Greg's bank account has a balance of $18.

▶ LeAnn thought of a number. First she added $^-3$ to the number, then doubled
the sum. The answer she got was $^-16$. Is LeAnn's number $^-1$ or $^-5$?

To find LeAnn's number, write and solve the equation:

$(n + {}^-3) \times 2 = {}^-16$ with *replacement set* $\{^-1, {}^-5\}$.

Let n = LeAnn's number.

> A replacement set is the
> set of numbers to be used
> for possible solutions of a
> mathematical sentence.

To solve an equation when given a replacement set, replace the
variable with each value of the replacement set and determine
the value that makes the equation a true statement.

$(n + {}^-3) \times 2 = {}^-16$, when $n = {}^-1$ $(n + {}^-3) \times 2 = {}^-16$, when $n = {}^-5$
$({}^-1 + {}^-3) \times 2 \stackrel{?}{=} {}^-16$ ◀—Replace n with given value.—▶ $({}^-5 + {}^-3) \times 2 \stackrel{?}{=} {}^-16$
$({}^-4) \times 2 \stackrel{?}{=} {}^-16$ ◀————Simplify.————▶ $({}^-8) \times 2 \stackrel{?}{=} {}^-16$
$^-8 = {}^-16$ false   ◀—Determine whether—▶ $^-16 = {}^-16$ true
true or false.

LeAnn thought of the number $^-5$.

Study these examples.

Solve: $x + {}^-14 = {}^-9$
$x + {}^-14 - {}^-14 = {}^-9 - {}^-14$ ◀—Isolate the variable.
$x = {}^+5$ ◀—Simplify.

Check: $x + {}^-14 = {}^-9$
$^+5 + {}^-14 = {}^-9$
$^-9 = {}^-9$ True

Solve: $^-3a = {}^+12$
$\dfrac{^-3a}{^-3} = \dfrac{^+12}{^-3}$ ◀—Isolate the variable.
$a = {}^-4$ ◀—Simplify.

Check: $^-3a = {}^+12$
$^-3 \cdot {}^-4 = {}^+12$
$^+12 = {}^+12$ True

Evaluate each expression when $a = {}^+5$, $b = {}^-4$, $c = {}^-2$, and $d = 0$.

1. $b \div c$ **2.** $a - b$ **3.** $a + b \cdot c$ **4.** $(b - d) \div c$

5. $\dfrac{ab}{2c}$ **6.** $a - \dfrac{b}{c}$ **7.** $cd - a$ **8.** $\dfrac{bd}{{}^-3c}$

9. $(a + b)^3 + c$ **10.** $bd - a^2$ **11.** $a^2 + bc$ **12.** $b \div (c \cdot d)$

Solve each equation. Use the replacement set $\{{}^+5, {}^-5, 0, {}^+25, {}^-25\}$.

13. $n - {}^+10 = {}^-15$ **14.** $n + {}^+10 = {}^-15$ **15.** $n + {}^-5 = {}^+20$

16. $n - {}^+5 = 0$ **17.** ${}^+25 = n + 0$ **18.** $n - {}^-25 = {}^+5$

Solve and check.

19. $b + {}^-4 = {}^-6$ **20.** $x - {}^+3 = {}^+11$ **21.** ${}^+5 + h = {}^-13$ **22.** ${}^+8t = {}^-104$

23. $\dfrac{y}{{}^-6} = {}^+9$ **24.** ${}^+15z = 0$ **25.** $\dfrac{d}{{}^-10} = 0$ **26.** ${}^+14 - g = {}^-1$

27. ${}^-9 + f = {}^-20$ **28.** ${}^+15 = \dfrac{v}{{}^+3}$ **29.** ${}^-33 = {}^+11r$ **30.** ${}^-243 = {}^-9p$

Write and solve an equation for the variable used.

31. A number z divided by 8 equals ${}^-20$.

32. ${}^-4$ less than a number y is ${}^-7$.

33. A number r increased by 15 equals ${}^-22$.

34. The product of a number d and ${}^-12$ is ${}^+60$.

Problem Solving

35. Richard scored ${}^-12$ points in a game. This was three times his previous score. What was his previous score?

36. Ann's bank account is overdrawn $17. The bank charges a fee, f, for the account being overdrawn. If Ann deposits $20, and the bank's fee is $15, how much money does Ann have in her account?

DO YOU REMEMBER? — Algebra

Write in order from least to greatest.

37. 0.28, 0.82, 0.2, 0.08

38. 0.472, 0.481, 0.399, 0.38

39. 2.57, 2.5, 2.48, 1.99

40. 8.4861, 0.9614, 0.0756, 0.8496

41. 59.221, 59.212, 59.122

42. 0.097765, 0.97765, 0.0907765

Temperature

▶ Temperature can be measured in degrees Fahrenheit (°F), or in degrees Celsius (°C).

The temperature was 15°C. It dropped 25°. What was the new temperature?

▶ To find the new temperature, n, add:

$^+15 + {}^-25 = n$

Think

Dropped 25° = $^-25°$

$^+15 + {}^-25 = {}^-10$

The new temperature was $^-10°C$.

The temperature was 10°F. It dropped to $^-15°F$. How many degrees did the temperature drop?

▶ To find the number of degrees, n, subtract:

$^-15 - {}^+10 = n$

Think

$-({}^+10) = {}^-10$

$^-15 + {}^-10 = {}^-25$

The temperature dropped 25 degrees.

▶ You can use formulas to *estimate* temperature.

$$°C \approx (°F - 30) \div 2 \quad | \quad °F \approx 2°C + 30$$

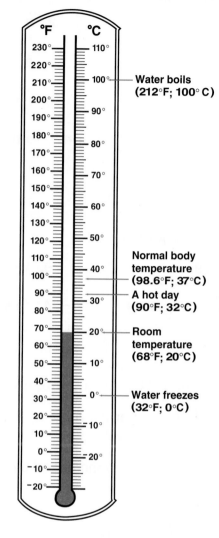

°F °C

230° — 110°
220° —
210° — 100° — Water boils (212°F; 100°C)
200° —
190° — 90°
180° —
170° — 80°
160° —
150° — 70°
140° — 60°
130° —
120° — 50°
110° —
100° — 40° — Normal body temperature (98.6°F; 37°C)
90° — 30° — A hot day (90°F; 32°C)
80° —
70° — 20° — Room temperature (68°F; 20°C)
60° —
50° — 10°
40° —
30° — 0° — Water freezes (32°F; 0°C)
20° —
10° — 10°
0° —
$^-10°$ — 20°
$^-20°$ —

Estimate 46°F to degrees Celsius.

$°C \approx (°F - 30) \div 2$
$= (46 - 30) \div 2$ ← Replace F with 46.
$= 8$ ← Simplify.

46°F is about 8°C.

Estimate $^-2°C$ to degrees Fahrenheit.

$°F \approx (2°C + 30)$
$= (2 \cdot {}^-2 + 30)$ ← Replace C with $^-2$.
$= 26$ ← Simplify.

$^-2°C$ is about 26°F.

Compute the new temperature.

	Starting Temperature	Change in Temperature	New Temperature
1.	35°C	rises 15°	?
2.	$^-5°C$	falls 10°	?
3.	0°C	drops 12°	?
4.	$^-8°C$	climbs 4°	?

Practice

Compute the temperature change.

	Starting Temperature	New Temperature	Change in Temperature
5.	⁻20°F	12°F	?
6.	3°F	⁻7°F	?
7.	19°F	23°F	?
8.	11°F	⁻9°F	?

Estimate the temperature in °C or in °F.
Watch for the degree unit.

9. 60°F   **10.** ⁻8°F   **11.** ⁻2°F   **12.** 74°F   **13.** 200°F

14. 7°C   **15.** ⁻21°C   **16.** ⁻4°C   **17.** 83°C   **18.** 62°C

19. 86°F   **20.** 6°F   **21.** ⁻4°F   **22.** 114°F   **23.** ⁻32°F

24. 75°C   **25.** 5°C   **26.** ⁻30°C   **27.** 35°C   **28.** ⁻10°C

Problem Solving

29. What is the difference between normal body temperature and the freezing point of water on the Celsius scale? on the Fahrenheit scale?

30. The boiling point of nitrogen is ⁻196°C. A miniature transistor conducts electricity that is 48°C above the boiling point of nitrogen. What temperature is this?

31. On one winter morning, the temperature in Boston was ⁻4°F. By noon, the temperature had gone up 10 degrees. What was the temperature in Boston at noon?

32. The normal July temperature in Toronto, Canada is 27°C. Estimate the temperature in °F.

DO YOU REMEMBER?

Match each definition with a word in the box.

33. a diagram used to find the prime factors of a number

34. a statement that two mathematical expressions are equal

35. a mathematical expression that contains one or more variables

36. the written form of a number that shows the place value of its digits

> equation
> standard form
> algebraic expression
> expanded form
> factor tree

Problem-Solving Strategy: Make a Table

The outside temperature at 11:00 P.M. is 14°F. The weather forecaster predicts that it will drop 5° each hour. Then the temperature will rise 3° each hour after 2 A.M. What will the temperature be at 6:00 A.M.?

 Read

Visualize yourself in the problem above as you reread it. List the facts and the question.

Facts: At 11:00 P.M. the temperature is 14°F.

The temperature drops 5° each hour until 2:00 A.M.

The temperature rises 3° each hour after 2:00 A.M.

Question: What will the temperature be at 6:00 A.M.?

 Plan

Make a table to record the hourly temperature change.

When the temperature drops, use a negative integer.

When the temperature rises, use a positive integer.

Solve

Complete the table.

Add ⁻5° (or subtract 5°) for each hour until 2:00 A.M.
Add 3° for each hour until 6:00 A.M.

Time	11:00	12:00	1:00	2:00	3:00	4:00	5:00	6:00
Temperature	⁺14°	⁺9°	⁺4°	⁻1°	⁺2°	⁺5°	⁺8°	⁺11°

$-5 \quad -5 \quad -5 \quad +3 \quad +3 \quad +3 \quad +3$

At 6:00 A.M. the temperature will be 11°F.

Check

Work backward to check. Subtract ⁺3° (or add ⁻3°) and add ⁺5°.

$(^{+}11°) + (^{-}3°) + (^{-}3°) + (^{-}3°) + (^{-}3°) + (^{+}5°) + (^{+}5°) + (^{+}5°) = {^{+}}14°$

Solve each problem. Make a table to help.

1. Henry saved $130 to buy a $250 bicycle. His dad paid him for doing chores each week. Henry received $10 the first week. For each additional week Henry received $4 more than the preceding week. How many weeks must he work to have enough money to pay for the bicycle?

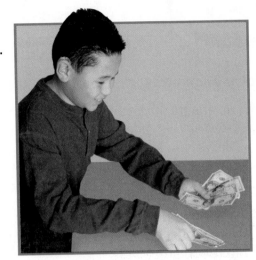

Read ▶ Visualize yourself in the problem as you reread it. List the facts and question.

Facts: amount saved—$130
cost of bicycle—$250
first week—$10
each week—$4 more than the preceding week

Question: How many weeks must he work to have enough money?

Plan ▶ Make a table. Add to find how long it will take to have at least $250.

Week	1st	2nd	3rd	4th
Amount	$130 + $10	$140 + $14	$154 + $18	$172 + ?

Solve ┄┄┄▸ **Check**

2. A baker uses 3 c of sugar, 3 c of flour, and 2 sticks of butter for each pound cake. How much of each ingredient is needed for 8 cakes?

3. Sue played a game in which she won 8 points and lost 5 points in each round. In which round did her score reach 15 points?

4. Adam inspected apples. He found 2 out of every 15 apples to be of poor quality. How many apples of poor quality could he expect to find in a shipment of 165 apples?

5. During an experiment Dana recorded the following temperatures: 22°C, 12°C, 15°C, 5°C, 8°C. If this pattern continues, predict the tenth temperature in the series.

°C
100—
90—
80—
70—
60—
50—
40—
30—
20—
10—
0—

Solve each problem and explain the method you used.

1. Scientists built earthquake stations at different elevations. One station is 75 m above sea level, and a second is 35 m below sea level. What is the difference in height between the two stations?

2. A submarine is at a depth of ⁻300 ft. What must happen for the submarine to reach sea level?

3. How many negative integers are between ⁻4 and ⁺4?

4. How many integers greater than ⁻10 are less than ⁻3?

5. A balloon is 218 m above sea level. A submersible is 220 m below sea level. Which is closer to sea level? How much closer?

6. A diamond-mine entrance begins at 75 ft above sea level. Workers discover diamonds 48 ft below sea level. How deep is the mine at that point?

7. The temperature change from 6 A.M. to 7 A.M. was ⁺3°C. If the temperature at 6 A.M. was ⁻2°C, what was the temperature at 7 A.M.?

8. A parachutist opens her parachute at an altitude of 5000 ft. Her change in altitude is ⁻25 ft per second.
   a. Write an equation to find her altitude h at a time after she opens her parachute.
   b. How far, written as an integer, has she descended in 12 seconds?
   c. What is her altitude 12 seconds after she opens her parachute?

9. To map the features of the ocean floor, scientists take several sonar readings. What is the average of these three readings they made: ⁻14,230 ft; ⁻14,246 ft; ⁻14,235 ft?

Use one or more of the strategies from the list or another strategy you know to solve each problem.

10. The temperature at 11:00 P.M. was 37°F. If it dropped 2°F every hour until 5:00 A.M. and then rose 4°F every hour after that, what was the temperature at 9:00 A.M. the next day?

11. Claire tripled a number and added ⁻14 to it. Her answer was ⁺4. What was her number?

12. A sonar device was positioned 100 m below the surface of the sea. The device was then lowered 175 m. What is the final depth of the device?

13. Each page of Derek's science scrapbook holds 12 pictures. If he has collected 151 pictures to put in his scrapbook, how many more pictures does he need to fill a page?

14. Each time a hot-air balloon rose 65 ft, a downdraft pushed it back down 35 ft. Its original altitude was 185 ft. What would be its altitude after the third downdraft?

15. Mr. Torres spent $85.50 for tickets to the National Aquarium for his family. The tickets cost $19.50 for each adult and $13.50 for each child. If three adults went to the aquarium, how many children went?

16. A scuba diver descended 30 m below the ocean surface, rose 17 m, and then descended 7 m. How far, as an integer, below the ocean surface is the diver?

> **Strategy File**
>
> **Use These Strategies**
> Write an Equation
> Guess and Test
> Interpret the Remainder
> Use More Than One Step
> Make a Table

Use the table for problems 17–19.

17. The wind was 40 mph and the wind chill was 21°F below zero. How much warmer was the air temperature?

18. How much colder does an air temperature of 30°F feel with winds at 30 mph than at 20 mph?

19. With winds at only 15 mph, an air temperature of 15°F feels 7°F colder than when the air temperature is 20°F. What is the wind chill at 15°F?

Wind Chill Table			
27	21	16	12
16	10	3	−3
9	2	−5	−11
4	−3	−10	−17
1	−7	−15	−22
−2	−10	−18	−25
−4	−12	−20	−27
−5	−13	−21	−29

Miles Per Hour (mph): 5, 10, 15, 20, 25, 30, 35, 40

Air Temperature (°F): 35, 30, 25, 20

Write Your Own

20. Write a problem that uses the data in the table. Have someone solve it.

Check Your Progress
Lessons 1–11

Express each as an integer. *(See pp. 150–151.)*

1. an increase of 14 dollars
2. a gain of 9 meters
3. 4 hours before arrival
4. a depth of 12 meters

Write the opposite and absolute value of each integer.

5. $^+15$
6. $^-13$
7. $^+22$
8. $^+7$
9. $^-1$

Compare. Write <, =, or >. *(See pp. 152–153.)*

10. $^-9$? $^+9$
11. $^-4$? $^-7$
12. $^+5$? $^-14$
13. $^-6$? $^-6$

Compute. *(See pp. 154–163.)*

14. $^+6 + {}^-3$
15. $^-4 + {}^+9$
16. $0 + {}^-5$
17. $^-7 + {}^-5$
18. $^+9 - {}^+5$
19. $^-6 - {}^-8$
20. $^+7 - {}^-11$
21. $0 - {}^+4$
22. $^-5 \times {}^-10$
23. $^-90 \div {}^+5$
24. $0 \times {}^-6$
25. $\frac{^-33}{^-3}$
26. $^+4 \times {}^-11$
27. $^-6 \times {}^+3$
28. $^+8 \times {}^-8$
29. $^-3 \times {}^+5$
30. $^+40 \div ({}^+95 + {}^-79) + {}^-214$
31. $^+37 + ({}^+8 - {}^+10)^2 \times {}^-3$

Solve each equation. Use the replacement set $\{^-3, 0, {}^+3\}$. *(See pp. 164–165.)*

32. $n - {}^+12 = {}^-15$
33. $n + {}^-15 = {}^-15$
34. $n - {}^-5 = {}^+8$
35. $n - {}^-3 = 0$
36. $^+3 = n + 0$
37. $n - {}^-3 = {}^+9$

Estimate the temperature in °C or in °F. *(See pp. 166–167.)*
Watch for the degree unit.

38. $^-12°F$
39. $50°F$
40. $^-32°F$
41. $40°C$
42. $^-20°C$

Problem Solving
(See pp. 168–171.)

43. The temperature was $^+12°C$ at noon. By nine o'clock it was $^-2°C$. How many degrees did the temperature drop?

44. The football team gained 23 yards on 1st down and were penalized 5 yards on 2nd down. What was the net result?

(See *Still More Practice*, p. 523.)

Inequalities in One Variable

You can solve an inequality in one variable and graph its solution on a number line.

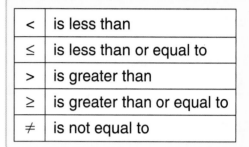

Remember:
An inequality is a statement that uses one of these symbols: $<$, $\leq$, $>$, $\geq$, or $\neq$.

<	is less than
≤	is less than or equal to
>	is greater than
≥	is greater than or equal to
≠	is not equal to

▶ Solving an addition or subtraction inequality is like solving an equation.

$x + 5 > 7$ ◀—— addition inequality

$x + 5 - 5 > 7 - 5$ ◀—Subtract 5 from both sides.

$x > 2$ ◀——————solution to the inequality

$y - {}^-5 \leq {}^+4$ ◀—— subtraction inequality

$y - {}^-5 + {}^-5 \leq {}^+4 + {}^-5$ ◀—Add $^-5$ to both sides.

$y \leq {}^-1$ ◀——————solution to the inequality

▶ To graph $x > 2$, place an open dot at 2 on the number line and then shade the number line to the right of 2.

▶ To graph $y \leq {}^-1$, place a solid dot at 1 on the number line and then shade the number line to the left of $^-1$.

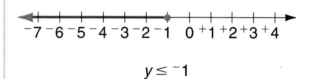

$x > 2$

$y \leq {}^-1$

- The open dot at 2 means that 2 is *not* a solution of $x > 2$.

- The green line with the arrow shows that all values *greater than* 2 are solutions of $x > 2$.

- The solid dot at $^-1$ means that $^-1$ is a solution of $y \leq {}^-1$.

- The red line with the arrow shows that all values *less than* $^-1$ are also solutions of $y \leq {}^-1$.

Some solutions of $x > 2$: $\{2\frac{1}{2}, 3, 7.4, \ldots\}$

Not solutions of $x > 2$: $\{\ldots, {}^-2, 0, 1.9, 2\}$

Some solutions of $y \leq {}^-1$: $\{\ldots, {}^-9, {}^-6, {}^-3\}$

Not solutions of $y \leq {}^-1$: $\{1.1, 6, 10, 35, \ldots\}$

Solve and graph the solution of each inequality. Then list three numbers that are solutions and three numbers that are not solutions.

1. $t - 34 > {}^-19$
2. $w + 21 \leq 45$
3. $19 + x \geq 14$
4. $s - 14 < 12$

5. $k - 5 \geq 8$
6. $p + 12 < 9$
7. $r + 88 \leq 92$
8. $v + 2 > {}^-6$

9. $a - 2 \leq {}^-4$
10. $z - 2 > 10$
11. $b - 4 < {}^-9$
12. $c + 6 \geq 0$

Chapter 5 Test

Write each as an integer.

1. a gain of 5 lb

2. 11 m backward

3. 17 floors down

Find the absolute value of the integer.

4. $|{}^-18|$

5. $|{}^+19|$

6. $|{}^-73|$

7. $|502|$

8. $|{}^-643|$

Arrange in order from least to greatest.

9. ${}^+9, {}^-9, 0$

10. ${}^-9, {}^+6, {}^-2$

11. ${}^-60, {}^+30, 0, {}^-70$

Compute.

12. ${}^-11 + {}^-7$

13. ${}^-8 + {}^+4$

14. ${}^+366 \div {}^+6$

15. ${}^+2448 \div {}^-24$

Evaluate each expression when $a = {}^+7$, $b = {}^-2$, $c = {}^-3$, and $d = 0$.

16. $b \times (c + a)$

17. $ad \div c$

18. $a + b \cdot c$

19. $(a - b)^2 \div c$

Solve and check.

20. $y \div {}^-6 = {}^+7$

21. ${}^+15z = 0$

22. ${}^-9 + f = {}^-25$

23. ${}^+17 - g = {}^-1$

Estimate the temperature in °C or in °F. Watch for the degree unit.

24. 70°F

25. ${}^-18$°F

26. ${}^-2$°C

27. 74°C

28. 90°C

Problem Solving

Use a strategy or strategies you have learned.

29. Andrew writes an integer pattern by adding ${}^+5$ and subtracting ${}^-2$ in order. The eighth number in the pattern is ${}^+20$. What number did he start with?

Tell About It

Explain how you solved the problem. Show all your work.

30. A geologist studied rock forms at a site 5 m below sea level. If he moves to a site 9 m higher, how far above or below sea level will he be?

Performance Assessment

31. Lee added the same integer to each number in the magic square at the left to get a new magic square. Find the integer and complete the square.

${}^+1$	${}^+2$	${}^-3$
${}^-4$	0	${}^+4$
${}^+3$	${}^-2$	${}^-1$

${}^+3$	${}^+4$	${}^-1$

Test Preparation

Choose the best answer.

1. Choose the short word name for the number.

687,400,000,000

   a. 687 million, 400 thousand
   b. 687 billion, 400 million
   c. 687 billion, 400 thousand
   d. 687 million, 200

2. Choose the quotient.

$0.36\overline{)0.12312}$

   a. 0.00342
   b. 0.0342
   c. 0.342
   d. not given

3. An expression for "2 less than x, divided by 3.5" is:

   a. $\dfrac{2-x}{3.5}$ **b.** $\dfrac{x-2}{3.5}$

   c. $x - \dfrac{2}{3.5}$ **d.** $2 - \dfrac{x}{3.5}$

4. Use $A = \dfrac{1}{2}bh$. Find b when $A = 30$ ft^2 and $h = 6$ ft.

   a. 12 ft
   b. 10 ft
   c. 8 ft
   d. 6 ft

5. When $x = 2$, $y = 5$, and $z = 6$, which expression has a value of 22?

   a. $4z - 2x + 3y$ **b.** $x(y + z)$

   c. $\dfrac{z}{x} + y$ **d.** $\dfrac{5z}{y - x}$

6. 113,707 subtracted from 509,911 is:

   a. 395,204
   b. 396,104
   c. 396,204
   d. 496,204

7. Estimate by rounding.

$$\begin{array}{r} \$529.47 \\ \times\ \ \ \ 623 \\ \hline \end{array}$$

   a. $30,000
   b. $36,000
   c. $300,000
   d. $500,000

8. Choose the product.

0.91×0.37

   a. 0.3367
   b. 1.28
   c. 33.67
   d. not given

9. A mathematical sentence for "10 more than one third of a number n is greater than 25" is:

   a. $10 - \dfrac{1}{3}n > 25$ **b.** $\dfrac{1}{3}n + 10 > 25$

   c. $\dfrac{n}{3} + 10 < 25$ **d.** $10 + \dfrac{1}{3} + n > 25$

10. Choose the equation that is solved by using the Subtraction Property of Equality.

   a. $\dfrac{x}{3} = 4.2$

   b. $x - 3 = 4.2$
   c. $4.2 = x - 3$
   d. $x + 3 = 4.2$

11. Which makes the number sentence true?

$|n| < 8$

   a. 10   **b.** $^-2$
   c. $^-8$ **d.** $^-10$

12. The product of 32,238 and 705 is:

   a. 2,227,790
   b. 2,727,790
   c. 22,727,090
   d. 22,727,790

13. Which statement is true?

    a. $|^-7| = ^-|7|$ **b.** $|^-7| = ^-(^-7)$
    c. $^-|^-7| = ^-(^-7)$ **d.** $^-|^-7| = |^-(^-7)|$

14. Add.

    $^-21 + (^-14)$
      a. $^-7$
      b. $^-35$
      c. 7
      d. 35

15. Estimate by using compatible numbers.

    $584{,}719 \div 329$
      a. 2000
      b. 3000
      c. 4000
      d. not given

16. Evaluate $3a^2 - 4b$ when $a = {}^-2$ and $b = 0$.

      a. $^-16$
      b. $^-12$
      c. 16
      d. 12

17. Simplify.

    $^-4 - (^-2 + 5) \times {}^-1$
      a. $^-7$
      b. $^-1$
      c. 1
      d. 7

18. Ray's aquarium holds 25 gallons of water. One gallon of water weighs 8.33 lb. What is the weight of the water if the aquarium is filled to the top?

    a. 180.25 lb   **b.** 200.25 lb
    c. 208.25 lb   **d.** 280.25 lb

19. Which does not name an integer?

      a. $^-35$ **b.** 0
      c. $\frac{3}{15}$ **d.** $\frac{10}{2}$

20. Subtract.

    $^-45 - 63$
      a. 108
      b. $^-108$
      c. 18
      d. $^-18$

21. Multiply.

    $\begin{array}{r} 8.005 \\ \times\ 5.32 \\ \hline \end{array}$
      a. 40.5866
      b. 41.5866
      c. 42.5866
      d. not given

22. Solve.

    $x - (7.65 + 3.18) = 4$
      a. $x = 6.83$
      b. $x = 10.83$
      c. $x = 14.83$
      d. not given

23. In scientific notation, 0.0000631 is:

      a. 6.31×10^6
      b. 6.31×10^5
      c. 6.31×10^{-5}
      d. 6.31×10^{-6}

24. The temperature at noon was 13°F. It dropped 17 degrees. What is the temperature now?

    a. 4°F   **b.** $^-13$°F
    c. $^-17$°F   **d.** $^-4$°F

Explain how you solved each problem. Show all your work.

25. Two groups of tourists flew to Japan. The first group took 4 hours less than the second to fly there. If the first group flew for 17 hours, how many hours did the second group fly?

26. A theater has 675 seats. There are three times as many seats in a row as there are rows. How many rows and how many seats are there?

Number Theory and Fractions

You may have thought there was no mathematics in pizza. Well, there is. It turns out there is mathematics in plain cheese pizzas, sausage pizzas, pepperoni pizzas, pineapple pizzas, teriyaki pizzas, and avocado pizzas, just to name a few. (Sometimes, it's just not good to take mathematics too seriously.)

From *Math for Smarty Pants* by
Marilyn Burns

In this chapter you will:

Investigate fractions, primes, and composites
Compare, order, and estimate fractions
Explore greatest common factor and least
  common multiple
Relate fractions, mixed numbers, and decimals
Identify terminating and repeating decimals
Solve problems by finding a pattern

Critical Thinking/Finding Together

The number of slices in the 1st giant pizza is a prime number between 10 and 20. The number of slices in the 2nd and 3rd giant pizzas together is a multiple of 5. If the total number of slices is 32, how many slices are there in the 1st pizza?

Divisibility

A number is divisible by another number if there is no remainder when you divide.

$$\begin{array}{r} 39 \\ 9\overline{)351} \\ -27 \\ \hline 81 \\ -81 \\ \hline 0 \end{array}$$

Since there is no remainder, 351 is *divisible* by 9.

▶ You can use the divisibility rules in the table below to help you determine if one number is divisible by another number.

Divisibility Rules	
A number is divisible by:	**if . . .**
2	it is an even number (ends in 0, 2, 4, 6, or 8)
3	the sum of its digits is divisible by 3
4	the last two digits form a number divisible by 4
5	the ones digit is 0 or 5
6	it is divisible by both 2 and 3
8	the last three digits form a number divisible by 8
9	the sum of its digits is divisible by 9
10	the last digit is 0

Study this example.

Determine whether 3024 is divisible by 2, 3, 4, 5, 6, 8, 9, and/or 10.

3024 ⟶ 4 is an even number.	3024 is divisible by 2.
3024 ⟶ 3 + 0 + 2 + 4 = 9 and 9 ÷ 3 = 3	3024 is divisible by 3.
3024 ⟶ 24 ÷ 4 = 6	3024 is divisible by 4.
3024 ⟶ 4 is not 0 or 5.	3024 is *not* divisible by 5.
3024 ⟶ 4 is an even number and 3 + 0 + 2 + 4 = 9 and 9 ÷ 3 = 3.	3024 is divisible by 6.
3024 ⟶ 24 ÷ 8 = 3	3024 is divisible by 8.
3024 ⟶ 3 + 0 + 2 + 4 = 9 and 9 ÷ 9 = 1	3024 is divisible by 9.
3024 ⟶ 4 is not 0.	3024 is *not* divisible by 10.

So 3024 is divisible by 2, 3, 4, 6, 8, and 9.

Tell whether the number is divisible by 2, 3, 4, 5, 6, 8, 9, and/or 10.

1. 333　　　**2.** 128　　　**3.** 225　　　**4.** 7535　　　**5.** 8289

6. 9410　　　**7.** 99,483　　　**8.** 67,704　　　**9.** 67,713　　　**10.** 67,722

11. 23,918　　　**12.** 35,932　　　**13.** 85,446　　　**14.** 40,620　　　**15.** 90,990

16. 17,934　　　**17.** 49,708　　　**18.** 77,075　　　**19.** 13,104　　　**20.** 486,890

21. 207,984　　　**22.** 352,860　　　**23.** 607,712　　　**24.** 581,889　　　**25.** 270,228

Find the missing digit or digits that would make each number divisible by the given number.

26. 3,95□; by 10

> **Think**
> The last digit must be **0** to be divisible by 10.

27. 17,84□; by 3　　　**28.** 243,05□; by 9　　　**29.** 698,39□; by 3 and by 9

30. 17,39□; by 5　　　**31.** 14,5□2; by 8　　　**32.** 13,□12; by 8 and by 3

33. 27,1□8; by 6　　　**34.** 20,71□; by 4　　　**35.** 502,7□5; by 3 and by 5

36. 37,6□3; by 9　　　**37.** 98□,124; by 6　　　**38.** 109,83□; by 4 and by 8

Problem Solving

39. Ms. Sutphin has 74,516 pennies. She wants to divide them equally among some containers. She has 10 containers, but does not need to use them all. How many containers could she use so there are no pennies left over?

40. Mr. Diaz wants to divide 4952 stickers equally among some teachers at school. He wants to give the stickers to at least 4 but no more than 10 teachers. To how many teachers can he give stickers so there are none left over? How many will each teacher get?

TEST PREPARATION

41. Which number is divisible by 4?

A 448,274
B 346,493
C 330,902
D 286,156

42. Which number is *not* divisible by 9?

F 34,947
G 38,999
H 55,026
J 80,973

Update your skills. See page 3.

Prime and Composite Numbers

▶ A **prime number** is a whole number greater than 1 that has *exactly two* factors, itself and 1.

Find all the factors of 11.

$$1 \times 11 = 11$$ Factors of 11: 1, 11

Since 11 has exactly two factors, it is a prime number.

▶ A **composite number** is a whole number greater than 1 that has *more than two* factors.

> The numbers 0 and 1 are neither prime nor composite.

Find all the factors of 25.

$$1 \times 25 = 25$$
$$5 \times 5 \ = 25$$ Factors of 25: 1, 5, 25

Since 25 has more than two factors, it is a composite number.

Practice

Tell whether each number is *prime, composite,* or *neither.*

1. 24	**2.** 35	**3.** 2	**4.** 9	**5.** 19
6. 21	**7.** 33	**8.** 11	**9.** 1	**10.** 0
11. 51	**12.** 26	**13.** 81	**14.** 100	**15.** 41
16. 207	**17.** 613	**18.** 127	**19.** 10,011	**20.** 37,311

Copy these statements in your Math Journal. Then tell whether each statement is true or false. Give an example to justify your answer.

21. Any whole number is either prime or composite.

22. No composite number is an even number.

23. All prime numbers are odd numbers.

24. Every even number greater than 2 is a composite number.

25. The product of two prime numbers is a prime number.

26. The sum of two prime numbers is a composite number.

Make and complete a table like the one below for the numbers 1–20. Use the table for exercises 27–35.

27. Which numbers are prime numbers?

28. Which numbers are composite numbers?

29. Which numbers have exactly three factors?

30. Which number has only one factor?

31. Which numbers have six factors?

Number	Factors	Number of Factors	Prime or Composite
1	1	1	neither
2	1, 2	?	prime
3	1, 3	?	?
17	?	?	?
18	?	?	?
19	?	?	?
20	?	?	?

32. Which number is a factor of all of the numbers?

33. Which numbers have both 2 and 3 as factors?

34. Which numbers have both 2 and 5 as factors?

35. Which numbers have both 4 and 8 as factors?

Problem Solving

36. Why is the number 1 neither prime nor composite?

37. Why is 2 the only even prime number?

38. Rita's locker number is a two-digit prime number. There are 25 lockers, numbered 1–20, in Rita's classroom. What are the possible numbers that could be Rita's locker number?

39. Carl ran 4 km every day for 5 days. Ken ran 3 km every day for 7 days. Was the total number of kilometers both Carl and Ken ran prime or composite? How do you know?

CRITICAL THINKING

Six is called a perfect number because it is the sum of all its factors, not including itself.

The factors of 6 are 1, 2, 3, 6.
$$1 + 2 + 3 = 6$$

40. Find another perfect number. Extend the table above to help you.

41. Are any prime numbers also perfect numbers? Explain.

42. Use the internet or reference books to define these two types of numbers: (a) deficient numbers and (b) abundant numbers. Discuss your results with the class.

Prime Factorization

Every composite number can be written as the product of prime factors. This is called prime factorization.

Find the prime factorization of 36.

▶ You can use a **factor tree** to find the prime factors.

- Start with the composite number.

- Choose *any* 2 factors.

- Continue factoring until all the branches show *prime* numbers.

- Arrange the prime factors in order from least to greatest.

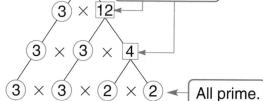

$$2 \times 2 \times 3 \times 3$$

The prime factorization of 36 is $2 \times 2 \times 3 \times 3$.

▶ You can use exponents to express the prime factorization of 36.　　$2^2 \times 3^2$

Remember:
$2 \times 2 = 2^2$
$3 \times 3 = 3^2$

▶ No matter which 2 factors you begin with, the prime factorization will always be the same.

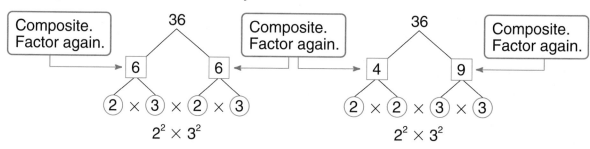

Practice

Express each in exponential form. Then find the product.

1. $5 \times 2 \times 2 \times 5$　　　　**2.** $2 \times 2 \times 2 \times 3$　　　　**3.** $11 \times 2 \times 11 \times 5$

4. $7 \times 3 \times 2 \times 7 \times 3$　　**5.** $5 \times 13 \times 5 \times 5$　　**6.** $2 \times 7 \times 2 \times 7$

Make a factor tree for each to find the prime factorization.

7. 45　　　　**8.** 64　　　　**9.** 72　　　　**10.** 88　　　　**11.** 48

Find the prime factorization and write in exponential form.

12. 32   **13.** 24   **14.** 50   **15.** 125   **16.** 63

17. 71   **18.** 44   **19.** 60   **20.** 100   **21.** 96

Prime Factorization Using Divisibility Rules

You can use the divisibility rules to help you find the prime factorization of larger numbers.

Find the prime factorization of 9450.

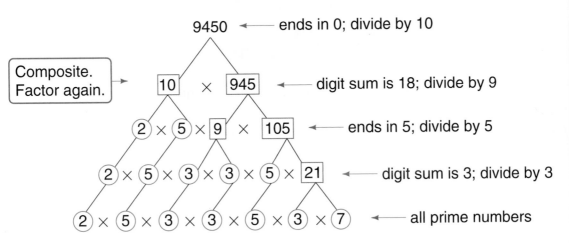

9450 ← ends in 0; divide by 10

Composite. Factor again. → 10 × 945 ← digit sum is 18; divide by 9

2 × 5 × 9 × 105 ← ends in 5; divide by 5

2 × 5 × 3 × 3 × 5 × 21 ← digit sum is 3; divide by 3

2 × 5 × 3 × 3 × 5 × 3 × 7 ← all prime numbers

So, the prime factorization of 9450 is $2 \times 3^3 \times 5^2 \times 7$.

Find the prime factorization. Use the divisibility rules and a factor tree to help.

22. 95   **23.** 114   **24.** 153   **25.** 390   **26.** 504

27. 189   **28.** 225   **29.** 540   **30.** 1215   **31.** 2916

Solve for _y_ to complete the prime factorization.

32. $2 \times y \times 3 = 12$ **33.** $2y = 82$ **34.** $117 = 3^2 \times y$

35. $2^3 \times y = 88$ **36.** $110 = y \times 5 \times 11$ **37.** $2^2 \times y \times 5 = 60$

Make two different factor trees for each number. Then write the prime factorization for each.

38. 70   **39.** 99   **40.** 120   **41.** 40

42. 48   **43.** 150   **44.** 84   **45.** 54

Equivalent Fractions

Fractions that name the same part of a whole or a set are called equivalent fractions. $\frac{1}{2}, \frac{2}{4}, \frac{3}{6}, \frac{4}{8}$ are equivalent.

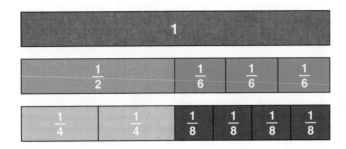

To find equivalent fractions, multiply or divide the numerator and denominator of the fraction by the *same* nonzero number. This does not change the value because it is the same as multiplying or dividing by 1.

$\frac{5}{6} = \frac{n}{18}$ .Think..........

$6 \times 3 = 18$

$\frac{5 \times 3}{6 \times 3} = \frac{15}{18}$

$\frac{5}{6} = \frac{15}{18}$

$\frac{5}{6}$ and $\frac{15}{18}$ are equivalent fractions.

$\frac{8}{32} = \frac{1}{r}$ .Think..........

$8 \div 8 = 1$

$\frac{8 \div 8}{32 \div 8} = \frac{1}{4}$

$\frac{8}{32} = \frac{1}{4}$

$\frac{8}{32}$ and $\frac{1}{4}$ are equivalent fractions.

In each exercise, which two figures show equivalent fractions? Explain your answer.

1. a.   b.   c.   d.

2. a.   b.   c.   d.

Write the missing term to complete the equivalent fraction.

3. $\dfrac{3}{4} = \dfrac{n}{12}$ 4. $\dfrac{1}{11} = \dfrac{a}{88}$ 5. $\dfrac{2}{9} = \dfrac{c}{81}$ 6. $\dfrac{2}{3} = \dfrac{q}{12}$ 7. $\dfrac{5}{7} = \dfrac{40}{f}$

8. $\dfrac{1}{8} = \dfrac{6}{b}$ 9. $\dfrac{1}{10} = \dfrac{3}{q}$ 10. $\dfrac{3}{11} = \dfrac{6}{s}$ 11. $\dfrac{9}{10} = \dfrac{r}{100}$ 12. $\dfrac{1}{25} = \dfrac{4}{d}$

13. $\dfrac{9}{30} = \dfrac{m}{10}$ 14. $\dfrac{4}{12} = \dfrac{t}{3}$ 15. $\dfrac{21}{28} = \dfrac{z}{4}$ 16. $\dfrac{40}{45} = \dfrac{x}{9}$ 17. $\dfrac{2}{6} = \dfrac{1}{h}$

18. $\dfrac{4}{k} = \dfrac{20}{25}$ 19. $\dfrac{6}{13} = \dfrac{24}{m}$ 20. $\dfrac{49}{e} = \dfrac{7}{8}$ 21. $\dfrac{x}{15} = \dfrac{36}{45}$ 22. $\dfrac{9}{16} = \dfrac{y}{144}$

Write two equivalent fractions for each fraction.

23. $\dfrac{5}{9}$ 24. $\dfrac{3}{5}$ 25. $\dfrac{1}{4}$ 26. $\dfrac{5}{10}$ 27. $\dfrac{6}{8}$

28. $\dfrac{3}{7}$ 29. $\dfrac{11}{15}$ 30. $\dfrac{9}{12}$ 31. $\dfrac{25}{75}$ 32. $\dfrac{8}{12}$

Complete the equivalent fractions.

33. $\dfrac{1}{3} = \dfrac{x}{6} = \dfrac{y}{18}$ 34. $\dfrac{3}{4} = \dfrac{s}{8} = \dfrac{t}{24}$ 35. $\dfrac{40}{64} = \dfrac{c}{16} = \dfrac{d}{8}$

36. $\dfrac{4}{5} = \dfrac{8}{a} = \dfrac{24}{b}$ 37. $\dfrac{1}{6} = \dfrac{2}{e} = \dfrac{6}{f}$ 38. $\dfrac{2}{7} = \dfrac{n}{14} = \dfrac{12}{p}$

39. $\dfrac{50}{75} = \dfrac{g}{15} = \dfrac{h}{3}$ 40. $\dfrac{48}{64} = \dfrac{12}{x} = \dfrac{3}{y}$ 41. $\dfrac{216}{252} = \dfrac{m}{42} = \dfrac{6}{n}$

42. $\dfrac{112}{144} = \dfrac{a}{36} = \dfrac{7}{b}$ 43. $\dfrac{25}{75} = \dfrac{5}{c} = \dfrac{1}{d}$ 44. $\dfrac{98}{441} = \dfrac{e}{63} = \dfrac{2}{f}$

CHALLENGE

45. I am equivalent to $\dfrac{2}{3}$. My numerator is 7 less than my denominator. What fraction am I?

46. I am equivalent to $\dfrac{36}{60}$. The sum of my numerator and my denominator is 24. What fraction am I?

6-5

Greatest Common Factor

▶ The **greatest common factor (GCF)** of two or more numbers is the greatest number that is a factor of all of the numbers.

Find the greatest common factor of 8, 12, and 20.

To find the GCF:

- List all the factors of each number.

8: 1, 2, 4, 8
12: 1, 2, 3, 4, 6, 12
20: 1, 2, 4, 5, 10, 20

- Find the common factors.

Common factors:
1, 2, 4

- Choose the greatest common factor.

The greatest common factor is 4.

The GCF of 8, 12, and 20 is 4.

▶ You can also refer to the greatest common factor of two or more numbers as the **greatest common divisor (GCD)**.

The GCD of 8, 12, and 20 is 4.

Think
4 divides evenly into 8, 12, and 20.

Practice

Write all the common factors for each set of numbers.

1. 8 and 24

2. 10 and 30

3. 15 and 35

4. 12 and 18

5. 16 and 20

6. 12 and 24

7. 30 and 18

8. 45 and 20

9. 4, 6, and 8

10. 6, 9, and 12

11. 5, 12, and 14

12. 6, 14, and 22

Find the GCF and the GCD of each set of numbers.

13. 6 and 12

14. 12 and 36

15. 8 and 10

16. 6 and 14

17. 9 and 30

18. 8 and 36

19. 24 and 42

20. 7 and 40

21. 8, 24, and 32

22. 5, 30, and 35

23. 15, 30, and 45

Find the GCF Using Prime Factorization

Find the GCF of 27 and 54.

- First use factor trees to find the prime factors of each number.

  Finding the prime factors of a number is called prime factorization.

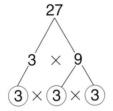
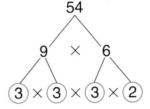

- Then multiply the prime factors that are common to both to find the GCF.

common to both

$27 = 3 \times 3 \times 3$ $54 = 2 \times 3 \times 3 \times 3$

$$3 \times 3 \times 3 = 27$$
GCF of 27 and 54: 27

Find the GCF. Use prime factorization.

24. 48 and 56   **25.** 64 and 96   **26.** 36 and 72   **27.** 80 and 100

28. 45 and 75   **29.** 39 and 104   **30.** 48 and 84   **31.** 100 and 125

32. 14, 49, and 70   **33.** 48, 80, and 112   **34.** 18, 54, and 90

Find a pair of numbers:

35. Between 10 and 20 that have 6 as their GCF.

36. Between 12 and 18 that have 4 as their GCF.

37. Between 15 and 30 that have 5 as their GCF.

38. Between 16 and 24 that have 8 as their GCF.

CRITICAL THINKING

39. Can the greatest common factor of 8 and 32 be greater than 8? Explain your reasoning.

Practice

Fractions in Simplest Form

A fraction is in **simplest form**, or **lowest terms**, when the numerator and denominator have no common factor other than 1.

Cass and Arti surveyed 32 classmates to find out when they did their homework. The results showed that 20 out of 32 ($\frac{20}{32}$) of the students did homework after dinner. Rename this fraction in simplest form.

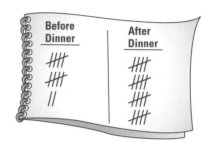

Before Dinner	After Dinner
Ⅲ Ⅲ Ⅱ	Ⅲ Ⅲ Ⅲ Ⅲ

To rename a fraction as an equivalent fraction in simplest form:

- Find the GCF of the numerator and the denominator.

$$\frac{20}{32} \longrightarrow \text{factors of 20: 1, 2, 4, 5, 10, 20}$$
$$\phantom{\frac{20}{32}} \longrightarrow \text{factors of 32: 1, 2, 4, 8, 16, 32}$$

GCF of 20 and 32: 4

- Divide the numerator and the denominator by their GCF.

$$\frac{20}{32} = \frac{20 \div 4}{32 \div 4} = \frac{5}{8}$$

$\frac{4}{4} = 1$, so the quotient is still equal to $\frac{20}{32}$.

The simplest form of $\frac{20}{32}$ is $\frac{5}{8}$.

Write the letter of the GCF of the numerator and the denominator of each fraction.

1. $\frac{3}{6}$ **a.** 1   **b.** 6   **c.** 3   **d.** 18

2. $\frac{7}{8}$ **a.** 7   **b.** 1   **c.** 8   **d.** 14

3. $\frac{10}{12}$ **a.** 10   **b.** 12   **c.** 2   **d.** 1

4. $\frac{25}{45}$ **a.** 25   **b.** 9   **c.** 5   **d.** 1

5. $\frac{80}{100}$ **a.** 20   **b.** 10   **c.** 50   **d.** 2

6. $\frac{11}{132}$ **a.** 1   **b.** 11   **c.** 132   **d.** 12

Is the fraction in lowest terms? Write *Yes* or *No*. If no, rename the fraction in simplest form.

7. $\frac{2}{3}$ 8. $\frac{1}{8}$ 9. $\frac{4}{8}$ 10. $\frac{5}{10}$ 11. $\frac{3}{10}$ 12. $\frac{1}{12}$

13. $\frac{7}{21}$ 14. $\frac{12}{25}$ 15. $\frac{10}{18}$ 16. $\frac{6}{21}$ 17. $\frac{12}{18}$ 18. $\frac{5}{24}$

19. $\frac{16}{27}$ 20. $\frac{9}{12}$ 21. $\frac{14}{35}$ 22. $\frac{24}{34}$ 23. $\frac{17}{36}$ 24. $\frac{18}{72}$

Rename each as a fraction in simplest form.

25. $\frac{18}{36}$ 26. $\frac{15}{40}$ 27. $\frac{16}{48}$ 28. $\frac{3}{18}$ 29. $\frac{16}{20}$ 30. $\frac{9}{45}$

31. $\frac{5}{55}$ 32. $\frac{12}{16}$ 33. $\frac{20}{50}$ 34. $\frac{21}{49}$ 35. $\frac{12}{24}$ 36. $\frac{12}{30}$

37. $\frac{12}{44}$ 38. $\frac{30}{55}$ 39. $\frac{14}{42}$ 40. $\frac{14}{18}$ 41. $\frac{5}{35}$ 42. $\frac{20}{32}$

43. $\frac{14}{20}$ 44. $\frac{16}{24}$ 45. $\frac{20}{32}$ 46. $\frac{9}{36}$ 47. $\frac{6}{27}$ 48. $\frac{16}{28}$

Problem Solving

Write each answer as a fraction in simplest form.

49. Lions spend about 20 hours a day sleeping. What part of their day do lions spend sleeping? What part of their day are they awake?

50. At the circus, 128 of the 160 animals are *not* lions. What part of the animals are lions?

CRITICAL THINKING

Write *sometimes*, *always*, or *never*. Give an example to justify your answer.

51. A fraction with 1 as a numerator is in simplest form.

52. A fraction with a prime number in the numerator is in simplest form.

53. A fraction with an even number in its numerator and denominator is in simplest form.

Mixed Numbers and Improper Fractions

When you compute with fractions, you must be able to express mixed numbers as improper fractions and vice versa.

An improper fraction has a value that *is equal to or is greater than* 1. It has a numerator *equal to or greater than* its denominator.

$$3\frac{1}{2} = \frac{7}{2}$$

▶ **To rename a mixed number as a fraction:**

- Multiply the whole number by the denominator.

- Add the product to the numerator.

- Write the sum over the denominator.

$$3\frac{1}{2} = \frac{(2 \times 3) + 1}{2} = \frac{7}{2}$$

improper fraction

▶ **To rename an improper fraction as a whole number or as a mixed number:**

- Divide the numerator by the denominator. Write the quotient as the whole number part.

- If there is a remainder, write it over the denominator and express the fraction in simplest form.

$$\frac{38}{4} = 4\overline{)38}\ \ \overset{9}{}\ \text{R2}$$

$$\frac{38}{4} = 9\frac{2}{4}$$

$$= 9\frac{1}{2}$$

Remember: Read $9\frac{1}{2}$ as nine *and* one half.

Study these examples.

$$\frac{18}{9} = 9\overline{)18}\ \overset{2}{} \longrightarrow \frac{18}{9} = 2$$

$$10\frac{5}{6} = \frac{(6 \times 10) + 5}{6} = \frac{60 + 5}{6} = \frac{65}{6}$$

Write the word name for each mixed number.

1. $7\frac{1}{2}$ 2. $8\frac{4}{5}$ 3. $5\frac{1}{10}$ 4. $22\frac{1}{8}$ 5. $1\frac{1}{20}$ 6. $11\frac{11}{12}$

Write as a mixed number.

7. eleven and one fourth

8. nine and nine tenths

9. sixteen and three fifths

10. thirty and two thirds

11. twenty and fifteen sixteenths

12. twenty-one and seven tenths

Express each mixed number as a fraction.

13. $4\frac{1}{4}$ 14. $2\frac{1}{2}$ 15. $1\frac{3}{8}$ 16. $2\frac{1}{8}$ 17. $3\frac{4}{5}$ 18. $5\frac{2}{7}$

19. $1\frac{1}{9}$ 20. $1\frac{1}{10}$ 21. $11\frac{1}{3}$ 22. $12\frac{1}{2}$ 23. $15\frac{1}{4}$ 24. $12\frac{2}{7}$

25. $1\frac{5}{8}$ 26. $5\frac{2}{3}$ 27. $8\frac{2}{9}$ 28. $10\frac{4}{5}$ 29. $7\frac{7}{8}$ 30. $19\frac{5}{7}$

Express each improper fraction as a whole number or a mixed number in simplest form.

31. $\frac{6}{5}$ 32. $\frac{9}{7}$ 33. $\frac{11}{8}$ 34. $\frac{5}{3}$ 35. $\frac{14}{2}$ 36. $\frac{48}{8}$

37. $\frac{12}{8}$ 38. $\frac{15}{9}$ 39. $\frac{44}{6}$ 40. $\frac{92}{10}$ 41. $\frac{88}{6}$ 42. $\frac{110}{5}$

43. $\frac{27}{6}$ 44. $\frac{19}{4}$ 45. $\frac{33}{10}$ 46. $\frac{29}{11}$ 47. $\frac{69}{13}$ 48. $\frac{121}{15}$

Problem Solving

49. A 14-foot board is divided into 4 equal parts. How long is each part?

50. A dessert recipe calls for $2\frac{3}{4}$ lb of butter. How many quarter-pound sticks of butter are needed for the recipe?

CRITICAL THINKING

51. Explain how each mixed number in the box can be simplified.

$$15\frac{10}{24} \qquad 15\frac{24}{24} \qquad 15\frac{25}{24}$$

Fraction Sense

To **estimate** if a fraction is close to 0, close to $\frac{1}{2}$, or close to 1, compare its numerator to its denominator.

▶ A fraction is **close to 0** when its numerator is much less than its denominator.

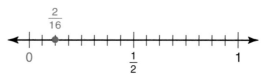

$\frac{2}{16}$ is close to 0 because 2 is much less than 16.

▶ A fraction is **close to $\frac{1}{2}$** when double its numerator is about equal to its denominator.

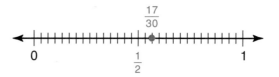

$\frac{17}{30}$ is close to $\frac{1}{2}$ because $17 \times 2 = 34$ and 34 is about equal to 30.

▶ A fraction is **close to 1** when its numerator is about equal to its denominator.

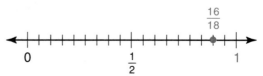

$\frac{16}{18}$ is close to 1 because 16 is about equal to 18.

Practice

Write the fraction that names each point.
Tell whether the fraction is close to 0, $\frac{1}{2}$, or 1.

1.

2.

3.

4.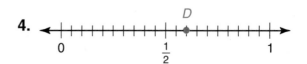

5.

6.

Use Compatible Numbers to Estimate

▶ You can replace the numerator and/or the denominator of a fraction with compatible numbers to estimate.

$\frac{1}{32}$ is about $\frac{0}{32}$ or 0.

$\frac{29}{62}$ is about $\frac{30}{60}$ or $\frac{1}{2}$.

$\frac{17}{31}$ is about $\frac{15}{30}$ or $\frac{1}{2}$.

$\frac{76}{78}$ is about $\frac{76}{76}$ or 1.

Practice

Tell whether the fraction is close to 0, $\frac{1}{2}$, or 1.
Use a number line or compatible numbers to help.

7. $\frac{1}{8}$ **8.** $\frac{2}{15}$ **9.** $\frac{6}{7}$ **10.** $\frac{13}{15}$ **11.** $\frac{7}{13}$ **12.** $\frac{8}{15}$

13. $\frac{13}{27}$ **14.** $\frac{17}{28}$ **15.** $\frac{1}{4}$ **16.** $\frac{3}{4}$ **17.** $\frac{30}{40}$ **18.** $\frac{25}{100}$

Complete. Write a fraction that is close to 0.

19. $\frac{a}{12}$ **20.** $\frac{b}{20}$ **21.** $\frac{c}{9}$ **22.** $\frac{1}{d}$ **23.** $\frac{7}{e}$ **24.** $\frac{12}{f}$

Complete. Write a fraction that is close to $\frac{1}{2}$.

25. $\frac{g}{7}$ **26.** $\frac{h}{25}$ **27.** $\frac{j}{15}$ **28.** $\frac{12}{k}$ **29.** $\frac{9}{m}$ **30.** $\frac{n}{42}$

Complete. Write a fraction that is close to 1.

31. $\frac{p}{7}$ **32.** $\frac{r}{30}$ **33.** $\frac{s}{14}$ **34.** $\frac{35}{t}$ **35.** $\frac{24}{v}$ **36.** $\frac{x}{100}$

DO YOU REMEMBER? — Algebra

Input these numbers. Write the product that comes out of the function machine.

37. 10 **38.** 9 **39.** 8

40. 7 **41.** 12 **42.** 11

in $\square \times 6$ out

Update your skills. See page 3.

6-9

Least Common Multiple

The planet Jupiter takes 12 years to make one complete revolution around the Sun. The planet Saturn takes 30 years to make one complete revolution around the Sun. If both planets are aligned tonight, how many years will it be before they have the exact same position in the sky again?

To find the number of years, you must find the **least common multiple (LCM)** of 12 and 30.

▶ The least common multiple of two or more numbers is the least number, except 0, that is a common multiple of both (or all) of the numbers.

Multiples of 12: 12, 24, 36, 48, 60, 72, . . .

Multiples of 30: 30, 60, 90, 120, 150, 180, . . .

Extend the list until you find a common multiple of the numbers.

The least common multiple (LCM) of 12 and 30 is 60.

So Jupiter and Saturn will have the exact same position in the sky in 60 years.

Practice

Find the LCM of each set of numbers.

1. 3, 4	**2.** 3, 6	**3.** 2, 5	**4.** 8, 24	**5.** 12, 15
6. 4, 10	**7.** 1, 9	**8.** 6, 5	**9.** 12, 10	**10.** 40, 16
11. 3, 4, 6	**12.** 1, 6, 7	**13.** 4, 5, 10	**14.** 4, 6, 8	
15. 5, 6, 12	**16.** 3, 9, 12	**17.** 8, 12, 36	**18.** 10, 18, 72	
19. 4, 6, 9	**20.** 5, 10, 15	**21.** 3, 5, 9	**22.** 8, 9, 10	

Find the LCM Using Prime Factorization

Find the LCM of 6, 18, and 24.

▶ To find the least common multiple using prime factorization:

- Write the prime factorization for each number.

$6 = 2 \times 3$

$18 = 2 \times 3 \times 3$

$24 = 2 \times 2 \times 2 \times 3$

> 3 appears two times.
> Write two 3s.

- Write each prime factor the greatest number of times it appears in any of the numbers. Then multiply the factors.

$2 \times 2 \times 2 \times 3 \times 3 = 72$

> 2 appears three times.
> Write three 2s.

So the least common multiple of 6, 18, and 24 is 72.

Practice

Find the LCM of each set of numbers. Use prime factorization.

23. 3, 7   **24.** 2, 3   **25.** 7, 21   **26.** 3, 9   **27.** 12, 4   **28.** 10, 5

29. 7, 2   **30.** 11, 5   **31.** 3, 15   **32.** 16, 32   **33.** 1, 9   **34.** 12, 1

35. 7, 8, 56   **36.** 8, 10, 40   **37.** 12, 48, 72   **38.** 8, 13, 52

39. 5, 9, 27   **40.** 9, 14, 16   **41.** 9, 15, 25   **42.** 4, 14, 49

BB: 4, 8, 12, 16, 20, 24, 28
T: 6, 12, 18, 24, 30

Problem Solving

43. A grasshopper and a frog start together and jump along the same path. The grasshopper always jumps 12 cm and the frog always jumps 15 cm. Will they ever land on the same spot again? Where?

LCM

44. In June, Al has a baseball game every 4th day starting June 4, and a tennis game every 6th day, beginning June 6. On which June days will he play both baseball and tennis?

on the 12th and 24th

CRITICAL THINKING

Tell whether the shortcuts below will help you find the least common multiple (LCM) of a pair of numbers. Explain using examples.

45. If both numbers are prime numbers, the LCM is the product of the two.

46. If one number is a factor of the other, the LCM is the greater of the two.

Compare Fractions

Compare: $\dfrac{11}{14}$? $\dfrac{13}{14}$

▶ To compare fractions with **like denominators**, compare the numerators. The fraction with the greater numerator is greater.

$$11 < 13 \rightarrow \dfrac{11}{14} < \dfrac{13}{14}$$

▶ You can also use a number line to compare.

$$\begin{array}{c} 0 \\ \hline \frac{0}{14} \quad \frac{5}{14} \quad \frac{11}{14} \quad \frac{13}{14} \frac{14}{14} \end{array}$$

| | | | 1 |

Remember: Values increase as you move right on a number line. Values decrease as you move left.

Compare: $\dfrac{7}{8}$? $\dfrac{3}{4}$

The least common denominator (LCD) of two or more fractions is the least common multiple (LCM) of their denominators.

▶ To compare fractions with **unlike denominators**:

$\dfrac{7}{8}$ Multiples of 8: 8, 16, . . .

• Find the least common denominator (LCD) of the fractions.

$\dfrac{3}{4}$ Multiples of 4: 4, 8, 12, 16, . . .

• Use the LCD to rename the fractions as equivalent fractions with the same denominator.

The LCD of $\dfrac{7}{8}$ and $\dfrac{3}{4}$ is 8.

$$\dfrac{3}{4} = \dfrac{?}{8} \rightarrow \dfrac{3 \times 2}{4 \times 2} = \dfrac{6}{8}$$

• Compare the numerators.

$7 > 6$, so $\dfrac{7}{8} > \dfrac{3}{4}$.

▶ You can also use a number line to compare fractions with unlike denominators.

$$\begin{array}{cccc} \frac{0}{4} & \frac{2}{4} & \frac{3}{4} & \frac{4}{4} \\ \hline \frac{0}{8} & \frac{4}{8} & \frac{6}{8} \; \frac{7}{8} & \frac{8}{8} \end{array}$$

So $\dfrac{7}{8} > \dfrac{3}{4}$.

Compare. Write <, =, or >. You can use a number line to help.

1. $\frac{7}{8}$? $\frac{5}{8}$ ___

2. $\frac{9}{20}$? $\frac{9}{20}$ ___

3. $\frac{14}{30}$? $\frac{26}{30}$ ___

4. $\frac{17}{21}$? $\frac{10}{21}$ ___

5. $\frac{12}{7}$? $\frac{16}{7}$ ___

6. $\frac{9}{8}$? $\frac{8}{8}$ ___

7. $\frac{22}{6}$? $\frac{32}{6}$ ___

8. $\frac{19}{19}$? $\frac{20}{19}$ ___

Rename each pair of fractions using the LCD as their denominator.

9. $\frac{3}{5}$ and $\frac{1}{4}$

10. $\frac{3}{4}$ and $\frac{1}{10}$

11. $\frac{7}{8}$ and $\frac{5}{6}$

12. $\frac{1}{2}$ and $\frac{2}{3}$

13. $\frac{1}{12}$ and $\frac{3}{24}$

14. $\frac{1}{3}$ and $\frac{4}{9}$

15. $\frac{5}{7}$ and $\frac{12}{49}$

16. $\frac{2}{5}$ and $\frac{4}{7}$

Compare. Write <, =, or >. You can use a number line to help.

17. $\frac{1}{4}$? $\frac{7}{16}$ ___

18. $\frac{7}{10}$? $\frac{3}{5}$ ___

19. $\frac{4}{21}$? $\frac{1}{7}$ ___

20. $\frac{6}{14}$? $\frac{2}{7}$ ___

21. $\frac{3}{5}$? $\frac{5}{8}$ ___

22. $\frac{4}{7}$? $\frac{6}{9}$ ___

23. $\frac{7}{12}$? $\frac{9}{15}$ ___

24. $\frac{10}{25}$? $\frac{7}{10}$ ___

25. $\frac{11}{16}$? $\frac{11}{16}$ ___

26. $\frac{4}{5}$? $\frac{12}{15}$ ___

27. $\frac{11}{20}$? $\frac{9}{15}$ ___

28. $\frac{11}{21}$? $\frac{22}{42}$ ___

Problem Solving

29. Jack rides his bicycle $\frac{1}{2}$ mile to the park. Jerry rides his bike $\frac{3}{10}$ mile to the park. Who travels farther? How do you know?

30. On a team project, Lisa does $\frac{12}{16}$ of the work and Mel does $\frac{3}{12}$. Who does less for the project? How do you know?

MENTAL MATH — Algebra

Compare. Write < or >. Look for fractions close to 0, $\frac{1}{2}$, or 1.

31. $\frac{6}{11}$? $\frac{5}{6}$ → $\frac{6}{11}$ is close to $\frac{1}{2}$; $\frac{5}{6}$ is close to 1; $\frac{6}{11} < \frac{5}{6}$

32. $\frac{11}{20}$? $\frac{9}{20}$ ___

33. $\frac{3}{32}$? $\frac{21}{32}$ ___

34. $\frac{15}{16}$? $\frac{17}{16}$ ___

35. $\frac{16}{17}$? $\frac{3}{7}$ ___

36. $\frac{10}{9}$? $\frac{5}{8}$ ___

37. $\frac{1}{11}$? $\frac{6}{13}$ ___

38. $\frac{7}{15}$? $\frac{8}{7}$ ___

39. $\frac{15}{31}$? $\frac{2}{30}$ ___

Order Fractions

Write these fractions in order from least to greatest: $1\frac{1}{4}$, $\frac{2}{3}$, $1\frac{5}{6}$.

$1\frac{1}{4}$ and $1\frac{5}{6}$ have whole numbers. $\frac{2}{3} < 1$, so it is the least number. Now compare and order the mixed numbers.

▶ To compare and order mixed numbers with unlike denominators:

- Compare the whole numbers.

  $1 = 1$

- Rename each fraction using the LCD.

  $1\frac{1}{4} \qquad 1\frac{5}{6}$ LCD is 12.

  $1\frac{3}{12} \qquad 1\frac{10}{12}$

- Compare the numerators.

  $\frac{3}{12} < \frac{10}{12}$, so $1\frac{3}{12} < 1\frac{10}{12}$

  $1\frac{1}{4} < 1\frac{5}{6}$

- Write the fractions in order from least to greatest.

  $\frac{2}{3}$, $1\frac{1}{4}$, $1\frac{5}{6}$

▶ The number line shows that $\frac{2}{3} < 1\frac{1}{4} < 1\frac{5}{6}$.

From least to greatest: $\frac{2}{3}$, $1\frac{1}{4}$, $1\frac{5}{6}$ From greatest to least: $1\frac{5}{6}$, $1\frac{1}{4}$, $\frac{2}{3}$

Study these examples.

Order from greatest to least.

$2\frac{1}{8}$, $2\frac{3}{4}$, $\frac{19}{8}$

$2\frac{1}{8}$, $2\frac{6}{8}$, $2\frac{3}{8}$

$\frac{19}{8} = 8\overline{)19} \; ^{2\frac{3}{8}}$

From greatest to least: $2\frac{3}{4}$, $\frac{19}{8}$, $2\frac{1}{8}$

$6\frac{5}{6}$, $6\frac{3}{5}$, $6\frac{2}{3}$

$6\frac{25}{30}$, $6\frac{18}{30}$, $6\frac{20}{30}$ LCD is 30.

From greatest to least: $6\frac{5}{6}$, $6\frac{2}{3}$, $6\frac{3}{5}$

Write in order from least to greatest.

1. $\dfrac{4}{5}, \dfrac{7}{10}, \dfrac{3}{4}$

2. $\dfrac{5}{12}, \dfrac{3}{8}, \dfrac{5}{6}$

3. $9\dfrac{3}{5}, 9\dfrac{5}{8}, 9\dfrac{7}{10}$

4. $7\dfrac{2}{9}, 7\dfrac{1}{3}, 7\dfrac{3}{4}$

Write in order from greatest to least.

5. $\dfrac{7}{12}, \dfrac{1}{2}, \dfrac{2}{3}$

6. $\dfrac{1}{4}, \dfrac{1}{3}, \dfrac{1}{5}$

7. $\dfrac{2}{5}, \dfrac{7}{10}, \dfrac{1}{3}$

8. $\dfrac{7}{12}, \dfrac{4}{5}, \dfrac{9}{10}$

9. $5\dfrac{4}{5}, 5\dfrac{3}{4}, 5\dfrac{7}{8}$

10. $2\dfrac{2}{3}, 3\dfrac{3}{4}, 2\dfrac{4}{5}$

11. $\dfrac{17}{18}, \dfrac{7}{9}, \dfrac{2}{3}$

12. $\dfrac{3}{7}, \dfrac{1}{2}, \dfrac{3}{14}$

13. $\dfrac{21}{9}, \dfrac{12}{9}, \dfrac{9}{12}$

14. $\dfrac{7}{6}, \dfrac{14}{5}, \dfrac{31}{10}$

15. $1\dfrac{2}{15}, \dfrac{18}{15}, 1\dfrac{4}{15}$

16. $\dfrac{21}{9}, 1\dfrac{5}{9}, \dfrac{8}{3}$

Problem Solving

17. Tony saw three pumpkins labeled $5\dfrac{3}{8}$ lb, $5\dfrac{1}{4}$ lb, and $5\dfrac{5}{16}$ lb. Which pumpkin was the heaviest? Explain.

18. If you put a jar $12\dfrac{3}{4}$ inches tall into a carton $12\dfrac{7}{12}$ inches high, will the jar stick out? Explain.

19. In a standing broad jump contest, the results were: Patty, $6\dfrac{5}{12}$ ft; Hank, $6\dfrac{3}{4}$ ft; and Terry, $6\dfrac{5}{6}$ ft. Who won the contest? Explain.

20. Which of these model cars can fit into the box? Explain.

a.
$1\dfrac{7}{8}$ in.

b.
$1\dfrac{5}{16}$ in.

c.
$1\dfrac{13}{16}$ in.

$1\dfrac{3}{8}$ in.

CRITICAL THINKING

Name three fractions in each region of the diagram.

21. A   22. B   23. C

24. D   25. E   26. F

27. G

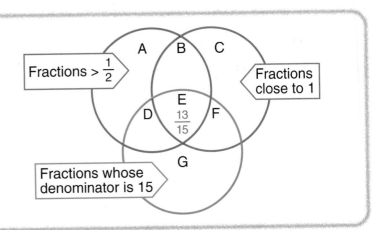

Fractions > $\dfrac{1}{2}$

Fractions close to 1

Fractions whose denominator is 15

Relate Fractions to Decimals

▶ Fractions and mixed numbers with denominators that are *powers of ten* can be renamed as decimals. The word names are the same.

$$\frac{7}{10} \quad 0.7 \qquad\qquad 3\frac{9}{100} \quad 3.09 \qquad\qquad \frac{41}{10,000} \quad 0.0041$$

| seven tenths | three and nine hundredths | forty-one ten thousandths |

| 1.0 | 1.1 | 1.2 | 1.3 | 1.4 | 1.5 | 1.6 | 1.7 | 1.8 | 1.9 | 2.0 |

| 1 | $1\frac{1}{10}$ | $1\frac{2}{10}$ | $1\frac{3}{10}$ | $1\frac{4}{10}$ | $1\frac{5}{10}$ | $1\frac{6}{10}$ | $1\frac{7}{10}$ | $1\frac{8}{10}$ | $1\frac{9}{10}$ | 2 |

1.7, $\frac{17}{10}$, and $1\frac{7}{10}$ all have the same value.
They all name one and seven tenths.

▶ **To rename fractions and mixed numbers with denominators that are powers of ten as decimals:**

- Read the given fraction. $\frac{8}{100}$ ⟶ eight hundredths

- Determine the decimal place. hundredths: ⟶ *two* decimal places

- Write an equivalent decimal. eight hundredths = 0.08

Practice

Choose the equivalent decimal or fraction.

1. $\frac{7}{100}$ **a.** 0.700   **b.** 0.07   **c.** 0.007   **d.** 700.7

2. $13\frac{28}{100}$ **a.** 13.28   **b.** 13.028   **c.** 13.0028   **d.** 0.1328

3. $\frac{109}{1000}$ **a.** 100.9   **b.** 0.0109   **c.** 0.109   **d.** 109.001

4. 8.09   **a.** $8\frac{9}{10}$ **b.** $8\frac{9}{100}$ **c.** $8\frac{9}{1000}$ **d.** $\frac{89}{100}$

5. 12.37   **a.** $12\frac{37}{1000}$ **b.** $123\frac{7}{10}$ **c.** $1\frac{237}{1000}$ **d.** $12\frac{37}{100}$

Write the word name. Then write the equivalent decimal or fraction.

6. $\frac{9}{10}$

7. $\frac{35}{100}$

8. $\frac{81}{1000}$

9. $\frac{71}{10,000}$

10. $6\frac{2}{10}$

11. $16\frac{19}{100}$

12. $4\frac{12}{1000}$

13. $9\frac{417}{1000}$

14. $\frac{2}{1000}$

15. $\frac{56}{10,000}$

16. 0.87

17. 0.022

18. 0.0563

19. 0.1578

20. 7.52

21. 8.009

22. 16.573

23. 37.069

24. 5.0005

25. 11.0011

Rename Improper Fractions as Decimals

▶ To rename improper fractions with denominators that are powers of ten as decimals:

- Rename the improper fraction as a mixed number.

$$\frac{628}{100} \longrightarrow 100)\overline{628} \quad 6\frac{28}{100}$$

- Rename the mixed number as a decimal.

$$6\frac{28}{100} = 6.28$$

Write the equivalent decimal or whole number.

26. $\frac{25}{10}$

27. $\frac{420}{100}$

28. $\frac{372}{10}$

29. $\frac{4620}{100}$

30. $\frac{5390}{1000}$

31. $\frac{1472}{1000}$

32. $\frac{7000}{1000}$

33. $\frac{20,000}{10,000}$

34. $\frac{34,000}{10,000}$

35. $\frac{79,500}{10,000}$

DO YOU REMEMBER?

Complete the sentences. Use the terms in the box.

36. Two fractions that name the same part of a whole or a set are __?__ .

37. A number is __?__ by another number if there is no remainder when you divide.

38. The __?__ of 4, 6, and 8 is 24.

divisible

LCM

equivalent

GCF

Rename Fractions as Decimals

Write $\frac{3}{4}$ as a decimal.

▶ **To rename a fraction as a decimal:**

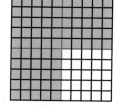

- Divide the numerator by the denominator.

$$4\overline{)3}$$

- Place a decimal point after the numerator and in the quotient.

$$4\overline{)3.}$$

- Divide. Add zeros as needed.

$$\begin{array}{r} 0.7\,5 \\ 4\overline{)3.0\,0} \end{array}$$

So $\frac{3}{4} = 0.75$.

Write $9\frac{1}{16}$ as a decimal.

▶ **To rename a mixed number as a decimal:**

- Separate the mixed number into a whole number part and a fraction part.

$$9\frac{1}{16} = 9 + \frac{1}{16}$$

- Rename the fraction part as a decimal.

$$\frac{1}{16} \longrightarrow \begin{array}{r} 0.0\,6\,2\,5 \\ 1\,6\overline{)1.0\,0\,0\,0} \end{array}$$

- Add the whole number part and the decimal.

$$9 + 0.0\,6\,2\,5 = 9.0\,6\,2\,5$$

So $9\frac{1}{16} = 9.0625$.

Practice

Write each fraction as a decimal.

1. $\frac{2}{5}$ **2.** $\frac{1}{2}$ **3.** $\frac{1}{4}$ **4.** $\frac{4}{5}$ **5.** $\frac{3}{8}$ **6.** $\frac{6}{15}$

7. $\frac{9}{20}$ **8.** $\frac{3}{50}$ **9.** $\frac{1}{20}$ **10.** $\frac{1}{25}$ **11.** $\frac{22}{50}$ **12.** $\frac{19}{20}$

13. $\frac{7}{8}$ **14.** $\frac{5}{32}$ **15.** $\frac{17}{25}$ **16.** $\frac{9}{200}$ **17.** $\frac{5}{16}$ **18.** $\frac{3}{250}$

Write each mixed number as a decimal.

19. $7\frac{4}{5}$ **20.** $15\frac{1}{2}$ **21.** $28\frac{3}{5}$ **22.** $12\frac{5}{8}$ **23.** $7\frac{3}{100}$

24. $9\frac{4}{1000}$ **25.** $11\frac{3}{50}$ **26.** $80\frac{3}{4}$ **27.** $44\frac{11}{20}$ **28.** $61\frac{1}{8}$

Shortcut for Renaming Fractions

Write $\frac{12}{25}$ as a decimal.

▶ When a fraction has a denominator that is a factor of 10, 100, 1000, . . . :

.Think...........
25 is a factor
of 100.

- Rename as an equivalent fraction with a denominator that is a power of ten.

$$\frac{12 \times 4}{25 \times 4} = \frac{48}{100}$$

- Read the fraction. Then write the decimal.

$$\frac{48}{100} = 0.48$$

forty-eight hundredths

So $\frac{12}{25} = 0.48$.

Write each fraction or mixed number as a decimal.
Use the shortcut whenever possible.

29. $\frac{3}{20}$ **30.** $\frac{7}{25}$ **31.** $7\frac{9}{10}$ **32.** $8\frac{3}{10}$ **33.** $\frac{32}{50}$

34. $\frac{11}{25}$ **35.** $\frac{5}{16}$ **36.** $\frac{25}{32}$ **37.** $9\frac{12}{20}$ **38.** $10\frac{3}{25}$

Problem Solving

Write each answer as a decimal.

39. Ann has nine tenths of a dollar. How much money does she have?

40. Allan has three fifths of a dollar. How much money does he have?

41. Roy has one and three fourths dollars. How much more money does he need to have $3.25?

42. Drew has three and two fifths dollars and Rita has four and one fourth dollars. How much more money does Rita have?

Rename Decimals as Fractions

Write 0.35 as a fraction in simplest form.

▶ **To rename a decimal as a fraction:**

- Read the given decimal.   0.35 → thirty-five hundredths

- Determine the denominator   The denominator is 100.
  of the fraction.

- Write an equivalent fraction.   thirty-five hundredths $= \dfrac{35}{100}$

- Simplify if necessary. $\dfrac{35}{100} = \dfrac{35 \div 5}{100 \div 5} = \dfrac{7}{20}$

So 0.35 $= \dfrac{7}{20}$.

Study this example.

Write 9.008 as a mixed number in simplest form.

$$9.008 \longrightarrow \text{nine and eight thousandths} \longrightarrow 9\frac{8}{1000}$$

$$\frac{8}{1000} = \frac{8 \div 8}{1000 \div 8} = \frac{1}{125}$$

So $9.008 = 9 + \dfrac{1}{125} = 9\dfrac{1}{125}$.

**Rename each decimal as a fraction or mixed number
in simplest form.**

1. $0.63 = \dfrac{?}{100}$

2. $0.05 = \dfrac{5}{?} = \dfrac{?}{20}$

3. $0.259 = \dfrac{?}{1000}$

4. $0.750 = \dfrac{750}{?} = \dfrac{?}{4}$

5. $8.7 = 8\dfrac{?}{10}$

6. $4.09 = 4\dfrac{9}{?}$

7. $2.627 = 2\dfrac{?}{1000}$

8. $5.500 = 5\dfrac{?}{1000} = 5\dfrac{?}{2}$

9. $38.03 = 38\dfrac{?}{?}$

Practice

Write each decimal as a fraction in simplest form.

10. 0.9   **11.** 0.07   **12.** 0.43   **13.** 0.77   **14.** 0.003

15. 0.127   **16.** 0.45   **17.** 0.36   **18.** 0.675   **19.** 0.325

20. 0.0033   **21.** 0.0009   **22.** 0.441   **23.** 0.101   **24.** 0.0500

Write each decimal as a mixed number in simplest form.

25. 1.09   **26.** 5.7   **27.** 11.31   **28.** 12.1   **29.** 2.5

30. 8.4   **31.** 9.16   **32.** 6.35   **33.** 1.055   **34.** 3.004

35. 6.0005   **36.** 8.0010   **37.** 3.375   **38.** 2.95   **39.** 20.0750

Rename each decimal as a fraction or mixed number in simplest form.

40. A tortoise travels 0.7 mile per hour.

41. An elephant can run at a speed of 24.5 miles per hour.

42. The height of a zebra may be 1.55 meters.

43. The height of a flower may be 0.44 meter.

Write the missing decimal, word name, or fraction.

	Decimal	Word Name	Fraction in Simplest Form
44.	4.7	four and seven tenths	?
45.	?	two hundred and six thousandths	?
46.	?	one thousand eleven ten thousandths	?
47.	101.003	?	?

Problem Solving

48. Mitch got 30 out of 40 questions correct on a test. What is his test score as a decimal?

49. Patty got 2 incorrect answers out of 20 on a test. What is her test score as a decimal?

50. Dov got 3 incorrect answers out of 15 on a quiz. If each answer was worth 2 points, would his decimal score be the same or different than if each answer was worth 1 point?

51. Jill got 3 incorrect answers out of 30 on a test. Her brother got 1 incorrect answer out of 10 on a different test. Who had a higher decimal score? Explain.

Terminating and Repeating Decimals

Alberto plays baseball for the Piney Creek Wildcats.
In his first 30 times at bat, he gets 10 hits.
Write his batting average as a decimal.

Rename $\frac{10}{30}$ as an equivalent decimal.

$$3\,0\overline{)1\,0.0\,0\,0\,0}\;\;^{0.3\,3\,3\,3\,\ldots}$$

No matter how many zeros you write in the dividend,
the division just keeps on going. When the same
digit(s) repeat in the quotient, you have a
repeating decimal.

Alberto's batting average is 0.3333 . . . , or 0.333
when rounded to the nearest thousandth.

▶ Every fraction can be renamed as a
terminating decimal or a repeating decimal.

A terminating decimal has a
definite number of decimal places.
When you divide, the remainder
is 0.

$$\frac{5}{8} \longrightarrow 8\overline{)5.0\,0\,0}\;\;^{0.6\,2\,5}$$

$$\frac{5}{8} = 0.6\,2\,5$$

A repeating decimal has one
or more digits that repeat
indefinitely. When you divide,
the remainder is never zero.

$$\frac{3}{11} \longrightarrow 1\,1\overline{)3.0\,0\,0\,0\,0}\;\;^{0.2\,7\,2\,7\,2\,\ldots}$$

$$\frac{3}{11} = 0.2\,7\,2\,7\,\ldots$$

▶ Repeating decimals may be written with a *bar* over
the digit or digits that repeat.

0.2727 . . . = $0.\overline{27}$ ◀——[bar]

5.13636 . . . = $5.1\overline{36}$ ◀——[bar]

.Think......................
The digits 2 and 7
repeat indefinitely.

.Think......................
The digits 3 and 6
repeat indefinitely. The
digit 1 does not repeat.

Rewrite each repeating decimal with a bar over the part that repeats.

1. 0.66666 . . .
2. 0.11111 . . .
3. 0.45454 . . .
4. 0.09090 . . .

5. 0.83333 . . .
6. 0.26666 . . .
7. 2.384848 . . .
8. 5.13232 . . .

Write each repeating decimal showing eight decimal places.

9. $0.\overline{1}$
10. $0.\overline{12}$
11. $0.1\overline{4}$
12. $0.2\overline{8}$

13. $5.\overline{3}$
14. $12.0\overline{6}$
15. $7.2\overline{7}$
16. $13.2\overline{17}$

Rename each fraction as a terminating or repeating decimal.

17. $\frac{1}{8}$
18. $\frac{13}{20}$
19. $\frac{5}{11}$
20. $\frac{1}{3}$
21. $\frac{3}{4}$

22. $\frac{2}{9}$
23. $\frac{7}{16}$
24. $\frac{5}{12}$
25. $\frac{11}{18}$
26. $\frac{1}{16}$

Rename each mixed number as a terminating or repeating decimal.

27. $4\frac{2}{5}$
28. $6\frac{1}{4}$
29. $12\frac{2}{3}$
30. $15\frac{2}{3}$
31. $1\frac{3}{8}$

32. $121\frac{1}{9}$
33. $33\frac{1}{3}$
34. $5\frac{5}{16}$
35. $28\frac{21}{36}$
36. $11\frac{13}{25}$

CRITICAL THINKING

Copy and complete each table. Write the equivalent decimal. Explain the patterns in your Math Journal.

	Fraction		Decimal
37.	$\frac{1}{9}$	$1 \div 9 =$	$0.\overline{1}$
38.	$\frac{2}{9}$		?
39.	$\frac{3}{9}$		?
40.	$\frac{4}{9}$		?

	Fraction	Decimal
41.	$\frac{1}{11}$	?
42.	$\frac{2}{11}$	?
43.	$\frac{3}{11}$	?
44.	$\frac{4}{11}$	?

Rational Numbers

Earl's Software	$+1\frac{1}{2}$
Ultimate Graphics	$^-2$
Pelican Steel	$^-3\frac{1}{4}$
BAC Stores	$^+2$
Clark Electronics	$^-\frac{3}{4}$
Mike's Bikes	$^+1$
Ellen Stores	$^+\frac{1}{8}$

A class is learning about the stock market. The table shows how the stocks performed in a one-week period. It shows how much the value of a stock rose ($^+$) or fell ($^-$) that week. A share of Earl's Software rose $^+1\frac{1}{2}$ points. A share of Ultimate Graphics fell $^-2$ points.

▶ You can use a number line to represent all of the positive and negative numbers.

The numbers $^-3\frac{1}{4}$, $^-2$, $\frac{^-3}{4}$, $\frac{^+1}{8}$, $^+1$, $^+1\frac{1}{2}$, and $^+2$ are rational numbers. 0 is also a rational number.

A **rational number** is a number that can be written in the form of a fraction $\frac{a}{b}$, where a and b are integers and $b \neq 0$.

.Think.....................................
All whole numbers are integers.
All integers are rational numbers.
....

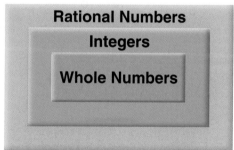

▶ You can write any rational number as a decimal. Compare the number line above with the one below.

Notice that $^-3\frac{1}{4} = ^-3.25$, $\frac{^-3}{4} = ^-0.75$, $\frac{^+1}{8} = ^+0.125$, and $^+1\frac{1}{2} = ^+1.5$.

▶ Every rational number has an opposite.

The opposite of $^+2\frac{1}{2}$ is $^-2\frac{1}{2}$.   The opposite of $\frac{^-3}{4}$ is $\frac{^+3}{4}$.

The opposite of $^+3.5$ is $^-3.5$.   The opposite of $^-0.2$ is $^+0.2$.

Identify the rational number that corresponds to the point on the number line.

1. *C*   2. *F*   3. *A*   4. *E*   5. *B*   6. *D*

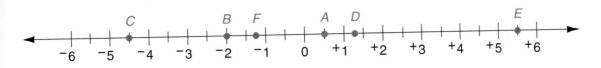

Write a rational number for each point.

7.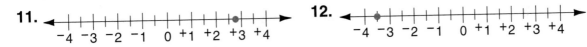

8.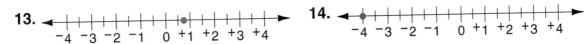

9.

10.

11.

12.

13.

14.

15.

16.

Write each rational number.

17. Express $^-4\frac{1}{2}$ as a decimal.

18. Express $^-2.5$ as a fraction.

19. Express $^+9\frac{1}{4}$ as a decimal.

20. Express $^+4.85$ as a fraction.

Write the opposite of each.

21. $^-5$ 22. $^+2\frac{1}{4}$ 23. $^-6.5$ 24. $\frac{^-1}{2}$ 25. 0.75   26. $3\frac{1}{2}$

Problem Solving

27. One day the price of a share of stock dropped $3\frac{1}{2}$ points. What rational number represents this loss?

28. The price of a share of stock rose $12\frac{1}{4}$. What rational number represents this gain?

Compare and Order Rational Numbers

Compare: $^-6$ __?__ $^-8\frac{1}{2}$

▶ You can use a number line to compare rational numbers.

The number farther to the right is the *greater* number.
$^-6$ is farther to the right.

So $^-6 > ^-8\frac{1}{2}$.

Compare: $^-3$ __?__ $\frac{^-4}{2}$

$^-3 \quad < \quad ^-2$

> Simplify to compare.
> $\frac{^-4}{2} = ^-4 \div 2 = ^-2$

So $^-3 < \frac{^-4}{2}$. ◀—— Look at the number line above: $^-3 < ^-2$

▶ Order from least to greatest: $0, \ ^+1\frac{1}{2}, \ ^-2.5$

From least to greatest: $^-2.5, \ 0, \ ^+1\frac{1}{2}$

Study these examples.

Compare: $^+9.17$ __?__ $^-8\frac{3}{4}$

$^+9.17 > ^-8\frac{3}{4}$

Order from least to greatest:
$^-6\frac{1}{4}, \ \frac{^-12}{3}, \ ^-6.9$

$^-6.9, \ ^-6\frac{1}{4}, \ \frac{^-12}{3}$

Order from greatest to least:
$\frac{^+11}{3}, \ ^+4.6, \ \frac{^-8}{4}$

$^+4.6, \ \frac{^+11}{3}, \ \frac{^-8}{4}$

Compare. Write < , = , or >. Use the number line.

$$\begin{array}{ccccccccccccccccccccccccc}
\leftarrow & | & | & | & | & | & | & | & | & | & | & | & | & | & | & | & | & | & | & | & | & | & | & | & | & \rightarrow \\
& ^-6 & & ^-5 & & ^-4 & & ^-3 & & ^-2 & & ^-1 & & 0 & & ^+1 & & ^+2 & & ^+3 & & ^+4 & & ^+5 & & ^+6
\end{array}$$

1. $\dfrac{^-1}{2}$? $\dfrac{^-3}{4}$

2. $^-0.5$? $^+0.75$

3. $^-3.5$? $^-4.25$

4. $^+3\dfrac{1}{4}$? $^+3\dfrac{1}{8}$

5. $^-4$? $\dfrac{^-6}{3}$

6. $^+2.5$? $^-3\dfrac{1}{2}$

7. $^-5\dfrac{1}{8}$? $^+4$

8. $^-6$? $^-5.75$

9. 0 ? $^-3.25$

10. $\dfrac{^+3}{4}$? 0

11. $\dfrac{^-8}{2}$? $^-4$

12. $\dfrac{^-1}{8}$? $^-0.125$

Write in order from least to greatest. Use the number line above to help.

13. $^-3,\ ^-4\dfrac{1}{2},\ 2$

14. $0,\ \dfrac{^-1}{2},\ 2\dfrac{1}{4}$

15. $5,\ 0,\ \dfrac{2}{1}$

16. $^-4,\ 3\dfrac{1}{4},\ ^-1.5$

17. $^-2.25,\ ^+0.25,\ ^-1.5$

18. $^-2\dfrac{1}{2},\ 2.5,\ ^-1\dfrac{1}{4}$

19. $\dfrac{1}{4},\ \dfrac{^-1}{4},\ 0$

20. $5\dfrac{1}{4},\ ^-1,\ ^-2\dfrac{3}{4}$

21. $\dfrac{6}{3},\ \dfrac{^-3}{4},\ ^-4$

22. $\dfrac{^-3}{4},\ \dfrac{2}{1},\ 1\dfrac{1}{4}$

23. $\dfrac{3}{2},\ ^-2\dfrac{1}{2},\ 3$

24. $\dfrac{^-4}{2},\ ^-1.5,\ ^-2\dfrac{1}{2}$

Problem Solving

25. Two metals were cooled to temperatures of $2\dfrac{1}{2}°\text{F}$ and $^-3\dfrac{3}{4}°\text{F}$. Which of the two is the greater temperature?

26. Over a 5-day period, a share of stock showed the following changes: $^-6\dfrac{1}{4},\ ^-2\dfrac{1}{2},\ ^+1\dfrac{3}{4},\ ^+1,$ and $\dfrac{^-1}{2}$. Which was the greatest gain? greatest loss?

MENTAL MATH — Algebra

Compare. Write < or >. Think of a number line.

27. $^-8.95$? $^+7\dfrac{3}{5}$

28. $^+6\dfrac{1}{4}$? $^-9.9$

29. $^-10.4$? $^-9\dfrac{2}{3}$

Order from least to greatest. Think of a number line.

30. $^+10.5,\ ^-15\dfrac{1}{6},\ ^+36$

31. $^-26\dfrac{1}{2},\ ^+12.5,\ ^-83\dfrac{1}{5}$

32. $^-8.91,\ ^-23\dfrac{5}{6},\ ^+23$

33. $^+62\dfrac{1}{4},\ ^+38.3,\ ^-287$

Problem-Solving Strategy:
Find a Pattern

Tim gave all his baseball cards to Walter. On the first day, he gave him 1 card. On each day after that, he gave him 3 times the number he had given him the day before. At the end of 4 days, Tim had given away all the cards he had. How many did he give to Walter in all?

 Read

Visualize yourself in the problem above as you reread it. List the facts and the question.

Facts: first day—1 card

each day after—3 times the number he gave the day before

after 4 days—all cards are given away

Question: How many cards did Tim give to Walter?

Plan

To find how many cards Tim gave to Walter, use the pattern rule × 3. Make a table to list the cards given away and the daily total. Multiply the number he gave away the day before by 3. To find the total, add the amount given away to the total of the day before. Look for a pattern.

Solve

Day	1st	2nd	3rd	4th
Walter received	1	$3 \times 1 = 3$	$3 \times 3 = 9$	$3 \times 9 = 27$
Tim's daily total	1	$1 + 3 = 4$	$4 + 9 = 13$	$13 + 27 = 40$

Tim gave Walter 40 baseball cards.

 Check

Begin with 40 cards and subtract the number Tim gave away each day.
Do you have 0 left on the 4th day? Yes.

$$40 - 1 - 3 - 9 - 27 \overset{?}{=} 0$$
$$39 \quad - 3 - 9 - 27 \overset{?}{=} 0$$
$$36 \quad - 9 - 27 \overset{?}{=} 0$$
$$27 \quad - 27 = 0 \qquad \text{The answer checks.}$$

Solve each problem. Find a pattern to help you.

1. In a science experiment, Joel discovered that his record of the changes in a liquid's temperature formed a pattern. In each of the first 3 minutes, the temperature increased 1.5° F; in each of the next 2 minutes, it decreased 0.75° F. Then this pattern repeated itself. If Joel started measuring the temperature at 50° F, how long would it take the temperature to reach 62° F?

Read Visualize yourself in the problem above as you reread it. List the facts and the question.

> **Facts:** each of first 3 min—increase 1.5° F
> each of next 2 min—decrease 0.75° F
> starting temperature—50° F
>
> **Question:** How long will it take the temperature to reach 62° F?

Plan To find how many minutes it will take to reach 62° F, make a table to list the time and degrees increased or decreased. Look for a pattern.

Solve .... **Check**

2. Alice makes a necklace with 24 red and white beads. If she creates a pattern of 1 red and 3 white beads, how many red beads will she use? how many white beads?

3. Find the next three terms in this sequence: $\frac{1}{8}, \frac{1}{2}, \frac{3}{8}, \frac{3}{4}, \frac{5}{8}$, 1. What is the pattern?

4. Hector caught 2 fish on Monday, 4 on Tuesday, 8 on Wednesday, 16 on Thursday, and so on. Following this pattern, how many fish did he catch on Saturday?

5. Crystal builds a tower out of blocks for her little brother. She uses 7 blocks. The edge of each block is $1\frac{1}{4}$ in. shorter than the edge of the block under it. If the bottom block is $9\frac{3}{4}$ in. on each edge, how long is the edge of the top block?

Problem-Solving Applications: Mixed Review

Solve each problem and explain the method you used.

1. Stella paints this pattern. What fraction, in simplest form, names the shaded region?

2. Dom has these tubes of paint: $\frac{1}{4}$ oz crimson, $\frac{2}{3}$ oz burnt sienna, $\frac{2}{5}$ oz black, and $\frac{6}{9}$ oz magenta. Which two tubes have the same amount of paint?

3. Milly has $\frac{19}{4}$ oz of white paint. Is this more than 5 ounces?

4. Julio's favorite brushes are the following lengths: $\frac{15}{2}$ in., $7\frac{1}{3}$ in., $7\frac{5}{9}$ in., and $\frac{31}{4}$ in. How would he arrange the brushes in order from shortest to longest?

5. One sheet of watercolor paper is 0.01 in. thick. Write 0.01 as a fraction.

6. Jeremiah has finished $\frac{5}{8}$ of his painting. Write this fraction as a decimal.

7. Stella's newest painting has an area of 156.25 in.² Write this decimal as a mixed number.

8. Becky has $3\frac{3}{4}$ quarts of paint thinner. She also has 7.5 pints of turpentine. Does she have more paint thinner or turpentine?

Use the table for problems 9–11.

9. Which two pencils are the same length?

10. What are the longest and shortest pencils?

11. Which pencils are close to 5 in. in length?

Color	Length
red	$6\frac{3}{4}$ in.
orange	7.8 in.
yellow	$5\frac{2}{5}$ in.
green	$\frac{11}{5}$ in.
blue	$7\frac{9}{10}$ in.
indigo	5.4 in.
violet	$\frac{40}{9}$ in.

Choose a strategy from the list or use another strategy you know to solve each problem.

12. A painting is $\frac{1}{4}$ in. longer than it is wide. Its length is 8.2 in. The frame is 2.7 in. thick. What is the width of the painting?

13. James folds a sheet of drawing paper in fourths, then in thirds, and then in half. Estimate into how many parts his paper is divided. Check your answer by following the folds.

14. Gary uses $\frac{3}{8}$ of a 10-oz tube of raw sienna to paint a fall landscape. He also uses $\frac{2}{5}$ oz of cadmium red for the same picture. How much more raw sienna than cadmium red does he use?

15. Joanne paints these three pictures. If she continues the pattern in a fourth picture, what fractional part of that picture will be shaded?

16. Every third day Fran goes to calligraphy class. Every fourth day she goes to pottery class. On March 1 Fran attends both classes. How many days that month will the 2 classes fall on the same day?

17. Gesso boards are advertised at 3 boards for $14.20. How much would Danielle pay for one gesso board?

Use the circle graph for problems 18–20.

18. What part of Abby's artworks are oil paintings?

19. What type of art makes up $\frac{1}{5}$ of Abby's work?

20. Abby did 5 charcoals this week. When these charcoals are added to the data from the graph, what part of her work will be charcoals?

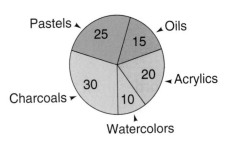

Abby's Artworks

Write About It

21. Write a problem modeled on problem 17. Have a classmate solve it.

Strategy File

Use These Strategies
Guess and Test
Write an Equation
Use a Graph
Find a Pattern
Interpret the Remainder
Use More Than One Step

Find the prime factorization and write in exponential form. *(See pp. 180–183.)*

1. 28 **2.** 30 **3.** 75 **4.** 84

Write the missing number to complete the equivalent fraction. *(See pp. 184–185.)*

5. $\frac{2}{3} = \frac{x}{9}$ **6.** $\frac{3}{4} = \frac{9}{y}$ **7.** $\frac{20}{90} = \frac{z}{9}$ **8.** $\frac{15}{45} = \frac{p}{3}$

9. $\frac{10}{13} = \frac{x}{65}$ **10.** $\frac{38}{44} = \frac{19}{t}$ **11.** $\frac{23}{69} = \frac{w}{3}$ **12.** $\frac{7}{11} = \frac{49}{s}$

Find the GCF of each pair of numbers. *(See pp. 186–187.)*

13. 3 and 27 **14.** 12 and 48 **15.** 21 and 35

16. 10, 14, and 34 **17.** 22, 33, and 55 **18.** 27, 63, and 81

Find the LCM of each pair of numbers. *(See pp. 194–195.)*

19. 3 and 5 **20.** 6 and 18 **21.** 4 and 15

22. 4, 7, and 8 **23.** 9, 12, and 15 **24.** 8, 24, and 36

Rename each as indicated. *(See pp. 188–191, 200–207.)*

25. $\frac{9}{45}$ in simplest form **26.** $4\frac{2}{3}$ as an improper fraction

27. $7\frac{3}{8}$ as a decimal **28.** 0.45 as a fraction in simplest form

29. $\frac{7}{15}$ as a decimal **30.** 9.6 as a mixed number in simplest form

31. $\frac{98}{16}$ as a mixed number **32.** $\frac{121}{132}$ in simplest form

Write in order from least to greatest. *(See pp. 196–199, 206–211.)*

33. $\frac{2}{9}, \frac{1}{3}, \frac{3}{4}$ **34.** $8\frac{5}{6}, 8\frac{7}{12}, 8\frac{3}{4}$ **35.** $\frac{-3}{2}, {}^-2.5, {}^-4$

Problem Solving

36. Marcia bought a bag of red, white, and blue balloons for the party. There were 49 balloons in the bag. If there are twice as many red as blue and half as many white as blue, how many of each color are in the bag? *(See pp. 178–179.)*

(See Still More Practice, p. 524.)

The Sieve of Eratosthenes

A Greek mathematician named Eratosthenes created a method for finding prime numbers. The method is called the Sieve of Eratosthenes. You can use it to find all of the prime numbers between 1 and 100.

1	2	3	4	5	6	7	8	9	10
11	12	13	14	15	16	17	18	19	20
21	22	23	24	25	26	27	28	29	30
31	32	33	34	35	36	37	38	39	40
41	42	43	44	45	46	47	48	49	50
51	52	53	54	55	56	57	58	59	60
61	62	63	64	65	66	67	68	69	70
71	72	73	74	75	76	77	78	79	80
81	82	83	84	85	86	87	88	89	90
91	92	93	94	95	96	97	98	99	100

Copy the table above. Then use it to complete the following.

1. Cross out 1, because it is neither prime nor composite.

2. Circle 2, the first prime number. Cross out every multiple of 2.

3. Circle 3, the second prime number. Cross out every multiple of 3, including those already crossed out.

4. Circle 5, the third prime number. Cross out every multiple of 5, including those already crossed out.

5. Circle 7, the fourth prime number. Cross out every multiple of 7, including those already crossed out. Circle the remaining numbers. The circled numbers are prime numbers.

6. Tell whether each number is prime or composite:

    a. 13   **b.** 37   **c.** 49   **d.** 57   **e.** 59   **f.** 84

7. Find prime numbers that complete each statement.

    a. $69 = \underline{\ ?\ } \times \underline{\ ?\ }$ **b.** $\underline{\ ?\ } + \underline{\ ?\ } = 66$

    c. $91 = \underline{\ ?\ } \times \underline{\ ?\ }$ **d.** $\underline{\ ?\ } - \underline{\ ?\ } = 76$

Chapter 6 Test

Find the prime factorization.

1. 34   **2.** 42   **3.** 90

Write three equivalent fractions for each.

4. $\frac{2}{5}$ **5.** $\frac{7}{9}$ **6.** $\frac{5}{6}$

Rename each as indicated.

7. $\frac{16}{48}$ in simplest form   **8.** $5\frac{1}{2}$ as an improper fraction

9. $7\frac{1}{8}$ as a decimal   **10.** 0.64 as a fraction in simplest form

11. $\frac{6}{11}$ as a decimal   **12.** $12\frac{1}{3}$ as a decimal

Compare. Write $<$, $=$, or $>$. Use a number line to help you.

13. $^-5$ ___?___ $^+2\frac{1}{2}$ **14.** $^-6.75$ ___?___ $^-7$ **15.** $^+2\frac{1}{8}$ ___?___ $^+\frac{17}{8}$

Problem Solving

Use a strategy or strategies you have learned.

16. Dawn makes a quilt pattern with 45 blue and yellow patches. If she uses 2 blue patches for every 3 yellow patches, how many blue patches will she use? how many yellow patches?

Tell About It

17. Lou Ann must choose a melon from those that weigh $4\frac{2}{5}$ lb, $4\frac{3}{10}$ lb, or $4\frac{1}{2}$ lb. If she wants to choose the heaviest, which melon should she choose? Explain.

Performance Assessment

Find a pair of numbers, if any, for each description.

18. Between 9 and 25 that have 8 as their GCF

19. Between 0 and 9 that have 1 as their GCF

20. Between 0 and 9 that have 8 as their GCF and their LCM

21. LCM is between 100 and 200 and their GCF is 64

Test Preparation

Choose the best answer.

1. Find the value of n.

$n = 13{,}024 \div 32$

- **a.** 40 R7
- **b.** 407
- **c.** 407 R25
- **d.** not given

2. 1000×0.6

- **a.** 0.600
- **b.** 60
- **c.** 600
- **d.** not given

3. $3 \times 0.4 \times 0.8$

- **a.** 0.096
- **b.** 0.96
- **c.** 9.6
- **d.** not given

4. $0.413 \div 0.01$

- **a.** 0.41300
- **b.** 4.13
- **c.** 41.3
- **d.** not given

5. $0.7\overline{)3.934}$

- **a.** 0.0562
- **b.** 0.562
- **c.** 5.62
- **d.** not given

6. Which is the GCF of 18 and 30?

- **a.** 3
- **b.** 6
- **c.** 9
- **d.** 90

7. Which is ordered greatest to least?

- **a.** $\frac{7}{10}, \frac{7}{8}, \frac{2}{3}$
- **b.** $\frac{9}{10}, \frac{2}{5}, \frac{2}{3}$
- **c.** $\frac{5}{6}, \frac{3}{4}, \frac{1}{2}$
- **d.** none of these

8. Which will give a terminating decimal as a quotient?

- **a.** $1 \div 2$
- **b.** $1 \div 3$
- **c.** $1 \div 7$
- **d.** $1 \div 9$

9.
$$\begin{array}{r} 4550 \\ \times\ \ 240 \\ \hline \end{array}$$

- **a.** 10,920
- **b.** 109,200
- **c.** 10,920,000
- **d.** not given

10. Estimate.

8.7×19.52

- **a.** 30
- **b.** 80
- **c.** 90
- **d.** 180

11.
$$\begin{array}{r} 21.7 \\ \times\ 0.04 \\ \hline \end{array}$$

- **a.** 0.868
- **b.** 8.68
- **c.** 86.8
- **d.** not given

12. Estimate.

$218.7 \div 3.9$

- **a.** 5
- **b.** 50
- **c.** 90
- **d.** 700

13. $0.07875 \div 0.75$

- **a.** 0.105
- **b.** 1.5
- **c.** 10.5
- **d.** not given

14. Which is equivalent to $2\frac{2}{5}$?

- **a.** 2.2
- **b.** 2.4
- **c.** 2.5
- **d.** 2.6

15. Which is equivalent to $3\frac{1}{4}$?

- **a.** $\frac{4}{3}$
- **b.** $\frac{13}{3}$
- **c.** $\frac{7}{4}$
- **d.** $\frac{13}{4}$

16. Rename $1\frac{2}{3}$ as a repeating decimal.

- **a.** $1.\overline{2}$
- **b.** $1.\overline{3}$
- **c.** $1.\overline{6}$
- **d.** $1.\overline{7}$

17. Choose the algebraic expression.

$\frac{1}{4}$ of a number, plus 35

   a. $\frac{35}{y} + \frac{1}{4}$ **b.** $y \div \frac{1}{4} + 35$

   c. $\frac{1}{y} + 35$ **d.** $\frac{1}{4} \cdot y + 35$

18. Which is the greatest number?

   a. 0.546   **b.** 0.5462
   c. 0.5478   **d.** 0.5593

19. Estimate by rounding.

   $49.34 - 5.72$

   a. about 41   **b.** about 43
   c. about 45   **d.** about 39

20. A car travels at a rate of 65 miles per hour. How many miles will it travel in 7 hours?

   a. 9.29 miles   **b.** 420 miles
   c. 455 miles   **d.** 650 miles

21. Amy and Marcus sell lemonade at the neighborhood swimming pool. Marcus has $\frac{2}{3}$ of a pitcher remaining, and Amy has $\frac{3}{4}$ of a pitcher. How much more lemonade does Amy have?

   a. $\frac{1}{8}$ more   **b.** $\frac{1}{9}$ more
   c. $\frac{1}{6}$ more   **d.** not given

22. What is $^-60 \div 6$?

   a. 12
   b. 10
   c. $^-10$
   d. $^-6$

23. What is the value of the underlined digit?   36.098$\underline{7}$24

   a. 7 thousandths
   b. 7 ten thousandths
   c. 7 hundred thousandths
   d. 7 millionths

24. Choose the standard form of 4.6×10^4.

   a. 4,600   **b.** 46,000
   c. 46   **d.** 460

25. Subtract: $^-3 - 7$

   a. $^-4$
   b. $^-10$
   c. 4
   d. 10

26. Michael and Emily each have to drive home from college. Michael's drive is 1,286 miles and Emily's drive is 245 miles. About how many times longer is Michael's drive than Emily's?

   a. 4   **b.** 8
   c. 6   **d.** 12

Tell About It

Explain how you solved the problem. Show all your work.

27. Jefferson Junior High has 25 days of school remaining until summer vacation. Williams Junior High has $\frac{4}{5}$ as many days remaining. Leesville Junior High has 1.2 times as many days as Jefferson until their summer vacation begins.

   a. How many days of school do Williams students have before summer vacation?

   b. How many more days of school do the students at Leesville have than Williams students have?

Fractions: Addition and Subtraction

$\dfrac{3}{4}$

$\dfrac{4}{5}$

$\dfrac{3}{8}$

$\dfrac{9}{12}$

Where is math in dinnertime?

One whole pizza pie:
Two toppings to choose.
Three slices with peppers: 3/8.
Four slices with pepperoni: 1/2.
(How many slices are plain?)

From *Math in the Bath* by
Sara Atherlay

In this chapter you will:

Explore addition properties
Estimate, add, and subtract fractions
Evaluate expressions and
  solve equations with fractions
Solve problems by working backward

Critical Thinking/Finding Together

Work with a classmate to write a pizza
problem similar to the problem above.
Use your favorite pizza toppings. Challenge
student pairs to solve the problem.

Addition Properties: Fractions

The properties of addition are true for whole numbers, decimals, and fractions. The properties can help you compute with fractions mentally.

▶ **Commutative Property of Addition:** $a + b = b + a$

$$\frac{1}{5} + \frac{2}{5} = \frac{2}{5} + \frac{1}{5}$$

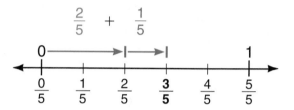

▶ **Associative Property of Addition:** $(a + b) + c = a + (b + c)$

$$(\frac{3}{8} + \frac{1}{8}) + \frac{2}{8} = \frac{3}{8} + (\frac{1}{8} + \frac{2}{8})$$

$$\frac{4}{8} + \frac{2}{8} = \frac{3}{8} + \frac{3}{8}$$

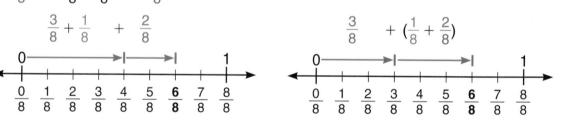

▶ **Identity Property of Addition:** $a + 0 = a$

$$\frac{1}{2} + 0 = \frac{1}{2}$$

$$\frac{1}{2} = \frac{1}{2}$$

▶ **Inverse Property of Addition:** $a + {}^-(a) = 0$

$$\frac{1}{2} + \frac{{}^-1}{2} = 0$$

$$0 = 0$$

Write *true* or *false* for each equation. If *false*, explain why.

1. $\frac{3}{9} + \frac{2}{9} = \frac{2}{9} + \frac{3}{9}$

2. $\frac{2}{3} + 0 = 0$

3. $(\frac{1}{12} + \frac{5}{12}) + \frac{2}{12} = \frac{1}{12} + (\frac{5}{12} - \frac{2}{12})$

4. $0 + \frac{7}{8} = \frac{7}{8}$

Name the property shown.

5. $\frac{1}{7} + \frac{3}{7} = \frac{3}{7} + \frac{1}{7}$

6. $0 + \frac{7}{12} = \frac{7}{12}$

7. $\frac{5}{9} + 0 = \frac{5}{9}$

8. $\frac{1}{8} + \frac{^-1}{8} = 0$

9. $\frac{1}{10} + (\frac{2}{10} + \frac{3}{10}) = (\frac{1}{10} + \frac{2}{10}) + \frac{3}{10}$

10. $\frac{2}{15} + (\frac{3}{15} + \frac{5}{15}) = \frac{2}{15} + (\frac{5}{15} + \frac{3}{15})$

11. $0 = \frac{^-4}{5} + \frac{4}{5}$

Find the value of the variable. Use the properties of addition.

12. $\frac{8}{9} + 0 = r$

13. $\frac{3}{10} + s = \frac{3}{10}$

14. $\frac{3}{20} + \frac{7}{20} = \frac{7}{20} + m$

15. $b + \frac{6}{7} = \frac{6}{7} + \frac{1}{7}$

16. $(\frac{1}{13} + \frac{3}{13}) + \frac{5}{13} = \frac{1}{13} + (g + \frac{5}{13})$

17. $\frac{3}{16} + (\frac{5}{16} + 0) = \frac{3}{16} + k$

18. $(\frac{6}{11} + \frac{1}{11}) + \frac{3}{11} = (\frac{1}{11} + y) + \frac{3}{11}$

19. $(0 + \frac{9}{20}) + \frac{3}{20} = \frac{9}{20} + z$

20. $\frac{1}{10} + \frac{3}{10} + \frac{5}{10} = \frac{5}{10} + \frac{1}{10} + d$

Problem Solving

Write an equation to solve each problem.

21. Jenny swam $\frac{1}{4}$ mile on Monday and $\frac{3}{4}$ mile on Tuesday. Bill swam $\frac{3}{4}$ mile on Monday and $\frac{1}{4}$ mile on Tuesday. Who swam farther in the two days?

22. Of the 7 sixth-grade classes, 2 are on the second floor. Of the 7 sixth-grade classes, none has a female teacher. What fraction names the sixth-grade classes that are on the second floor or have a female teacher?

DO YOU REMEMBER?

Tell whether each number is divisible by 2, 3, 4, 5, 6, 8, 9, and/or 10.

23. 101

24. 295

25. 682

26. 678

27. 480

28. 1611

29. 79,643

30. 53,995

31. 814,350

32. 652,248

Estimate Sums and Differences

A package of cheese weighs $\frac{9}{16}$ pound. Brittany needs 1 pound of cheese. If she buys two packages, will she have enough cheese?

To find the approximate amount of cheese in two packages, estimate: $\frac{9}{16}$ lb + $\frac{9}{16}$ lb.

▶ **To estimate the sum (or difference) of fractions:**

- Round each fraction to 0, $\frac{1}{2}$, or 1.

- Add (or subtract) the rounded numbers.

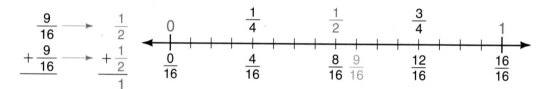

$$\frac{9}{16} \longrightarrow \frac{1}{2}$$
$$+\frac{9}{16} \longrightarrow +\frac{1}{2}$$
$$\overline{\phantom{+\frac{9}{16}}} \qquad \overline{1}$$

Brittany will have enough cheese.

.Think......................................

$\frac{9}{16}$ is a little more than $\frac{1}{2}$.

So $\frac{9}{16}$ + $\frac{9}{16}$ is a little more than 1.
....

Study these examples.

Tell whether the sum or difference is close to 0, $\frac{1}{2}$, or 1.

$\frac{1}{5} + \frac{3}{7}$	$\frac{7}{12} - \frac{1}{9}$	$\frac{11}{12} - \frac{8}{10}$
↓ ↓	↓ ↓	↓ ↓
$0 + \frac{1}{2} = \frac{1}{2}$	$\frac{1}{2} - 0 = \frac{1}{2}$	$1 - 1 = 0$

$\frac{1}{5} + \frac{3}{7}$ is close to $\frac{1}{2}$. | $\frac{7}{12} - \frac{1}{9}$ is close to $\frac{1}{2}$. | $\frac{11}{12} - \frac{8}{10}$ is close to 0.

Match each exercise to its estimated sum or difference in the box.

1. $\frac{1}{5} + \frac{8}{9}$

2. $\frac{6}{7} + \frac{11}{12}$

3. $\frac{9}{10} - \frac{5}{8}$

4. $\frac{6}{13} - \frac{8}{18}$

a. $1 + 1 = 2$

b. $1 - \frac{1}{2} = \frac{1}{2}$

c. $\frac{1}{2} - \frac{1}{2} = 0$

d. $0 + 1 = 1$

Estimate the sum or difference.

5. $\frac{1}{11} + \frac{4}{9}$

6. $\frac{15}{16} - \frac{1}{10}$

7. $\frac{2}{9} + \frac{5}{6}$

8. $\frac{11}{12} + \frac{12}{14}$

9. $\frac{7}{15} - \frac{1}{10}$

10. $\frac{18}{20} - \frac{13}{24}$

11. $\frac{3}{11} - \frac{1}{6}$

12. $\frac{1}{9} + \frac{4}{10}$

13. $\frac{9}{10} + \frac{1}{6} + \frac{3}{8}$

14. $\frac{1}{9} + \frac{1}{7} + \frac{1}{2}$

15. $\frac{15}{16} + \frac{5}{8} + \frac{4}{9} + \frac{3}{25}$

Estimate with Mixed Numbers

To estimate the sum (or difference) of mixed numbers:

- Round each mixed number to the nearest whole number.
- Add (or subtract) the rounded numbers.

$$8\frac{1}{5} \longrightarrow 8$$
$$+9\frac{5}{8} \longrightarrow +10$$
$$\overline{18} \longleftarrow \text{estimated sum}$$

$$15\frac{1}{2} \longrightarrow 16$$
$$-9\frac{9}{10} \longrightarrow -10$$
$$\overline{6} \longleftarrow \text{estimated difference}$$

Estimate the sum or difference.

16. $7\frac{2}{3}$
$+4\frac{3}{4}$

17. $9\frac{1}{3}$
$-3\frac{5}{12}$

18. $16\frac{1}{8}$
$+13\frac{8}{9}$

19. $12\frac{1}{2}$
$-4\frac{7}{10}$

20. $10\frac{1}{6}$
$-9\frac{8}{9}$

21. $15\frac{3}{4} - \frac{9}{10}$

22. $19\frac{2}{15} + \frac{6}{7}$

23. $12\frac{3}{5} + \frac{10}{12} + 9\frac{8}{15}$

Problem Solving

24. Antonio needs at least 15 pounds of chicken for a dinner party. He buys three packages: $3\frac{1}{4}$ lb, $4\frac{3}{7}$ lb, and $5\frac{2}{3}$ lb. Will this be enough chicken? Explain.

Add Fractions

Felix tapes together horizontally three pieces of paper. They measure $\frac{9}{16}$ in., $\frac{7}{8}$ in., and $\frac{3}{4}$ in. How long is the taped piece?

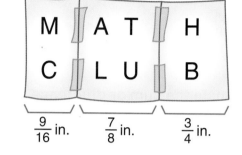

$\frac{9}{16}$ in. $\frac{7}{8}$ in. $\frac{3}{4}$ in.

To find the length, n, of the taped piece, add: $\frac{9}{16}$ in. $+ \frac{7}{8}$ in. $+ \frac{3}{4}$ in. $= n$.

First estimate:

$$\frac{9}{16} + \frac{7}{8} + \frac{3}{4} \longrightarrow \frac{1}{2} + 1 + 1 = 2\frac{1}{2}.$$

Then add.

▶ **To add fractions:**

- Find the least common denominator (LCD) of the fractions.

  Multiples of 16: 16, 32, 48, 64, . . .
  Multiples of 8: 8, 16, 24, 32, . . .
  Multiples of 4: 4, 8, 12, 16, . . .
  The LCD is 16.

  Think
  The (LCD) of $\frac{9}{16}$, $\frac{7}{8}$, and $\frac{3}{4}$ is the least common multiple (LCM) of the denominators.

- Rename each fraction as an equivalent fraction with the LCD as the denominator.

  $$\frac{9}{16} = \frac{9}{16}$$
  $$\frac{7}{8} = \frac{7 \times 2}{8 \times 2} = \frac{14}{16}$$
  $$+\frac{3}{4} = \frac{3 \times 4}{4 \times 4} = \frac{12}{16}$$

- Add. Express the sum in simplest form.

  $$\frac{35}{16} = 2\frac{3}{16}$$
  $$n = 2\frac{3}{16}$$

The taped piece of paper is $2\frac{3}{16}$ in. long.

Think
$2\frac{3}{16}$ is close to the estimate of $2\frac{1}{2}$.

Find the LCD for each set of fractions.

1. $\dfrac{2}{3}, \dfrac{3}{4}$ 2. $\dfrac{5}{12}, \dfrac{5}{6}$ 3. $\dfrac{7}{8}, \dfrac{1}{6}$ 4. $\dfrac{1}{2}, \dfrac{1}{4}, \dfrac{1}{8}$ 5. $\dfrac{1}{3}, \dfrac{5}{9}, \dfrac{1}{2}$

Estimate and then add. Write each answer in simplest form.

6. $\dfrac{1}{2}$
  $+\dfrac{1}{3}$

7. $\dfrac{1}{4}$
  $+\dfrac{2}{5}$

8. $\dfrac{1}{8}$
  $+\dfrac{5}{6}$

9. $\dfrac{1}{12}$
  $+\dfrac{1}{3}$

10. $\dfrac{4}{5}$
  $+\dfrac{1}{20}$

11. $\dfrac{8}{15}$
  $+\dfrac{1}{3}$

12. $\dfrac{7}{9}$
  $+\dfrac{1}{2}$

13. $\dfrac{5}{7}$
  $+\dfrac{3}{8}$

14. $\dfrac{3}{10}$
  $+\dfrac{1}{6}$

15. $\dfrac{2}{9}$
  $+\dfrac{7}{12}$

16. $\dfrac{3}{8}$
  $+\dfrac{5}{24}$

17. $\dfrac{4}{9}$
  $+\dfrac{1}{5}$

18. $\dfrac{1}{4}$
  $\dfrac{1}{3}$
  $+\dfrac{1}{2}$

19. $\dfrac{11}{20}$
  $\dfrac{2}{5}$
  $+\dfrac{1}{2}$

20. $\dfrac{1}{6}$
  $\dfrac{1}{9}$
  $+\dfrac{1}{9}$

21. $\dfrac{3}{4}$
  $\dfrac{1}{6}$
  $+\dfrac{1}{2}$

22. $\dfrac{3}{20}$
  $\dfrac{1}{5}$
  $+\dfrac{3}{10}$

23. $\dfrac{5}{6}$
  $\dfrac{5}{8}$
  $+\dfrac{7}{24}$

Compare. Use <, =, or >.

24. $\dfrac{1}{5} + \dfrac{3}{10}$? $\dfrac{1}{2}$ 25. $\dfrac{4}{7} + \dfrac{1}{2}$? $\dfrac{13}{14}$ 26. $\dfrac{1}{6} + \dfrac{4}{9}$? $\dfrac{2}{3}$ 27. $\dfrac{7}{9} + \dfrac{1}{10}$? 1

Problem Solving

28. In water, sound travels about $\dfrac{9}{10}$ mi in a second. How far will it travel in 2 seconds?

29. Three fifths of the 2nd floor is used for hallways and $\dfrac{3}{20}$ for offices. What part of the floor is used for both?

30. On Friday Hector skied $\dfrac{7}{16}$ mi and then $\dfrac{5}{8}$ mi. On Saturday he skied $\dfrac{2}{5}$ mi and then $\dfrac{3}{10}$ mi. On which day did Hector ski farther?

31. Mia has 1 cup of milk that she wants to use. She uses $\dfrac{1}{4}$ c, $\dfrac{1}{3}$ c, and $\dfrac{3}{8}$ c in three recipes. Did Mia use the entire cup?

DO YOU REMEMBER?

Write as a mixed number in simplest form.

32. $\dfrac{18}{4}$ 33. $\dfrac{11}{5}$ 34. $\dfrac{29}{6}$ 35. $\dfrac{76}{8}$ 36. $\dfrac{57}{9}$ 37. $\dfrac{85}{20}$

Add Mixed Numbers

A stock gained $1\frac{3}{8}$ points on Monday and $2\frac{1}{8}$ points on Tuesday. What was the total gain for the two days?

To find the total gain, s, add: $1\frac{3}{8} + 2\frac{1}{8} = s$.

First estimate: $1\frac{3}{8} + 2\frac{1}{8}$.

$$1 + 2 = 3$$

Then add.

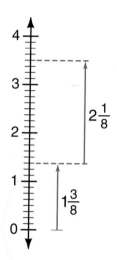

▶ **To add mixed numbers with *like* denominators:**

- Add the fractions.

- Add the whole numbers.

- Express the sum in simplest form.

$$1\frac{3}{8}$$
$$+\,2\frac{1}{8}$$
$$3\frac{4}{8} = 3\frac{1}{2} \leftarrow \boxed{\text{simplest form}}$$
$$s = 3\frac{1}{2}$$

The total gain of the stock was $3\frac{1}{2}$ points.

.Think......................................
$3\frac{1}{2}$ is close to the estimate of 3.
....

▶ **To add mixed numbers with *unlike* denominators:**

- Find the LCD of the fractions.

- Rename each fraction as an equivalent fraction with the LCD as the denominator.

- Add. Express the sum in simplest form.

$$14\frac{1}{10} = 14\frac{3}{30}$$
$$+\,26\frac{1}{15} = 26\frac{2}{30}$$
$$= 40\frac{5}{30} = 40\frac{1}{6} \leftarrow$$

.Think..................
LCD of 10
and 15 is 30.
....

$\boxed{\text{simplest form}}$

Study these examples.

$$\begin{array}{r} 17 \\ +\,9\frac{3}{16} \\ \hline 26\frac{3}{16} \end{array}$$

$\boxed{\text{Add whole numbers. Bring down the fraction.}}$

$$11\frac{5}{8} = 11\frac{5}{8}$$
$$+\,5\frac{3}{4} = 5\frac{6}{8}$$
$$16\frac{11}{8} = 16 + 1\frac{3}{8} = 17\frac{3}{8}$$

$\boxed{\text{Rename the sum.}}$

Complete the addition.

1. $4\frac{1}{6} = 4\frac{?}{24}$
   $+3\frac{1}{4} = 3\frac{?}{24}$
   _____
   $7\frac{?}{24} = 7\frac{?}{12}$

2. $8\frac{4}{5}$
   $+ 9\frac{1}{5}$
   _____
   $17\frac{?}{?} = \underline{\quad ?}$

3. $7\frac{7}{20} = 7\frac{?}{?}$
   $+4\frac{4}{5} = 4\frac{16}{?}$
   _____
   $11\frac{?}{20} = 12\frac{?}{20}$

Add. Estimate to help.

4. $6\frac{2}{9}$
   $+3\frac{2}{9}$

5. $6\frac{1}{7}$
   $+8\frac{3}{7}$

6. $4\frac{1}{6}$
   $+2\frac{3}{8}$

7. $1\frac{5}{6}$
   $+2\frac{1}{3}$

8. $2\frac{2}{5}$
   $+3\frac{1}{10}$

9. $6\frac{2}{3}$
   $+7\frac{2}{5}$

10. $14 + 7\frac{5}{9}$

11. $9\frac{3}{8} + 4$

12. $8\frac{7}{12} + \frac{5}{12}$

13. $16\frac{1}{8} + 7\frac{7}{8}$

14. $12\frac{7}{10} + 23\frac{7}{30}$

15. $25\frac{7}{18} + 15\frac{1}{6}$

16. $3\frac{7}{8} + 3\frac{1}{2}$

17. $8\frac{3}{4} + 6\frac{1}{3}$

18. $6\frac{11}{16} + 12\frac{3}{4}$

19. $18\frac{3}{4} + 20\frac{2}{3}$

20. $10\frac{9}{20} + 8\frac{3}{4}$

21. $15\frac{5}{6} + 12\frac{7}{9}$

22. $9\frac{3}{7} + 6\frac{2}{7} + 4\frac{1}{7}$

23. $6\frac{1}{2} + 3\frac{1}{3} + 4\frac{5}{6}$

24. $4\frac{3}{5} + 2\frac{3}{10} + 1\frac{1}{2}$

25. $7\frac{1}{2} + 4\frac{2}{3} + 5\frac{7}{12}$

26. $5\frac{1}{5} + 4\frac{3}{10} + 2\frac{3}{4}$

27. $3\frac{1}{3} + 2\frac{5}{8} + \frac{1}{4}$

Problem Solving

28. It takes $1\frac{2}{3}$ gal for paint repairs in the den and $1\frac{1}{2}$ gal for the kitchen. How much paint is that in all?

29. A butcher sold packages of meat weighing $1\frac{2}{3}$ lb and $5\frac{3}{4}$ lb. What was the total weight of the meat?

MENTAL MATH

Add. Look for sums of 1.

30. $\frac{1}{2} + \frac{3}{4} + \frac{1}{2}$

31. $5\frac{1}{4} + 6\frac{2}{3} + 11\frac{3}{4}$

32. $\frac{1}{4} + 7\frac{3}{4} + \frac{1}{5}$

33. $2\frac{6}{8} + 9 + 3\frac{1}{4}$

34. $\frac{2}{3} + 1\frac{1}{5} + 7\frac{5}{15}$

35. $8\frac{1}{6} + 9\frac{1}{7} + 2\frac{5}{6}$

7-5

Subtract Fractions

The chart shows the fractional part of family income spent on food for five countries. How much greater is the fractional part for China than for the U.S.A.?

To find how much greater, p, subtract:

$$\frac{1}{2} - \frac{1}{10} = p.$$

First estimate: $\frac{1}{2} - \frac{1}{10} \longrightarrow \frac{1}{2} - 0 = \frac{1}{2}.$

Then subtract.

Family Income Spent on Food	
India	$\frac{2}{5}$
China	$\frac{1}{2}$
Mexico	$\frac{4}{15}$
Japan	$\frac{1}{6}$
U.S.A.	$\frac{1}{10}$

▶ **To subtract fractions:**

- Find the LCD of the fractions.

- Rename each fraction as an equivalent fraction with the LCD as the denominator.

- Subtract. Express the difference in simplest form.

$$\frac{1}{2} = \frac{1 \times 5}{2 \times 5} = \frac{5}{10}$$

$$-\frac{1}{10} \qquad = \frac{1}{10}$$

$$\frac{4}{10} = \frac{2}{5}$$

$$p = \frac{2}{5}$$

simplest form

Think
LCD of 2 and 10 is 10.

Think
$\frac{2}{5}$ is close to the estimate of $\frac{1}{2}$.

The fractional part of China's family income spent on food is $\frac{2}{5}$ greater than that of the U.S.A.'s.

Estimate and then subtract. Write each answer in simplest form.

1. $\frac{3}{4}$
    $-\frac{5}{8}$

2. $\frac{5}{6}$
    $-\frac{1}{2}$

3. $\frac{7}{10}$
    $-\frac{1}{5}$

4. $\frac{1}{5}$
    $-\frac{1}{25}$

5. $\frac{1}{2}$
    $-\frac{3}{10}$

6. $\frac{3}{4}$
    $-\frac{2}{3}$

7. $\frac{7}{8}$
    $-\frac{5}{6}$

8. $\frac{1}{2}$
    $-\frac{2}{5}$

9. $\frac{6}{7}$
    $-\frac{1}{2}$

10. $\frac{3}{8}$
    $-\frac{1}{10}$

Practice

Find the difference.

11. $\dfrac{7}{8} - \dfrac{4}{5}$

12. $\dfrac{3}{10} - \dfrac{7}{30}$

13. $\dfrac{4}{11} - \dfrac{8}{22}$

14. $\dfrac{25}{48} - \dfrac{3}{8}$

Use Related Sentences to Solve Equations with Fractions

You can use related addition or subtraction sentences to find missing fractions in some equations.

$n + \dfrac{1}{5} = \dfrac{4}{5}$

$n = \dfrac{4}{5} - \dfrac{1}{5}$ ← related subtraction sentence

$n = \dfrac{3}{5}$

$a - \dfrac{1}{3} = \dfrac{5}{9}$

$a = \dfrac{5}{9} + \dfrac{1}{3}$ ← related addition sentence

$a = \dfrac{5}{9} + \dfrac{3}{9} = \dfrac{8}{9}$

Use a related sentence to find the missing fraction or whole number.

15. $n + \dfrac{1}{8} = \dfrac{7}{8}$

16. $y - \dfrac{1}{6} = \dfrac{1}{6}$

17. $m + \dfrac{1}{3} = \dfrac{1}{2}$

18. $z - \dfrac{1}{9} = \dfrac{1}{18}$

19. $p - \dfrac{5}{6} = \dfrac{3}{8}$

20. $t + \dfrac{3}{5} = \dfrac{5}{6}$

21. $c - 0 = \dfrac{3}{5}$

22. $d + 0 = \dfrac{5}{12}$

23. $f - 3\dfrac{1}{2} = 3\dfrac{1}{2}$

24. $g - 1\dfrac{1}{4} = \dfrac{3}{4}$

25. $\dfrac{2}{3} = r - \dfrac{1}{3}$

26. $\dfrac{7}{8} = b + \dfrac{7}{16}$

Problem Solving Use the table on page 230 for problems 27–28.

27. How much greater is the fractional part of family income spent on food for China than for Japan?

28. How much greater is the fractional part of family income spent on food for India than for Mexico?

29. Mr. Baumbach plans to leave his estate to four charities. One charity gets $\dfrac{1}{4}$ of his estate, the second gets $\dfrac{1}{16}$, and the third gets $\dfrac{3}{8}$. How much does the fourth charity get? Explain your answer.

CRITICAL THINKING

Write a word problem with two fractions so that the:

30. sum is $\dfrac{1}{2}$

31. difference is $\dfrac{1}{8}$

32. difference is $\dfrac{12}{45}$

Subtract Mixed Numbers

From a $7\frac{7}{12}$-ft piece of rope, Ray cut off $3\frac{5}{12}$ ft. How much rope was left?

To find how much rope was left, m, subtract:
$7\frac{7}{12} - 3\frac{5}{12} = m.$

First estimate: $7\frac{7}{12} - 3\frac{5}{12} \longrightarrow 8 - 3 = 5$

Then subtract.

▶ **To subtract mixed numbers with *like* denominators:**

- Subtract the fractions.

- Subtract the whole numbers.

- Express the difference in simplest form.

$$\begin{array}{r} 7\frac{7}{12} \\ -3\frac{5}{12} \\ \hline 4\frac{2}{12} = 4\frac{1}{6} \end{array}$$ ← simplest form

$$m = 4\frac{1}{6}$$

Ray has $4\frac{1}{6}$ ft of rope left.

.....Think.....
$4\frac{1}{6}$ is close to the estimate of 5.

▶ **To subtract mixed numbers with *unlike* denominators:**

- Find the LCD of the fractions.

- Rename each fraction as an equivalent fraction with the LCD as the denominator.

- Subtract. Express the difference in simplest form.

$$\begin{array}{r} 8\frac{5}{6} = 8\frac{10}{12} \\ -4\frac{3}{4} = 4\frac{9}{12} \\ \hline 4\frac{1}{12} \end{array}$$

.....Think.....
LCD of 6 and 4 is 12.

simplest form

▶ When the fraction in the minuend *is less than* the fraction in the subtrahend, rename the minuend. Then subtract.

minuend ⟶ $6\frac{1}{4}$ ⟶ $\boxed{\begin{aligned} 6\frac{1}{4} &= 5 + 1 + \frac{1}{4} \\ &= 5 + \frac{4}{4} + \frac{1}{4} = 5\frac{5}{4} \end{aligned}}$ ⟶ $\begin{array}{r} 5\frac{5}{4} \\ -4\frac{3}{4} \\ \hline 1\frac{2}{4} = 1\frac{1}{2} \end{array}$

subtrahend ⟶ $-4\frac{3}{4}$

Estimate and then subtract. Write each answer in simplest form.

1. $6\frac{4}{9}$
   $-4\frac{1}{9}$

2. $7\frac{5}{8}$
   $-3\frac{3}{8}$

3. $5\frac{3}{4}$
   $-1\frac{3}{4}$

4. $2\frac{9}{10}$
   $-2\frac{9}{10}$

5. $9\frac{1}{8}$
   $-3\frac{5}{8}$

6. $11\frac{5}{7}$
   $-9\frac{6}{7}$

7. $9\frac{1}{3} - 1\frac{5}{6}$

8. $13\frac{1}{6} - 9\frac{3}{4}$

9. $10\frac{2}{5} - 3\frac{7}{10}$

10. $11\frac{1}{4} - 6\frac{2}{3}$

11. $8\frac{1}{6} - 3\frac{3}{4} + 2\frac{1}{2}$

12. $9\frac{1}{12} - 5\frac{3}{8} - 1\frac{3}{4}$

13. $6\frac{1}{2} + 7\frac{1}{3} - 8\frac{1}{4}$

Subtract Mixed Numbers and Whole Numbers

$9\frac{3}{4}$
-3
$\overline{\quad}$
$6\frac{3}{4}$

Subtract whole numbers. Bring down the fraction.

$9 = 8\frac{4}{4}$
$-3\frac{3}{4} = 3\frac{3}{4}$
$\overline{\qquad}$
$5\frac{1}{4}$

$9 = 8 + 1$
$= 8 + \frac{4}{4}$
$= 8\frac{4}{4}$

Find the difference.

14. $7\frac{3}{5}$
    -4
    $\overline{\quad}$

15. $11\frac{1}{8}$
    -6
    $\overline{\quad}$

16. 14
    $-8\frac{2}{9}$
    $\overline{\quad}$

17. 6
    $-2\frac{1}{12}$
    $\overline{\quad}$

18. $8\frac{1}{2}$
    $-1\frac{1}{2}$
    $\overline{\quad}$

19. $10\frac{4}{7}$
    $-7\frac{4}{7}$
    $\overline{\quad}$

20. $10 - 1\frac{1}{4}$

21. $9 - 1\frac{1}{9}$

22. $7\frac{1}{2} - 7$

23. $15\frac{1}{5} - 15$

Problem Solving

24. There are $16\frac{1}{3}$ yd of material on a bolt. If $5\frac{3}{4}$ yd are used, how much material is left on the bolt?

25. Tricia usually works 40 hours a week. Last week she was absent $6\frac{1}{4}$ hours. How many hours did she work?

DO YOU REMEMBER?

Match each number sentence below with an addition property in the box.

26. $\frac{1}{8} + \frac{^-1}{8} = 0$

27. $(\frac{7}{9} + \frac{5}{8}) + \frac{1}{4} = \frac{7}{9} + (\frac{5}{8} + \frac{1}{4})$

28. $\frac{2}{3} + 0 = \frac{2}{3}$

29. $\frac{3}{5} + \frac{11}{15} = \frac{11}{15} + \frac{3}{5}$

Associative Property of Addition
Commutative Property of Addition
Identity Property of Addition
Inverse Property of Addition

Mental Math: Addition and Subtraction

You can add and subtract fractions and mixed numbers mentally
by using the three strategies below.

▶ **Compute the whole-number
part and then the fraction part.**

$$8\frac{7}{\boxed{8}} - 5\frac{5}{\boxed{8}} = 3\frac{2}{8} = 3\frac{1}{4}$$

Think
The denominators are alike.
$$(8-5) + (\frac{7}{8} - \frac{5}{8})$$

▶ **Look for sums of 1.**

$$5\frac{\boxed{1}}{\boxed{6}} + 2\frac{\boxed{5}}{\boxed{6}} + \frac{1}{3} = 8\frac{1}{3}$$

Think
$$\frac{1}{6} + \frac{5}{6} = 1$$

▶ **Compensate by "adding on"
and then subtracting.**

$$10 - 3\frac{5}{8} = 6\frac{3}{8}$$

Think
$$3\frac{5}{8} + \frac{\boxed{3}}{\boxed{8}} = 4$$

Subtract 4, then add $\frac{3}{8}$.

$$10 - 4 = 6 \text{ and } 6 + \frac{\boxed{3}}{\boxed{8}} = 6\frac{3}{8}$$

Study these examples.

$$7 - 4\frac{7}{16} = n$$

Think
$$4\frac{7}{16} + \frac{\boxed{9}}{\boxed{16}} = 5$$

$$7 - 5 = 2 \text{ and } 2 + \frac{\boxed{9}}{\boxed{16}} = 2\frac{9}{16}$$

So $7 - 4\frac{7}{16} = 2\frac{9}{16}$.

$$3\frac{1}{4} - 1\frac{1}{2} = n$$

Think
$$1\frac{1}{2} + \frac{\boxed{1}}{\boxed{2}} = 2$$

$$3\frac{1}{4} - 2 = 1\frac{1}{4} \text{ and } 1\frac{1}{4} + \frac{\boxed{1}}{\boxed{2}} = 1\frac{3}{4}$$

So $3\frac{1}{4} - 1\frac{1}{2} = 1\frac{3}{4}$.

Compute mentally. Find the whole-number part and then the fraction part.

1. $8\frac{2}{3} - 5\frac{1}{3}$

2. $6\frac{7}{8} - 2\frac{5}{8}$

3. $10\frac{1}{12} + 1\frac{7}{12}$

4. $12\frac{1}{16} + 8\frac{7}{16}$

5. $10\frac{3}{8} - 4\frac{1}{8} + 2$

6. $9\frac{7}{15} - 3\frac{2}{15} - 4$

Compute mentally. Look for sums of 1.

7. $6\frac{1}{3} + 8\frac{2}{3} + 7$

8. $2\frac{3}{8} + 1\frac{5}{8}$

9. $5\frac{1}{4} + 1\frac{1}{4} + \frac{1}{2}$

10. $1\frac{1}{16} + 5\frac{1}{2} + 2\frac{3}{16} + 2\frac{1}{4}$

11. $3\frac{1}{12} + 7\frac{7}{12} + 8\frac{1}{3}$

12. $3\frac{1}{3} + 6\frac{4}{5} + 10\frac{2}{3} + 3\frac{1}{5}$

13. $9\frac{3}{4} + 5\frac{6}{11} + 6\frac{1}{4}$

Compensate to compute mentally.

14. $8 - 4\frac{1}{3}$

15. $12 - 10\frac{5}{6}$

16. $5\frac{1}{3} - \frac{2}{3}$

17. $7\frac{2}{5} - \frac{3}{5}$

18. $22\frac{1}{4} - 13\frac{3}{4}$

19. $10\frac{3}{8} - 7\frac{5}{8}$

Problem Solving

20. Fred mixes $3\frac{1}{2}$ cups of flour, $1\frac{1}{4}$ cups of sugar, $\frac{2}{3}$ cup of rye flour, and $\frac{1}{3}$ cup of wheat flour. Will the ingredients fit into a 6-cup bowl? Explain.

21. Angela cuts $5\frac{3}{8}$ yards of ribbon from a 10-yard spool to make centerpieces. She orders more ribbon when there is less than 3 yards on the spool. Should she order more ribbon now? Explain.

DO YOU REMEMBER?

Rename each fraction as a decimal.

22. $\frac{1}{15}$

23. $\frac{2}{15}$

24. $\frac{3}{15}$

25. $\frac{4}{15}$

26. $\frac{5}{15}$

27. $\frac{6}{15}$

28. $\frac{7}{15}$

29. $\frac{8}{15}$

30. $\frac{9}{15}$

31. $\frac{10}{15}$

32. $\frac{11}{15}$

33. $\frac{12}{15}$

34. What fractions are repeating decimals? terminating decimals?

Addition and Subtraction Expressions with Fractions

Mark mixed a solution of $1\frac{3}{4}$ L of colored water, $2\frac{1}{3}$ L of salt water, and some liters of lemon juice. What algebraic expression represents the amount of mixed solution?

Let j represent the liters of lemon juice.

$$\underset{\substack{\text{colored}\\\text{water}}}{1\frac{3}{4}} \quad + \quad \underset{\substack{\text{salt}\\\text{water}}}{2\frac{1}{3}} \quad + \quad \underset{\substack{\text{lemon}\\\text{juice}}}{j}$$

If Mark mixed $\frac{1}{4}$ L of lemon juice, how many liters of solution did he make?

To determine how many liters of solution Mark made, evaluate the expression:

$1\frac{3}{4} + 2\frac{1}{3} + j$, when $j = \frac{1}{4}$.

$1\frac{3}{4} + 2\frac{1}{3} + \frac{1}{4}$ ← Replace j with $\frac{1}{4}$.

$(1\frac{3}{4} + \frac{1}{4}) + 2\frac{1}{3}$ ← Use the Commutative and Associative Properties.

$\quad 2 \quad + 2\frac{1}{3}$ ← Simplify using the order of operations.

$\quad 4\frac{1}{3}$

> Commutative means "order."
> Associative means "grouping."

Mark made $4\frac{1}{3}$ L of solution.

Study this example.

Evaluate: $f + 4\frac{4}{5} + g + 6\frac{1}{3}$, when $f = 5\frac{2}{3}$ and $g = 2\frac{2}{5}$.

$5\frac{2}{3} + 4\frac{4}{5} + 2\frac{2}{5} + 6\frac{1}{3}$ ← Replace f with $5\frac{2}{3}$ and g with $2\frac{2}{5}$.

$(5\frac{2}{3} + 6\frac{1}{3}) + (4\frac{4}{5} + 2\frac{2}{5})$ ← Use the Commutative and Associative Properties.

$\quad 12 \quad + \quad 7\frac{1}{5}$ ← Simplify using the order of operations.

$\quad 19\frac{1}{5}$

Evaluate each expression for the given values. Use the properties of addition.

1. $5\frac{1}{2} + n$, when $n = 3\frac{1}{4}$

2. $7\frac{1}{8} - y$, when $y = 0$

3. $1\frac{1}{6} + r + 1\frac{2}{5}$, when $r = 1\frac{3}{4}$

4. $k - 10\frac{1}{10} + 0$, when $k = 14\frac{2}{3}$

5. $9\frac{1}{6} + \frac{5}{6} - m$, when $m = \frac{1}{2}$

6. $1\frac{1}{2} + s + 6\frac{3}{4}$, when $s = 1\frac{3}{8}$

7. $f - 1\frac{3}{5} + g$, when $f = 2\frac{1}{4}$ and $g = 5\frac{1}{2}$

8. $5 + 3\frac{3}{8} + d + 2\frac{5}{8}$, when $d = 6\frac{1}{6}$

Simplify each expression. Use mental math and the properties of addition.

9. $5\frac{2}{5} + 3\frac{3}{5} + 6\frac{1}{4}$

10. $8\frac{1}{8} + 4\frac{1}{4} + 5\frac{7}{8}$

11. $0 + 11\frac{2}{5}$

12. $9\frac{1}{6} + 0$

13. $7\frac{1}{2} + 6 + 4\frac{1}{4}$

14. $3\frac{3}{4} + 2\frac{1}{2} + 11$

15. $12\frac{1}{4} + 5\frac{1}{8} + 2\frac{1}{2}$

16. $9\frac{1}{2} + 4\frac{3}{7} + 1\frac{1}{4}$

17. $(\frac{1}{2} + 2\frac{3}{5}) + 1\frac{1}{2}$

18. $8\frac{1}{4} + (4\frac{1}{9} + \frac{3}{4})$

19. $3\frac{1}{2} + (1\frac{1}{4} - 1\frac{1}{4})$

20. $(2\frac{1}{5} - 2\frac{1}{5}) + (3\frac{2}{3} + 1\frac{1}{4})$

Problem Solving

Write and evaluate an expression for each situation.

21. A stock started at $16\frac{1}{4}$ points. It gained $3\frac{2}{3}$ points and then lost some points. If the stock lost $2\frac{1}{2}$ points, how many points is the stock worth?

22. Rich's photo album has $3\frac{5}{12}$ pages of family photos, some pages of photos of pets, and $6\frac{1}{2}$ pages of photos of friends. If there are $1\frac{1}{3}$ pages of photos of pets, how many pages are there altogether?

TEST PREPARATION

23. Anton used $1\frac{2}{3}$ c of milk to make cupcakes and $\frac{4}{5}$ c to make cookies. If he used $2\frac{1}{3}$ c for bread, how much milk in all did he use?

   a. $1\frac{2}{3} + \frac{4}{5} - 2\frac{1}{3}$

   b. $1\frac{2}{3} + \frac{4}{5} + 2\frac{1}{3}$

   c. $2\frac{1}{3} - 1\frac{2}{3} - \frac{4}{5}$

   d. $1\frac{2}{3} + \frac{4}{5} = 2\frac{1}{3}$

Addition and Subtraction Equations with Fractions

Jackie bought some almonds and $\frac{1}{8}$ lb of cashews. She bought $\frac{7}{8}$ lb of nuts in all. How many pounds of almonds did she buy?

To find how many pounds of almonds, a, write and solve the equation: $a + \frac{1}{8} = \frac{7}{8}$. ◄

> Let a represent the weight of almonds.

$$a + \frac{1}{8} - \frac{1}{8} = \frac{7}{8} - \frac{1}{8}$$ ◄ Subtract $\frac{1}{8}$ from both sides to isolate the variable.

$$a = \frac{6}{8} = \frac{3}{4}$$ ◄ Simplify.

Think
Solve equations with fractions the same way as equations with whole numbers.

Check by replacing a with $\frac{3}{4}$. $\frac{3}{4} + \frac{1}{8} \overset{?}{=} \frac{7}{8} \rightarrow \frac{6}{8} + \frac{1}{8} \overset{?}{=} \frac{7}{8} \rightarrow \frac{7}{8} = \frac{7}{8}$ True

Jackie bought $\frac{3}{4}$ lb of almonds.

► You can add a variable to both sides to solve an equation.

$$\frac{6}{7} - k = \frac{2}{7}$$ ◄ k is subtracted from $\frac{6}{7}$.

$$\frac{6}{7} - k + k = \frac{2}{7} + k$$ ◄ Add k to both sides.

> **Inverse Property of Addition**
> $k - k = 0$

$$\frac{6}{7} = \frac{2}{7} + k$$ ◄ Simplify.

$$\frac{6}{7} - \frac{2}{7} = \frac{2}{7} + k - \frac{2}{7}$$ ◄ Subtract $\frac{2}{7}$ from both sides to isolate the variable.

$$\frac{4}{7} = k + \frac{2}{7} - \frac{2}{7}$$ ◄ Use the Commutative Property of Addition to rewrite $\frac{2}{7} + k$ as $k + \frac{2}{7}$.

$$\frac{4}{7} = k, \text{ or } k = \frac{4}{7}$$

Study this example.

$$w + \frac{3}{5} + \frac{4}{5} = 3\frac{4}{5}$$ ◄ Simplify by adding the numbers on one side.

$$w + 1\frac{2}{5} = 3\frac{4}{5}$$

$$w + 1\frac{2}{5} - 1\frac{2}{5} = 3\frac{4}{5} - 1\frac{2}{5}$$ ◄ Subtract $1\frac{2}{5}$ from both sides to isolate the variable.

$$w = 2\frac{2}{5}$$

Solve and check.

1. $\frac{7}{9} - y = \frac{2}{9}$

2. $\frac{5}{8} + k = 3\frac{1}{8}$

3. $2\frac{3}{10} - g = 1\frac{1}{5}$

4. $d - \frac{3}{5} = \frac{4}{5}$

5. $h - 1\frac{5}{8} = 3\frac{1}{8}$

6. $x - \frac{4}{7} = \frac{5}{14}$

7. $t + 2\frac{1}{6} = 7\frac{11}{12}$

8. $10\frac{1}{2} - u = 8\frac{3}{8}$

9. $p + 1\frac{3}{5} = 3\frac{3}{10}$

10. $w - 2\frac{1}{4} = 4\frac{5}{12}$

11. $10\frac{5}{6} = s + 3\frac{5}{8}$

12. $2\frac{1}{6} = v - 7\frac{4}{9}$

Problem Solving

Choose the correct equation to solve each problem. Then solve.

13. Brit buys some peanuts and $2\frac{1}{4}$ pounds of walnuts. He buys $5\frac{1}{8}$ pounds of nuts in all. How many pounds of peanuts does Brit buy?

 a. $p + 2\frac{1}{4} = 5\frac{1}{8}$

 b. $p + 5\frac{1}{8} = 2\frac{1}{4}$

 c. $p = 2\frac{1}{4} + 5\frac{1}{8}$

14. Roger had $3\frac{1}{2}$ pounds of grapes. He gave some to Catie. Now Roger has $1\frac{3}{4}$ pounds of grapes. How many pounds of grapes did he give to Catie?

 a. $3\frac{1}{2} + g = 1\frac{3}{4}$

 b. $3\frac{1}{2} - g = 1\frac{3}{4}$

 c. $1\frac{3}{4} - 3\frac{1}{2} = g$

15. Becca had some flour. She used $1\frac{3}{4}$ pounds of the flour to make ornaments. Now she has $2\frac{1}{2}$ pounds of flour. How much flour did Becca have to begin with?

 a. $f - 1\frac{3}{4} = 2\frac{1}{2}$

 b. $f + 1\frac{3}{4} = 2\frac{1}{2}$

 c. $f = 2\frac{1}{2} - 1\frac{3}{4}$

16. Liam made $\frac{2}{3}$ cup of red icing, $\frac{3}{4}$ cup of white icing and the rest of blue icing. Liam made $2\frac{1}{2}$ cups of icing altogether. How many cups of blue icing did Liam make?

 a. $b - \frac{2}{3} + \frac{3}{4} = 2\frac{1}{2}$

 b. $b - \frac{2}{3} - \frac{3}{4} = 2\frac{1}{2}$

 c. $\frac{2}{3} + \frac{3}{4} + b = 2\frac{1}{2}$

CHALLENGE — Algebra

Solve and check.

17. $r + \frac{2}{5} + \frac{3}{10} = 2\frac{7}{10}$

18. $b - \frac{3}{8} + \frac{4}{5} = 9\frac{1}{10}$

19. $4\frac{1}{3} + e + 2\frac{5}{6} - 1\frac{3}{6} = 9\frac{1}{3}$

Problem-Solving Strategy:
Work Backward

Mrs. Kline bought a bolt of fabric. She used $4\frac{3}{4}$ yd to make a dress and $2\frac{3}{8}$ yd for a jacket. After buying $1\frac{1}{8}$ yd more, she had $6\frac{1}{2}$ yd left to make two pairs of pants. How much fabric was on the bolt she bought?

Read

Visualize yourself in the problem above as you reread it. List the facts and the question.

Facts: She used $4\frac{3}{4}$ yd and $2\frac{3}{8}$ yd.
   She bought $1\frac{1}{8}$ yd more.
   She had $6\frac{1}{2}$ yd left.

Question: How much fabric was on the bolt she bought?

Plan

Begin with the amount of fabric she had left ($6\frac{1}{2}$ yd) and *work backward*. Subtract the extra amount she bought and add the amounts she used to find the amount of fabric, m, on the bolt.

$$6\frac{1}{2} \text{ yd} - 1\frac{1}{8} \text{ yd} + 2\frac{3}{8} \text{ yd} + 4\frac{3}{4} \text{ yd} = m$$

   left   bought   used   used   amount on bolt

Solve

Add or subtract in order from left to right.

$$6\frac{1}{2} \text{ yd} - 1\frac{1}{8} \text{ yd} + 2\frac{3}{8} \text{ yd} + 4\frac{3}{4} \text{ yd} = m$$

Think
$$6\frac{4}{8} - 1\frac{1}{8} = 5\frac{3}{8}$$

$$5\frac{3}{8} \text{ yd} + 2\frac{3}{8} \text{ yd} + 4\frac{3}{4} \text{ yd} = m$$

Think
$$7\frac{6}{8} = 7\frac{3}{4}$$

$$7\frac{3}{4} \text{ yd} + 4\frac{3}{4} \text{ yd} = m$$

Think
$$11\frac{6}{4} = 12\frac{2}{4} = 12\frac{1}{2}$$

$$12\frac{2}{4} \text{ yd} = 12\frac{1}{2} \text{ yd}$$

There was $12\frac{1}{2}$ yd of fabric on the bolt.

Check

Begin with the first amount and compute by working *forward*:

$$12\frac{1}{2} \text{ yd} - 4\frac{3}{4} \text{ yd} - 2\frac{3}{8} \text{ yd} + 1\frac{1}{8} \text{ yd} = 6\frac{1}{2} \text{ yd}$$

Solve. Use the Work Backward strategy.

1. After losing $2\frac{1}{2}$ lb in each of the first 2 weeks of March and gaining $1\frac{3}{8}$ lb in each of the next 2 weeks, Ted's prizewinning piglet weighed 110 lb. How much did his piglet weigh on March 1?

Read Visualize yourself in the problem as you reread it. List the facts and the question.

Facts: $2\frac{1}{2}$ lb lost each of the first 2 weeks

$1\frac{3}{8}$ lb gained each of the next 2 weeks

110 lb is its final weight.

Question: How much did the piglet weigh on March 1?

Plan Begin with the piglet's final weight of 110 lb and *work backward*. Subtract the pounds it gained and add the pounds it lost to find its weight on March 1.

Think

$$110 \text{ lb} - 1\frac{3}{8} \text{ lb} - 1\frac{3}{8} \text{ lb} + 2\frac{1}{2} \text{ lb} + 2\frac{1}{2} \text{ lb}$$

Solve **Check**

2. At the end of one school day, Ms. Dinger had 17 crayons left. She remembered giving out 14 crayons in the morning, getting back 12 crayons at recess, and giving out 11 crayons after lunch. How many crayons did Ms. Dinger have at the start of the day?

3. Jason was given his allowance on Sunday. On Monday he bought a book for $2.95. On Tuesday Kurt paid Jason the $3.50 he owed him. Jason now has $6.05. How much was his allowance?

4. Lee wrote a 2-digit number. She divided it by 9, added 24, and doubled the result. Her final answer was 64. What number did Lee write?

5. Rita bought some peaches. She used $3\frac{2}{3}$ lb to make peach cobbler. Then she used $\frac{5}{6}$ lb in fruit salad. After her neighbor gave her $2\frac{1}{2}$ lb from her tree, she had $3\frac{1}{4}$ lb. How many pounds of peaches did she buy?

Read **Plan** **Solve** **Check**

Solve each problem and explain the method used.

1. Ms. Carson's class makes silk flowers for a craft fair. A silk rose is $12\frac{1}{2}$ in. long. A silk lily is 15 in. long. How much longer is the lily?

2. Marissa cuts petals out of red ribbon. One of the petals is $\frac{9}{16}$ in. long, another is $\frac{13}{16}$ in. long, and a third is $1\frac{5}{16}$ in. long. How many inches of ribbon does she cut for all three petals?

3. Paul cuts wire stems for the flowers. He has a piece of wire 12 in. long. He cuts a stem $9\frac{1}{2}$ in. long. How much wire does he have left?

4. Paul uses $\frac{2}{3}$ yard of green tape to wrap one stem and $\frac{3}{4}$ yard of green tape to wrap another. How much tape does he use in all?

5. Gloria made a wreath using $4\frac{2}{3}$ yards of green ribbon and $5\frac{3}{4}$ yards of yellow ribbon. How much ribbon did she use?

6. José made a flower arrangement that measured $18\frac{5}{16}$ in. tall. It was a little too tall, so he cut $2\frac{1}{2}$ in. off the stems. How tall was the finished arrangement?

7. At the fair, $\frac{1}{5}$ of the class worked the booth. Another $\frac{2}{3}$ of the class had created the flowers. The remaining part of the class decorated the booth. What part of the class decorated the booth?

8. Mr. McCauley's class made wicker baskets for the craft fair. Each basket is $6\frac{1}{8}$ in. tall and $2\frac{5}{16}$ in. wider than it is tall. How wide are the baskets?

Choose a strategy from the list or use another strategy you know to solve each problem.

Strategy File

Use These Strategies
Work Backward
Use More Than One Step
Use a Diagram
Find a Pattern
Use Simpler Numbers
Write an Equation
Make a Table

9. Dan started with a 36-in. strip of wicker. He cut two $11\frac{5}{8}$-in. pieces. Does he have enough left over to cut two $6\frac{1}{2}$-in. pieces?

10. Ben cut wicker strips to make a basket. He cut two $8\frac{3}{4}$-in. strips and one $6\frac{1}{2}$-in. strip from one long piece. He had $\frac{5}{8}$ in. of wicker left over. How long was the original piece of wicker?

11. Write the next five numbers in this series:
$\frac{23}{24},\ \frac{11}{12},\ \frac{21}{24},\ \frac{5}{6},\ \frac{19}{24},\ \frac{3}{4}.$

12. Mr. Cortez spent $10.25 of his money on wicker each week for 2 weeks. Next he collected $4.65 and $6.70 from students. Then he had $45.53 to spend. How much money did he have originally?

13. Nedra made a basket handle using three pieces of wicker. The first piece was 9 in. long, the second was $\frac{1}{2}$ in. longer than the first, and the third was $\frac{3}{4}$ in. shorter than the second. How much wicker did she use?

Use the diagram for problems 14–16.

14. How much wider is the thick wicker than the thin?

15. Jason makes a basket using the medium width wicker. The basket is as tall as 8 strips of the wicker. Is the basket taller than 4 inches?

16. Arlene's basket is 9 strips tall. The pattern is thin, thick, thick, thin, thick, thick, and so on. How tall is Arlene's basket?

Widths of Wicker

$\frac{5}{16}$ in.

Thin Wicker

$\frac{7}{16}$ in.

Medium Wicker

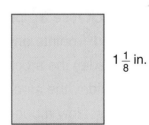

$1\frac{1}{8}$ in.

Thick Wicker

Write Your Own

17. Plan a wicker basket of your own. Then write a problem about it. Have a classmate solve it.

Estimate the sum or difference.   (See pp. 224–225.)

1. $\dfrac{5}{9} + \dfrac{3}{7}$

2. $\dfrac{14}{15} - \dfrac{7}{8}$

3. $9\dfrac{1}{6} - 7\dfrac{1}{2}$

4. $12\dfrac{9}{10} + 11\dfrac{6}{7}$

Add or subtract. Estimate to help.   (See pp. 226–233.)

5. $\begin{array}{r} \dfrac{1}{2} \\ +\dfrac{1}{3} \\ \hline \end{array}$

6. $\begin{array}{r} 4\dfrac{1}{8} \\ +6\dfrac{3}{8} \\ \hline \end{array}$

7. $\begin{array}{r} \dfrac{1}{3} \\ -\dfrac{1}{4} \\ \hline \end{array}$

8. $\begin{array}{r} 4\dfrac{5}{7} \\ -1\dfrac{2}{7} \\ \hline \end{array}$

9. $\begin{array}{r} 5 \\ -1\dfrac{1}{2} \\ \hline \end{array}$

10. $\begin{array}{r} 10 \\ -2\dfrac{3}{4} \\ \hline \end{array}$

11. $14\dfrac{3}{10} - 1\dfrac{1}{3}$

12. $1\dfrac{3}{8} + 19\dfrac{2}{3}$

13. $10 - 1\dfrac{1}{10}$

14. $4\dfrac{3}{7} - 1\dfrac{1}{6}$

15. $4\dfrac{1}{4} + 1\dfrac{1}{2} + 2\dfrac{3}{8}$

16. $\dfrac{1}{8} + 3\dfrac{2}{3} + 3\dfrac{7}{8}$

17. $15\dfrac{3}{8} - 9\dfrac{7}{8}$

Compute. Use mental math and the properties of addition. (See pp. 222–223, 234–235.)

18. $\dfrac{1}{4} + \dfrac{1}{4}$

19. $5\dfrac{1}{6} + (3\dfrac{1}{2} - 3\dfrac{1}{2})$

20. $7\dfrac{1}{4} + 3\dfrac{1}{2}$

Evaluate each expression for the given values.   (See pp. 236–237.)

21. $7\dfrac{3}{8} - n$, when $n = 3\dfrac{1}{8}$

22. $r + 5\dfrac{1}{3} + 2\dfrac{3}{5}$, when $r = 1\dfrac{2}{5}$

23. $7\dfrac{3}{4} + c + 1\dfrac{1}{4} - d$, when $c = 3\dfrac{2}{6}$ and $d = 2\dfrac{3}{8}$

Solve and check.   (See pp. 238–239.)

24. $a + \dfrac{1}{6} + \dfrac{5}{6} = 7\dfrac{1}{3}$

25. $3\dfrac{3}{7} + y = 8\dfrac{2}{3}$

26. $w - 8\dfrac{3}{4} = 9\dfrac{7}{12}$

Problem Solving
(See pp. 240–243.)

27. A stock rose $3\dfrac{1}{4}$ points on Tuesday. It fell $1\dfrac{3}{4}$ points on Wednesday. On Thursday the stock rose $4\dfrac{1}{8}$ points. By Friday the stock was worth $28\dfrac{1}{2}$ points. How much was the stock worth on Monday?

28. A veterinarian recommended that Troy put his cat on a diet. The first week the cat lost $1\dfrac{3}{4}$ lb. The second week she gained $\dfrac{1}{2}$ lb. The third and fourth weeks she lost $2\dfrac{3}{4}$ lb each. If the cat's weight after four weeks was 12 lb, how much did the cat weigh before the diet began?

(See *Still More Practice*, p. 525.)

Logic: Statements and Negations

In logic, the negation of a statement is formed by denying the original statement. When a statement is true, its negation is false. When a statement is false, its negation is true.

Statement		Negation	
A square is round.	False	A square is not round.	True
Seven is an odd number.	True	Seven is not an odd number.	False
All squares have 5 sides.	False	No squares have 5 sides.	True

Tell whether each is a negation of the statement: "A triangle has 4 sides." Write *Yes* or *No.*

1. A triangle does not have 4 sides.

2. A square has 4 sides.

Tell whether the statement is true or false. Then write the negation of the statement and tell whether it is true or false.

3. A whole number is an integer.

4. All decimals are rational numbers.

5. All squares have 4 sides.

6. Sixteen is a prime number.

7. No circles have 3 sides.

8. No prime numbers are even.

9. A fraction cannot be renamed as a decimal.

10. An odd number is not divisible by 4.

11. Fractions can be added if they are like fractions.

12. The product of a fraction and zero is zero.

Write a statement and its negation for each description.

13. A statement about adding fractions or mixed numbers whose statement is true and negation is false.

14. A statement about subtracting fractions or mixed numbers whose statement is false and negation is true.

Chapter 7 Test

Add or subtract. Estimate to help you.

1. $\frac{7}{12} + \frac{13}{24}$

2. $\frac{5}{6} - \frac{1}{5}$

3. $2\frac{1}{5} + 4\frac{3}{5}$

4. $9\frac{5}{7} - 8\frac{2}{7}$

5. $8\frac{3}{5} + 6\frac{1}{3}$

6. $5\frac{5}{7} + 4$

7. $4\frac{3}{8} - 1\frac{1}{7}$

8. $1\frac{1}{2} + 2\frac{1}{3} + 1\frac{5}{6}$

9. $12 - 1\frac{1}{8}$

10. $15\frac{9}{10} - 14\frac{1}{3}$

Compute. Use the addition properties when possible.

11. $2\frac{4}{5} + (1\frac{1}{3} - 1\frac{1}{3})$

12. $(\frac{1}{4} + 5\frac{3}{8}) + 3\frac{3}{4}$

13. $2\frac{1}{2} + 4 + 1\frac{1}{4}$

Evaluate each expression for the given values.

14. $2\frac{5}{6} - n$, when $n = 1\frac{1}{2}$

15. $4\frac{5}{8} + c + 2\frac{1}{8}$, when $c = 1\frac{2}{5}$

Solve and check.

16. $a + \frac{1}{4} = \frac{1}{2}$

17. $t + 1\frac{1}{2} = 3\frac{1}{2}$

18. $n - \frac{3}{8} = \frac{5}{16}$

Problem Solving

Use a strategy or strategies you have learned.

19. Javier received a paycheck on Friday. From the paycheck he bought a CD for $12.95 and a book for $8.65. Then Macy paid Javier the $4.00 she owed him. Javier now has $48.60. How much was his paycheck?

Tell About It

Explain how you solved the problem. Show all your work.

20. Laura wrote a 3-digit number. She doubled it, added 150, divided by 100, and added 6. Her final result was 10. What number did Laura write?

Performance Assessment

Solve the problems and explain your methods.

21. Eduardo wrote a fraction problem: He chose a fraction or a mixed number, added $\frac{1}{4}$, and subtracted $2\frac{1}{2}$. In the same pattern, Eduardo got these numbers:

$\underline{\ ?\ }, 8\frac{5}{8}, 6\frac{1}{8}, 6\frac{3}{8}, 3\frac{7}{8}, \underline{\ ?\ }, \underline{\ ?\ }$

What are the sixth and seventh numbers in this sequence? With what number did Eduardo start?

Test Preparation

Choose the best answer.

1. Round 378,642,133,002 to the nearest ten million.

    a. 380,000,000,000
    b. 378,600,000,000
    c. 378,640,000,000
    d. 378,642,000,000

2. An expression for "5 more than x, multiplied by 6" is:

    a. $(x + 5) \times 6$ **b.** $(x - 5) \times 6$
    c. $5 + (x \times 6)$ **d.** $5 \times (x + 6)$

3. Which statement is true?

    a. $|{}^-4| = {}^-|4|$
    b. $|{}^-4| = {}^-({}^-4)$
    c. ${}^-|{}^-4| = {}^-({}^-4)$
    d. ${}^-|{}^-4| = |{}^-({}^-4)|$

4. Which makes the inequality true?

$|n| > 6$

    a. ${}^-5$ **b.** ${}^-2$
    c. ${}^-8$ **d.** ${}^-6$

5. Use $A = \frac{1}{2}bh$. Find b when $A = 60 \text{ ft}^2$ and $h = 8$ ft.

    a. 120 ft
    b. 15 ft
    c. 8 ft
    d. 6 ft

6. 714,288 subtracted from 800,379 is:

    a. ${}^-86,091$ **b.** 86,091
    c. 86,451   **d.** 196,551

7. Estimate by rounding.

$$3611.42 \times 268$$

    a. 600,000
    b. 800,000
    c. 1,200,000
    d. 12,000,000

8. Which is the greatest number?

    a. 0.00189   **b.** 0.01890
    c. 0.10890   **d.** 0.18900

9. Choose the product.

0.91×0.37

    a. 0.3367
    b. 1.28
    c. 33.67
    d. not given

10. Choose the product of 14,027 and 245.

    a. 154,297   **b.** 3,436,615
    c. 2,800,000   **d.** 3,460,115

11. Choose the number sentence that represents the Commutative Property of Addition.

    a. $\frac{3}{5} + \frac{1}{2} + \frac{1}{5} = n$
    b. $\frac{3}{5} + \frac{1}{5} = \frac{1}{5} + \frac{3}{5}$
    c. $\frac{3}{5} + 0 = \frac{3}{5}$
    d. $\frac{3}{5} + \frac{{}^-3}{5} = 0$

12. When $x = \frac{1}{3}$ and $y = \frac{1}{2}$, which expression has a value of $\frac{5}{12}$?

    a. $x + y - \frac{5}{12}$ **b.** $x + y + \frac{5}{12}$
    c. $x - y + \frac{5}{12}$ **d.** $x - y - \frac{5}{12}$

13. Evaluate $2a^3 - 5b$, when $a = 3$ and $b = 5$.

    a. $^-7$
    b. 29
    c. 79
    d. 235

14. Choose the scientific notation of 53,000.

    a. 5.3×10^4
    b. 5.3×10^5
    c. 53×10^4,
    d. 53×10^5

15. Add.

$^-18 + {}^-3$

    a. 21
    b. 15
    c. $^-15$
    d. $^-21$

16. Simplify:

$6\frac{2}{5} + 4\frac{1}{2} + 1\frac{3}{5}$

    a. 11
    b. $11\frac{1}{2}$
    c. $12\frac{1}{2}$
    d. not given

17. A chef used $2\frac{3}{4}$ lb of strawberries, $1\frac{1}{2}$ lb of grapes, and $3\frac{5}{8}$ lb of bananas. How many pounds of fruit did the chef use?

    a. $6\frac{9}{14}$ lb   **b.** $6\frac{7}{8}$ lb
    c. $7\frac{1}{8}$ lb   **d.** $7\frac{7}{8}$ lb

18. Which does *not* name an integer?

    a. $\frac{6}{3}$
    b. 0
    c. $\frac{^-1}{2}$
    d. $^-14$

19. Add.

$^-13 + 26$

    a. $^-39$
    b. $^-13$
    c. 13
    d. 39

20. Solve.

$y + (9 - 4.28) = 18$

    a. $y = 12.72$
    b. $y = 13.28$
    c. $y = 22.72$
    d. not given

21. Simplify:

$^-10 + (^-6 - 7) \times {}^-2$

    a. 46
    b. 16
    c. $^-16$
    d. $^-46$

22. The temperature at noon was 6°F. It dropped 8 degrees. What is the temperature now?

    a. $^-14$°F   **b.** $^-2$°F
    c. 2°F   **d.** 14°F

Tell About It

Explain how you solved the problem. Show all your work.

23. Dana spends half of her money on a new book. She then spends half of the money she has left on lunch. Then Dana buys a bus pass with half of the remaining money. After these three purchases, Dana has $2.25 left. How much money did she have to begin with?

Fractions: Multiplication, Division, and Probability

We are just about to go home when Rebecca remembers the special birthday cupcakes her mom made.

There are 24 **KIDS** in the class.
Rebecca has 24 **CUPCAKES**.

X So what's the problem?

Rebecca wants Mrs. Fibonacci to have a cupcake, too.

Everyone is going crazy trying to figure out what fraction of a cupcake each person will get.

I'm the first to figure out the answer.

I raise my hand and tell Mrs. Fibonacci I'm allergic to cupcakes.

**EVERYONE (24) believes me and gets ONE (1) cupcake.
NO ONE (0) has to figure out fractions.**

From *Math Curse* by
Jon Scieszka and Lane Smith

In this chapter you will:

Estimate and find products and
   quotients of fractions and
   mixed numbers
Learn about multiplication and division
   expressions and equations with fractions
Find the probability of simple and
   compound events
Make predictions based on probability
Solve problems by using a diagram

Critical Thinking/Finding Together

In a group of 50 people, $\frac{3}{5}$ are male
and $\frac{1}{5}$ of the males wear glasses.
How many of the males wear glasses?
How many females wear glasses?

Multiply Fractions by Fractions

Ms. Amazing is a great magician. She can take a red rope that is $\frac{3}{8}$ yd long and change $\frac{2}{3}$ of it into a blue rope. How long is the blue part of the rope?

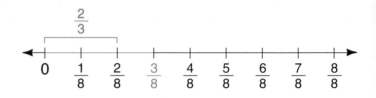

To find how long the blue part of the rope, *n*, is,

multiply: $\frac{2}{3} \times \frac{3}{8}$ yd = *n*.

▶ **To multiply a fraction by a fraction:**

- Multiply the numerators.
  Then multiply the denominators.

$$\frac{2}{3} \times \frac{3}{8} = \frac{2 \times 3}{3 \times 8}$$

- Write the product in simplest form.

$$= \frac{6}{24} = \frac{6 \div 6}{24 \div 6} = \frac{1}{4}$$

The blue part of the rope is $\frac{1}{4}$ yd long.

simplest form

▶ **You can also use the greatest common factor (GCF) to multiply a fraction by a fraction.**

- Divide *any* numerator and denominator by their GCF.

$$\frac{2}{3} \times \frac{3}{8} = \frac{\overset{1}{\cancel{2}}}{\underset{1}{\cancel{3}}} \times \frac{\overset{1}{\cancel{3}}}{\underset{4}{\cancel{8}}}$$

GCF of 2 and 8: 2
GCF of 3 and 3: 3

- Multiply the numerators.
  Then multiply the denominators.
  The product will be in simplest form.

$$= \frac{1 \times 1}{1 \times 4}$$

$$= \frac{1}{4}$$

simplest form

Study these examples.

$$\frac{4}{15} \times \frac{5}{6} = \frac{\overset{2}{\cancel{4}}}{\underset{3}{\cancel{15}}} \times \frac{\overset{1}{\cancel{5}}}{\underset{3}{\cancel{6}}}$$

$$= \frac{2 \times 1}{3 \times 3} = \frac{2}{9}$$

simplest form

Draw a diagram to illustrate $\frac{2}{3} \times \frac{3}{4}$.

Then write a multiplication sentence.

$$\frac{2}{3} \times \frac{3}{4} = \frac{6}{12} = \frac{1}{2}$$

$\left.\frac{2}{3}\right\{$

$\frac{3}{4}$

Multiply. Use the GCF to simplify whenever possible.

1. $\dfrac{7}{18} \times \dfrac{3}{5}$
2. $\dfrac{12}{20} \times \dfrac{5}{6}$
3. $\dfrac{5}{9} \times \dfrac{2}{3}$
4. $\dfrac{3}{4} \times \dfrac{2}{9}$
5. $\dfrac{7}{12} \times \dfrac{1}{7}$

6. $\dfrac{9}{16} \times \dfrac{4}{5}$
7. $\dfrac{4}{21} \times \dfrac{1}{8}$
8. $\dfrac{14}{18} \times \dfrac{2}{3}$
9. $\dfrac{24}{50} \times \dfrac{10}{12}$
10. $\dfrac{1}{9} \times \dfrac{1}{10}$

11. $\dfrac{9}{10} \times \dfrac{1}{2} \times \dfrac{2}{9}$
12. $\dfrac{5}{8} \times \dfrac{2}{3} \times \dfrac{7}{10}$
13. $\dfrac{3}{4} \times \dfrac{1}{6} \times \dfrac{2}{5}$

14. $\dfrac{5}{12} \times \dfrac{4}{5} \times \dfrac{2}{3}$
15. $\dfrac{4}{5} \times \dfrac{1}{2} \times \dfrac{3}{8}$
16. $\dfrac{3}{5} \times \dfrac{5}{7} \times \dfrac{7}{9} \times \dfrac{9}{11}$

Draw a diagram to illustrate each product. Then write a multiplication sentence. Explain your diagram.

17. $\dfrac{3}{4} \times \dfrac{1}{5}$
18. $\dfrac{5}{8} \times \dfrac{1}{3}$
19. $\dfrac{3}{7} \times \dfrac{5}{6}$
20. $\dfrac{8}{10} \times \dfrac{1}{2}$
21. $\dfrac{7}{8} \times \dfrac{3}{4}$

Problem Solving

22. Harold is following a cookie recipe. The recipe calls for $\dfrac{1}{2}$ cup of butter. If Harold wants to make $\dfrac{1}{2}$ as many cookies as the recipe allows for, how much butter should he use?

23. Ebony lifts weights $\dfrac{3}{4}$ hour a day 5 days a week. Adam lifts weights $\dfrac{1}{2}$ as long 2 days a week and twice as long 3 days a week. How many hours does Adam lift weights each week?

24. In water, sound travels approximately $\dfrac{9}{10}$ of a mile per second. How far does sound travel in $\dfrac{1}{3}$ second?

25. A can holds $\dfrac{7}{8}$ qt of water. How much water is in the can when it is $\dfrac{2}{3}$ full? when it is $\dfrac{3}{4}$ full?

26. Of the students in the sophomore class, $\dfrac{2}{5}$ have cameras; $\dfrac{1}{4}$ of the students with cameras join the photography club. What fraction of the students in the sophomore class does not join the photography club?

CRITICAL THINKING

Is each product correct? Write *Yes* or *No*. If no, explain the error made, then write the correct product.

27. $\dfrac{3}{5} \times \dfrac{10}{13} = \dfrac{6}{13}$
28. $\dfrac{4}{9} \times \dfrac{1}{9} = \dfrac{4}{1}$
29. $\dfrac{7}{11} \times \dfrac{1}{7} = \dfrac{8}{18}$
30. $\dfrac{1}{8} \times \dfrac{1}{6} = \dfrac{1}{14}$

Multiply Fractions and Whole Numbers

Nancy uses $\frac{2}{3}$ ft of silk to make a bow for a package. How much silk is needed for 4 bows?

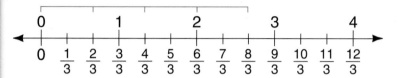

To find the amount of silk needed, s, multiply: $4 \times \frac{2}{3}$ ft $= s$.

► **To multiply a fraction and a whole number:**

- Rename the whole number as a fraction with a denominator of 1.

$$4 \times \frac{2}{3} = \frac{4}{1} \times \frac{2}{3}$$

- Multiply the numerators. Then multiply the denominators.

$$= \frac{4 \times 2}{1 \times 3}$$

- Write the product in simplest form.

$$= \frac{8}{3} = 2\frac{2}{3} \longrightarrow s = 2\frac{2}{3}$$

Nancy needs $2\frac{2}{3}$ ft of silk.

Study these examples.

Multiply: $3 \times \frac{1}{4}$

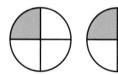

$3 \times \frac{1}{4} = \frac{3}{1} \times \frac{1}{4}$

$\quad = \frac{3 \times 1}{1 \times 4} = \frac{3}{4}$

$3 \times \frac{1}{4} = \frac{3}{4}$

Find: $\frac{3}{5}$ of $9.50

Remember: "of" means "times."

$$\frac{3}{5} \times \$9.50 = \frac{3}{\overset{\;}{\underset{1}{5}}} \times \frac{\overset{1.90}{\cancel{9.50}}}{1}$$

$$= \frac{3 \times 1.90}{1 \times 1} = \frac{5.70}{1} = 5.70$$

$\frac{3}{5} \times \$9.50 = \$5.70$

Remember: Rename a whole number as a fraction with a denominator of 1 before you multiply.

Multiply.

1. $4 \times \frac{3}{4}$

2. $10 \times \frac{3}{5}$

3. $18 \times \frac{1}{3}$

4. $24 \times \frac{1}{12}$

5. $25 \times \frac{4}{5}$

6. $20 \times \frac{3}{10}$

7. $9 \times \frac{3}{4}$

8. $27 \times \frac{1}{2}$

9. $\frac{5}{6} \times 18$

10. $\frac{7}{9} \times 45$

11. $\frac{4}{5} \times 12$

12. $\frac{3}{7} \times 9$

Find the product.

13. $\frac{1}{2}$ of 12

14. $\frac{1}{8}$ of 40

15. $\frac{2}{3}$ of 9

16. $\frac{3}{4}$ of 44

17. $\frac{1}{9}$ of 3

18. $\frac{3}{8}$ of 4

19. $\frac{5}{6}$ of 20

20. $\frac{3}{8}$ of 18

21. $\frac{2}{5}$ of $2

22. $\frac{5}{6}$ of $3.60

23. $\frac{1}{2}$ of $107.50

24. $\frac{2}{3}$ of $2.70

Problem Solving

25. David is making 12 flags for the parade. Each flag requires $\frac{2}{3}$ yd of material. How many yards of material are needed?

26. Rori budgets $\frac{3}{10}$ of her $540 weekly income for rent. How much money is not budgeted for rent each week?

27. Sociologists have determined that $\frac{2}{5}$ of the people in the world are shy. A personnel manager is interviewing 150 people. How many of these people might be shy?

28. A mathematics exam contains 75 questions. Amos answers $\frac{4}{5}$ of the questions correctly. How many questions does he answer incorrectly?

29. Of the 24 players on the football team, $\frac{1}{4}$ are first-year players and $\frac{1}{3}$ are second-year players. How many of the players are in their first or second year?

CHALLENGE — Algebra

Find the whole-number value for each variable.

30. $\frac{1}{a} \cdot 48 = 3$

31. $\frac{1}{b} \cdot 96 = 12$

32. $\frac{1}{c} \cdot 100 = 4$

33. $\frac{e}{7} \cdot 56 = 32$

34. $\frac{f}{6} \cdot 42 = 35$

35. $\frac{d}{9} \cdot 99 = 88$

Properties of Multiplication

The properties of multiplication can help you multiply with fractions.

Commutative Property: $a \times b = b \times a$

$$\frac{2}{5} \times \frac{5}{6} = \frac{5}{6} \times \frac{2}{5}$$

$$\frac{\cancel{2}^{1}}{\cancel{5}_{1}} \times \frac{\cancel{5}^{1}}{\cancel{6}_{3}} = \frac{\cancel{5}^{1}}{\cancel{6}_{3}} \times \frac{\cancel{2}^{1}}{\cancel{5}_{1}}$$

> **Think** "order"

$$\frac{1}{3} = \frac{1}{3}$$

Associative Property: $(a \times b) \times c = a \times (b \times c)$

$$\left(\frac{1}{3} \times \frac{1}{2}\right) \times 14 = \frac{1}{3} \times \left(\frac{1}{2} \times 14\right)$$

$$\frac{1}{\cancel{6}_{3}} \times \frac{\cancel{14}^{7}}{1} = \frac{1}{3} \times \frac{\cancel{14}^{7}}{\cancel{2}_{1}}$$

> **Think** "grouping"

$$\frac{7}{3} = \frac{7}{3}$$

Identity Property: $a \times 1 = 1 \times a = a$

$$\frac{4}{7} \times 1 = \frac{4}{7}$$

> **Think** "same"

$$1 \times \frac{4}{7} = \frac{4}{7}$$

Zero Property: $a \times 0 = 0 \times a = 0$

$$\frac{3}{4} \times 0 = 0$$

> **Think** "0 product"

$$0 \times \frac{3}{4} = 0$$

Distributive Property of Multiplication Over Addition: $a \times (b + c) = (a \times b) + (a \times c)$

$$\frac{1}{2} \times \left(\frac{4}{5} + \frac{2}{5}\right) = \left(\frac{1}{2} \times \frac{4}{5}\right) + \left(\frac{1}{2} \times \frac{2}{5}\right)$$

> **Think** "same factor across addends"

$$\frac{1}{\cancel{2}_{1}} \times \frac{\cancel{6}^{3}}{5} = \left(\frac{1}{\cancel{2}_{1}} \times \frac{\cancel{4}^{2}}{5}\right) + \left(\frac{1}{\cancel{2}_{1}} \times \frac{\cancel{2}^{1}}{5}\right)$$

$$\frac{3}{5} = \frac{2}{5} + \frac{1}{5}$$

$$\frac{3}{5} = \frac{3}{5}$$

Find the value of *n*. Use the properties of multiplication.

1. $\frac{1}{5} \times \frac{3}{4} = \frac{3}{4} \times n$

2. $\frac{3}{8} \times n = \frac{3}{8}$

3. $n \times \frac{5}{6} = \frac{5}{6}$

4. $\frac{1}{2} \times n = 0$

5. $\frac{1}{3} \times 0 = n \times \frac{1}{3}$

6. $\frac{7}{10} \times n = \frac{2}{3} \times \frac{7}{10}$

7. $\frac{1}{4} \times \left(\frac{1}{5} \times \frac{1}{6}\right) = \left(\frac{1}{4} \times n\right) \times \frac{1}{6}$

8. $n \times \left(4 + \frac{1}{3}\right) = \left(\frac{1}{2} \times 4\right) + \left(\frac{1}{2} \times \frac{1}{3}\right)$

Reciprocals (Multiplicative Inverses)

Two numbers with a product of 1 are called reciprocals or multiplicative inverses of each other.

$$\frac{3}{4} \times \frac{4}{3} = \frac{\overset{1}{\cancel{3}}}{\cancel{4}} \times \frac{\overset{1}{\cancel{4}}}{\cancel{3}} = \frac{1}{1} = 1 \leftarrow \boxed{\frac{3}{4} \text{ and } \frac{4}{3} \text{ are reciprocals.}}$$

$$6 \times \frac{1}{6} = \frac{\overset{1}{\cancel{6}}}{1} \times \frac{1}{\cancel{6}} = \frac{1}{1} = 1 \leftarrow \boxed{6 \text{ and } \frac{1}{6} \text{ are reciprocals.}}$$

▶ **To find the reciprocal of a number:**

- Write the number as a fraction.

  $10 = \frac{10}{1}$

- *Invert* the fraction by exchanging the position of the numerator and the denominator.

  $\frac{10}{1} \diagdown \frac{1}{10}$

- Check. Multiply the reciprocals to verify that their product is 1.

  $\frac{\overset{1}{\cancel{10}}}{1} \times \frac{1}{\cancel{10}} = \frac{1}{1} = 1$ $\boxed{10 \text{ and } \frac{1}{10} \text{ are reciprocals.}}$

$\boxed{\text{Inverse Property of Multiplication } \frac{a}{b} \times \frac{b}{a} = 1, \text{ where } a, b \neq 0.}$

Write the reciprocal of each number.

9. 15 **10.** 9 **11.** $\frac{1}{7}$ **12.** $\frac{11}{12}$ **13.** $\frac{7}{4}$ **14.** $\frac{12}{5}$

Explain how using properties or reciprocals can make these computations easier. Then compute.

15. $\frac{3}{5} \times 14 \times \frac{1}{2}$

16. $\frac{3}{4} \times \frac{7}{12} \times 0$

17. $(\frac{1}{4} \times \frac{7}{8}) \times 16$

18. $(46 \times \frac{1}{9}) \times 9$

19. $\frac{7}{8} \times (\frac{8}{7} \times 33)$

20. $\frac{4}{5} \times (9 \times \frac{5}{4})$

21. $\frac{5}{7} \times \frac{5}{8} \times \frac{14}{25}$

22. $14 \times \frac{14}{15} \times 15$

23. $\frac{3}{7} \times 9 \times 21$

24. Explain in your Math Journal why:

a. 0 does not have a reciprocal. **b.** 1 has itself as its reciprocal.

Multiply Mixed Numbers

The weight of water is $62\frac{1}{2}$ lb per cubic foot. What is the weight of $2\frac{4}{5}$ cubic feet of water?

To find the weight of $2\frac{4}{5}$ cubic feet of water, w, multiply: $2\frac{4}{5} \times 62\frac{1}{2}$ lb $= w$.

First estimate by rounding:

$2\frac{4}{5} \times 62\frac{1}{2} \longrightarrow 3 \times 63 = 189$

Then multiply.

▶ **To multiply with mixed numbers:**

- Rename both factors as fractions greater than or equal to one.

- Simplify using the GCF where possible.

  GCF of 14 and 2: 2
  GCF of 5 and 125: 5

- Multiply the numerators. Then multiply the denominators.

- Rename the product as a whole or mixed number when needed.

$$2\frac{4}{5} \times 62\frac{1}{2} = \frac{14}{5} \times \frac{125}{2}$$

$$= \frac{\overset{7}{\cancel{14}}}{\underset{1}{\cancel{5}}} \times \frac{\overset{25}{\cancel{125}}}{\underset{1}{\cancel{2}}}$$

$$= \frac{7 \times 25}{1 \times 1}$$

$$= \frac{175}{1} = 175$$

The weight of $2\frac{4}{5}$ cubic feet of water is 175 lb.

Think
175 lb is close to the estimate of 189 lb.

Study these examples.

$$\frac{2}{3} \times 3\frac{3}{8} = \frac{2}{3} \times \frac{27}{8}$$

Think
Estimate: $1 \times 3 = 3$

$$= \frac{\overset{1}{\cancel{2}}}{\underset{1}{\cancel{3}}} \times \frac{\overset{9}{\cancel{27}}}{\underset{4}{\cancel{8}}} = \frac{9}{4} = 2\frac{1}{4}$$

$$9 \times 5\frac{2}{3} = \frac{9}{1} \times \frac{17}{3}$$

Think
Estimate: $9 \times 6 = 54$

$$= \frac{\overset{3}{\cancel{9}}}{1} \times \frac{17}{\underset{1}{\cancel{3}}} = \frac{51}{1} = 51$$

Estimate each product by rounding.

1. $7\frac{2}{3} \times 4\frac{1}{4}$

2. $9\frac{1}{5} \times 3\frac{7}{12}$

3. $8 \times 9\frac{7}{8}$

4. $7\frac{1}{2} \times 10$

5. $\frac{5}{6} \times 32\frac{4}{7}$

6. $75\frac{1}{10} \times \frac{3}{5}$

7. $12\frac{1}{4} \times 5\frac{1}{4}$

8. $15\frac{7}{8} \times 1\frac{5}{9}$

Multiply. Estimate to help you.

9. $\frac{2}{3} \times 2\frac{1}{2}$ 10. $\frac{3}{4} \times 2\frac{2}{3}$ 11. $3\frac{1}{7} \times 4\frac{2}{3}$ 12. $2\frac{2}{5} \times 3\frac{1}{6}$

13. $2\frac{1}{10} \times \frac{6}{7}$ 14. $5\frac{5}{8} \times \frac{5}{9}$ 15. $1\frac{1}{6} \times 9$ 16. $3\frac{1}{8} \times 12$

17. $8\frac{1}{6} \times 3\frac{3}{7}$ 18. $3\frac{1}{9} \times 2\frac{1}{7}$ 19. $\frac{3}{4}$ of $2\frac{2}{3}$ 20. $\frac{5}{9}$ of $2\frac{1}{4}$

21. $6 \times 5\frac{3}{5} \times 1\frac{2}{3}$ 22. $6\frac{2}{3} \times 7 \times 1\frac{1}{5}$ 23. $2\frac{1}{6} \times 5\frac{1}{3} \times 1\frac{7}{8}$

Compare. Write <, =, or >.

24. $2\frac{1}{2} \times 3\frac{1}{4}$? $2\frac{1}{4} \times 3\frac{1}{2}$ 25. $1\frac{2}{3} \times 3\frac{1}{4}$? $3\frac{1}{4} \times 1\frac{2}{3}$

26. $3\frac{3}{5} \times 1\frac{1}{2}$? $2\frac{1}{2} \times 1\frac{3}{4}$ 27. $6\frac{1}{4} \times 2\frac{1}{4}$? $3\frac{1}{2} \times 4\frac{1}{8}$

Find the value of n. Use the properties of multiplication.

28. $n \times 1 = 3\frac{1}{2}$ 29. $n \times 4\frac{1}{5} = 4\frac{1}{5} \times 5$ 30. $1\frac{1}{3} \times n = 0$

31. $(n \times \frac{1}{2}) \times 4 = \frac{1}{3} \times (\frac{1}{2} \times 4)$ 32. $25(\frac{2}{5} + \frac{8}{15}) = (25 \times \frac{2}{5}) + (25 \times n)$

Problem Solving

33. One serving of meat is about $3\frac{1}{2}$ oz. If a person eats 2 servings a day, how many ounces of meat is this?

34. Round steak contains $3\frac{1}{2}$ servings per pound. How many servings are there in 10 lb of round steak?

35. The weight of water is $62\frac{1}{2}$ lb per cubic foot. What is the weight of $5\frac{1}{3}$ cubic feet of water?

36. A long-playing record makes $33\frac{1}{3}$ revolutions per minute. If it plays for 42 min, how many revolutions does it make?

MENTAL MATH

Find each product.

37. $5 \times 4\frac{1}{4}$ $5 \times (4 + \frac{1}{4}) = (5 \times 4) + (5 \times \frac{1}{4}) = 20 + \frac{5}{4} = 20 + 1\frac{1}{4} = 21\frac{1}{4}$

38. $7 \times 9\frac{2}{7}$ 39. $3 \times 6\frac{1}{3}$ 40. $9 \times 5\frac{5}{18}$ 41. $4 \times 2\frac{3}{8}$

Meaning of Division

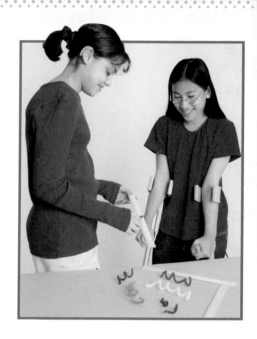

Each loop in a spring takes $\frac{3}{8}$ in. of wire. How many loops can be made from 3 in. of wire?

To find how many loops, n, can be made, divide: $3 \div \frac{3}{8} = n$.

.Think..........................
How many $\frac{3}{8}$s are in 3?
....

You can use a *diagram* to help you divide 3 by $\frac{3}{8}$.

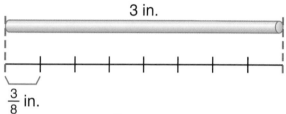

3 in.

$\frac{3}{8}$ in.

Count the number of $\frac{3}{8}$ in. units. There are 8 units. So $3 \div \frac{3}{8} = 8$.

Eight $\frac{3}{8}$-in. loops can be made from 3 in. of wire.

Study these examples.

Write a division sentence for each diagram.

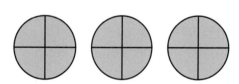

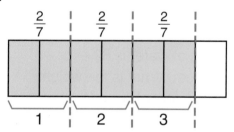

.Think..........................
How many $\frac{1}{4}$s are in 3?
....

3 wholes divided into fourths make 12 equal parts.

Division sentence: $3 \div \frac{1}{4} = 12$

.Think..........................
How many $\frac{2}{7}$s are in $\frac{6}{7}$?
....

1 whole is divided into sevenths. There are three $\frac{2}{7}$s in $\frac{6}{7}$.

Division sentence: $\frac{6}{7} \div \frac{2}{7} = 3$

Write a division sentence for each diagram.

1.

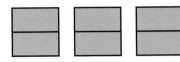

How many halves are in 3?

2.

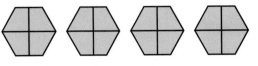

How many fourths are in 4?

3.

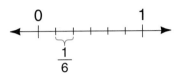

How many $\frac{1}{6}$s are in $\frac{5}{6}$?

4.

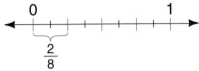

How many $\frac{2}{8}$s are in $\frac{6}{8}$?

5.

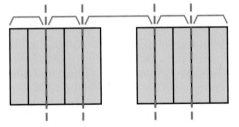

6.

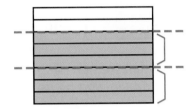

7.

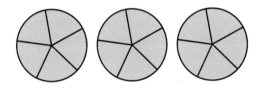

8.

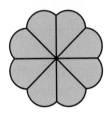

Draw a diagram to show each division. Write each quotient. Explain how your drawing illustrates the division.

9. $4 \div \frac{1}{2}$ **10.** $3 \div \frac{1}{3}$ **11.** $\frac{4}{5} \div \frac{1}{5}$ **12.** $\frac{8}{10} \div \frac{2}{10}$

13. $2 \div \frac{2}{6}$ **14.** $3 \div \frac{3}{7}$ **15.** $1 \div \frac{1}{6}$ **16.** $1 \div \frac{3}{6}$

Write About It

17. Draw diagrams to help you divide by the unit fractions in these exercises: (a) $2 \div \frac{1}{2}$; (b) $1 \div \frac{1}{3}$; (c) $3 \div \frac{1}{5}$.

> A unit fraction is a fraction with a numerator of 1.

18. Write a rule in your Math Journal that tells what happens when you divide a whole number by a unit fraction.

Divide Fractions by Fractions

Eduardo discovered a short way to divide fractions by examining some division sentences and the related multiplication sentences.

	Division Sentence	Multiplication Sentence
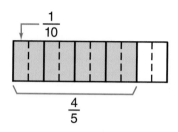	$\dfrac{4}{5} \div \dfrac{1}{10} = 8$	$\dfrac{4}{\cancel{5}} \times \dfrac{\cancel{10}^{\,2}}{1} = \dfrac{8}{1} = 8$
	$\dfrac{3}{5} \div \dfrac{1}{10} = 6$	$\dfrac{3}{\cancel{5}} \times \dfrac{\cancel{10}^{\,2}}{1} = \dfrac{6}{1} = 6$
	$\dfrac{9}{10} \div \dfrac{1}{10} = 9$	$\dfrac{9}{\cancel{10}} \times \dfrac{\cancel{10}^{\,1}}{1} = \dfrac{9}{1} = 9$

reciprocals

Eduardo concluded that *dividing by a fraction* gives the same result as *multiplying by its reciprocal*.

▶ **To divide a fraction by a fraction:**

- Multiply by the reciprocal of the divisor.

- Simplify using the GCF, where possible. Then multiply the numerators and the denominators.

- Rename the product as a whole or mixed number when needed.

reciprocals

$$\dfrac{3}{4} \div \dfrac{1}{16} = \dfrac{3}{4} \times \dfrac{16}{1}$$

$$= \dfrac{3}{\cancel{4}_{1}} \times \dfrac{\cancel{16}^{\,4}}{1} = \dfrac{3 \times 4}{1 \times 1}$$

$$= \dfrac{12}{1} = 12$$

whole number

Study these examples.

$$\dfrac{7}{20} \div \dfrac{1}{5} = \dfrac{7}{20} \times \dfrac{5}{1}$$

Reciprocal of $\dfrac{1}{5}$ is 5, or $\dfrac{5}{1}$.

$$= \dfrac{7}{\cancel{20}_{4}} \times \dfrac{\cancel{5}^{\,1}}{1} = \dfrac{7}{4} = 1\dfrac{3}{4}$$

mixed number

$$\dfrac{11}{14} \div \dfrac{11}{12} = \dfrac{11}{14} \times \dfrac{12}{11}$$

$$= \dfrac{\cancel{11}^{\,1}}{\cancel{14}_{7}} \times \dfrac{\cancel{12}^{\,6}}{\cancel{11}_{1}}$$

$$= \dfrac{6}{7} \quad \longleftarrow \text{fraction}$$

Write the value of each variable.

1. $\frac{9}{13} \div \frac{3}{5} = \frac{9}{13} \times \frac{5}{3} = a$

2. $\frac{12}{25} \div \frac{3}{10} = \frac{12}{25} \times \frac{10}{3} = b$

3. $\frac{3}{7} \div \frac{1}{14} = \frac{3}{7} \times \frac{x}{y} = z$

4. $\frac{1}{8} \div \frac{1}{16} = \frac{p}{r} \times \frac{16}{1} = s$

Solve for n. Draw a diagram to help you.

5. $\frac{1}{2} \div \frac{1}{4} = n$

6. $\frac{2}{5} \div \frac{1}{10} = n$

7. $\frac{1}{4} \div \frac{1}{16} = n$

8. $\frac{1}{2} \div \frac{1}{10} = n$

9. $n = \frac{7}{8} \div \frac{1}{8}$

10. $n = \frac{5}{6} \div \frac{1}{6}$

11. $n = \frac{6}{8} \div \frac{3}{8}$

12. $n = \frac{6}{16} \div \frac{2}{16}$

Find the quotient.

13. $\frac{5}{8} \div \frac{5}{8}$

14. $\frac{2}{5} \div \frac{2}{5}$

15. $\frac{5}{24} \div \frac{5}{12}$

16. $\frac{6}{13} \div \frac{3}{26}$

17. $\frac{2}{9} \div \frac{1}{3}$

18. $\frac{1}{8} \div \frac{1}{5}$

19. $\frac{16}{25} \div \frac{3}{5}$

20. $\frac{9}{28} \div \frac{3}{7}$

21. $\frac{14}{15} \div \frac{8}{9}$

22. $\frac{9}{10} \div \frac{6}{7}$

23. $\frac{1}{6} \div \frac{1}{11}$

24. $\frac{1}{11} \div \frac{1}{6}$

 **Write a division sentence.**

25. How many $\frac{1}{16}$s are there in $\frac{3}{8}$?

26. How many $\frac{1}{100}$s are there in $\frac{1}{10}$?

27. How many $\frac{1}{8}$-ft strips can Eric cut from a $\frac{1}{2}$-ft piece of wood?

28. How many $\frac{1}{16}$-yd strips can Karen cut from a $\frac{3}{4}$-yd piece of leather?

29. If $\frac{13}{6}$ is divided by a certain fraction $\frac{x}{y}$, the result is $\frac{2}{3}$. What is $\frac{x}{y}$?

30. Ms. Appell bought $\frac{1}{3}$ bushel of apples. She used $\frac{3}{4}$ of the apples to make applesauce. What part of a bushel did she use for applesauce?

31. Explain why the quotient of $5 \div \frac{2}{3}$ is not a whole number.

Estimate Quotients of Fractions and Mixed Numbers

▶ You can compare the dividend and the divisor to determine if the quotient of two fractions *is less than 1* or *is greater than 1.*

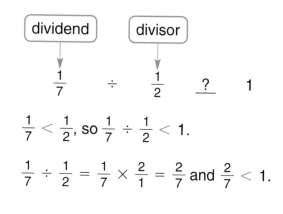

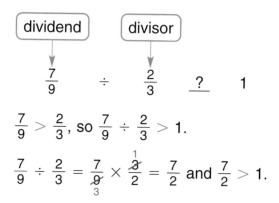

- When the dividend is less than the divisor, the quotient is less than 1.
- When the dividend is greater than the divisor, the quotient is greater than 1.

▶ You can round mixed numbers to the nearest compatible whole numbers to help you estimate quotients.

Estimate: $9\frac{5}{6} \div 2\frac{1}{3}$.

Think
$9\frac{5}{6} > 2\frac{1}{3}$, so the quotient is greater than 1.

$9\frac{5}{6} \div 2\frac{1}{3}$

$10 \div 2 = 5$ ← estimated quotient

Estimate: $3 \div 11\frac{1}{2}$.

Think
$3 < 11\frac{1}{2}$, so the quotient is less than 1.

$3 \div 11\frac{1}{2}$

$3 \div 12 = \frac{3}{12} = \frac{1}{4}$ ← estimated quotient

Compare the dividend and the divisor to determine whether the quotient is less than 1 or is greater than 1. Write < or >. Then find the quotient.

1. $\frac{6}{7} \div \frac{3}{7}$ _?_ 1

2. $\frac{2}{5} \div \frac{4}{5}$ _?_ 1

3. $\frac{1}{3} \div \frac{1}{10}$ _?_ 1

4. $\frac{1}{15} \div \frac{1}{12}$ _?_ 1

5. $\frac{3}{7} \div \frac{3}{11}$ _?_ 1

6. $\frac{4}{5} \div \frac{4}{9}$ _?_ 1

7. $\frac{2}{3} \div \frac{3}{4}$ _?_ 1

8. $\frac{7}{8} \div \frac{5}{6}$ _?_ 1

9. $\frac{5}{9} \div \frac{7}{18}$ _?_ 1

10. $\frac{17}{36} \div \frac{5}{12}$ _?_ 1

11. $\frac{11}{12} \div \frac{3}{7}$ _?_ 1

12. $\frac{4}{9} \div \frac{9}{10}$ _?_ 1

13. $\frac{1}{8} \div \frac{3}{7}$ _?_ 1

14. $\frac{3}{10} \div \frac{9}{11}$ _?_ 1

15. $\frac{5}{6} \div \frac{4}{5}$ _?_ 1

16. $\frac{3}{8} \div \frac{5}{7}$ _?_ 1

Estimate. Round each mixed number to the nearest compatible whole number.

17. $8\frac{1}{3} \div 1\frac{5}{6}$

18. $9\frac{3}{4} \div 4\frac{3}{4}$

19. $11 \div 1\frac{7}{8}$

20. $17 \div 2\frac{1}{4}$

21. $6\frac{1}{8} \div 9\frac{2}{5}$

22. $3\frac{8}{9} \div 12\frac{1}{9}$

23. $11\frac{1}{2} \div \frac{11}{12}$

24. $\frac{7}{8} \div 9\frac{1}{2}$

Compare. Write < or >. Use estimation to help you.

25. $3 \div \frac{1}{12}$ _?_ 1

26. $\frac{1}{2} \div \frac{3}{7}$ _?_ 1

27. $2 \div \frac{1}{10}$ _?_ $\frac{1}{10} \div 2$

28. $9 \div 3$ _?_ $9 \div 3\frac{1}{3}$

29. $\frac{7}{8} \div 1\frac{1}{2}$ _?_ $1\frac{1}{2} \div \frac{7}{8}$

30. $10\frac{5}{6} \div 2\frac{3}{8}$ _?_ $9\frac{5}{6} \div 1\frac{3}{8}$

Problem Solving

31. If $2\frac{7}{9}$ yd of material is cut into 5 pieces of the same length, about how long is each piece?

32. A piece of wire $\frac{3}{5}$ yd long is to be cut into 6 pieces of the same length. About how long is each piece?

33. About how much will each person get if 10 people share $12\frac{1}{2}$ qt of strawberries equally?

CRITICAL THINKING

34. When the dividend stays the same and the divisor increases, what happens to the quotient?

35. Write in your Math Journal whether your conclusion in exercise 34 is true for whole numbers, decimals, and fractions. Explain.

Divide with Whole and Mixed Numbers

A curtain requires $2\frac{3}{5}$ yd of material. How many curtains can be made from 39 yd of material?

To find how many curtains, c, divide: $39 \div 2\frac{3}{5} = c$.

First estimate by using compatible numbers: $39 \div 3 = 13$. Then divide.

▶ **To divide with whole numbers and mixed numbers:**

- Rename the whole number as a fraction with a denominator of 1 and the mixed number as a fraction greater than one.

$$39 \div 2\frac{3}{5} = \frac{39}{1} \div \frac{13}{5}$$

- Multiply by the reciprocal of the divisor. Simplify using the GCF where possible.

$$= \frac{\overset{3}{\cancel{39}}}{1} \times \frac{5}{\underset{1}{\cancel{13}}}$$

- Multiply the numerators. Then multiply the denominators.

$$= \frac{3 \times 5}{1 \times 1} = \frac{15}{1}$$

- Write the quotient in simplest form.

$$= 15$$

$$c = 15$$

Fifteen $2\frac{3}{5}$-yd curtains can be made from 39 yd of material.

........**Think**........
15 is close to the estimate of 13.

Study these examples.

> When dividing with fractions, whole numbers, and mixed numbers, rename the whole numbers and mixed numbers as fractions.

Divide: $1\frac{3}{4} \div 6 = w$.

$$1\frac{3}{4} \div 6 = \frac{7}{4} \times \frac{1}{6}$$

$$= \frac{7 \times 1}{4 \times 6} = \frac{7}{24}$$

$$w = \frac{7}{24}$$

Divide: $1\frac{1}{2} \div \frac{1}{6} = v$.

$$1\frac{1}{2} \div \frac{1}{6} = \frac{3}{2} \div \frac{1}{6}$$

$$= \frac{3}{\underset{1}{\cancel{2}}} \times \frac{\overset{3}{\cancel{6}}}{1} = \frac{3 \times 3}{1 \times 1}$$

$$= \frac{9}{1} = 9$$

$$v = 9$$

Divide: $7\frac{1}{3} \div 1\frac{5}{6} = t$.

$$7\frac{1}{3} \div 1\frac{5}{6} = \frac{22}{3} \div \frac{11}{6}$$

$$= \frac{\overset{2}{\cancel{22}}}{\underset{1}{\cancel{3}}} \times \frac{\overset{2}{\cancel{6}}}{\underset{1}{\cancel{11}}} = \frac{2 \times 2}{1 \times 1}$$

$$= \frac{4}{1} = 4$$

$$t = 4$$

Find the value of each variable to complete the division.

1. $4\frac{2}{3} \div 6 = \frac{e}{3} \div \frac{f}{1}$

   $= \frac{e}{3} \times \frac{1}{f} = n$

2. $10\frac{1}{2} \div 1\frac{1}{2} = \frac{21}{2} \div \frac{i}{j}$

   $= \frac{21}{2} \times \frac{j}{i} = y$

Divide. Estimate to help you.

3. $9 \div \frac{3}{7}$

4. $36 \div \frac{6}{7}$

5. $27 \div \frac{3}{5}$

6. $8 \div \frac{8}{9}$

7. $\frac{5}{6} \div 10$

8. $\frac{4}{9} \div 8$

9. $\frac{11}{12} \div 22$

10. $\frac{7}{15} \div 42$

11. $32 \div 1\frac{1}{7}$

12. $6 \div 2\frac{1}{4}$

13. $26 \div 3\frac{1}{2}$

14. $84 \div 5\frac{1}{4}$

15. $2\frac{1}{3} \div \frac{1}{6}$

16. $3\frac{1}{2} \div \frac{1}{3}$

17. $5\frac{1}{4} \div \frac{11}{16}$

18. $11\frac{2}{3} \div \frac{7}{8}$

19. $5\frac{2}{3} \div 1\frac{1}{3}$

20. $5\frac{1}{7} \div 2\frac{1}{7}$

21. $4\frac{4}{5} \div 1\frac{1}{5}$

22. $3\frac{1}{4} \div 1\frac{1}{2}$

Compare. Write <, =, or >.

23. $16 \div \frac{8}{9}$ __?__ $10 \div \frac{1}{2}$

24. $\frac{1}{3} \div 3\frac{3}{10}$ __?__ $\frac{2}{3} \div 6\frac{3}{5}$

25. $8 \div \frac{3}{4}$ __?__ $6 \div \frac{3}{4}$

26. $2\frac{1}{7} \div 15$ __?__ $2\frac{1}{3} \div \frac{1}{3}$

Problem Solving

27. How many $\frac{2}{3}$-cup sugar bowls can be filled from 10 cups of sugar?

28. At a rate of $22\frac{1}{2}$ ft per hour, how long will it take an insect to walk 90 ft?

29. After driving 240 mi, $\frac{3}{5}$ of a trip was completed. How long was the total trip? How many miles were left to drive?

30. How many boards $1\frac{1}{4}$ ft long can be cut from a board $9\frac{7}{8}$ ft long? How much of a $1\frac{1}{4}$-ft board is left over?

31. A $\frac{1}{2}$-ton weight is to be lifted equally by 5 people. How many pounds must each person lift? (*Hint:* 1 ton = 2000 pounds.)

CHALLENGE

Divide.

32. $21 \div \frac{3}{16} \div 2\frac{2}{3}$

33. $1\frac{1}{3} \div 5 \div 2\frac{3}{5}$

34. $3\frac{1}{3} \div 2\frac{1}{2} \div 1\frac{1}{3}$

Order of Operations with Fractions

You can use the order of operations to simplify mathematical expressions with fractions.

Simplify: $(3\frac{1}{3} - 1\frac{1}{3})^2 + 1\frac{1}{2}$.

Order of Operations
1. Grouping symbols
2. Exponents
3. × or ÷ left to right
4. + or − left to right

$(3\frac{1}{3} - 1\frac{1}{3})^2 + 1\frac{1}{2}$ ← Compute within parentheses first.

$(2)^2 \quad + 1\frac{1}{2}$ ← Compute exponents next.

$4 \quad + 1\frac{1}{2}$ ← Compute + or − last.

$5\frac{1}{2}$

So $(3\frac{1}{3} - 1\frac{1}{3})^2 + 1\frac{1}{2} = 5\frac{1}{2}$.

Check.

(3 Unit 1 n 3 d − 1 Unit 1 n 3 d)

∧ 2 + 1 Unit 1 n 2 d Enter = $5\frac{1}{2}$

Study these examples.

Simplify: $(\frac{2}{3})^2 - \frac{1}{5} \times \frac{1}{2}$.

Think
$(\frac{2}{3})^2 = \frac{2}{3} \times \frac{2}{3} = \frac{4}{9}$

$(\frac{2}{3})^2 - \frac{1}{5} \times \frac{1}{2}$ ← Compute exponents first.

$\frac{4}{9} - \frac{1}{5} \times \frac{1}{2}$ ← Multiply next.

$\frac{4}{9} - \frac{1}{10}$ ← Subtract last.

$\frac{40}{90} - \frac{9}{90} = \frac{31}{90}$

Simplify: $2 \times \frac{1}{3} \div 0.25$.

Think
$0.25 = \frac{1}{4}$

$2 \times \frac{1}{3} \div 0.25$ ← Compute × or ÷ left to right.

$\frac{2}{3} \div \frac{1}{4}$ ← Multiply first. Then divide.

$\frac{2}{3} \times \frac{4}{1} = \frac{8}{3} = 2\frac{2}{3}$

Simplify each mathematical expression.

1. $6 \times \frac{1}{2} \div (\frac{1}{4})^2$

2. $9 \times \frac{1}{3} \div (\frac{1}{2})^3$

3. $\frac{5}{6} + \frac{1}{6} - 0.5$

4. $\frac{4}{9} - \frac{1}{9} + \frac{2}{3}$

5. $\frac{1}{8} + 0.5 \times 16$

6. $1\frac{2}{3} - 6 \times (\frac{1}{6})^2$

Simplify. Check with a calculator.

7. $(1\frac{1}{4} \times 4) - (\frac{1}{3})^2$

8. $(8 \div 1\frac{1}{3}) + 6^2$

9. $(1\frac{2}{3} \times 1\frac{1}{2}) \div 5$

10. $(10 \div 1\frac{2}{3}) \times \frac{7}{8}$

11. $(\frac{2}{3})^2 \times (1\frac{1}{2} + 1\frac{3}{4})$

12. $1\frac{1}{3} \times (2\frac{1}{2} - 1\frac{1}{4})^2$

Distributive Property Over Subtraction

Distributive Property Over Subtraction $a \times (b - c) = (a \times b) - (a \times c)$

$$\frac{4}{5} \times (10 - \frac{5}{8}) = (\frac{4}{5} \times 10) - (\frac{4}{5} \times \frac{5}{8})$$

$$\frac{4}{5} \times 9\frac{3}{8} = (\frac{4}{5} \times \frac{10}{1}) - (\frac{4}{5} \times \frac{5}{8})$$

$$\overset{1}{\underset{1}{\frac{4}{5}}} \times \overset{15}{\underset{2}{\frac{75}{8}}} = (\overset{2}{\underset{1}{\frac{4}{5}}} \times \frac{10}{1}) - (\overset{1}{\underset{1}{\frac{4}{5}}} \times \overset{1}{\underset{2}{\frac{5}{8}}})$$

$$\frac{15}{2} = 8 - \frac{1}{2}$$

$$7\frac{1}{2} = 7\frac{1}{2}$$

Simplify using the Distributive Property.

13. $\frac{1}{8} \times (8 - \frac{8}{11})$

14. $\frac{1}{6} \times (12 - \frac{3}{5})$

15. $\frac{1}{3} \times (15 - \frac{3}{8})$

16. $\frac{3}{4} \times (4 - \frac{1}{3})$

17. $\frac{8}{9} \times (18 - \frac{1}{4})$

18. $\frac{3}{7} \times (14 - \frac{1}{9})$

MENTAL MATH

Use compatible numbers to estimate each product.

19. $\frac{5}{6}$ of 43 $\longrightarrow$ $\frac{5}{6}$ of 42 $\frac{1}{6} \times \frac{42}{1} = 7$, so $\frac{5}{6}$ of 42 $= 5 \times 7 = 35$

20. $\frac{2}{3}$ of 25

21. $\frac{3}{4}$ of 198

22. $\frac{1}{8}$ of $76

23. $\frac{1}{3}$ of $3.95

Fractions with Money

A package of copier paper costs $1.50.
Leroy bought a package for $\frac{3}{4}$ of the cost.
How much did Leroy pay?

To determine how much Leroy paid, p,
find: $\frac{3}{4}$ of $1.50 = p$.

First estimate: $\frac{3}{4}$ of $1.50 \longrightarrow \frac{3}{4}$ of $1.60

$\frac{1}{4}$ of $1.60 = $.40, so $\frac{3}{4}$ of $1.60 = $1.20.

Then compute.

$$\frac{3}{4} \text{ of } \$1.50 = \frac{3}{4} \times \$1.50 \qquad \boxed{\text{Remember: "of" means "times."}}$$

$$= \frac{3}{4} \times \frac{\$1.50}{1}$$

$$= \frac{3 \times \$1.50}{4 \times 1} = \frac{\$4.50}{4}$$

$$\begin{array}{r} \$1.125 = \$1.13 \\ 4\overline{)\$4.500} \end{array}$$

$\uparrow$
$\boxed{\text{Round to the nearest cent.}}$

$$= \$1.13$$

$$p = \$1.13$$

Leroy paid $1.13.

Think

$1.13 is close to the estimate of $1.20.

Study this example.

Divide: $8.75 ÷ $1\frac{1}{4} = d$.

$$\$8.75 \div 1\frac{1}{4} = \frac{\$8.75}{1} \div \frac{5}{4} = \frac{\$8.75}{1} \times \frac{4}{5} \quad \boxed{\text{Multiply by the reciprocal.}}$$

$\boxed{\text{Rename as fractions.}}$

$$= \frac{\overset{\$1.75}{\cancel{\$8.75}}}{1} \times \frac{4}{\underset{1}{\cancel{5}}} = \frac{\$7.00}{1} = \$7.00$$

$$d = \$7.00$$

Compute. Round to the nearest cent when necessary.

1. $\frac{1}{2}$ of $46
2. $\frac{1}{5}$ of $85
3. $\frac{1}{3}$ of $6.09
4. $\frac{1}{4}$ of $8.32

5. $\frac{3}{4}$ of $70
6. $\frac{2}{5}$ of $86
7. $\frac{2}{3}$ of $21.50
8. $\frac{3}{8}$ of $16.50

9. $3.50 $\div$ $3\frac{1}{2}$
10. $5.50 $\div$ $1\frac{2}{3}$
11. $36.75 $\div$ $3\frac{3}{4}$
12. $11.20 $\div$ $1\frac{1}{3}$

13. $14.90 $\div$ $2\frac{1}{2}$
14. $11.40 $\div$ $1\frac{1}{5}$
15. $6.65 $\div$ $1\frac{3}{4}$
16. $56 $\div$ $\frac{7}{8}$

Problem Solving

17. Hiro wants to sell the bicycle he bought originally for $220 for $\frac{3}{5}$ of that price. What is the selling price of the bicycle?

18. Mary Ann bought a computer marked $950 for $\frac{3}{4}$ of the price. How much did she pay?

19. Joni paid $8.75 for a $3\frac{1}{2}$-square-foot rug. How much is that per square foot?

20. John bought a roast that weighed $4\frac{1}{2}$ lb for $12.60. How much is that per pound?

21. Dennis spent $\frac{1}{4}$ of his $18 weekly allowance. How much money does he have left?

22. A $35 dress in a store is marked "$\frac{1}{4}$ off." What is the new price of the dress?

23. Mr. Bucks has $44,000 to divide among three local charities and five international charities. He gives the first local charity $\frac{1}{2}$, the second local charity $\frac{1}{5}$, and the third local charity $\frac{1}{8}$ of the money. How much money is left for the international charities? What fractional part of the money is that?

DO YOU REMEMBER?

Match each definition with a term in the box.

24. the whole numbers and their opposites

25. part of a region, an object, or a set

26. a number with a decimal point separating the ones from the tenths place

27. a number having a whole number part and a fraction part

> decimal
> whole number
> integers
> fraction
> mixed number

Multiplication and Division Expressions with Fractions

Miguel cuts a piece of wood into $\frac{2}{3}$-foot-long pieces. If the piece of wood is 6 ft long, how many $\frac{2}{3}$-ft pieces in all will he cut?

To find how many pieces, write and evaluate a division expression:

$s \div \frac{2}{3}$, when $s = 6$. ← Let s represent the length of the original piece of wood.

$s \div \frac{2}{3}$

$6 \div \frac{2}{3} = \frac{6}{1} \div \frac{2}{3}$ ← Replace the variable with the given value.

$= \frac{\overset{3}{\cancel{6}}}{1} \times \frac{3}{\underset{1}{\cancel{2}}}$ ← Multiply by the reciprocal of the divisor. Then simplify if possible.

$= \frac{3 \times 3}{1 \times 1}$ ← Multiply the numerators. Then multiply the denominators.

$= \frac{9}{1} = 9$ ← Write the quotient in simplest form.

$s = 9$

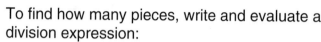

Miguel will cut nine $\frac{2}{3}$-foot-long pieces of wood.

Study these examples.

Evaluate:

$\frac{t}{7}$, when $t = 6\frac{4}{5}$.

$\frac{t}{7} = \frac{6\frac{4}{5}}{7}$ ← fraction bar means ÷

$6\frac{4}{5} \div 7 = \frac{34}{5} \div \frac{7}{1}$

$= \frac{34}{5} \times \frac{1}{7}$

$= \frac{34 \times 1}{5 \times 7} = \frac{34}{35}$ ← value

Evaluate:

$r + 7\frac{2}{9} \div s$, when $r = \frac{2}{3}$ and $s = \frac{5}{12}$.

$r + 7\frac{2}{9} \div s = \frac{2}{3} + \frac{65}{9} \div \frac{5}{12}$

$= \frac{2}{3} + \frac{\overset{13}{\cancel{65}}}{\underset{3}{\cancel{9}}} \times \frac{\overset{4}{\cancel{12}}}{\underset{1}{\cancel{5}}} = \frac{2}{3} + \frac{13 \times 4}{3 \times 1}$

$= \frac{2}{3} + \frac{52}{3} = \frac{54}{3}$

$= 18$ ← value

Evaluate each expression.

1. $\frac{3}{5}z$, when $z = \frac{3}{8}$

2. $c \div \frac{7}{12}$, when $c = \frac{7}{9}$

3. $2\frac{3}{4}t$, when $t = \frac{8}{11}$

4. $m \div \frac{9}{10}$, when $m = 5\frac{2}{5}$

5. $7h$, when $h = \frac{10}{21}$

6. $x \div \frac{8}{9}$, when $x = 14$

7. $6\frac{7}{8}y$, when $y = \frac{8}{15}$

8. $3\frac{2}{3} \div z$, when $z = 2\frac{4}{9}$

9. $7\frac{1}{8}b$, when $b = 1\frac{13}{19}$

10. $(a + b) \div \frac{1}{6}a$, when $a = \frac{2}{3}$ and $b = \frac{1}{12}$

11. $c + \frac{1}{2}d$, when $c = 2\frac{1}{6}$ and $d = \frac{2}{3}$

12. $(x - y)z \div y$, when $x = \frac{3}{4}$, $y = \frac{3}{8}$, and $z = \frac{3}{10}$

13. $m + (p + s) \div s$, for $m = 1\frac{1}{2}$, $p = \frac{3}{5}$, and $s = \frac{2}{3}$

Problem Solving

Write and evaluate an expression that could be used to solve the problem.

14. Three eighths of the students in Kaitlyn's math class are in science class together. If 32 students are in Kaitlyn's math class, how many are in science class together?

15. Regina cuts a board into 31 pieces of equal length. If the board is $7\frac{3}{4}$ ft long, how long is each piece that Regina cuts?

16. Mr. Ruiz buys some pounds of ground beef for a cookout. He uses the beef to make $\frac{1}{4}$-pound hamburgers. If Mr. Ruiz buys $3\frac{1}{2}$ lb of ground beef, how many hamburgers does Mr. Ruiz make?

17. Michael burns some calories per hour when skiing. He skis for $4\frac{1}{2}$ h before lunch and $1\frac{1}{4}$ h afterward. If he burns 610 calories per hour, how many calories in all does he burn?

18. Aurora has some dog food. She feeds her dog $1\frac{1}{4}$ cans each day. If she has $8\frac{3}{4}$ cans of dog food, how many days will the food last?

TEST PREPARATION

Evaluate each expression. Choose the correct answer.

19. $5\frac{5}{8}g$, when $g = 3\frac{1}{5}$

  A $1\frac{97}{128}$ B $15\frac{1}{8}$

  C 18   D not given

20. $ab \div c$, when $a = 1\frac{3}{8}$, $b = 2\frac{4}{5}$, and $c = \frac{3}{4}$

  F $5\frac{2}{15}$ G $5\frac{4}{55}$

  H $5\frac{2}{25}$ J not given

Multiplication and Division Equations with Fractions

Sadie deposits $\frac{3}{5}$ of the money she earned last month in her savings account. If she deposits $75, how much did Sadie earn last month?

To find how much, write and solve the equation:

$\frac{3}{5}t = \$75.$ ← Let t represent the amount Sadie earned last month.

$\frac{3}{5}t \div \frac{3}{5} = \$75 \div \frac{3}{5}$ ← Divide both sides by $\frac{3}{5}$, using the Division Property of Equality.

$t = \$75 \times \frac{5}{3}$ ← Multiply by the reciprocal of $\frac{3}{5}$.

$t = \$\overset{25}{\cancel{75}} \times \frac{5}{\underset{1}{\cancel{3}}}$ ← Simplify.

$t = \$125$ ← solution

Check by replacing t with 125: $\frac{3}{5}t = \$75 \rightarrow \frac{3}{5} \cdot \$125 \overset{?}{=} \$75 \rightarrow \$75 = \$75$

Sadie earned $125 last month.

Study these examples.

Solve: $y \div 2\frac{1}{3} = 3\frac{3}{7}.$

$y \div 2\frac{1}{3} \times 2\frac{1}{3} = 3\frac{3}{7} \times 2\frac{1}{3}$ ← Isolate the variable.

$y = 3\frac{3}{7} \times 2\frac{1}{3}$ ← Compute to solve.

$y = \frac{\overset{8}{\cancel{24}}}{\cancel{7}} \times \frac{\overset{1}{\cancel{7}}}{\cancel{3}} = \frac{8}{1}$

$y = 8$

Solve: $\frac{1}{3}g + \frac{1}{3}g = \frac{8}{9}.$

$\frac{2}{3}g = \frac{8}{9}$ ← Combine like terms.

$\frac{2}{3}g \div \frac{2}{3} = \frac{8}{9} \div \frac{2}{3}$ ← Isolate the variable.

$g = \frac{8}{9} \times \frac{3}{2}$ ← Compute to solve.

$g = \frac{\overset{4}{\cancel{8}}}{\underset{3}{\cancel{9}}} \times \frac{\overset{1}{\cancel{3}}}{\underset{1}{\cancel{2}}} = \frac{4}{3}$

$g = 1\frac{1}{3}$

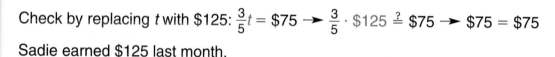

Solve for x.

1. $\frac{5}{8}x = 95$

2. $20x = \frac{10}{13}$

3. $x \div \frac{8}{9} = 21$

4. $x \div 9 = 9\frac{2}{3}$

5. $x \div 11\frac{7}{9} = 18$

6. $5x = 5\frac{5}{8}$

7. $2\frac{7}{10}x = 21$

8. $x \div \frac{2}{3} = \frac{6}{7}$

9. $\frac{4}{5}x = \frac{2}{3}$

10. $x \div \frac{7}{12} = 3\frac{3}{7}$

11. $10\frac{4}{5}x = \frac{9}{10}$

12. $x \div 6\frac{7}{8} = 1\frac{5}{11}$

13. $\frac{8}{15}x = 1\frac{1}{9}$

14. $x \div 7\frac{1}{2} = 13\frac{1}{4}$

15. $8\frac{4}{9}x = 1\frac{1}{3}$

16. $2x + \frac{1}{2}x = 25$

Temperature Conversions

You can use formulas to **convert** between temperatures in degrees Celsius (°C) and in degrees Fahrenheit (°F).

Conversion Formulas

$$°C = \frac{5}{9}(°F - 32) \qquad °F = \frac{9}{5}°C + 32$$

▶ Convert ⁻13°F to °C.
Use the formula:

$$°C = \frac{5}{9}(°F - 32)$$

$$= \frac{5}{9}(^-13 - 32) \leftarrow \text{Replace } F \text{ with } ^-13.$$

$$= ^-25 \leftarrow \text{Simplify.}$$

$$^-13°F = ^-25°C$$

▶ Convert 45°C to °F.
Use the formula:

$$°F = \frac{9}{5}°C + 32$$

$$= \frac{9}{5} \cdot 45 + 32 \leftarrow \text{Replace } C \text{ with } 45.$$

$$= 113 \leftarrow \text{Simplify.}$$

$$45°C = 113°F$$

Convert the temperature to °C or to °F. Watch for the degree unit.

17. 32°F

18. ⁻31°F

19. 23°F

20. ⁻49°F

21. ⁻30°C

22. 5°C

23. ⁻10°C

24. 50°C

Problem Solving

25. Jabaar deposits $\frac{2}{3}$ of the money he earned last month in his savings account. If he deposits $48, how much did he earn?

26. Kendra divides a package of trail mix into $\frac{1}{4}$-cup servings. She fills $7\frac{1}{2}$ bags. How many cups of trail mix did she have to begin with?

DO YOU REMEMBER?

Find each sum.

27. ⁻24 + ⁺24

28. ⁻18 + ⁻18

29. ⁺50 + ⁺16

30. ⁺38 + ⁻33

Probability

Probability is a measure of the likelihood of an event.
The probability of an event is any number from 0 to 1.
A probability of 0 means an event is impossible.
A probability of 1 means an event is certain to occur.

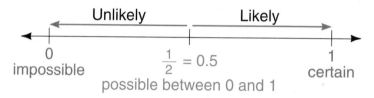

▶ When you use a formula to find probability you are finding **theoretical probability**.

Theoretical probability can be defined by the formula:

$$P(E) = \frac{\text{number of favorable outcomes}}{\text{total number of possible outcomes}}$$

▶ Each number on the spinner is one possible **outcome**, or result of spinning the spinner. The **sample space** or the set of all possible outcomes is {1, 3, 5, 7, 9}.

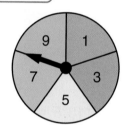

Use the spinner to find each theoretical probability.

$P(2) = \frac{0}{5} = 0$	$P(\text{odd number}) = \frac{5}{5} = 1$	$P(7) = \frac{1}{5} = 0.2$
impossible	certain	possible

Complementary Events	Mutually Exclusive Events
Two events, E and *not* E, are complementary if both events cannot occur at the same time. The sum of their likelihood of occurring is 1.	Two events, A and B, that have no outcomes in common, are called mutually exclusive, or **disjoint events**.

<table>
<tr><td>

$$P(E) + P(\text{not } E) = 1$$

$$
\begin{aligned}
P(\text{not } 7) &= 1 - P(7) \\
&= 1 - \frac{1}{5} \\
&= \frac{4}{5} = 0.8
\end{aligned}
$$

</td><td>

$$P(A \text{ or } B) = P(A) + P(B)$$

$$
\begin{aligned}
P(< 5 \text{ or } > 7) &= P(< 5) + P(> 7) \\
&= \frac{2}{5} + \frac{1}{5} = \frac{3}{5} \\
&= 0.6
\end{aligned}
$$

</td></tr>
</table>

Use the spinner to find the probability of each event.
Are the events in ex. 3, 4, and 8 mutually exclusive?
If not, tell why.

1. $P(1)$
2. $P(\text{not } 2)$
3. $P(4 \text{ or } 6)$
4. $P(4 \text{ or odd})$

5. $P(< 7)$
6. $P(> 6)$
7. $P(\text{odd})$
8. $P(\text{even or } 2)$

Find the probability of each event, E.
Then find the probability
of its complement.

.Think..
$P(E)$ is the complement of $P(\text{not } E)$.
$P(\text{not } E)$ is the complement of $P(E)$.
....

A number is selected from 1 through 10.

9. $P(\text{prime})$
10. $P(\text{multiple of } 5)$
11. $P(\text{divisible by } 3)$
12. $P(\text{factor of } 10)$

Experimental Probability

When you find the probability of an event by doing an experiment,
you are finding experimental probability. The greater the number of
trials you do in an experiment, the closer the experimental probability
gets to the theoretical probability.

Experimental probability can be defined by the formula:

$$\text{Exp } P(E) = \frac{\text{number of times favorable outcomes occur}}{\text{number of trials in the experiment}}$$

A trial is each time you
do the experiment.

Experiment: A coin is tossed repeatedly. The results
are recorded as 53 heads, 47 tails.

Find Exp $P(H)$ and Exp $P(T)$. Then compare the values
with the theoretical probabilities of $P(H)$ and $P(T)$.

$\text{Exp } P(H) = \frac{53}{100} = 0.53$

.Think..
$53 + 47 = 100$ trials
....

$\text{Exp } P(T) = \frac{47}{100} = 0.47$

$P(H) = \frac{1}{2} = 0.5$

$P(T) = \frac{1}{2} = 0.5$

$0.53 > 0.5$

$0.47 < 0.5$

Find the experimental probability of each event.
Then compare it with the theoretical probability.

Experiment:
Roll a 1–6 number cube.

Outcome	1	2	3	4	5	6
No. of Times	8	11	10	11	8	12

13. $\text{Exp } P(1)$
14. $\text{Exp } P(3)$
15. $\text{Exp } P(4)$
16. $\text{Exp } P(3 \text{ or } 6)$

Compound Events

In a school election there are 4 candidates for president and 2 candidates for vice president. How many possible president/vice president outcomes are there?

Finding the number of possible president/vice president outcomes is an example of a compound event. A compound event is a combination of two or more single events.

Label the candidates for president P1, P2, P3, and P4. Label the candidates for vice president V1 and V2.

▶ One way of finding possible outcomes is to draw a tree diagram.

President	Vice President	Outcome
P1	V1	(P1, V1)
	V2	(P1, V2)
P2	V1	(P2, V1)
	V2	(P2, V2)
P3	V1	(P3, V1)
	V2	(P3, V2)
P4	V1	(P4, V1)
	V2	(P4, V2)

▶ Another way of finding possible outcomes is to make a table.

	Vice President	
	V1	**V2**
P1	(P1, V1)	(P1, V2)
P2	(P2, V1)	(P2, V2)
P3	(P3, V1)	(P3, V2)
P4	(P4, V1)	(P4, V2)

President

There are 8 president/vice president possible outcomes.

▶ You can also find the number of possible outcomes by using the Counting Principle.

> ### The Counting Principle
>
> If one event has *m* possible outcomes and a second event has *n* possible outcomes, then there are *m* × *n* total possible outcomes for the two events together.

president		vice president		president/vice president outcomes
4	×	2	=	8

Draw a tree diagram or make a table and use the Counting Principle to find the number of possible outcomes. List all possible outcomes.

1. Toss a penny and roll a 1–6 number cube.

2. Spin the spinner and choose a marble without looking.

3. Make a sandwich with 5 different types of bread and 2 different fillings.

4. Put together an outfit from a selection of 4 shirts, 2 pairs of pants, and 2 sweaters.

Independent and Dependent Events

A bag contains 10 cubes: 5 red, 3 blue, and 2 green. Pick 2 cubes from the bag without looking. What is the probability of picking a blue cube and then a red cube?

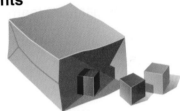

To find P(blue, red), multiply: P(blue) $\times$ P(red)

▶ Pick the first cube. Return it to the bag. Then pick the second cube. These events are independent events.

The first event does not affect the second event.

> If A and B are independent events, $P(A, B) = P(A) \times P(B)$.

$$P(\text{blue, red}) = P(\text{blue}) \times P(\text{red}) = \frac{3}{\overset{}{\underset{2}{10}}} \times \frac{\overset{1}{5}}{10} = \frac{3}{20}$$

▶ Pick the first cube. Do not return it to the bag. Then pick the second cube. These events are dependent events.

The first event does affect the second event.

> If A and B are dependent events, $P(A, B) = P(A) \times P(B \text{ after } A)$.

$$P(\text{blue, red}) = P(\text{blue}) \times P(\text{red}) = \frac{\overset{1}{3}}{\underset{2}{10}} \times \frac{\overset{1}{5}}{\underset{3}{9}} = \frac{1}{6} \quad \boxed{1 \text{ less cube in bag}}$$

Find the probability: (a) if the first choice is replaced; and (b) if the first choice is not replaced.

Experiment: Pick one marble from a box containing 3 yellow (Y) marbles, 2 white (W) marbles, and 1 red (R) marble. Then pick a second marble.

5. P(R, Y)

6. P(Y, R)

7. P(Y, W)

8. P(R, Y or W)

Permutations and Combinations

Two students from a team of 4 will go to the city math contest. How many different teams can be formed?

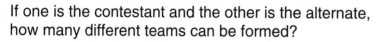

To find how many teams, make an organized list.

Let A, B, C, and D represent each of the four students.

I. Order does not matter:

AB   AC   AD   BC   BD   CD ◄─ 6 teams

Six teams can be formed.

If one is the contestant and the other is the alternate, how many different teams can be formed?

AB ≠ BA

II. Order matters: AB BA   AC CA   AD DA   BC CB   BD DB   CD DC ◄─ 12 teams

When order matters, as in team II, you are counting **permutations**.
When order does not matter, as in team I, you are counting **combinations**.

▶ You can also use the Counting Principle to find permutations and combinations.

A. Three out of 5 students can win an essay contest. How many different ways can the winners be selected?

To find the number of ways, find the number of permutations since the order matters.

choices for 1st place		choices for 2nd place		choices for 3rd place		total number of ways
5	×	4	×	3	=	60

There are 60 ways of selecting the winners.

B. Tony can only take 3 out of 5 subjects offered during the marking period. How many different ways can he choose the subjects he will take?

To find the numbers of ways, find the number of combinations since the order does not matter.

Find the number of permutations of the items.	Find the number of arrangements for each combination.	Divide to eliminate duplicate combinations.
5 × 4 × 3 = 60	3 × 2 × 1 = 6	60 ÷ 6 = 10

Tony has 10 ways of choosing the three subjects.

Tell whether or not order matters in each situation.
Write *Yes* or *No*. If yes, explain why.

1. a phone number being dialed

2. items checked off in a list

3. four group members selected from a class

4. three runners awarded first-, second-, and third-place medals in a marathon

5. six people randomly selected for a survey

6. digits in the number of an address

7. coins put into a vending machine

8. four digits in a password

Tell how many permutations and combinations can be made.

9. three of the digits 3, 5, 7, and 9

10. four of the letters A, B, C, D, and E

11. two of the letters *A, B, C, D*, and *E*

12. two of the digits 3, 5, 7, and 9

Problem Solving

13. A novel, an art book, a history book, and a math book are lined up on a shelf. In how many ways can they be arranged?

14. Mike, Jim, and Sam are going to the movies. They want to sit together in the same row. How many different seating orders are possible?

15. If 5 people want to be seated, in how many ways can 4 of them be seated on a bench that seats 4?

16. From 2 girls and 3 boys, how many committees of 3 can be formed?

17. Ms. Malik has 4 plants to put into 3 plant pots. In how many ways can she pot 3 plants?

18. There are 6 problems on a math final exam. Students must choose 3 problems to solve. How many ways can they choose the problems?

CHALLENGE

$5 \times 4 \times 3 \times 2 \times 1$ can be written as 5! and is read "five factorial."
5! = 120

Evaluate each expression.

19. 3!

20. 4!

21. 2!

22. 6!

23. 7!

24. How would you use the factorial notation to express the number of ways in which 4 objects can be arranged in a row? 8 objects? 10 objects? *n* objects?

Predictions and Probability

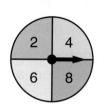

In 1000 spins, predict how many times the spinner will land on 6.

To predict how many times, use *theoretical probability*.

- Find the theoretical probability of the spinner landing on 6.

$$P(6) = \frac{\text{favorable outcomes}}{\text{possible outcomes}} = \frac{1}{4}$$

- Multiply the probability by the number of trials.

$$\frac{1}{4} \times 1000 = \frac{1}{\cancel{4}} \times \frac{\overset{250}{\cancel{1000}}}{1} = 250$$

Based on the probability of $\frac{1}{4}$, you can predict the spinner will land on 6 about 250 out of 1000 spins.

▶ You can also use *experimental probability* to make predictions.

Paul spun a 4-section spinner 40 times. The results are shown in the table at the right. Based on his experimental results, how many times can Paul expect a result of blue in the next 100 spins?

Color	Spins
blue	16
yellow	8
red	10
orange	6

To predict how many times, use *experimental probability*.

- Find the experimental probability of spinning blue.

$$\text{Exp. } P(\text{blue}) = \frac{\text{number of favorable outcomes}}{\text{total number of possible trials}} = \frac{16}{40} = \frac{2}{5}$$

- Multiply 100 by the experimental probability

$$\frac{2}{\cancel{5}} \times \overset{20}{\cancel{100}} = \frac{40}{1} = 40$$

Paul can expect to spin blue 40 times in his next 100 spins.

In 2000 spins, predict the number of times the spinner above would land on each of the following.

1. number > 5 **2.** number < 4 **3.** number between 2 and 8

4. Explain how you made your predictions in exercises 1–3.

Practice

Use the experimental results to predict how many times you can expect to randomly select the tile given the number of selections.

Tiles	Times Selected
Red	25
Black	20
Blue	22
Green	33

5. red tile, 60 times

6. green tile, 200 times

7. black tile, 150 times

8. blue tile, 700 times

Odds

Odds are a way of measuring the chance of success against the chance of failure.

Odds in favor of an event:

$$\frac{\text{number of favorable outcomes}}{\text{number of unfavorable outcomes}}$$

Odds against an event:

$$\frac{\text{number of unfavorable outcomes}}{\text{number of favorable outcomes}}$$

Use the spinner to find the odds in favor of and the odds against the spinner landing on an even number.

odds in favor of an even number $= \frac{2}{3}$

odds against an even number $= \frac{3}{2}$

2 favorable outcomes: 2, 4

3 unfavorable outcomes: 1, 3, 5

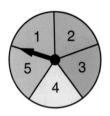

Find the odds in favor of and the odds against rolling the given number of a 1–6 number cube.

9. a multiple of 3   **10.** an odd number   **11.** a factor of 5   **12.** not 4

Problem Solving

Use the table for exercises 15–16.

13. A bag contains the letters A, B, C, D, and E. A letter is picked from the bag at random. What are the odds in favor of picking a vowel?

14. Each guest will select a prize from a bag. Of the 25 prizes, 12 are pens and 8 are pencils. What are the odds against selecting a pen or a pencil?

15. Find the probability that a lightbulb will last less than 900 hours.

16. Predict how many lightbulbs out of 500,000 will last longer than 899 hours.

Life of Bulbs in Hours	No. of Bulbs
600–699	102
700–799	95
800–899	108
900–999	195

17. Eve has a spinner with two colors, red and green. If the odds of spinning a green are $\frac{1}{2}$, on which color is the spinner more likely to land, red or green? Explain.

Problem-Solving Strategy:
Use a Diagram

There are 27 bowling balls for rent that are black, speckled, or both. If 12 are black and 24 are speckled, what fractional part of the bowling balls are both black and speckled?

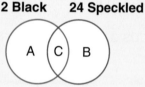

Read

Visualize yourself in the problem above as you reread it. List the facts and the question.

Facts: 27 bowling balls
12 are black
24 are speckled

Question: What fractional part of the bowling balls are both black and speckled?

Plan

Make a Venn diagram and list the facts.
Let A represent black bowling balls.
Let B represent speckled bowling balls.
Let C represent black speckled bowling balls.

12 Black   24 Speckled

A (C) B

To find the number of bowling balls that are both black and speckled (C), subtract 27 from the sum of 12 and 24. $(12 + 24) - 27 = C$

Then write a fraction to show the number of black speckled bowling balls out of all the balls.

$\dfrac{C}{27}$ $\dfrac{\text{number of black speckled}}{\text{total number of bowling balls}}$

.·**Think**·.
$\dfrac{C}{27} = ?$

Solve

$(12 + 24) - 27 = C$
$\quad 36 \quad - 27 = 9$

$\dfrac{9}{27} = \dfrac{1}{3}$

One third of the bowling balls are both black and speckled.

Black
12

$\begin{array}{c} 12 \\ -9 \\ \hline 3 \end{array}$ 9 $\begin{array}{c} 24 \\ -9 \\ \hline 15 \end{array}$

Speckled
24

Check

Add the number of bowling balls in each region:

$A + B + C \overset{?}{=} 27$ $A + C \overset{?}{=} 12$ $C + B \overset{?}{=} 24$
$3 + 15 + 9 \overset{?}{=} 27$ $3 + 9 \overset{?}{=} 12$ $9 + 15 \overset{?}{=} 24$
$\qquad\qquad 27 = 27$ $\qquad 12 = 12$ $\qquad 24 = 24$

Your answer checks.

Solve by using a Venn diagram.

1. The school paper lists the names of the 18 baseball players, 20 volleyball players, and 16 soccer players. One person belongs to all three teams. One third of the baseball players and 4 of the volleyball players also belong to the soccer team. How many students play only soccer?

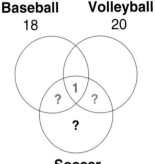

Baseball   **Volleyball**
18   20

1

?   ?

?

Soccer
16

Read ▸ Visualize yourself in the problem above as you reread it. List the facts and the question.

       Facts: 18 baseball players
                   20 volleyball players
                   16 soccer players
                   1 student plays on all three teams.
                   $\frac{1}{3}$ of the baseball players also play soccer.
                   4 volleyball players also play soccer.

       Question: How many students play only soccer?

Plan ▸ To find the number who play both soccer and baseball, multiply: $\frac{1}{3} \times 18 = 6$.

       Use the Venn diagram and subtract to find the number in each overlapping region.
       $6 - 1 = \underline{\ ?\ }$ and $4 - 1 = \underline{\ ?\ }$

       Then solve for the number who play only soccer.
       $16 - (1 + ? + ?) = \underline{\ ?\ }$ soccer only

Solve ┈┈┈▸ **Check**

2. There are 26 shops at the minimall. One third of the 12 shops that provide services also provide goods. How many shops provide only goods?

3. At a buffet table, ham, chicken, and beef were being served. Of the 200 guests, 70 ate ham, 100 ate chicken, 85 ate beef, 25 ate ham and beef, and 30 ate chicken and ham. One tenth of the guests ate all three. How many guests ate only ham?

4. While on vacation 50 people could opt to fish, scuba dive, and/or water ski. Of the group, 35 went fishing, 32 went scuba diving, 14 tried water skiing, 21 tried both fishing and scuba diving, 4 tried only water skiing, and 10 did all three. How many went only fishing? only scuba diving?

Read ⟩ **Plan** ⟩ **Solve** ⟩ **Check**

Solve each problem and explain the method you used.

1. Hanley's Farm Stand sets out $\frac{2}{5}$ bushel of apples. If $\frac{1}{2}$ of the apples are sold in the first hour the stand is open, what part of a bushel is left?

2. Solomon can pick $\frac{5}{8}$ bushel of grapes each hour. How many bushels can he pick in 7 hours?

3. An apple cake recipe calls for $2\frac{2}{3}$ cups of apple slices. Each apple supplies about $\frac{2}{3}$ cup of slices. How many apples are needed to make the cake?

4. Geraldine picked $4\frac{1}{2}$ quarts of strawberries. Lonnie picked $\frac{3}{4}$ as much as Geraldine. How many quarts of strawberries did Lonnie pick?

5. How many half-pint containers did Pat use to package $10\frac{1}{2}$ pints of raspberries?

6. A pound of plums costs $1.05. How much do $3\frac{1}{5}$ lb cost?

7. How many $\frac{2}{5}$-lb slices can be cut from a 15-lb watermelon?

8. The Pumpkin Pickers have won the coin toss at the beginning of the County Vegetable-Picking Race for the last three years. What is the probability that they will win the coin toss at the beginning of the next race?

9. From a bag of 1 yellow, 2 green, and 2 red peppers, Don chooses 2 peppers at random. What is the probability that he will choose a red and a yellow pepper if the first pepper is replaced? if the first pepper is *not* replaced?

10. How many $\frac{1}{2}$-gal containers can be filled from a $25\frac{1}{2}$-gal keg of cider?

11. Maya picks $\frac{3}{4}$ bushel of peaches in $\frac{2}{3}$ hour. How many bushels can she pick in one hour?

Choose a strategy from the list or use another strategy you know to solve each problem.

12. Tami's cookie jar has 8 oatmeal cookies, 5 lemon cookies, and 3 raisin cookies. What is the probability of selecting a lemon cookie in one random draw from the cookie jar?

13. Hanley's has $\frac{7}{8}$ bushel of peaches when the farm stand opens in the morning. By noon, $\frac{1}{4}$ of the peaches are left. What part of the bushel of peaches was sold in the morning?

14. The stand sells $\frac{1}{2}$ quart of berries for $1.49. Do $2\frac{3}{4}$ quarts of berries cost more than $10?

15. Lynn's snack bag contains only red and green grapes. The number of green grapes is 5 more than the number of red grapes. If the probability of randomly selecting a green grape is $\frac{10}{15}$, how many red grapes are in the bag? green grapes?

16. A customer buys a $2\frac{5}{8}$-lb melon for $1.05. Would a $4\frac{1}{2}$-lb melon cost more than $2?

17. By 11 A.M. Kathy had sold $\frac{1}{6}$ of the 5-lb bags of pears. Between 11 A.M. and 4 P.M. she sold 2 dozen more bags. If she had 11 bags left at 4 P.M., how many bags did she have when the stand opened?

Strategy File

Use These Strategies
Use More Than One Step
Use Simpler Numbers
Use a Diagram
Work Backward

Use the diagram for problems 18–20.

Anne, Bill, Carol, Derek, and Emmy each bought berries.

18. Who bought only strawberries?

19. How many people bought raspberries?

20. Who bought both strawberries and raspberries?

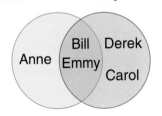

21. Make up your own problem modeled on problem 16 above. Then have a classmate solve it.

Check Your Progress
Lessons 1–18

Multiply. Simplify using the GCF whenever possible. *(See pp. 250–255.)*

1. $\frac{5}{6} \times \frac{3}{4}$ **2.** $18 \times \frac{2}{3}$ **3.** $\frac{2}{9}$ of 3   **4.** $\frac{6}{11} \times \frac{33}{42}$ **5.** $\frac{4}{5} \times \frac{3}{7}$

Find the value of *n*. Name the property of multiplication used.

6. $\frac{5}{6} \times \frac{6}{5} = n$ **7.** $n \times (8 \times \frac{2}{3}) = (\frac{1}{4} \times 8) \times \frac{2}{3}$

8. $n \times \frac{3}{5} = \frac{3}{5}$ **9.** $\frac{2}{11} \times (5 + \frac{11}{14}) = (\frac{2}{11} \times n) + (\frac{2}{11} \times \frac{11}{14})$

Estimate. Then multiply or divide. *(See pp. 256–267.)*

10. $4\frac{1}{5} \times 2\frac{2}{3}$ **11.** $2\frac{4}{7} \times 3\frac{1}{2}$ **12.** $8 \div 3\frac{1}{5}$ **13.** $10\frac{2}{5} \div 2\frac{1}{6}$

Compute. *(See pp. 268–269.)*

14. $\frac{1}{3}$ of $48   **15.** $\frac{3}{5}$ of $12.75   **16.** $36.40 $\div 1\frac{1}{7}$ **17.** $8 $\div \frac{4}{5}$

Evaluate. *(See pp. 270–271.)*

18. $(m + n) \div \frac{2}{5}n$, when $m = \frac{3}{10}$ and $n = \frac{1}{5}$ **19.** $x + \frac{1}{2}y$, when $x = \frac{1}{6}$ and $y = \frac{2}{3}$

Convert the temperature to °C or to °F. *(See pp. 272–273.)*
Watch for the degree unit.

20. $^-10°C =$ **21.** $^-30°C =$ **22.** $41°F =$ **23.** $122°F =$

Find the probability of each event and the complementary event. *(See pp. 274–279.)*

Experiment: A number is randomly selected from the numbers 1 through 6.

24. P(prime)   **25.** P(multiple of 3)   **26.** $P(> 6)$ **27.** P(divisible by 2)

Problem Solving
(See pp. 276–285.)

28. A box contains 3 red marbles, 1 black marble, and 2 white marbles. Choose one marble at random, without replacing it. Then pick another marble. What is the probability that you would pick a black marble, then a red marble?

29. How many four-digit numbers can you make using the digits 0, 2, 4, and 6 if repetition of digits is not permitted?

(See Still More Practice, p. 526.)

Complex Fractions

Complex fractions have a fraction as a term in the numerator or denominator, or both.

$$\dfrac{\frac{2}{5}}{10} \qquad \dfrac{^-32}{\frac{4}{5}} \qquad \dfrac{\frac{3}{4}}{\frac{7}{8}} \qquad \dfrac{\frac{1}{2}+\frac{2}{5}}{25} \qquad \dfrac{\frac{3}{8}+\frac{1}{4}}{\frac{5}{16}-\frac{1}{2}}$$

A complex fraction can be simplified to an integer, a fraction, or a mixed number.

▶ To simplify a complex fraction, divide the numerator by the denominator.

Simplify: $\dfrac{^-30}{\frac{2}{3}}$.

$$\dfrac{^-30}{\frac{2}{3}} = ^-30 \div \frac{2}{3}$$
$$= \frac{\overset{-15}{\cancel{^-30}}}{1} \times \frac{3}{\cancel{2}}$$
$$= \frac{^-15 \times 3}{1 \times 1}$$
$$= \frac{^-45}{1} = ^-45 \quad \boxed{\text{integer}}$$

Simplify: $\dfrac{\frac{3}{4}}{\frac{7}{8}}$.

$$\dfrac{\frac{3}{4}}{\frac{7}{8}} = \frac{3}{4} \div \frac{7}{8}$$
$$= \frac{3}{\cancel{4}} \times \frac{\overset{2}{\cancel{8}}}{7}$$
$$= \frac{3 \times 2}{1 \times 7}$$
$$= \frac{6}{7} \quad \boxed{\text{fraction}}$$

Simplify: $\dfrac{\frac{3}{8}+\frac{1}{4}}{\frac{5}{16}-\frac{1}{2}}$.

$$\dfrac{\frac{3}{8}+\frac{1}{4}}{\frac{5}{16}-\frac{1}{2}} = \left(\frac{3}{8}+\frac{1}{4}\right) \div \left(\frac{5}{16}-\frac{1}{2}\right)$$
$$= \left(\frac{3}{8}+\frac{2}{8}\right) \div \left(\frac{5}{16}-\frac{8}{16}\right)$$
$$= \frac{5}{8} \div \frac{^-3}{16} = \frac{5}{\cancel{8}} \times \frac{\overset{2}{\cancel{16}}}{^-3}$$
$$= \frac{5 \times 2}{1 \times ^-3} = \frac{10}{^-3}$$
$$= ^-3\frac{1}{3} \quad \boxed{\text{mixed number}}$$

Simplify each complex fraction.

1. $\dfrac{\frac{2}{3}}{8}$

2. $\dfrac{8}{\frac{2}{5}}$

3. $\dfrac{\frac{3}{7}}{\frac{9}{10}}$

4. $\dfrac{^-21}{\frac{7}{8}}$

5. $\dfrac{\frac{5}{9}}{^-3}$

6. $\dfrac{\frac{^-7}{10}}{\frac{^-5}{12}}$

7. $\dfrac{\frac{1}{12}+\frac{1}{3}}{\frac{3}{8}+\frac{5}{24}}$

8. $\dfrac{\frac{1}{5}-\frac{1}{25}}{\frac{1}{2}-\frac{2}{5}}$

9. $\dfrac{\frac{5}{6}-\frac{7}{8}}{\frac{2}{9}+\frac{7}{12}}$

Chapter 8 Test

Multiply or divide. Estimate to help you.

1. $\frac{7}{8} \times \frac{6}{35} \times \frac{5}{9}$

2. $5\frac{2}{5} \times 3\frac{1}{3}$

3. $6\frac{2}{3} \times 1\frac{1}{5}$

4. $\frac{7}{10}$ of $20

5. $\frac{7}{8} \div \frac{5}{16}$

6. $7\frac{5}{7} \div \frac{9}{14}$

7. $7\frac{1}{2} \div 3\frac{3}{4}$

8. $9 \div 1\frac{1}{3}$

Evaluate.

9. $(c + d) \div \frac{1}{6}c$, when $c = \frac{1}{2}$ and $d = \frac{1}{12}$

10. $x \div \frac{1}{2}y$, when $x = 2\frac{1}{6}$ and $y = \frac{2}{3}$

Solve and check.

11. $\frac{3}{8}x = 15$

12. $5x = \frac{10}{13}$

13. $x \div \frac{5}{9} = 20$

14. $x \div 14 = 3\frac{2}{7}$

Convert the temperature to °C or to °F. Watch for the degree unit.

15. $5°C =$

16. $50°C =$

17. $23°F =$

18. $^-49°F =$

Use spinners A and B.

19. For spinner A find: **a.** P(1 or 4)   **b.** P(not 2)

20. Spin A and then spin B. List all possible outcomes.

21. In 600 spins, predict how many times spinner B will land on 6, 7, or 8.

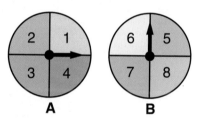

A   B

Problem Solving

Use a strategy you have learned.

22. In a 9-room house, 6 rooms are tiled, 2 rooms are painted, and 1 room is both tiled and painted. How many rooms are not tiled or painted?

Tell About It

Explain how you solved the problem. Show all your work.

23. If the digits cannot repeat, how many ways are there to pick a three-digit PIN (personal identification number)?

Performance Assessment

Find the error or errors in each computation. Explain.

24. $\frac{4}{5} \div \frac{5}{4} \times 0$

$= (\frac{4}{5} \div \frac{5}{4}) \times 0$

$= 1 \times 0$

$= 1$

25. $19 \times \frac{19}{20} \times \frac{20}{19}$

$= (\frac{1}{19} \times \frac{19}{20}) \times (\frac{19}{1} \times \frac{20}{19})$

$= \frac{1}{20} \times 20$

$= 1$

Test Preparation

Choose the best answer.

1. Which shows the standard form of 2 trillion, 14 million, 800 thousand?

   a. 2,014,800
   b. 2,014,000,800,000
   c. 2,014,800,000
   d. 2,000,014,800,000

2. Estimate.

   9,879,632
   +   763,986

   a. 9,700,000
   b. 10,700,000
   c. 11,700,000
   d. 9,000,000,000

3. Find the difference.

   2,729,000 − 409,026

   a. 2,320,026
   b. 2,320,974
   c. 2,320,984
   d. not given

4. Which shows greatest to least?

   a. 1.88; 1.8; 1.08; 1.008
   b. 1.8; 1.88; 1.08; 1.008
   c. 1.008; 1.88; 1.08; 1.8
   d. none of these

5. Find the difference.

   $\frac{11}{12}$
   $-\frac{2}{3}$

   a. $\frac{1}{4}$
   b. $\frac{5}{6}$
   c. $1\frac{1}{9}$
   d. not given

6. How much more than 2×10^3 is 2500?

   a. 500
   b. 2300
   c. 3000
   d. 5500

7. Which shows the decimal 0.8741 rounded to its greatest nonzero place?

   a. 1
   b. 0.9
   c. 0.874
   d. 0.87

8. Find the sum.

   $4.56 + $.56 + $44

   a. $5.56
   b. $49.12
   c. $104.56
   d. not given

9. Find the difference.

   68 − 0.054

   a. 0.014
   b. 67.46
   c. 67.946
   d. not given

10. Which shows least to greatest?

    a. $2\frac{2}{5}, 2\frac{2}{3}, 2\frac{1}{4}$
    b. $2\frac{2}{3}, 2\frac{2}{5}, 2\frac{1}{4}$
    c. $2\frac{1}{4}, 2\frac{2}{3}, 2\frac{2}{5}$
    d. none of these

11. Find the value of m:

    $m - \frac{2}{3} = \frac{4}{5}$

    a. $\frac{2}{15}$
    b. $\frac{3}{4}$
    c. $\frac{8}{15}$
    d. $1\frac{7}{15}$

12. Which is greater than 3 but less than $6\frac{1}{2}$?

    a. $5 + 1\frac{3}{4}$
    b. $1\frac{1}{2} + 1\frac{1}{2}$
    c. $9\frac{1}{9} - 5\frac{5}{12}$
    d. $20 - 17\frac{1}{3}$

13. Which is true?

    a. $^-5 \div {^+1} > {^+8} \div {^+2}$
    b. $^-2 \times {^+3} < {^+4} \times {^-2}$
    c. $^-7 + {^+6} < {^-3} + 0$
    d. $^+10 - {^-4} > {^-12} - {^+17}$

14. Find the value of n: $2\frac{1}{4} \times 3 = n$.

    a. $\frac{3}{4}$ **b.** $2\frac{3}{4}$

    c. $6\frac{3}{4}$ **d.** not given

15. Twice a number n is 7. What is the number?

    a. 3.5   **b.** 14   **c.** 28   **d.** not given

16. A coin is tossed and a number cube with faces labeled 1 through 6 is rolled. Find $P(\text{H, even})$.

    a. $\frac{1}{4}$ **b.** $\frac{1}{2}$ **c.** $\frac{1}{8}$ **d.** 1

17. Connie had $82.50. She spent $\frac{4}{5}$ of it on a shirt. About how much did she have left?

    a. $16   **b.** $20
    c. $25   **d.** not given

18. Find the prime factorization of 36.

    a. 1×36
    b. 6×6
    c. 9×4
    d. not given

19. Find the quotient: $\frac{4}{5} \div \frac{2}{5}$.

    a. 2   **b.** $\frac{8}{25}$

    c. $\frac{2}{5}$ **d.** not given

20. Thirty-five fewer than a number is 35. What is the number?

    a. 0   **b.** 35   **c.** 70   **d.** not given

21. A jar contains 1 blue, 2 red, and 2 green marbles. If one marble is drawn at random 50 times and is replaced each time, how many times can you expect to draw green?

    a. 2   **b.** 10   **c.** 20   **d.** not given

22. Paulo needs $5\frac{1}{3}$ yd of material to make a curtain of certain size. How many such curtains can he make if he has 78 yd of material?

    a. 16 curtains   **b.** 15 curtains
    c. 14 curtains   **d.** not given

**Explain how you solved each problem.
Show all your work.**

23. A factory makes CD players. The table shows that it produces 29 CD players during the first 4 days of production.

Day (d)	1	2	3	4
Number of CD players (n)	8	15	22	29

    a. What pattern do you see in the 1st row of the table? 2nd row?

    b. Predict the number of CD players produced in the first 12 days of production. Upon what do you base your prediction?

    c. Write an expression to show how you can get the numbers in the 2nd row of the table from the numbers in the 1st row.

Data and Statistics

Lunch Time

Oh, for a piece of papaya,
or a plate of beef lo mein—

Oh, for a bowl of Irish stew,
or fresh paella from Spain—

Oh, for a forkful of couscous,
or a chunk of Jarlsberg cheese—

Oh, for some lasagna,
or a bowl of black-eyed peas—

Of all the tasty foods
That I would love to try,

I sit here and wonder
why, oh why,
Mama packed me
this liverwurst on rye.

Lee Bennett Hopkins

In this chapter you will:

Survey, collect, organize, report, and
  interpret data
Learn about bias in surveys
Apply measures of central tendency and range
Investigate stem-and-leaf plots, box-and-
  whisker plots, double bar and line graphs,
  histograms, and circle graphs
Recognize misleading statistics
Solve problems by making an organized list

Critical Thinking/Finding Together

Research each of the foods mentioned in the
poem. Make organized lists to find the number
of two-food combinations you can make.

Surveys

Iris wanted to know whether the students in her school think that it is a good idea to make the school day longer. She decided to conduct a survey.

A survey is a method of gathering information about a group. Surveys are usually made up of questions or other items that require responses.

To conduct a survey:

- Write and ask questions to determine the opinions on the topic.
- Record the responses.
- Organize the data in a table or graph.

Iris surveyed the school population that included:

- the same number of students from each grade
- the same number of boys as girls
- students from various ethnic backgrounds

Iris asked this question of 30 students: *Do you think the school day should be longer? Answer Yes, No, or Not Sure.*

Responses: Yes—8 students   No—18 students   Not Sure—4 students

She presented her findings in both a pictograph and a bar graph.

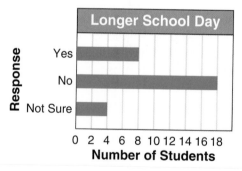

From her survey, Iris predicted that most students in her school do not think that the school day should be longer.

The bar graph shows the results of a survey about favorite types of movies. Use the graph to answer the questions.

1. Write a survey question that could be used to obtain the data.

2. How many more people chose science fiction than adventure?

3. How many people in all were surveyed?

4. What fractional part of those surveyed chose drama?

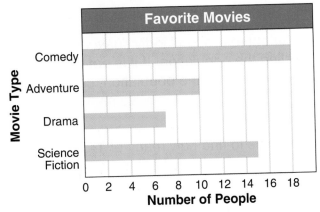

The pictograph shows the results of a survey about favorite drinks. Use the graph to answer the questions.

5. Write a survey question that could be used to obtain the data.

6. How many of those surveyed did not choose soda or iced tea as their favorite?

7. What fractional part of those surveyed chose either lemonade or orange juice?

8. You are ordering drinks for 200 people. Based on the results of the survey, how many of each drink would you order?

9. If you surveyed your class, do you think that most students would favor the same drink? Explain.

10. Survey your class to test your prediction in exercise 9. Present your data in a bar graph or pictograph.

11. Write a paragraph comparing your data with the data displayed above in the pictograph. Was your prediction correct?

CRITICAL THINKING

12. Nancy makes predictions from survey data that she collects about a favorite holiday from people in a shopping mall. Name three things that can affect the accuracy of Nancy's predictions and explain why they would.

Samples

▶ The entire group of individuals or objects considered for a survey is called the population. If it is not practical to survey an entire population, a small part of the population, called a sample, is used. A sample is said to be a representative sample if it has characteristics similar to the entire population.

John wants to find how many of 14,000 voters in a town are likely to vote for Candidate A. Explain whether a survey of the population or a sample is better.

John should use a sample since it is not practical to survey the entire population.

If the population changed to only 50 voters, John can survey the population. Given time, each member of the population could be surveyed individually.

▶ There are different ways of selecting a sample:

- Random sampling — Each individual or object in the given population has an equal chance of being chosen. A representative sample can be provided by random sampling.
  Example: 50 voters whose names are chosen, without looking, from a box containing all voters' names.

- Convenience sampling — Each individual or object is chosen because they are available and accessible.
  Example: The first 50 voters to arrive at a polling place are surveyed.

- Responses to a survey — Each individual is given an oral interview or written questionnaire.
  Example: Some voters might mail completed survey forms to the researcher.

Practice

For each survey question, tell whether you would survey the *population* or use a *sample*. Explain.

1. What section of the newspaper do subscribers read first?

2. Where do the students in your class want to go on a field trip?

3. What is the most popular car of the people in your city?

4. What is the favorite animal of students in your school?

5. What is the favorite movie of the people working in the video store?

6. Who is the favorite counselor of the students at summer camp?

Tell whether the sample is *likely* or *unlikely* to be a representative sample of the whole population. If unlikely, explain why.

7. Palo wants to find the favorite beach of the swim team members. He writes each member's name on a craft stick and chooses 10 names randomly.

8. To find the favorite hobbies of the students at school, Joanna asks the members of the chess club.

Tell which method of selecting a sample is used. Write *random sampling*, *convenience sampling*, or *responses to a survey*.

9. Philip chooses one name from each page of the phone book.

10. Rhianne distributes a questionnaire and tallies the results she gets back.

11. Mickey e-mails a list of questions to everyone in school. He records the results from the people who reply.

12. Elena questions people as they are leaving the bookstore.

Use Samples to Predict

You can use data from a sample to predict data for an entire population.

A lake is estimated to have a fish population of 1000. Ten out of 50 fish are trout. Based on this sample, predict about how many fish in the lake are trout.

- Set up an equation.

$$\text{sample} \longrightarrow \frac{10 \text{ trout}}{50 \text{ fish in all}} = \frac{n \text{ trout}}{1000 \text{ fish in all}} \longleftarrow \text{population}$$

- Find equivalent fractions to solve for *n*.

$$\frac{10 \times 20}{50 \times 20} = \frac{200}{1000}$$

$$n = 200$$

Think.............
50 × 20 = 1000
....

Out of about 1000 fish in the lake, about 200 are trout.

Predict the number of *yes* responses from the population.

13. population: 1000 voters
sample: 250 voters
yes responses from sample: 175

14. population: 500 students
sample: 20 students
yes responses from sample: 8

Write About It

15. Dr. Phillips samples 30 students to find the average distance students live from school. His results indicate an average distance of 2.2 mi. The actual average distance students live from school is 1.9 mi. Dr. Phillips used a random sample. Explain why the average distance from the survey is different from the actual average distance.

16. What results would Dr. Phillips get if he randomly sampled another 30 students?

Bias in Surveys

▶ When you collect data in a survey, your sample should represent the whole population. If certain groups from the population are not represented in the sample, then the sample is a biased sample.

To determine which sports television programs are the most popular in a city, a survey is made by selecting and interviewing people at random on a street corner. Outside of which location would the interviewer be most likely to find a biased sample? Explain.

A. a sports arena   **B.** a concert hall   **C.** a park

Sample from A is most likely to be biased in favor of sports programming.

▶ Sometimes, questions are biased. A biased question suggests or leads to a specific response or excludes a certain group.

Roger and Gino want to find out the favorite spectator sports of the students in school. Roger asks, *Don't you think soccer is the most fun sport to watch?* Gino asks, *Which sport do you think is the most fun to watch?* Whose question is biased?

Roger's question is biased toward soccer.

▶ Data displays can be biased and influence how results are interpreted. Look at these graphs.

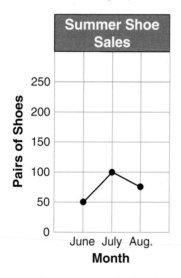

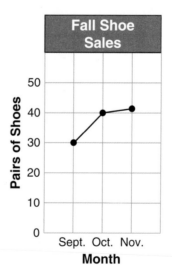

Shoe sales appear to be lower in summer than in fall. Look carefully at the intervals on the vertical axes and you will see that is not true.

Write whether one would be most likely to find a biased sample for the survey at each location. Write *Yes* or *No*. Explain.

1. Favorite food; Italian restaurant

2. Favorite holiday; shopping mall

3. Favorite sport; football game

4. Favorite music; park

Write whether the question is *biased* or *unbiased*. Explain.

5. What is your favorite kind of cereal?

6. Is gym your favorite school subject?

7. Do you think corn flakes are the best cereal?

8. Is pizza your best choice for lunch?

Explain how the data displays can influence how the results are interpreted.

9.

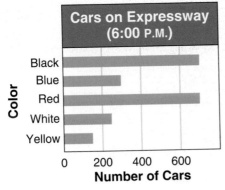
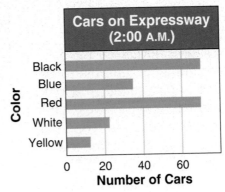

Problem Solving

A survey about type of phone preference, land line or cell phone, was made. Use the table for problems 10–11.

10. How may sample A be biased? Give an example in which that bias may be eliminated.

11. Which sample may be the least biased? Explain.

Sample	How Selected
A	Every 20th number in a phone directory is called.
B	People walking in a park are randomly chosen and asked questions.

CRITICAL THINKING

12. Suppose you need to find out the favorite vacation spot of the students in school. If you cannot survey everyone, explain how you could sample the population so that the sample is least likely to be biased. Then write one question you could ask that would be biased and one question that would not be biased. Explain why you think your biased question is biased.

Record and Interpret Data

Daria's gym teacher wanted to find out how fast most sixth graders could run the 100-meter dash. The recorded times, in seconds, are shown below.

14.2	14.4	13.9	14.9	14.4	13.8	14.4	14.3	13.8	14.2
14.6	13.7	15.1	13.9	14.0	13.8	14.4	15.4	15.2	13.8
14.4	14.1	14.2	13.7	14.2	14.4	14.6	14.1	15.1	13.8

▶ To *record* and *organize* the data, Daria makes a cumulative frequency table. She groups the data by range of time and uses tally marks to record the running times within each range of times. Then she counts the tallies to find the frequency and shows a running total of data to find the cumulative frequency.

Running Times: 100-m Dash			
Speed (seconds)	Tally	Frequency	Cumulative Frequency
13.6–14.0	̶H̶t̶ ̶H̶t̶	10	10
14.1–14.5	̶H̶t̶ ̶H̶t̶ ///	13	23◄
14.6–15.0	///	3	26◄
15.1–15.5	////	4	30◄

$$10 + 13 = 23$$
$$23 + 3 = 26$$
$$26 + 4 = 30 \longleftarrow \text{total frequency}$$

Daria concluded that most students could run the race in 14.5 seconds or less.

▶ Rico records the same data in this ungrouped frequency table that includes a row for relative frequency. Relative frequency compares the frequency of a category to the total frequency.

Speed (seconds)	13.7	13.8	13.9	14.0	14.1	14.2	14.3	14.4	14.6	14.9	15.1	15.2	15.4
Tally	//	̶H̶t̶	//	/	//	////	/	̶H̶t̶ /	//	/	//	/	/
Frequency	2	5	2	1	2	4	1	6	2	1	2	1	1
Relative Frequency	0.07	0.17	0.07	0.03	0.07	0.13	0.03	0.20	0.07	0.03	0.07	0.03	0.03

$$2 \div 30 = 0.07$$

He concluded that 14.4 seconds (0.20 of the total frequency) was the time most frequently run for the 100-meter dash.

Copy and complete the table. Use the completed table for exercises 6–9.

Distances: Standing Long Jump			
Distance (meters)	Tally	Frequency	Cumulative Frequency
1. 1.1–1.3	~~HHT~~ /	?	?
2. 1.4–1.6	?	11	?
3. 1.7–1.9	?	5	?
4. 2.0–2.2	//	?	?
5. 2.3–2.5	//	?	?

6. How many long jumps were recorded?

7. Within which interval do most jumps fall?

8. How many more students jumped from 1.4 m to 1.6 m than from 1.7 m to 1.9 m?

9. Write a conclusion about the long-jump data shown in the table.

Some sixth-grade students at Owens School participated in the softball throw. The numerical data below show the distances thrown, in meters.

10. Organize the data in an ungrouped frequency table. Include a relative frequency column.

Softball Throw: Grade 6							
21	20	28	21	24	20	22	28
20	28	26	24	21	23	28	26
29	23	29	20	23	20	21	28

11. How many softball throws were recorded?

12. Which distance was thrown most often? Which was thrown exactly 4 times?

13. Write a conclusion about the data in the table. Select two distances thrown and compare them to all the distances.

CHALLENGE

14. Conduct a softball throw (distances to nearest meter or nearest yard) with the students in your mathematics or physical education class (as in exercises 10–13 above).

   a. Collect the data and make a cumulative frequency table.

   b. Write the three best conclusions you can make about the data in your cumulative frequency table.

Apply Measures of Central Tendency and Range

The mean, median, and mode of a data set are called measures of central tendency. They indicate where the greatest number of the data set is concentrated. The range represents the spread between the greatest and the least values of the data set.

Gloria keeps a record of the number of sit-ups she does each day.

To describe Gloria's data, you can use the mean, median, mode, or range.

Day	S	M	T	W	Th	F	S
Number of Sit-ups	28	30	30	37	35	40	45

- The **mean** of a data set of n numbers is the sum of the numbers divided by n.

$$\frac{28 + 30 + 30 + 37 + 35 + 40 + 45}{7} = \frac{245}{7} = 35$$

mean

The mean, 35, shows the number of sit-ups Gloria would do each day if the total number of sit-ups were evened out.

- The **median** of a data set is the middle number when the data are arranged in order.

28 30 30 35 37 40 45

median

For an even number of data, the median is the average of the two middle numbers.

12, 13, 14, 15, → median $= \frac{13 + 14}{2} = 13.5$

The median, 35, shows that the number of days Gloria did less than 35 sit-ups equals the number of days she did more than 35.

- The **mode** of a data set is the number that occurs most frequently.

28, 30, 30, 35, 37, 40, 45

mode

Sometimes a data set has no mode or has more than one mode.

29, 33, 35, 31, 30, 32 has no mode.

28, 31, 31, 29, 36, 29, 35 has two modes: 31 and 29.

The mode, 30, shows that Gloria does 30 sit-ups more frequently than any other number of sit-ups.

- The **range** is the difference between the greatest and the least values in a data set.

$45 - 28 = 17$ ← range

The range, 17, shows how far the data is spread out from the greatest number of sit-ups to the least number of sit-ups.

Find the mean, median, mode, and range for each set of data. Then use each measure to describe the data set.

1.

Ana's Reading Test Scores				
70	110	90	70	60

2.

Bob's Daily Expenses				
$4.50	$4.95	$4.80	$6.25	$4.25

The Most Representative Measure

The measure that is closest to most of the data in the set most accurately describes the data.

The daily temperatures in °F last week were 98°, 97°, 94°, 75°, 74°, 97°, and 95°. Would mean, median, or mode best describe these data? Explain.

Mean: 90°; median: 95°; mode: 97°; since the median and the mode are close to most of the data, the median or the mode most accurately describe the data.

For each data set, find the mean, median, and mode. Tell which measure is most useful for describing the data. Explain why.

3. Ray scored 15, 7, 5, 3, 9, and 15 points in 6 basketball games. He wants to show that he is a valuable player.

4. Ed wants to know the average amount of gas he uses in a week. In the past 3 weeks, he used 5 gal, 7 gal, and 30 gal.

5. Ana spent 5 min, 2h, 6h, 1h, and 6 h using the Internet for the past 5 days. She wants to consider how much time she spends on the Internet.

6. The Lim's collected donations of $175, $210, $125, $50, $10, $24, and $50 for flood victims. They want to show that they are good fundraisers.

Problem Solving

Use the information in the table for exercises 7–8.

Annual Salaries: F. H. Murphy Co.	
$20,000	$30,000
$325,000	$26,000
$32,000	$26,000
$30,000	$28,000
$28,000	$30,000

7. Does the mean, median, or mode most accurately describe the average salary of F. H. Murphy Co. employees? Explain.

8. How would the mean, median, and mode be affected if the greatest salary is changed to $3,000,000?

TEST PREPARATION

9. Which data set has more than one mode?

  A 2, 2, 4, 6, 7, 9   **B** 2, 2, 6, 7, 9

  C 2, 2, 4, 6, 9, 9   **D** 2, 3, 4, 6, 9

10. In which data set are the mean, median, and mode all the same value?

  F 1, 3, 3, 3, 5   **G** 1, 1, 1, 2, 5

  H 1, 1, 2, 5, 6   **J** 1, 1, 3, 5, 10

Analyze Data

High temperatures of the last nine days were 2°C, 3°C, 1°C, 3°C, 5°C, 10°C, 4°C, 4°C, and 3°C. Kathy organizes the data in a line plot. A line plot is a graph that uses Xs to show data on a number line.

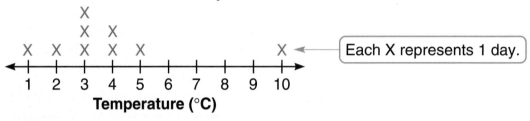

High Temperatures of the Last Nine Days

Each X represents 1 day.

- **Clusters** are places on the line plot where several Xs occur very close together. There is a data cluster from 3°C to 4°C.

- **Gaps** are large places on the line plot where no data occurs. A gap exists between 5°C and 10°C.

- **Outliers** are numbers set apart from the rest of the data. A set of data may have no outliers or it may have one or more outliers. 10°C is an outlier of the data set.

▶ Outliers can affect the measures of central tendency of a data set.

- Find the mean, median, and mode of the above data set.

Mean: $\dfrac{2 + 3 + 1 + 3 + 5 + 10 + 4 + 4 + 3}{9} = \dfrac{35}{9} \approx 3.9$ → mean ≈ 3.9°C

Median: 1, 2, 3, 3, 3, 4, 4, 5, 10 → median = 3°C

Mode: 1, 2, 3, 3, 3, 4, 4, 5, 10 → mode = 3°C

- Find the mean, median, and mode of the above data set *without* the outlier.

Mean: $\dfrac{2 + 3 + 1 + 3 + 5 + 4 + 4 + 3}{8} = \dfrac{25}{8} \approx 3.1$ → mean ≈ 3.1°C

Median: 1, 2, 3, 3, 3, 4, 4, 5 → median = $\dfrac{3 + 3}{2} = 3$°C

Mode: 1, 2, 3, 3, 3, 4, 4, 5 → mode = 3°C

When the outlier is not included in the data set, the mean decreases by 0.8 degree. The median and the mode are not changed.

Use the line plot for exercises 1–6.

1. What score is an outlier?

2. Where is there a gap?

3. Around what score do the data cluster?

4. Find the mean, median, and mode of the data set.

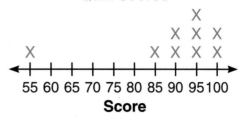

Quiz Scores

5. Find the mean, median, and mode of the scores without the outlier.

6. Describe what effect the outlier has on the mean, the median, and the mode.

Use the line plot for exercises 7–8.

7. Identify any clusters, gaps, and outliers of the data set.

8. Describe what effect the outliers have on the mean, median, and mode.

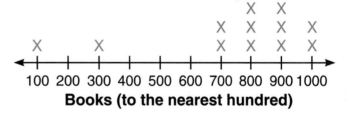

School Library Book Collections

Make a line plot for each set of data. Identify any clusters, gaps, and outliers.

9.

Daily Low Temperatures
26°F, 25°F, 24°F, 29°F, 28°F, 21°F, 10°F

10.

Number of Stories in Town Buildings
3, 3, 1, 1, 8, 6, 6, 4, 3, 23, 7, 9

11.

Meghan's Math Test Scores
85 80 90 95 90 100 90 70 85 80 90 100 95 90 90

12.

Len's Bowling Scores
93, 96, 93, 106, 95, 95, 97, 98, 100, 94

DO YOU REMEMBER?

13. $8 \div \frac{2}{3}$

14. $\frac{5}{6} \div \frac{3}{4}$

15. $5\frac{5}{8} \div \frac{5}{12}$

16. $6\frac{2}{3} \div 7\frac{1}{2}$

Box-and-Whisker Plots

The data set shows student scores from a 120-point reading test. A box-and-whisker plot can be used to show the data distribution.

Scores		
50	60	80
100	90	70
70	110	90

A box-and-whisker plot includes a number line that shows the **extremes** (greatest and least) numbers, the median, and the **quartile** divisions. A box is drawn on top of the second and third quartiles. The **whiskers** show the first and fourth quartiles.

▶ **To make a box-and-whisker plot:**

- Order the data from least to greatest.

- Find the *median*. Then find the *upper* and *lower* quartiles, which are the middle values of each half of the data.

- Display the extremes, quartiles, and median as points above a number line.

- Draw a *box* that ends at the lower and upper quartiles. Then draw a vertical line segment through the box at the median.

- Draw horizontal line segments, called *whiskers*, from the ends of the box to the lower and upper extremes.

- Write a title for the plot.

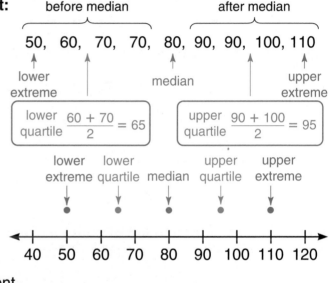

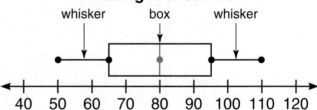

Reading Test Scores

Use the box-and-whisker plot above.

1. How many quartiles or values are needed to divide the data into four parts?

2. Which characteristic of a box-and-whisker plot can be used to determine the range of the data?

3. About how much of the data are in the box?

4. If each score was tripled, how would the shape of the box change?

Use the box-and-whisker plot for exercises 5–6.

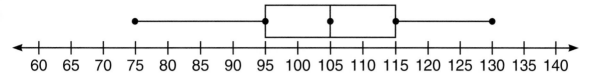

60 65 70 75 80 85 90 95 100 105 110 115 120 125 130 135 140

5. What are the extremes of the data?

6. What is the median of the data? the upper and lower quartiles?

Make a box-and-whisker plot for each set of data.

7.

Science Quiz Scores
35, 30, 20, 25, 30, 25, 15, 45, 50, 30

8.

Math Test Scores
97, 76, 84, 112, 93, 68, 88

Problem Solving

The box-and-whisker plot shows how many bottles and cans each of 11 students collected for the recycling project.

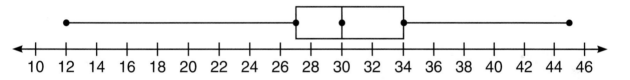

10 12 14 16 18 20 22 24 26 28 30 32 34 36 38 40 42 44 46

9. What does each part of the plot represent, including the points and each part of the box?

10. What would happen to the box if the numbers 36 and 39 were added?

11. Write 11 possible combinations of the number of cans collected and the number of bottles collected by each student to equal the amounts that the box-and-whisker plot represents.

MENTAL MATH

Use mental math to find the median, lower quartile, upper quartile, and range for each set of data.

12. 10, 20, 30, 40, 50

13. 25, 30, 32, 50, 60, 100, 200, 225

14. 19, 40, 60, 75, 85, 88, 98, 99

15. 1000, 1200, 1400, 1750, 1900, 1900, 1920

Stem-and-Leaf Plots

Some of the tallest buildings in Baltimore, Maryland, are listed in the table below. You can organize and display the same data in a stem-and-leaf plot. A stem-and-leaf plot is a convenient way to organize numerical data so that the numbers themselves make up the display.

Building	Number of Floors
Legg Mason Building	40
Blaustein Building	30
Harbour Court	28
250 W. Pratt St.	24
Bank of America Building	37
Commerce Place	31
Wachovia Tower	24
Fallon Federal	28
World Trade Center	32
Tremont Plaza Hotel	37
Charles Center South	25

▶ **To make a stem-and-leaf plot:**

- Draw a chart and label two columns as *Stem* and *Leaf*, as shown. The front-end digits of the data are the *stems*. Write them in order in the stem column.

- The *leaves* are the ones digits. Write each leaf to the right of its stem in the leaf column.

- Rewrite the leaves in order from least to greatest.

- Write a *Key* to show the meaning of each piece of data in the plot. Then write a *title* for the plot.

Stem	Leaf
2	8 4 4 8 5
3	0 7 1 2 7
4	0

Heights of Buildings in Baltimore, Maryland (No. of Floors)

Stem	Leaf
2	4 4 5 8 8
3	0 1 2 7 7
4	0

Key: 2│8 represents 28

Range: 40 − 24 = 16
Median: Count to find the (middle) number, 30.
Mode: There are 3 modes—24, 28, and 37.

Use the plot to answer the questions.

1. The heights of how many buildings are shown?

2. How many floors are there in the tallest building?

3. How many buildings have 40 or more floors?

4. What are the range, the median, and the mode of the data?

Heights of Some Buildings in Charlotte, North Carolina (No. of Floors)	
Stem	**Leaf**
6	0
4	0 2
3	2 2 2
2	4 7

Use the data in the box to complete the stem-and-leaf plot. Then answer the questions.

5.
Stem	Leaf
5	? ? ?
4	? ? ? ?
3	? ? ? ? ? ?
2	? ?

Heights of Some Buildings in Denver, Colorado (No. of Floors)
56   54   52   43   41   40
36   35   31   32   34   42
32   28   26

6. What are the range, the median, and the mode of the data?

7. Write a statement that summarizes the results that the plot shows.

Make a stem-and-leaf plot for each set of data. Find the range, median, and mode of the data.

8.
Lions' Basketball Scores
49   54   66   51   81   72   77
52   56   48   53   65   63

9.
High March Temperatures (in °F)
42°   66°   26°   44°   31°   60°
52°   79°   45°   38°   64°   42°
83°   21°   38°

10.
Ages of the First Twenty-One United States Presidents at Their Inaugurations
57   61   57   57   58   57   61   54   68   51   49
64   50   48   65   52   56   46   54   49   50

Write About It

11. Use the stem-and-leaf plot you made in exercise 10 to explain the data about

a. the ages of the first 21 United States presidents at their inaugurations.

b. how many of the 21 presidents were younger than 60 years of age at their inaugurations.

Line Graphs

Mr. Fleury, owner of Pizzas Unlimited, records pizza sales for 6 days.

Day	Mon.	Tues.	Wed.	Thurs.	Fri.	Sat.
Pizzas Sold	100	90	80	60	40	30

Mr. Fleury displayed his sales in a line graph.
A line graph is used to show changes in data over time.

▶ To make a line graph:
   • Draw horizontal and vertical axes on grid paper. Label the axes.
   • Use the data from the table to choose an appropriate scale (intervals of 10).
   • Start at 0 and label equal intervals of the scale on the vertical axis.
   • Label the horizontal axis by day.
   • Graph the points on the grid.
   • Connect the points with line segments.
   • Write a title for the graph.

▶ To determine a trend, look for a rise (the data show an increase) or a fall (the data show a decrease) in the line between two points.

   The number of pizzas sold decreased each day.

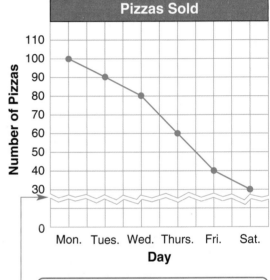

The broken scale indicates that part of the scale is missing.

Researchers conducted a survey and concluded that of every 50 pizzas ordered, people will request extra cheese on 9 of them.

▶ Use a line graph to compare two quantities, such as the number of pizzas ordered and the number of pizzas with extra cheese. As the number of pizzas ordered increases, the number of pizzas with extra cheese also increases.

   From left to right, the line slopes upward.

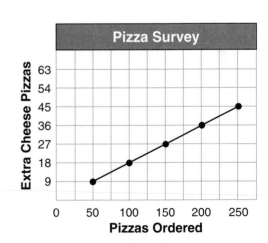

Copy and complete the graph to show the data in the table.

1.

School Fair Profits	
Year	Profit (in dollars)
2005	850
2004	740
2003	700
2002	620
2001	525
2000	585

School Fair Profits

Amount (dollars)

850
800
750
700
650
600
550
500
0

2000 2001 2002 2003 2004 2005

Year

Use the completed line graph for exercises 2–5.

2. What does each interval on the vertical scale represent?

3. What trend does the graph show?

4. By how much did profits increase from 2003 to 2005?

5. What is the range of the profits? What is the mean (average) profit?

Problem Solving

6. A certain clock loses 3 minutes every 12 hours as shown in the table. Draw a line graph of the data and determine if the line slopes upward or downward. Explain why this happens.

Number of Hours	12	24	36	48	60
Time Lost (minutes)	3	6	9	12	15

CRITICAL THINKING

Use the given line graph.

7. As *b* increases, what happens to *c*?

8. As *c* decreases, what happens to *b*?

9. If $c = 75$, what is the value of *b*?

10. Predict the value of *b* if $c = 165$.

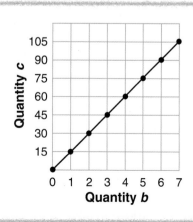

Quantity *c*

105
90
75
60
45
30
15

0 1 2 3 4 5 6 7

Quantity *b*

Double Line Graphs

Stock at Sam's Shirts		
Month	**T-Shirts**	**Sweatshirts**
Jan.	275	225
Feb.	375	175
Mar.	350	200
Apr.	450	250
May	410	310
June	400	300
July	350	250
Aug.	300	175
Sept.	500	260

Sam's Shirts sells T-shirts and sweatshirts. The owner recorded in a table how many T-shirts and sweatshirts were in stock during a 9-month period. He then displayed the results in a double line graph.

A double line graph compares two sets of data over time. The data sets are graphed separately on the same grid. The key shows which line graph represents each data set.

▶ To make a double line graph:

- Draw horizontal and vertical axes on grid paper.

- Choose an appropriate scale for both sets of data.

- Label both axes. On the vertical axis, mark equal intervals beginning with 0. On the horizontal axis, write the categories.

- Choose two different colors and make a key to show what each color represents.

- Plot a point for each data item. Join the points with line segments.

- Write a title for the graph.

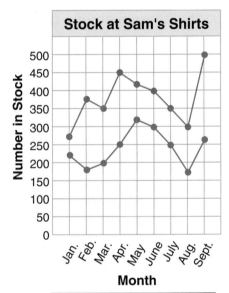

Stock at Sam's Shirts

Number in Stock

Month

Key: T-shirts ———
Sweatshirts ———

Use the double line graph above.

1. Describe the change in T-shirt stock from April to August.

2. Describe the change in sweatshirt stock between February and May.

3. When was the total stock of T-shirts and sweatshirts the greatest? When was the total stock the least?

4. When was the difference between the stock of T-shirts and sweatshirts the greatest? When was it the least?

5. Why might stocks of both T-shirts and sweatshirts increase greatly from August to September?

Use the given graph.

6. In which city was the average temperature 68° in June? How do you know?

7. During which month(s) was the difference in average temperature in the two cities the greatest? the least? Explain how you found your answer.

8. During which months is the difference in average temperature less than 20°? Explain how you found your answer.

9. Describe the general trend you see in each city's average monthly temperature.

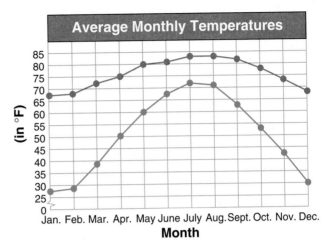

Average Monthly Temperatures

(in °F)

Jan. Feb. Mar. Apr. May June July Aug. Sept. Oct. Nov. Dec.

Month

Key: Miami ⎯⎯⎯
       Chicago ⎯⎯⎯

Make a double line graph for each data set.

10.

Stock at Sam's Shirts		
Month	Jeans	Shorts
Oct.	525	175
Nov.	425	225
Dec.	450	210
Jan.	475	200
Feb.	480	185

11.

Average Height (in cm)		
Age	Boys	Girls
12	150	152
13	157	157
14	163	160
15	169	162
16	174	162

Use your graphs from exercises 10–11.

12. When was the difference between the stock of jeans and shorts the greatest? When was it the least?

13. When was the total stock of jeans and shorts the greatest? When was the total stock the least?

14. At what ages are boys taller than girls?

15. At what ages are the average heights of boys and girls the same?

CHALLENGE

16. Choose two cities that you would like to visit and the month you would like to visit each. Then research and record in a double line graph the daily high temperature in each city for one week.

Double Bar Graphs

The owner of Kim's Shirts recorded in a table the daily shirt sales for five days. She then displayed the results in a double bar graph.

A double bar graph compares two related sets of data. Each set of data is graphed separately, but on the same grid. The key explains which set of data is shown by each bar graph.

Daily Shirt Sales at Kim's		
Day	**T-Shirts**	**Sweatshirts**
Monday	60	40
Tuesday	70	45
Wednesday	40	35
Thursday	55	40
Friday	80	60

▶ To make a double bar graph:

- Draw horizontal and vertical axes on grid paper.

- Choose an appropriate scale for both sets of data.

- Label both axes. On the vertical axis, mark equal intervals beginning with 0. On the horizontal axis, write the categories.

- Choose your colors and make a key to show what each color represents.

- Draw a bar for each value of data.

- Write a title for the graph.

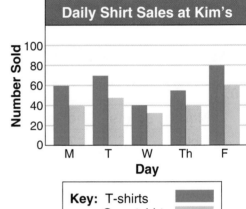

Use the double bar graph above.

1. How many more T-shirts than sweatshirts were sold on Monday?

2. On which day were the most T-shirts sold? the most sweatshirts?

3. Which day had the greatest number of total sales? the least number of total sales?

4. On which day was there the least difference between T-shirts sales and sweatshirts sales?

5. What can you say about the sale of T-shirts from Wednesday to Friday? Explain your answer.

6. How would you summarize the data about shirts sales shown by the graph?

Use the given graph.

7. How many calories do men use when running for an hour? when walking for an hour?

8. How many calories do women use when sleeping for an hour? when sitting for an hour?

9. What can you conclude about the number of calories used by men and by women when doing the five activities?

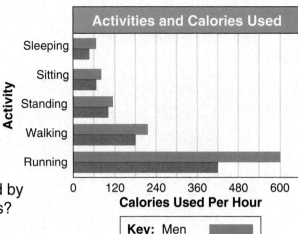

Activities and Calories Used

Activity: Sleeping, Sitting, Standing, Walking, Running

Calories Used Per Hour: 0, 120, 240, 360, 480, 600

Key: Men, Women

Make a double bar graph for each data set. Then answer exercises 12–13.

10.

Favorite T-Shirt Colors		
Color	Girls	Boys
white	4	7
red	8	8
blue	12	8
green	11	6
yellow	7	11

11.

Swimsuit Sales		
Month	Two-Piece	One-Piece
April	$2,400	$2,100
May	$3,200	$4,600
June	$5,600	$5,800
July	$5,900	$6,000
August	$5,100	$4,800

12. What T-shirt colors are favored by more boys than girls? by the same number of boys and girls?

13. When was the total sale of two-piece and one-piece swimsuits the greatest? When was the total sale the least?

CRITICAL THINKING

A scatter plot is a graph that shows whether there is a correlation, or relationship, between two sets of data. If the data cluster around a line that is drawn from lower left to upper right, there is a positive correlation. If the line that is drawn is from upper left to lower right, there is a negative correlation. If a line cannot be drawn, there is no correlation.

14. What correlation, if any, do you see between temperature and time?

15. Over what period of time was the temperature at or below 53°F?

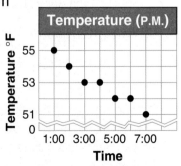

Temperature (P.M.)

Temperature °F: 55, 53, 51, 0

Time: 1:00, 3:00, 5:00, 7:00

Misleading Graphs and Statistics

When data presented in a graph affects the impression the graph makes, the representation is considered biased. Examine the two graphs below.

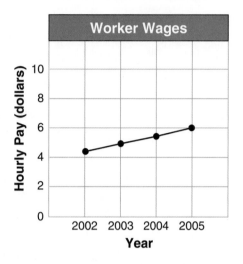

Both graphs show the same information about worker hourly pay. Although both show that wages have increased, the graph at the right gives the impression that wages have increased more rapidly. What causes this?

Look at the vertical scale of each graph. The *expanded scale* on the graph at the right creates the impression of a faster rate of increase.

Study this example.

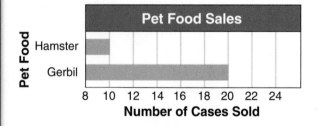

This graph is *misleading*. Although gerbil food sales are *twice* those of hamster food sales, the graph gives the impression that the difference is much greater because the scale does not start at 0.

Practice

Use the graphs above for exercises 1–2.

1. It is time for a new labor contract. Which line graph would you use if you represented labor? Which would you use if you represented management? Explain.

2. Why does the bar graph give the impression that gerbil food sales are about 6 times as great as hamster food sales? Draw an accurate bar graph for the data.

The table and graphs show the number of exercise DVDs sold during a 5-month period.

Month	Jan.	Feb.	Mar.	Apr.	May
Sales (hundreds)	7.5	10	12	14	16

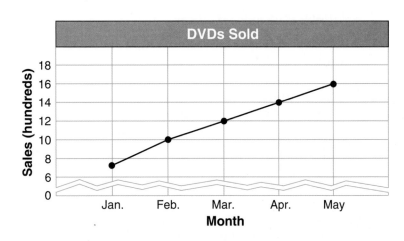

3. Do both graphs show the same data?

4. Which graph would someone use who wants to convince you that the sales of exercise DVDs have risen dramatically?

5. Why do you get a different impression about the data from the two graphs?

The graph at the right shows sales of pet-training DVDs.

6. How many pet-training DVDs were sold in 2004? in 2005?

7. What is misleading about this graph?

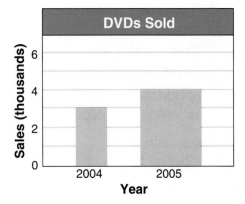

Write About It

8. Will had the following test scores: 55, 70, 88, 56, 88, 71, 62. He told his friend, "My most typical score was 88" (the mode). Explain why Will's statement is misleading.

9. An advertiser said, "Nine out of 10 dentists agree. Glomb works best." Explain why this statement might be misleading.

Histograms

Ms. Eilhardt organized the data shown at the right. First she made a frequency table.

Heights of Ms. Eilhardt's Students (in inches)					
52	57	59	59	50	59
51	52	49	60	56	50
55	58	53	52	51	54
50	54	53	58	57	67
55	57	58	56	57	58

▶ To make a frequency table:

- Choose a reasonable interval to group the data.

  > Since the data span from 49 to 67, use 5 intervals of 4 inches.

- Tally the data for each interval and record the frequencies.

Height (in.)	Tally	Frequency
49–52	卌 IIII	9
53–56	卌 III	8
57–60	卌 卌 II	12
61–64		0
65–68	I	1

Then Ms. Eilhardt made a histogram from the same table. A **histogram** is a graph that shows the *frequency* of equal intervals of data. In a histogram, the intervals must not overlap. There are no spaces between the bars of a histogram, unless there is an interval with a frequency of 0.

▶ To make a histogram:

- Use the frequency table to choose and label a scale on the vertical axis for the frequencies.

- Label the horizontal axis, listing the intervals in order.

- Draw bars (with no space between them) to show the frequency of each interval.

- Write a title for the histogram.

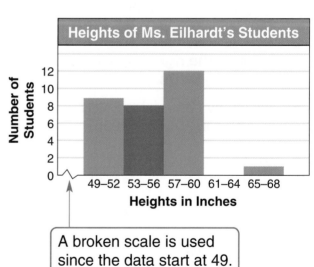

A broken scale is used since the data start at 49.

In which height group are most of Ms. Eilhardt's students?

▶ To find which group, look for the tallest bar and read the interval it represents.

Most of Ms. Eilhardt's students are from 57–60 inches tall.

Make a frequency table for the given data.
Then copy and complete the histogram.

1.

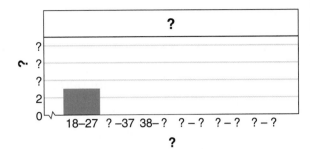

Weights of Kennel Dogs (in lb)
37 63 40 77 44 56 35
18 33 24 29 31 26 58
65 72 75 60 31 42 60

Make a frequency table and a histogram for each set of data.

2.

Number of Jumping Jacks Completed in One Minute
45 38 29 77 20 57 42 62 76
73 79 67 47 37 57 56 62 55
69 54 59 53 54 63 51 58 54

3.

Lengths of Bait Worms (in cm)
5 12 10 17   9 11 11 17 13
13   8 10 10 16 20 14   7 12
9 11   6 11   9 10 15 11 10
10 15   9 16 14 12   8   8 12

4.

Ages of People at the Pool
1 32   6 12 35 56 10   3 10
11   5 42   2   7 38 95 61   5
1   6 11 37   5   7 12 12 12

5.

Minutes Students Spent Outdoors Last Weekend
35 10 36 53 32   20 30 40   35
31 51 30 23   9 123 37 45   34
27   0 33 29 35   23 31 37 115

Problem Solving

Use the histogram for exercises 6–9.

6. How many students were surveyed?

7. Which interval of days did most students spend riding bikes last spring and summer?

8. Which interval has the least frequency?

9. Make a frequency table for the histogram. Explain how you made your table.

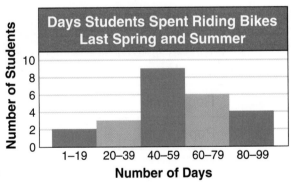

Write About It

10. Explain how a histogram is different from a bar graph.

11. How would the histogram on page 316 change if Ms. Eilhardt used intervals of 2 inches? intervals of 7 inches?

Interpret Circle Graphs

A circle graph shows how different parts of a set of data compare to the whole set. Many circle graphs display the fraction that corresponds to each part of the whole.

Shapiro's Marketing conducted a survey of music preferences on the basis of store sales of CDs. The circle graph at the right shows the fraction of the 200 people surveyed who purchased each type of music.

Music Preferences

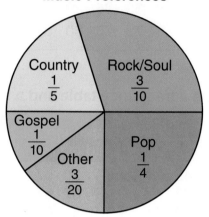

To find out how many of the 200 people chose country music, find $\frac{1}{5}$ of 200.

$$\frac{1}{5} \times \frac{200}{1} \longrightarrow \frac{1}{\overset{1}{\cancel{5}}} \times \frac{\overset{40}{\cancel{200}}}{1} = 40$$

So 40 people chose country music.

> Remember: A circle graph shows *parts of a whole*.
> The parts may be given as fractions or percents.

Practice

Use the circle graph above.

	Type of Music	Fraction	Number of People
1.	Country	$\frac{1}{5}$	40
2.	Rock/Soul	?	?
3.	Pop	?	?
4.	Gospel	?	?
5.	Other	?	?

6. Together, what part of the people surveyed chose either pop or country? pop or rock/soul? pop, country, or rock/soul?

7. Shapiro's conducted the same survey last month with 250 people and got the same fractions. Will the circle graph look the same or different? Explain.

Use the circle graph at the right.

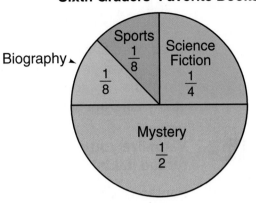

Sixth Graders' Favorite Books

8. There are 64 students in the sixth grade at Whitman School. How many favor mystery books?

9. How many sixth graders chose science fiction books?

10. What fractional part of the sixth graders prefer books that are *not* science fiction?

11. How many more sixth graders chose mystery books than sports books?

12. Which two types of books do one fourth of the sixth graders favor? Which two types do three fourths of the sixth graders favor?

13. Explain how the circle graph would differ if 8 of the sixth graders chose science fiction books instead of mystery books.

Use the circle graph at the right.

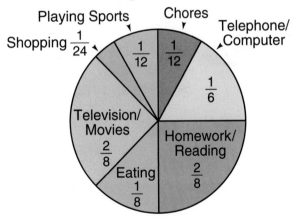

Teenager's Weekend

14. About how many weekend hours do teenagers spend playing sports?

15. About how many more weekend hours do teenagers spend reading and doing homework than they spend eating?

16. To which two sets of activities do teenagers devote the same amount of weekend time? how much time?

CRITICAL THINKING

Use the circle graph titled Teenager's Weekend.

17. How many times greater is a teenager's television and movie time than his or her shopping time?

18. On graph paper, construct a different kind of appropriate graph that shows the number of hours (not the fractional part) that a teenager spends on each activity in four weekends. Give your graph a title and label all of its parts.

Problem-Solving Strategy:
Make an Organized List

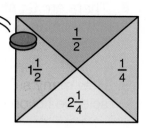

Frank designed this math game for his class. It is played by tossing a marker twice onto the board and finding the sum of the two addends on which the marker lands. How many different sums are possible?

Read

Visualize yourself in the problem above as you reread it. List the facts and the question.

Facts: A marker is tossed 2 times.
Possible addends — $\frac{1}{2}$, $\frac{1}{4}$, $2\frac{1}{4}$, $1\frac{1}{2}$

Question: How many different sums are possible?

Plan

Since a marker is tossed twice, you can get the same addend or 2 different addends. To find the possible sums, *make an organized list*. Eliminate duplicate sums with the same addends.

Remember:
A marker can land twice on the same addend.

Solve

Addend	$\frac{1}{2}$	$\frac{1}{2}$	$\frac{1}{2}$	$\frac{1}{2}$	$\frac{1}{4}$	$\frac{1}{4}$	$\frac{1}{4}$	$\frac{1}{4}$
+ Addend	$+\frac{1}{2}$	$+\frac{1}{4}$	$+2\frac{1}{4}$	$+1\frac{1}{2}$	$+\frac{1}{2}$	$+\frac{1}{4}$	$+2\frac{1}{4}$	$+1\frac{1}{2}$
Sum	1	$\frac{3}{4}$	$2\frac{3}{4}$	2	$\frac{3}{4}$	$\frac{1}{2}$	$2\frac{1}{2}$	$1\frac{3}{4}$

Think

$$\frac{1}{2} + \frac{1}{4} = \frac{1}{4} + \frac{1}{2}$$

Addend	$2\frac{1}{4}$	$2\frac{1}{4}$	$2\frac{1}{4}$	$2\frac{1}{4}$	$1\frac{1}{2}$	$1\frac{1}{2}$	$1\frac{1}{2}$	$1\frac{1}{2}$
+ Addend	$+\frac{1}{2}$	$+\frac{1}{4}$	$+2\frac{1}{4}$	$+1\frac{1}{2}$	$+\frac{1}{2}$	$+\frac{1}{4}$	$+2\frac{1}{4}$	$+1\frac{1}{2}$
Sum	$2\frac{3}{4}$	$2\frac{1}{2}$	$4\frac{1}{2}$	$3\frac{3}{4}$	2	$1\frac{3}{4}$	$3\frac{3}{4}$	3

There are 10 different possible sums.

Check

Use a tree diagram to be sure all possible combinations are listed.

Solve. Make an organized list to help you.

1. The nursery has 6 evergreen trees to be used in landscaping the park. There are 4 different areas where the trees can be put. In how many ways can the trees be placed so that each area has at least one tree?

Read Visualize yourself in the problem above as you reread it. List the facts and the question.

Facts: 6 evergreen trees
4 different areas

Question: In how many ways can the trees be placed so that each area has at least one tree?

Plan Make an organized list of 4 different park areas and trees to go into each.
(Make as many combinations as possible with 6 trees in 4 areas.)

Solve ......▶ **Check**

2. How many different four-digit numbers can you make using the digits 0, 1, 2, and 3 if repetition of a digit is not permitted?

3. Jason's dad has a yellow shirt, a pink shirt, and a blue shirt; a pair of black slacks and a pair of tan slacks; a pin-striped sport coat and a black sport coat. How many different three-piece outfits can he make?

4. If you spin each dial once, how many different combinations of numbers and letters can be made from spinning a dial marked 4, 7, and 9 and spinning a dial marked *A, B, C, D,* and *E*?

5. In a bowling game you have 2 chances to knock down the 10 pins. How many different ways can the pins be knocked down if with every 2 tries all 10 pins are knocked down?

6. How many different three-digit numbers can you make using the digits 0, 1, and 2 if repetition of digits *is* permitted?

Problem-Solving Applications: Mixed Review

Read ⟩ **Plan** ⟩ **Solve** ⟩ **Check**

Solve each problem and explain the method you used.

1. In their last 8 basketball games, the Johnston Jump Shots score these points: 85, 62, 74, 71, 81, 65, 81, and 57. Find the mean, median, mode, and range. Which measure gives the most useful information about how well the Johnston Jump Shots can shoot? Explain.

2. Make a line plot for this data set: 33, 43, 47, 44, 42, 46, and 46. Identify any clusters, gaps, and outliers and then explain how the outlier affects the mean in this data set.

3. Make a box-and-whisker plot for this data set: 11, 14, 15, 11, 2, 3, 5, 2, 7, 6, 3, 10, and 9. Find the extremes, the median, and the lower and upper quartiles.

4. If three fifths of 50 students in a random survey said basketball is their favorite sport, predict how many of 350 students do *not* favor basketball.

Use the stem-and-leaf plot for problems 5–7.

5. Find the mean, median, mode, and range of the Victors' scores.

6. If the Victors won each game in which their score was higher than the mean of all of their scores, how many games did they win?

7. Last season, the Victors scored a total of 24 less points in the same number of games. What was their mean score last season?

Victors' Scores	
Stem	**Leaf**
9	2
8	3 8
7	0 3 3 5 8
6	2 8 9
5	7

Use the line graph for problems 8–10.

8. Which team had the greater mean score in February?

9. Which team had a mean score of 62 in March?

10. Over the four months, which team had the greater mean score?

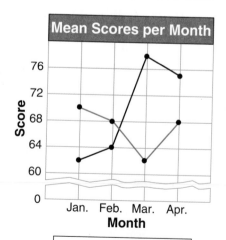

Mean Scores per Month

Key: —— Jump Shots
—— Zoomers

Choose a strategy from the list or use another strategy you know to solve each problem.

11. There are 5 teams in the local basketball league: the Jump Shots, the Zoomers, the Victors, the Hoopsters, and the Towers. Each season, every team plays every other team twice. How many games are played in a season?

12. In the first game of the season, the Towers scored 3 points less than twice the Hoopsters' score. If the Towers scored 89 points, what did the Hoopsters score?

13. Janine scored the following points in the first 5 games: 24, 29, 20, 28, and 19. How many points must Janine score in the sixth game to keep her median and mean scores the same?

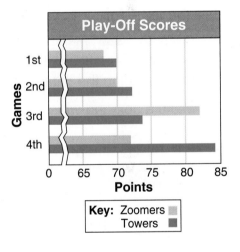

Use the bar graph for problems 14–16.

14. Which team scored more points in the first game?

15. Which game had the greatest point spread between the winning and losing scores?

16. Which team won 3 out of 4 of the play-off games?

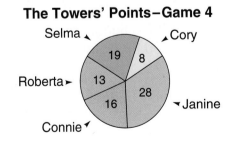

Use the circle graph for problems 17–19.

17. Which two players together scored one fourth of the points in Game 4?

18. What part of the team's points did Janine score?

19. What was the mean score per player for the players in game 4?

20. Have each student write a problem modeled on the circle graph above. Then have a classmate solve it.

Tell which method of selecting a sample is used: *random,* *convenience,* **or** *survey.* **Which sample is biased?** *(See pp. 292–297.)*

1. The first 20 people in line at a basketball game were surveyed.

2. Lea tallied the results from a questionnaire that she had distributed.

3. People in a mall are randomly chosen and asked questions.

Use the table for exercises 4–6. *(See pp. 298–303, 306–307, 314–315.)*

4. Make a cumulative frequency table with 3 intervals.

5. Find the relative frequency of each interval.

6. Make a line plot, a stem-and-leaf plot, and a histogram for the data set.

Students' Heights (in inches)
70 67 62 64 70 63 68
65 62 71 70 60 64 66
63 62 71 63 62 69

Use the table for exercises 7–8. *(See pp. 300–301, 304–305.)*

7. Find the mean, median, mode, and range of the data set. Tell which measure is most useful for describing the data. Explain.

8. Make a box-and-whisker plot for the data set.

Math Scores
81 81 32 81 83
82 88 87 83 82

Make a double line graph for this table. *(See pp. 310–311, 318–319.)*

9.

Doris Ann's Weekend Jobs					
Weekend	**1**	**2**	**3**	**4**	**5**
Frame Making	15	10	10	9	10
Frame Painting	3	11	15	14	7

Use the circle graph for exercises 10–11.

10. What fractional part of Martha's monthly budget is used for clothing and contributions?

11. What two parts comprise $\frac{3}{4}$ of Martha's monthly budget?

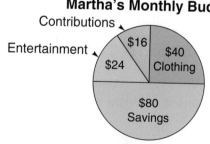

Martha's Monthly Budget

Problem Solving

12. Monica has 4 picture stamps: a fish, a flag, flowers, and berries. How many different ways can Monica arrange her 4 stamps in a row in her album?

13. Reword the survey question *Should skateboarders be allowed to endanger people by doing stunts on city sidewalks?* to remove bias.

(See Still More Practice, p. 527.)

Triple Line and Bar Graphs

A triple line graph and a triple bar graph are used to compare three sets of data. Each set of data is graphed separately, but on the same grid.

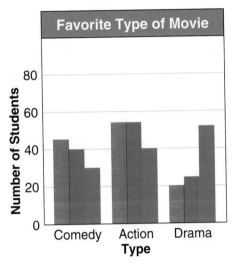

Use the graphs above.

1. On which day were the most sandwiches sold?

2. On which two days were the same number of salads sold?

3. On which day did the three foods have equal sales? How is this shown in the graph?

4. On Monday, which food was most popular? least popular?

5. Which type of movie was least preferred by Grade 6?

6. In which grade did the fewest students prefer comedy?

7. Which type of movie was liked by the same number of 6th and 7th graders?

8. In which grade did the greatest number of students prefer drama?

Chapter 9 Test

Use the table for exercises 1–3.

1. Organize the data in a cumulative frequency table with 5 intervals.

2. Find the relative frequency of each interval.

Pages Read: Grade 6							
31	20	38	31	24	30	12	38
20	18	36	34	21	33	38	36
34	23	39	30	43	30	31	28

3. Make a line plot, a stem-and-leaf plot, a histogram, and a box-and-whisker plot of the data.

Make a double line graph.

4.

Number of Books Sold				
Month	Jan.	Feb.	Mar.	Apr.
History	100	125	100	90
Psychology	175	180	170	120

5. Find the mean, median, and mode of the number of books sold each month in exercise 4. Which best describes the data? Explain.

Problem Solving

Use a strategy you have learned.

6. Carrie has 4 pennies dated 1976, 1971, 1966, and 1962. How many different ways can she arrange the pennies in a row so that the two pennies made in the 1970s are not next to each other?

Tell About It

Explain how you solved the problem. Show all your work.

7. In a random survey of 60 students, $\frac{2}{5}$ said they walk to school. Based on this sample, how many of the 350 students in the school do not walk to school?

Performance Assessment

Use the pictograph for problems 8–9.

8. If the number of dogs owned by 6th graders increases by 6 and the number owned by 5th graders decreases by 5, what would be the total number of dogs owned by all students?

9. Name three things that affect the accuracy of the survey.

Survey: Number of Dogs Owned	
3rd grade	🐶 🐶 🐶
4th grade	🐶 🐶 🐶 🐶 🐶
5th grade	🐶 🐶 🐶
6th grade	🐶 🐶 🐶 🐶 🐶

Key: Each  = 2 dogs.

Test Preparation

Choose the best answer.

1. Which statement is true?

   a. $\dfrac{1}{4} < \dfrac{1}{3}$ **b.** $^-\dfrac{1}{4} > \dfrac{1}{3}$

   c. $^-\dfrac{1}{2} > ^-\dfrac{1}{4}$ **d.** $\dfrac{1}{2} < ^-\dfrac{1}{3}$

2. Which is the prime factorization of 100?

   a. $1 \cdot 100$
   b. $10 \cdot 10$
   c. $1 \cdot 2 \cdot 5 \cdot 10 \cdot 20 \cdot 50 \cdot 100$
   d. $2 \cdot 2 \cdot 5 \cdot 5$

3. Which number is equivalent to 6.95×10^{-4}?

   a. 0.000695   **b.** 0.00695
   c. 0.0695   **d.** 69,500

4. Use $\{^-2, ^-1, 0, 1, 2\}$ to make $x + ^-8 = ^-10$ true.

   a. $^-2$ **b.** 2
   c. $^-2, ^-1, 0, 1, 2$ **d.** 0, 1, and 2

5. When $x = 2$, $y = 5$, and $z = 6$, which expression has a value of 8?

   a. $4z - 2x + 3y$ **b.** $x(y + z)$
   c. $\dfrac{z}{x} + y$ **d.** $\dfrac{5z}{y - x}$

6. What is 113,707 subtracted from 509,911?

   a. 395,204   **b.** 396,104
   c. 396,204   **d.** 496,204

7. Evaluate $x^2 - 2y^3$ for $x = ^-5$ and $y = ^-3$.

   a. $^-29$
   b. $^+43$
   c. $^+79$
   d. $^+243$

8. Which expression does not name an integer?

   a. $^-8$ **b.** 0
   c. $\dfrac{3}{12}$ **d.** $^-\dfrac{15}{5}$

9. Which is true of $(^-5)(^-8)$?

   a. The product is negative.
   b. The product is positive and less than 1.
   c. The product is positive and greater than 40.
   d. The product is a whole number.

10. Which are a pair of like terms?

   a. $9x$ and $7y$ **b.** $9x$ and $7x$
   c. $9x$ and $7x^2$ **d.** ^-9x and ^-9y

11. Choose the equation that is solved by using the Addition Property of Equality.

   a. $\dfrac{x}{3} = 4.2$ **b.** $3x = 4.2$
   c. $4.2 = x - 3$ **d.** $x + 3 = 4.2$

12. Which makes the number sentence true?

$|x| < 10$

   a. 10   **b.** $^-12$
   c. $^-8$ **d.** $^-10$

13. What is the product of 32,238 and 705?

   a. 2,227,790   **b.** 2,727,790
   c. 22,727,090   **d.** 22,727,790

14. Choose the value of $3a - (^-16)$, when $a = ^-6$.

   a. 2
   b. 3
   c. $^-3$
   d. $^-2$

15. If the probability of an event is 0, then

    a. it is certain.
    b. it is impossible.
    c. it is probable but certain.
    d. it is probable but not impossible.

16. A marble is selected from among 5 red and 4 blue marbles, replaced, then a second marble is selected. $P(\text{red, red}) = $?

    a. $\dfrac{5}{9} \cdot \dfrac{5}{9}$ **b.** $\dfrac{5}{9} + \dfrac{4}{9}$

    c. $\dfrac{5}{9} \cdot \dfrac{3}{8}$ **d.** $\dfrac{5}{9} + \dfrac{3}{8}$

17. Choose the quotient.

$$2\dfrac{1}{3} \div \dfrac{2}{3}$$

    a. $2\dfrac{2}{9}$ **b.** $2\dfrac{2}{3}$

    c. $3\dfrac{1}{2}$ **d.** $3\dfrac{1}{6}$

18. The temperature was ⁻15°F at 7:00 A.M. It rose 25 degrees by noon and then dropped 8 degrees by 5:00 P.M. What was the temperature at 5:00 P.M.?

    a. 12°F   **b.** 10°F
    c. 2°F   **d.** ⁻2°F

19. Suppose that E is an event in a sample space. Which cannot be true?

    a. $P(E) = 0.75$ **c.** $P(E) = \dfrac{7}{9}$

    b. $P(E) = 0.33$ **d.** $P(E) = 1.2$

20. Which value of x will make the mean of the data below equal to 6?

$$\{3, 3, 4, 5, 6, 7, 8, x\}$$

    a. $x = 8$ **b.** $x = 12$
    c. $x = 16$ **d.** $x = 48$

21. Choose the value of n.

$$n - 3 = 5\dfrac{7}{9}$$

    a. $n = 8\dfrac{7}{9}$ **b.** $n = 2\dfrac{4}{9}$

    c. $n = 2\dfrac{1}{3}$ **d.** $n = 1\dfrac{4}{9}$

22. In a survey that asked if they preferred soccer or tennis, 7 out 10 people chose soccer. Based on the results of the survey, how many people would you predict to choose tennis out of a group of 1000 people?

    a. 700 people   **b.** 300 people
    c. 70 people   **d.** 30 people

Tell About It

Explain how you solved each problem. Show all your work.

23. The graph shows the speed of a bicycle after 5, 10, 15, 20 minutes.

    a. What type of graph is it?

    b. After riding for exactly 10 min, what was the speed of the bike?

    c. Section B to C shows no change in speed. What other section shows no change?

    d. Which section(s) show where the bike is going uphill? downhill? Explain your answer.

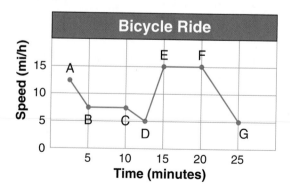

Bicycle Ride

Geometry

COMPASS

It stands
on bright silver leg,
toe sharp and pointed.

The other leg draws
a perfect circle
like a skater gracefully
tracing
half a figure eight
on paper ice.

Its silver skirt above
measures out inches

–two–three–four–

widening spheres
of mathematical perfection.

Georgia Heard

In this chapter you will:

Measure, draw, and classify
    angles
Learn geometric constructions
Classify polygons and solid figures
Explore circles, transformations,
    symmetry, and tessellations
Identify congruent and similar polygons
Solve problems by logical reasoning

Critical Thinking/Finding Together

Is one half of a figure eight congruent
to the other half? Is a figure eight
symmetrical? Does it tessellate?

Measure and Draw Angles

An **angle** is a plane figure formed by two rays with a common endpoint. Each ray is a **side** of the angle, and the endpoint is the **vertex** of the angle.

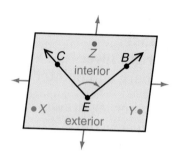

sides: $\overrightarrow{EC}$, $\overrightarrow{EB}$ **vertex:** E
angle: $\angle CEB$ or $\angle BEC$ or $\angle E$
Plane XYZ contains $\angle CEB$.

An angle separates a plane into three sets of points: the angle itself, the points in the **interior** of the angle, and the points in the **exterior** of the angle.

Point Z is in the interior of $\angle CEB$.
Points X and Y are in the exterior of $\angle CEB$.

Angles are measured in **degrees** (°).
A **protractor** is used to measure or draw an angle.

▶ **To measure $\angle XYZ$:**

- Using the inner scale, place the center mark of the protractor on the vertex of the angle, Y, with $\overrightarrow{YX}$ pointing to 0°.

- Read the measure of the angle where $\overrightarrow{YZ}$ crosses the protractor.

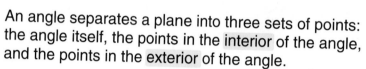

$$m\angle XYZ = 55°$$

measure of $\angle XYZ$

▶ **To draw an angle of 140°:**

- Draw a base ray, $\overrightarrow{MN}$. Use the outer scale.

- Place the center mark of the protractor on M with $\overrightarrow{MN}$ pointing to 0°.

- Mark P at 140°.

- Draw $\overrightarrow{MP}$.

Mark P at the 140° point on the protractor.

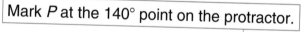

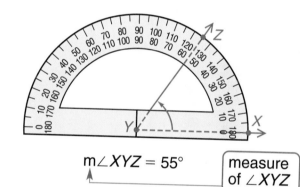

$$m\angle NMP = 140°$$

measure of $\angle NMP$

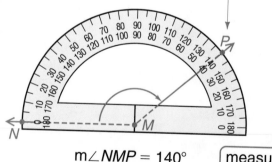

Name the points that are in the interior and the points that are in the exterior of the given angle. Then find the measure of the angle.

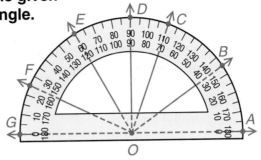

1. ∠AOE
2. ∠AOC
3. ∠AOD
4. ∠GOB
5. ∠GOE
6. ∠EOC

Use a protractor to draw each angle.

7. 40°
8. 75°
9. 90°
10. 135°
11. 5°
12. 180°

Estimate the measure of each angle. Then use a protractor to find the exact measure.

13.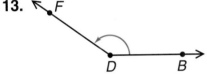

14.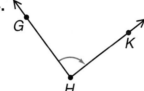

15.

Find the measure of the angle formed by the hands of a clock at the given time.

16. 9:00
17. 2:00
18. 6:00
19. 11:00
20. 8:00

Problem Solving

21. How many different angles are in the given figure? Name the angles.

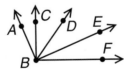

Write About It

In your Math Journal:

22. Explain which student described the figure correctly.

    Deven: Two lines intersect at a point.

    Ivette: There are two angles with the same vertex.

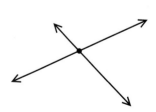

23. Draw two angles with the same vertex that do not form intersecting lines. Explain the steps you use.

Lines and Angles

▶ Lines that do not intersect may or may not lie in the same plane. They are either **parallel** or **skew**.

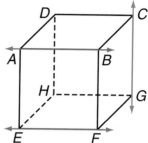

- $\overleftrightarrow{AB}$ and $\overleftrightarrow{EF}$ are in the same plane. They are parallel lines.

  $\overleftrightarrow{AB} \parallel \overleftrightarrow{EF}$

  is parallel to

- $\overleftrightarrow{AB}$ and $\overleftrightarrow{CG}$ are in different planes. They are skew lines.

▶ Angles can be classified according to their degree measures.

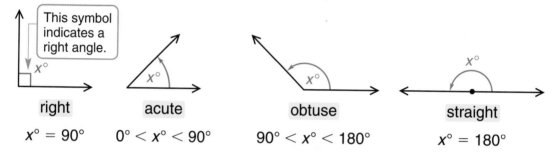

This symbol indicates a right angle.

right	acute	obtuse	straight
$x° = 90°$	$0° < x° < 90°$	$90° < x° < 180°$	$x° = 180°$

▶ **Perpendicular lines** are two lines in the same plane that intersect to form right angles.

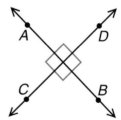

$\overleftrightarrow{AB} \perp \overleftrightarrow{CD}$

  is perpendicular to

Use the figure at the right.

1. Name a line that is parallel to the given line.

   a. $\overleftrightarrow{AC}$ b. $\overleftrightarrow{EF}$

   c. $\overleftrightarrow{AD}$ d. $\overleftrightarrow{AB}$

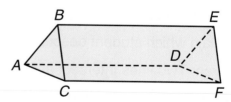

2. Name all the lines that form a pair of skew lines with $\overleftrightarrow{AD}$.

**Classify each angle as *right, acute, obtuse,* or *straight.*
Use a protractor to check.**

3.

4.

5.

6.

Bisectors

▶ The midpoint of a segment is the point that divides the segment into two congruent segments. Segments that are equal in length are called congruent segments.

Point M is the midpoint of $\overline{PQ}$.

P •——|——•——|——• Q
M

$\overline{PM} \cong \overline{QM}$ ⎣ is congruent to ⎦

▶ A segment bisector is any line, ray, or segment that intersects a segment at its midpoint. If a segment bisector is also perpendicular to the segment, it is called the perpendicular bisector of the segment.

Line s is a segment bisector of $\overline{AB}$. A •——|——•——|——• B
M

Line t is a perpendicular bisector of $\overline{CD}$. C •——||——⌐•——||——• D
N

▶ Angles that are equal in measure are called congruent angles.

An angle bisector is the ray that divides a given angle into two congruent angles.

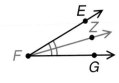

$\overrightarrow{FZ}$ is the angle bisector of $\angle EFG$. $\angle EFZ \cong \angle ZFG$

Write *True* or *False*. If false, explain why. Use the figure at the right.

7. $\overline{AM} \cong \overline{MB}$

8. $\overleftrightarrow{MC} \perp \overleftrightarrow{MD}$

9. $\angle AMC \cong \angle CMB$

10. M is the midpoint of $\overleftrightarrow{CE}$.

11. $\overrightarrow{MD}$ bisects $\angle CMB$.

12. $m\angle AME = 90°$

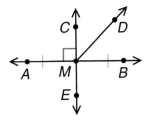

Draw a figure for each description.

13. $\overrightarrow{BQ}$ is the bisector of $\angle PBS$.

14. $\overline{AY}$ bisects $\overline{BX}$ at P.

15. $\overleftrightarrow{AB}$ is the perpendicular bisector of $\overline{XY}$.

16. $\overleftrightarrow{MN} \perp \overleftrightarrow{QR}$

Angle Pairs

Pairs of angles can be classified according to their degree measures or sides.

▶ **Complementary angles** are two angles whose measures have a sum of 90°. Each angle is said to be the **complement** of the other.

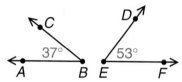

∠ABC and ∠FED are complementary angles.

37° + 53° = 90°

▶ **Supplementary angles** are two angles whose measures have a sum of 180°. Each angle is said to be the **supplement** of the other.

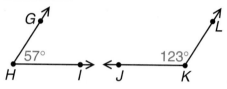

∠GHI and ∠LKJ are supplementary angles.

57° + 123° = 180°

▶ **Adjacent angles** are two angles that are in the same plane and share a common side and a common vertex, but have no interior points in common.

∠1 and ∠2 are adjacent angles.

▶ When the noncommon sides of two adjacent angles are opposite rays, the angles form a **linear pair**. The angles of a linear pair are supplementary.

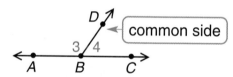

∠3 and ∠4 are a linear pair.
m∠3 + m∠4 = 180°

▶ **Vertical angles** are two congruent angles formed by intersecting lines. Their sides are pairs of opposite rays.

∠AED and ∠BEF are vertical angles.
So are ∠DEB and ∠AEF.

∠AED ≅ ∠BEF
∠AEF ≅ ∠BED

Study these examples.

Find the value of x.

43° + x = 90°
$x = 47°$

x + 75° = 180°
$x = 105°$

3x = 45°
$x = 15°$

Are ∠1 and ∠2 adjacent angles? Write _Yes_ or _No_. If no, explain why.

1.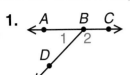

2.

3.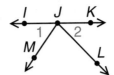

4.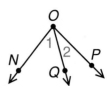

Are ∠1 and ∠2 vertical angles? Write _Yes_ or _No_. If no, explain why.

5.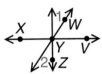

6.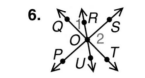

7.

8.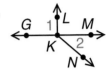

Write whether the angle pairs are _complementary angles_, _supplementary angles_, or _neither_.

9. 60°, 30°

10. 130°, 50°

11. 113°, 67°

12. 110°, 90°

13. 90°, 90°

14. 179°, 1°

15. 45°, 45°

16. 97°, 93°

Find the value of _x_.

17.

18.

19.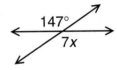

Problem Solving

20. Two angles are supplementary and congruent. What is the degree measure of each angle?

21. Two vertical angles are complementary. What is the degree measure of each angle?

22. In the figure, $\overleftrightarrow{CB} \perp \overleftrightarrow{AJ}$ at _D_. If $\overrightarrow{DM}$ bisects ∠BDJ, what is the measure of each angle?

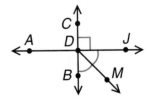

    a. ∠JDM   **b.** ∠CDB   **c.** ∠CDA

    d. ∠CDM   **e.** ∠ADM   **f.** ∠JDA

TEST PREPARATION

23. In which figure is the measure of ∠a _not_ 35°?

    A    **B** 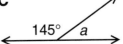   **C** 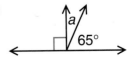   **D**

Update your skills. See page 18.

Angles of Parallel Lines

A line that intersects two or more lines at different points is called a **transversal**. In many cases, those lines are parallel. In the figure at the right, $\overleftrightarrow{AB}$ and $\overleftrightarrow{CD}$ are intersected by transversal t.

The **interior angles** are $\angle 3$, $\angle 4$, $\angle 5$, and $\angle 6$.

The **exterior angles** are $\angle 1$, $\angle 2$, $\angle 7$, and $\angle 8$.

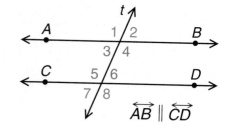

▶ Special names are given to the pairs of angles formed by the transversal.

Corresponding angles are a pair of nonadjacent angles, one interior and one exterior, that are both on the same side of the transversal.

Corresponding angles of parallel lines are congruent.

Corresponding angles:
$\angle 1$ and $\angle 5$; $\angle 2$ and $\angle 6$; $\angle 3$ and $\angle 7$; $\angle 4$ and $\angle 8$.
So, $\angle 1 \cong \angle 5$, $\angle 2 \cong \angle 6$, $\angle 3 \cong \angle 7$, and $\angle 4 \cong \angle 8$.

Alternate interior angles are a pair of nonadjacent interior angles on opposite sides of the transversal.

Alternate interior angles of parallel lines are congruent.

Alternate interior angles:
$\angle 3$ and $\angle 6$; $\angle 4$ and $\angle 5$.

So, $\angle 3 \cong \angle 6$ and $\angle 4 \cong \angle 5$.

Alternate exterior angles are a pair of nonadjacent exterior angles on opposite sides of the transversal.

Alternate exterior angles of parallel lines are congruent.

Alternate exterior angles:
$\angle 1$ and $\angle 8$; $\angle 2$ and $\angle 7$.

So, $\angle 1 \cong \angle 8$ and $\angle 2 \cong \angle 7$.

Study this example.

In the figure, $\ell \parallel n$ and $m\angle 1 = 40°$. Find the measure of each indicated angle.

a. $m\angle 2 = 140°$ ← $\angle 1$ and $\angle 2$ are supplementary.

b. $m\angle 3 = 40°$ ← $\angle 1$ and $\angle 3$ are vertical angles.

c. $m\angle 5 = 40°$ ← $\angle 3$ and $\angle 5$ are alternate interior angles.

d. $m\angle 6 = 140°$ ← $\angle 2$ and $\angle 6$ are corresponding angles.

e. $m\angle 7 = 40°$ ← $\angle 1$ and $\angle 7$ are alternate exterior angles.

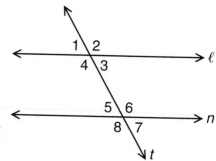

Identify each pair of angles as *alternate interior*, *alternate exterior*, *corresponding* angles, or *none of these*.

1. ∠6 and ∠10
2. ∠7 and ∠9
3. ∠6 and ∠12
4. ∠5 and ∠10
5. ∠8 and ∠12
6. ∠8 and ∠10

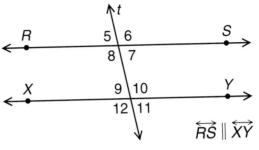

$\overleftrightarrow{RS} \parallel \overleftrightarrow{XY}$

Use the figure to find each measure.

7. m∠5 when m∠3 = 80°
8. m∠2 when m∠6 = 150°
9. m∠8 when m∠3 = 65°
10. m∠7 when m∠1 = 75°
11. m∠4 when m∠5 = 60°

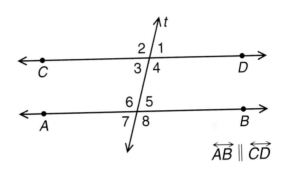

$\overleftrightarrow{AB} \parallel \overleftrightarrow{CD}$

Problem Solving

12. In the figure below, $\overleftrightarrow{AB} \parallel \overleftrightarrow{CD}$. $\overleftrightarrow{EF}$ and $\overrightarrow{GF}$ are transversals. If m∠4 = 80° and m∠5 = 40°, find the measures of the remaining angles.

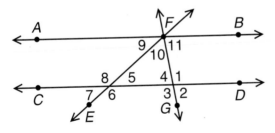

13. In the figure below, points A, B, and E are on the same line. $\overrightarrow{BD} \parallel \overrightarrow{AC}$. If m∠A = 65° and m∠C = 80°, find m∠CBE.

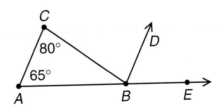

CHALLENGE

14. In the figure at the right, $\overleftrightarrow{AB} \parallel \overleftrightarrow{CD}$, $\overleftrightarrow{EF}$ intersects $\overleftrightarrow{AB}$ at G and $\overleftrightarrow{CD}$ at H, and $\overline{MH}$ bisects ∠CHG. Find m∠MHC.

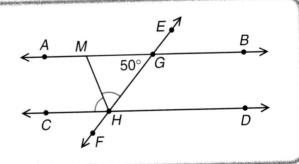

Line Constructions

A **construction** is a geometric drawing that is made using only an unmarked **straightedge** and a **compass**. A compass is a geometric tool used to draw a circle or a part of a circle, called an **arc**.

▶ To construct a line segment, *CD*, congruent to a given line segment, *AB*:

Given: $\overline{AB}$

Step 1	**Step 2**	**Step 3**
Draw a ray with endpoint *C*.	Open the compass to the length of $\overline{AB}$.	With the same compass setting, put the compass point on *C*. Construct an arc that intersects the ray. Label the intersection *D*. $\overline{CD} \cong \overline{AB}$

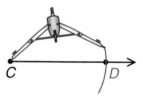

▶ To construct the perpendicular bisector of a line segment, *AB*:

Given: $\overline{AB}$

Step 1	**Step 2**	**Step 3**
Put the compass point on point *A* and construct an arc. Be sure the opening is greater than $\frac{1}{2}\,\overline{AB}$. Keep the same compass setting for Step 2.	Put the compass point on point *B* and construct an arc. Label the points where the two arcs intersect as *X* and *Y*.	Draw $\overleftrightarrow{XY}$. Label the intersection of $\overline{AB}$ and $\overleftrightarrow{XY}$ as point *M*. $\overleftrightarrow{XY}$ is the perpendicular bisector of $\overline{AB}$. Point *M* is the midpoint of $\overline{AB}$.

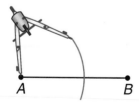

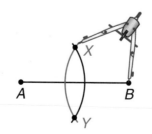

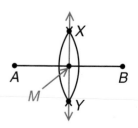

Trace each line segment. Then construct a line segment congruent to each.

1. R •——————• S

2. C •——————• D

3. X •——————• Y

Trace each line segment. Then construct the perpendicular bisector of each line segment.

4. O •——————• M

5. T •——————• N

6. F •——————• H

Construct Perpendicular Lines

▶ To construct a perpendicular to a given line, *m*, at a given point, *P*, on *m*:

Given:

Step 1: Place the compass tip on *P*. Construct arcs intersecting line *m* at the two points, *A* and *B*.

Step 2: Widen the compass to construct two intersecting arcs above point *P*, one with the center at *A* and one with the center at *B*. Label the intersection *C*.

Step 3: Draw $\overleftrightarrow{CP}$. $\overleftrightarrow{CP} \perp m$

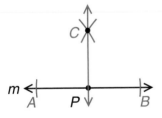

▶ To construct a perpendicular to a given line, *m*: from a given point, *P*, not on *m*:

• *P*

Given:

Step 1: Place the compass tip on *P*. Construct arcs intersecting line *m* at the two points, *A* and *B*.

Step 2: Using the same compass setting, construct two intersecting arcs, one with the center at *A* and another with the center at *B*. Label the intersection *C*.

Step 3: Draw $\overleftrightarrow{CP}$. $\overleftrightarrow{CP} \perp m$

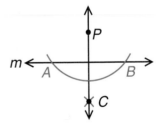

Trace each figure and construct a perpendicular line to ℓ through *P*.

7. ←—•—————————→ ℓ
       P

8. • *P*

       ←——————————————→ ℓ

CRITICAL THINKING

9. Draw a line and pick two points on the line. Construct a perpendicular line at each point. What do you discover?

Constructions with Angles

Elmira is making a class pennant.
She uses a compass to construct an
angle congruent to the angle drawn.

▶ **To construct an angle *DEF*
congruent to angle *ABC*:**

Step 1

Put the compass point
on *B*. Construct an arc
that intersects both rays
of the angle at *P* and *Q*.

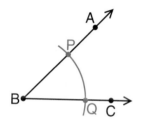

Step 2

Use a straightedge
to draw a ray with
endpoint *E*. With the
compass point on *E*
and the same compass
opening as in Step 1,
construct an arc that
intersects the ray at *F*.

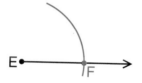

Step 3

Open the compass to
measure the length
PQ. With the same
compass opening and
the compass point on *F*,
construct an arc that
intersects the other arc
at *D*. Draw $\overrightarrow{ED}$.

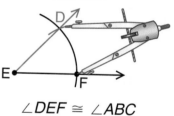

∠*DEF* ≅ ∠*ABC*

**Use unlined paper to trace each of the angles.
Then construct an angle congruent to each.**

1.

2.

3.

Construct the indicated angles.

4. Draw an angle with each given measure: 70° and 135°.

  a. Construct an angle congruent to each.

  b. Construct the supplement of each angle.

Construct an Angle Bisector

You can use a compass and a straightedge to bisect an angle.

▶ **To construct the bisector of ∠XYZ:**

Step 1	**Step 2**	**Step 3**
Put the compass point on *Y*. Construct an arc that intersects both rays of the angle. Label the points of intersection *A* and *B*.	Open the compass to measure the length of arc *AB*. With the same compass opening and the compass point on *A*, construct an arc inside the angle.	With the same compass opening and the compass point on *B*, construct an arc that intersects the other arc. Label the point of intersection *P*. Draw $\overrightarrow{YP}$.

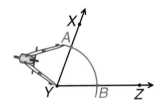 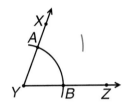 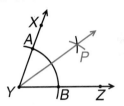

$\overrightarrow{YP}$ is the bisector of ∠XYZ.

Draw each angle described. Then construct the angle bisector of each.

5. acute angle **6.** obtuse angle **7.** right angle

Practice

Problem Solving

8. The measure of ∠*CAB* is 160°. Draw ∠*CAB* and construct $\overrightarrow{AX}$ such that $\overrightarrow{AX}$ bisects ∠*CAB*. Then find m∠*CAX* and m∠*XAB*.

9. The measure of ∠*RST* is 45°. Draw ∠*RST* and construct ∠*MNP* such that ∠*MNP* ≅ ∠*RST*. What is the measure of ∠*MNP*?

DO YOU REMEMBER?

Match each definition with a term in the box.

| double bar graph |
| event |
| graph |
| sample |
| double line graph |

10. compares two sets of data over time

11. a pictorial representation of data

12. a set of one or more outcomes of a probability experiment

13. a segment of population selected for study to predict characteristics of the whole

10-7

Polygons

A polygon is a closed plane figure made up of line segments that intersect only at their endpoints and in such a way that no two segments are on the same line. You can classify a polygon by its number of sides.

Polygon	Number of Sides
triangle	3
quadrilateral	4
pentagon	5
hexagon	6
heptagon	7
octagon	8
nonagon	9
decagon	10
dodecagon	12

Polygons
When all of the sides of a polygon are congruent and all of the angles are congruent, the polygon is a regular polygon.

regular triangle | regular quadrilateral

In general, if a polygon has *n* sides, you call it an *n*-gon. A polygon of 16 sides is a 16-gon.

► A diagonal of a polygon is a line segment that connects two vertices and is *not* a side.

$\overline{AC}, \overline{AD}, \overline{BD}, \overline{BE}, \overline{CE}$ are diagonals of pentagon *ABCDE*.

Every pentagon, whether it is regular or not regular, has five diagonals.

► You can draw some of the diagonals of a polygon to help you decide if the polygon is convex or concave.

convex polygon — diagonals do not have any points outside the polygon; *JKLMNO* is a convex hexagon.

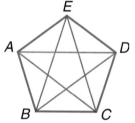

concave polygon — one or more diagonals have points outside the polygon; *PRSTUV* is a concave hexagon. Diagonal $\overline{PU}$ is outside the hexagon.

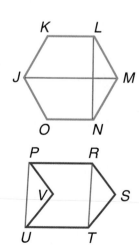

Tell whether the polygon is *regular* or *not regular*. Then tell whether it is *convex* or *concave*. Explain your answers.

1.
2.
3.
4.

5.
6.
7.
8.

Draw each polygon and find its number of sides or vertices to complete the table.

	Name	Number of Sides	Number of Vertices
9.	heptagon	7	?
10.	nonagon	?	9
11.	decagon	10	?
12.	dodecagon	12	?

Find the number of diagonals in each polygon.

13. quadrilateral   **14.** hexagon   **15.** heptagon   **16.** octagon

17. In your answers for exercises 13–16, does it matter if the polygons are convex or concave? Explain.

Draw the polygon described. Then draw and name its diagonals.

18. hexagon *JKLMNO*

19. a quadrilateral *WXYZ* with no right angles

20. concave pentagon *ABCDE*

21. regular triangle *NRT*

DO YOU REMEMBER?

Solve each equation.

22. $c + 98 = 180$

23. $\frac{4}{9} + d = \frac{2}{3}$

24. $a + 110 = 180$

25. $b + 2.75 = 3.60$

26. $^-310 + a = {}^-360$

27. $165 + c = 180$

Triangles

► Triangles are classified by the lengths of their sides and/or by the measures of their angles.

Sides

equilateral triangle (A)—all sides congruent
isosceles triangle (B)—two sides congruent
scalene triangle (C)—no sides congruent

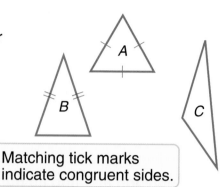

Matching tick marks indicate congruent sides.

Angles

acute triangle (D)—three acute angles
obtuse triangle (E)—one obtuse angle
right triangle (F)—one right angle

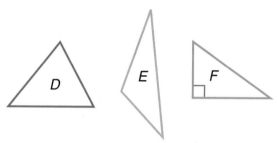

► Triangles can also be classified by both the lengths of their sides and by the measures of their angles.

Both Sides and Angles

isosceles right triangle (G)—two sides congruent and one right angle

scalene obtuse triangle (H)—no sides congruent and one obtuse angle

Practice

Draw an example of each type of triangle on dot paper.

1. isosceles   **2.** acute   **3.** obtuse   **4.** scalene

5. right   **6.** equilateral   **7.** isosceles obtuse   **8.** scalene acute

Classify each triangle by the measure of its sides and by the measure of its angles.

9.
17 mm / 75° / 25 mm
65°   40°
27 mm

10.
10 m / 60° / 10 m
60°   60°
10 m

11.
40 cm / 106° / 40 cm
37°   37°
60 cm

12.
60° / 5 m
3 m
30°
4 m

Use a protractor and a centimeter ruler to measure the sides and angles of each triangle. Then classify the triangle by its sides and angles.

13.

14.

15.

16.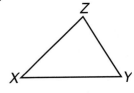

17. What did you discover about the relationship between the angle and side measures of a triangle?

Construct Congruent Triangles

Congruent triangles have exactly the same size and the same shape.
Given: △XYZ

Construct △ABC congruent to △XYZ.

Step 1	**Step 2**	**Step 3**
Open the compass to measure the length of $\overline{XY}$. Draw a line ℓ and on the line, construct $\overline{AB} \cong \overline{XY}$.	Open the compass to measure the length of $\overline{XZ}$. From point A, construct an arc. Open the compass to the length of YZ. From point B, construct an arc that intersects the other arc.	Label the point where the two arcs intersect as point C. Draw $\overline{AC}$ and $\overline{BC}$. $\triangle ABC \cong \triangle XYZ$

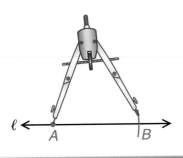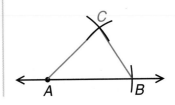

Draw the triangle indicated. Then construct a triangle congruent to it.

18. equilateral △DEF   **19.** obtuse △JKL   **20.** right △PQR

CRITICAL THINKING   *Algebra*

Suppose the sides of a triangle have each of the given measures. Classify each triangle.

21. y, y, y **22.** $a, 1.25a, 1.25a$ **23.** $3x, 3x, 3x$

Quadrilaterals

Quadrilaterals are four-sided polygons. They can be classified according to the special properties of their sides or angles.

A **trapezoid** is a quadrilateral with exactly one pair of parallel sides.

$\overline{BC} \parallel \overline{AD}$

A **parallelogram** is a quadrilateral with two pairs of parallel congruent sides. Opposite sides as well as opposite angles are congruent.

$\overline{MN} \parallel \overline{OP}$
$\overline{MO} \parallel \overline{NP}$

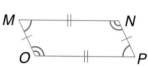

A **rectangle** is a parallelogram with four right angles.

$\overline{ST} \parallel \overline{UV}$
$\overline{SU} \parallel \overline{TV}$

A **square** is a parallelogram with four right angles and four congruent sides.

$\overline{EF} \parallel \overline{GH}$
$\overline{EG} \parallel \overline{FH}$

A **rhombus** is a parallelogram with four congruent sides.

$\overline{JK} \parallel \overline{LR}$
$\overline{JL} \parallel \overline{KR}$

▶ The diagram below shows how the different types of quadrilaterals are related.

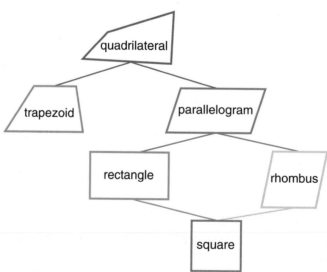

Complete the table. Write *Yes* or *No* for each description.

	Description	Trapezoid	Parallelogram	Rectangle	Square	Rhombus
1.	all sides congruent	?	?	?	?	?
2.	4 right angles	?	?	?	?	?
3.	opposite sides parallel	?	?	?	?	?
4.	opposite sides congruent	?	?	?	?	?

Construct a Parallelogram

To construct parallelogram *ABCD*:

Step 1	Step 2	Step 3
Draw $\overline{AB}$ and $\overline{AD}$. Open the compass to the length of $\overline{AB}$. From point *D*, construct an arc.	Open the compass to the length of $\overline{AD}$. From point *B*, construct an arc.	Label the point where the two arcs intersect as point *C*. Draw $\overline{BC}$ and $\overline{CD}$. *ABCD* is a parallelogram.
	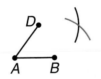	

Construct the figure described.

5. parallelogram *WXYZ*

6. parallelogram *MNOP*

7. rhombus *EFGH* with each side 3 cm long

8. rectangle *CDBA* with length of 4 cm and width of 2 cm

Explain why each statement is true. Draw a picture to help.

9. A square is a rhombus.

10. A trapezoid is *not* a parallelogram.

11. A square is a rectangle.

12. Some quadrilaterals are parallelograms.

Angles of Triangles and Quadrilaterals

The angles determined by the sides of a triangle are called its interior angles, or simply, its angles.

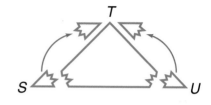

▶ If you tear off two angles of a triangle and place the pieces next to the third angle, the angles would form a straight angle. Thus, the **sum of the measures of the interior angles of any triangle is 180°.**

In $\triangle PQR$ at the right, if m∠P = 55° and m∠Q = 25°, what is m∠R?

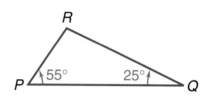

m∠P + m∠Q + m∠R = 180°
 55° + 25° + m∠R = 180°
      80°   + m∠R = 180° ← Simplify.
 80° − 80°   + m∠R = 180° − 80° ← Subtract 80° to
          m∠R = 100° ← Simplify. isolate m∠R.

▶ If you draw one diagonal of a quadrilateral, as shown at the right, you form two triangles. Thus, the **sum of the measures of the interior angles of a quadrilateral is** 2 × 180°, or **360°.**

In the figure at the right, find m∠E.

m∠E + m∠F + m∠G + m∠H = 360°
m∠E + 90° + 50° + 85° = 360°
          m∠E + 225° = 360° ← Simplify.
    m∠E + 225° − 225° = 360° − 225° ← Subtract 225° to
          m∠E = 135° ← Simplify. isolate m∠E.

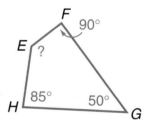

Study this example.

Find the measure of each angle in the given figure.

x + 85° + 135° + 35° = 360° ← The sum of the measures
          x + 255° = 360°   of the interior angles of a
              x = 105°   quadrilateral is 360°.

y + 105° = 180° ← ∠y and ∠x
      y = 75°   are supplementary.

z + 70° + 75° = 180° ← The sum of the measures of the
   z + 145° = 180°   interior angles of a triangle is 180°.
        z = 35°

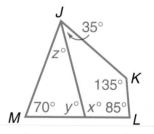

Find the measure of the third angle of each triangle.

1.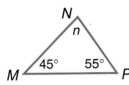

2.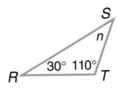

3.

4.

5. $\angle D = 43°$, $\angle T = 29°$, $\angle F =$ __?__

6. $\angle W = 16°$, $\angle B = 5°$, $\angle U =$ __?__

Find the measure of the fourth angle of the quadrilateral.

7. $\angle A = 85°$, $\angle B = 85°$, $\angle C = 65°$, $\angle D =$ __?__

8. $\angle E = 65°$, $\angle F = 90°$, $\angle G = 90°$, $\angle H =$ __?__

9. $\angle Q = 89°$, $\angle R = 67°$, $\angle S = 102°$, $\angle T =$ __?__

Find the value of *n* in each quadrilateral.

10.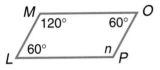

11.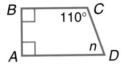

12.

Find the value of each variable.

13.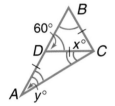

14.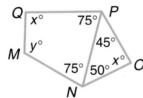

15.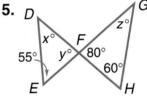

Problem Solving

16. Two angles of a triangle are congruent and the measure of the third angle is 120°. Find the measure of one the congruent angles.

17. In parallelogram *ABCD*, the measure of $\angle ABC$ is 165°. Find the measure of $\angle C$.

CRITICAL THINKING

If you extend a side of a triangle, you form an exterior angle of the triangle.

18. $\angle ACD$ is an exterior angle of $\triangle ABC$. Find the measure of $\angle ACD$. Explain how you found your answer.

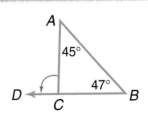

Angles of Polygons

An interior angle of a convex polygon is an angle determined by two consecutive sides of the polygon.

In the figure, $\angle ABC$ is an interior angle.

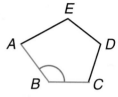

The following table shows how you can find the sum of the interior angles of a convex polygon by drawing all the diagonals from one vertex.

Interior Angles of a Polygon			
Polygon	Number of Sides	Number of Triangles Formed	Sum of the Measures of the Interior Angles
pentagon	5	$5 - 2 = 3$	$3 \times 180° = 540°$
hexagon	6	$6 - 2 = 4$	$4 \times 180° = 720°$
octagon	8	$8 - 2 = 6$	$6 \times 180° = 1080°$
n-gon	n	$n - 2$	$(n - 2) \times 180°$

> The sum of the measures of the interior angles of a convex polygon with n sides is $(n - 2) \times 180°$.

Study these examples.

Find the sum of the measures of the interior angles of a dodecagon.

A dodecagon has 12 sides. The sum of the measures of the interior angles is:

$$= (12 - 2) \times 180°$$
$$= 10 \times 180°$$
$$= 1800°$$

In the figure, find m$\angle A$.

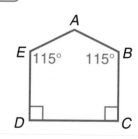

$$m\angle A + 115° + 90° + 90° + 115° = (5 - 2) \times 180°$$
$$m\angle A + 410° = 540°$$
$$m\angle A = 130°$$

Find the number of triangles formed by the diagonals from one vertex of each polygon.

1. heptagon　　　　**2.** nonagon　　　　**3.** quadrilateral　　　　**4.** decagon

5. hexagon　　　　**6.** octagon　　　　**7.** 15-gon　　　　**8.** 17-gon

Find the sum of the measures of the interior angles of each polygon.

9. decagon　　　　**10.** hexagon　　　　**11.** nonagon　　　　**12.** heptagon

13. 11-gon　　　　**14.** 18-gon　　　　**15.** 13-gon　　　　**16.** 20-gon

Find the value of the variable in each polygon.

17.
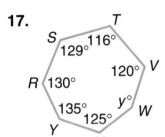

18.
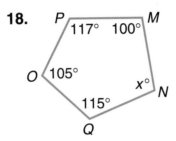

19.
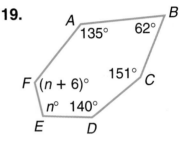

Problem Solving

20. The measures of four interior angles of a pentagon are 115°, 92°, 107°, and 83°. Find the measure of the fifth interior angle.

21. Five interior angles of a hexagon each have a measure of 110°. What is the measure of the sixth interior angle?

CHALLENGE — Algebra

A fractal is an endlessly repeating pattern containing shapes that are like the whole but of different sizes throughout. You can build fractals from plane figures by iteration, the process of repeating over and over again.

22. The figures below show a developing fractal from a square by repeating the iteration process two times. Look for a pattern and find the number of shaded squares that would be in stage 4.

Stage 1

Stage 2

Stage 3

Circles

A **circle** is a set of points in a plane, all of which are the same distance from a given point, called the **center**. A circle is named by its center.

Point P is the center of circle P.

A **radius** (*plural:* radii) is a line segment from the center of a circle to a point on the circle. $\overline{PK}$, $\overline{PL}$, and $\overline{PA}$ are radii of circle P.

A **central angle** has its vertex at the center of the circle. $\angle APC$ and $\angle IPL$ are central angles of circle P.

A **chord** is a line segment with its endpoints on the circle. $\overline{AC}$ is a chord.

A **diameter** is a chord that passes through the center of a circle. $\overline{CI}$ and $\overline{AG}$ are diameters.

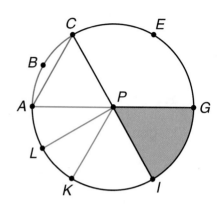

> The length of the diameter (d) is twice the length of the radius (r).
>
> $$d = 2 \times r \qquad r = d \div 2$$

An **arc** is a part of a circle, with all of its points on the circle. An arc that connects the endpoints of a diameter has a measure of 180° and is a **semicircle**. A **minor arc** is an arc with a measure less than 180°. A **major arc** is an arc with a measure greater than 180°. $\overparen{AB}$ is an arc of circle P.

$\overparen{ACG}$ is a semicircle.	$\overparen{ABC}$ is a minor arc.	$\overparen{CKE}$ is a major arc.
m $\overparen{ACG}$ = 180°	m $\overparen{ABC}$ < 180°	m $\overparen{CKE}$ > 180°

A **sector** of a circle is the region bounded by two radii and their intercepted arc. The shaded region is a sector of circle P.

Use the circle for exercises 1–9.

1. What is the center of the circle?

2. What is $\overline{IJ}$ called?

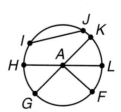

3. Name two diameters of the circle.

4. Name all the radii shown in the circle.

5. Name two central angles of the circle.

6. What is the curved part of the circle that joins point G and point F called?

7. Name two minor arcs and two major arcs.

8. Name all the semicircles shown.

9. What is the region bounded by $\overline{KA}$, $\overparen{KL}$, and $\overline{LA}$ called?

For each statement, write *always*, *sometimes*, or *never*.

10. All radii of a circle have the same length.

11. Some arcs are line segments.

12. Chords are diameters.

13. All circles are regular polygons.

14. A central angle has its vertex on the circle.

15. The longest chord of any circle is its diameter.

Use a compass to construct a circle. Then do the following:

16. Draw and label the diameter $\overline{AB}$.

17. Draw any point C on the circle.

18. Draw the chords $\overline{AC}$ and $\overline{BC}$.

19. Name the figure you have drawn.

Construct a Regular Polygon

You can construct a regular polygon by using a circle.

To construct a regular hexagon, follow these steps.

> A regular polygon has congruent sides and congruent angles.

Step 1	**Step 2**	**Step 3**
Use a compass to construct a circle. Put the compass point anywhere on the circle. With the same radius as the circle, construct an arc that intersects the circle at point *A*.	With the same radius as the circle, put the compass point at *A* and construct another arc that intersects the circle at point *B*.	Repeat Step 2 all the way around the circle. Label the points of intersection *C, D, E,* and *F*. With a straightedge, draw the segments joining the points. *ABCDEF* is a regular hexagon.

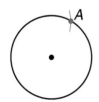 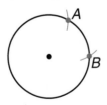 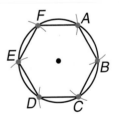

Construct each regular polygon by using a circle. Explain your process.

20. an equilateral triangle

21. a square

22. a regular dodecagon

Problem Solving

23. Alex draws circle *O* with a diameter of 12 inches. What is the length of a radius of the circle *O*?

24. Circle *X* has two intersecting diameters, $\overline{AB}$ and $\overline{CD}$. If m∠*AXC* = 75°, what are the measures of the other three central angles?

Congruent and Similar Polygons

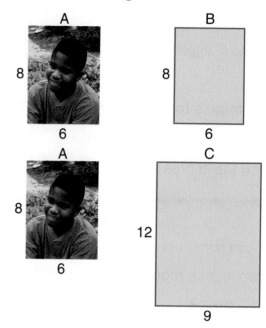

A

B

8

8

6

6

A

C

8

12

6

9

The students in Class 6-B are matting their photos (polygon *A*) for gifts to their grandparents. There are two mat sizes: 6 x 8 (polygon *B*) and 9 x 12 (polygon *C*). How might the class describe the photo and the mats?

Polygons A and B are **congruent**. **Congruent polygons** have exactly the same size and same shape.

Polygons A and C are **similar**. **Similar polygons** have the same shape. They may or may *not* have the same size.

▶ The **corresponding parts** (matching sides and matching angles) of congruent polygons are congruent.

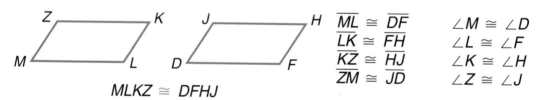

Z _____ K   J _____ H $\overline{ML} \cong \overline{DF}$ $\angle M \cong \angle D$

                                     $\overline{LK} \cong \overline{FH}$ $\angle L \cong \angle F$

M _____ L   D _____ F $\overline{KZ} \cong \overline{HJ}$ $\angle K \cong \angle H$

                                     $\overline{ZM} \cong \overline{JD}$ $\angle Z \cong \angle J$

MLKZ $\cong$ *DFHJ*

▶ The **corresponding angles** (matching angles) of similar polygons are congruent.

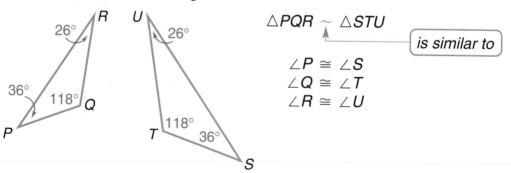

R   U

26°   26°

36°

118°   Q

P

118°   36°

T   S

$\triangle PQR \sim \triangle STU$

is similar to

$\angle P \cong \angle S$

$\angle Q \cong \angle T$

$\angle R \cong \angle U$

Parallelograms *MLKZ* and *DFHJ* are congruent and therefore similar. Triangles *PQR* and *STU* are similar but *not* congruent.

Do the polygons appear to be *similar*, *congruent*, or *neither*? Explain your answer.

1.

2.

3.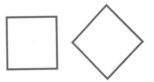

4.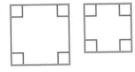

5.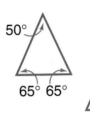

6.

Name the corresponding congruent parts.

$\triangle ABC \cong \triangle DEF$

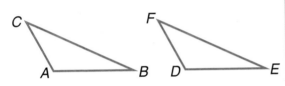

7. $\overline{AB} \cong$ _?_

8. $\angle A \cong$ _?_

9. $\overline{BC} \cong$ _?_

10. _?_ $\cong \angle E$

11. _?_ $\cong \overline{FD}$

12. $\angle C \cong$ _?_

Quadrilateral *MXOP* ~ Quadrilateral *GCEK*

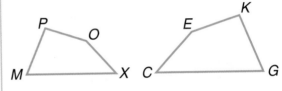

13. $\angle X \cong$ _?_

14. $\angle G \cong$ _?_

15. $\angle P \cong$ _?_

16. _?_ $\cong \angle E$

Problem Solving

17. In the figures below, $ABCDE \cong OPQMN$. Find the lengths of $\overline{PO}$ and $\overline{QM}$ and the measures of $\angle P$ and $\angle O$.

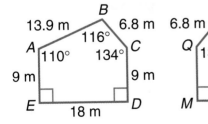

18. In the figures below, $\triangle RSP \sim \triangle LMO$. Find the measures of $\angle P$ and $\angle L$.

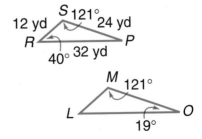

Transformations

In a plane, a geometric transformation moves a geometric figure to a new position in one of three ways. Each transformed figure is the image of the original figure.

- translation (or slide) — Every point of a figure moves the same distance and in the same direction along a line.

- reflection (or flip) — A figure is flipped over a line of reflection so that its *mirror image* is formed.

- rotation (or turn) — A figure is turned around a center point.

Translation (Slide)

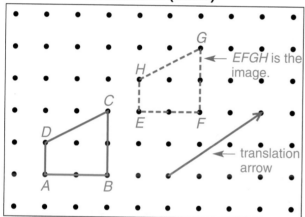

Reflection (Flip)

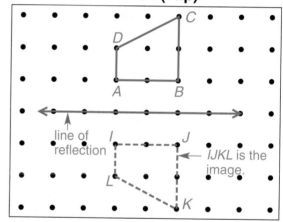

The translation arrow shows that ABCD is moved 3 units right and 2 units up.
Translation image EFGH ≅ ABCD.

ABCD is flipped over the line of reflection to form its mirror image.
Reflection image IJKL ≅ ABCD.

Rotation (Turn)

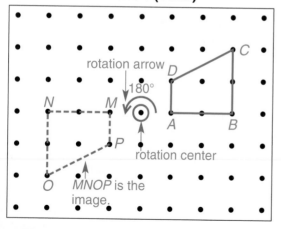

The rotation arrow shows that ABCD is rotated (or turned) one-half turn counterclockwise around the rotation center.
Rotation image MNOP ≅ ABCD.

Think
Half turn is 180°.

Copy each figure on dot paper. Draw a translation, reflection, and rotation image of each figure.

1.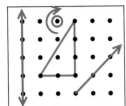

2.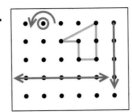

3.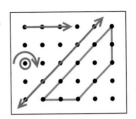

Write *True* or *False* for each statement. If false, explain why. Draw transformations on dot paper to help.

4. The distance between pairs of corresponding points of an original figure and its translation image is the same.

5. A translation, reflection, or rotation does not change the shape of a figure but may change its size.

6. Corresponding sides of a transformed figure (translation, reflection, or rotation) and its image are parallel.

7. In a reflection, corresponding points of the figure and its image are the same distance from the line of reflection.

8. You can flip a figure twice to get a half turn.

Problem Solving

9. Draw a 270° clockwise rotation of the given figure.

10. Describe this transformation.

CHALLENGE

A glide reflection is a translation followed by a reflection.

Decide whether the transformation of the first triangle into the second triangle is a *reflection*, *translation*, or a *glide reflection*.

11. △CDE ⟶ △FHI   12. △CDE ⟶ △PNM

13. △MNJ ⟶ △EDC   14. △PQM ⟶ △KJN

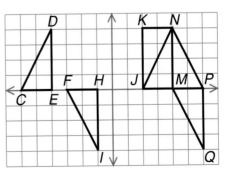

Symmetry

When figures can be reflected or rotated and the result is the original figure, these figures have **symmetry**.

Types of Symmetry		
Reflection Symmetry	**Rotational Symmetry**	**Point Symmetry**
A figure has **reflection symmetry** if a line, called a **line of symmetry**, can be drawn through the figure so that the part of the figure on one side of the line is the mirror image of the part on the other side.	A figure has **rotational symmetry** if the figure coincides with itself when rotated in either direction $n°$, where n is less than a full turn ($n < 360°$), about a fixed point.	A figure has **point symmetry** if there is a central point so that the part of the figure on one side of the central point is the reflection of the part on the other side.

<table>
<tr><td></td><td></td><td>180°-rotational symmetry is also point symmetry.</td></tr>
</table>

Reflection Symmetry column:

△ vertical line of symmetry   K horizontal line of symmetry

diagonal line of symmetry   vertical, horizontal, and diagonal lines of symmetry

Rotational Symmetry column:

72° 72° 72° 72° 72°

$72°(\frac{1}{5}\text{-turn})$
rotational symmetry

120° 120° 120°

$120°(\frac{1}{3}\text{-turn})$
rotational symmetry

Point Symmetry column:

S N

□ ⌐ ⌐

Study these examples.

<table>
<tr>
<td>T O O T

The word has reflection symmetry.</td>
<td>1961

The number has rotational (180°) symmetry and point symmetry.</td>
<td>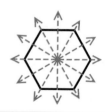

The figure has reflection, rotational, and point symmetry.</td>
</tr>
</table>

**Name all the lines of symmetry for each figure. Write *vertical,
horizontal,* or *diagonal*. Trace the figure and draw all lines of symmetry.**

1.

2.

3.

4.

**Each figure has rotational symmetry about point *O*. Tell the smallest turn,
or the number of degrees, that will rotate the figure onto itself.**

5.

6.

7.

8.

Does each figure have point symmetry? Write *yes* or *no*.

9.

10.

11.

12.

**Tell which words and numbers have *reflection,
rotational,* or *point* symmetry.**

13. ODD   14. 8118   15. SWIMS   16. 1001

17. Shirley printed the last three letters
of the English alphabet in block capital
letters. Which letters have point
symmetry? rotational symmetry?
reflection symmetry? no symmetry?

18. Danny cuts all along all the lines of
symmetry of his square cake. Will he
be able to give each of his 10 friends
a piece of cake? Explain.

Write About It

19. Draw a figure on a grid or dot paper to show each kind of symmetry.
Describe the symmetry.

Tessellations

Interesting patterns are often used on floors, wallpaper, and fabrics. The designs are often made of polygons.

A design like the one shown at the right is called a tessellation.

A tessellation is made from congruent figures placed so that they completely cover a surface without overlapping or leaving gaps.

Many polygons will form a tessellation. Follow these steps to form a tessellation made of squares.

> A tessellation may contain one or more different types of polygons.

- Draw square *ABCD* on dot paper.

- Turn *ABCD* one-half turn clockwise around the midpoint (halfway point) of $\overline{BC}$. You get square 2.

- Turn square 2 one-half turn clockwise around the midpoint of its side to get square 3.

- Turn square 3 one-half turn clockwise around the midpoint of its side to get square 4.

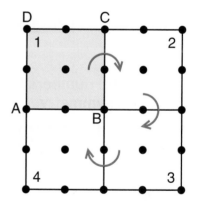

Copy the figure on dot paper and continue to draw half-turn images. You should see that a square tessellates (covers) the plane.

Study these examples.

All parallelograms tessellate.

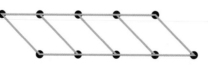

Circles do not tessellate. There are gaps.

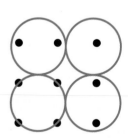

Draw these polygons on dot paper. Try to make a tessellation using each polygon.

1.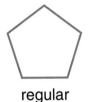
regular
pentagon

2.
regular
hexagon

3.
regular
heptagon

4.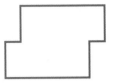
octagon

5. Which of the polygons above could not be used for a tessellation?

Use each figure to create a tessellation on dot paper.

6.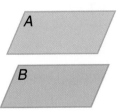

7.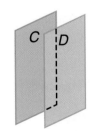

8.

9.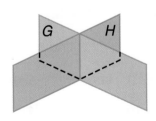

Problem Solving

10. If all triangles tessellate, do all quadrilaterals tessellate?

11. Can you tessellate a plane using a combination of squares and equilateral triangles? Explain.

12. Create your own tessellation by using a combination of polygons.

CRITICAL THINKING

Planes can be parallel, intersecting, or perpendicular.

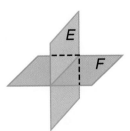

13. Which pairs of planes shown above are parallel? intersecting? perpendicular?

14. How do you describe parallel planes? intersecting planes?

Solid Figures

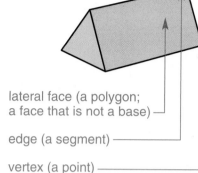

The model at the right is an example of a solid figure. Solid figures are three-dimensional. Their parts are not all contained in the same plane.

Solid figures formed by *flat* plane surfaces are called polyhedra.

Polyhedra are named by the shape of their base.

lateral face (a polygon; a face that is not a base)

edge (a segment)

vertex (a point)

▶ Prisms: polyhedra having polygons as parallel congruent bases joined by rectangular faces.

parallel congruent bases

triangular prism

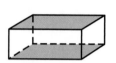

rectangular prism

pentagonal prism

▶ Pyramids: polyhedra having one polygon as a base and triangular faces that share a common vertex.

triangular pyramid

rectangular pyramid

hexagonal pyramid

▶ Not polyhedra: solid figures having curved surfaces.

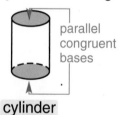

parallel congruent bases

cylinder

one base

cone

sphere

Is the figure a prism or a pyramid? Tell how many faces, edges, and vertices it has. (*Hint:* The bases are also faces.)

1.

2.

3.

4.

Tell which solid figure(s) can have a base like the one named.

5. equilateral triangle   **6.** circle   **7.** rectangle   **8.** square

Write *True* or *False*. If false, explain why.

9. A prism has 5 or more surfaces, or faces.

10. Prisms, pyramids, and spheres are polyhedra.

11. A pyramid has 3 or more surfaces, or faces.

12. A cube is a special type of rectangular pyramid.

Net of a Solid Figure

A triangular prism opens up to the net at the right. A net is a flat pattern that folds into a solid figure.

The net:
- has 2 triangular bases.
- has 3 rectangular faces between the bases.
- has 6 vertices and 9 edges.

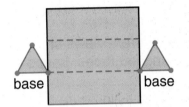
base   base

Use the solid figures below to answer exercises 13–14.

A

B

C

D

E

13. Name each figure above.

14. Draw the net for each figure.

Problem Solving

15. Steve made a net from two trapezoids and four rectangles. Name the solid figure for the net he made.

16. Margaret made a net from four triangles. Name the solid figure for her net.

CRITICAL THINKING   Algebra

17. Make a table listing the number of edges, faces, and vertices for each solid figure in exercises 1–4 on page 362. Write an equation to describe the relationship between the number of edges and the sum of the vertices and faces of a polyhedron.

Views of Solid Figures

Lance has a solid figure in his hand. He looks at it from different views, and draws a picture of each view. What solid figure does Lance have?

Top View   Front View   Side View   Bottom View

The different views show that there are square and rectangular faces. Lance has a rectangular prism.

▶ What solid figure has these views?

Top View   Front View   Side View

This figure is a triangular pyramid.

▶ Using cubes, Sam built a figure that looks like this. You can build a model to see and draw the front view, top view, right view, and left view of this figure.

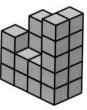

Front View   Top View

Right View   Left View

Name the solid figure that has these views.

1. Top View   Front View

2. Top View   Front View

Draw the top, front, and side views of each figure.

3.

4.

5.

6.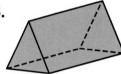

7.

8.

9.

10.

Problem Solving

11. Ronna cut the top off of a cone. She drew the top, front, and side views of the new solid figure. Draw the top, front, and side views that Ronna saw.

12. Felipe cut a sphere in half. He drew the top, bottom, and front views of the new solid figure. Draw the top, bottom, and front views that Felipe saw.

13. Danny puts a tower that is 5 cubes high in the middle of a base that is 3 cubes long by 3 cubes wide. Draw the top view and the front view of Danny's building.

14. Julie builds a base that is 5 cubes long by 5 cubes wide. On top of that she places another base that is 5 cubes long and 4 cubes wide. On top of that she places a third base that is 5 cubes long and 3 cubes wide. Draw the top, front, and side views of Julie's building.

DO YOU REMEMBER?

Solve and check.

15. $17 + y = 90$

16. $j - 329 = 477$

17. $45x = 405$

18. $z \div 13 = 95$

19. $f + 2.47 = 0.05$

20. $22.5 - m = 3.91$

21. $1\frac{1}{5}u = 10$

22. $6\frac{1}{6} \div w = 18\frac{1}{2}$

Problem-Solving Strategy:
Logical Reasoning

Helen has to choose two different polygons to complete this analogy. Which two polygons should she choose?

2 diagonals are to a __?__ as 9 diagonals are to a __?__ .

Read ▶ **Visualize yourself in the problem above as you reread it. List the facts and the question.**

Facts: a polygon with 2 diagonals
a polygon with 9 diagonals

Question: Which two polygons should she choose?

Plan ▶ To complete the analogy, first draw some polygons and then count the number of diagonals.

Polygon				
Number of Diagonals	0	2	5	?

+ 2   + 3   + ?

Solve ▶ A square is a quadrilateral.
A square has 2 diagonals.
All quadrilaterals have 2 diagonals.

Look at the pattern in the table.

What number should be added to 5 to find the number of diagonals in a hexagon? 4

5 + 4 = 9   number of diagonals in a hexagon

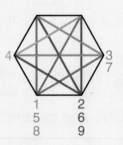

So 2 diagonals are to a quadrilateral as 9 diagonals are to a hexagon.

Check ▶ Draw and count the number of diagonals in a hexagon.

Solve each problem. Use logical reasoning to help you.

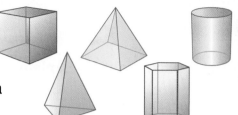

1. Ms. Geldof wants to place these five solids in a row so that no two prisms or pyramids are side by side. From the left, the fourth figure should have six congruent faces. The square pyramid should be to the right of the figure with a curved surface. What is the order of the solids?

Read ▶ Visualize yourself in the problem above as you reread it. List the facts and the question.

> **Facts:** No two prisms or pyramids are to be side by side.
> fourth figure—6 congruent faces
> square pyramid—to the right of the figure
> with a curved surface
>
> **Question:** What is the order of the solids?

Plan ▶ Use the clues in the problem and logical reasoning to find the correct order.

?	?	?	?	?
1st	2nd	3rd	4th	5th

▶ **Solve** ·········▶ **Check** ▶

2. An acute angle is to an equilateral triangle as a right angle is to a ? .

3. Abby, Kara, Ed, and Ben each drew a different pattern. Match each person with the pattern each drew if Ben's pattern has exactly 6 right triangles, Abby's has 6 squares and 4 pentagons, and Ed's has 12 trapezoids and 8 right triangles. Which pattern did each person draw?

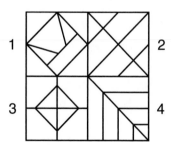

4. Find two ways Rose can complete this analogy: 180° is to a triangle as ? ° is to a ? .

5. Find two ways Larry can complete this analogy: 7 is to 49 as 5 is to ? .

6. Use polygons and geometric solids to make up your own analogies.

Problem-Solving Applications: Mixed Review

Read ▶ Plan ▶ Solve ▶ Check

Solve each problem. Explain the method you used.

Ms. Widsky's class created a class pennant with this design:

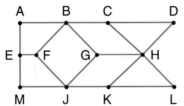

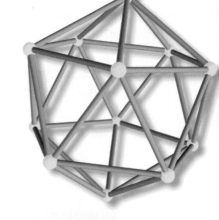

1. Classify quadrilateral *GHKJ.* What is the sum of the measures of its angles?

2. Identify one acute angle, one right angle, and one obtuse angle.

3. Is △*HKL* scalene, isosceles, or equilateral? Is it acute, right, or obtuse? Explain.

4. Name 2 pairs of alternate interior angles if $\overline{AD} \parallel \overline{ML}$.

Which of the following pairs of angles are adjacent? complementary? supplementary? Which of the angles form a linear pair?

5. ∠*CHG,* ∠*GHK*   6. ∠*KLH,* ∠*HDC*

7. ∠*MJF,* ∠*GJF*   8. ∠*LHD,* ∠*DHC*

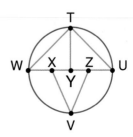

9. The four faces of a sculpture are equilateral triangles. The base is a rectangle. What shape is the sculpture?

10. The class creates these four floor plans. Which two plans are congruent? Which three are similar?

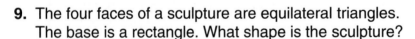
A

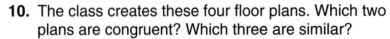
B

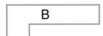
C

D

Use the diagram for problems 11–12.

11. Ms. Widsky's class designed a circular rug like the one at the right. Name two chords.

12. Name two central angles in this pattern. Are they acute, obtuse, or right?

Choose a strategy from the list or use another strategy you know to solve each problem.

13. Mr. Gray's class creates a logo that has six line segments. In the logo, you can find a trapezoid, two right triangles, and a square. Draw one possible design for the logo.

Strategy File

Use These Strategies
Logical Reasoning
Make an Organized List
More Than One Solution
Use More Than One Step
Use a Diagram
Write an Equation

14. Greg is making designs with exactly three interlocking figures. He can choose from circles, squares, triangles, and trapezoids. He can use one or more than one of the figures. How many combinations can he use to make his designs?

15. 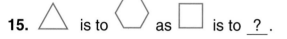 is to ___ as ___ is to ? .

16. Each right triangle in the figure at the right has an area of 30 square inches. Each obtuse triangle has an area of 16.5 square inches. What is the area of the entire figure?

17. Four students each draw a rhombus, a square, a rectangle, or a trapezoid. No shape is drawn twice. Meg and Bill draw more than 2 right angles. Bill and Lyle's shapes have 4 congruent sides. What shape does Zack draw?

18. Bill measures the angles of a quadrilateral. He finds that two angles measure 55° and 87°. What is the sum of the measures of the other two angles?

Use the diagram for problems 19–22.

19. What is the measure of $\angle MNR$?

20. The measures of $\angle SOR$ and $\angle ORS$ are equal. What is each measure?

21. What is the measure of $\angle NRO$? (Notice that $\angle QRS$ is a straight angle.)

22. Are $\angle PRN$ and $\angle RNO$ congruent? Why?

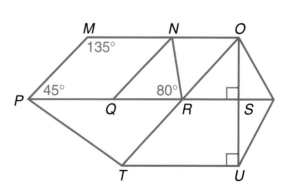

Use the figure below right for ex. 1–5. Classify each angle as *right, acute, obtuse,* or *straight.* Then use a protractor to find the exact measure of each angle. *(See pp. 330–335.)*

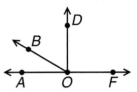

1. ∠DOF
2. ∠AOF
3. ∠AOB
4. ∠BOF
5. Which angles are complementary? supplementary?

Use the figure at the right to name the angles. *(See pp. 336–337.)*

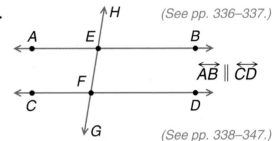

6. the corresponding angle to ∠AEH
7. the alternate interior angle to ∠BEF
8. the alternate exterior angle to ∠GFD

$\overleftrightarrow{AB} \parallel \overleftrightarrow{CD}$

Use a compass and a straightedge. *(See pp. 338–347.)*

9. Trace ∠ABC on unlined paper. Then construct ∠DEF ≅ ∠ABC.

10. Bisect ∠DEF from exercise 10.

Find the value of the variable in each polygon. *(See pp. 348–351, 354–365.)*

11.

12.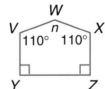

13.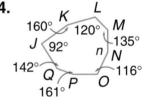

14.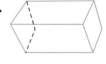

Draw the translation, reflection, and rotation image. Use dot paper.

Draw a net for the solid figure.

15.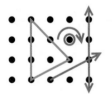

16.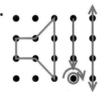

17.

18.

Problem Solving *(See pp. 352–353, 366–369.)*

19. Mel colors $\frac{1}{2}$ of a circle red. He then marks off a sector with a central angle of 40° and colors it blue. What is the measure of the central angle of the sector that is not red nor blue?

20. Complete the analogy and explain your answer: A rectangle is to a pentagonal prism as a _?_ is to a hexagonal pyramid.

(See *Still More Practice,* p. 528.)

Networks

A **network** is a set of points connected by segments or arcs, called **paths**. If it is possible to draw or trace each segment or arc exactly once without lifting a pencil from paper, then the network is **traversable**. A point at which the segments or arcs intersect is called a **vertex** (plural: *vertices*), or a corner.

A vertex is **even** if there are an even number of paths at a vertex.
A vertex is **odd** if there are an odd number of paths at a vertex.

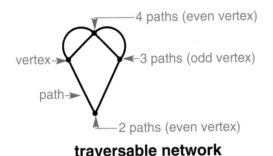

- 4 paths (even vertex)
- vertex→ ←3 paths (odd vertex)
- path→
- 2 paths (even vertex)

traversable network

not traversable network

Use the networks below.

A

B

C

D

E

F

G

1. How many even vertices are in each network? odd vertices?

2. Trace each network. Which are traversable?

3. Look for a pattern for traversable networks in the number of odd vertices. How many odd vertices are in a traversable network?

4. Use the pattern to draw three traversable networks.

5. Use the same pattern to draw three more networks that are not traversable.

Draw or construct as indicated.

1. Draw a parallelogram with congruent sides.

2. Draw vertical angles with measures 120° each.

3. Draw a right scalene triangle.

4. Construct $\overleftrightarrow{JK} \perp \overleftrightarrow{TV}$.

5. Construct the bisector of $\angle ABC$ with m$\angle ABC = 130°$.

6. Construct $\overline{AB} \cong \overline{CD}$

Use the figures to find the value of each variable.

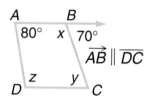

7. x

8. y

9. z

10. a

11. b

12. c

$\overline{NH} \parallel \overline{RO}$

$\overrightarrow{AB} \parallel \overline{DC}$

Identify each for circle O.

13. diameter

14. 2 chords

15. 2 minor arcs

16. 3 radii

17. 2 central angles

18. a semicircle

Name the type of transformation. Write *reflection, translation,* or *rotation.*

19.

20.

21.

Problem Solving

Use a strategy you have learned.

22. $\triangle RST$ is a right triangle. $\angle S$ is a right angle, and m$\angle R = 43°$. What is the sum of the measures of $\angle R$ and $\angle S$? What is the measure of $\angle T$?

Tell About It

Explain how you solved the problem. Show all your work.

23. $\triangle MNO \cong \triangle PQD$ with $\overline{MN} \cong \overline{PQ}$, $\overline{NO} \cong \overline{QD}$, and $\overline{MO} \cong \overline{PD}$. If m$\angle M +$ m$\angle N = 95°$, what is m$\angle D$?

Performance Assessment

Draw each solid figure to solve. Explain your reasoning.

24. Four students each draw one solid figure: a cylinder, cone, rectangular pyramid, or triangular prism. No solid figure is drawn twice. Sue and Ted draw at least one circle. Ann draws at least one triangle. What solid figure does Jim draw?

Test Preparation

Choose the best answer.

1. Simplify: $\frac{1}{4} + \frac{5}{8} \times 2$

   a. $\frac{7}{8}$ **b.** $1\frac{1}{2}$ **c.** 3   **d.** not given

2. 0.91×0.37

   a. 0.3367   **b.** 1.28

   c. 33.67   **d.** not given

3. What part of Ed's budget is spent on food and housing?

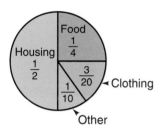

   a. $\frac{1}{6}$

   b. $\frac{1}{4}$

   c. $\frac{2}{3}$

   d. $\frac{3}{4}$

4. Choose the measure of $\angle A$.

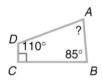

   a. 75°
   b. 85°
   c. 110°
   d. 175°

5. The stem-and-leaf plot shows the number of floors in several buildings. How many buildings have fewer than 40 floors?

   a. 2
   b. 6
   c. 8
   d. 12

Stem	Leaf
5	0 1
4	2 2 3 4
3	4 5 5 6
2	0 1 1 2

6. $2\frac{2}{3} = j - 2\frac{1}{6}$ $j = \underline{?}$

   a. $\frac{1}{3}$ **b.** $4\frac{1}{3}$ **c.** $4\frac{5}{6}$ **d.** not given

7. $2\frac{3}{8} \div \frac{1}{4}$

   a. 2   **b.** $9\frac{1}{2}$

   c. $12\frac{3}{8}$ **d.** not given

8. Spin each spinner one time. What is P(even, M)?

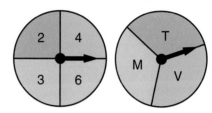

   a. $\frac{1}{12}$

   b. $\frac{1}{7}$

   c. $\frac{1}{4}$

   d. $\frac{7}{12}$

9. Which solid figure has 5 faces, 6 vertices, and 9 edges?

   a. triangular pyramid   **b.** rectangular prism
   c. hexagonal prism   **d.** triangular prism

10. According to the graph, how many favorite sandwiches were chosen?

   a. 13
   b. 46
   c. 48
   d. 50

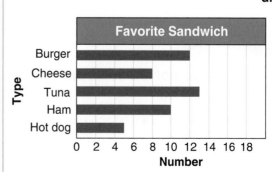

11. What type of angle is a 150° angle?

    a. acute   **b.** obtuse
    c. right   **d.** straight

12. Round 962,847.4512 to its greatest place.

    a. 900,000   **b.** 950,000
    c. 960,000   **d.** 1,000,000

13. Choose the number in standard form.

4.5×10^4

    a. 450
    b. 4,500
    c. 45,000
    d. 450,000

14. Divide.

$0.75 \div 1000$

    a. 0.075
    b. 0.0075
    c. 0.00075
    d. 0.000075

15. Fiona's scores in six games were 27, 41, 32, 22, 36, 22. What is the median of her scores?

    a. 19
    b. 22
    c. 29.5
    d. 30

16. Which polygon has 12 vertices?

    a. quadrilateral   **b.** decagon
    c. nonagon   **d.** dodecagon

17. Choose the equation.

Six more than twice a number is 9.

    a. $6n \times 2 = 9$ **b.** $2 \times 9 + 6 = n$
    c. $2n + 6 = 9$ **d.** $6 \times 2n = 9$

18. Evaluate the expression, when $a = {}^+5, \quad b = {}^-1, \text{ and } c = {}^-2.$

$b \times (c + a)$

    a. ${}^-3$
    b. ${}^+3$
    c. ${}^-7$
    d. ${}^+7$

19. Which is a curve that joins any two points on a circle?

    a. sector   **b.** arc
    c. chord   **d.** radius

20. A bowl contains 100 beads. If $P(\text{black}) = \frac{3}{5}$ and $P(\text{red}) = \frac{2}{5}$, how many black beads are in the bowl?

    a. 40
    b. 60
    c. 80
    d. 120

**Explain how you solved each problem.
Show all your work.**

21. In problem 15, if Fiona's next score is 30, which statistic will change: range, mean, median, or mode?

22. Use this set of numbers: 22, 23, 29, 31, 34, 41. Can you include a seventh number in this set so that the range, mean, median, and mode do *not* change? Explain your answer.

Ratio, Proportion, and Percent

We've got a tree in our yard. It grows about six feet every year.

If I had grown at the same speed, I'd now be almost fifty feet tall! I wouldn't really mind, except that I'd never get clothes to fit.

From *Counting on Frank*
by Rod Clement

In this chapter you will:

Simplify ratios and rates
Write and solve proportions
Learn about scale drawings,
    maps, and similar figures
Relate percents, fractions,
    and decimals
Solve problems by combining
    strategies

Critical Thinking/Finding Together

Suppose that you grew at a rate of 6 feet per year. About how many inches tall would you be today?

11-1

Ratio

A ratio is a way of comparing two numbers or quantities, *a* and *b*, by division. The numbers, *a* and *b*, are called the terms of the ratio.

▶ A ratio can be written in three forms.

Word form:　　a to b
Ratio form:　　$a : b$

Fraction form:　$\dfrac{a}{b}$

> Each form is read as "the ratio of *a* to *b*."

▶ You can write a ratio to compare two amounts— a part to a part, a part to a whole, or the whole to a part.

The picture above shows the following ratios:

Type	Comparisons	Word Form	Ratio Form	Fraction Form
part to part	the number of fashion magazines to the number of news magazines	3 to 5	3 : 5	$\dfrac{3}{5}$
part to whole	the number of sports magazines to the total number of magazines	2 to 10	2 : 10	$\dfrac{2}{10}$
whole to part	the total number of magazines to the number of fashion magazines	10 to 3	10 : 3	$\dfrac{10}{3}$

▶ You can simplify ratios by dividing both terms by their greatest common factor (GCF).

　　　　　　2 to 20
　　2 ÷ 2 to 20 ÷ 2 ◀—— Divide terms by 2.
　　　　　　1 to 5 ◀—— Simplify.

Practice

Use the bar graph. Write each ratio in three ways.

1. news magazines to sports magazines

2. home magazines to fashion magazines

3. all magazines to home magazines

4. sports and hobby magazines to all magazines

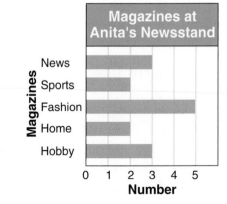

Magazines at Anita's Newsstand

Write each ratio in simplest form.

5. 4 to 12   **6.** 5 to 10   **7.** 8 : 12   **8.** 9 : 15   **9.** 10 : 6

10. $\dfrac{3}{15}$ **11.** $\dfrac{12}{16}$ **12.** $\dfrac{27}{36}$ **13.** $\dfrac{36}{27}$ **14.** $\dfrac{50}{30}$

15. $\dfrac{21}{63}$ **16.** $\dfrac{36}{45}$ **17.** $\dfrac{10}{25}$ **18.** $\dfrac{5}{20}$ **19.** $\dfrac{12}{18}$

Write each ratio of coupons redeemed in simplest form.

The table shows the number of coupons redeemed per household in a recent year.

20. Spain to Italy   **21.** Italy to U.K.

22. France to U.K.   **23.** Spain to Belgium

24. U.K. to Spain   **25.** U.S.A. to Canada

Country	Coupons Redeemed
U.S.A.	81
Canada	33
Belgium	19
U.K.	16
Italy	4
Spain	2
France	1

Find the baseball batting average to complete the table. Use a calculator to help.

1 6 ÷ 1 2 2 Enter = [0.1311475] ⟶ 0.131

26.

Hits	16	43	27	38	25	29	36
Times at Bat	122	201	166	154	179	111	182
Average	0.131	?	?	?	?	?	?

Problem Solving

27. Jo has 2 quarters and 1 nickel in her pocket. Her dad gives her $1.45. What is the ratio of change in Jo's pocket to the total amount she has?

CRITICAL THINKING

Write a ratio in simplest form. (*Hint:* Use like units for each ratio.)

28. 1 inch to 1 foot ⟶ ....Think.... 1 ft = 12 in. ⟶ 1 to 12

29. 1 quart to 1 gallon   **30.** 1 yard to 1 inch   **31.** 1 quart to 1 pint

32. 1 day to 1 hour   **33.** 1 half dollar to 2 quarters   **34.** 4 nickels to 1 quarter

Equivalent Ratios

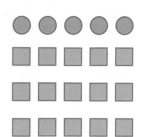

Equivalent ratios have the same value.
Equivalent ratios can be written as *equivalent fractions*.

The ratio of circles to squares is 5 to 15.
Write an equivalent ratio for 5 to 15.

To write an equivalent ratio:

- Write the given ratio as a fraction.

  $\dfrac{5}{15}$ ← number of circles
  ← number of squares

- *Multiply* or *divide* both the numerator and the denominator by the same nonzero number.

  $\dfrac{5 \div 5}{15 \div 5}$ ⎤ Divide both terms by the same nonzero number.

- Express the result as a fraction.

An equivalent ratio for 5 to 15 is 1 to 3. $\dfrac{5 \div 5}{15 \div 5} = \dfrac{1}{3}$

▶ You can use equivalent ratios to solve problems.

At 1 table Sue Ann can place 6 chairs. How many chairs can she place at 3 tables?

To find the number of chairs, *n*, write equivalent ratios.

$$\frac{1 \text{ table}}{6 \text{ chairs}} = \frac{3 \text{ tables}}{n \text{ chairs}}$$

$$\frac{1 \times 3}{6 \times 3} = \frac{3}{18}$$

So Sue Ann can place 18 chairs at 3 tables.

Study this example.

Write three equivalent ratios for 1 : 8.

$1 : 8 = \dfrac{1}{8} \rightarrow \dfrac{1}{8} = \dfrac{1 \times 2}{8 \times 2} = \dfrac{2}{16}$ $\dfrac{1}{8} = \dfrac{1 \times 3}{8 \times 3} = \dfrac{3}{24}$ $\dfrac{1}{8} = \dfrac{1 \times 4}{8 \times 4} = \dfrac{4}{32}$

$\dfrac{2}{16}, \dfrac{3}{24},$ and $\dfrac{4}{32}$ are equivalent ratios for 1 : 8.

Write three equivalent ratios for each.

1. $\dfrac{5}{8}$
2. $\dfrac{3}{4}$
3. $\dfrac{8}{40}$
4. $\dfrac{4}{9}$
5. $\dfrac{32}{24}$

Write the letter of the ratio that is equivalent to the given ratio.

6. 7 to 10
   a. 30 to 21
   b. $\dfrac{14}{20}$
   c. $\dfrac{13}{20}$
   d. $\dfrac{10}{7}$

7. 3 : 2
   a. $\dfrac{6}{4}$
   b. $\dfrac{10}{12}$
   c. $\dfrac{15}{20}$
   d. 2 to 3

Which ratios are equivalent? Write = or ≠.

8. $\dfrac{6}{8}$? $\dfrac{18}{24}$
9. $\dfrac{1}{3}$? $\dfrac{3}{1}$
10. $\dfrac{15}{1}$? $\dfrac{30}{15}$
11. $\dfrac{25}{45}$? $\dfrac{5}{9}$

Find the value of each variable.

12. $\dfrac{2}{8} = \dfrac{1}{n}$
13. $\dfrac{15}{18} = \dfrac{y}{6}$
14. $\dfrac{5}{6} = \dfrac{r}{12}$
15. $\dfrac{7}{4} = \dfrac{21}{h}$

16. $\dfrac{21}{27} = \dfrac{7}{a}$
17. $\dfrac{16}{20} = \dfrac{e}{5}$
18. $\dfrac{8}{1} = \dfrac{24}{f}$
19. $\dfrac{4}{7} = \dfrac{i}{28}$

20. $\dfrac{18}{6} = \dfrac{3}{c}$
21. $\dfrac{11}{d} = \dfrac{11}{1}$
22. $\dfrac{12}{36} = \dfrac{g}{3}$
23. $\dfrac{36}{9} = \dfrac{4}{k}$

24. $\dfrac{20}{16} = \dfrac{10}{x} = \dfrac{5}{4}$
25. $\dfrac{28}{24} = \dfrac{m}{12} = \dfrac{7}{?}$
26. $\dfrac{18}{12} = \dfrac{9}{v} = \dfrac{w}{z}$
27. $\dfrac{36}{48} = \dfrac{l}{12} = \dfrac{u}{t}$

Problem Solving

28. There are 6 boxes of fruit drink in 1 package. How many boxes are in 7 packages?

29. There are 60 pencils in 4 boxes. How many pencils are in 1 box?

30. You can fit 72 books on 3 shelves of a bookcase. How many books can you fit on 1 shelf?

31. The ratio of boys to girls in the math club is 2 to 3. There are 10 boys in the club. How many girls are in the club?

CHALLENGE

32. Lola has a collection of old magazines, comic books, and paperback novels. The ratio of magazines to comic books is 2 to 5, and the ratio of paperback novels to comic books is 1 to 3. If Lola has 6 magazines, how many paperback novels does she have? Explain how you solve the problem.

Rates

A rate is a ratio that compares two quantities with different units of measure. A unit rate is a rate that has 1 unit as its second term, or denominator.

Rates are used almost every day. For example, average speeds and prices are often given as rates.

▶ Moya ran 18 miles at a steady pace in 3 hours. Her average speed can be expressed as a ratio:

$$\frac{18 \text{ miles}}{3 \text{ hours}} \qquad 18 \text{ miles} : 3 \text{ hours} \qquad 18 \text{ miles in 3 hours}$$

To find how many miles Moya ran in 1 hour, x, use equivalent ratios.

$$\frac{18 \text{ miles}}{3 \text{ hours}} = \frac{x \text{ miles}}{1 \text{ hour}} \qquad \frac{18 \div 3}{3 \div 3} = \frac{6}{1}$$

> 6 miles in 1 hour is called a unit rate.

Moya ran 6 miles in 1 hour, or 6 miles per hour.

▶ Four ballpoint pens cost $2.20. This rate of cost can be given as a ratio.

$$\frac{4 \text{ pens}}{\$2.20} \qquad 4 \text{ pens} : \$2.20 \qquad 4 \text{ pens for } \$2.20$$

To find the cost of one pen, p, use equivalent ratios.

$$\frac{\text{total number of units}}{\text{total price}} = \frac{1 \text{ unit}}{\text{price of 1 unit}}$$

$$\frac{4 \text{ pens}}{\$2.20} = \frac{1 \text{ pen}}{p} \qquad \frac{4 \quad \div 4}{\$2.20 \div 4} = \frac{1}{\$.55}$$

> A unit price is the cost of one item.

One pen costs $.55.

Write each as a unit rate.

1. $\dfrac{12 \text{ books}}{2 \text{ cartons}} = \dfrac{x \text{ books}}{1 \text{ carton}}$

2. $\dfrac{20 \text{ cats}}{4 \text{ bowls}} = \dfrac{x \text{ cats}}{1 \text{ bowl}}$

3. $\dfrac{9 \text{ feet}}{18 \text{ hours}} = \dfrac{x \text{ foot}}{y \text{ hours}}$

4. $\dfrac{50 \text{ miles}}{5 \text{ hours}} = \dfrac{x \text{ miles}}{y \text{ hour}}$

5. $\dfrac{100 \text{ km}}{10 \text{ L}} = \dfrac{x \text{ km}}{1 \text{ L}}$

6. $\dfrac{2 \text{ boys}}{2 \text{ wagons}} = \dfrac{x \text{ boy}}{y \text{ wagon}}$

Find the unit rate or unit price.

7. 28 kilometers in 4 hours

8. 24 inches in 2 hours

9. 6 records for $30

10. 5 envelopes for $1.50

11. 120 feet in 8 seconds

12. 8 discs for $6.00

Use the unit rate or unit price to find the value of *x*.

13. 3 miles in 1 hour
    x miles in 6 hours

14. 1 card for $.35
    x cards for $1.05

15. 50 miles in 1 hour
    x miles in 4 hours

16. 2 books in 1 week
    x books in 3 weeks

17. 22 miles on 1 gallon
    x miles on 16 gallons

18. 1 apple for $.30
    x apples for $1.80

Problem Solving

19. Three rides on the roller coaster cost $2.25. How much does one ride cost?

20. What is the cost of one pencil if a box of 8 pencils sells for $.96?

21. A 5-lb watermelon costs $2.50. At the same rate per pound, how much would a 10-lb watermelon cost?

22. During the first hour 250 tickets to a concert were sold. At this rate how long will it be before 1500 tickets are sold?

23. Tyrone rode his bicycle 8 miles in one hour. At the same rate, how long will it take him to ride 44 miles?

24. If a package of 175 sheets of paper costs $1.55, how much do 3 packages cost?

DO YOU REMEMBER?

Solve and check.

25. $n + \dfrac{2}{3} = \dfrac{5}{3}$

26. $n + \dfrac{3}{8} = 5\dfrac{7}{8}$

27. $n + 1\dfrac{1}{5} = 2\dfrac{3}{10}$

28. $n - \dfrac{4}{9} = \dfrac{7}{9}$

29. $n - 1\dfrac{5}{8} = \dfrac{3}{8}$

30. $n - \dfrac{4}{7} = \dfrac{9}{14}$

31. $\dfrac{4}{5}n = \dfrac{2}{3}$

32. $5n = 1\dfrac{5}{8}$

33. $10n = \dfrac{5}{13}$

Proportions

A proportion is an equation that shows two ratios are equivalent.

John made trail mix using 2 cups of nuts and 6 cups of dried fruit. Marcy used 3 cups of nuts and 9 cups of dried fruit. Are the two mixes the same?

To determine if the two mixes are the same, check if the ratios form a proportion.

$$\frac{2 \text{ c nuts}}{6 \text{ c dried fruit}} \overset{?}{=} \frac{3 \text{ c nuts}}{9 \text{ c dried fruit}}$$

▶ There are two ways to check if two ratios form a proportion.

- Write the ratios as fractions in simplest form.
  If the fractions are the same, the ratios are equivalent.

$$\frac{2}{6} \overset{?}{=} \frac{3}{9} \longrightarrow \frac{2}{6} = \frac{1}{3} \text{ and } \frac{3}{9} = \frac{1}{3} \longrightarrow \frac{1}{3} = \frac{1}{3}$$

$\frac{2}{6} = \frac{3}{9}$ is a proportion because both ratios equal one third.

- Use the cross-products rule:
  Two ratios form a proportion if their *cross products* are equal.

The product of the extremes is equal to the product of the means.

extremes
$$a : b = c : d \longrightarrow a \times d = b \times c$$
means

| 2 and 9 are the extremes. | $\frac{2}{6} \overset{?}{\underset{\nearrow}{\times}} \frac{3}{9}$ | 6 and 3 are the means. |

$$2 \times 9 \overset{?}{=} 6 \times 3$$
$$18 = 18$$

Cross-Products Rule

$a : b = c : d$ when $b, d \neq 0$

$$\frac{a}{b} = \frac{c}{d} \longleftarrow \text{Write the ratios in fraction form.}$$

$$\frac{a}{b} \times \frac{d}{c} = \frac{c}{d} \times \frac{d}{c} \longleftarrow \text{Multiply both sides by } \frac{d}{c}.$$

$$\frac{a \times d}{b \times c} = 1 \longleftarrow \frac{c}{d} \text{ and } \frac{d}{c} \text{ are multiplicative inverses.}$$

$$a \times d = b \times c \longleftarrow \text{Numerator and denominator are equal since their quotient is 1.}$$

The trail mixes are the same because the ratios form a proportion.

Use equivalent fractions or the cross-products rule to determine if the ratios form a proportion.

1. $\frac{1}{5} \overset{?}{=} \frac{6}{10}$

2. $\frac{3}{4} \overset{?}{=} \frac{7}{5}$

3. $\frac{2}{1} \overset{?}{=} \frac{10}{5}$

4. $\frac{6}{10} \overset{?}{=} \frac{18}{30}$

5. $\frac{7}{4} \overset{?}{=} \frac{14}{18}$

6. $\frac{6}{60} \overset{?}{=} \frac{10}{90}$

7. $\frac{7}{5} \overset{?}{=} \frac{49}{35}$

8. $\frac{8}{5} \overset{?}{=} \frac{40}{50}$

Find the missing term to form a proportion.

9. $\frac{7}{3} = \frac{28}{n}$

10. $\frac{5}{1} = \frac{15}{n}$

11. $\frac{12}{21} = \frac{n}{7}$

12. $\frac{15}{18} = \frac{n}{36}$

13. $\frac{3}{4} = \frac{n}{8}$

14. $\frac{9}{10} = \frac{81}{n}$

15. $\frac{n}{1} = \frac{14}{7}$

16. $\frac{32}{36} = \frac{8}{n}$

Choose the two equivalent ratios. Write a proportion.
Check by showing the cross products.

17. $\frac{4}{5}, \frac{20}{25}, \frac{5}{4}$

18. $\frac{1}{12}, \frac{24}{21}, \frac{40}{35}$

19. $\frac{9}{5}, \frac{36}{30}, \frac{36}{20}$

20. $\frac{20}{10}, \frac{2}{1}, \frac{4}{5}$

21. $\frac{9}{81}, \frac{9}{27}, \frac{1}{9}$

22. $\frac{7}{6}, \frac{7}{16}, \frac{14}{32}$

23. $6:2, 3:1, 10:5$

24. $8:4, 4:2, 3:1$

25. $10:15, 12:18, 14:16$

Problem Solving

26. Leonard's cat catches 3 mice every 2 days. Francine's cat catches 10 mice every 6 days. Do the two cats catch mice at the same rate? Explain.

27. George Ferris constructed the first Ferris wheel. It was about 250 ft high and almost 800 ft around. Name four equivalent ratios that compare the height of the wheel to the distance around it.

CRITICAL THINKING — Algebra

If $\frac{a}{b} = \frac{c}{d}$ and a, b, c, and d are nonzero numbers, determine whether each statement is *true* or *false* for given values of a, b, c, and d. Give an example to support your answer.

28. $\frac{b}{a} = \frac{d}{c}$

29. $\frac{a}{c} = \frac{b}{d}$

30. $\frac{a}{a+b} = \frac{c}{c+d}$

31. $\frac{a+b}{b} = \frac{c+d}{c}$

Solve Proportions

You can use the cross-products rule to solve a proportion.

Solve the proportion: $\dfrac{n}{25} = \dfrac{6}{5}$.

Method 1

Find the cross products. The product of the extremes is equal to the product of the means.

Extremes   Means

$\dfrac{n}{25} = \dfrac{6}{5} \longrightarrow n \times 5 = 25 \times 6$

$5n \div 5 = 150 \div 5$

$n = 30$

Method 2

Multiply each side of the proportion by the reciprocal.

$\dfrac{n}{25} = \dfrac{6}{5} \longrightarrow \dfrac{n}{\overset{1}{\cancel{25}}} \times \dfrac{\overset{1}{\cancel{25}}}{1} = \dfrac{6}{\underset{1}{\cancel{5}}} \times \dfrac{\overset{5}{\cancel{25}}}{1}$

$n = 30$

Check by substituting the solution for n.

Check: $\dfrac{30}{25} \overset{?}{=} \dfrac{6}{5} \longrightarrow 30 \times 5 \overset{?}{=} 25 \times 6 \longrightarrow 150 = 150$

Study these examples.

Extremes   Means

$\dfrac{30}{n} \underset{\times}{\times} \dfrac{6}{5} \longrightarrow 30 \times 5 = n \times 6$

$150 = 6n$

$150 \div 6 = 6n \div 6$

$25 = n$ or $n = 25$

Check: $\dfrac{30}{25} \overset{?}{=} \dfrac{6}{5} \longrightarrow \dfrac{6}{5} = \dfrac{6}{5}$

Extremes   Means

$3 : 8 = n : 24 \longrightarrow 3 \times 24 = 8 \times n$

$72 = 8n$

$72 \div 8 = 8n \div 8$

$9 = n$ or $n = 9$

Check: $\dfrac{3}{8} \overset{?}{=} \dfrac{9}{24} \longrightarrow \dfrac{3}{8} = \dfrac{3}{8}$

Complete to find the missing term in each proportion.

1. $\dfrac{n}{6} = \dfrac{5}{3} \longrightarrow n \times 3 = 6 \times 5$

$3n \div \underline{\ ?\ } = 30 \div \underline{\ ?\ }$

$n = \underline{\ ?\ }$

2. $\dfrac{8}{n} = \dfrac{32}{40} \longrightarrow 8 \times 40 = n \times 32$

$320 \div \underline{\ ?\ } = 32n \div \underline{\ ?\ }$

$\underline{\ ?\ } = n$

Find the missing term in each proportion.

3. $\dfrac{n}{12} = \dfrac{5}{20}$ **4.** $\dfrac{n}{10} = \dfrac{3}{5}$ **5.** $\dfrac{n}{3} = \dfrac{7}{21}$ **6.** $\dfrac{6}{5} = \dfrac{24}{n}$

7. $\dfrac{4}{n} = \dfrac{16}{36}$ **8.** $\dfrac{2}{n} = \dfrac{14}{28}$ **9.** $\dfrac{12}{4} = \dfrac{18}{n}$ **10.** $\dfrac{5}{15} = \dfrac{n}{12}$

11. $\dfrac{n}{16} = \dfrac{3}{6}$ **12.** $\dfrac{n}{9} = \dfrac{5}{9}$ **13.** $\dfrac{n}{7} = \dfrac{6}{2}$ **14.** $\dfrac{18}{48} = \dfrac{n}{8}$

Find the value of *n*.

15. $4 : 5 = n : 10$ **16.** $6 : n = 3 : 9$ **17.** $n : 8 = 5 : 5$

18. $9 : 8 = 18 : n$ **19.** $n : 12 = 18 : 9$ **20.** $13 : 5 = n : 15$

21. $n : 6 = 0.4 : 12$ **22.** $9 : 4 = 2.7 : n$ **23.** $17 : 3 = n : 1.5$

Select the two ratios that form a proportion.
Check by showing the cross products.

24. $\dfrac{1}{2}, \dfrac{1}{4}, \dfrac{2}{4}$ **25.** $\dfrac{3}{5}, \dfrac{9}{15}, \dfrac{6}{9}$ **26.** $\dfrac{2}{3}, \dfrac{3}{9}, \dfrac{1}{3}$

27. $\dfrac{4}{6}, \dfrac{2}{5}, \dfrac{8}{12}$ **28.** $\dfrac{5}{8}, \dfrac{20}{32}, \dfrac{15}{16}$ **29.** $\dfrac{3}{10}, \dfrac{9}{10}, \dfrac{9}{30}$

CRITICAL THINKING   Algebra

Is the given value of *n* reasonable?
Explain your answer.

30. $\dfrac{3}{7} = \dfrac{n}{140}$ No, 6 is not reasonable.

     $n \approx 6$ $\dfrac{3}{7} \approx \dfrac{1}{2}$ so $\dfrac{n}{140}$ should be $\approx \dfrac{1}{2}$.

31. $\dfrac{33}{60} = \dfrac{n}{40}$ **32.** $\dfrac{32}{160} = \dfrac{1}{n}$ **33.** $\dfrac{100}{250} = \dfrac{n}{5}$ **34.** $\dfrac{35}{n} = \dfrac{0.2}{0.4}$

    $n \approx 30$ $n \approx 5$ $n \approx 7.5$ $n \approx 7\dfrac{1}{2}$

Write Proportions

At the given rate, how many gallons would Meghan use on a 3600-mile trip?

Average Miles Per Gallon	
Meghan	30
Ann	35
Harold	37
Paco	38.5

▶ To find the number of gallons, t, write and solve a proportion.

When you write a proportion, be sure that the two equivalent ratios compare similar things.

• Write two equal rates of miles to gallons.

miles per gallon → $\dfrac{30 \text{ miles}}{1 \text{ gallon}} = \dfrac{3600 \text{ miles}}{t \text{ gallons}}$ ← total miles in t gallons

Think
Miles per gallon means miles per 1 gallon.

• Use the cross-products rule to solve the proportion.

$\dfrac{30}{1} \diagup\!\!\!\!\times \dfrac{3600}{t}$

$30 \times t = 1 \times 3600$

$30t \div 30 = 3600 \div 30$ ← Apply the Division Property of Equality.

$t = 120$

• Check.

$\dfrac{30}{1} = \dfrac{3600}{t} \longrightarrow \dfrac{30}{1} \overset{?}{=} \dfrac{3600}{120} \longrightarrow 30 \times 120 \overset{?}{=} 1 \times 3600 \longrightarrow 3600 = 3600$

Meghan would use 120 gallons on a 3600-mile trip.

▶ There are many ways to set up a proportion as long as the equivalent ratios compare similar things.

gallons → $\dfrac{1}{30} = \dfrac{t}{3600}$ ← miles

short trip → $\dfrac{30}{3600} = \dfrac{1}{t}$ ← long trip

Practice

Use the table above to write and solve a proportion to find the number of gallons of gasoline for each trip.

1. Harold, 185 miles
2. Ann, 1050 miles
3. Paco, 3080 miles

Write a proportion. Then solve.

4. If apples sell at 3 for $.75, how many apples can be bought for $4.25?

5. If 12 calculators cost $60, what will 4 calculators cost?

6. If rent for 2 weeks is $750, how much rent is paid for 6 weeks?

7. If 5 CDs cost $60, how much would a dozen CDs cost?

Distance, Speed, Time, and Proportion

Speed, or rate (r), is the ratio of distance (d) to time (t). You can use a proportion to solve for distance or time.

Voyager I travels through space at about 38,600 mph. At that rate, about how far would Voyager I travel in a half hour?

Voyager I would travel about 19,300 miles in a half hour.

$$r = \frac{d}{t}$$

$$\frac{38{,}600 \text{ mi}}{1 \text{ h}} = \frac{d \text{ mi}}{0.5 \text{ h}}$$

$$38{,}600 \times 0.5 = 1 \times d$$

$$19{,}300 \quad = \quad d$$

Problem Solving

Use the formula relating distance, speed, and time to write and solve a proportion.

8. How far will a motorboat travel in 5 h if it travels 35 mi in 1 h?

9. A train takes 1 hour to go 75 miles. How long will it take the train to go 450 miles?

10. How long does it take a car to travel 510 miles at a rate of 68 miles per hour?

11. A dragonfly can travel 58 km per hour. At this speed, how long would it take this insect to fly 87 km?

12. Chin delivers 4 newspapers in 5 min. At this rate, how many newspapers can he deliver in one hour?

13. Catherine spent $2\frac{1}{2}$ hours writing 3 pages of her report. At this rate, how long will it take her to write a 15-page report?

14. A rocket sled traveled a record of 10 300 km in one hour. At this rate, how long would the vehicle take to travel 2575 km?

15. An electronic car traveled a record of 321.8 mi in one hour. At this rate, how far would it travel in 15 min?

TEST PREPARATION

16. A cake recipe calls for 1.5 cups of milk and 3 cups of flour. Ann made a mistake and used 5 cups of flour. How many cups of milk should she use to keep the proportion correct?

   A 1.75 cups   **B** 2.25 cups

   C 2 cups   **D** 2.5 cups

17. A rocket car travels at a rate of 640 miles per hour. At this rate, how much time would it take for the car to travel 384 miles?

   F 36 min   **G** 256 min

   H 245 min   **J** 1.7 h

Practice

Proportions and Similar Figures

The lengths of the corresponding sides of similar figures are in proportion.

$ABCD \sim WXYZ$

$$\frac{AB}{WX} = \frac{BC}{XY} = \frac{CD}{YZ} = \frac{AD}{WZ}$$

$$\frac{6}{9} = \frac{2}{3} = \frac{6}{9} = \frac{2}{3}$$

$$\frac{6 \div 3}{9 \div 3} = \frac{2}{3} = \frac{6 \div 3}{9 \div 3} = \frac{2}{3}$$

$$\frac{2}{3} = \frac{2}{3} = \frac{2}{3} = \frac{2}{3}$$

> Similar figures have the same shape and their corresponding angles are congruent.

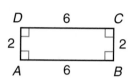

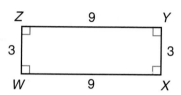

Study this example.

What is the length of $\overline{GF}$?

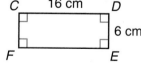

$\triangle EFG \sim \triangle PQR$

$$\frac{EG}{PR} = \frac{GF}{RQ} \rightarrow \frac{9}{18} = \frac{m}{24} \leftarrow \text{Write a proportion.}$$

$$9 \times 24 = 18 \times m \leftarrow \text{Use the cross-products rule.}$$

$$216 = 18m$$

$$216 \div 18 = 18m \div 18 \leftarrow \text{Apply the Division Property of Equality.}$$

$$12 = m$$

The length of $\overline{GF}$ is 12 cm.

Write the lengths of the corresponding sides in a proportion for each pair of similar figures.

1.
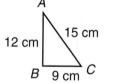

2.
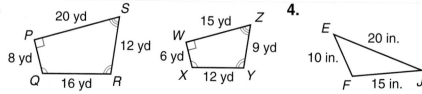

3.

4.
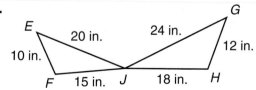

The figures in each pair are similar. Write and solve a proportion to find the length of each missing side.

5.

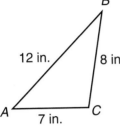

6.

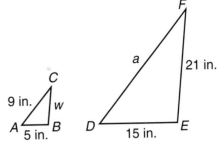

7.

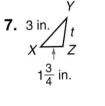
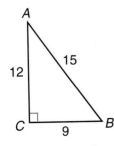

8.

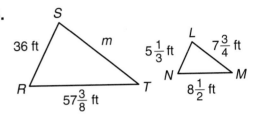

Problem Solving

9. Rex draws two similar trapezoids with the longer bases 12 cm and 15 cm in length. If the length of the shorter base of the smaller trapezoid is 4 cm, how long is the shorter base of the larger trapezoid?

10. Danielle draws two triangles. The first triangle has sides that are 7, 10, and 13 inches long. The second triangle has sides that are 10.5, 15, and 19.5 inches long. Are the triangles similar? Explain.

11. $\triangle ABC \sim \triangle DGF$. $\overline{AC}$, $\overline{AB}$, and $\overline{DF}$ are 3 cm, 5 cm, and 9 cm long, respectively. How many times the length of $\overline{CB}$ is the length of $\overline{FG}$?

12. The lengths, in inches, of the sides of a triangle are 5, 8, and 11. If the shortest side of a similar triangle has a length of 10 inches, what is the length of its longest side?

CHALLENGE — Algebra

Find the value of n.

13. $\triangle ABC \sim \triangle DEF$.

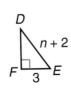

14. $\triangle ABC \sim \triangle ADE$.

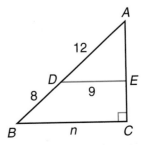

Use Proportions

Proportions in similar triangles can be useful for indirect measurement, such as finding heights of objects that are too large to be measured directly.

To solve shadow problems, you can draw a pair of similar right triangles.

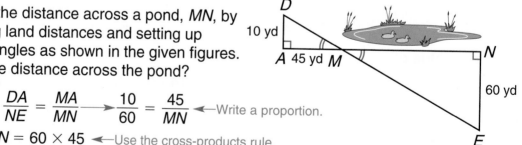

taller structure
light ray
shadow cast by taller structure

shorter structure
light ray
shadow cast by shorter structure

A 6-ft-tall person is standing near a tree. If the person's shadow is 10 ft long and the tree's shadow is 20 ft long, what is the height of the tree?

To find the height of the tree, h, draw a pair of similar right triangles. Then write and solve a proportion.

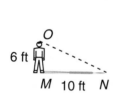

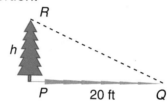

$$\triangle MNO \sim \triangle PQR$$

$\dfrac{6}{h} = \dfrac{10}{20}$ ←—Write a proportion.

$6 \times 20 = 10h$ ←—Use the cross-products rule.

$120 \div 10 = 10h \div 10$ ←—Apply the Division Property of Equality.

$12 = h$

The tree is 12 ft tall.

Study this example.

Gil found the distance across a pond, MN, by measuring land distances and setting up similar triangles as shown in the given figures. What is the distance across the pond?

$\dfrac{DA}{NE} = \dfrac{MA}{MN} \longrightarrow \dfrac{10}{60} = \dfrac{45}{MN}$ ←—Write a proportion.

$10MN = 60 \times 45$ ←—Use the cross-products rule.

$10MN \div 10 = 2700 \div 10$ ←—Apply the Division Property of Equality.

$MN = 270$

The distance across the pond is 270 yards.

Write a proportion. Then solve.

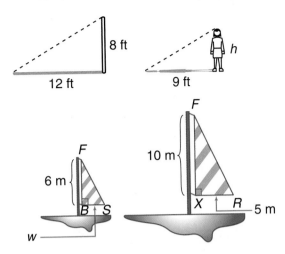

1. An 8-foot electricity pole casts a 12-foot shadow. At the same time, Ruth Ann casts a 9-foot shadow. How tall is Ruth Ann?

2. Similar triangular sails are raised on two sailboats. If the larger sail is 5 m wide and 10 m high and the smaller sail is 6 m high, how wide is the smaller sail?

3. A 6-ft-tall person casts a shadow 15 ft long. At the same time, a nearby tower casts a shadow 100 ft long. Find the height of the tower.

4. What is the height of a vertical pole that casts a shadow 8 ft long at the same time that a 12-ft-high vertical pole casts a shadow 3 ft long?

5. A mailbox that is 1 meter tall casts a shadow 4 meters long, while a lamppost casts a shadow 24 meters long. How tall is the lamppost?

6. A lamppost is 6.5 meters high. Next to it, a 1.2-meter-high mailbox casts a shadow 4.8 meters long. How long is the shadow of the lamppost?

7. A triangular sail has sides of 10 ft, 24 ft, and 26 ft. If the shortest side of a similar sail measures 6 ft, what is the measure of its longest side?

8. The heights of two signal poles are 20 feet and 30 feet, respectively. If the shorter pole casts a shadow of 8 feet, how long is the taller pole's shadow?

9. A surveyor determines the width of a river by setting up similar triangles as shown in the given figure.
   $\triangle AEC \sim \triangle BED$ with $AC = 89.5$ ft, $CE = 20$ ft, and $DE = 80$ ft. What is the width of the river BD?

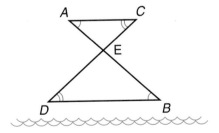

CRITICAL THINKING — *Algebra*

10. On the school softball team, there are 3 boys for every 4 girls. If the team has 21 members, how may boys does it have? how many girls?

11. A football team has 6 players who play offense for every 5 who play defense. There are 33 players on the team. How many players play offense? how many play defense?

Scale Drawings and Maps

A scale drawing is a drawing of a real object but is smaller than (a reduction of) or larger than (an enlargement of) the object. Measurements on a scale drawing are proportional to measurements of the real object.

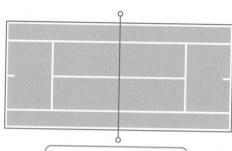

Scale: 1 in. = 32 ft

A scale is a ratio of the scale drawing to the actual measure. The scale 1 in. = 32 ft on this drawing of a tennis court means that 1 in. on the drawing represents 32 ft on the actual tennis court.

$$\frac{1 \text{ in.}}{32 \text{ ft}} \longleftarrow \text{measure in drawing}$$
$$\phantom{\frac{1 \text{ in.}}{32 \text{ ft}}} \longleftarrow \text{actual measure}$$

The scale length of the tennis court is $2\frac{7}{16}$ in. What is the actual length of the tennis court?

To find the actual length of the tennis court, n, write a proportion and use the cross products to solve.

$$\frac{\text{Scale measure}}{\text{Actual measure}} = \frac{\text{Scale length}}{\text{Actual length}} \longrightarrow \frac{1 \text{ in.}}{32 \text{ ft}} = \frac{2\frac{7}{16} \text{ in.}}{n \text{ ft}}$$

$$\frac{1}{32} \diagup\!\!\!\!= \frac{2\frac{7}{16}}{n} \longrightarrow 1 \times n = 32 \times 2\frac{7}{16} \longrightarrow n = \frac{\overset{2}{\cancel{32}}}{1} \times \frac{39}{\underset{1}{\cancel{16}}} = 78$$

The actual length of the tennis court is 78 feet.

Copy and complete the table. Use the scale: 1 in. = 10 ft.

	Rooms	Scale Length	Scale Width	Actual Length	Actual Width
1.	Dining Room	$1\frac{1}{2}$ in.	1 in.	?	?
2.	Kitchen	$1\frac{1}{4}$ in.	$\frac{3}{4}$ in.	?	?
3.	Living Room	2 in.	$1\frac{3}{4}$ in.	?	?

Measure the scale distance on the map to the nearest 0.5 cm. Then use a proportion to find the actual distance.

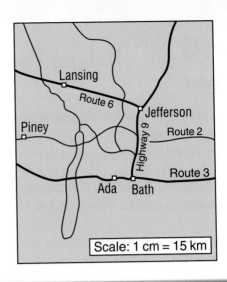

4. Between Lansing and Jefferson

5. Between Jefferson and Bath

6. Between Ada and Bath

7. Using Route 6 and Highway 9, about how far is it between Lansing and Bath? between Lansing and Ada?

Enlarged Models

Scale drawings are also used to compare measures of very small objects to a model that is enlarged.

The picture of the ladybug is an enlargement in which 1 cm represents 1 mm.

Scale model is larger than the real object.

Scale: 1 cm = 1 mm

Use the scale drawing of the ladybug to answer each question.

8. What is the scale length of the ladybug's body?

9. What is the actual length of the ladybug's body?

10. What is the scale width of the ladybug's body? Measure to the nearest 0.5 cm.

Write About It

11. Use a string and a metric ruler to find these distances on the map at the top of the page: (a) scale distance between Lansing and Piney along Route 6, Highway 9, and Route 2; (b) "straight line" distance between Lansing and Piney. Compare your measurements in (a) and (b).

12. Find the actual distances in (a) and (b) and compare them. Explain your method.

Relate Percents to Fractions

A **percent** is a ratio that compares a number to 100.
Percent means "per hundred" or "out of 100."
The symbol for percent is **%**.

In the grid, 25 out of 100 squares are red.
You can express this ratio as:

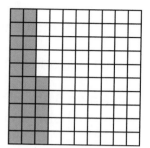

Ratio	Fraction	Percent
25 to 100	$\dfrac{25}{100}$	25%
25 : 100		

▶ To rename a fraction as a percent:

Use equivalent fractions:

- Write an equivalent fraction with a denominator of 100.

- Write the fraction as a percent.

$$\frac{4}{5} = ?$$

$$\frac{4}{5} = \frac{4 \times 20}{5 \times 20} = \frac{80}{100} = 80\%$$

So $\dfrac{4}{5} = 80\%$.

Use a proportion:

- Write the fraction as one ratio and $n : 100$ as the other ratio.

- Solve the proportion and write the percent symbol (%) next to the value of n.

$$\frac{3}{25} = ?$$

$$\frac{3}{25} = \frac{n}{100}$$

$$\frac{3}{25} \diagdown \frac{n}{100} \longrightarrow 3 \times 100 = 25n$$

$$\frac{300}{25} = \frac{25n}{25}$$

$$12 = n$$

So $\dfrac{3}{25} = 12\%$.

▶ To rename a percent as a fraction:

- Drop the percent symbol. Then write the given percent as the numerator and 100 as the denominator.

- Write the fraction in simplest form.

$$36\% = \frac{?}{}$$

$$36\% \longrightarrow \frac{36}{100}$$

$$\frac{36}{100} = \frac{36 \div 4}{100 \div 4} = \frac{9}{25}$$

.Think......
: GCF = 4 :
....

So $36\% = \dfrac{9}{25}$.

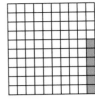

**Write a ratio to show the part of the grid that is shaded.
Then write the ratio as a percent.**

1.

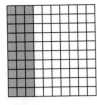

$$\frac{?}{100} = \underline{\ ?\ }\%$$

2.

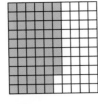

$$\frac{?}{100} = \underline{\ ?\ }\%$$

3.

$$\frac{?}{100} = \underline{\ ?\ }\%$$

Write each percent as a ratio and a fraction.

4. 70%   **5.** 46%   **6.** 11%   **7.** 5%   **8.** 8%

9. 27%   **10.** 30%   **11.** 92%   **12.** 71%   **13.** 89%

Write as a fraction in simplest form.

14. 75%   **15.** 28%   **16.** 66%   **17.** 80%   **18.** 13%

19. 37%   **20.** 64%   **21.** 22%   **22.** 15%   **23.** 78%

Write as a percent.

24. $\frac{53}{100}$ **25.** $\frac{71}{100}$ **26.** $\frac{6}{10}$ **27.** $\frac{1}{2}$ **28.** $\frac{1}{4}$

29. $\frac{1}{5}$ **30.** $\frac{3}{5}$ **31.** $\frac{7}{25}$ **32.** $\frac{16}{40}$ **33.** $\frac{42}{60}$

Percents on a Number Line

You can use a number line to show how percents are related to fractions.

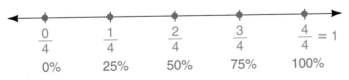

Draw a number line to show each percent. Write each percent as a fraction.

34. 12%   **35.** 80%   **36.** 45%   **37.** 22%   **38.** 64%

Problem Solving

39. Of 100 students, 59 are soccer players. What percent of the students are soccer players? What percent are not soccer players?

40. Of 150 basketball players surveyed, 108 are over six feet tall. What percent are over six feet tall? What percent are not over six feet tall?

Relate Percents to Decimals

Approximately 65% of the people of Virginia live in urban areas. Write this percent as a decimal.

To write 65% as an equivalent decimal, use the meaning of percent.

Richmond ★

▶ To rename a percent as an equivalent decimal:

- Rename the percent as a fraction with a denominator of 100.

| % means *per hundred.* |

- Write the fraction as a decimal.

Percent	Fraction	Decimal
65%	$\frac{65}{100}$	0.65

So 65% = 0.65.

▶ To rename a decimal as an equivalent percent:

- Rename the decimal as a fraction with a denominator of 100.

| % means *hundredths.* |

- Write the fraction as a percent.

Decimal	Fraction	Percent
0.32	$\frac{32}{100}$	32%

▶ You can use a shortcut and may need to write zero(s) to write a percent as a decimal or a decimal as a percent.

- Drop the percent (%) symbol. Then move the decimal point two places to the left.

Percent		Decimal
65% →	.65. →	0.65
2% →	.02. →	0.02

- Move the decimal two places to the right. Then write the percent (%) symbol.

Decimal		Percent
0.32 →	0.32. →	32%
0.6 →	0.60. →	60%

Practice

Write as a decimal.

1. 27%   **2.** 36%   **3.** 59%   **4.** 6%   **5.** 1%

Write as a percent.

6. 0.20   **7.** 0.35   **8.** 0.02   **9.** 0.07   **10.** 0.2

Find the percent, decimal, and fraction equivalents
to complete each table. Then write the percents in
each table in order from least to greatest.

	Percent	Decimal	Fraction
11.	10%	?	?
12.	50%	?	?
13.	?	0.4	?
14.	35%	?	?

	Percent	Decimal	Fraction
15.	?	0.85	?
16.	28%	?	?
17.	?	0.44	?
18.	?	?	$\frac{3}{10}$

Problem Solving

Use the double line graph to answer
each question.

19. Write a decimal for the percent
approval of each candidate in April.

20. Write a fraction in simplest
form for the percent approval
of each candidate in May.

21. How many people out of 100
approved of Candidate A
in February? Candidate B?

22. What is the difference of the
approval ratings in June?

23. Assuming the trends of the graph
continue, what ratings would you
expect the candidates to have in July?

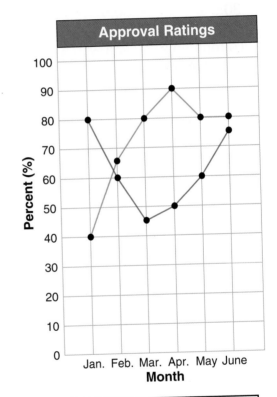

Approval Ratings

Key: Candidate A ——
Candidate B ——

MENTAL MATH — Algebra

Compare. Write <, =, or >.

24. 0.12 __?__ 1.2%

25. 0.08 __?__ 80%

26. 0.15 __?__ 15%

27. 0.47 __?__ 4.7%

28. 3.9 __?__ 39%

29. 0.086 __?__ 8.6%

Decimals, Fractions, and Percents

Some percents are *not* whole numbers.

30.5% of the grid is shaded.
30.5% is greater than 30% and is less than 31%.

Decimal percents like 30.5% can be renamed as equivalent decimals by dividing by 100. This moves the decimal point *two places* to the left.

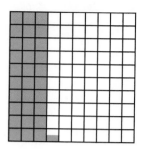

Percent	Decimal
30.5% ⟶ .30.5 ⟶	0.305

Percent means *hundredths*.

▶ To rename a fraction with a denominator that is not a factor of 100 as a percent, you can use a proportion or division.

Use a proportion:

- Write the fraction as one ratio and $n : 100$ as the other ratio.
- Solve the proportion.
- Write the percent symbol (%) next to the value of n.

$$\frac{3}{8} = ?$$

$$\frac{3}{8} = \frac{n}{100}$$

$$\frac{3}{8} \times \frac{n}{100} \longrightarrow 3 \times 100 = 8n$$

$$\frac{300}{8} = \frac{8n}{8}$$

$$37\frac{1}{2} = n$$

So $\frac{3}{8} = 37\frac{1}{2}\%$.

Use division:

- Rename the fraction as a decimal. Divide the numerator by the denominator to the hundredths place. Write the remainder as a fraction.
- Write the decimal as a percent.

$$\frac{2}{3} = ?$$

$$\frac{2}{3} \longrightarrow \begin{array}{r} 0.66 \\ 3\overline{)2.00} \\ -18 \\ \hline 20 \\ -18 \\ \hline 2 \end{array} \longrightarrow 0.66\frac{2}{3}$$

$$0.66\frac{2}{3} \longrightarrow 66\frac{2}{3}\%$$

So $\frac{2}{3} = 66\frac{2}{3}\%$.

▶ You can use a number line to relate fractions, decimals, and percents.

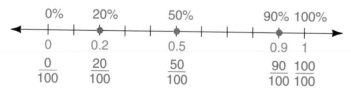

Each tick mark on the number line has a value of 0.1, $\frac{1}{10}$, or is 10% greater than the value to its left.

Write as a decimal.

1. 48.5%   **2.** 53.2%   **3.** 20.1%   **4.** 8.07%   **5.** 2.16%

6. 2%   **7.** 4%   **8.** 73.02%   **9.** 84.20%   **10.** 59.99%

Write as a percent.

11. $\frac{7}{8}$ **12.** $\frac{9}{16}$ **13.** $\frac{7}{16}$ **14.** $\frac{24}{30}$ **15.** $\frac{42}{60}$

16. $\frac{1}{8}$ **17.** $\frac{1}{16}$ **18.** $\frac{16}{40}$ **19.** $\frac{30}{32}$ **20.** $\frac{44}{64}$

Write as a fractional percent.

21. $\frac{5}{6}$ **22.** $\frac{1}{6}$ **23.** $\frac{1}{3}$ **24.** $\frac{1}{8}$ **25.** $\frac{2}{11}$

26. $\frac{3}{17}$ **27.** $\frac{1}{7}$ **28.** $\frac{1}{9}$ **29.** $\frac{7}{8}$ **30.** $\frac{5}{8}$

Order Rational Numbers

You can use a number line to order fractions, decimals, and percents.

Order from least to greatest: $\frac{3}{4}$, 0.4, 70%.

- Rename the rational numbers as all percents, or all fractions or decimals.

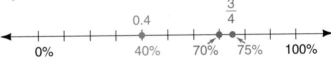

$$\frac{3}{4} = \frac{3 \times 25}{4 \times 25} = \frac{75}{100} = 75\%$$

$$0.4 = \frac{4}{10} = \frac{4 \times 10}{10 \times 10} = \frac{40}{100} = 40\%$$

From least to greatest, the order is 0.4, 70%, $\frac{3}{4}$.

Order each set from least to greatest on a number line.
Show how you changed from fractions and decimals to percents.

31. 65%, 0.9, $\frac{3}{4}$ **32.** 10%, 0.45, $\frac{11}{20}$ **33.** 0.65, 90%, $\frac{1}{50}$ **34.** 0.09, 43%, $\frac{9}{25}$

Problem Solving

35. Of the students in Shiva's class, 0.5 eat lunch from home, $\frac{1}{5}$ eat the school lunch, and 30% eat from the salad bar. Which kind of lunch do the greatest number of students eat?

36. Of the students at school, 40% walk or ride a bike to school, $\frac{9}{20}$ ride a bus to school, and 15% ride in a car to school. Which way of getting to school do the fewest number of students use?

Percents Greater Than 100%

A bicycle is 125% of its original value. This means that the bicycle is 25% more than its original value.

100% of something means the *whole*.

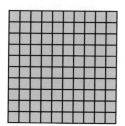

125% of something means 25% *more than the whole.*

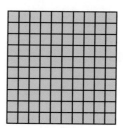 

A percent *greater than 100%* can be renamed as an equivalent decimal or as an equivalent mixed number.

▶ **To rename a percent greater than 100% as an equivalent *decimal*:**

- Drop the percent symbol (%).

- Move the decimal point *two* places to the left.

$$125\% = 1.25. = 1.25$$

▶ **To rename a percent greater than 100% as an equivalent *mixed number*:**

- Drop the percent symbol (%).

- Write the number as the numerator and 100 as the denominator.

- Express the fraction in simplest form.

$$125\% = \frac{125}{100} = 1\frac{25 \div 25}{100 \div 25} = 1\frac{1}{4}$$

Write each as a decimal.

1. 175%	**2.** 220%	**3.** 440%	**4.** 350%	**5.** 101%
6. 205%	**7.** 432%	**8.** 500%	**9.** 355%	**10.** 816%
11. 200%	**12.** 550%	**13.** 625%	**14.** 130%	**15.** 760%

Practice

Write each as a mixed number in simplest form.

16. 141%   **17.** 110%   **18.** 350%   **19.** 520%   **20.** 116%

21. 212%   **22.** 484%   **23.** 150%   **24.** 275%   **25.** 680%

26. 268%   **27.** 497%   **28.** 720%   **29.** 805%   **30.** 945%

31. 520%   **32.** 702%   **33.** 215%   **34.** 380%   **35.** 262.5%

Explain the meaning of each statement.

36. The population of Maple Grove is 300% of what it was 10 years ago.

37. This year the school librarian ordered 120% of the books she ordered last year.

38. Mr. Mendoza's salary is 150% of what it was 2 years ago.

39. Kevin's sweater is 100% wool.

Problem Solving

40. This year the cost of a bicycle is 35% higher than it was last year. What percent of last year's price is this year's price?

41. Mr. Ortega spends 13% of his budget for car repairs. What percent of his budget is used for other purposes?

42. After repairs a bicycle can be sold for twice the price at which it was purchased. The bicycle would then be worth what percent of its purchase price?

43. In a public survey, 78% of the questionnaires sent out by a store were returned. What percent of the questionnaires sent out were *not* returned?

CHALLENGE

Express each percent as a fraction in simplest form.

44. $7\frac{1}{2}\% = 7.5\% = \frac{7.5}{100} = \frac{7.5 \times 10}{100 \times 10} = \frac{75}{1000} = \frac{3}{40}$

45. $8\frac{4}{5}\%$ **46.** $10\frac{3}{4}\%$ **47.** $15\frac{1}{2}\%$ **48.** $5\frac{1}{8}\%$ **49.** $16\frac{2}{5}\%$

11-14 Percents Less Than 1%

Sometimes a percent *is less than 1%*.

A group of 600 students takes a test. Only 3 students get a perfect score. What percent of the group gets a perfect score?

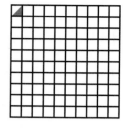

To find the percent, rename $\frac{3}{600}$ as an equivalent percent.

$$\frac{3}{600} \rightarrow 600\overline{)3.000}^{\,0.005} \rightarrow 0.00.5 = 0.5\%$$

So 0.5% of the group gets a perfect score.

> 0.5% or $\frac{1}{2}\%$ means $\frac{1}{2}$ of 1 out of 100.

▶ You can use the meaning of percent to rename a decimal or fraction as an equivalent percent less than 1%.

$$0.25\% = 0.25 \div 100 = 0.0025 = \frac{25}{10,000} = \frac{1}{400}$$

> % means *per hundred*.

$$\frac{1}{4}\% = \frac{\frac{1}{4}}{100} = \frac{1}{4} \div \frac{100}{1} = \frac{1}{4} \times \frac{1}{100} = \frac{1}{400}$$

Study these examples.

Write 0.15% as an equivalent fraction.

$$0.15\% = 0.15 \div 100 = 0.0015$$

$$= \frac{15}{10,000} = \frac{3}{2000}$$

So $0.15\% = \frac{3}{2000}$.

Write $\frac{1}{8}\%$ as an equivalent decimal.

$$\frac{1}{8}\% = \frac{\frac{1}{8}}{100} = \frac{1}{8} \div \frac{100}{1}$$

$$= \frac{1}{8} \times \frac{1}{100} = \frac{1}{800}$$

$$\frac{1}{800} \rightarrow 800\overline{)1.00000}^{\,0.00125}$$

So $\frac{1}{8}\% = 0.00125$.

Practice

Express each as a percent.

1. 0.001
2. 0.0026
3. $\frac{3}{1000}$
4. $\frac{1}{800}$
5. $\frac{4}{2000}$
6. $\frac{2}{500}$

7. 0.0031
8. $\frac{1}{200}$
9. 0.0006
10. $\frac{3}{4000}$
11. $\frac{5}{8000}$
12. $\frac{35}{10,000}$

Express each as an equivalent decimal.

13. 0.7%   **14.** 0.2%   **15.** 0.23%   **16.** $\frac{1}{5}$%   **17.** $\frac{3}{8}$%   **18.** $\frac{3}{4}$%

19. 0.3%   **20.** 0.58%   **21.** 0.26%   **22.** $\frac{4}{25}$%   **23.** $\frac{3}{20}$%   **24.** $\frac{9}{100}$%

Express each as an equivalent fraction.

25. 0.3%   **26.** 0.8%   **27.** 0.64%   **28.** $\frac{1}{10}$%   **29.** $\frac{12}{25}$%   **30.** $\frac{7}{8}$%

31. 0.7%   **32.** 0.05%   **33.** 0.54%   **34.** $\frac{5}{16}$%   **35.** $\frac{4}{15}$%   **36.** $\frac{3}{7}$%

Write in order from least to greatest.

37. 1.5, 0.3%, 155%, 0.004, $\frac{1}{200}$

38. 158%, $1\frac{5}{8}$, 0.005, 0.6%, $\frac{1}{100}$

39. $\frac{1}{50}$, 0.05, 0.2%, 150%, 1.55

40. 19%, 0.7, $\frac{1}{80}$, 2.5, 192%

Problem Solving

41. A total of 500 students enter the Science Fair. Of those students, 4 are awarded a trip to Science Camp. What percent of the group is awarded a trip to Science Camp?

42. Of the 750 people at the beach yesterday, only 3 forgot to put on sunscreen. What percent of the people at the beach forgot to put on sunscreen?

43. Jason has 675 stamps in his collection. Of those stamps, 5 are from foreign countries. To the nearest hundredth, what percent of Jason's stamps are *not* from foreign countries?

44. Abby is reading a 925-page book. So far she has read 9 pages. To the nearest hundredth, what percent of the book has Abby left to read?

DO YOU REMEMBER?

Match each definition with a term in the box.

| complementary angles |
| alternate interior angles |
| corresponding angles |
| vertical angles |
| supplementary angles |

45. two angles whose measures total 90°

46. two nonadjacent angles formed by two intersecting lines

47. a pair of nonadjacent interior angles on opposite sides of the transversal

48. a pair of nonadjacent angles, one interior and one exterior, that are both on the same side of the transversal

Problem-Solving Strategy:
Combine Strategies

Leon bought some stamps. He used 6 of them to mail a package. He gave 50% of what was left to Mira. Then he had 15 stamps. How many stamps did Leon buy?

Read

Visualize yourself in the problem above as you reread it. List the facts and the question.

Facts: Leon bought some stamps.
He used 6 stamps.
He gave away 50% of what was left.
He then had 15.

Question: How many stamps did Leon buy?

Plan

Some problems can be solved by combining strategies.

To find the number of stamps Leon bought, Work Backward and Write and Solve Equations.

Let n = number of stamps Leon had left.
Let t = number of stamps Leon bought.

$15 = 50\%$ of n and $n + 6 = t$

Solve

$$15 = 50\% \text{ of } n$$
$$15 = \frac{1}{2} \times n$$
$$15 \times 2 = \frac{n}{2} \times 2$$
$$30 = n$$

Think
$50\% = \frac{1}{2}$
"of" means $\times$.

Leon had 30 stamps left.

$$n + 6 = t \longrightarrow 30 + 6 = t$$
$$36 = t$$

So Leon bought 36 stamps.

Check

Begin with 36 stamps.

$$\underset{\text{bought}}{36} - \underset{\text{used}}{6} = \underset{\text{left}}{30} \quad \text{and} \quad 50\% \times \underset{\text{left}}{30} = 15$$

Solve. Combine strategies to help you.

1. A business office mailed 24 packages last week. Each package weighed $1\frac{1}{2}$ lb. For every 3 packages mailed special delivery, 5 packages were bulk rate. How many packages were mailed special delivery?

Read → Visualize yourself in the problem above as you reread it. List the facts and the question.

> **Facts:** 24 packages mailed
> $1\frac{1}{2}$ lb—weight of each package
> packages—3 special delivery
> 5 bulk rate

> **Question:** How many packages were mailed special delivery?

Plan → This is a *multistep problem* and it contains extra information. Use more than one step. First find the sum of $3 + 5$, then write and solve a proportion.

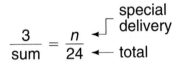

$$\frac{3}{\text{sum}} = \frac{n}{24}$$

special delivery ← n

total ← 24

Solve ⋯⋯→ **Check**

2. Ann's birthday is a dozen days after Ron's. Ron's birthday is in May but it is after May 15th. The sum of the digits of the date is 5 and it falls on a Sunday. What is the day and date of Ann's birthday?

3. The ratio of the length of a side of square *AXRD* to the length of a side of square *TVBN* is 2 to 7. If the perimeter of *TVBN* is 84 cm, what is the area of each square?

4. Of the 630 students at South School, three fifths are girls. Four out of every 7 boys can swim. How many boys can swim?

5. Brittany mailed this puzzle to a math magazine. Solve the problems she made up.

   a. What is the ratio of the sum of the numbers outside the parallelogram to the sum of the numbers inside the circle?

   b. What is the missing number if the ratio of the missing number to the sum of the numbers inside the parallelogram equals 40%?

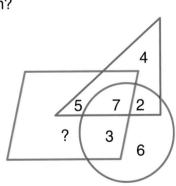

Problem-Solving Applications: Mixed Review

Solve each problem and explain the method you used.

1. Mr. Barry teaches a cooking class every Saturday. The ratio of students to stoves is 4 : 1. There are 5 stoves in the classroom. How many students are in the class?

2. What is the ratio of a cup to a pint?

3. The lessons are paid for at the rate of 4 lessons for $50. How much does each lesson cost?

4. Last week, the class prepared granola. The ratio of rolled oats to raisins was 5 : 2. The class used 25 cups of rolled oats. How many cups of raisins did the class use?

5. Peg added 1 cup of almonds for every 3 cups of oats in her granola. Mark added 3 cups of almonds for every 9 cups of oats in his granola. Did Peg and Mark add the same ratio of almonds to oats?

6. If 12 ounces of almonds cost $2, how much do 18 ounces of almonds cost?

7. Out of every 100 recipes Mr. Barry teaches, 15 include peanut butter. What percent of the recipes include peanut butter?

8. Of all Mr. Barry's recipes, 90% are healthful. Write this percent as a decimal.

9. One student notices that $\frac{1}{5}$ of the recipes taught can be classified as side dishes. Of the remaining dishes, one half are chicken dishes. What percent of the recipes are neither side nor chicken dishes?

10. Of the calories in a banana bread, 75% comes from carbohydrates. What part of the calories does not come from carbohydrates?

Solve. Combine strategies to help you.

11. Ann and Greg each made lemonade. Ann used 10 lemons for every 1 quart of water. Greg used 5 lemons for every pint of water. Did the two friends use equal ratios of lemons to water?

Strategy File

Use These Strategies
Write an Equation
Use a Graph
Use More Than One Step
Work Backward
Make a Table

12. The ratio of beans to rice in a recipe is 3 : 4. Jake cooks 2 cups of rice and 5 pounds of chicken. How many cups of beans should he use?

13. The class has 18 baking sheets. Each sheet holds 1 dozen cookies. A batch of cookie batter makes 3 dozen cookies. The class fills all of the sheets with cookies. Then they sell bags of 6 cookies each at a bake sale. How many bags of cookies did they make?

14. Lindsey and her sisters are baking pies to take to their family reunion. They plan to bake one cherry pie and two apple pies for every 14 people attending. How many pies will they bake for 126 people?

15. Tara made some snack bars. She ate 8 of them. She gave Paul 50% of the bars that were left. Then she had 11 bars. How many snack bars did she make?

Use the circle graph for problems 16–19.

16. What part of the trail mix is raisins?

17. What is the ratio of apricots to raisins?

18. Sue makes a batch of trail mix using 1 cup of granola. Will she use more than $\frac{1}{2}$ cup of apricots?

Trail Mix Ingredients

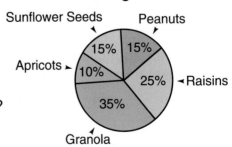

Write Your Own

19. Use the data in the circle graph to write a problem. Then solve it.

Check Your Progress
Lessons 1–16

Write each ratio in simplest form. *(See pp. 376–377.)*

1. 8 : 12

2. 6 to 45

3. $\dfrac{45}{60}$

4. $\dfrac{78}{100}$

Find the missing term in each proportion. *(See pp. 378–379, 382–385.)*

5. $\dfrac{n}{7} = \dfrac{5}{21}$

6. $\dfrac{4}{n} = \dfrac{20}{15}$

7. $\dfrac{12}{28} = \dfrac{n}{14}$

8. $\dfrac{n}{1.2} = \dfrac{3}{2}$

Write a proportion. Then solve. *(See pp. 386–389.)*

9. $\triangle ABC \sim \triangle DEF$
Find the value of *n*.

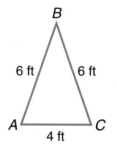

Find the actual measurements. *(See pp. 390–393.)*

10. Actual length

11. Actual width

Scale: 1 cm = 40 km

Write as an equivalent percent. *(See pp. 394–399.)*

12. $\dfrac{3}{4}$

13. $\dfrac{24}{30}$

14. $\dfrac{5}{9}$

15. 0.72

16. 0.9

Write as an equivalent decimal. *(See pp. 396–403.)*

17. 29%

18. $\dfrac{3}{5}$%

19. 47.5%

20. 0.2%

21. 534%

Write as an equivalent fraction or mixed number in simplest form *(See pp. 394–395, 400–403.)*

22. 80%

23. 0.04%

24. 48%

25. 340%

26. 605%

Problem Solving
(See pp. 380–381, 390–391.)

27. Sixteen cans of corn sell for $12.00. Find the unit cost. Explain the method you used to solve the problem.

28. A road map uses a scale of 3 in. = 9 mi. Find the distance between the cities if the map distance is 15 in.

(See *Still More Practice*, p. 529.)

Pythagorean Theorem

In about 500 B.C., Pythagoras, a Greek mathematician, proved that a certain pattern exists in all right triangles.

A right triangle has a 90° angle. The side opposite the 90° angle is called the hypotenuse. The remaining sides are called legs.

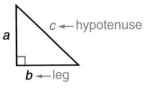

Pythagorean Theorem
In a right triangle, the sum of the squares of the lengths of the legs, a and b, is equal to the square of the length of the hypotenuse, c.

$$a^2 + b^2 = c^2$$

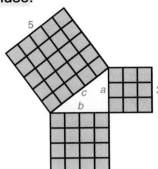

$$a^2 + b^2 = c^2$$
$$3^2 + 4^2 = 5^2$$

▶ When you know the lengths of any two sides of a right triangle, use the Pythagorean Theorem to find the length of the third side.

Find the length of the hypotenuse of a right triangle whose legs measure 6 cm and 8 cm.

$$a^2 + b^2 = c^2$$ Substitute the given values of
$$6^2 + 8^2 = c^2$$ ← the variables.
$$36 + 64 = c^2$$ ← Solve for c.
$$100 = c^2$$
$$\sqrt{100} = c$$
$$10 = c$$

So the hypotenuse is 10 cm long.

The length of the hypotenuse of a right triangle is 17 ft. If the length of one leg is 15 ft, find the length of the other leg.

$$a^2 + b^2 = c^2$$ Substitute the given values of
$$15^2 + b^2 = 17^2$$ ← the variables.
$$225 + b^2 = 289$$ ← Solve for b.
$$225 + b^2 - 225 = 289 - 225$$
$$b^2 = 64$$
$$b = \sqrt{64}$$
$$b = 8$$

So the other leg is 8 ft long.

Find the length of the missing side of each right triangle.

1. legs: 10 cm
   24 cm
   hypotenuse = _?_ cm

2. legs: 9 in.
   _?_ in.
   hypotenuse: 15 in.

3. legs: _?_ m
   12 m
   hypotenuse: 13 m

Problem Solving

4. The diagonal of a rectangle is 15 mm. If the length of the rectangle is 12 mm, what is the width?

5. Raul walks 30 m north and then 16 m east. How far is he from the starting point?

Chapter 11 Test

Write each ratio or rate in simplest form.

1. 4 to 8
2. 9 to 15
3. 20 : 30
4. 24 : 39

Find the missing term in each proportion.

5. $\dfrac{n}{9} = \dfrac{10}{15}$

6. $\dfrac{6}{n} = \dfrac{18}{12}$

7. $n : 2 = 0.9 : 3$

Write a proportion. Then solve.

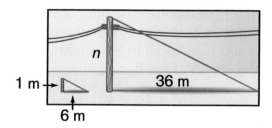

8. A vertical meterstick casts a 6-m shadow while a telephone pole casts a 36-m shadow. How tall is the telephone pole?

Find the actual measurements.

9. Scale length: $1\dfrac{3}{4}$ in.
   Scale: 1 in. = 20 yd

10. Scale width: 3.5 cm
    Scale: 1 cm = 100 km

Write as a percent.

11. $\dfrac{3}{25}$

12. 0.47

13. 2.03

14. $\dfrac{7}{8}$

Write as a decimal and as a fraction (or mixed number) in simplest form.

15. 40%

16. 0.02%

17. 475%

18. 148%

Problem Solving

Use a strategy you have learned.

19. Out of every 9 students in the school activity club, there are 2 boys. If there are 35 girls in the activity club, how many boys are in it?

Tell About It

20. Use a 10 × 10 grid to create a design that is 20% one color, 32% another color, and 5.5% a third color. Which percent of your design is *not* colored? How do you know?

Performance Assessment

Use <, =, or > to compare. Explain your answers.

21. 15 : 100 __?__ 16%

22. 49% __?__ $\dfrac{51}{100}$

23. 5.5% __?__ $\dfrac{11}{200}$

Test Preparation

Choose the best answer.

1. Choose the product.

   12.5×1000

   a. 125   b. 1250
   c. 12,500   d. not given

2. Compare.

   $25\% \; \underline{\;?\;} \; \dfrac{28}{100}$ a. <   b. =
   c. >   d. cannot tell

3. Rename as a percent.

   $\dfrac{3}{25}$

   a. 3%   b. 6%
   c. 9%   d. 12%

4. Which kind of graph shows the upper and lower quartiles?

   a. stem-and-leaf   b. line plot
   c. box-and-whisker   d. circle graph

5. Choose the bisector of $\angle MPR$.

   a. $\overrightarrow{PQ}$
   b. $\overrightarrow{MR}$
   c. $\overrightarrow{PR}$
   d. $\overrightarrow{PM}$

6. Divide.

   $10\dfrac{2}{5} \div 2\dfrac{1}{6}$

   a. $3\dfrac{1}{6}$ b. $4\dfrac{4}{5}$
   c. $8\dfrac{1}{5}$ d. not given

7. Which decimals are in order, least to greatest?

   a. 0.3, 0.32, 0.03
   b. 0.32, 0.3, 0.03
   c. 0.03, 0.3, 0.32
   d. not given

8. Choose the quotient.

   $0.36\overline{)0.12312}$

   a. 0.00342   b. 0.0342
   c. 0.342   d. not given

9. Find the value of n.

   $\dfrac{n}{9} = \dfrac{28}{63}$ a. 4   b. 7
   c. 35   d. 44

10. What is the range of the set of data?

    26, 32, 49, 21, 28, 16

    a. 16   b. 21
    c. 33   d. 49

11. A card is drawn and not replaced. Then a second card is drawn. How many outcomes are there?

    a. 5   b. 10
    c. 20   d. 25

12. Which is *not* a central angle?

    a. $\angle ABD$
    b. $\angle CBD$
    c. $\angle DBC$
    d. $\angle CDB$

13. Compute.

    $18 \div (3\dfrac{3}{5} - 1\dfrac{4}{5})$

    a. $8\dfrac{2}{11}$ b. 10
    c. $3\dfrac{1}{5}$ d. not given

14. What is 30,700,000 in scientific notation?

    a. $(3 \times 10^7) + (7 \times 10^5)$
    b. 30.7×10^6
    c. 3.07×10^8
    d. not given

15. Compute.

$^+7 - {}^-10$

    a. $^+17$
    b. $^-17$
    c. $^-2$
    d. not given.

16. Seven out of 10 people surveyed preferred basketball over baseball. In a survey of 1000 people, how many would you expect to choose basketball?

    a. 70   **b.** 300
    c. 500   **d.** 700

17. Which figure does not tessellate the plane?

    a. parallelogram   **b.** regular hexagon
    c. circle   **d.** square

18. A number decreased by 6 is 3. What is the number?

    a. 2   **b.** 3
    c. 10   **d.** not given

19. A map scale sets 1 cm = 10 km. What is the actual distance between the two cities that are 3.5 cm apart on the map?

    a. 0.35 km   **b.** 35 km
    c. 350 km   **d.** not given

20. What is the mode of the set of data?

8.8, 2.5, 8.8, 3.1, 2.5, 8.8

    a. 2.5
    b. 8.8
    c. 3.1
    d. no mode

21. Joe has 4 shirts, 3 pairs of pants, and 3 sweaters. How many shirt-pant-sweater outfits can he put together?

    a. 36   **b.** 21
    c. 10   **d.** 7

22. Subtract.

$70 - 0.85$

    a. 0.15   **b.** 69.15
    c. 70.85   **d.** not given

23. A car traveled 110 miles in 2 hours. How many miles per hour did the car average?

    a. 220 mph   **b.** 55 mph
    c. 50 mph   **d.** not given

24. Find the sum of the measures of the interior angles of a polygon of 13 sides.

    a. 2700°   **b.** 2340°
    c. 1980°   **d.** 65°

Explain how you solved the problem. Show all your work.

25. You and four friends are planning a vacation. All expenses are to be shared equally.

    a. Complete the table below. How much in all will you each spend for the vacation?

Expenses	Total Amount	Individual Share
Housing	$1575	?
Food	$250	$50
Recreation	$400	?

    b. You plan to take $550 in cash with you. After the above expenses, what percent of your money will you have left? (*Hint:* % = dollar amount left ÷ total cash taken)

    c. After the above expenses, what percent of your $550 will you have spent?

Percent Applications

SKY

Decimal point
meteors
streak
through
the night—

Fractions
of moonbeams
gleam
white-bright—

Percentages
of stars
seem
to multiply—

in the
finite
dramatic
mathematic-filled
sky.

Lee Bennett Hopkins

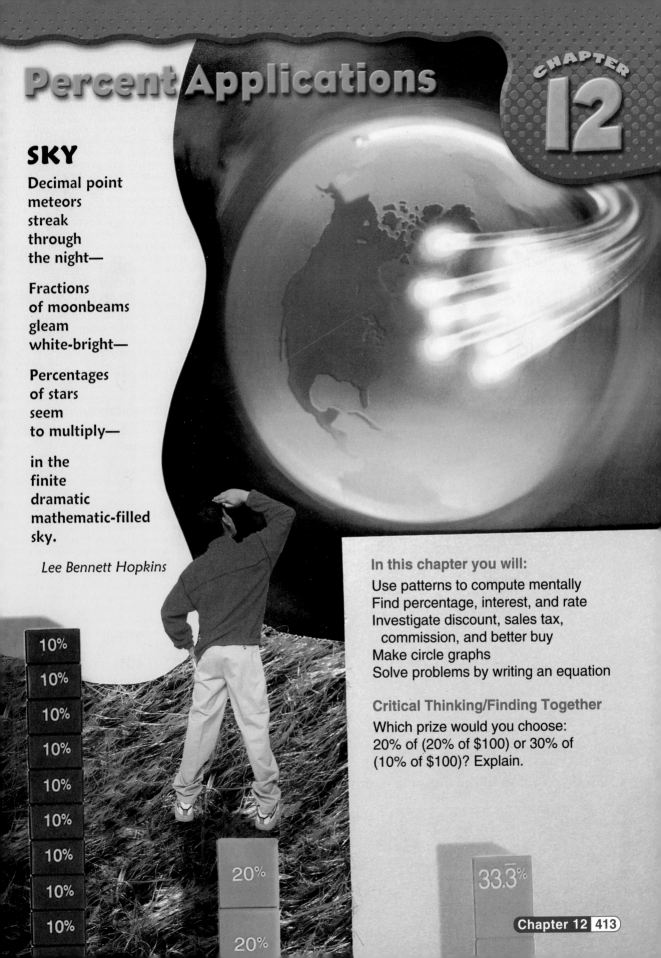

In this chapter you will:

Use patterns to compute mentally
Find percentage, interest, and rate
Investigate discount, sales tax,
   commission, and better buy
Make circle graphs
Solve problems by writing an equation

Critical Thinking/Finding Together

Which prize would you choose:
20% of (20% of $100) or 30% of
(10% of $100)? Explain.

Mental Math: Percent

Here are some percents that are equivalent to common fractions.

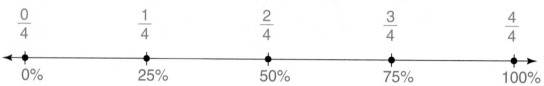

$\frac{0}{4}$	$\frac{1}{4}$	$\frac{2}{4}$	$\frac{3}{4}$	$\frac{4}{4}$
0%	25%	50%	75%	100%

Study the pattern for these percents and common fractions.

$10\% = \frac{1}{10}$ $\qquad$ $20\% = \frac{2}{10}$ or $\frac{1}{5}$

$30\% = \frac{3}{10}$ $\qquad$ $40\% = \frac{4}{10}$ or $\frac{2}{5}$

$50\% = \frac{5}{10}$ or $\frac{1}{2}$ $\qquad$ $60\% = \frac{6}{10}$ or $\frac{3}{5}$

$70\% = \frac{7}{10}$ $\qquad$ $80\% = \frac{8}{10}$ or $\frac{4}{5}$

$90\% = \frac{9}{10}$ $\qquad$ $100\% = \frac{10}{10}$ or $\frac{5}{5}$ or 1

▶ To find a percent of a number mentally, use common fractions.

> Remember: "of" means "times."

Find the value of n.

25% of $36 = n$.

$\frac{1}{4}$ of $36 = n$

$\frac{1}{\underset{1}{\cancel{4}}} \times \overset{9}{\cancel{36}} = 9$

.Think......
$25\% = \frac{1}{4}$
....

So $n = 9$.

40% of $35 = n$.

$\frac{2}{5}$ of $35 = n$

$\frac{2}{\underset{1}{\cancel{5}}} \times \overset{7}{\cancel{35}} = 14$

.Think......
$40\% = \frac{2}{5}$
....

So $n = 14$.

Find the value of the variable. Compute mentally.

1. $\frac{1}{5}$ of $30 = 6$, so 20% of $30 = n$.

2. $\frac{1}{20}$ of $40 = 2$, so 5% of $40 = c$.

3. $\frac{2}{5}$ of $30 = 12$, so 40% of $30 = a$.

4. $\frac{3}{20}$ of $40 = 6$, so 15% of $40 = r$.

Find the value of the variable. Compute mentally.

5. $\frac{3}{5}$ of 30 = 18, so 60% of 30 = y.

6. $\frac{3}{10}$ of 30 = 9, so 30% of 30 = h.

7. $\frac{1}{4}$ of 44 = c, so 25% of 44 = e.

8. $\frac{1}{2}$ of 44 = t, so 50% of 44 = m.

9. $\frac{3}{4}$ of 44 = x, so 75% of 44 = y.

10. $\frac{1}{10}$ of 30 = p, so 10% of 30 = z.

More Percents and Common Fractions

Study these percents and common fractions.

$12\frac{1}{2}\% = \frac{1}{8}$

$37\frac{1}{2}\% = \frac{3}{8}$

$62\frac{1}{2}\% = \frac{5}{8}$

$87\frac{1}{2}\% = \frac{7}{8}$

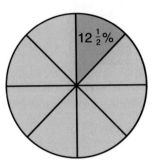

$16\frac{2}{3}\% = \frac{1}{6}$

$33\frac{1}{3}\% = \frac{2}{6} = \frac{1}{3}$

$66\frac{2}{3}\% = \frac{4}{6} = \frac{2}{3}$

$83\frac{1}{3}\% = \frac{5}{6}$

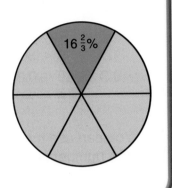

Find the percent of the number. Compute mentally.

11. $12\frac{1}{2}\%$ of 16

Think: $\frac{1}{8}$ of 16 = b

12. $33\frac{1}{3}\%$ of 60

Think: $\frac{1}{3}$ of 60 = f

13. 20% of 100

Think: $\frac{1}{5}$ of 100 = j

14. $37\frac{1}{2}\%$ of 56

Think: $\frac{3}{8}$ of 56 = m

15. 80% of 20

Think: $\frac{4}{5}$ of 20 = n

16. 60% of 45

Think: $\frac{3}{5}$ of 45 = v

17. 30% of 60 = x

18. $66\frac{2}{3}\%$ of 60 = i

19. $62\frac{1}{2}\%$ of 16 = o

20. $87\frac{1}{2}\%$ of 88 = c

21. 75% of 48 = d

22. 70% of 70 = e

23. $83\frac{1}{3}\%$ of 24 = w

24. 90% of 90 = l

25. 100% of 90 = q

Percent Sense

Which is greater:

3% of 100 or 30% of 100?

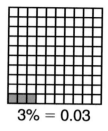 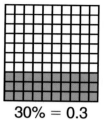

The pictures show that

30% of 100 > 3% of 100.

0.3 × 100 > 0.03 × 100

30 > 3

3% = 0.03   30% = 0.3

Which is less:

30% of 60 or 30% of 80?

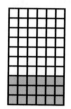 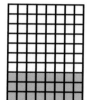

The pictures show that

30% of 60 < 30% of 80.

0.3 × 60 < 0.3 × 80

18 < 24

▶ You can use mental math to estimate what percent one number is of another.

Math class is 55 minutes long.
Ten minutes are used to check homework.
True or *False*: 10 minutes is more than 50% of the class time.

Is $\frac{10}{55}$ > 50%?

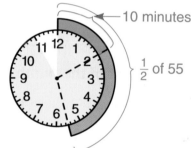

10 minutes

$\frac{1}{2}$ of 55

.Think.........

50% is $\frac{1}{2}$. $\frac{1}{2}$ of 55 is more than $\frac{1}{2}$ of 50, which is 25.

10 minutes is less than 50% of the class time.

The statement is *false*.

Compare. Use < or >.

1. 50% of 20 _?_ 50% of 40

2. 20% of 30 _?_ 20% of 10

3. 2% of 40 _?_ 2% of 80

4. 3% of 10 _?_ 3% of 4

5. $33\frac{1}{3}$% of 30 _?_ $33\frac{1}{3}$% of 3

6. $16\frac{2}{3}$% of 12 _?_ $16\frac{2}{3}$% of 60

Compare. Use < or >.

7. 3% of 60 __?__ 30% of 60

8. 62% of 40 __?__ 52% of 40

9. 19% of 300 __?__ 29% of 300

10. 86% of 50 __?__ 66% of 50

11. $16\frac{2}{3}$% of 12 __?__ $66\frac{2}{3}$% of 12

12. $83\frac{1}{3}$% of 24 __?__ $33\frac{1}{3}$% of 24

13. $37\frac{1}{2}$% of 16 __?__ $\frac{1}{8}$ of 16

14. $\frac{7}{8}$ of 40 __?__ $62\frac{1}{2}$% of 40

Write *True* or *False* for each situation. Explain your answer.
Draw a picture to help you.

Tina has one half hour for lunch.
She finishes in 20 minutes.

15. Tina uses exactly 50%
of her lunchtime to eat.

16. Tina uses less than 50%
of her lunchtime to eat.

17. Tina uses more than 50%
of her lunchtime to eat.

Alberto allots one hour to deliver
newspapers. He finishes in 45 minutes.

18. Alberto uses more than 50%
of his newspaper time.

19. Alberto uses more than 25%
of his newspaper time.

20. Alberto uses less than 100%
of his newspaper time.

Forty students are in the class.
Fourteen receive A's.

21. 50% of the students receive A's.

22. Less than 50% receive A's.

23. Less than 25% receive A's.

Ninety animals are in the shelter.
Thirty are adopted.

24. 50% of the animals are adopted.

25. More than 25% are adopted.

26. More than 50% are *not* adopted.

Write About It

27. There are 6 ducks in the pond at the park. This is 10% of the
ducks in the park. True or False: 100 ducks are in the park.

a. Shade a ten-by-ten grid to show 6 ducks
and a different ten-by-ten grid to show
10% of 100 ducks. Compare the two shadings.

b. Does 10% of 100 = 6? Is the statement above
true or false? How many ducks are in
the park? (*Hint:* 10% of __?__ = 6.)

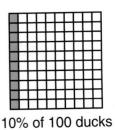

10% of 100 ducks

Percentage of a Number

Find: 45% of 360 = p.

- First estimate the **percentage** (or part) of a number, using **benchmark percents**. Benchmark percents are commonly known and frequently used percents such as 10%, 25%, and 50% and their common fractions.

45% of 360 ⟶ 50% of 360

$$\frac{1}{\underset{1}{2}} \times \overset{180}{\cancel{360}} = 180$$

45% of 360 ≈ 180

.Think..........
45% ≈ 50%
50% = $\frac{1}{2}$
....

- Then use a formula to find the percentage, p, of a number.

rate (r) × base (b) = percentage (p) ⟶ **$r \times b = p$**

Rename the percent (rate) as a *decimal* or as a *fraction*. Then solve.

As a Decimal

$r \times b = p$

45% of 360 = p

0.45 × 360 = p

162 = p

As a Fraction

$r \times b = p$

45% of 360 = p

$\frac{45}{100} \times 360 = p$

$\frac{9}{\underset{1}{20}} \times \frac{\overset{18}{360}}{1} = p$

162 = p

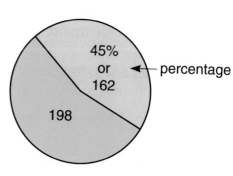

45%
or
162 ⟵ percentage

198

So 45% of 360 = 162.

.Think..........................
162 is close to the estimate of 180.
....

Study this example.

Find: 78% of $24.

- First estimate.

75% of $24

$$\frac{3}{\underset{1}{4}} \times \overset{\$6}{\$24} = \$18$$

78% of $24 ≈ $18

.Think.......
78% ≈ 75%
and 4 and 24
are compatible
numbers.
....

- Then solve.
78% of $24 = p

0.78 × $24 = p

$18.72 = p

.Think..........
$18.72 is close
to the estimate
of $18.
....

So 78% of $24 = $18.72.

Use the formula and decimals to solve for the variable.

1. 30% of 60 = a

2. 50% of 32 = d

3. 75% of 80 = g

4. 25% of 44 = b

5. 10% of $18 = e

6. 20% of $70 = h

7. 5% of 800 = c

8. 6% of 700 = f

9. 35% of 120 = i

Use the formula and fractions to solve for the variable.

10. 40% of 20 = j

11. 60% of 60 = m

12. 75% of 120 = p

13. 15% of 40 = k

14. 2% of $8.00 = n

15. 3% of $5.00 = q

16. 56% of 400 = l

17. 88% of 250 = o

18. 95% of 240 = r

Percentage Using Proportions

In the basketball game between the sixth and seventh grades, 62.5% of 24 free throws were made. How many free throws were made?

To find how many free throws, write a proportion and solve.
Let n = the number of free throws made.

part $\longrightarrow$ $\dfrac{n}{24} = \dfrac{62.5}{100}$ $\longleftarrow$ part
whole $\longrightarrow$ $\phantom{\dfrac{n}{24} = \dfrac{62.5}{100}}$ $\longleftarrow$ whole

$$\dfrac{n}{24} \diagdown \dfrac{62.5}{100}$$
$$100n = 24 \times 62.5$$
$$100n \div 100 = 1500 \div 100$$
$$n = 15$$

So 15 free throws were made.

Use a proportion to find the percentage of the number.

19. 40% of 25

20. 25% of 96

21. 80% of 90

22. 55% of 200

23. 76% of 475

24. 12% of 625

25. 37.5% of 56

26. 62.5% of 320

27. 87.5% of 480

MENTAL MATH

Find the percentage of the number.

28. 150% of 4   100% of 4 = 4; 50% of 4 = $\frac{1}{2}$ of 4 = 2; 4 + 2 = 6

29. 150% of 80

30. 110% of 200

31. 250% of 600

Find the Rate

Of 125 baseball players named most valuable players, 24 were also batting champions. What percent (or rate) of the 125 baseball players were also batting champions?

batting champs | players

To find the percent (or rate), find 24 out of 125.

First estimate: 25 out of $125 = \dfrac{25}{125} = \dfrac{1}{5}$ or 20%.

Then use one of these two methods to find the percent, or rate, r, that one number is of another.

Method 1

- Use the formula $r \times b = p$ and solve for r.

$$r \times b = p \longrightarrow \dfrac{p}{b} = r$$
$$\dfrac{24}{125} = r$$

- Rename the fraction as a decimal.

$$125\overline{)24.000} \quad 0.192$$

- Rename the decimal as a percent.

$$19.2\% = r$$

Method 2

- Write a proportion.

part $\longrightarrow \dfrac{24}{125}$ ⤬ $\dfrac{n}{100} \longleftarrow$ part
whole $\longrightarrow$ $\phantom{\dfrac{24}{125}}$ $\phantom{\dfrac{n}{100}} \longleftarrow$ whole

- Solve the proportion.

$$24 \times 100 = 125n$$
$$2400 \div 125 = 125n \div 125$$
$$19.2 = n$$

$$\dfrac{n}{100} = \dfrac{19.2}{100} = 19.2\%$$

So 19.2% were batting champions.

Think
19.2% is close to the estimate of 20%.

Study this example.

What percent of 8 is 20?

$$\dfrac{20}{8} = r \longrightarrow r = 2.5 = 250\%$$

Think
20 is greater than 8.
The percent is greater than 100%.

Check: $250\% \times 8 = 2.50 \times 8 = 20$

Find the percent or rate. Estimate first.

1. What percent of 5 is 3?

2. What percent of 80 is 400?

3. What percent of 100 is 11?

4. What percent of 900 is 243?

5. 90 is what percent of 120?

6. 60 is what percent of 240?

7. What percent of 180 is 63?

8. What percent of 140 is 91?

9. What percent of 20 is 25?

10. What percent of 10 is 80?

11. 4.4 is what percent of 80?

12. 4.6 is what percent of 50?

13. 475 is what percent of 950?

14. 30 is what percent of 8?

15. 2 is what percent of 16?

16. 5 is what percent of 40?

17. 15 is what percent of 6?

18. 20 is what percent of 25?

19. 28 is what percent of 35?

20. 125 is what percent of 50?

Problem Solving

21. At the school picnic, 30 of the 50 teachers came by car. What percent of the teachers came by car?

22. In the basketball game, 12 baskets were made in 25 attempts. What percent of the baskets were made?

23. Janet earned $420 at the golf course last summer. She put 70% of her earnings in the bank. How much money did she spend?

24. This year the price of a baseball glove is 105% of last year's price of $40. What is the price this year?

25. Of 125 players in the marching band, 44 are also in the school orchestra. What percent of the marching band members are not in the school orchestra?

Write About It

26. Explain how to find the value of each variable, the percent of student population for each grade. The total student population is 240.

    Grade 5 = f%   Grade 6 = s%

    Grade 7 = v%   Grade 8 = e%

Student Population

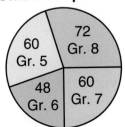

Find the Original Number

Of the people at the bowling alley, 45% play for the bowling league. There are a total of 9 bowling league players. How many people are at the bowling alley?

To find how many people, the original number or **base**, write and solve an equation or a proportion.

$$\text{percentage} = \text{rate} \times \text{base} \longrightarrow p = r \times b$$
$$\text{original number (total number)} \longrightarrow$$

45% of *what number* is 9?

Let *b* equal the total number of people.

- Write and solve an equation.

$$45\% \text{ of } b = 9$$
$$0.45b = 9$$
$$0.45b \div 0.45 = 9 \div 0.45 \longleftarrow \text{Divide both sides by 0.45.}$$
$$b = 20$$

45% of 20 is 9.

- Write and solve a proportion.

$$\frac{\text{part}}{\text{whole}} \longrightarrow \frac{45}{100} \diagup\!\!\!\!\diagdown \frac{9}{b} \longleftarrow \frac{\text{part}}{\text{whole}}$$

$$45b = 900$$
$$45b \div 45 = 900 \div 45$$
$$b = 20$$

So there are 20 people at the bowling alley.

Study these examples.

25% of Marlo's savings is in a shoebox under her bed. The shoebox has $45 in it. How much has Marlo saved in all?

Let *s* = total savings.

$$25\% \text{ of } s = \$45$$
$$\frac{1}{4}s = \$45$$
$$\frac{1}{4}s \times \frac{4}{1} = \$45 \times \frac{4}{1}$$
$$s = \$180$$

Marlo has saved $180 in all.

If Mike's savings of $268.80 is 42% of his savings goal, what amount of money does Mike want to save?

.....**Think**..........
42% = 0.42

$$42\% \text{ of } s = \$268.80$$
$$0.42s = \$268.80$$
$$\frac{0.42s}{0.42} = \frac{\$268.80}{0.42}$$
$$s = \$640$$

Mike wants to save $640.

Find the original number. Explain the method you used.

1. 65% of *x* is 650
2. 90% of *a* is 765
3. 50% of *d* is 155
4. 45% of *u* is $54
5. 30% of *h* is $18.60
6. 72% of *y* is $1872
7. 88% of *l* is 6600
8. 19% of *j* is 152
9. 7.1% of *b* is 142
10. 83% of *z* is $2075
11. 65% of *p* is 451.75
12. 21% of *g* is $10.50
13. 22% of *t* is 550
14. 46% of *e* is 296.7
15. 90% of *k* is 225.36
16. $12\frac{1}{2}$% of *f* is 95
17. $16\frac{2}{3}$% of *c* is 776
18. $83\frac{1}{3}$% of *u* is 4610

Compare. Use <, =, or >.

19. 25% of *y* is 110.5

    20% of *r* is 81.6

    y _?_ *r*

20. 4.2% of *c* is 15.12

    22.8% of *m* is 84.36

    c _?_ *m*

21. $62\frac{1}{2}$% of *j* is 375

    $33\frac{1}{3}$% of *n* is 200

    j _?_ *n*

Problem Solving

22. Of the people in the theater, 5% have seen the movie before. If there are 8 people who have seen the movie before, how many people have *not* seen the movie before?

23. Of the animals at the preserve, 4% are babies. If there are 6 baby animals at the preserve, how many animals are *not* babies?

24. 30% of Howard's rock collection is in a box. The rest of it is on shelves. If Howard has 27 rocks in the box, how many rocks does he have in his collection?

25. 18% of the people at the park brought picnic lunches with them. If 9 people brought picnic lunches, how many people were at the park?

26. Tracey has saved $56.25. That is 4.5% of what she wants to save. How much does Tracey want to save?

27. Riley loaned his brother $273. That is 5.25% of Riley's savings account. How much did Riley have in his account?

TEST PREPARATION

Find the original number. Choose the best answer.

28. 38% of *q* is 458.66.

    A 12.07   B 174.2908
    C 1207   D 17,429.08

29. 19% of *v* is 106.4.

    F 5.6   G 20.216
    H 560   J 2021.6

Percent Problems

The population of Manchester is 25,100.
Twenty-three percent of the population attends school.
How many people in Manchester attend school?

To find how many, find 23% of 25,100.

▶ To find a percentage of a number, use $r \times b = p$.

- First estimate: 23% of 25,100 ⟶ 25% of 24,000

$$\frac{1}{4} \times 24,\!000 = 6000$$

(with $\overset{6000}{24,\!000}$ and $\underset{1}{4}$)

- Then solve: 23% of 25,100 = p

$$0.23 \times 25,100 = p$$

$$5773 = p$$

.Think......................
5773 is close to
the estimate of 6000.

So 5773 people in Manchester attend school.

Manchester Middle School has 960 students enrolled.
Six hundred seventy-two of these students ride the
bus to school. What percent of the students ride
the bus to school?

To find the percent, find 672 out of 960.

▶ To find the percent one number is of another, use $\frac{p}{b} = r$.

- First estimate: $\dfrac{672}{960} \longrightarrow \dfrac{700}{1000} = \dfrac{70}{100} = 70\%$

- Then solve: $\dfrac{672}{960} = r$ $960\overline{)672.00}$ ← 0.70

$$70\% = r$$

.Think......................
70% is the same as the estimate.

So 70% of the students ride the bus to school.

Problem Solving

Solve. Explain the method you used.

1. The population of Newton is 1460. Twenty percent of the people in Newton read the local newspaper. How many people read the local newspaper?

2. There are 360 animals in the New City Zoo. Fifteen percent of the animals are monkeys. How many animals in the New City Zoo are *not* monkeys?

3. Jeff used 10 oranges to make juice this morning. There were 25 oranges in the bag. What percent of the oranges in the bag did he use?

4. There are 16 teenagers in Sarah's neighborhood. Four of them are available to baby-sit. What percent of the teenagers are *not* available to baby-sit?

5. A report states that 72% of 1250 middle school students enjoy playing team sports. How many of the middle school students enjoy playing team sports?

6. There are 860 students in sixth grade. Two hundred fifteen of them play basketball. What percent of the students in sixth grade do not play basketball?

7. The Girl Scouts want to collect 500 pounds of old newspapers. They have already collected 150 pounds. What percent of their goal have they *not* reached?

8. On a typical day at Emerson Middle School, 6% of the 650 students are absent. How many students are present on a typical day?

9. Thirty percent of the people in the park rent rowboats. If 270 people rent rowboats, how many people are in the park?

10. Margaret spent $15 dollars on souvenirs on her vacation. If that was 5% of the cost of her trip, how much did her vacation cost?

11. Out of each 2500 pairs of athletic shoes imported from Asia, about how many pairs come from each country?

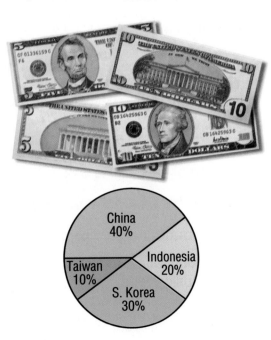

China 40%

Indonesia 20%

Taiwan 10%

S. Korea 30%

Discount and Sale Price

A discount is a reduction of the list, or regular, price of an item. The rate of discount is given as a percent.

The sale price is the difference between the list price and the discount.

> • Discount = Rate of Discount × List Price
> $$D = R \times LP$$
>
> • Sale Price = List Price − Discount
> $$SP = LP - D$$

Some CDs at Posio's Music World regularly sell for $15 each. This week they are being sold at a 15% discount. What is the discount? What is the sale price?

▶ To find the discount, D, write an equation and solve for the discount.

$$D = 15\% \text{ of } \$15.00$$
$$D = 0.15 \times \$15.00$$
$$D = \$2.25$$

The discount on each CD is $2.25.

▶ To find the sale price, SP, write an equation and solve for the sale price.

$$SP = \$15.00 - \$2.25$$
$$SP = \$12.75$$

The sale price of each CD is $12.75.

Find the discount and sale price.

1. 15% discount of a $13 CD at Posio's Music World

2. 20% discount of a $500 entertainment system at LP Electronics

Find the discount and sale price.

	Item	List Price	Rate of Discount	Discount	Sale Price
3.	Radio	$130	20%	?	?
4.	Big Screen TV	$3200	10%	?	?
5.	Headset	$33	15%	?	?
6.	CD Player	$180	12%	?	?

Use a Proportion to Find Discount

DVD Player

A DVD player with a regular price of $495 is marked to sell at 30% off. What is the discount?

sale price — discount — 30% — ?

Regularly $495

"30% off" means a discount rate of 30%.

To find the discount, write and solve a proportion.
Let D = the discount.

part → $\dfrac{D}{\$495} \times \dfrac{30}{100}$ ← part
whole → $\phantom{\dfrac{D}{\$495}}$ ← whole

$$100D = \$495 \times 30$$
$$100D \div 100 = \$14{,}850 \div 100$$
$$D = \$148.50$$

The discount is $148.50.

Problem Solving

7. The rate of discount on a $47 clock radio is 20%. Find the discount and sale price.

8. The rate of discount on a $12 CD is 15%. Find the discount and sale price.

9. How much is saved on a $625 television set at a 25%-off sale?

10. What is the sale price of a $150 CD player marked 15% off?

11. Carlos has $25 to spend at the music store. He wants a CD that regularly lists for $24. The rate of discount on the CD is $33\frac{1}{3}$%. After buying the CD, how much money does Carlos have left to spend?

12. Find the answer to problem 11 using a rate of discount of $12\frac{1}{2}$%.

Write About It

13. An item for $60 is discounted 20%. At a special sale, Joan receives an additional 20% discount. Will that be the same as a 40% discount of the item? Explain.

Sales Tax and Total Cost

A sales tax is the amount of tax added to the price of an item by a state or local government. The rate of sales tax is given as a percent.

The total cost is the sum of the marked, or list, price and the tax.

> - Sales Tax = Rate of Sales Tax × Marked Price
> $$T = R \times MP$$
> - Total Cost = Marked Price + Sales Tax
> $$TC = MP + T$$

A remote control toy costs $224.50, plus 5% sales tax. Find the sales tax and total cost of the toy.

▶ To find the sales tax, T, write and solve an equation or a proportion.

- First estimate: 5% of $220 = $\frac{1}{20} \times \$220 = \$11$

- Then use one of these methods to find the sales tax.

Method 1	Method 2
Write and solve an equation.	Write and solve a proportion.

Method 1

Write and solve an equation.

$T = $ 5% of $224.50.

$T = $ 5% × $224.50

$T = \$11.225 \approx \$11.23$

Method 2

Write and solve a proportion.

part ⟶ $\dfrac{T}{\$224.50}$ ⤫ $\dfrac{5}{100}$ ⟵ part
whole ⟶ ⟵ whole

$100T = \$224.50 \times 5$

$100T \div 100 = \$1122.50 \div 100$

$T = \$11.225 \approx \$11.23$

The sales tax is $11.23.

....Think....
: $11.23 is close to the estimate of $11. :

▶ To find the total cost, TC, write and solve the equation: $TC = \$224.50 + \$11.23.$

$$TC = \$224.50 + \$11.23$$

$$TC = \$235.73$$

The total cost of the toy is $235.73.

Find the sales tax and total cost of each item.

1. $23.40 sneakers, 5% sales tax

2. $59.75 camera, 4% sales tax

Use the tables below for exercises 3–10. The rate of sales tax is 6%.

Item	Price
Calculator	$88.25
Video Game	$12.95
Blank CDs	2 for $7.50

Item	Price
Color Film	1 roll for $6.50
CD Player	$62.75
Skateboard	$49

3. Find the sales tax on 2 blank CDs.

4. Find the sales tax on a skateboard.

5. Find the total cost of a CD player.

6. Find the total cost of a calculator.

7. Find the sales tax on 2 rolls of color film.

8. Find the sales tax on 4 blank CDs.

9. Janell buys 3 video games. Find her change from a $50 bill.

10. Find the total cost in exercise 8 if the rate of sales tax is $6\frac{1}{2}\%$.

11. Kurt buys a calculator and a CD player. How much does he spend altogether?

12. Greg buys a pair of gloves that are priced at $19.50. If he pays 6% sales tax, how much does Greg pay for the gloves?

Problem Solving

13. A $220 bicycle is on sale at 20% off. The rate of sales tax is 5%. What is the total cost of the bicycle?

14. Jean paid $11.25 for her new shirt on sale. The discount was 10%. What was the original price of the shirt?

CHALLENGE — Algebra

Find the marked price.

15. a DVD player
    total cost: $206
    rate of sales tax: 3%

16. an amplifier
    total cost: $318
    rate of sales tax: 6%

17. a CD
    total cost: $13
    rate of sales tax: 4%

18. a stereo
    total cost: $844
    rate of sales tax: 5.5%

Better Buy

A regular-size box of 12-oz dog food sells for $1.50.
A 15-oz jumbo-size box sells for $1.71. Which is the
better buy?

To decide which is the better buy, find the unit price or
unit cost for 1 oz of each type of dog food. Then compare them.

Regular Size	**Jumbo Size**

Regular Size

Let c = the cost of 1 oz.

$$\frac{12}{\$1.50} = \frac{1}{c}$$

$$12 \times c = \$1.50 \times 1$$

$$12c \div 12 = \$1.50 \div 12$$

$$c = \underline{\$.125} \approx \$.13$$

Jumbo Size

Let n = the cost of 1 oz.

$$\frac{15}{\$1.71} = \frac{1}{n}$$

$$15 \times n = \$1.71 \times 1$$

$$15n \div 15 = \$1.71 \div 15$$

$$n = \underline{\$.114} \approx \$.11$$

Unit cost (cost per oz)

Compare: $.114 < $.125

Think
11¢ is less than 13¢.

The jumbo size is the better buy.
Its unit cost is less than the unit cost
of the regular-size dog food.

Which is the better buy? Explain.

Practice

1. Drinking Glasses:
   4 for $1.80
   6 for $2.40

2. Corn:
   6 ears for 96¢
   8 ears for $1.12

3. Detergent:
   2 lb box for $1.26
   5 lb box for $3.05

4. Cereal:
   12 oz box for $1.74
   15 oz box for $2.04

5. Napkins:
   100 count for $.99
   145 count for $1.10

6. Party Favors:
   10 for $1.50
   30 for $4.45

Estimation and Better Buy

Estimate to decide which is the better buy, a bag of apples or 6 individual apples.

Estimate the unit cost of 1 apple in the bag of apples.

$$6\overline{)\$1.29} \rightarrow 6\overline{)\$1.20} = \$.20$$

6 for $1.29
or
30¢ each

Use compatible numbers to estimate.

Each apple in the bag costs about 20¢. The bag of apples is the better buy.

Estimate to decide which is the better buy.

7. 5 cakes of soap for $1.49
1 cake of soap for 25¢

8. Bag of a dozen lemons for $2.50
Lemons: 15¢ each

9. Picture frames: 2 for $5.67
Picture frames: $2.45 each

10. 3 boxes of crackers for $4.19
Crackers: $1.50 per box

Practice

Problem Solving

11. At Rosada's Market, a 10-oz can of mushrooms sells for 40¢ and a 6-oz can sells for 30¢. Which is the better buy?

12. A package of 6 coasters is marked $1.44 and a package of 8 of the same coasters is marked $1.76. Which is the better buy?

13. An 8-oz can of peaches costs $.68. A 14-oz can costs $1.05. Which is the better buy?

14. A 12-oz box of Crispy Cereal costs $2.10 and the 15-oz box of the same cereal costs $2.94. Which is the better buy?

Write About It

**Which is the better buy? Explain.
Show all your work.**

15. Sweaters in Store A marked $18.50 at a 30%-off sale; the same sweaters in Store B marked $19.00 at a $\frac{1}{3}$-off sale

16. Skirts in Store C marked $32.00 at a 15% discount; the same skirts in Store D marked $44.00 at a $\frac{1}{4}$-off sale

Algebra 12-10

Commission

Commission is the amount of money that a salesperson is paid for selling a product or service. The rate of commission is given as a percent.

A salesperson works on straight commission if the commission is the only pay he or she receives.

- Commission = Rate of Commission × Total Sales
$$C = R \times TS$$
- Total Earnings = Salary + Commission
$$TE = S + C$$

Marvella receives a weekly salary of $200 and makes a $3\frac{1}{2}$% commission on all of her clothing sales. What is her commission on sales of $6500? What are her total earnings for the week?

▶ Use one of the following two methods to find her commission, C.

Method 1

- Write and solve an equation.

$$C = 3\frac{1}{2}\% \text{ of } \$6500$$

$$C = 0.035 \times \$6500$$

$$C = \$227.50$$

Method 2

- Write and solve a proportion.

$$\text{part} \longrightarrow \frac{C}{\$6500} \bowtie \frac{3\frac{1}{2}}{100} \longleftarrow \text{part} \atop \longleftarrow \text{whole}$$

$$100C = \$6500 \times 3.5$$

$$100C \div 100 = \$22{,}750 \div 100$$

$$C = \$227.50$$

Marvella's commission is $227.50.

▶ To find the total earnings, TE, write an equation and solve for the total earnings.

$$TE = \$200 + \$227.50$$
$$TE = \$427.50$$

Marvella's total earnings for the week are $427.50.

Find the commission and the total earnings.

1. Salary = $100
Amount sold = $550
Rate of commission = 4%

2. Salary = $120
Amount sold = $480
Rate of commission = 2%

3. Salary = $350
Amount sold = $5000
Rate of commission = 1.5%

4. Salary = $400
Amount sold = $6500
Rate of commission = $4\frac{1}{2}$%

Problem Solving

Use the advertisement for ex. 9–11.

5. Find the commission Ms. Levine receives for selling electronic equipment worth $13,000 if her rate of commission is 4%.

6. Ms. Velarde sold $825 worth of cosmetics last year. Her rate of commission was 6%. What was her commission?

7. Mr. Jenkins sells major appliances at an $8\frac{1}{2}$% commission rate. Last month his total sales were $9675. How much commission did he make?

8. Ms. Farber had carpet sales of $15,215 last month. Her rate of commission is 3%. What is her commission?

9. Vicente plans to take a job at Hoody's Auto at a salary of $550 per month. If his total sales for the first month are $20,000, find his earnings for the month.

WANTED-
Auto Salesperson,
Hoody's Auto,
Experienced Only
Salary Plus
4% Commission
on Sales

10. Stella anticipates total monthly auto sales at Hoody's of $37,500. With a regular salary of $550 per month, how much would she make in salary plus commission?

11. Jamal is offered a choice of jobs at Hoody's:
(a) regular monthly salary of $550 plus 4% commission; or
(b) straight commission of $7\frac{1}{2}$% on all sales.
If Jamal expects monthly sales of $20,000, which is the better offer? Explain in your Math Journal.

CHALLENGE — Algebra

12. Aboul's boss offers him a $5\frac{1}{2}$% commission on all sales. What must Aboul's total monthly sales be in order to receive a $2200 commission?

Simple Interest

Principal (*p*) is the amount of money borrowed, or deposited.

Simple Interest (*I*) is the amount of money to be paid by the borrower on the principal, or the amount of money paid to the depositor on the principal, for a stated period of time, in years. The rate of interest (*r*) is the percent of interest paid.

Mr. McPherson borrowed $1000 to be paid back in 3 years. The bank charges a simple interest rate of 5%. How much interest will Mr. McPherson pay at the end of 3 years? What will be the total amount due on the loan?

GREAT RATES!

Earn 6.5% per year on a minimum deposit of $5,000.00.

Open One Today!

Pay 5% per year on a personal loan of $1000.00.

Ask Us Today!

TWO GREAT RATES

▶ To find the simple interest due, use the formula $I = prt$.

$$I = prt$$
$$I = \$1000 \times 0.05 \times 3$$
$$I = \$150$$

I = amount of simple interest
p = principal
r = rate of interest
t = time in years

Mr. McPherson will pay $150 in simple interest.

▶ To find the total amount due, add the principal plus simple interest.

Amount due = Principal + Simple Interest
= $1000 + $150
= $1150

The total amount due on Mr. McPherson's loan will be $1150.

Study these examples.

Polly deposits $7000 at a simple interest rate of 6.5% for 5 years in her savings account. Find the interest she will earn.

$$I = prt$$
$$I = \$7000 \times 0.065 \times 5$$
$$I = \$2275$$

Polly will earn $2275 interest at the end of 5 years.

Dillon puts $1200 at a simple interest rate of $7\frac{1}{2}$% for $3\frac{1}{2}$ years into his savings. How much interest will he earn?

$$I = prt$$
$$I = \$1200 \times 0.075 \times 3.5$$
$$I = \$315$$

Dillon will earn $315 interest at the end of $3\frac{1}{2}$ years.

Find the simple interest, *I*, for each loan.

1. $5000 at 5% for 5 years

2. $2500 at 7% for 7 years

3. $9000 at 6.5% for $8\frac{1}{2}$ years

4. $7000 at 5.2% for 9 years

5. $6210 at 4.8% for 3 years

6. $4280 at 2.5% for 3.5 years

Find the simple interest earned for each number of years.
Round to the nearest cent when necessary.

	Principal	Rate	3 years	5 years	$7\frac{1}{2}$ years	10 years
7.	$495	7.6%				
8.	$5230	1.9%				
9.	$9500	8.4%				
10.	$4065	2.1%				

Problem Solving

11. Elizabeth borrows $1500 at a simple interest rate of 3% for 3 years. At the end of the loan, how much principal and interest will she have paid back?

12. Gerard borrows $12,000 at a simple interest rate of 5.9% for 4 years. At the end of the loan, how much principal and interest will he have paid back?

13. Abby deposits $750 in a new savings account and earns a simple interest rate of 6%. At the end of 5 years, how much money is in the account if she never makes any more deposits or withdrawals?

14. Aidan deposits $925 in a new savings account and earns a simple interest rate of 5.5%. At the end of $3\frac{1}{2}$ years, how much money is in the account if he never makes any more deposits or withdrawals?

15. Pete saves $1275 at a simple interest rate of 5% for 5 years. Sharon saves $1175 at a simple interest rate of 7% for 5 years. At the end of 5 years, who has earned more interest? how much more?

16. Greg borrows $1975 at a simple interest rate of 5% for 3 years. Linda borrows $1975 at a simple interest rate of 4.5% for 4 years. Who pays more interest at the end of their loan? how much more?

DO YOU REMEMBER?

Write as a percent.

17. $\frac{17}{25}$

18. $\frac{37}{100}$

19. $\frac{23}{50}$

20. $\frac{9}{25}$

21. $\frac{7}{20}$

22. $\frac{3}{4}$

12-12

Make Circle Graphs

Hakan surveyed the students in his class to find the number of television sets in each home. You can help Hakan make a circle graph to display his results.

Number of TVs Per Home	Number of Homes	Percent of Total	Angle Measure
1	6	20%	72°
2	12	?	?
3	9	?	?
4 or more	3	?	?
Totals	30	100%	360°

In a circle graph, the whole represents 100% or 360°.

Materials: straightedge, paper, pencil, protractor, compass

Step 1 Copy the table above onto your own paper.

Step 2 Complete the Percent of Total column in Hakan's table by solving proportions.

Find what *percent* of the total number of homes, 30, is represented by 6 homes.

$$\text{part} \rightarrow \frac{6}{30} \underset{\text{whole} \rightarrow}{\times} \frac{n}{100} \leftarrow \text{part (\%)} \atop \leftarrow \text{whole (\%)}$$

$$6 \times 100 = 30n$$
$$600 \div 30 = 30n \div 30$$
$$20 = n$$

So $\frac{6}{30} = \frac{n}{100} = 20\%$

Does the Percent of Total column add up to 100%? If not, check your work with a calculator.

Step 3

Complete the Angle Measure column in Hakan's table.

Since there are 360° in a circle, multiply each of the percents by 360° to find the degrees in each section of the circle graph. Find the number of degrees that 20% (homes with 1 TV) represents.

Let d = number of degrees.

20% of 360° = d

$\frac{1}{5} \times 360° = d$

$72° = d$

Think
One angle of the circle graph should be 72°.

Does the Angle Measure column add up to 360°? If not, check your work.

Step 4
Use your compass to draw a large circle. Draw radius $\overline{PA}$ of the circle.

Step 5
Place the center mark of your protractor on P and draw a central angle of 72°, as shown.

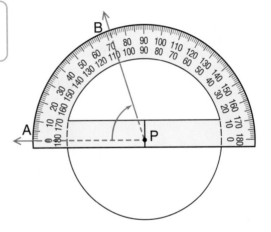

Step 6
Draw the other central angles. Use the degrees in Step 3. Start your next angle using radius $\overline{PB}$.

Step 7
Label each section of the graph with 1 TV, 2 TVs, and so on. Give your graph a title.

Communicate

1. Change the number of homes in your table, in order, from 6, 12, 9, 3 to 9, 30, 6, 15. Discuss with your class and then draw a circle graph for the new data.

2. Carl had 3 hours of homework last weekend. He spent the following amount of time on each subject: math, 30 min; science, 60 min; spelling, 15 min; social studies, 45 min; English, 30 min. Construct a circle graph and discuss the results with your class.

Problem-Solving Strategy:
Write an Equation

A disposable digital camera costs $29.95 plus 5% sales tax. Find the sales tax and total cost of the camera.

Read

Visualize yourself in the problem above as you reread it. List the facts and the question.

Facts: camera cost—$29.95
           rate of sales tax— 5%

Question: What is the sales tax and the
          total cost of the camera?

$29.95

Plan

To find the sales tax, multiply the marked price by the rate of sales tax.

Write a percent equation: Let T represent the sales tax.
                               T = rate of sales tax × marked price
                               T =   5%   × $29.95

To find the total cost, add the   Let TC represent the total cost.
sales tax to the marked price. TC = marked price + sales tax
                                    TC = $29.95   + T

Solve

$T = 5\% \times \$29.95$

$$
\begin{array}{r}
\overset{4\;\;4\;\;2}{} \\
\$\,2\,9.9\,5 \\
\times\quad 0.0\,5 \\
\hline
\$\,1.4\,9\,7\,5 \approx \$1.50
\end{array}
$$

Round to the nearest cent.

The sales tax is $1.50.

$TC = \$29.95 + \$1.50 = \$31.45$

The total cost is $31.45.

Check

Since Total Cost = Marked Price + Sales Tax, check if the total cost is greater than the marked price.

Solve each problem. Write an equation to help you.

1. There are 90 animals on Henley's farm. Of these animals, 60% are cows. How many of the animals are cows?

Read Visualize yourself in the problem above as you reread it. List the facts and the question.

Facts: 90 animals
            60% cows

Question: How many of the animals are cows?

Plan Draw and label a diagram.
Look at the diagram.
Write a percent equation.
Let *n* represent the number of cows.

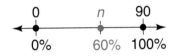

Number of cows	=	Percent of cows	×	All animals
n	=	60%	×	90

Solve .... **Check**

2. The school principal received 240 complimentary tickets to a concert. She gave 5% of the tickets to Ms. DeSilva's class. How many tickets did Ms. DeSilva's class receive?

3. The school received a delivery of 700 textbooks. Of these, 140 are math books. What percent of the delivery are math books?

4. There are 1250 students in the middle school. Of this number, 30% are in sixth grade. How many students are in sixth grade?

5. A swimming pool that costs $850 is on sale for $637.50. What is the rate of discount on the pool?

6. Mr. Schultz sold 3 cars for the following amounts: $11,995, $30,985, and $22,175. If his rate of commission on these 3 sales was 4%, what was his commission for all 3 cars?

7. Of the 750 children who went to the fair, 600 had yogurt. What percent of the children did *not* have yogurt?

Solve each problem and explain the method you used.

1. Of the 25 food booths at the Elm Street Fair, 20% serve vegetarian meals. How many booths serve vegetarian meals?

2. The Golden Dragon restaurant serves 375 meals at the fair. Of those, 40% are lo mein. How many lo mein meals are served?

3. The Mexican Hat serves tacos at the fair. The usual price for one taco is $2.60. For the fair, the store discounts the price by 35%. How much is one taco at the fair?

4. Marissa works for 5 hours at the Mexican Hat. She spends 40% of her time cooking and the rest serving. How much time does she spend serving?

5. It costs $350 to rent a booth at the fair. This year, 15% of the rental fee is donated to city charities. How much money is donated to city charities for each booth rented?

6. Of 150 booths at the fair, 45 feature games. What percent of the booths feature games?

7. The Children's Hospital sells T-shirts at the fair. Each T-shirt costs $8.00 plus 6.5% sales tax. What is the total cost of one T-shirt?

8. For each $8.00 T-shirt, the hospital earns $4.80. What percent of the selling price is profit?

9. The Potter's Place sells mugs at the fair. A mug that usually costs $15 sells at the fair for $11.25. By what percent is the usual price reduced?

10. The Potter's Place sells these percentages of goods at the fair: 30% mugs   20% bowls   15% vases
                     15% plates   10% wind chimes   10% miniature animals
Make a circle graph to show this data.

Choose a strategy from the list or use another strategy you know to solve each problem.

11. At one game booth, 10 players use air pumps to fill balloons. The first two players to pop their balloons win prizes. What percent of the players win prizes?

12. The ring-toss booth gives giant stuffed animals as prizes. At the beginning of the day, the booth had 220 animals. So far, 75% of the animals have been won. Of the remaining stuffed animals, 15 are pandas. How many are not pandas?

13. Of 48 spaces on a game wheel, 10 show a fish. A player who spins a fish wins a goldfish. Are the chances of winning a goldfish better than 25%?

14. Glittering Prizes sells earrings. It sells 25% of its earrings by the end of the day. If it has 51 pairs left, how many pairs did it have to start with?

15. A pair of earrings sells for $6.75. The local sales tax is 6.5%. Necklaces have a marked price of $8.50. What is the total price for a necklace?

16. Wanda's Wickerware sells 50% of its baskets before noon. It sells 80% of the remaining baskets before 5:00. At 5:00, it has 10 baskets left. How many baskets did the store have at the beginning of the day?

Strategy File

Use These Strategies
Write an Equation
Use More Than One Step
Work Backward
Use a Graph

Use the bar graph for problems 17–20.

17. What percent of this year's booths sell clothing?

18. Which type of booth increased by 100% between last year's fair and this year's fair?

19. By how many did the number of booths increase this year?

20. Last year, 60% of the game booths gave away stuffed animals. How many booths gave away stuffed animals last year?

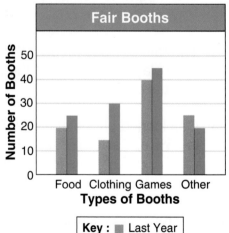

Fair Booths

Number of Booths — Types of Booths
Food Clothing Games Other

Key : ▦ Last Year
      ▦ This Year

Find the percentage of the number. *(See pp. 414–419.)*

1. 25% of 20
2. 3% of $7.20
3. 52% of 60
4. $33\frac{1}{3}$% of 48
5. 62.5% of 800
6. 150% of 40

Find the percent or rate. *(See pp. 420–421.)*

7. What percent of 8 is 2?
8. What percent of 100 is 12?
9. 48 is what percent of 192?
10. 2.2 is what percent of 40?

Find the sales tax and total cost of each item. *(See pp. 428–429.)*

11. $35.20 radio, 5% sales tax
12. $500 refrigerator, $6\frac{1}{2}$% sales tax

Estimate to decide which is the better buy. *(See pp. 430–431.)*

13. 3 pairs of socks for $2.08
    1 pair of socks for 60¢
14. Dozen oranges for $3.15
    Oranges: 25¢ each

Draw a circle graph of the favorite pets of a Grade 6 class. *(See pp. 436–437.)*

15. Dog: 40 students   Bird: 5 students   Fish: 15 students
    Cat: 30 students   Other: 10 students

Problem Solving
(See pp. 420–427, 432–435, 438–441.)

16. Seventeen percent of the 500 pages of a magazine contain photos. How many pages contain photos?

17. This year the price of a calculator is 110% of last year's price of $50. What is the price this year?

18. The rate of discount on a $560 DVD player is 15%. Find the discount and the sale price.

19. Find the commission on sales of $2000 if the rate of commission is 8%.

20. Carl loaned his sister $375. That is 15% of Carl's savings. How much did Carl have in savings?

21. Judy borrows $1200 at 4% simple interest for 2 years. At the end of the loan, how much principal and interest must she pay?

22. Mr. Kirkpatrick's regular salary is $1500 per month. His rate of commission is 4%. How much does he make in a month when his total sales are $10,000?

(See Still More Practice, p. 530.)

Percent Change

Percent change is the ratio of the change to the original price expressed as a percent.

A $25 shirt is on sale for $20. What is the percent decrease in price?

```
0%                              d   100%
◄─●─────────────────────────────●───●─►
  $0                           $20  $25
```

▶ To find the **percent decrease**, use a proportion.

Let d = rate of decrease

$$\underset{\text{original price}}{\underset{}{\text{decrease}}} \quad \frac{\$25 - \$20}{\$25} = \frac{d}{100}$$ ◄── Subtract the sale price from the original price to find the amount of decrease.

$$\frac{\$5}{\$25} = \frac{d}{100} \longrightarrow \$5 \times 100 = \$25d \longrightarrow \frac{\$500}{\$25} = \frac{\$25d}{\$25} \longrightarrow 20 = d$$

So $\dfrac{\$5}{\$25} = \dfrac{d}{100} = 20\%$

The decrease in price is 20%.

Last month the skateboard that Joe wanted cost $40. This month the skateboard costs $50. What is the percent increase in price?

▶ To find the **percent increase**, use a proportion.

Let i = rate of increase

$$\underset{\text{original price}}{\underset{}{\text{increase}}} \quad i = \frac{\$50 - \$40}{\$40}$$ ◄── Subtract the original price from the new price to find the amount of increase.

$$i = \frac{\$10}{\$40}$$

$$i = 0.25 = 25\%$$

The increase in price is 25%.

Find the percent decrease or increase.

1. $45 decreased by $9

2. $85 decreased by $42.50

3. 120 decreased by 54

4. 828 decreased by 289.8

5. 316 decreased by 28.44

6. $32 increased by $8

7. $62 increased by $18.60

8. 648 increased by 486

9. 153 increased by 15.3

Find the percent change. Explain whether it is a decrease or increase.

10. from $346 to $269.88

11. from 1295 to 1036

12. from $1022 to $715.40

13. from $525 to $603.75

14. from 3950 to 4937.5

15. from $9696 to $12,895.68

Chapter 12 Test

Find the percentage of the number.

1. 50% of 44

2. 4% of $6.00

3. 34% of 500

Find the percent or rate.

4. What percent of 25 is 5?

5. 78 is what percent of 120?

Estimate to decide which is the better buy.

6. 4 loaves of bread for $4.99
1 loaf of bread for $1.50

7. 5 puzzles for $4.45
1 puzzle for 95¢

Find the commission and total earnings.

8. Salary = $250
Amount sold = $640
Rate of commission = 5%

9. Salary = $400
Amount sold = $3500
Rate of commission = $4\frac{1}{2}\%$

Draw a circle graph of Mr. Lapid's monthly budget.

10. Food $500   Transportation $200   Mortgage payment $800
Utilities $100   Miscellaneous $400

Problem Solving

Use a strategy or strategies you have learned.

11. There are 520 students in the sixth grade. Forty-five percent are girls. How many are girls?

12. The rate of discount on a $14.80 CD is 25%. Find the sale price.

Tell About It

Explain how you solved each problem. Show all your work.

13. Which is the better buy: $28 pants at 20% off or the same pants for $32 at a $\frac{1}{4}$-off sale?

14. If Ann gave a 15% tip on a restaurant bill of $46, how much was the tip?

Performance Assessment

Answer each question and explain your answer.

15. Which is the better discount: 15% off the list price or $15 off every $100 you spend?

16. Is 100% off always a good buy? When is 15% off the list price *not* a good buy?

Test Preparation

Choose the best answer.

1. Which ratio is equal to $\frac{7}{10}$?

    a. 14 : 10   **b.** 21 : 30
    c. 28 : 30   **d.** 21 : 40

2. Rename as a decimal.

  12.8%

    a. 12.8   **b.** 1.28
    c. 0.128   **d.** 0.0128

3. If two lines intersect and form congruent adjacent angles, then the lines are:

    a. congruent   **b.** parallel
    c. perpendicular   **d.** skew

4. Which statement is correct?

    a. 55% > 0.75   **b.** 0.017 > 4%
    c. 87% < 0.85   **d.** 0.73 < 78%

5. As a decimal, $\frac{5}{8}$ is equal to:

    a. 0.625
    b. 0.655
    c. 1.5
    d. 1.6

6. What is the m∠R in △RST?

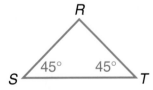

    a. 40°
    b. 90°
    c. 180°
    d. 200°

7. Find the value of n.

$$\frac{8}{3} = \frac{n}{15}$$

    a. $n = 5$ **b.** $n = 24$
    c. $n = 40$ **d.** $n = 120$

8. Rename as a mixed number in simplest form.

  275%

    a. $1\frac{3}{4}$ **b.** $2\frac{2}{3}$
    c. $2\frac{3}{4}$ **d.** $2\frac{75}{100}$

9. Solve for x.

  $^{-}12 + x = {}^{+}5$

    a. $x = {}^{-}17$ **b.** $x = {}^{-}7$
    c. $x = {}^{+}7$ **d.** $x = {}^{+}17$

10. Evaluate $\frac{5}{6} + a \times 2\frac{1}{2}$ when $a = 9\frac{1}{3}$.

    a. $25\frac{5}{12}$ **b.** $24\frac{1}{6}$
    c. $23\frac{1}{3}$ **d.** $12\frac{2}{3}$

11. Simplify the expression.

  $(12 \times 9) \div 3 + 4(7 - 15)$

    a. $^{-}68$
    b. $^{-}4$
    c. $^{+}4$
    d. $^{+}68$

12. If the temperature in Buffalo is 23°F, what is the temperature in °C? [Use the formula $C = \frac{5}{9}(F - 32)$.]

    a. $^{-}45$°C
    b. $^{-}5$°C
    c. 45°C
    d. 5°C

13. Which shows rational numbers ordered from least to greatest?

a. $\dfrac{^-3}{4}, -1\dfrac{2}{3}, +1\dfrac{1}{6}, \dfrac{^+5}{6}$

b. $\dfrac{^-3}{4}, -1\dfrac{2}{3}, \dfrac{^+5}{6}, +1\dfrac{1}{6}$

c. $-1\dfrac{2}{3}, \dfrac{^-3}{4}, +1\dfrac{1}{6}, \dfrac{^+5}{6}$

d. $-1\dfrac{2}{3}, \dfrac{^-3}{4}, \dfrac{^+5}{6}, +1\dfrac{1}{6}$

14. Victoria has $7.25. After she lends money to Ada, she has $4.85 left. How much money did Victoria lend to Ada?

a. $2.40   b. $3.60
c. $4.85   d. $12.10

15. A restaurant bill is $34.50. What is a reasonable estimate for a 15% tip?

a. $6.50   b. $6.00
c. $5.00   d. $4.50

16. The product of 8 and a number is 72. What is the number?

a. 9   b. 576
c. 80   d. not given

17. Norma reads 120 pages in 3 hours. At that rate, how many pages can she read in 9 hours?

a. 1080   b. 360 pages
c. 40 pages   d. 27 pages

18. Chris bought $7\dfrac{1}{3}$ yd of cloth. She gave Judy $\dfrac{3}{4}$ yd. How much cloth does Chris have left?

a. $3\dfrac{1}{3}$ yd

b. $6\dfrac{5}{12}$ yd

c. $6\dfrac{7}{12}$ yd

d. $8\dfrac{1}{12}$ yd

19. If two complementary angles have measures $(3x - 10)°$ and $(2x + 10)°$, then what is the value of x?

a. 18   b. 20
c. 22   d. 36

20. A sweater is on sale for 24% off the original price. If the original price is $56, what is the selling price?

a. $13.44   b. $40
c. $42.56   d. $70

21. Cesar drives 150 miles in $2\dfrac{1}{2}$ hours. At this rate, how far can he drive in 4 hours?

a. 240 miles   b. 250 miles
c. 350 miles   d. 400 miles

22. If $\overrightarrow{BD}$ is the angle bisector of $\angle ABC$, $m\angle ABD = 48°$ and $m\angle DBC = (2x + 18)°$, then what is the value of x?

a. 15   b. 20
c. 28   d. 33

Tell About It

Explain how you solved the problem. Show all your work.

23. A ribbon 56 cm long is cut into two pieces. One of the pieces is three times longer than the other. Find the lengths, in centimeters, of both pieces of ribbon.

24. Suppose there are 125 boys attending a school of 400 students. In a survey of 50 girls in that school, 10 said they have a part-time job. Based on this sample, predict about how many girls in the school have a part-time job.

Measurement

Joan Benoit
1984 U.S. Olympic Marathon Gold Medalist

During the third mile
not the eighteenth as expected
she surged ahead
leaving behind the press
of bodies, the breath
hot on her back
and set a pace
the experts claimed
she couldn't possibly keep
to the end.

Sure, determined,
moving to an inner rhythm
measuring herself against herself
alone in a field of fifty
she gained the twenty-six miles
of concrete, asphalt and humid weather
and burst into the roar of the crowd
to run the lap around the stadium
at the same pace
once to finish the race
and then again in victory

and she was still fresh
and not even out of breath
and standing.

Rina Ferrarelli

In this chapter you will:

Relate decimals and metric units
Rename and compute metric and
    customary units
Investigate perimeter,
    circumference, and area formulas
Compute surface area and volume
Rename and compute customary
    units and time
Decompose figures to solve problems
Solve problems using drawings
    and formulas

Critical Thinking/Finding Together

The 2003 Special Olympics World
Summer Games were held in Dublin,
Ireland. Research and report to the
class the results for three sports in
these Games. Discuss measurement
used for each sport.

Measure Metric Length

▶ You can use a **centimeter ruler** to measure length to the nearest centimeter or millimeter.

| 1 meter(m) = 10 decimeters (dm) |
| 1 m = 100 centimeters (cm) |
| 1 m = 1000 millimeters (mm) |
| 1 kilometer (km) = 1000 m |

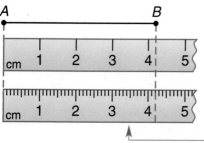

On this ruler, the distance from one tick mark to the next is 1 millimeter:
1 cm = 10 mm.

Think
$\overline{AB}$ is about 4 cm long.
$\overline{AB}$ is 42 mm long.

▶ You can use a **meterstick** to measure greater lengths, widths, or heights.

You would need 1000 metersticks laid end to end to measure a 1-kilometer long bridge.

▶ Metric units of length are related by **powers of 10**. Each unit has *ten* times the value of the next unit to its *right* and *one-tenth* the value of the next unit to its *left*.

thousands	hundreds	tens	ones	tenths	hundredths	thousandths
1000	100	10	1	0.1	0.01	0.001
kilometer (km)	hectometer (hm)	dekameter (dam)	meter (m)	decimeter (dm)	centimeter (cm)	millimeter (mm)

Multiply by a power of 10 to rename larger units as smaller units.

7 km = __?__ m
7 km = (7 × 1000) m = 7000 m

Divide by a power of 10 to rename smaller units as larger units.

240 cm = __?__ m
240 cm = (240 ÷ 100) m = 2.4 m

▶ To rename one metric unit to another (short way):

• Count the number of places from the known unit to the new unit in the table.

• Move the decimal point the same number of places in the same direction.

30.5 m = __?__ km

From meters to kilometers, move 3 places left.

30.5 m = 0.030.5 km

30.5 m = 0.0305 km

Measure each line segment to the nearest centimeter and to the nearest millimeter.

1. •————————•

2. •————————————•

3. •————•

Draw each quadrilateral described. Then draw and measure its diagonals.

4. square *ABCD* with
   AB = 5 cm

5. rhombus *EFGH* with
   EF = 25 mm

6. regular quadrilateral *MNOP*
   with *MN* = 44 mm

7. concave quadrilateral *QRST*
   with *QR* = 2.5 cm, *RS* = 3.5 cm

8. For which quadrilaterals in exercises 4–7 are
   the diagonals congruent? Explain your answer.

Rename each unit of measure. Use the tables on page 448 to help you.

9. 6 cm = __?__ mm

10. 7 m = __?__ cm

11. 9.7 km = __?__ m

12. 11 mm = __?__ cm

13. 453 dm = __?__ km

14. 34 dm = __?__ m

Compare. Use <, =, or >.

15. 0.45 m __?__ 45 cm

16. 4.8 cm __?__ 0.48 mm

17. 257 cm __?__ 25.7 dm

Problem Solving

18. One piece of electrical wire is 35 mm
    long. A second piece is 34.9 cm long.
    Which piece is longer? Explain.

19. Last year City X reported 1.65 m of
    rain. City Y reported 131.5 cm of rain.
    Which city had more rain? Explain.

20. The jogging track is 4.8 km long.
    Laura knows that her jogging stride is
    about 1 m in length. How many of her
    strides would cover the distance
    around the track once?

21. A strip of metal is 420 cm long. How
    many 1.4 cm strips can be cut from it?
    How many 14 mm strips can be cut
    from it? Explain how you found your
    answers.

DO YOU REMEMBER?

Multiply or divide as indicated.

22. 11 × 1000

23. 7.6 × 100

24. 120 ÷ 100

25. 5.8 ÷ 100

26. 0.48 ÷ 10

27. 5.732 ÷ 100

28. 0.06 × 10

29. 15.2 × 1000

Update your skills. See page 21.

Measure Metric Capacity and Mass

Capacity is the amount a container can hold. The most commonly used metric units of capacity are the liter (L), milliliter (mL), and kiloliter (kL).

$$1 \text{ L} = 1000 \text{ mL}$$
$$1 \text{ kL} = 1000 \text{ L}$$

Mass is the amount of matter in an object. The milligram (mg), gram (g), kilogram (kg), and metric ton (t) are the most commonly used metric units of mass.

$$1 \text{ g} = 1000 \text{ mg}$$
$$1 \text{ kg} = 1000 \text{ g}$$
$$1 \text{ t} = 1000 \text{ kg}$$

► You can rename metric units of capacity and mass the same way as you rename metric units of length.

thousands	hundreds	tens	ones	tenths	hundredths	thousandths
1000	100	10	1	0.1	0.01	0.001
kiloliter (kL)	hectoliter (hL)	dekaliter (daL)	liter (L)	deciliter (dL)	centiliter (cL)	milliliter (mL)
kilogram (kg)	hectogram (hg)	dekagram (dag)	gram (g)	decigram (dg)	centigram (cg)	milligram (mg)

Multiply by a power of 10 to rename larger units as smaller units.

$$0.001 \text{ kL} = \underline{} \text{ L}$$

$$0.001 \text{ kL} = (0.001 \times 1000) \text{ L} = 1 \text{ L}$$

Divide by a power of 10 to rename smaller units as larger units.

$$355 \text{ mL} = \underline{} \text{ L}$$

$$355 \text{ mL} = (355 \div 1000) \text{ L} = 0.355 \text{ L}$$

Study these examples.

$$5.85 \text{ kg} = \underline{} \text{ g}$$

$$5.85 \text{ kg} = (5.85 \times 1000) \text{ g} = 5850 \text{ g}$$

$$87{,}226 \text{ kg} = \underline{} \text{ t}$$

$$87{,}226 \text{ kg} = (87{,}226 \div 1000) \text{ t} = 87.226 \text{ t}$$

$$6014 \text{ g} = \underline{} \text{ kg}$$
$$6014 \text{ g} = 6.014. \text{ kg}$$
$$6014 \text{ g} = 6.014 \text{ kg}$$

> **Think**
> Move the decimal point 3 places to the left.

$$8.6 \text{ L} = \underline{} \text{ mL}$$
$$8.6 \text{ L} = 8.600. \text{ mL}$$
$$8,6 \text{ L} = 8600 \text{ mL}$$

> **Think**
> Move the decimal point 3 places to the right.

Practice

Rename each unit of measure.

1. $11 \text{ L} = \underline{} \text{ mL}$

2. $4000 \text{ L} = \underline{} \text{ kL}$

3. $72.5 \text{ mL} = \underline{} \text{ L}$

4. $14 \text{ kg} = \underline{} \text{ g}$

5. $3000 \text{ mg} = \underline{} \text{ g}$

6. $45\,000 \text{ g} = \underline{} \text{ kg}$

7. $9.1 \text{ L} = \underline{} \text{ kL}$

8. $4.025 \text{ g} = \underline{} \text{ mg}$

9. $200 \text{ dg} = \underline{} \text{ g}$

Rename each unit of measure. Use the tables on page 450 to help you.

10. 0.45 L = _?_ mL

11. 543 cL = _?_ hL

12. 19.2 dag = _?_ dg

13. _?_ g = 621 mg

14. _?_ mL = 0.768 L

15. _?_ kg = 1389 mg

16. 125 cL = _?_ L

17. 19 g = _?_ mg

18. 5635 mL = _?_ L

Compare. Use < , = , or > .

19. 24 L _?_ 240 mL

20. 7.3 kL _?_ 7300 L

21. 4000 mL _?_ 0.4 L

22. 24 g _?_ 240 mg

23. 6.6 kg _?_ 6600 g

24. 6550 mg _?_ 6.55 g

25. 6.7 kg _?_ 6700 g

26. 8575 mL _?_ 8.5 L

27. 2000 mg _?_ 20 g

28. 3 L _?_ 3100 mL

29. 3.225 kg _?_ 3225 g

30. 15.5 kg _?_ 16 t

Problem Solving

31. A can of condensed soup has a capacity of 325 mL. How many liters of soup is this?

32. The mass of a bicycle is about 10 kg. How many grams is the mass of the bicycle?

33. If 1000 copies of a report are sent out, each with a mass of 5500 g, how many metric tons is the report?

34. A can holds 354 mL of juice. How many liters of juice are there in a carton of 8 cans?

35. A glass container has a capacity of 7500 mL. How much more or less than 75 L can the glass container hold? Explain.

36. Colette's softball bat is 75 cm long. It has a mass of 112 g for every 10 cm of length. What is the total mass of Colette's bat?

37. Alice has the following amounts of orange juice in separate containers: 355 mL, 0.001 kL, and 125 cL. How many liters of orange juice does she have in all the containers?

TEST PREPARATION

38. Conrad buys 2 L of apple juice. He drinks 250 mL with lunch. How many milliliters are left?

    A 2480 mL   **C** 248 mL
    B 1750 mL   **D** 175 mL

39. Nelda measures the mass of a rock and finds out that it is 0.15 kg. What is the mass of the rock in grams?

    F 1.5 g   **H** 150 g
    G 15 g   **J** 1500 g

13-3

Measure Customary Length

▶ You can use an inch ruler to measure the length of an object to the nearest inch or nearest part of an inch.

The length of $\overline{AB}$ is:

- 1 in. to the nearest in.

- $1\frac{1}{2}$ in. to the nearest $\frac{1}{2}$ in.

- $1\frac{1}{4}$ in. to the nearest $\frac{1}{4}$ in.

- $1\frac{3}{8}$ in. to the nearest $\frac{1}{8}$ in.

- $1\frac{5}{16}$ in. to the nearest $\frac{1}{16}$ in.

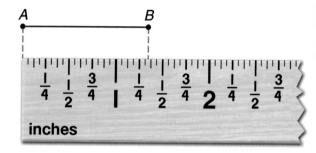

▶ These tools are used to measure lengths in customary units:

inch ruler— measures objects that are shorter in length, width, or height

| 12 inches (in.) = 1 foot (ft) |
| 3 feet = 1 yard (yd) |
| 5280 ft or 1760 yd = 1 mile (mi) |

yardstick— measures greater lengths, widths, or heights, such as the width of your classroom

odometer—measures distances, such as the number of miles between two cities

▶ Multiply and divide to rename customary units of length.

Multiply to rename larger units as smaller units.

$2\frac{1}{2}$ mi = __?__ yd **Think** 1 mi = 1760 yd

$2\frac{1}{2}$ mi = $(2\frac{1}{2} \times 1760)$ yd

$= \frac{5}{2} \times \frac{\overset{880}{\cancel{1760}}}{1}$ yd
  $\underset{1}{}$

Divide to rename smaller units as larger units.

102 in. = __?__ ft **Think** 12 in. = 1 ft

102 in. = $(102 \div 12)$ ft

$= 8$ ft 6 in.

$\frac{6}{12}$ or $\frac{1}{2}$ ft

Find the missing value to complete each proportion.

1. **a.** 1 foot (ft) : 12 inches (in.) = 3 feet : __?__ inches

   b. 3 feet : __?__ yard (y) = 6 feet : 2 yards

   c. 1760 yards : 1 mile (mi) = __?__ feet : 1 mile

Rename each unit of measure. Use the table on page 452 to help you.

2. 40 ft = __?__ yd

3. 114 in. = __?__ ft

4. 23,760 ft = __?__ mi

5. $4\frac{1}{2}$ mi = __?__ ft

6. $7\frac{1}{4}$ ft = __?__ in.

7. $6\frac{2}{3}$ yd = __?__ ft

8. 8 ft 9 in. = __?__ in. (*Hint:* 8 ft 9 in. means 8 ft + 9 in.)

9. 7 yd 2 ft = __?__ in.

10. 2 mi 40 ft = __?__ ft

11. $1\frac{1}{2}$ mi 60 yd = __?__ ft

Compare. Use <, =, or >.

12. 15 yd __?__ 50 ft

13. 18 ft __?__ 200 in.

14. 25,000 ft __?__ 5 mi

15. 96 in. __?__ $2\frac{2}{3}$ yd

16. $2\frac{1}{2}$ yd __?__ 2700 ft

17. 40 in. __?__ $3\frac{1}{4}$ ft

18. 49 ft __?__ 16 yd 2 ft

19. 294 in. __?__ 24 ft 6 in.

Use a ruler to measure each segment to the nearest 1 in., $\frac{1}{2}$ in., $\frac{1}{4}$ in., $\frac{1}{8}$ in., and $\frac{1}{16}$ in.

20. R •————————————• P

21. X •————————————————————• Y

22. A •————————• B

23. M •—————————• N

Problem Solving

24. A rug is $7\frac{1}{2}$ ft long. How many yards long is the rug?

25. Kate's backyard is 16 yd long and $14\frac{1}{2}$ yd wide. How many feet wide is the backyard?

13-4

Measure Customary Capacity and Weight

Customary units of capacity include fluid ounces (fl oz), cups (c), pints (pt), quarts (qt), and gallons (gal).

1 c = 8 fl oz
1 pt = 2 c
1 qt = 2 pt
1 gal = 4 qt

Weight is a measure of how heavy an object is. Customary units of weight include ounces (oz), pounds (lb), and tons (T).

1 lb = 16 oz
1 T = 2000 lb

► You can rename customary units of capacity and weight the same way you rename customary units of length.

120 fl oz = __?__ c

120 fl oz = (120 ÷ 8) c

= 15 c

Think
8 fl oz = 1 c

$18\frac{1}{4}$ pt = __?__ c

$18\frac{1}{4}$ pt = $(18\frac{1}{4} \times 2)$ c

$= \frac{73}{\overset{}{\underset{2}{4}}} \times \frac{\overset{1}{2}}{1}$ c

$= 36\frac{1}{2}$ c

Think
1 pt = 2 c

Remember: Multiply to rename larger units as smaller units.
Divide to rename smaller units as larger units.

Study these examples.

$5\frac{1}{2}$ gal = __?__ qt

$5\frac{1}{2}$ gal = $(5\frac{1}{2} \times 4)$ qt

$= \frac{11}{\underset{1}{2}} \times \frac{\overset{2}{4}}{1}$ qt

= 22 qt

Think
1 gal = 4 qt

30 oz = __?__ lb

30 oz = (30 ÷ 16) lb

= 1 lb 14 oz

$= 1\frac{7}{8}$ lb

Think
16 oz = 1 lb

14 oz = $\frac{14}{16}$ lb
or $\frac{7}{8}$ lb

Practice

Find the missing value to complete each proportion.

1. a. 1 quart (qt) : 2 pints (pt) = 5 quarts : __?__ pints

b. 16 ounces (oz) : __?__ pound (lb) = 64 ounces : 4 pounds

c. 2000 pounds (lb) : 1 ton (T) = 5000 pounds : __?__ tons

Rename each unit of measure. Use the tables on page 454 to help you.

2. 8 gal = ___?___ qt

3. 80 oz = ___?___ lb

4. 50 fl oz = ___?___ c

5. $2\frac{1}{2}$ lb = ___?___ oz

6. $7\frac{3}{4}$ pt = ___?___ fl oz

7. $10\frac{1}{8}$ lb = ___?___ oz

8. 8 c 2 fl oz = ___?___ fl oz

9. 16 lb 5 oz = ___?___ oz

10. 15 T 920 lb = ___?___ lb

11. 19 qt = ___?___ gal ___?___ qt

12. 17 c = ___?___ pt ___?___ c

13. 1 lb 48 oz = ___?___ lb

Compare. Use <, =, or >.

14. 7 gal ___?___ 29 qt

15. 4.5 T ___?___ 10,000 lb

16. 33 pt ___?___ 16 qt 1 pt

17. 10 c ___?___ 6 pt

18. 7 pt 5 c ___?___ 19 c

19. $6\frac{1}{2}$ lb ___?___ 103 oz

20. 5 gal 5 qt ___?___ 20 qt

21. 54 oz ___?___ 3 lb 7 oz

22. 7 pt 5 c ___?___ 19 c

Problem Solving

23. How much more than a gallon is 7 quarts?

24. How much less than a pound is 13 ounces?

25. At $.49 a pint, what is the cost of 24 qt of milk?

26. At $.59 a quart, what is the cost of 3 gal of syrup?

27. Which weighs more: a 12-oz jar of fruit jelly or a $\frac{3}{4}$-lb jar of jam?

28. How many pint containers can be filled from 24 gal of juice?

Write About It

29. Conduct an experiment to find out how much liquid you drink in a week (5 days). Follow these steps:

- Estimate the number of cups of liquid you drink in one week.

- As closely as you can, each day record to the nearest whole number of cups of liquid that you drink.

- Find the total for the week and compare it with your estimate.

- Discuss your results with the class. Then work together to find (a) the number of fluid ounces and (b) the number of gallons for your class.

Compute Customary Units

▶ **To *add* or *subtract* customary units:**

- Add or subtract *like* units.

- Regroup to rename one unit to another, as needed.

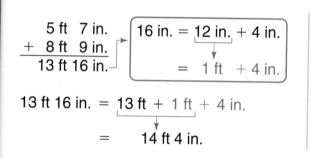

$$\begin{array}{r} 5 \text{ ft} \quad 7 \text{ in.} \\ + \quad 8 \text{ ft} \quad 9 \text{ in.} \\ \hline 13 \text{ ft} \ 16 \text{ in.} \end{array}$$

$\boxed{16 \text{ in.} = 12 \text{ in.} + 4 \text{ in.} \\ = 1 \text{ ft} + 4 \text{ in.}}$

13 ft 16 in. = 13 ft + 1 ft + 4 in.

= 14 ft 4 in.

$$\begin{array}{r} {}^{8} \ \ {}^{5} \\ \cancel{9} \text{ gal } \cancel{1} \text{ qt} \\ - \ 4 \text{ gal } 3 \text{ qt} \\ \hline 4 \text{ gal } 2 \text{ qt} \end{array}$$

9 gal 1 qt

= 8 gal + 1 gal + 1 qt

= 8 gal + 4 qt + 1 qt

= 8 gal 5 qt

▶ **To *multiply* with customary units:**

- Multiply by each unit.

- Regroup to rename one unit to another.

Think
12 in. = 1 ft

$$\begin{array}{r} 9 \text{ ft } 4 \text{ in.} \\ \times \qquad 3 \\ \hline 27 \text{ ft } 12 \text{ in.} = 27 \text{ ft} + 1 \text{ ft} \\ = 28 \text{ ft} \end{array}$$

or

- Rename all units as like units.

- Multiply.

- Regroup.

9 ft 4 in. = (9 × 12) in. + 4 in.
= 108 in. + 4 in. = 112 in.

112 in. × 3 = 336 in.

= (336 ÷ 12) ft

= 28 ft

▶ **To *divide* with customary units:**

- Rename all units as like units.

- Divide.

- Regroup.

Think
1 lb = 16 oz

3 lb 8 oz ÷ 2 = ___?___

3 lb 8 oz = (3 × 16) oz + 8 oz
= 48 oz + 8 oz = 56 oz

56 oz ÷ 2 = 28 oz

= (28 ÷ 16) lb

= 1 lb 12 oz

Add.

1. 8 ft 4 in.
   + 3 ft 10 in.

2. 7 yd 1 ft
   + 7 yd 2 ft

3. 10 yd 24 in.
   + 10 yd 16 in.

4. 2 gal 3 qt
   + 1 gal 3 qt

5. 6 lb 10 oz
   + 9 lb 12 oz

6. 6 pt 3 c
   + 3 pt 1 c

Subtract.

7. 10 yd 2 ft
   − 6 yd 2 ft

8. 3 ft 8 in.
   − 1 ft 10 in.

9. 4 yd 10 in.
   − 3 yd 11 in.

10. 5 gal 3 qt
    − 2 gal 1 qt

11. 8 qt 3 c
    − 4 qt 4 c

12. 10 lb 8 oz
    − 6 lb 9 oz

Multiply.

13. 2 ft 3 in.
    × 2

14. 6 yd 2 ft
    × 4

15. 4 yd 16 in.
    × 5

16. 7 × 9 gal 3 qt

17. 6 × 8 qt 3 pt

18. 6 × 7 lb 6 oz

Divide.

19. 4 yd 1 ft ÷ 3

20. 2 mi 5 yd ÷ 5

21. 3 gal 1 pt ÷ 2

22. 2 lb 1 oz ÷ 3

23. 3 qt 1 pt ÷ 7

24. 16 ft 8 in. ÷ 5

Problem Solving

25. A 16-in. piece is cut off the end of a board 1 yd 2 in. long. How long is the board now?

26. A leaking water pipe loses $1\frac{1}{2}$ cups of water an hour. How many gallons of water does it lose in a day?

CHALLENGE

Compute.

27. 7 yd 1 ft 8 in.
    − 4 yd 2 ft 4 in.

28. 5 gal 3 qt 1 pt
    + 2 gal 4 qt 3 pt

29. 3 mi 1760 yd 100 ft
    + 4 mi 1760 yd 250 ft

30. 3 mi 6 yd 2 ft ÷ 5

31. 4 × 9 qt 2 pt 1 c

32. 20 × 7 mi 140 yd 50 ft

Compute with Time

Tim's watch reads 8:55 A.M. If he plans to go to lunch at 12:00 P.M., how much longer must he wait?

To find how much time longer, find the elapsed time from 8:55 A.M. to 12:00 P.M. You may use mental math or subtract using paper and pencil.

60 seconds (s) = 1 minute (min)
60 min = 1 hour (h)
24 h = 1 day (d)
7 days = 1 week (wk)
12 months (mo) = 1 year (y)
365 d = 1 y
100 y = 1 century (cent.)

Mental Math

From 8:55 A.M. to 9:00 A.M. is 5 min.
From 9:00 A.M. to 12:00 P.M. is 3 h.
The elapsed time is 3 h 5 min.

Tim must wait 3 h 5 min.

Paper and Pencil

$$\begin{array}{r} 12{:}00 \\ -\ \ 8{:}55 \end{array} \longrightarrow \begin{array}{r} \overset{5\ \ 10}{1\ 1{:}6\ 0} \\ -\ \ 8{:}5\ 5 \\ \hline 3{:}0\ 5 \end{array}$$

Regroup 1 h as 60 min.

3:05 = 3 h 5 min

▶ You can add to find the ending time of an event.

Pam boards the bus from her home at 12:15 P.M. If it takes 1 h 55 min to reach her destination, at what time will Pam reach her destination?

To find the time, t, add: 12 h 15 min + 1 h 55 min = t.

$$\begin{array}{r} 12 \text{ h } 15 \text{ min} \\ +\ \ 1 \text{ h } 55 \text{ min} \\ \hline 13 \text{ h } 70 \text{ min} \end{array} = 14 \text{ h } 10 \text{ min} \longrightarrow 2{:}10 \text{ P.M.}$$

Pam reaches her destination at 2:10 P.M.

Study these examples.

$$\begin{array}{r} \overset{2\quad\ \ 80}{3 \text{ min } 20 \text{ s}} \\ -2 \text{ min } 35 \text{ s} \\ \hline 0 \text{ min } 45 \text{ s} \end{array} = 45 \text{ s}$$

$$\begin{array}{r} 8 \text{ wk } 2 \text{ d} \\ \times \qquad 4 \\ \hline 32 \text{ wk } 8 \text{ d} \end{array} = 33 \text{ wk } 1 \text{ d}$$

3 y 8 mo ÷ 2
44 mo ÷ 2 = 22 mo
22 mo = 1 y 10 mo

Find the elapsed time.

1. from 3:15 P.M. to 6:30 P.M.

2. from 5:55 A.M. to 7:30 A.M.

3. from 10:30 A.M. to 3:15 P.M.

4. from 9:20 A.M. to 1:30 P.M.

5. from 5:16 A.M. to 9:35 A.M.

6. from 6:22 A.M. to 2:10 P.M.

Rename each unit of time. Use the table on page 458 to help you.

7. 2 y 3 mo = ? mo   **8.** 650 y = ? cent.   **9.** 3 d 2 h = ? h

10. 2½ h = ? min   **11.** 1250 s = ? min ? s   **12.** 758 d = ? y ? wk

Compute.

13. 6 h 25 min   **14.** 3 d 18 h   **15.** 2 y 5 mo 12 d   **16.** 33 min 15 s ÷ 5
      − 2 h 40 min   + 1 d 15 h   ×   3

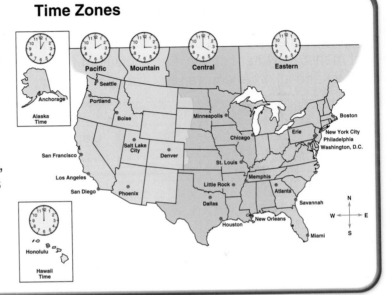

Time Zones

The United States is divided into six time zones. From time zone to time zone, it is one hour earlier as you travel west, and one hour later as you travel east.

When it is 3:00 A.M. in Denver, Colorado, it is 2:00 A.M. in Los Angeles, California.

When it is 4:00 P.M. in Dallas, Texas, it is 5:00 P.M. in New York City, New York.

It is 9:00 A.M. in Denver, Colorado. Write the time in each city.

17. Portland, OR   **18.** St. Louis, MO   **19.** Miami, FL   **20.** Anchorage, AK

21. Honolulu, HI   **22.** Seattle, WA   **23.** Boise, ID   **24.** Washington, DC

Problem Solving

25. Julio's clock read 9:45 P.M. when he arrived home after a 10 h 30 min trip. What time did he leave?

26. At 4:55 P.M. in Honolulu a flight to Houston departs. It arrives at 6:43 A.M. Houston time. How long is the flight?

CRITICAL THINKING

Use reference books to learn about the 24-hour clock. Then write the 24-hour clock times. 3:00 P.M. = 15:00

27. 4:15 A.M.   **28.** 3:25 P.M.   **29.** 12:40 A.M.

Relate Customary and Metric Units

While traveling in Italy, Mr. Santos bought an 80-cm long leather belt as a gift. His friends wear 30-in., 34-in., and 36-in. belts. Which of them would the belt fit?

To find who the belt would fit, rename: 80 cm = _?_ in.

▶ You can rename between customary and metric units of measure the same way as you rename units within the customary or metric system.

The table below shows the equivalents between customary and metric units of measure. Note that only the equivalent for inches and centimeters is exact and all other equivalents are approximate.

Customary and Metric Unit Equivalents		
Length	**Capacity**	**Weight/Mass**
1 in. = 2.54 cm	1 fl oz ≈ 30 mL	1 oz ≈ 28.35 g
1 m ≈ 39.37 in.	1 L ≈ 1.06 qt	1 kg ≈ 2.2 lb
1 mi ≈ 1.61 km	1 gal ≈ 3.79 L	1 metric ton (t) ≈ 1.102 T

80 cm = (80 ÷ 2.54) in.

80 cm ≈ 31.5 in.

The belt would fit the one who wears a 30-in. belt.

> **Think**
> A centimeter is a smaller unit than an inch, so divide.
> 2.54 cm = 1 in.

Study these examples.

25 gal ≈ _?_ L

25 gal ≈ (25 × 3.79) L

25 gal ≈ 94.75 L

> **Think**
> 1 gal > 1 L, so multiply.
> 1 gal ≈ 3.79 L

24 lb ≈ _?_ kg

24 lb ≈ (24 ÷ 2.2) kg

24 lb ≈ 11.36 kg

> **Think**
> 1 lb < 1 kg, so divide.
> 2.2 lb ≈ 1 kg

Find the missing value to complete each proportion.

1. a. 1 mile (mi) : 1.61 kilometers (km) = 3 mile : _?_ kilometers

b. 1 liter (L) : 1.06 quarts (qt) = 5 liters : _?_ quarts

c. 1 metric ton (t) : 1.102 tons (T) = 10 metric tons : _?_ tons

d. 39.37 inches (in.) : 1 meter (m) = 150 inches : _?_ meters

Rename each unit of measure. Round to the nearest hundredth.
Use the table on page 460 to help you.

2. 12 in. = __?__ cm

3. 12 yd ≈ __?__ m

4. 2 mi ≈ __?__ km

5. 20 qt ≈ __?__ L

6. 20 fl oz ≈ __?__ mL

7. 20 qal ≈ __?__ L

8. 30 lb ≈ __?__ kg

9. 30 oz ≈ __?__ g

10. 30 T ≈ __?__ t

11. 5 cm ≈ __?__ in.

12. 5 m ≈ __?__ yd

13. 5 km ≈ __?__ mi

14. 100 L ≈ __?__ qt

15. 100 mL ≈ __?__ fl oz

16. 100 L ≈ __?__ gal

17. 55.5 kg ≈ __?__ lb

18. 55.5 g ≈ __?__ oz

19. 55.5 t ≈ __?__ T

Compare. Use <, =, or >.

20. 4 m __?__ 12 ft

21. 38 km __?__ 30 mi

22. 20 in. __?__ 50.8 cm

23. 3.25 gal __?__ 12 L

24. 100 L __?__ 27 gal

25. 5 fl oz __?__ 160 mL

26. 10 lb __?__ 5 kg

27. 3 oz __?__ 70 g

28. 10 t __?__ 12 T

Problem Solving

29. A perfumery uses customary and metric units of measure. Which contains more, a 500-mL bottle or a bottle with 0.5 qt? Explain.

30. While traveling in Canada, Richard stopped at a gas station and bought 32 L of gas. About how many gallons of gas did he buy?

31. Anna's car weighs about 3000 pounds. About how many kilograms does the car weigh?

DO YOU REMEMBER?

Use a vocabulary word in the box to complete each sentence.

32. A __?__ is when a figure is moved without changing its size or shape.

33. A __?__ is a flat pattern that folds into a solid figure.

34. A __?__ is a solid, or space, figure whose faces are polygons.

polyhedron
proportion
transformation
sample
net

13-8

Perimeter

Rita uses 54.6 m of fencing to enclose a play area for her dogs. The play area is in the shape of a polygon, shown at the right. She painted all but one side of the fence. How many meters of fencing does Rita have left to paint?

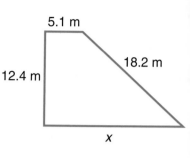

To find how many meters of fencing left, x, write and solve the equation:

sum of the lengths of sides	is equal to	perimeter

$12.4 \text{ m} + 5.1 \text{ m} + 18.2 \text{ m} + x = 54.6 \text{ m}$

Think
Add like units of measure.

$12.4 + 5.1 + 18.2 + x = 54.6$

$35.7 + x = 54.6$ ← Simplify.

$35.7 - 35.7 + x = 54.6 - 35.7$ ← Subtract 35.7 to isolate the variable.

$x = 18.9$ ← Simplify.

Rita has 18.9 m of fencing left to paint.

▶ For some polygons, you can use formulas to find perimeter.

- Square or Rhombus → $P = 4s$, where $s =$ length of side

- Rectangle → $P = 2\ell + 2w$ or $P = 2(\ell + w)$, where $\ell =$ length and $w =$ width

- Regular Polygon → $P = ns$, where $n =$ number of congruent sides, and $s =$ length of one side

$\frac{5}{6}$ yd

$1\frac{1}{6}$ yd

$P = 2(\ell + w)$
$= 2(1\frac{1}{6} \text{ yd} + \frac{5}{6} \text{ yd})$
$= 4 \text{ yd}$

4.1 cm

$P = 5s$
$= 5(4.1 \text{ cm})$
$= 20.5 \text{ cm}$

▶ To find the perimeter of a more complex figure, break it down into simpler figures and then add the lengths of its actual sides.

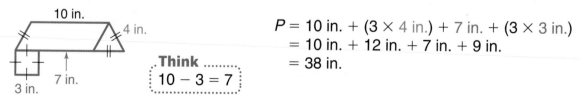

10 in.

4 in.

3 in.   7 in.

Think
$10 - 3 = 7$

$P = 10 \text{ in.} + (3 \times 4 \text{ in.}) + 7 \text{ in.} + (3 \times 3 \text{ in.})$
$= 10 \text{ in.} + 12 \text{ in.} + 7 \text{ in.} + 9 \text{ in.}$
$= 38 \text{ in.}$

Find the perimeter of each polygon.

1.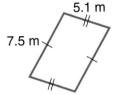
5.1 m
7.5 m

2.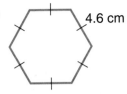
4.6 cm

3.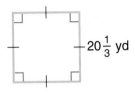
$20\frac{1}{3}$ yd

4. Rectangle
$\ell = 23.2$ cm
$w = 8.6$ cm

5. Square
$s = 27\frac{1}{4}$ ft

6. Regular heptagon
$s = 45$ in.

7.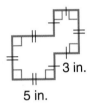
3 in.
5 in.

8.
12 m
4 m
8 m
6 m

9.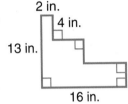
2 in.
4 in.
13 in.
16 in.

Find the length of each unknown side.

10.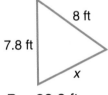
8 ft
7.8 ft
x
$P = 22.8$ ft

11.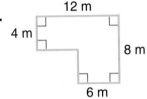
y
6.5 in.
2.8 in.
8.6 in.
$P = 23.1$ in.

12.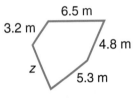
6.5 m
3.2 m
4.8 m
z
5.3 m
$P = 26.6$ m

Problem Solving

13. Find the perimeter of a triangle with sides measuring 25 mm, 2.8 cm, and 1.9 cm.

14. Find the perimeter of a quadrilateral with sides measuring $9\frac{1}{3}$ yd, 18 ft, $4\frac{1}{2}$ yd, and 45 in.

15. At $2.95 per foot, what is the cost of fencing for a rectangular garden that is 20 ft wide and $30\frac{1}{2}$ ft long?

16. How many meters of fringe are needed to border a triangular pennant 125 cm on a side?

CRITICAL THINKING

Measure the lengths of the sides of each polygon to the nearest $\frac{1}{8}$ in. Then find the perimeter of each polygon.

17.

18.

Area of Rectangles and Squares

The area of a polygon is the number of square units that cover its surface. The square units may be square centimeters, square meters, square inches, and so on.

1 square unit

Area of a Square
Area = side × side
$A = s \times s = s^2$

Area of a Rectangle
Area = length × width
$A = \ell \times w = \ell w$

What is the area of a square mirror that measures 9.5 cm on each side?

First estimate: 10 cm × 10 cm = 100 cm²
Then find the area.

$A = s \times s$

$A = 9.5$ cm × 9.5 cm

$A = 90.25$ cm²

9.5 cm

The area of the mirror is 90.25 cm².

.Think.....
90.25 cm² is close to 100 cm².

What is the area of a wall that measures $16\frac{2}{3}$ ft by $10\frac{1}{2}$ ft?

First estimate: 17 ft × 11 ft = 187 ft²
Then find the area.

$A = \ell \times w$

$A = 16\frac{2}{3}$ ft × $10\frac{1}{2}$ ft

$A = \dfrac{\overset{25}{\cancel{50}}}{\underset{1}{3}}$ ft × $\dfrac{\overset{7}{\cancel{21}}}{\underset{1}{2}}$ ft = 175 ft²

$10\frac{1}{2}$ ft

$16\frac{2}{3}$ ft

The area of the wall is 175 ft².

.Think.....
175 ft² is close to 187 ft².

▶ To find the area of more complex figures divide the figure into squares and rectangles.

The dashed red lines show how the figure can be divided into rectangles.

• Find the area of each rectangle and square.

Rectangle *ABCI*: $A = 4$ m × 8 m = 32 m²
Square *DEJI*: $A = (3$ m$)^2 = 9$ m²
Rectangle *IFGH*: $A = 8$ m × 2 m = 16 m²

• Add to find the area of the entire figure.
$A = 32$ m² + 9 m² + 16 m² = 57 m²

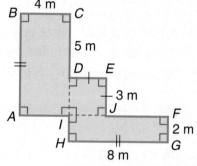

Study this example.

Find the area of a rectangle that is $3\frac{1}{4}$ feet by 24 inches.

Rename units as feet.
24 inches = 2 feet

$A = \ell \times w$

$A = 3\frac{1}{4} \times 2 \longrightarrow A = \dfrac{13}{\underset{2}{\cancel{4}}} \times \overset{1}{\cancel{2}} \longrightarrow A = 6\frac{1}{2}$ ft²

Use formulas to find the areas. Estimate to help.

1.

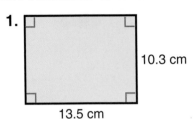

10.3 cm

13.5 cm

2.

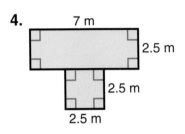

$1\frac{1}{2}$ yd

$1\frac{1}{2}$ yd

3.

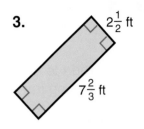

$2\frac{1}{2}$ ft

$7\frac{2}{3}$ ft

4.

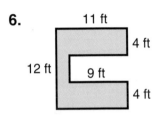

7 m

2.5 m

2.5 m

2.5 m

5.

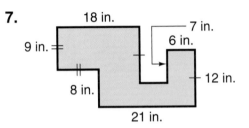

4 in.

$1\frac{1}{3}$ in.

4 in.

$1\frac{1}{3}$ in.

$1\frac{1}{3}$ in.

4 in.

6.

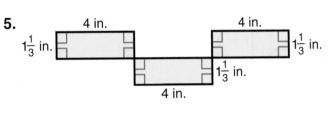

11 ft

4 ft

12 ft

9 ft

4 ft

7.

18 in.

7 in.

9 in.

6 in.

8 in.

12 in.

21 in.

Problem Solving

Draw a diagram and use a formula to solve each problem.

8. Find the total area of 8 rectangular wooden panels if each measures 5.2 cm by 7.6 cm.

9. How many 4-in. square tiles are needed to cover an 8 ft by 16 ft wall? (*Hint:* 1 ft^2 = 144 in.^{2})

10. How many square yards of carpeting are needed to cover a floor that is 9 ft wide and 15 ft long? (*Hint:* 9 ft^2 = 1 yd^2)

11. A rectangular floor is 7.5 ft long. It is 4 times as wide as it is long. How many square yards of vinyl are needed to cover this floor?

CHALLENGE — Algebra

Find each missing dimension. Use Guess and Test.

12. Area of square: 144 in.^{2}
Find the length of a side.

$s \times s$ = 12 in. $\times$ 12 in. = 144 in.^{2}

s = 12 in.

13. Area of square: 625 cm^2
Find the length of a side.

14. Area of rectangle: 276 m^2
Width = 12 m
Find the length.

Area of Triangles and Parallelograms

Robin discovered the area formulas for triangles and parallelograms using the area of a rectangle.

▶ **Right Triangle**

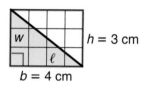

$h = 3$ cm

$b = 4$ cm

The base (*b*) and the height (*h*) of the right triangle correspond to the length and the width of the rectangle.

Think
The area of the right triangle is half the area of the rectangle.

$A = \dfrac{1}{2} \times b \times h$

$A = \dfrac{1}{\overset{}{2}} \times \dfrac{\overset{2}{4}}{\underset{1}{1}} \text{ cm} \times \dfrac{3}{1} \text{ cm}$

$A = 6 \text{ cm}^2$

Area of Triangle: $A = \dfrac{1}{2} \times b \times h$

$$A = \dfrac{1}{2}bh$$

Any side of a triangle can serve as the base.
The height is the length of the perpendicular segment from the base to the opposite vertex.

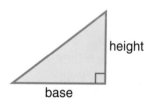

height

base

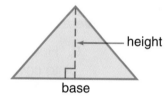

height

base

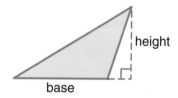

height

base

▶ **Parallelogram**

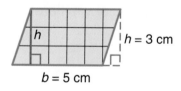

h

$h = 3$ cm

$b = 5$ cm

The base (*b*) and the height (*h*) of the parallelogram correspond to the length and the width of the rectangle.

Think
The area of the parallelogram is equal to the area of the rectangle.

Area of Parallelogram: $A = b \times h$

$$A = bh$$

$A = b \times h$

$A = 5 \text{ cm} \times 3 \text{ cm}$

$A = 15 \text{ cm}^2$

Any side of a parallelogram can serve as the base.

Find the area of each triangle.

1.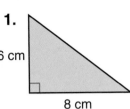
6 cm
8 cm

2.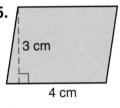
8 ft
10 ft

3.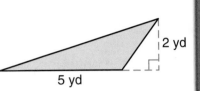
30 cm
12 cm

4.
2 yd
5 yd

Find the area of each parallelogram.

5.
3 cm
4 cm

6.
12 in.
18 in.

7.
15 mm
7.5 mm

8.
$1\frac{4}{5}$ yd
$1\frac{2}{3}$ yd

Find the area of each triangle and parallelogram to complete each table.

	Area of Triangle		
	Base	**Height**	**Area**
9.	10 ft	5 ft	?
10.	8.4 m	5.1 m	?
11.	$5\frac{1}{2}$ yd	9 yd	?

	Area of Parallelogram		
	Base	**Height**	**Area**
12.	4 cm	6 cm	?
13.	8.1 m	12 m	?
14.	$6\frac{1}{3}$ ft	3 ft	?

Problem Solving

15. Find the area of a triangular traffic sign with a base of 40 cm and height of 60 cm.

16. Find the area of a parallelogram-shaped pennant with a base of 2 yd and height of 15 ft.

17. The area of a parallelogram is 24 in.^{2} and the height is 8 in. Find the length of the base.

18. An isosceles right triangle has area of 98 cm^2. Find the length of each leg.

CHALLENGE

19. Find the length and width of a rectangle that has an area of 64 ft^2, with the least perimeter possible. Explain how you found your answer.

Area of Trapezoids

Two congruent trapezoids put together, as in the figure below, form a parallelogram.

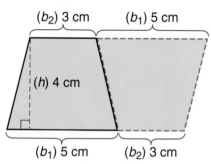

(b_2) 3 cm (b_1) 5 cm

(h) 4 cm

(b_1) 5 cm (b_2) 3 cm

Notice that:
• the original trapezoid has 2 bases: the lower base, b_1, and the upper base, b_2.
• the height, h, is a perpendicular line segment connecting the 2 parallel bases.
• by rotating the original trapezoid 180°, you can form a parallelogram.

Area of parallelogram = bh
$$= (b_1 + b_2)\, h \longleftarrow \text{Substitute } (b_1 + b_2) \text{ for } b.$$

The area of the original trapezoid is one half the area of the parallelogram. So, the area of a trapezoid = $\frac{1}{2}(b_1 + b_2)\, h$.

> The formula for the area of a trapezoid:
> Area = $\frac{1}{2} \times (\text{base}_1 + \text{base}_2) \times \text{height}$
> $A = \frac{1}{2}(b_1 + b_2)\, h$

▶ To find the area of the trapezoid above:

$$A = \frac{1}{2}(b_1 + b_2)\, h$$

$$A = \frac{1}{2}(5 \text{ cm} + 3 \text{ cm})\, 4 \text{ cm} \longleftarrow \text{Substitute } b_1 = 5 \text{ cm}, b_2 = 3 \text{ cm}, \text{ and } h = 4 \text{ cm}.$$

$$A = \frac{1}{\overset{}{\underset{1}{2}}}(\overset{4}{8} \text{ cm})\, 4 \text{ cm}$$

$$A = 16 \text{ cm}^2$$

Study these examples.

15 in.

5 in.

25 in.

$$A = \frac{1}{2}(b_1 + b_2)\, h$$

$$A = \frac{1}{2}(25 \text{ in.} + 15 \text{ in.})\, 5 \text{ in.}$$

$$A = \frac{1}{\underset{1}{2}} \times \frac{\overset{20}{40}}{1} \times \frac{5}{1}$$

$$A = 100 \text{ in.}^2$$

8 m

70 dm

9 m

$$A = \frac{1}{2}(b_1 + b_2)\, h$$

$$A = \frac{1}{2}(9 \text{ m} + 8 \text{ m})\, 7 \text{ m}$$

$$A = \frac{1}{2}(17 \text{ m})\, 7 \text{ m}$$

$$A = 59.5 \text{ m}^2$$

Think
Rename 70 dm as meters.
70 dm = 7 m

Find the area of each trapezoid.

1.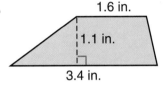
21 yd
4 yd
12 yd

2.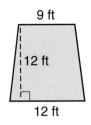
9 ft
12 ft
12 ft

3.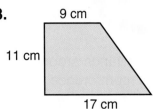
9 cm
11 cm
17 cm

4.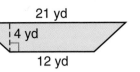
1.6 in.
1.1 in.
3.4 in.

5.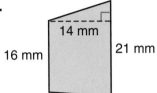
14 mm
16 mm
21 mm

6.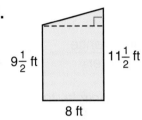
$9\frac{1}{2}$ ft
$11\frac{1}{2}$ ft
8 ft

Problem Solving

7. Danica makes a quilt in the shape of a trapezoid. The longer base is 15 ft long and the shorter base is 12 ft long. The height is 8 ft. The quilt cost her $0.65 per square foot to make. How much did it cost Danica to make the quilt?

8. Les builds a patio in the shape of a trapezoid. The parallel bases are 14 ft and 16 ft long. The distance between the bases (the height) is 13 ft. The patio cost $1.25 per square foot. How much did it cost Les to make his patio?

9. A trapezoid has a shorter base that is 19 in. long and a longer base that is 23 in. long. The area of the trapezoid is 105 in.² What is the height of the trapezoid?

10. A trapezoid has a shorter base that measures 6.2 cm and a longer base that measures 7.5 cm. The area of the trapezoid is 30.14 cm². What is the height of the trapezoid?

DO YOU REMEMBER?

Find the simple interest, *I*, for each loan.

11. $2000 at 3% for 2 years

12. $9400 at 5% for 3 years

13. $7500 at 4.5% for 3 years

14. $7080 at 6% for 5 years

15. $38,000 at 7% for 9 years

16. $85,500 at 3.9% for 7 years

13-12

Circumference

The distance around a circle is called the circumference (*C*) of the circle.

Lynn uses a string to measure around the circle at the right and uses a metric ruler to measure the length of the string. Then she finds the ratio of circumference to diameter.

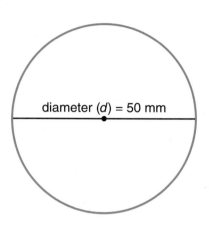

diameter (*d*) = 50 mm

$$\frac{\text{circumference}}{\text{diameter}} \approx \frac{157 \text{ mm}}{50 \text{ mm}} \approx 3.14$$

For every circle, the ratio of the circumference, *C*, to the length of the diameter (*d*) is close to 3.14. Mathematicians use the Greek letter π (pi) to name this ratio. π is a nonterminating, nonrepeating decimal and is an irrational number.

.Think.........
$\pi \approx 3.141592653589793 \ldots$

▶ You can use formulas to find the approximate circumference of a circle.

To find circumference when the length of a diameter, *d*, is given:

Use $C = \pi d$.

Use $\pi = 3$ to estimate.

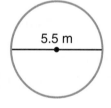

5.5 m

First estimate:
$C \approx 3 \times 6 \text{ m} \approx 18 \text{ m}$

Then solve.

$C = \pi \times d$

$C \approx 3.14 \times 5.5 \text{ m}$

$C \approx 17.27 \text{ m}$

.Think.........
17.27 m is close to the estimate of 18 m.

To find circumference when the length of a radius, *r*, is given:

Use $C = 2\pi r$.

3 yd

.Think.........
$d \approx 2 \times r$ or $r = d \div 2$

First estimate:
$C \approx 3 \times (2 \times 3 \text{ yd}) \approx 18 \text{ yd}$

Then solve.

$C = 2 \times \pi \times r$

$C \approx 2 \times 3.14 \times 3 \text{ yd}$

$C \approx 18.84 \text{ yd}$

.Think.........
18.84 yd is close to the estimate of 18 yd.

Use π = 3 to estimate the circumference. Then use 3.14 for π to find the circumference of each circle.

1.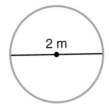
2 m

2.
4 ft

3.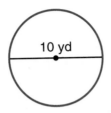
10 yd

4.
8.5 in.

Use the Fractional Value for π

You can use the fraction $\frac{22}{7}$ as an approximate value for π to find the circumference of a circle.

$$\frac{22}{7} \approx 3.14$$

$C = 2 \times \pi \times r$

$C \approx \frac{\overset{1}{\cancel{2}}}{1} \times \frac{22}{\underset{1}{\cancel{7}}} \times \frac{\overset{1}{\cancel{7}}}{\underset{1}{\cancel{2}}}$ ft ◄— $3\frac{1}{2}$ ft $= \frac{7}{2}$ ft

$C \approx 22$ ft

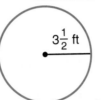
$3\frac{1}{2}$ ft

Find the circumference. Use $\frac{22}{7}$ for π.

5. $d = 7$ ft

6. $r = 14$ cm

7. $d = 21$ in.

8. $d = 35$ mm

9. $d = 1\frac{3}{4}$ ft

10. $d = 1\frac{2}{5}$ yd

11. $r = \frac{1}{2}$ yd

12. $r = 2\frac{1}{4}$ ft

Problem Solving

13. The diameter of Earth measures about 13 000 km. What is its approximate circumference?

14. A wheel has a diameter of 72 cm. How far will a point on the wheel travel in 3 complete turns?

CHALLENGE

Find the perimeter of each complex figure.

15.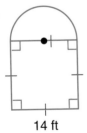
14 ft

16.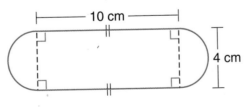
10 cm
4 cm

17.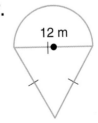
12 m

Area of a Circle

You can use the formulas for circumference of a circle and area of a parallelogram to help you find the formula for the area of a circle.

The sections of the circle at the right have been rearranged to approximate a parallelogram.

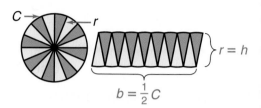

$A = b \times h$ ← Use the formula for the area of a parallelogram.

$= \frac{1}{2} C \times r$ ← Substitute $b = \frac{1}{2} C$ and $h = r$.

$= \frac{1}{2}(2\pi r) \times r$ ← Substitute $C = 2\pi r$.

$= \pi r^2$ ← Simplify.

> **Area of a Circle:** $A = \pi r^2$

▶ Find the area of the circular piece of wood.

First estimate: $A = \pi r^2$

$$A \approx 3 \times (10 \text{ ft})^2 \approx 3 \times 100 \text{ ft}^2$$

$$\approx 300 \text{ ft}^2$$

.Think.
Think: $r = 18 \text{ ft} \div 2 = 9 \text{ ft}$

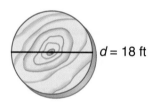

$d = 18$ ft

Then find the area using 3.14 for π.

$A = \pi r^2$

$$\approx 3.14 \times (9 \text{ ft})^2 \approx 3.14 \times 81 \text{ ft}^2$$

$$\approx 254.34 \text{ ft}^2$$

.Think.
254.34 ft² is close to the estimate of 300 ft².

Study these examples.

Find the area.

42 yd

.Think.
$r = 42 \text{ yd} \div 2$
$= 21 \text{ yd}$

Estimate: $A \approx 3 \times (20 \text{ yd})^2 = 1200 \text{ yd}^2$

Then solve: $A = \pi \times (21 \text{ yd})^2$

$$A \approx \frac{22}{\overset{}{\underset{1}{7}}} \times \frac{\overset{3}{21}}{1} \text{ yd} \times \frac{21}{1} \text{ yd}$$

$$A \approx 1386 \text{ yd}^2$$

Find the area of the shaded region.

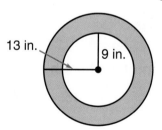

13 in.   9 in.

A = area of big circle − area of small circle

$$\approx 3.14 \times (13 \text{ in.})^2 - 3.14 \times (9 \text{ in.})^2$$

$$\approx 530.66 \text{ in.}^2 - 254.34 \text{ in.}^2$$

$$\approx 276.32 \text{ in.}^2$$

Find the area. Use 3.14 or $\frac{22}{7}$ for π. Estimate to help.

1.
5 ft

2.
10 m

3.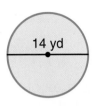
14 yd

4. $r = 3$ in. **5.** $r = 10$ cm **6.** $r = 7$ km **7.** $r = 14$ m

8. $d = 40$ yd **9.** $d = 35$ mm **10.** $r = 28$ ft **11.** $r = 36$ km

12. $r = 0.6$ m **13.** $r = 1.5$ cm **14.** $r = 3\frac{1}{2}$ yd **15.** $d = 21$ ft

Find the area of the shaded region.

16.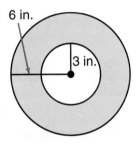
6 in.
3 in.

17.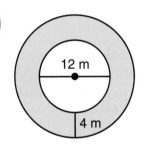
12 m
4 m

18.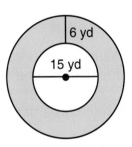
6 yd
15 yd

Problem Solving

19. A designer has a circular piece of canvas with a radius that measures 50 cm. Find its area.

20. The length of a diameter of a metal jar lid is 4.2 cm. Find its area.

21. A circular rug is 4 m across. What is the distance around the rug?

22. A circular metal part for a machine has a radius 0.1 mm long. Find the total area of 100 of these parts.

MENTAL MATH

Find the area of each circle in terms of π.

23. $r = 2$ cm $\rightarrow A = \pi r^2 \rightarrow A = \pi(2$ cm$)^2 \rightarrow A = 4\pi\,cm^2$

24. $r = 5$ ft **25.** $r = 7$ yd **26.** $r = 9$ in. **27.** $r = 10$ m

Surface Area of Cubes, Rectangular Prisms, and Cylinders

The surface area of a solid figure is the sum of the areas of all its faces. To find the surface area of a polyhedron, look at its net.

Find the surface area of a cube that measures $2\frac{1}{2}$ ft on an edge.

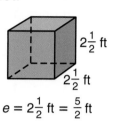

$2\frac{1}{2}$ ft

$2\frac{1}{2}$ ft

$e = 2\frac{1}{2}$ ft $= \frac{5}{2}$ ft

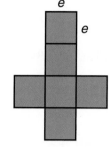

e

e

▶ **To find the surface area of a cube:**

> **Surface Area of a Cube**
> $S = 6e^2$

• Find the area of one square face.

$$A = \frac{5}{2} \text{ ft} \times \frac{5}{2} \text{ ft} = \frac{25}{4} \text{ ft}^2$$

• Multiply the area by 6 since all six faces of a cube are congruent.

$$S = \frac{\overset{3}{\cancel{6}}}{1} \times \frac{25}{\underset{2}{\cancel{4}}} \text{ ft}^2 = 37\frac{1}{2} \text{ ft}^2$$

The surface area of the cube is $37\frac{1}{2}$ ft².

Find the surface area of a rectangular prism that measures 10 cm long, 3 cm wide, and 5 cm high.

$h = 5$ cm

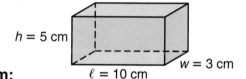

$w = 3$ cm

$\ell = 10$ cm

▶ **To find the surface area of a rectangular prism:**

> **Surface Area of a Rectangular Prism**
> $S = 2\ell w + 2wh + 2\ell h$

top	
back	
side	bottom	side
front	

w

• Find the area of one of each parallel faces and then double the area.

h

• Find the sum of the areas.

ℓ

Area of top and bottom faces →	2(10 cm × 3 cm) =	60 cm²
Area of side faces →	2(3 cm × 5 cm) =	30 cm²
Area of front and back faces →	2(10 cm × 5 cm) =	+ 100 cm²
Surface Area (S) =		190 cm²

The surface area of the rectangular prism is 190 cm².

Find the surface area of each cube.

1.
4 cm

2.
0.6 m

3.
5 ft

4.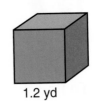
1.2 yd

5. $e = 15$ in.   **6.** $e = 8$ m   **7.** $e = 2.1$ cm   **8.** $e = 1\frac{1}{3}$ yd

Find the surface area of each rectangular prism.

9.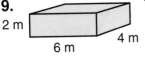
2 m   6 m   4 m

10.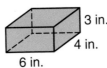
3 in.   4 in.   6 in.

11. $\ell = 9$ ft
$w = 2\frac{1}{3}$ ft
$h = 1\frac{1}{2}$ ft

12. $\ell = 5$ m
$w = 1.4$ m
$h = 5.9$ m

Surface Area of a Cylinder

Find the surface area of a cylinder with a base that has a radius of 2 in. and a height of 4 in.

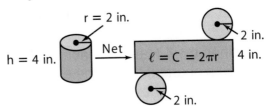

$h = 4$ in.   Net $\ell = C = 2\pi r$ $r = 2$ in.   2 in.   4 in.   2 in.

Surface Area = (2 × area of circular base) + (area of rectangular surface)
            = $(2 \times \pi r^2)$ + $(2\pi r \times h)$

> height of prism = width of rectangle

$S \approx 2 \times 3.14 \times (2 \text{ in.})^2 + 2 \times 3.14 \times 2 \text{ in.} \times 4 \text{ in.}$
$\approx 25.12 \text{ in.}^2 + 50.24 \text{ in.}^2$
$\approx 75.36 \text{ in.}^2$

> **Surface Area of a Cylinder**
> $S = 2\pi r^2 + 2\pi rh$

The surface area of the cylinder is 75.36 in.².

Find the surface area of each cylinder. Use 3.14 for π.

13.
4 in.   7 in.

14.
7 cm   9 cm

15.
13 yd   8 yd

16.
10.3 m   6.6 m

Problem Solving

17. Ed will paint the walls and ceiling of a room that is 14 ft wide by 15 ft long by 8 ft high. What is the surface area of the room?

18. Cans made by a local canning company are 6.4 cm in diameter and 12.5 cm high. How much aluminum is needed to make 100 cans?

Surface Area of Pyramids and Triangular Prisms

▶ **To find the surface area of a square pyramid:**

- Open the pyramid to form its net.
- Find the area of each of its 5 faces.
- Add the areas to get the surface area.

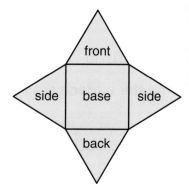

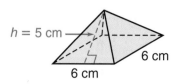

Area of base $= 6 \text{ cm} \times 6 \text{ cm} = 36 \text{ cm}^2$

Area of faces $= 4(\frac{1}{2}) (6 \text{ cm} \times 5 \text{ cm}) = +60 \text{ cm}^2$

Surface Area (S) $= 96 \text{ cm}^2$

> In this square pyramid, the 4 triangular faces are congruent.

When the 4 triangular faces of a square pyramid are congruent, use a shortcut to find the surface area. Find the area of one triangular face, multiply by 4, and add that to the area of the square base.

$S = 4 (A_{triangle}) \qquad + A_{square}$

$\quad = 4 \times \frac{1}{2} (6 \text{ cm} \times 5 \text{ cm}) + (6 \text{ cm})^2$

$\quad = \quad 60 \text{ cm}^2 \qquad\qquad + 36 \text{ cm}^2$

$\quad = \quad 96 \text{ cm}^2$

▶ **To find the surface area of a triangular prism:**

- Open the prism to form its net.
- Find the area of each of its 5 faces.
- Add the areas to get the total area.

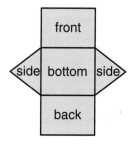

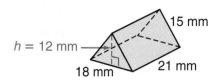

> In this triangular prism, the triangular bases are congruent and the front and back rectangular faces are congruent.

Area of bottom face $= 18 \text{ mm} \times 21 \text{ mm} = 378 \text{ mm}^2$

Area of rectangular front and back faces $= 2 (21 \text{ mm} \times 15 \text{ mm}) = 630 \text{ mm}^2$

Area of triangular bases $= 2 \times \frac{1}{2} (18 \text{ mm} \times 12 \text{ mm}) = + 216 \text{ mm}^2$

Surface Area (S) $= 1224 \text{ mm}^2$

Find the surface area of each figure.

1.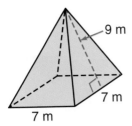
9 m
7 m
7 m

2.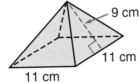
9 cm
11 cm
11 cm

3.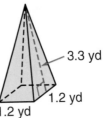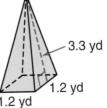
3.3 yd
1.2 yd
1.2 yd

4.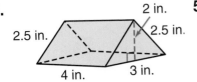
2 in.
2.5 in.
2.5 in.
4 in.
3 in.

5.
6 ft
4 ft
12 ft
5 ft   5 ft

6.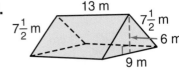
13 m
$7\frac{1}{2}$ m
$7\frac{1}{2}$ m
6 m
9 m

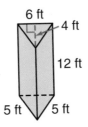

Problem Solving

Draw a diagram and solve.

7. Randolph makes a doorstop in the shape of a pyramid. The base of the pyramid is a square with 4-in. sides and triangular faces 4 in. tall. Randolph wants to cover the pyramid with felt. What is the surface area that he needs to cover?

8. The name tags on the library tables are shaped like triangular prisms. The triangular faces of the prisms have 5-cm bases, 6-cm sides, and heights of 5.45 cm. The rectangular faces of the prisms are 12 cm long. What is the surface area of each name tag?

9. Sheila makes a pyramid with a 5.5-in. square base. Each triangular face has a height of 7.8 in. Angie makes a pyramid with a 6.5-in. square base. Each triangular face has a height of 6.8 in. Whose pyramid has the greater surface area? by how many square inches?

10. David makes a triangular prism. The triangular faces of the prism have 5-ft bases. The sides of the triangles are 10.31 ft long, and their heights are twice the length of the bases. The lengths of the rectangular faces are twice the height of the triangular faces. What is the surface area of David's prism?

Write About It

11. Explain how to find the surface area of a triangular prism that has equilateral triangles as its bases.

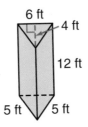
Practice

Volume of Prisms

The volume of a solid figure is the number of *cubic units* that it contains. The cubic units may be cubic centimeters, cubic inches, cubic meters, cubic feet, and so on.

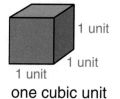

1 unit
1 unit
1 unit
one cubic unit

▶ You can count the cubes to find the volume of a cube or a rectangular prism.

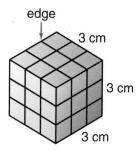

edge
3 cm
3 cm
3 cm

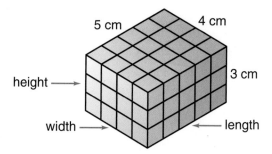

5 cm   4 cm
height →
width →
3 cm
← length

The large cube has 3 × 3 or 9 cubes in each layer, and there are 3 layers of cubes. The volume is 27 cm^3.

The rectangular prism has 5 × 4 or 20 cubes in each layer, and there are 3 layers of cubes. The volume is 60 cm^3.

▶ You can use formulas to find the volume of cubes and rectangular prisms.

Volume of a Cube
$V = $ edge $\times$ edge $\times$ edge
$V = e^3$

Volume of a Rectangular Prism
$V = $ length $\times$ width $\times$ height
$V = \ell w h$

Find the volume of the cube.

$V = e^3$

$V = (0.3 \text{ m})^3$

$V = 0.027 \text{ m}^3$

0.3 m

The volume of the cube is 0.027 m^3.

Find the volume of the rectangular prism.

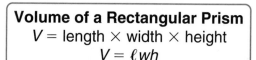

6 ft
8 ft
$10\frac{1}{2}$ ft

$V = \ell w h$

$V = \dfrac{\overset{}{21}}{\underset{1}{2}} \text{ ft} \times \dfrac{\overset{4}{8}}{1} \text{ ft} \times \dfrac{6}{1} \text{ ft}$

$V = 504 \text{ ft}^3$

The volume of the rectangular prism is 504 ft^3.

Find the volume of each cube.

1.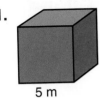
5 m

2.
10 mm

3.
0.8 cm

4. $e = 4$ in.

5. $e = 0.7$ dm

6. $e = 1\frac{1}{2}$ ft

Find the volume of each rectangular prism.

7.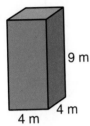
9 m
4 m
4 m

8.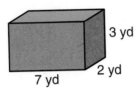
3 yd
2 yd
7 yd

9.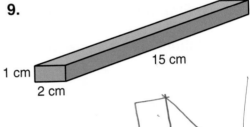
1 cm
2 cm
15 cm

10. $\ell = 3$ cm
$w = 4$ cm
$h = 5$ cm

11. $\ell = 5$ yd
$w = \frac{1}{2}$ yd
$h = 2\frac{1}{5}$ yd

12. $\ell = 5.2$ m
$w = 5$ m
$h = 6.4$ m

Problem Solving

13. Find the volume of a swimming pool that is 50 m long, 20 m wide, and 5 m deep.

14. A moving van is 12 m long, 3.5 m wide, and 3.8 m high. What is the volume of the van?

15. A storage room is shaped like a cube. It measures 5 m on each edge. What is the total volume of 10 storage rooms?

16. The inside of a cubical box measures 12 ft on each edge. How many cubes, each measuring 1 ft on each edge, will fit inside the box?

17. What happens to the volume of a cube if the length of an edge is doubled? tripled? Give examples to support your answers.

CRITICAL THINKING

Two rectangular prisms are similar solids if the ratios of the lengths of their corresponding edges are equal.

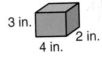
3 in.
4 in.
2 in.

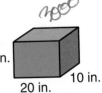
15 in.
20 in.
10 in.

18. Are the given rectangular prisms similar? Explain.

19. How does the volume of the smaller rectangular prism compare to the volume of the larger prism? Explain.

Volume of Triangular Prisms and Cylinders

You can use the formula $V = Bh$ where B is the base area and h is the height, to find the volume of triangular prisms and cylinders.

Find the volume of the triangular prism at the right.

▶ **To find the volume of a triangular prism:**

> **Volume of a Triangular Prism**
> $$V = Bh = (\tfrac{1}{2} bh)\, h$$

10 in.

height of prism

base of triangle ▶ 5 in.　4 in.

height of triangle

- Find the area of the triangular base, B.

- Multiply the area of the base, B, by the height of the prism, h. The product is the volume, V.

$B = \dfrac{1}{2} bh$

$= \dfrac{1}{2} \times 5 \text{ in.} \times 4 \text{ in.} = 10 \text{ in.}^2$

$V = Bh$
$= 10 \text{ in.}^2 \times 10 \text{ in.} = 100 \text{ in.}^3$

The volume of the triangular prism is 100 in.^{3}.

Find the volume of a cylinder that has a radius of 2 in. and a height of 8 in.

▶ **To find the volume of a cylinder:**

> **Volume of a Cylinder**
> $$V = Bh = (\pi r^2)\, h$$

$r = 2$ in.

$h = 8$ in.

- Find the area of the circular base, B.

$A = \pi r^2$
$\approx 3.14 \times (2 \text{ in.})^2 \approx 12.56 \text{ in.}^2$

- Multiply the area of the base, B, by the height of the prism, h. The product is the volume, V.

$V = Bh$
$\approx 12.56 \text{ in.}^2 \times 8 \text{ in.} \approx 100.48 \text{ in.}^3$

The volume of the cylinder is about 100.48 in.^{3}.

Find the volume of each triangular prism.

1.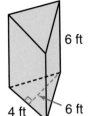
6 ft
4 ft · 6 ft

2.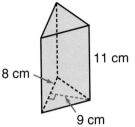
11 cm
8 cm
9 cm

3.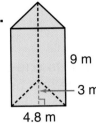
9 m
3 m
4.8 m

4.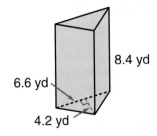
8.4 yd
6.6 yd
4.2 yd

5.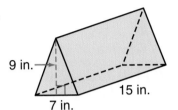
9 in.
15 in.
7 in.

6.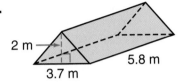
2 m
5.8 m
3.7 m

7.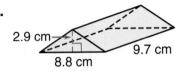
2.9 cm
9.7 cm
8.8 cm

Find the volume of each cylinder, to the nearest tenth.

8.
4 ft
7 ft

9.
1.5 m
0.9 m

10.
66 mm
46 mm

11.
5 in.
9 in.

12. $r = 3$ in.
$h = 6$ in.

13. $r = 4$ ft
$h = 10$ ft

14. $r = 5$ in.
$h = 12$ in.

15. $d = 6$ yd
$h = 8$ yd

Problem Solving

16. The height of a triangular prism is 6.5 cm and the area of its base is 24 cm². Find its volume.

17. The height of a triangular prism doubles. What happens to the volume?

18. The volume of a triangular prism is 84 cubic inches. The area of the base is 12 square inches. What is the height of the prism?

19. Caden says that the volume of a cylinder that has a diameter of 8 cm and a height of 14 cm is about 2813.44 cm³. Is Caden correct? If not what is the error?

Write About It

20. How is finding the volume of a cylinder and finding the volume of a triangular prism alike? How is it different?

Volume of Pyramids

The volume of a pyramid is equal to one-third the volume of a prism that has the same base and height.

The rectangular prism and the square pyramid below have congruent bases and have the same height. Find the volume of each.

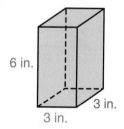

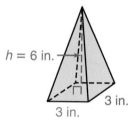

Volume of rectangular prism

$$V = \ell\, w\, h$$
$$= 3 \text{ in.} \times 3 \text{ in.} \times 6 \text{ in.}$$
$$= 54 \text{ in.}^3$$

Volume of square pyramid

$$V = \frac{1}{3}\ell\, w\, h$$
$$= \frac{1}{3}(3 \text{ in.} \times 3 \text{ in.} \times 6 \text{ in.})$$
$$= \frac{1}{3}(54 \text{ in.}^3) = 18 \text{ in.}^3$$

The volume of a pyramid is one third the product of the area of the base and the height of the pyramid.

Volume of a Pyramid

$$V = \frac{1}{3}Bh$$

Study these examples.

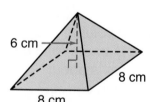

$$V = \frac{1}{3}Bh$$
$$= \frac{1}{3}(8 \text{ cm})^2 \times 6 \text{ cm}$$
$$= 128 \text{ cm}^3$$

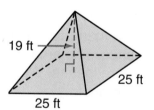

$$V = \frac{1}{3}Bh$$
$$= \frac{1}{3}(25 \text{ ft})^2 \times 19 \text{ ft}$$
$$= 3958\frac{1}{3} \text{ ft}^3$$

Find the volume of each pyramid.

1.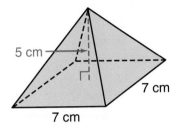
5 cm
7 cm
7 cm

2.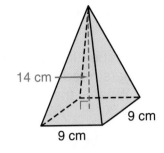
14 cm
9 cm
9 cm

3.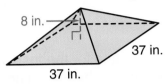
8 in.
37 in.
37 in.

4.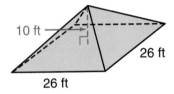
10 ft
26 ft
26 ft

5.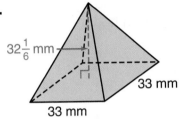
$32\frac{1}{6}$ mm
33 mm
33 mm

6.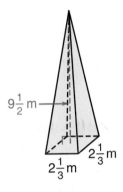
$9\frac{1}{2}$ m
$2\frac{1}{3}$ m
$2\frac{1}{3}$ m

Problem Solving

7. A pyramid has an 8-in. square base. The height of the pyramid is 1 ft. Find the volume.

8. Find the volume of a square pyramid if the edge of the base measures 100 dm and the height is 15 m.

9. The volume of Len's square pyramid is 21 yd³. The pyramid's height is 7 yd. How many yards long are the sides of the square base?

10. How many cubic feet of space are occupied by a pyramid-shaped tent with a 9-ft square base and a height of 8 ft?

11. The volume of Annabelle's square pyramid is $83\frac{1}{3}$ in.³. The sides of the pyramid's square base are each 5 inches long. What is the height of the pyramid?

Write About It

12. Explain how you would find the volume of the triangular pyramid at the right.

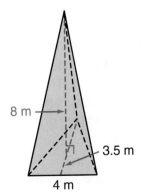
8 m
3.5 m
4 m

Use Formulas to Solve Problems

The stage for the fashion show is shaped like the diagram shown at the right. The show planners need to order carpeting to cover the stage floor. What is the area of the floor that needs to be carpeted?

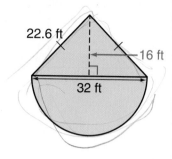

22.6 ft

16 ft

32 ft

Notice that the stage is shaped like a triangle attached to a semicircle.

To find the area of the floor, first find the area of the triangle and the area of the semicircle. Then find the sum of the areas.

- Find the area of the triangle.

$$A = \frac{1}{2} bh$$
$$= \frac{1}{2} (32 \text{ ft} \times 16 \text{ ft}) = 256 \text{ ft}^2$$

- Find the area of the semicircle.

$$A = \frac{1}{2} (\pi r^2) \longleftarrow \text{The area of a semicircle is half the area of a circle.}$$
$$A \approx \frac{1}{2} \times 3.14 \times (16 \text{ ft})^2$$
$$\approx 401.92 \text{ ft}^2$$
$$\approx 402 \text{ ft}^2 \longleftarrow \text{Round to the nearest whole number.}$$

- Find the surface area, S, by adding the two areas.

$$S = 256 \text{ ft}^2 + 402 \text{ ft}^2$$
$$= 658 \text{ ft}^2$$

So, the area of the floor that needs to be carpeted is about 658 square feet.

Problem Solving Use the figure above for exercise 1.

1. A ribbon banner will be attached around the outside border of the stage. How many feet of ribbon are needed? (Round to the nearest whole number.)

2. Originally, the show planners were going to have a stage shaped like a triangle attached to a rectangle. The triangle would have been the same size. The rectangle would have had the same length as the diameter of the semicircle and the same width as the radius of the semicircle. What would the area of a stage shaped like that be?

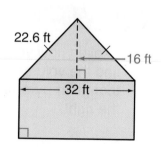

22.6 ft

16 ft

32 ft

Problem Solving

3. At the far end of the park there is a meditation garden. A new semicircular entrance to the garden will be added. What is the total area of the new garden?

37 ft

44 ft

New Entrance

4. A swimming pool is surrounded by a rectangular walkway. A committee decides to redo the walkway. What is the total area that needs to be redone?

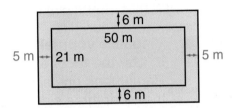

6 m
50 m
5 m ↔ 21 m ↔ 5 m
6 m

5. Erika is reseeding the horse pasture. The pasture is shaped like a rectangle, with semicircles at each end. If it costs $0.85 to reseed 1 square yard, how much will it cost to reseed the pasture?

39 yd

95 yd

6. The walkway around the back half of the bandstand will be removed and replaced with a hedge. How many square feet of walkway will be removed?

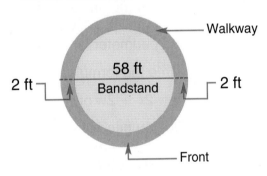

Walkway

58 ft
Bandstand
2 ft
2 ft

Front

7. Mr. McAllister is going to paint the front of his barn. How many square feet does he need to cover with paint?

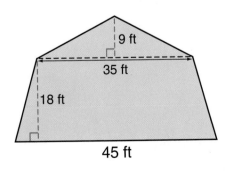

9 ft
35 ft
18 ft
45 ft

8. The triangular sign at the entrance to the park will be enlarged by placing a 1 foot border around each side. What will be the area of the new sign?

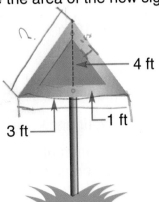

4 ft
3 ft
1 ft

Problem-Solving Strategy:
Use Drawings/Formulas

Larry wants to fence in a rectangular garden that is 10 m by 4 m. If he uses 10 m of his house as one side, how much fencing does he need to buy for the other three sides?

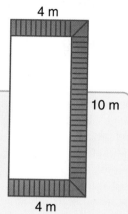

4 m

10 m

4 m

Read

Visualize yourself in the problem as you reread it. List the facts and the question.

Remember, one side is the house and the other three sides are fencing.

Facts: 10 m length
4 m width

Question: How much fencing is needed?

Plan

Look at the diagram.

To find the amount of fencing needed to go *around* the garden, will you need to know the area or the perimeter? Perimeter

Write the formula for perimeter of a rectangle.

$P = 2\ell + 2w$ or $P = 2(\ell + w)$

Do you need fencing around the *four* sides of the garden? No. One of the lengths is the house, so rewrite the formula using 1 length and 2 widths.

$P = \ell + 2w$

> Remember: One side of the house serves as the other length.

Solve

$P = 10\text{ m} + 2 \times 4\text{ m}$
$P = 10\text{ m} + 8\text{ m}$
$P = 18\text{ m}$

Larry will need 18 m of fencing.

Check

Is your answer reasonable?

The amount of fencing should be 10 m less than the perimeter of a 10 m by 4 m rectangle.

Solve. Draw a diagram and write a formula.

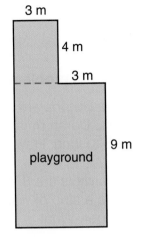

3 m

4 m

3 m

9 m

playground

1. The new town playground has the measurements shown in the drawing. What is the total area of the playground?

Read ▶ Visualize yourself in the problem above as you reread it. List the facts and the question.

      Facts: Playground measurements shown in diagram—9 m, 3 m, 4 m, 3 m

      Question: What is the total area of the playground?

Plan ▶ Divide the playground into 2 rectangles.

      Use the formula $A = \ell w$ to find the area of each. Then add:

      Area = (4 m × 3 m) + (9 m × 6 m)

▶ **Solve** ⋯⋯⋯▶ **Check**

2. A storage box in the shape of a cube measures 1.4 m on each edge. What is the total volume of 20 storage boxes?

3. How many feet of fencing are needed to enclose a circular swimming pool that has a 25-ft diameter if there is a 2.5-ft deck between the edge of the pool and the fence?

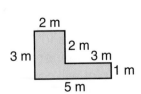

4. A children's square wading pool has a side of 5 ft. How many cubic feet of water are needed to fill the pool 1.5 ft deep?

5. Mr. Graycloud fenced in a part of his backyard for his dog. Find the area of the dog's yard. The dimensions are shown in the drawing.

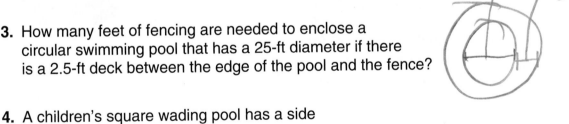

2 m

3 m

2 m
3 m

1 m

5 m

6. Cathy used gold trim around the edge of both the circle and the square at right. About how many centimeters of trim did Cathy use?

6 cm

Solve each problem and explain the method you used.

1. The Durans are renovating their apartment. Mrs. Duran measures a strip of wallpaper 2.5 m long. How many millimeters long is it?

2. The walls are 8 ft 10 in. high. Mrs. Duran cuts a strip of wallpaper that is 16 in. longer. What is the length of the strip?

3. Regina is refinishing an old wooden trunk. It measures $3\frac{1}{2}$ ft long by 2 ft wide by $1\frac{1}{2}$ ft high. What is its volume?

4. Regina will cover all surfaces of the trunk in problem 3 with translucent paper. How much paper will she need?

5. The living room is a rectangle with one side that measures 3.6 m and another side that measures 4.27 m. What is the perimeter of the living room?

6. The length of a radius of one paint can lid is 9.5 cm. What is the circumference of the lid?

7. Mr. Duran worked in the apartment for 7 h 20 min on Saturday and 5 h 47 min on Sunday. How much longer did he work on Saturday?

8. The dining alcove has this triangular shape. What is the area of the dining alcove floor?

9. Regina wants to paint the dining alcove floor with copper paint. The label says that 1 pint will cover 8000 in.^{2} Will she need more than 1 pint to cover the floor? (*Hint:* 144 in.^{2} = 1 ft^2)

Dining Alcove

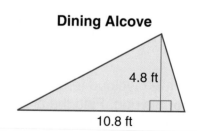

4.8 ft

10.8 ft

10. Alvin buys a can of paint that has a diameter of 4 in. and a height of 6 in. Find its volume.

Choose a strategy from the list or use another strategy you know to solve each problem.

11. Ed paints Regina's room. He uses $\frac{3}{4}$ qt of lavender paint for the trim. How many fluid ounces of paint does he use?

12. Ed uses $\frac{1}{4}$ gal of white paint on the bedroom walls and $\frac{1}{3}$ gal of the same paint in the parents' room. How much paint is left in the 1-gallon container?

13. The Durans buy a circular rug for the bathroom. The rug has a circumference of about 12.56 ft. Estimate its diameter.

14. Mr. Duran has 3 boards that are each 7 ft 9 in. long. If he uses them to build 15 ft 8 in. of shelving, will he have enough left over to build a flower box that uses 6 ft 3 in. of board?

15. The hallway is a rectangle with a length of 14.5 ft and a width of 5.25 ft. Roberto estimates that they will need about 70 ft² of carpeting to cover the hallway floor. Is his estimate reasonable?

16. Regina buys a paperweight shaped like a triangular prism for her desk. Its base measures 3 cm on a side and has a height of 2 cm. If the paperweight is 5 cm in height, what is its volume?

Strategy File

Use These Strategies
Use More Than One Step
Use Drawings/Formulas
Use Simpler Numbers
Write an Equation

Use the drawings for problems 17–20.

17. What is the perimeter of Alvin's room?

18. What is the area of Regina's room?

19. Is the perimeter of Regina's room greater or less than 32 ft? Explain.

20. Is the area of Alvin's room greater or less than the area of Regina's room? by how much?

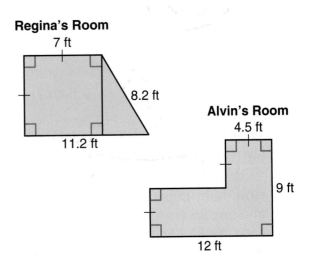

Regina's Room
7 ft
8.2 ft
11.2 ft

Alvin's Room
4.5 ft
9 ft
12 ft

Check Your Progress
Lessons 1–21

Rename each unit of measure. *(See pp. 448–461.)*

1. 40 m = __?__ km

2. 1.5 cm = __?__ mm

3. 8000 mL = __?__ L

4. 4.8 kg = __?__ g

5. 30 in. = __?__ ft

6. $3\frac{1}{4}$ gal = __?__ qt

7. 64 oz = __?__ lb

8. 20 lb ≈ __?__ kg

9. 5 km ≈ __?__ mi

Measure the line segment to the nearest centimeter and millimeter.

10. ●────────────●

Compute.

11.   7 ft 5 in.
    + 6 ft 9 in.

12.   9 h 35 min
    − 2 h 40 min

Find the perimeter or circumference and area. *(See pp. 462–473.)*

13.
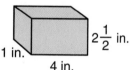
3.2 m
10 m

14.
8.5 ft
3 ft
16 ft

15.
4 in.
8 in.
6 in.
9.5 in.

16.
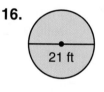
21 ft

Find the surface area and volume. *(See pp. 474–485.)*

17.
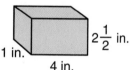
$2\frac{1}{2}$ in.
1 in.
4 in.

18.
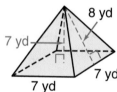
8 yd
7 yd
7 yd
7 yd

19.
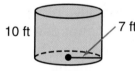
10 ft
7 ft

Problem Solving
(See pp. 484–485, 486–489.)

20. What is the area of a parallelogram with $b = 12$ cm and $h = 9.5$ cm?

21. Find the surface area and volume of a cube with $e = 1\frac{1}{2}$ ft.

22. What is the perimeter of a rectangular lawn 30 yd long and 25 yd wide?

23. Find the area of a square mirror 5.2 dm on each side.

24. How many cubic centimeters are in a box 85 cm long, 25 cm wide, and 120 cm deep?

25. A dog is tied to a pole by a 15-m leash. What is the area in which the dog can run?

(See *Still More Practice*, p. 531.)

Logic: Conjunctions and Disjunctions

In logic, two statements can be combined to form a compound statement using *and*, or a compound statement using *or.*

It is raining and I am leaving.   It is raining or I am leaving.

▶ A compound statement using *and* is called a conjunction.
It is true only when *both* original statements are *true.*

A right angle measures 90°   and   a straight angle measures 180°.   True

| True | | True |

▶ A compound statement using *or* is called a disjunction.
It is true when *both* of the original statements are *true*
or when *one* of the original statements is *true.*

A rhombus has 4 sides   or   a square has 4 sides.   True

| True | | True |

Eleven is a prime number   or   eleven is a composite number.   True

| True | | False |

A rectangle is a space figure   or   a prism is a plane figure.   False

| False | | False |

**Write a conjunction statement and a disjunction statement
for each exercise. Then tell whether each is *True* or *False.***

1. A robin is a bird.
A dime is worth exactly 5¢.

2. A boat can float.
A plane can fly.

3. Eighteen is a prime number.
One is a composite number.

4. $144 \div 12 = 12$
$56 \times 5 = 280$

5. $2400 + 80 = 2320$
$75 - 69 = 6$

6. $(17 - 3) \times 4 = 5$
$147 < 58 + 83$

Rename each unit of measure.

1. 6.5 km = ___?___ m

2. 14.2 mm = ___?___ cm

3. 23 L = ___?___ mL

4. 58.3 L = ___?___ kL

5. 5 kg = ___?___ g

6. 9 t = ___?___ kg

7. 12 cm ≈ ___?___ in.

8. 48 L ≈ ___?___ gal

9. $5\frac{1}{4}$ lb = ___?___ oz

Measure the line segment to the nearest $\frac{1}{8}$ in. and $\frac{1}{16}$ in.

10.
A   X

Find the perimeter and area.

11.
6 yd, 3 yd

12.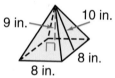
8 in.   12 in.
4 in.
16 in.

Find the surface area and volume.

13.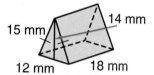
15 mm, 14 mm, 12 mm, 18 mm

14.
31 cm
14 cm

15.
9 in.   10 in.
8 in.
8 in.

Problem Solving

Use a strategy or strategies you have learned.

16. Which has a greater volume: a safe in the shape of a rectangular prism that is 6 ft wide, 6 ft long, and 2 ft deep or a cubical safe that measures 4 ft on each edge? How much greater?

Tell About It

17. What happens to the area or volume if you double each dimension in the following formulas: $A = \ell \times w$; $A = \frac{1}{2} \times b \times h$; $V = \ell \times w \times h$? Explain.

Performance Assessment

Solve each problem.

18. The perimeter of a rectangle is 60 yd. The length is twice the width. Find the length and width of the rectangle.

19. The area of a rectangle is 128 yd². The length is twice the width. Find the length and width of the rectangle.

Test Preparation

Choose the best answer.

1. $8.2 \text{ g} = \underline{\ ?\ } \text{ kg}$

    a. 0.0082
    b. 0.082
    c. 820
    d. 8200

2. The number 1.56×10^{-2} is equivalent to

    a. 156
    b. 0.156
    c. 0.0156
    d. 0.00156

3. What is the sum of the measures of the interior angles of an octagon?

    a. 360°
    b. 1080°
    c. 1440°
    d. 1880°

4. If the height of a trapezoid measures 10 cm and the bases measure 12 cm and 14 cm, what is the area of the trapezoid?

    a. 130 cm²   **b.** 200 cm²
    c. 230 cm²   **d.** 260 cm²

5. What is the circumference of a circle that has a diameter of 12 ft? (Use 3.14 for π.)

    a. 12 ft   **b.** 18.84 ft
    c. 37.68 ft   **d.** 113.04 ft

6. Which set of numbers is ordered from least to greatest?

    a. $-1\frac{1}{4}, 0.41, 0.3, \frac{5}{2}$

    b. $\frac{5}{2}, -1\frac{1}{4}, 0.3, 0.41$

    c. $0.41, 0.3, -1\frac{1}{4}, \frac{5}{2}$

    d. $-1\frac{1}{4}, 0.3, 0.41, \frac{5}{2}$

7. Billy bought supplies for $40. If the sales tax is 7%, what was the total cost?

    a. $2.80
    b. $37.20
    c. $42.80
    d. $47.00

8. If $a = 2$ and $b = {}^{-}7$, what is the value of $|a| - |b|$?

    a. 5
    b. 9
    c. ⁻5
    d. ⁻9

9. Find the surface area.

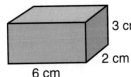

    a. 24 cm²
    b. 36 cm²
    c. 72 cm²
    d. 84 cm²

10. Rose has a table in the shape of a pentagon. Beth has a hexagonal table. What is the ratio of the number of sides of Beth's table to the number of sides of Rose's table?

    a. $5:7$ **b.** $5:6$
    c. $6:5$ **d.** $6:7$

11. What is the value of y in the equation $y + 195 = 276$?

    a. 1.4   **b.** 81
    c. 90   **d.** 471

12. Rename as a mixed number in simplest form.

    275%

    a. $1\frac{3}{4}$

    b. $2\frac{2}{3}$

    c. $2\frac{3}{4}$

    d. $2\frac{75}{100}$

13. The circle graph shows how the Dey family spends its income each month. What is the degree measure of the central angle that represents the percentage of income spent on food?

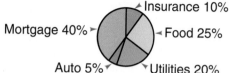

Insurance 10%

Mortgage 40%

Food 25%

Auto 5%

Utilities 20%

a. 25°
b. 50°
c. 90°
d. 360°

14. Bob chooses an integer at random from 1 to 6. What is the probability that the integer he chooses is a prime number?

a. $\frac{5}{6}$ b. $\frac{4}{6}$

c. $\frac{3}{6}$ d. $\frac{2}{6}$

15. Which letter has line symmetry but *not* point symmetry?

a. T   b. H

c. N   d. S

16. The weights of all students in Grade 6 are arranged from least to greatest. Which measure of central tendency separates the top half of the data set from the bottom half?

a. mean   b. median
c. mode   d. not given

17. A rocket car travels at a rate of 640 mph. How much time would it take for the car to travel 384 mi at this rate?

a. 36 min   b. 256 min
c. 245 min   d. 1.7 h

18. In △BCD, m∠C = 70°, m∠CDE = 130°, and side $\overline{BD}$ is extended to A and to E. Find m∠CBA.

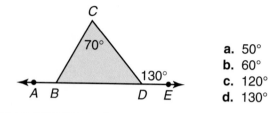

a. 50°
b. 60°
c. 120°
d. 130°

19. Mary bought a CD that cost $18.99 and paid $20.51, including sales tax. What was the rate of the sales tax?

a. 8%   b. 5%
c. 3%   d. 2%

20. If the temperature in Boston is 23°F, what is the temperature in degrees Celsius? [Use the formula $C = \frac{5}{9}(F - 32)$.]

a. ⁻5°C   b. ⁻45°C
c. 5°C   d. 45°C

21. In a certain quadrilateral, two opposite sides are parallel and the other two opposite sides are *not* congruent. The quadrilateral could be a

a. rhombus   b. square
c. parallelogram   d. trapezoid

22. The sum of Rob's age and Ann's age is 33 years. If Ann's age is represented by x, Rob's age is represented by

a. 33 − x   b. x − 33
c. x + 33   d. 33x

Explain how you solved each problem. Show all your work.

23. Carrie's sailboat has two sails that are similar triangles. The larger sail has sides of 10 ft, 24 ft, and 26 ft. If the shortest side of the smaller sail is 6 ft, what is the perimeter of the smaller sail?

24. How much greater is the volume of a cubical storage bin $4\frac{1}{2}$ ft on each edge than a sandbox that is 6 ft long, 5 ft wide, and 2 ft deep?

More Concepts in Algebra

Praise Song for a Drummer

The drum drums health,
The drum drums wealth,
He takes his wife six hundred thousand cowries.
The drum drums health,
The drum drums wealth,
He takes his son six hundred thousand cowries.
The drum drums health,
The drum drums wealth,

Mary Smith, translator

In this chapter you will:

Solve two-step equations and graph transformations
Learn about functions and algebraic patterns
Solve problems using more than one method

Critical Thinking/Finding Together

Research the use of the cowrie as money in Africa and elsewhere. Jamal owed Bob $27. From the $28 he earned from a part-time job, Jamal bought a $9 book and gave the rest to Bob toward his debt. If one cowrie = $.95, about how many cowries is his debt now?

14-1

Two-Step Equations

Mario ordered two large plain pizzas for delivery and paid a total of $21, including a $3 tip. How much did each pizza cost?

To find how much, write and solve a two-step equation. A two-step equation involves two operations.

Let p represent the cost of one pizza.

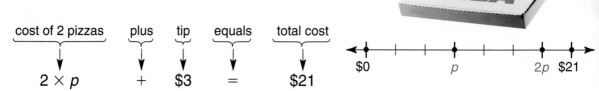

cost of 2 pizzas	plus	tip	equals	total cost
$2 \times p$	$+$	$\$3$	$=$	$\$21$

$2p + \$3 - \$3 = \$21 - \$3$ ◄—— Subract $3 from both sides.

$\qquad 2p = \$18$ ◄—— Simplify.

$\qquad 2p \div 2 = \$18 \div 2$ ◄—— Divide both sides by 2.

$\qquad p = \$9$ ◄— solution

Check: $2p + \$3 = \$21 \longrightarrow 2 \times \$9 + \$3 \overset{?}{=} \$21$ ◄—— Substitute $9 for p.

$\qquad \$21 = \$21$ True

Each pizza cost $9.

Study these examples.

Solve: $\frac{x}{7} + 1.2 = 8.2$

$\frac{x}{7} + 1.2 - 1.2 = 8.2 - 1.2$

$\qquad \frac{x}{7} = 7$

$\qquad \frac{x}{7} \cdot 7 = 7 \cdot 7$

$\qquad x = 49$

Check: $\frac{49}{7} + 1.2 \overset{?}{=} 8.2$

$\qquad 8.2 = 8.2$ True

Solve: $\frac{60}{n} - 2.4 = 27.6$

$\frac{60}{n} - 2.4 + 2.4 = 27.6 + 2.4$

$\qquad \frac{60}{n} = 30$

$\qquad \frac{60}{n} \cdot n = 30 \cdot n$

$\qquad 60 = 30n$

$\qquad 60 \div 30 = 30n \div 30$

$\qquad 2 = n$

Check: $\frac{60}{2} - 2.4 \overset{?}{=} 27.6$

$\qquad 27.6 = 27.6$ True

Solve and check.

1. $7z + 4 = 46$

2. $8i - 5 = 43$

3. $65 + 9e = 173$

4. $6.4u - 12 = 84$

5. $66.7 = 4.7h + 15$

6. $0.2\,m - 13 = 20.75$

7. $\dfrac{y}{6} + 14 = 51$

8. $\dfrac{j}{7} - 12 = 79$

9. $\dfrac{q}{12} + 65 = 90$

10. $\dfrac{117}{s} - 5 = 4$

11. $14 = \dfrac{7}{10}b + 8$

12. $\dfrac{9}{t} + 10 = 37$

13. $\dfrac{3y}{10} - 3 = 12$

14. $\dfrac{4x}{3} + 1.2 = 2.4$

15. $4.2 = 9.2 + 3r - 7.1$

Problem Solving

Write an equation, then solve.

16. If three times a certain number is increased by 5, the sum is 23. Find the number.

17. Eleven subtracted from twice a number is equal to 7. Find the number.

18. Two tenths less than five times a certain number is equal to 0.09. Find the number.

19. Six thousandths more than half a certain number is equal to 0.03. Find the number.

20. Five dollars more than half the price of a book is equal to $20. What is the full price of the book?

21. Brenda bought 12 bagels. She paid a total of $5.13, including a 75¢ discount. What was the cost per bagel?

22. A meteorologist says that the 52°F temperature is 8° less than twice the average high temperature for the day. What is the day's average high temperature?

23. In the auditorium, there are 15 equal rows of seats on the floor, and 45 seats in the balcony. There is a total of 420 seats. How many seats are in each row on the floor?

DO YOU REMEMBER?

Find the area of each figure.

24.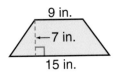
9 in.
7 in.
15 in.

25.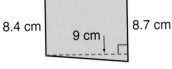
8.4 cm
9 cm
8.7 cm

26.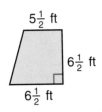
$5\frac{1}{2}$ ft
$6\frac{1}{2}$ ft
$6\frac{1}{2}$ ft

Addition and Subtraction Equations with Integers

From 9:00 P.M. to 6:00 A.M., the temperature rose 7 degrees Celsius. At 6:00 A.M., it was 2°C. What was the temperature at 9:00 P.M.?

To find the temperature at 9:00 P.M., write and solve an equation.

Let t represent the temperature at 9:00 P.M.

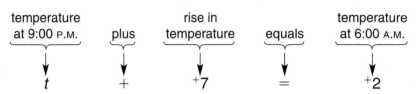

temperature at 9:00 P.M.	plus	rise in temperature	equals	temperature at 6:00 A.M.
t	$+$	$^+7$	$=$	$^+2$

$$t + {}^+7 = {}^+2$$
$$t + {}^+7 - {}^+7 = {}^+2 - {}^+7 \quad \longleftarrow \text{Subract } {}^+7 \text{ from both sides.}$$
$$t = {}^-5 \longleftarrow \boxed{\text{solution}}$$

Check: $^-5 + {}^+7 \overset{?}{=} {}^+2 \quad \longleftarrow \text{Substitute } {}^-5 \text{ for } t.$
$$^+2 = {}^+2 \quad \text{True}$$

The temperature at 9:00 P.M. was $^-5°C$.

Remember:
Adding or subtracting the same amount from both sides of a true equation results in a true statement.

Study these examples.

Solve: $n - {}^+16 = {}^-40$

$$n - {}^+16 + {}^+16 = {}^-40 + {}^+16$$
$$n = {}^-24$$

Check: $^-24 - {}^+16 \overset{?}{=} {}^-40$
$$^-40 = {}^-40 \quad \text{True}$$

Solve: $h + {}^-11 + {}^-4 = {}^-9$

$$h + {}^-11 + {}^-4 = {}^-9$$
$$h + {}^-15 = {}^-9$$
$$h + {}^-15 - {}^-15 = {}^-9 - {}^-15$$
$$h = {}^+6$$

Check: $^+6 + {}^-11 + {}^-4 \overset{?}{=} {}^-9$
$$^-9 = {}^-9 \quad \text{True}$$

Complete each step to solve and check each equation.

1. $$w + {}^+9 = {}^+51$$
$$w + {}^+9 - \underline{\ ?\ } = {}^+51 - \underline{\ ?\ }$$
$$w = \underline{\ ?\ }$$

Check: $\underline{\ ?\ } + {}^+9 \overset{?}{=} {}^+51$
$$\underline{\ ?\ } = {}^+51$$

2. $$f - {}^+14 = {}^-8$$
$$f - {}^+14 + \underline{\ ?\ } = {}^-8 + \underline{\ ?\ }$$
$$f = \underline{\ ?\ }$$

Check: $\underline{\ ?\ } - {}^+14 \overset{?}{=} {}^-8$
$$\underline{\ ?\ } = {}^-8$$

Solve and check.

3. $r + {}^-7 = {}^-19$

4. $y - {}^+85 = {}^-74$

5. $j + {}^+45 = {}^-9$

6. $g - {}^-17 = {}^+39$

7. $u + {}^-41 = {}^-52$

8. $d - {}^+61 = {}^+38$

9. ${}^-43 = c + {}^+69$

10. ${}^-50 = q - {}^-29$

11. ${}^+17 = p + {}^-69$

12. $a + {}^+13 + {}^+15 = {}^-75$

13. ${}^-23 + x + {}^+17 = {}^-96$

14. ${}^-33 + y = {}^-39 - {}^+87$

15. $r - ({}^+24 + {}^+8) = {}^-57$

16. ${}^-46 = z - ({}^-30 + {}^+76)$

Problem Solving

Write an equation and then solve.

17. Seven more than a number is ${}^-18$. Find the number.

18. Eighteen less a number is ${}^-80$. Find the number.

19. A number decreased by ${}^-8$ is ${}^-21$. Find the number.

20. When ${}^-4$ is added to the sum of ${}^-5$ and a number, the result is ${}^-7$. Find the number.

21. From 4:00 P.M. to 3:00 A.M., the temperature dropped 6 degrees Fahrenheit. At 3:00 A.M., the temperature was ${}^-4°F$. What was the temperature at 4:00 P.M.?

22. Jill played a card game with red negative cards and yellow positive cards. After she drew 4 yellow cards, her score was ${}^+11$. What was her score before she drew the 4 yellow cards?

23. From 6:30 A.M. to 4:30 P.M. on Monday, the temperature rose 12°C. From 4:30 P.M. on Monday to 5:45 A.M. on Tuesday, the temperature dropped 7°C. The temperature at 5:45 A.M. on Tuesday was ${}^-2°C$. What was the temperature at 6:30 A.M. on Monday?

24. Mateo played the same card game that Jill played in problem 22. He drew some cards. After he drew 7 red cards, he gave back 2 yellow cards. His final score was ${}^-3$. What was his score before he drew the 7 red cards?

CHALLENGE Algebra

Solve and check.

25. $h - {}^+2.3 = {}^-6.1 + {}^-2.2$

26. ${}^-5.6 + m = {}^-1.4 - {}^+2.2$

27. $c - ({}^+1.72 + {}^+3.28) = {}^-9$

28. ${}^-8.9 = k - ({}^-2.6 + {}^+1.7)$

Multiplication and Division Equations with Integers

Over a 9-month period, Gina's stocks showed an average loss of ⁻$16 per month. What was the total loss in Gina's stocks for that 9-month period?

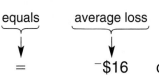

| 1d 1wk 1mo 3mo 6mo 1y (2y) |
| 16 |
| 13 |
| 10 |
| 7 |
| May Sept. Jan. May Sept. Jan. |
| Markets closed |

To find the total amount, write and solve an equation.

Let t represent the total loss.

total loss	divided by	number of months	equals	average loss
t	÷	9	=	⁻$16

or $\dfrac{t}{9} = {}^-\$16$

$$\dfrac{t}{9} = {}^-\$16$$

$\dfrac{t}{9} \cdot 9 = {}^-\$16 \cdot 9$ ⟵ Multiply both sides by 9.

$t = {}^-\$144$ ⟵ solution

Check: $\dfrac{{}^-\$144}{9} \overset{?}{=} {}^-\$16$ ⟵ Substitute ⁻$144 for t.

$^-\$16 = {}^-\$16$ True

Remember:
• The product or quotient of two integers having the *same sign* is *positive*.
• The product or quotient of two integers having *different signs* is *negative*.

The total loss for Gina's stocks over a 9-month period was ⁻$144.

Study these examples.

Solve: $^-3m = {}^+48$

$^-3m \div {}^-3 = {}^+48 \div {}^-3$

$m = {}^-16$

Check: $^-3(^-16) \overset{?}{=} {}^+48$

$^+48 = {}^+48$ True

Solve: $^+7f + {}^-13 = {}^-90$

$^+7f + {}^-13 - {}^-13 = {}^-90 - {}^-13$

$^+7f = {}^-77$

$^+7f \div {}^+7 = {}^-77 \div {}^+7$

$f = {}^-11$

Check: $^+7(^-11) + {}^-13 \overset{?}{=} {}^-90$

$^-90 = {}^-90$ True

Complete each step to solve and check each equation.

1.
$$^-5a = {}^+135$$
$$^-5a \div \underline{\ ?\ } = {}^+135 \div \underline{\ ?\ }$$
$$a = \underline{\ ?\ }$$

Check: $^-5 \times \underline{\ ?\ } \overset{?}{=} {}^+135$
$$\underline{\ ?\ } = {}^+135$$

2.
$$k \div {}^-6 = {}^-18$$
$$k \div {}^-6 \times \underline{\ ?\ } = {}^-18 \times \underline{\ ?\ }$$
$$k = \underline{\ ?\ }$$

Check: $\underline{\ ?\ } \div {}^-6 \overset{?}{=} {}^-18$
$$\underline{\ ?\ } = {}^-18$$

Solve and check.

3. $^-7r = {}^-49$

4. $^+25j = {}^-125$

5. $y \div {}^+15 = {}^-4$

6. $g \div {}^-17 = {}^-9$

7. $^+12 = u \div {}^-11$

8. $^-16d = {}^+80$

9. $c \div {}^+23 = {}^+3$

10. $^+14q = {}^+56$

11. $^-17c + {}^-42 = {}^+43$

12. $^+8t - {}^-96 = {}^+64$

13. $^-29 = {}^+77g + {}^+125$

14. $\frac{b}{^+4} - {}^+16 = {}^-78$

15. $^-42 = \frac{w}{^-11} + {}^-35$

16. $\frac{e}{^-12} - {}^-14 = {}^-36$

17. $x \div {}^+25 + {}^-24 = {}^+1$

18. $^+4 = {}^-160 + {}^+4k$

19. $^-21h - {}^-13 = {}^-134$

Problem Solving

Write an equation and then solve.

20. When a number is divided by $^-9$, the result is $^-11$. What is the number?

21. When a number is multiplied by $^+15$, the result is $^-165$. What is the number?

22. Eight more than $^-3$ times a certain number is equal to $^-1$. What is the number?

23. When 7 is subtracted from twice a certain number, the result is $^-25$. What is the number?

24. After a starting temperature of $^+9°C$, the temperature changed in equal increments for each of 7 days. The temperature at the end of the 7 days was $^-5°C$. How much did the temperature change each day?

25. Over a 9-month period, Bo's store showed a total loss of $^-\$190$. This included 8 months of losses and one month with a profit of $^+\$18$. What integer represents the average monthly loss in the 8 unprofitable months?

TEST PREPARATION

Solve for x. Choose the best answer.

26. $^+12x - {}^-108 = {}^+336$

    A $x = {}^+37$ **B** $x = {}^+19$

    C $x = {}^-19$ **D** $x = {}^-37$

27. $\frac{x}{^-46} + {}^-17 = {}^-28$

    F $^-2070$ **G** $^-506$

    H $^+2070$ **J** $^+506$

Functions and Ordered Pairs

One of the tallest persons in medical history was Robert Wadlow, born in Alton, Illinois, in 1918. On his 13th birthday, he stood 7 ft $1\frac{3}{4}$ in. By age 17, he had reached more than 8 ft in height.

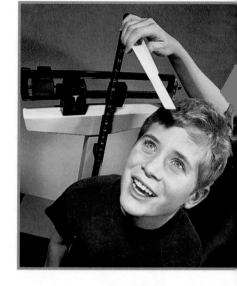

The function table below shows his height in inches as a function of his age. A **function** is a set of **ordered pairs** (x, y) in which there is only one y-value for each x-value.

Age in years (x)	5	8	10	20
Height in inches (y)	64	72	77	103

The pairs of numbers in the table can be written as ordered pairs (x, y).

(5, 64)   (8, 72)   (10, 77)   (20, 103) ← These ordered pairs do not have an obvious rule that relates the second number in the pair to the first number.

▶ You can write ordered pairs for a function because they are related in a specific way, called the **function rule**. The ordered pairs below are related by the rule: $y = x + {}^+3$.

Rule: $y = x + {}^+3$		
x	y	Ordered Pair
$^+6$	$^+6 + {}^+3 = {}^+9$	$(^+6, {}^+9)$
0	$0 + {}^+3 = {}^+3$	$(0, {}^+3)$
$^-2$	$^-2 + {}^+3 = {}^+1$	$(^-2, {}^+1)$

Use the function rule to complete each function table.

1.

Rule: $y = x + {}^+5$		
x	y	Ordered Pair
$^-6$	?	?
$^+12$	?	?
$^+48$	?	?

2.

Rule: $y = x - {}^+4$		
x	y	Ordered Pair
$^-12$	?	?
$^+4$	?	?
$^+73$	?	?

Practice

Use the function rule to find the value of *y* in each ordered pair.

	Function Rule	Ordered Pairs			
3.	$y = x + {}^+4$	$(^-11, y)$	$(0, y)$	$(^+6, y)$	$(^+9, y)$
4.	$y = x - {}^+8$	$(^-20, y)$	$(^-12, y)$	$(^+8, y)$	$(^+35, y)$
5.	$y = {}^-3x$	$(^+10, y)$	$(0, y)$	$(^-3, y)$	$(^-15, y)$
6.	$y = x \div {}^+2$	$(^-40, y)$	$(^-26, y)$	$(^-14, y)$	$(0, y)$

Use the function rule to complete each function table.

7. $d = 5r$

r	3	5	9	1	10	12
d	?	?	?	?	?	?
(*r, d*)	?	?	?	?	?	?

8. $d = r \div 3$

r	6	12	21	15	36	48
d	?	?	?	?	?	?
(*r, d*)	?	?	?	?	?	?

9.

Rule: $y = {}^-2 (x + {}^+5)$		
x	*y*	Ordered Pair
$^-4$	?	?
$^-6$	?	?
$^+8$	?	?

10.

Rule: $y = {}^+2 (x + {}^-7)$		
x	*y*	Ordered Pair
$^-9$	?	?
$^+11$	?	?
0	?	?

The approximate age of a lobster can be found from its weight. Copy and complete the function table. Then write a rule relating *x* and *y*.

11.

Weight in pounds, *x*	2	3	4	5	6
Age in years, *y*	14	21	28	?	?
(*x, y*)	(2, 14)	?	?	?	?

CHALLENGE Algebra

12. Complete the table at the right.
Explain how to find the *x*-values.

x	?	?	?	?
$y = 3x - 1$	5	8	11	14

Graph Ordered Pairs

A coordinate plane, or grid, is formed by a horizontal and vertical number line, called coordinate axes.

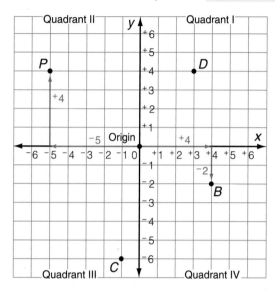

The horizontal axis is the *x*-axis.

The vertical axis is the *y*-axis.

The point at which the two axes intersect is called the origin.

The axes divide the coordinate plane into four quadrants.

▶ An ordered pair (*x, y*) locates a point on a coordinate plane. The numbers, *x* and *y*, are called coordinates.

> The coordinates of the *origin* are (0, 0).

▶ To graph, or locate, a point on a grid:

- Start at (0, 0). Move *right* or *left* the number of units indicated by the *x-coordinate*. The ⁺sign tells you to move right and the ⁻sign tells you to move left.

- Then, from that point, move *up* or *down* the number of units indicated by the *y-coordinate*. The ⁺sign tells you to move up and the ⁻sign tells you to move down.

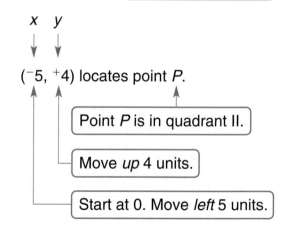

Study these examples.

(⁺4, ⁻2) locates point *B*.	(⁻1, ⁻6) locates point *C*.	(⁺3, ⁺4) locates point *D*.
right *down* 4 2	*left* *down* 1 6	*right* *up* 3 4
Point *B* is in quadrant IV.	Point *C* is in quadrant III.	Point *D* is in quadrant I.

Use the grid for exercises 1–19.
Name the ordered pair for each point.

1. D   2. I   3. B

4. G   5. M   6. J

7. H   8. L   9. E

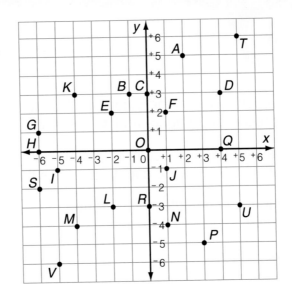

Name the point for each
ordered pair.

10. ($^-$4, $^+$3)   11. ($^+$1, $^+$2)

12. ($^+$3, $^-$5)   13. (0, $^-$3)

14. ($^+$4, 0)   15. ($^-$5, $^-$6)

Name the points located in the given quadrant or axis.

16. quadrant I   17. quadrant II   18. quadrant III

19. quadrant IV   20. x-axis   21. y-axis

Problem Solving

22. Annette graphed point A on a coordinate plane at ($^-$2, $^+$1). From point A, she went right 5 units to graph point B. From point B, she went left 1 unit and down 3 units to graph point C. From point C, she went left 5 units to graph point D. She connected the points to form a figure. What are the coordinates of each point? What figure did Annette form?

23. Billy graphed point M on a coordinate plane at ($^+$2, 0). From point M, he went right 6 units to graph point N. From point N, he went left 2 units and up 5 units to graph point O. From point O he went left 2 units to graph point P. He connected the points to form a figure. What are the coordinates of each point? What figure did Billy form?

Write About It

Graph each set of points on a coordinate plane. Then connect them.

24. a. A($^+$2, $^+$2), B($^+$8, $^+$2), C($^+$5, $^+$8);
    b. D($^+$4, $^+$3), E($^+$6, $^+$3), F($^+$5, $^+$5);
    c. G($^-$8, $^+$2), H($^-$2, $^+$2), I($^-$5, $^+$8)

25. a. M($^+$3, $^-$3), N($^+$7, $^-$3), O($^+$7, $^-$7), P($^+$3, $^-$7);
    b. Q($^-$7, $^-$3), R($^-$3, $^-$3), S($^-$3, $^-$7), T($^-$7, $^-$7);
    c. W($^-$4, $^-$4), X($^-$6, $^-$4), Y($^-$6, $^-$6), Z($^-$4, $^-$6)

26. What relationships exist among the figures you drew for exercise 24? for exercise 25? Discuss with the class.

Graph Reflections and Translations

A **reflection** is a transformation that flips a figure over a line called a **line of reflection**. A figure and its reflection are congruent.

You can draw the reflection of a plane figure on a coordinate plane. When you reflect a figure, you can flip it across the *x*-axis or the *y*-axis.

The figure you get after a transformation is the **image** of the original figure. Use **prime notation**, *P′*, to identify an image point. Read *P′* as "*P* prime."

▶ Graph $P(^+2, ^+3)$ and its reflection across the *x*-axis. Write the coordinates of its reflection.

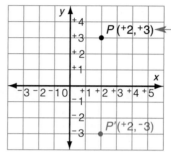

P is 3 units *above* the *x*-axis, so *P′* is 3 units *below* the *x*-axis.

$P(^+2, ^+3) \longrightarrow P'(^+2, ^-3)$

▶ Graph the reflection of △*ABC* across the *y*-axis. Use prime notation to write the coordinates of its reflection.

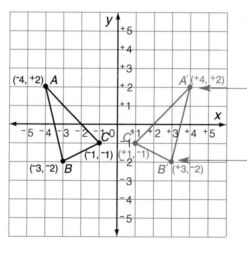

A is 4 units to the *left* of the *y*-axis, so *A′* is 4 units to the *right* of the *y*-axis.

Reflect the other vertices. Draw △*A′B′C′*.

$A(^-4, ^+2), B(^-3, ^-2), C(^-1, ^-1) \longrightarrow A'(^+4, ^+2), B'(^+3, ^-2), C'(^+1, ^-1)$

Practice

Graph each point and its reflection across the indicated axis. Use prime notation to write the coordinates of its reflection.

1. $A(^+4, ^+6)$, *x*-axis

2. $B(^+5, ^-7)$, *x*-axis

3. $C(^-1, ^-3)$, *x*-axis

4. $D(^+8, ^+2)$, *y*-axis

5. $E(^-4, ^+9)$, *y*-axis

6. $F(^-10, ^-5)$, *y*-axis

7. $G(0, ^+9)$, *x*-axis

8. $H(^-14, 0)$, *y*-axis

9. $K(^-5, ^+9)$, *x*-axis

Graph each triangle and its reflection across the indicated axis.
Use prime notation to write the coordinates of its reflection.

10. $Q(^+2, ^+2)$, $R(^+4, ^+5)$, $S(^+6, ^+2)$;
x-axis

11. $M(^-4, ^+5)$, $N(^-7, ^+3)$, $P(^-2, ^+3)$;
y-axis

Graph Translations

A translation is a transformation that moves every point of a figure the same distance and in the same direction. You can translate a figure on a coordinate plane by sliding it horizontally, vertically, or both.

▶ Translate $P(^+2, ^+3)$ right 3 units and up 4 units. What are the coordinates of the image P'?

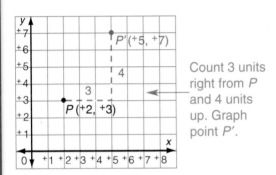

Count 3 units right from P and 4 units up. Graph point P'.

The coordinates of P' are $(^+5, ^+7)$.

▶ Translate $\triangle ABC$ down 6 units. Use prime notation to write the translation.

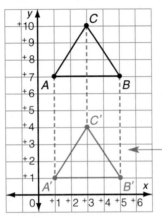

Translate each vertex 6 units down. Label the new vertices A', B', and C'. Connect the points.

$A(^+1, ^+7)$, $B(^+5, ^+7)$, $C(^+3, ^+10)$ ⟶
$A'(^+1, ^+1)$, $B'(^+5, ^+1)$, $C'(^+3, ^+4)$

Graph each point and its translation on the same coordinate grid.
Use prime notation to write the coordinates of its translation.

12. $A(^+5, ^+4)$ left 3 units, up 2 units

13. $B(^-3, ^+1)$ right 6 units, down 4 units

14. $C(^+7, ^-10)$ left 5 units, down 5 units

15. $D(^-9, ^-2)$ right 2 units, up 2 units

16. $E(^-5, ^+2)$, $F(^-2, ^+1)$, $G(^-6, ^-1)$, up 3 units

17. $X(^-1, ^-3)$, $Y(^-2, ^+2)$, $Z(^+2, 0)$, left 3 units, up 1 unit

Graph each figure and its image on the same coordinate grid.
Then tell whether the transformation is a *reflection* or a *translation*.

18. $J(^-3, 0)$, $K(0, ^+3)$, $L(^+3, 0)$, $M(0, ^-3)$
$J'(^-2, ^-2)$, $K'(^+1, ^+1)$, $L'(^+4, ^-2)$,
$M'(^+1, ^-5)$

19. $U(^+2, ^+2)$, $V(^+2, ^+6)$, $W(^+7, ^+6)$, $X(^+9, ^+2)$
$U'(^+2, ^-2)$, $V'(^+2, ^-6)$, $W'(^+7, ^-6)$,
$X'(^+9, ^-2)$

Graph Rotations

A rotation is a transformation that turns a figure about a point in either a clockwise or in a counterclockwise direction. The point around which a figure rotates is called the center of rotation.

To describe a rotation, tell whether the turn is clockwise or counterclockwise and the number of degrees through which the figure is turned.

A rotation of 90° is a quarter turn.
A rotation of 180° is a half turn.
A rotation of 270° is a three-quarter turn.

▶ You can draw a rotation of a point $P(x, y)$ counterclockwise about the origin on a coordinate plane.
The rotation image point $P'(x, y)$ is:

- $(^-y, x)$ if the rotation is 90°.
  $P(^+3, ^-1) \longrightarrow P'(^+1, ^+3)$

> A 90°-rotation changes the sign of the y-coordinate and then reverses the order of the coordinates.

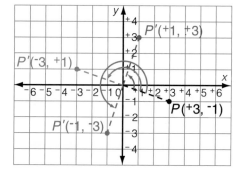

- $(^-x, ^-y)$ if the rotation is 180°.
  $P(^+3, ^-1) \longrightarrow P'(^-3, ^+1)$

> A 180°-rotation changes the signs of both x- and y-coordinates.

- $(y, ^-x)$ if the rotation is 270°.
  $P(^+3, ^-1) \longrightarrow P'(^-1, ^-3)$

> A 270°-rotation changes the sign of the x-coordinate and then reverses the order of the coordinates.

▶ You can rotate △*OAB* 90° counterclockwise about the origin.

$O(0, 0)$, $A(^+3, 0)$, $B(^+3, ^+4) \longrightarrow$
$O'(0, 0)$, $A'(0, ^+3)$, $B'(^-4, ^+3)$

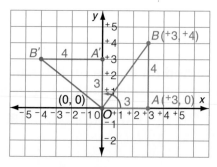

Rotate each vertex 90° counterclockwise. Label the new vertices *O'*, *A'*, and *B'*. Connect the points.

Rotate each point counterclockwise about the origin on a coordinate grid. Use prime notation to write the coordinates of its rotation.

1. $A(^+2, ^+7)$, 90°

2. $B(^-5, ^-3)$, 180°

3. $C(^+4, ^-11)$, 270°

4. $D(^-6, ^-1)$, 90°

5. $E(0, ^+5)$, 180°

6. $F(^-8, 0)$, 270°

Use the given graph for exercises 7–9.

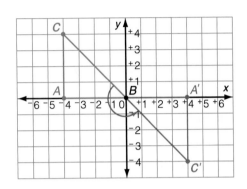

7. Give the coordinates of the vertices of triangle *ABC*.

8. Give the coordinates of the rotation image of triangle *ABC*.

9. Describe the rotation of triangle *ABC*.

Graph each figure and its image on the same coordinate grid. Then describe its rotation.

10. $E(0, 0)$, $F(^-3, 0)$, $G(^-3, ^+5)$
    $E'(0, 0)$, $F'(0, ^+3)$, $G'(^+5, ^+3)$

11. $M(^-3, ^-5)$, $N(^-5, ^-1)$, $P(0, 0)$
    $M'(^+3, ^+5)$, $N'(^+5, ^+1)$, $P'(0, 0)$

12. $R(^+2, ^+3)$, $S(0, ^+6)$, $T(^+2, ^+6)$
    $R'(^-3, ^+2)$, $S'(^-6, 0)$, $T'(^-6, ^+2)$

13. $A(0, 0)$, $B(^+6, 0)$, $C(^+6, ^+2)$, $D(0, ^+2)$
    $A'(0, 0)$, $B'(^-6, 0)$, $C'(^-6, ^-2)$, $D'(0, ^-2)$

Graph each triangle and its image on the same coordinate grid. Use prime notation to write the coordinates of its rotation.

14. $Q(0, 0)$, $R(^-3, 0)$, $S(^-3, ^-4)$,
    rotate 90° counterclockwise
    about the origin

15. $W(^-3, ^-5)$, $X(^-6, ^-5)$, $Y(^-3, ^-2)$,
    rotate 180° counterclockwise
    about the origin

CRITICAL THINKING

Use the triangles in exercises 14–15.

16. Rotate △*QRS* 90° *clockwise* about the origin. What did you discover?

17. Rotate △*WXY* 180° *clockwise* about the origin. What did you discover?

Graph Functions

You can use a rule or equation to make a function table and use ordered pairs to graph points on a coordinate plane.

Graph the function $y = 3x + 4$ on a coordinate plane using integer values from $^{-}3$ to 0.

▶ **To graph a function on a coordinate plane:**

- Make a function table.
    - Substitute values for x in the rule or equation.
    - Find the corresponding y-values.
    - Write an ordered pair for each x- and y-value.
- Graph each ordered pair.
- Connect the points.

x	$y = 3x + 4$	(x, y)
$^{-}3$	$3(^{-}3) + 4 = ^{-}9 + 4 = ^{-}5$	$(^{-}3, ^{-}5)$
$^{-}2$	$3(^{-}2) + 4 = ^{-}6 + 4 = ^{-}2$	$(^{-}2, ^{-}2)$
$^{-}1$	$3(^{-}1) + 4 = ^{-}3 + 4 = ^{+}1$	$(^{-}1, ^{+}1)$
0	$3(0) + 4 = \ 0 + 4 = ^{+}4$	$(0, ^{+}4)$

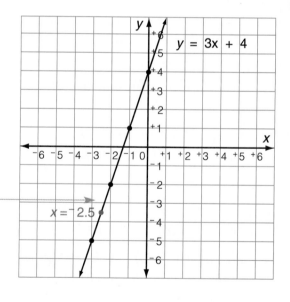

The graph of the function
$y = 3x + 4$.

$y = 3x + 4$ is a linear function, the ordered pairs, (x, y), for the equation are points that form a straight line.

▶ You can also use the graph of $y = 3x + 4$ to estimate the value of y for a given value of x.

Estimate the value of y when $x = ^{-}2.5$.

When $x = ^{-}2.5$, $y \approx ^{-}3.5$.

Copy and complete each function table. Then graph the ordered pairs on a coordinate plane. Is the function a linear function?

1. $y = x + {}^-2$

x	$y = x + {}^-2$	(x, y)
$^+2$	?	?
$^+1$	?	?
0	?	?
$^-1$	?	?

2. $y = 2x + 1$

x	$y = 2x + 1$	(x, y)
$^+2$	?	?
$^+1$	?	?
0	?	?
$^-1$	?	?

Make a function table using integer values from $^-2$ to $^+2$ for x and graph each function on a coordinate plane. Then use the graph to find the value of y when $x = {}^+3$.

3. $y = x - 4$ **4.** $y = 3x - 2$ **5.** $y = 2x$ **6.** $y = {}^-2x$

Solutions of Linear Functions

$(^-3, {}^-5)$ and $(0, {}^+4)$ are solutions of $y = 3x + 4$. When you substitute for x and y, you get a true statement.

$(^-3, {}^-5)$ $\quad y = 3x + 4$
$\quad\uparrow\quad\uparrow\quad\ ^-5 = 3(^-3) + 4$
$\quad x\quad y\quad\ ^-5 = {}^-9 + 4$
$\qquad\qquad\quad\ ^-5 = {}^-5$ True

$(0, {}^+4)$ $\quad y = 3x + 4$
$\ \uparrow\quad\uparrow\quad\ ^+4 = 3(0) + 4$
$\ x\quad y\quad\ ^+4 = 0 + 4$
$\qquad\qquad\ ^+4 = {}^+4$ True

---

7. Give three solutions for each equation in exercises 3–6. Explain how you found your answers.

Problem Solving

8. Suppose that the old town clock loses exactly 5 minutes every day. The function table shows the minutes lost after a given number of days. Write an equation for the function and find how many minutes are lost in 22 days. How many days will it take to lose 200 minutes?

x (Days)	y (Minutes Lost)
1	$^-5$
2	$^-10$
3	$^-15$
4	$^-20$
5	$^-25$

9. For each $9 tie shipped by Tie World, the mailing charge is $2. Use x for the number of ties shipped. Write a linear function for finding the total cost, y.

10. The number of *inches* in a length, y, is a function of the number of yards, x. Make a function table for this function using any five values for x. Write an equation for the function table.

Algebraic Patterns

A **sequence** is an ordered set of numbers that follow a pattern. Each number in a sequence is called a **term**. Write . . . to show that a sequence continues indefinitely.

Study these sequences.

A. 2, 4, 6, 8, 10, 12, . . .
Start at 2. Add 2 repeatedly.

B. 4, 8, 16, 32, 64, 128, . . .
Start at 4. Multiply by 2 repeatedly.

C. 1, 2, 4, 5, 10, 11, 22, 23, 46, . . .
Start at 1. Add 1, then double; add 1, then double; and so on.

For each sequence above, you found the next term by first finding a pattern, and then using the pattern to make a **conjecture** about the next term.

▶ **Triangular** and **square numbers** are sequences of whole numbers. Each number can be represented by an arrangement of dots.

A. The first two triangular numbers are 1 and 3. What are the next two triangular numbers?

B. The first two square numbers are 1 and 4. What are the next two square numbers?

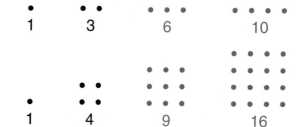

Practice

Find the next two terms in each sequence. Describe the pattern.

1. 3, 9, 27, 81, . . .

2. 10, 8, 6, 4, . . .

3. 21, 25, 29, 33, . . .

4. $1, \frac{1}{2}, \frac{1}{4}, \frac{1}{8}, \ldots$

5. $1, \frac{1}{2}, \frac{1}{3}, \frac{1}{4}, \ldots$

6. $1, \frac{1}{4}, \frac{1}{9}, \frac{1}{16}, \ldots$

7. 2.5, 3, 3.5, 4, . . .

8. 0.1, 0.8, 1.5, 2.2, . . .

9. 61, 54.5, 48, 41.5, . . .

10. 200, 100, 50, 25, . . .

11. 81, 27, 9, 3, . . .

12. 0.1, 0.01, 0.001. 0.0001 . . .

**Find the next three terms in each sequence.
Describe the pattern.**

13. 1, 2, 4, 7, 11, 16, . . .   **14.** 1, 2, 6, 24, 120, . . .   **15.** 1, ⁻1, 2, ⁻2, 3, . . .

16. 1, 2, 6, 7, 21, 22, 66, . . . **17.** 1, 3, 2, 6, 5, 15, . . .   **18.** 1, 3, ⁻6, ⁻4, 8, 10, . . .

**Use the arrangement of dots on page 512 to complete
each table. Look for a pattern.**

19.

Triangular Numbers	
Number	**Number of Dots**
5th	?
6th	?
7th	?
8th	?

20.

Square Numbers	
Number	**Number of Dots**
5th	?
6th	?
7th	?
8th	?

21. What is the tenth triangular number?   **22.** What is the twentieth square number?

Problem Solving

23. For the past 4 years, Ariel has grown 2 in. every year. He is now 16 years old and is 5 ft 10 in. tall. He figures that when he is 22 years old, he will be 6 ft 10 in. tall. What would you tell Ariel about his conjecture?

24. Cynthia rides a bus to school. On the first day the trip to school took 25 min, on the second day, 24 min, on the third day, 26 min, and on the fourth day, 25 min. What conjecture would you make about the time for Cynthia's trip to school?

25. The first three pentagonal numbers are shown. Draw a diagram to represent the next pentagonal number.

1   5   12

CRITICAL THINKING ── Algebra

Draw the next figure in each sequence.

26.

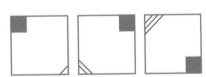

27.

Problem-Solving Strategy: Use More Than One Strategy

Michael's puppy was no more than 5 inches long at birth. Michael knows that 1 inch is equal to 2.54 centimeters. How many centimeters long was the puppy?

Read

Visualize yourself in the problem as you reread it. List the facts and the question.

Facts: Puppy is no more than 5 inches long at birth.

Question: How many centimeters long was the puppy?

Plan

To find how many centimeters long, *write an equation* or *make a graph*.

Let *x* represent the number of inches and *y* represent the number of centimeters.

Notice that each *y*-value is 2.54 times the corresponding *x*-value. So the equation $y = 2.54x$ can be used to find the length in centimeters for any length in inches.

number of inches, *x*	1	2	3	4
number of centimeters, *y*	2.54	5.08	7.62	10.16

Solve

For 5 inches of length, $x = 5$. Then $y = 2.54 \cdot 5 = 12.7$. So 5 inches = 12.7 centimeters.

Michael's puppy was no more than 12.7 cm long.

Check

You can also use a graph to find the *y*-value when the *x*-value is 5.

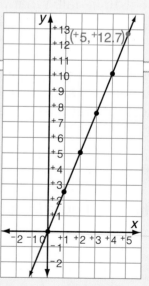

- Graph the data in the table. Then connect the points.

- Extend the line as needed. Then use the graph to find the value of y when $x = 5$. When $x = 5$, $y \approx 13$. Michael's puppy was no more than 13 cm long.

Solve each problem. Be sure that you find all possible solutions.

1. Tosha weighs 18 kilograms and Corey weighs no more than 13 kilograms. How many more *pounds* does Tosha weigh than Corey? Explain. Use 1 kilogram ≈ 2.2 pounds.

Read > Visualize yourself in the problem as you reread it. List the facts and the question.

Facts: Tosha weighs 18 kilograms.
Corey weighs 13 kilograms.
1 kilogram ≈ 2.2 pounds.

Question: How many more *pounds* does Tosha weigh than Corey?

Plan > First find how many more kilograms Tosha weighs than Corey: 18 kg − 13 kg = 5. Tosha weighs 5 more kilograms than Corey.

Then *write an equation.*

Let x represent the number of kilograms and y represent the number of pounds. Since 1 kilogram ≈ 2.2 pounds, then $y = 2.2x$.

Solve ....> **Check**

2. Elliot needs no less than 225 grams of flour for a recipe. He buys $\frac{1}{2}$ pound of flour. Elliot knows that 1 ounce ≈ 28.35 grams. Does he buy enough flour? Explain.

3. Liz bought a case containing 16 liters of club soda. She needs no more than 64 cups of club soda for Friday night's dance. Liz knows that 1 liter ≈ 4.2 cups. How many extra cups of club soda did Liz buy?

4. The distance from Tim's mailbox to his neighbor's mailbox is no more than 7 meters. Tim knows that 1 meter ≈ 3.3 feet. How many feet from his neighbor's mailbox is Tim's mailbox? how many yards?

5. Luisa's living room is no less than 4 meters long. How many *feet* long is Luisa's living room? Use 1 meter ≈ 1.1 yards. Explain.

6. Carl's bathroom sink holds no more than 3 liters of water. How many pints of water does Carl's sink hold? Use 1 liter ≈ 1.06 quarts. Explain.

7. Jamie lives 5 miles from school. Students who live 10 or more kilometers from school are on the second bus route. Is Jamie on the second bus route? Explain. Use 1 mile ≈ 1.6 kilometers.

Problem-Solving Applications: Mixed Review

Read 〉 **Plan** 〉 **Solve** 〉 **Check**

Solve each problem and explain the method you used.

Members of the Turbo-Math Club write equations for each other.

1. Sherman writes this equation:
   $\frac{w}{4} + 22 = 36$. What is the value of w?

2. Sarah writes this equation:
   $3d \div d = 3$. Does this equation have one unique solution? Explain.

3. $\triangle ABC$ has coordinates $A(^+2, {}^-4)$, $B(^+6, {}^+6)$, and $C(^+7, {}^+2)$. A translation maps point A to $A'(^-3, {}^+6)$. Find the coordinates of B' and C' under this translation.

4. Oxanna notices that these two equations both include the variable f: $f + 72 = 89$, $2f = 34$. Does f have the same value in each equation?

5. Ray solves this equation: $g \div 5 = 15$. Then he finds the value of h in this equation: $h \times g = 75$. What is the value of h?

6. Find the value of j in this equation: $(j - 10) + 27 = 27$.

7. Which equation has a solution greater than 55? less than or equal to 8? $16 = \frac{a}{2} + 12$; $16 = \frac{c}{2} - 12$.

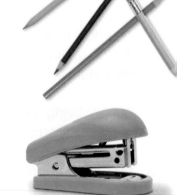

8. The ages of the four Kelly children form a sequence. If the ages of the three youngest are 9 months, $3\frac{1}{2}$ years, and $6\frac{1}{4}$ years, how old is the eldest?

9. The ages of Mrs. Lane (x) and her daughter (y) are related by the equation $y = \frac{5}{6}x - 16\frac{1}{2}$. Mrs. Lane is 27 years old. How old is her daughter?

Choose one or more strategies to solve each problem.

10. Iris wrote this riddle: "I am a number that is exactly four times the number of fluid ounces in a cup. What number am I?"

Strategy File

Use These Strategies
Write an Equation
Guess and Test
More Than One Solution
Logical Reasoning
Use More Than One Step
Use More Than One Strategy
Make a Graph

11. James thinks of a number. Sarah asks, "Are there any even digits? Is the number greater than 50? Is it divisible by 3? Is it less than 36?" James answers "no" to each of her questions. What number is he thinking of?

12. Edna has a favorite two-digit number. The sum of the digits is 9. The difference between the digits is 1. What are the two possibilities for Edna's favorite number?

13. The Math Club newsletter is twice as long as the French Club newsletter, which is one third as long as the Science Club newsletter. The Science Club newsletter is 6 pages long. How long is the Math Club newsletter?

14. The width of a rectangle is w and its length is 4 more than twice its width, or $2w + 4$. Ann writes the perimeter as $(w + 2w + 4) + (w + 2w + 4)$. Is Ann correct? Give three different values for w, $2w + 4$, and the perimeter.

15. Andrew plotted point K on a coordinate grid at $(^-3, ^+1)$. From point K, he went right 8 units to plot point L. From point L, he went up 2 units and left 2 units to plot point M. From point M, he went left 4 units to plot point N. He then connected the points to form a figure. What are the coordinates of each point? What figure did Andrew form? What is the area of the figure?

Write Your Own

16. Use $x, y,$ and z to represent students who play baseball, basketball, and soccer. Make up a problem modeled on problem 15. Write and solve the equation.

Check Your Progress
Lessons 1–11

Solve and check. *(See pp. 496–501.)*

1. $^-26 + a = {}^-47$

2. $21 = 17 + 2n$

3. $^-15z = {}^-240$

4. $9 = \dfrac{q}{12} + 5$

5. $\dfrac{d}{15} - {}^+3 = {}^-2$

6. $\dfrac{4x}{3} + 21 = 17$

7. $a + {}^+3 + {}^+10 = {}^-25$

8. $^-27 = r - ({}^+4 + {}^+9)$

9. $^-13 + y = {}^-19 - {}^+17$

Graph the points on a coordinate plane. *(See pp. 502–505.)*

10. $K({}^+2, {}^+7)$

11. $L({}^-2, {}^-4)$

12. $M({}^+6, {}^-8)$

13. $N({}^-1, {}^+6)$

14. $O({}^-5, 0)$

15. $P(0, {}^+6)$

16. $Q(0, 0)$

17. $R({}^-5, {}^-5)$

Name the point(s) in exercises 10–17 located in each quadrant.

18. quadrant I

19. quadrant II

20. quadrant III

21. quadrant IV

Graph each triangle and its image on the same coordinate grid. Use prime notation to write the coordinates of its image. *(See pp. 506–509.)*

22. $S(0, {}^+1)$, $T({}^+4, {}^+1)$, $U({}^+2, {}^+4)$
Rotate 180° counterclockwise about the origin.

23. $V({}^-4, {}^+5)$, $W({}^-4, {}^+2)$, $X({}^-1, {}^+3)$
Reflect across the *x*-axis.

Make a function table using integer values from $^-2$ to $^+2$ for *x*. Then graph each function on a coordinate plane. *(See pp. 510–511.)*

24. $y = x + {}^-2$

25. $y = x + {}^-3$

26. $y = {}^-x$

Find the next two terms in each sequence. Describe the pattern. *(See pp. 512–513.)*

27. 5, 10, 20, 40, . . .

28. 15, 12, 9, 6, . . .

29. 11, 17, 23, 29, . . .

30. $1, \dfrac{1}{3}, \dfrac{1}{9}, \dfrac{1}{27}, \ldots$

31. $1, \dfrac{1}{3}, \dfrac{1}{5}, \dfrac{1}{7}, \ldots$

32. $1, \dfrac{1}{4}, \dfrac{1}{6}, \dfrac{1}{8}, \ldots$

Problem Solving
(See pp. 514–517.)

33. A birdbath holds 4 liters of water. About how many quarts does it hold? Use 1 L ≈ 1.1 qt.

34. Alicia doubled the sum of two negative integers. Her answer was $^-6$. Find the addends.

(See Still More Practice, p. 532.)

Slope

Slope is the measure of steepness of a line.

You can find the slope of a line by picking two points on the line and finding the ratio:

$$\text{slope } (m) = \frac{\text{change in } y\text{-value}}{\text{change in } x\text{-value}} = \frac{y_2 - y_1}{x_2 - x_1} = \frac{\text{rise}}{\text{run}}$$

What is the slope of the line that passes through the points $(^+1, ^+7)$ and $(^+4, ^+1)$?

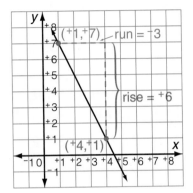

▶ To find the slope, m, of a line:

- Subtract the first y-coordinate from the second y-coordinate. Write the difference in the numerator.
- Subtract the first x-coordinate from the second x-coordinate. Write the difference in the denominator.

$$m = \frac{y_2 - y_1}{x_2 - x_1} = \frac{^+1 - ^+7}{^+4 - ^+1} = \frac{^-6}{^+3} = ^-2$$

So the slope of the line containing $(^+1, ^+7)$ and $(^+4, ^+1)$ is $^-2$.

Find the slope of the line that passes through the given points.

1. $(^+1, ^+4)$ and $(^+5, ^+8)$
2. $(^-2, 0)$ and $(0, ^-6)$
3. $(^-3, ^+9)$ and $(^+2, ^-1)$

4. $(^+2, ^-7)$ and $(^-2, ^+5)$
5. $(^-3, ^-2)$ and $(^-1, ^+12)$
6. $(^+1, ^+4)$ and $(^-1, ^+12)$

7. $(^-10, ^+5)$ and $(^-2, ^-3)$
8. $(^-9, ^-2)$ and $(^-1, ^-6)$
9. $(^-17, ^+2)$ and $(^-2, ^-3)$

Find the slope of the line.

10.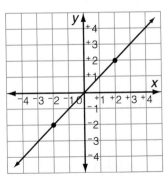
11.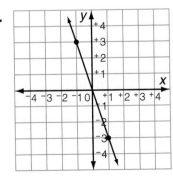
12.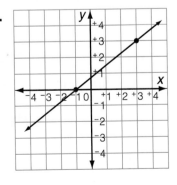

Graph each equation and then find the slope.

13. $y = ^-5x$
14. $y = ^+4x - 9$
15. $y = ^-2x + ^-3$

Chapter 14 Test

Solve and check.

1. $m - {}^+12 = {}^-13 + {}^-23$

2. ${}^-5c + {}^-5 = {}^-15$

3. ${}^-25 = {}^+4y - {}^-3$

4. $\dfrac{9a}{126} = 3$

5. $3 = \dfrac{s}{4} - 6$

6. $\dfrac{t}{3} + 12 = 39$

Graph each triangle and its image on the same coordinate grid. Then use prime notation to write the coordinates of its image.

7. $A({}^+4, {}^+1)$, $B({}^+3, {}^+5)$, $C({}^-3, {}^+2)$
   Translate 5 units left and 2 units down.

8. $C({}^+2, {}^-3)$, $D({}^+4, {}^+1)$, $E({}^+6, {}^-1)$;
   rotate 90° counterclockwise about the origin.

Make a function table using integer values from ${}^-2$ to ${}^+2$ for x. Then graph each function on a coordinate grid.

9. $y = x + 6$

10. $x + y = 11$

11. $y = 3x + 4$

Find the next two terms in each sequence. Describe the pattern.

12. 85, 79, 73, 67, . . .

13. 25, 29, 33, 37, . . .

14. ${}^-1, {}^-3, {}^-9, {}^-27,$ . . .

Problem Solving

Use a strategy you have learned.

15. Square $ABCD$ has vertices $A({}^+2, {}^+3)$, $B({}^+2, {}^-3)$, and $C({}^-4, {}^+3)$. What are the coordinates of vertex D? What is the area of $ABCD$?

Tell About It

Explain how you solved the problem. Show all your work.

16. Without graphing, how can you tell if the point $({}^+3, {}^-1)$ is on the graph of the equation $y = x + {}^-4$?

Performance Assessment

17. **a.** Graph the points in a coordinate grid:
    $A({}^+1, {}^+5)$, $B({}^+2, {}^+2)$, $C({}^+2, {}^+8)$, $D({}^+3, {}^+1)$, $E({}^+3, {}^+9)$, $F({}^+6, 0)$, $G({}^+6, {}^+10)$, $H({}^+7, {}^-1)$, $I({}^+7, {}^+11)$, $J({}^+9, {}^+1)$, $K({}^+9, {}^+9)$, $L({}^+10, {}^+2)$, $M({}^+10, {}^+8)$, $N({}^+11, {}^+5)$

    b. Which of the points do not fit the same pattern as the others?

    c. If you continue graphing points that fit the pattern, what figure would you get?

CHAPTER 1 ....

Practice 1-1

Write in expanded form.

1a. 83,007,100   **b.** 5.008407

Round each number to its greatest place (nonzero place for decimals) or to the nearest cent.

2a. 67,824   **b.** $18.375   **c.** 8.0957

Order from least to greatest.

3. 47,396,000; 47,963,000; 47,369,000

4. 0.2954; 0.0298; 0.29504; 0.29054

Estimate the sum or difference.

5a.   27.14   **b.**   0.275   **c.**   43.09
   $+31.762$ $+3.8$ -17.8

Use a related sentence to find the missing number or decimal.

6a. $n + 86 = 132$ **b.** $n - 0.03 = 0.7$

Compute. Watch for + and − signs.

7a.   9,392,738   **b.**   73
    $+3,678,907$ -8.92

8a. $341,086 - 87,794$ **b.** $\$80 - \$35.97$

Problem Solving

9. Which country has the greatest area—Brazil: 3,284,426 square miles; Canada: 3,851,787 square miles; or the United States: 3,623,420 square miles? the least?

10. Luis drove from New York to Chicago. The odometer read 32,949 when he started. It read 33,751 when he reached Chicago. How far did Luis travel?

11. Find the sum of 8.35, 9.046, 0.7185, 30, and 6.02.

12. Ed ran 9.75 mi on Friday and 13.6 mi on Saturday. How much farther did he run on Saturday?

CHAPTER 2 ....

Practice 2-1

Write each product in exponential form.

1. $4 \times 4 \times 4$ **2.** $8 \times 8 \times 8 \times 8 \times 8 \times 8 \times 8$

3. $10 \times 10 \times 10 \times 10 \times 10 \times 10$

4. $200 \times 200 \times 200 \times 200$

Find the product.

5a. 40×700 **b.** 500×8000 **c.** 186×300

6a. 508×720 **b.** 709×5309 **c.** $650 \times \$38.75$

7a.   917   **b.**   8236   **c.** $795.03
   $\times\ 38$ $\times\ 79$ $\times\ 28$

8a.   4752   **b.**   30,817   **c.** $39.87
   $\times\ 809$ $\times\ 450$ $\times\ 506$

9a. 1000×0.463 **b.** $910 \times 546,019$

Estimate the product.

10a. 917×380 **b.** 6.24×11.86 **c.** 5477×3819

Write the standard numeral.

11. $(6 \times 10^5) + (4 \times 10^3) + (2 \times 10^2) + (5 \times 1)$

12a. 5^3 **b.** 3^5 **c.** 9.14×10^4

Problem Solving

13. If a meteor travels 1899 miles per minute, how far will the meteor travel in 2 hours?

14. The interior temperature of the sun is about 35,000,000°F. Write this temperature in expanded form using exponents.

15. A large city has 375 office buildings. There is an average of 425 offices in each building. About how many offices are there in the city?

16. Snow fell at a rate of 0.6 cm per hour. At that rate, how much snow fell in 5 hours?

17. The distance from Pluto to the Sun is about 5,910,000,000 km. Write the number in scientific notation.

CHAPTER 3

Practice 3-1

Estimate the quotient.

1a. $31\overline{)3371}$ **b.** $297\overline{)6143}$

2a. $87\overline{)\$180,000}$ **b.** $117\overline{)\$54,000}$

Divide. Use R to write remainders.

3a. $40\overline{)1200}$ **b.** $200,000 \div 400$

4a. $5\overline{)7826}$ **b.** $9\overline{)3618}$ **c.** $3\overline{)\$75.21}$

5a. $29\overline{)5007}$ **b.** $82\overline{)6173}$ **c.** $12\overline{)4624}$

6a. $15\overline{)\$2208.75}$ **b.** $326\overline{)1313}$

7a. $730\overline{)25,550}$ **b.** $417\overline{)12,510}$

Evaluate each expression.

8a. $3 \cdot x \cdot 4$, when $x = 6$ **b.** $425 \div y$, when $y = 5$

9a. $56 \cdot 3201$ **b.** $0.5 \times 6 \times 20.7$

Tell whether each of the following numbers is divisible by 2, 3, 4, 5, 6, 8, 9, or 10.

10a. 36,720   **b.** 3,255,075   **c.** 76,269,804

Problem Solving

11. Every morning, 35,875 riders use public transportation to get to school or work. If a bus can hold 53 riders, estimate how many busloads of riders there are each morning.

12. Minnesota has an area of 86,943 square miles and 87 counties. What is the average number of square miles per county?

13. Kareem's Computer Store buys 19 pieces of Spelling Tutor software. The bill is $711.55. What is the average cost of each piece of software?

14. Two hundred fourteen bags of concrete mix weigh 11,984 lb. How much does one bag weigh?

Practice 3-2

Divide.

1a. $36.3 \div 10$ **b.** $18.6 \div 100$

2a. $25.2 \div 1000$ **b.** $7 \div 1000$

3a. $3\overline{)0.783}$ **b.** $9\overline{)1.917}$ **c.** $4\overline{)\$32.48}$

4a. $0.3\overline{)93}$ **b.** $0.8\overline{)\$4.00}$ **c.** $0.19\overline{)38}$

5a. $0.05\overline{)2.113}$ **b.** $2.4\overline{)1.8}$

6a. $0.03\overline{)8.124}$ **b.** $0.6\overline{)1.803}$

7a. $22.6\overline{)20.34}$ **b.** $0.28\overline{)1.225}$

Estimate the quotient.

8a. $35.81 \div 5.9$ **b.** $\$394 \div 79.05$

9a. $\$57.59 \div 8.1$ **b.** $0.8 \div 0.199$

10a. $\$22.32 \div 3.1$ **b.** $\$30.15 \div 16.2$

Translate each word phrase as an algebraic expression. Use x as a variable.

11a. the product of 405 and a number

     b. the quotient of 735 and a number

Problem Solving

12. If 8 copies of a novel cost $38.00, find the price of one novel.

13. Golf balls are on sale for $15.69 per dozen. Determine the price of one golf ball. Round your answer to the nearest cent.

14. A section of highway 3.87 miles long is being rebuilt. If the workers can complete 0.03 mile per day, how many days will it take them to complete the job?

15. A metal worker cuts an aluminum bar into segments that measure 3.625 cm. How many segments can be cut from a bar 87 cm long?

16. What number multiplied by 0.7 will give the same product as 5.6 multiplied by 0.8?

CHAPTER 4

Practice 4-1

Compute.

1a. $3 + 7 \times 9 - 5$ **b.** $(8 \div 2) \times (7 + 9) \times 10^2$

2a. $9 \times 6 \div 3 + 17 - 8$ **b.** $39 - 3 \times 4 \div 3$

Translate as an algebraic expression or equation.

3. the difference between y and 16

4. c divided by 4 is 10.

Evaluate each expression.

5a. $27 + 3ab^2$, when   **b.** $(x - 1)^2 + y \div z$, when
$a = 4$ and $b = 2$ $x = 6$, $y = 25$, and $z = 5$

Solve and check.

6a. $x + 9.373 = 21.627$ **b.** $t - 360.48 = 721.37$

7a. $c \times 36 = 9$ **b.** $d \div 3 = 1.8941$

Use the Volume formula, $V = \ell \times w \times h$, or the Perimeter formula, $P = 2(\ell + w)$, to find each missing dimension.

8. $V = 3750$ ft³, $\ell = 50$ ft, $w = \underline{\ ?\ }$ ft, $h = 3$ ft

9. $P = 48$ yd, $\ell = 14$ yd, $w = \underline{\ ?\ }$ yd

Problem Solving

Translate into an equation. Then solve.

10. A number decreased by 7 is 30. Find the number.

11. 45 is equal to the product of a number and 3. Find the number.

12. Ed bought 4 cans of peas at 2 for $1.79, 3 cans of pears at $.69 each, and 5 cans of corn at 3 cans for $2.07. How much did he spend?

CHAPTER 5

Practice 5-1

Write the integer that matches each letter on the number line.

1a. J   **b.** K   **c.** L   **d.** M

Express each as an integer.

2a. loss of 8 lb   **b.** 7 degrees warmer

3a. 50 ft below sea level **b.** $25 raise

Name the opposite of each integer.

4a. $^-5$ **b.** $^+8$ **c.** $^-16$ **d.** $^+7$

Compare. Write $<$ or $>$.

5a. $^+6 \ \underline{\ ?\ } \ ^-6$ **b.** $^-3 \ \underline{\ ?\ } \ ^-7$

6a. $0 \ \underline{\ ?\ } \ ^-2$ **b.** $^-5 \ \underline{\ ?\ } \ ^+1$

7a. $^-6 \ \underline{\ ?\ } \ ^-1$ **b.** $^+8 \ \underline{\ ?\ } \ ^-10$

Compute.

8a. $^+3 + \ ^+8$ **b.** $^-2 + \ ^+5$ **c.** $^-7 + \ ^-8$

9a. $^+6 - \ ^-5$ **b.** $^-8 - \ ^-9$ **c.** $^-5 - \ ^+3$

10a. $^+10 - \ ^+4$ **b.** $^+3 - \ ^-3$ **c.** $^+8 - \ ^+12$

11a. $^-8 \times \ ^-15$ **b.** $^-52 \div \ ^+4$ **c.** $^-1 \div \ ^-1$

Estimate the temperature in °C or in °F. Watch for the degree unit.

12a. °70F   **b.** $^-18$°F   **c.** $^-22$°F

13a. 17°C   **b.** $^-2$°C   **c.** $^-34$°C

Problem Solving

14. Arrange in order from least to greatest: $^-5$; $^-8$; $^+3$; $^-4$; 0.

15. The price of a stock fell 8 points on Monday and rose 3 points on Tuesday. Find the total change over both days.

16. The temperature was $^-16$°F. It dropped 7 degrees. Find the new temperature.

17. An archaeological site is 3 m above sea level. A discovery is made 4 m higher. How far above or below sea level is the discovery?

CHAPTER 6

Practice 6-1

Write a fraction for each point.

1a. R   **b.** P

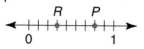

Complete.

2a. $\frac{5}{7} = \frac{n}{28}$ **b.** $\frac{4}{9} = \frac{24}{n}$ **c.** $\frac{18}{n} = \frac{2}{5}$

Write each fraction in simplest form.

3a. $\frac{18}{27}$ **b.** $\frac{15}{21}$ **c.** $\frac{16}{40}$

Compare. Write <, =, or >.

4a. $\frac{17}{23}$? $\frac{7}{23}$ **b.** $\frac{5}{6}$? $\frac{9}{10}$

5a. $\frac{7}{8}$? $\frac{49}{56}$ **b.** $\frac{1}{2}$? $\frac{3}{5}$

Write in order from least to greatest.

6a. $\frac{2}{3}, \frac{1}{5}, \frac{5}{6}$ **b.** $\frac{5}{9}, \frac{1}{4}, \frac{5}{12}$

7a. $1\frac{7}{12}, 1\frac{1}{2}, 1\frac{2}{3}$ **b.** $2\frac{2}{5}, 2\frac{2}{3}, 2\frac{2}{15}$

Tell whether each is *prime* or *composite*.

8a. 9   **b.** 19   **c.** 49

Find the prime factorization and write in exponent form.

9a. 26   **b.** 40   **c.** 56

Problem Solving

10. Which fraction is close to $\frac{1}{2}$: $\frac{6}{11}, \frac{13}{15}, \frac{1}{5}$?

11. Of 24 dogs, 9 are beagles, 5 are collies, and the rest are poodles. What fractional part are poodles?

12. Marla ate $\frac{3}{8}$ of a melon. Leah ate $\frac{2}{3}$ of a melon. Who ate more?

13. List all the prime numbers between 20 and 30.

14. Which is farthest: $7\frac{4}{5}$ mi, $7\frac{3}{4}$ mi, or $7\frac{7}{10}$ mi?

Practice 6-2

Find the GCF of each pair of numbers.

1a. 8 and 12   **b.** 15 and 24

2a. 10 and 45   **b.** 7 and 28

Find the LCM of each pair of numbers.

3a. 7 and 10   **b.** 8 and 12

4a. 6 and 15   **b.** 14 and 42

Rename as an improper fraction.

5a. $3\frac{2}{3}$ **b.** $9\frac{7}{10}$ **c.** $5\frac{1}{4}$

Rename as a fraction in simplest form.

6a. 0.54   **b.** 0.05   **c.** 0.75

Rename as a decimal.

7a. $4\frac{7}{8}$ **b.** $\frac{1}{6}$ **c.** $5\frac{2}{3}$

8a. $\frac{9}{16}$ **b.** $3\frac{4}{100}$ **c.** $6\frac{1}{8}$

Write each rational number for each point.

9.

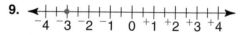

10.

11. Find a pair of numbers between 12 and 24 whose GCF is 5.

12. Find a pair of numbers between 1 and 10 whose LCM is 8.

13. A carton holds 10 music boxes. Write a mixed number in simplest form to show how many cartons would be filled by 46 music boxes.

14. Write the quotient of 1 divided by 9 as a repeating decimal.

15. Is $\frac{54}{110}$ a little more than $\frac{1}{2}$? Write *Yes* or *No*. Explain.

Practice 7-1

Add or subtract. Write each answer in simplest form.

a. $\dfrac{5}{9} + \dfrac{4}{9}$ **b.** $\dfrac{7}{8} - \dfrac{5}{8}$ **c.** $\dfrac{11}{16} - \dfrac{5}{16}$

a. $\dfrac{7}{8} + \dfrac{3}{4}$ **b.** $\dfrac{1}{3} + \dfrac{5}{6}$ **c.** $\dfrac{9}{10} - \dfrac{1}{2}$

a. $(\dfrac{3}{14} + \dfrac{3}{14}) + \dfrac{6}{7}$ **b.** $\dfrac{7}{12} - \dfrac{1}{4}$

Estimate the sum or difference.

a. $\dfrac{5}{7} + \dfrac{9}{10}$ **b.** $\dfrac{9}{16} - \dfrac{1}{7}$ **c.** $\dfrac{11}{12} - \dfrac{5}{9}$

a. $9\dfrac{2}{3} + 3\dfrac{1}{8}$ **b.** $7\dfrac{1}{5} + 7\dfrac{5}{6}$ **c.** $19\dfrac{1}{9} + 9\dfrac{7}{8}$

a. $12\dfrac{1}{5} - 7\dfrac{2}{3}$ **b.** $41\dfrac{1}{2} - 19\dfrac{5}{7}$ **c.** $10\dfrac{1}{3} - 3\dfrac{3}{4}$

Compute. Use the addition properties.

7a. $1\dfrac{2}{3} + (\dfrac{1}{6} + \dfrac{1}{6})$ **b.** $3\dfrac{1}{2} + 5 + 2\dfrac{1}{4}$

8a. $\dfrac{9}{10} - (\dfrac{1}{5} + \dfrac{2}{5})$ **b.** $2\dfrac{1}{4} + 2\dfrac{1}{3} + \dfrac{1}{4}$

Problem Solving

9. How much is $\dfrac{1}{6}$ increased by $\dfrac{1}{4}$?

10. Find the sum of $\dfrac{1}{7}$, $\dfrac{4}{21}$, and $\dfrac{2}{3}$.

11. Anita is a runner on the school track team. Upon reaching the $\dfrac{7}{8}$-mi marker of the $1\dfrac{1}{2}$-mi track, how much farther must she run to get to the end of the track?

12. The sum of n and $1\dfrac{3}{4}$ is 4. Find the value of n.

13. Ethan spent $1\dfrac{7}{8}$ h working on a model airplane. Then he spent $2\dfrac{1}{6}$ h raking leaves. About how much time did Ethan spend on those two activities?

14. From the sum of $\dfrac{7}{10}$ and $\dfrac{3}{5}$, subtract $\dfrac{2}{3}$.

Practice 7-2

Add or subtract. Write each answer in simplest form.

1a.
$$2\dfrac{2}{3}$$
$$+3\dfrac{1}{5}$$

b.
$$6\dfrac{5}{8}$$
$$+3\dfrac{1}{2}$$

c.
$$12\dfrac{1}{6}$$
$$+\;8\dfrac{4}{5}$$

2a.
$$3\dfrac{3}{4}$$
$$-1\dfrac{1}{2}$$

b.
$$9\dfrac{1}{3}$$
$$-6\dfrac{1}{2}$$

c.
$$11$$
$$-\;8\dfrac{3}{7}$$

3a.
$$7\dfrac{4}{7}$$
$$-5\dfrac{5}{6}$$

b.
$$4$$
$$-2\dfrac{2}{3}$$

c.
$$8\dfrac{1}{3}$$
$$-5\dfrac{3}{4}$$

Evaluate each expression.

4a. $a + b + 4\dfrac{11}{21}$, when $a = 3\dfrac{1}{7}$ and $b = 5\dfrac{2}{3}$

4b. $x - y$, when $x = 16$ and $y = 3\dfrac{5}{6}$

Solve and check.

5a. $c + \dfrac{2}{3} = \dfrac{11}{12}$ **b.** $t + 2\dfrac{1}{3} = 5\dfrac{1}{3}$

6a. $q - \dfrac{3}{5} = \dfrac{1}{15}$ **b.** $m - 3\dfrac{2}{5} = 7$

Problem Solving

7. Add $2\dfrac{5}{6}$ to the difference between 5 and $2\dfrac{7}{12}$.

8. A team practiced $2\dfrac{1}{2}$ h before lunch and then $1\dfrac{3}{4}$ h after lunch. What is the total time it practiced?

9. A recipe calls for $3\dfrac{1}{3}$ c of white flour, $1\dfrac{1}{4}$ c of whole wheat flour, and $\dfrac{1}{2}$ c of rice flour. Find the total amount of flour in the recipe.

10. Jeannette has three jump ropes: $6\dfrac{1}{2}$ ft, $9\dfrac{2}{3}$ ft, and $7\dfrac{1}{8}$ ft. Estimate the total length.

11. On Monday, a certain stock opened at $67\dfrac{1}{8}$ points. By Friday its value was 80 points. Find its increase in value.

12. Ted weighed $145\dfrac{1}{2}$ lb. After 2 months of dieting, he weighed $136\dfrac{1}{3}$ lb. How much weight did he lose?

13. Mary needs $6\dfrac{2}{5}$ yd of ribbon. She has $4\dfrac{3}{4}$ yd. How much more ribbon does she need?

Practice 8-1

Multiply. Use the GCF whenever possible.

1a. $\frac{3}{4} \times \frac{5}{6} \times \frac{7}{10}$ **b.** $\frac{9}{10}$ of 80

2a. $3\frac{4}{5} \times 1\frac{7}{8} \times 2\frac{1}{2}$ **b.** $5 \times \frac{7}{8} \times 3\frac{1}{4}$

Complete. Name the property of multiplication used.

3a. $\frac{3}{7} \times n = 0$ **b.** $\frac{7}{8} \times \frac{9}{10} = n \times \frac{7}{8}$

4a. $\frac{9}{11} \times 1 = n$

b. $(\frac{1}{2} \times \frac{1}{3}) \times \frac{5}{8} = \frac{1}{2} \times (n \times \frac{5}{8})$

Write the reciprocal of each number.

5a. $\frac{3}{4}$ **b.** 8   **c.** $2\frac{1}{3}$

Divide.

6a. $10\frac{2}{3} \div 1\frac{1}{9}$ **b.** $4\frac{1}{7} \div 2$ **c.** $\$10 \div 3\frac{1}{3}$

7a. $7 \div \frac{1}{4}$ **b.** $21 \div \frac{7}{8}$ **c.** $\frac{3}{4} \div 6$

Evaluate each expression.

8a. $4\frac{7}{8} t$, when $t = \frac{4}{5}$ **b.** $n \div 1\frac{2}{3}$, when $n = 5\frac{4}{}$

Solve for n.

9a. $n \div \frac{9}{10} = 3$ **b.** $6n = 22$

Problem Solving

10. Jason has saved $80. He spent $\frac{3}{4}$ of it on a new camera. How much did the camera cost?

11. A sofa was on sale for $\frac{1}{3}$ off the regular price of $360. Find the sale price of the sofa.

12. Lia bought $\frac{3}{4}$ yd of felt. She used $\frac{5}{6}$ of it to make a banner. How much of the felt did she use for the banner?

13. Which has the greater product: $3\frac{1}{2} \times \frac{1}{3}$ or $6\frac{1}{4} \times \frac{4}{5}$?

Practice 8-2

Compute. Use the order of operations rules.

1a. $6 \times \frac{3}{4} + \frac{1}{2}$ **b.** $\frac{2}{3} + \frac{1}{3} \times (9 + 6)$

2a. $9 \div \frac{2}{3} - \frac{7}{12}$ **b.** $\frac{3}{4} - \frac{5}{6} \div (2 + 8)$

Use a coin and the spinner for problems 3–4.

3. Make a tree diagram to list all possible outcomes.

4. Find the probability.
   a. P (heads, 6)
   b. P (tails, <5)

Use a number cube labeled 1–6 to find the probability of each event.

5a. P (1 or 3)   **b.** P (7)   **c.** P (1 through 6)

Problem Solving

6. A $7\frac{1}{2}$-ft board is cut into pieces that are $\frac{5}{6}$ ft long. How many pieces can be cut?

7. The price of cashew nuts is $9.75 for $1\frac{1}{2}$ lb. What is the price of 1 lb?

8. Bill has $9\frac{1}{3}$ c of blueberries. He is using half of them to make blueberry tarts. If each tart will have $\frac{2}{3}$ c of blueberries, how many tarts can Bill make?

9. In a survey of 36 sixth graders, 16 have braces. Predict how many wear braces among the school district's 720 sixth graders.

10. A card is chosen from a bag containing cards labeled A, B, C, D, E. Then a second card is chosen. If the first card is not replaced, find $P(B, D)$ and $P(A, C$ or $E)$.

A jar contains 2 red marbles, 4 green marbles, and 4 white marbles. One marble is drawn at random. Find the probability.

11a. P (green)   **b.** P (red) **c.** P (blue)

12a. P (red or white)   **b.** P (*not* blue)

13. If 6 people want to be seated, in how many ways can 4 of them be seated on a bench that seats 4?

14. From 3 girls and 2 boys, how many teams of 3 can be formed?

Practice 9-1

Use the double line graph for problems 1–3.

1. Find the temperature at the summit at 7 A.M.

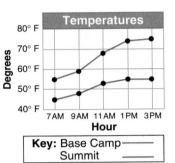

Temperatures

Degrees: 80° F, 70° F, 60° F, 50° F, 40° F

Hour: 7 AM 9 AM 11 AM 1 PM 3 PM

Key: Base Camp ———
Summit ———

2. Estimate the difference in temperatures at 9 A.M.

3. Between what hours did the temperatures change least?

Use the given data for problems 4–6.

Ages of Guests at a Party

19	48	67	11	45
29	11	44	11	36
28	12	10	39	11
35	12	18	40	11

4. Organize the data in a frequency table.

5. Use the data to make:
   a. a line plot
   b. a stem-and-leaf plot

6. Find the mode, range, and median of the data in problem 4.

7. In 5 games, Jan scored 15, 18, 20, 12, and 20 points. What is her mean score?

8. Ali's scores on her first four math tests were 98, 84, 88, and 92. What score must she make on the fifth test to have the mean of the five tests equal 90?

9. The table shows how many people saw the circus. Make a double bar graph to display the data.

Attendance

Days	Matinee	Evening
Sun.	350	450
Mon.	100	150
Tue.	125	250
Wed.	300	350

10. High temperature readings during one 5-day period were 72, 63, 70, 68, and 77 degrees Fahrenheit. Give the range, median, mean, and mode for this set of data.

Practice 9-2

Write whether you would be most likely to find a biased sample for the survey at each location. Write *Yes* or *No*. Explain.

1. Favorite music: concert hall

2. Favorite food: Chinese restaurant

3. Favorite TV show: shopping mall

4. Favorite sport: park

Use the circle graph for problems 5–8.

5. Which sport is most popular?

Sports Club Membership

Softball — $\frac{1}{3}$
Tennis — $\frac{1}{8}$
Soccer — $\frac{3}{8}$
Volleyball — $\frac{1}{6}$

6. What fractional part of the members prefer soccer or softball?

7. There are 96 members in the Sports Club. How many prefer softball?

8. Of the 96 members, which sport is preferred by exactly 12 members?

Use the given data for ex. 9–11.

9. What are the extremes of the data?

10. What is the median of the data? the upper and lower quartiles?

11. Make a box-and-whisker plot for this data.

Student Math Grades

| 75 | 80 | 90 | 79 | 82 |
| 93 | 79 | 88 | 95 | 88 |

12. Make a frequency table and a histogram for this data.

Number of Pets per Class in Parker Elementary

7	3	5	10	12
4	6	8	6	13
9	4	7	3	5
11	8	5	9	10

CHAPTER 10

Practice 10-1

Use a protractor to draw an angle of the given measure.

1a. 70°   **b.** 135°   **c.** 15°

Classify each angle as *right*, *acute*, *obtuse*, or *straight*. Estimate its measure.

2a.   **b.**   **c.**

Determine whether the polygon is *concave* or *convex*. Then classify the polygon by the number of sides.

3a.   **b.**   **c.**

Complete each statement.

4. If ∠ABC measures 43°, its complement measures ? .

5. If ∠XYZ measures 56°, its supplement measures ? .

Problem Solving

6. Draw an 80° angle. Then construct its bisector.

7. Draw hexagon *KLMNOP*. Then draw and name its diagonals.

8. Draw an isosceles right triangle. Label each angle by its measure.

9. In triangle *QRS*, ∠Q = 39° and ∠R = 76°. Find the measure of ∠S.

10. Explain the difference between an equilateral triangle and a scalene triangle. Use a drawing.

11. Construct a line *CD* perpendicular to line *AB* at point *P* on $\overleftrightarrow{AB}$.

12. One of the angles of an isosceles triangle measures 68°. What are the measures of the other angles of the triangle?

Practice 10-2

Identify each quadrilateral.

1a.   **b.**   **c.**

2a.   **b.**

Identify each solid figure.

3a.   **b.**   **c.**

4a.   **b.**   **c.**

Tell whether the figures are congruent. Write *Yes* or *No*.

5a.   **b.**

Which polygon is similar to *ABCD*?

6.   **a.**   **b.**

Problem Solving

7. Draw circle *P*. Label chord $\overline{AB}$ that is a diameter. Draw central angle *APR* that is an obtuse angle.

8. Name a regular polygon that cannot be used alone in a tessellation.

9. Name the solid figure that has 6 square faces, 8 vertices, and 12 edges.

10. △ABC is congruent to △XYZ. Use a drawing to show this.

11. Use dot paper. Draw rhombus *MNOP*. Then draw its reflection, rhombus *ABCD*, over a vertical line.

12. Which quadrilateral does *not* necessarily have opposite angles of equal measure?

13. Figure *A* is similar to figure *B*. Figure *B* is *not* similar to figure *C*. Is it possible that figure *A* is similar to figure *C*? Draw pictures to support your answer.

Practice 11-1

Write each ratio in simplest form.

1a. 5 to 15   **b.** 4 to 24   **c.** 8 to 56

2a. 30 : 60   **b.** 27 : 42   **c.** 75 : 125

Find the missing term in each proportion.

3a. $\dfrac{5}{7} = \dfrac{25}{n}$ **b.** $\dfrac{3}{12} = \dfrac{n}{4}$ **c.** $\dfrac{1}{30} = \dfrac{1}{n}$

4a. $n : 3 = 0.5 : 5$ **b.** $2.6 : 1.7 = n : 10.2$

Write a proportion. Then solve.

5. △ABC is similar to △XYZ. Find the value of n.

Using the word EXCELLENT, write each ratio:

6a. E's to all letters   **b.** consonants to vowels

7a. Ls to Es   **b.** vowels to consonants

Problem Solving

8. Lucinda got 18 out of 20 spelling words correct on her quiz. What is the ratio of correctly spelled words to all words on the quiz?

9. The ratio of teachers to students at Hickory School is 1 : 23. There are 25 teachers at the school. How many students are at the school?

10. Four blank tapes cost $6.60. Find the cost per tape.

11. Laverne rode her bike 9 mi in 1 h. At that rate, how long will it take her to ride 30 mi?

12. If 2 dozen pencils cost $3.60, what will 3 pencils cost?

13. LeRoy makes 5 out of every 8 free throws at basketball practice. At that rate, how many free throws can he expect to make in 64 tries?

Practice 11-2

Write as a percent.

1a. 43 to 100   **b.** 7 to 100   **c.** 0.75

2a. 0.5   **b.** $\dfrac{1}{4}$ **c.** $\dfrac{7}{25}$

Write as a decimal and as a fraction or mixed number in simplest form.

3a. 30%   **b.** 5%   **c.** 81%

4a. 37.5%   **b.** 625%   **c.** 187%

5a. 150%   **b.** 1000%   **c.** 0.3%

Find the actual measurements.

6a. Scale width: $1\dfrac{1}{4}$ in.   **b.** Scale length: 4.5 cm
   Scale: $\dfrac{1}{2}$ in. = 10 mi   Scale: 1 cm = 120 km

Problem Solving

7. In an enlarged model, 1 cm = 2 mm. A width of 5 cm is how many millimeters?

8. A road map uses a scale of 1 cm = 75 km. Find the map distance between two cities if the actual distance is 37.5 km.

9. A 9-ft telephone pole casts a 3-ft shadow. At the same time of day, Franny stands beside the pole. If she is 6 ft tall, how long is her shadow?

10. Spanish is spoken by 65 out of 100 people who work for a company. What percent of the workers speak Spanish?

11. Mrs. Gill spends 27% of her monthly income on rent and utilities. What percent of her monthly income is available for other purposes?

12. In a survey, 78% of the people said they approved of the idea of a new highway. What percent of the people did *not* approve?

13. In a ball-throwing contest, Jan scored 30 hits out of 35 tries. Al scored 0.85 of his throws and Roy's rate was 85.5%. Who had the best record?

REINFORCEMENT

Practice 12-1

Compute mentally.

1a. 10% of 90   **b.** 50% of 60

2a. $33\frac{1}{3}$% of 75   **b.** 75% of 16

Compare. Use < or >.

3. 27% of 50 _?_ 20% of 50

4. 60% of 80 _?_ 60% of 160

Find the percentage of the number.

5a. 45% of $900   **b.** 8% of $125

Find the percent or rate.

6. What percent of 40 is 16?

7. 57.6 is what percent of 96?

Problem Solving

8. Pam's soccer team won 15 out of 24 games. What percent of the games did Pam's team win?

9. Mel's Market sells oranges two ways: 5 for $.95 or 25¢ each. Which is the better buy?

10. In the football game, 62.5% of 24 passes wer completed. How many passes were completed

11. There are 360 members of the health club. $66\frac{2}{3}$% are adults; the rest are students. How many health club members are adults?

12. Of the 48 new library books, 12 are paperbacks. What percent are paperbacks?

13. The price of a personal stereo is 120% of last year's price of $35. Find the current price.

Practice 12-2

Compute the discount and sale price.

1a. basketball: $36   **b.** ice skates: $120
   rate of discount: 20%   rate of discount: 35%

2a. swimsuit: $40   **b.** skateboard: $99
   rate of discount: 25%   rate of discount: $33\frac{1}{3}$%

Find the sales tax and total cost.

3a. hat: $15   **b.** belt: $9.50
   sales tax: 6%   sales tax: 5%

4a. car: $12,500   **b.** motorcycle: $4,800
   sales tax: $5\frac{1}{4}$%   sales tax: $4\frac{1}{2}$%

Problem Solving

5. Maureen earns a 4% commission on computer sales. Find her earnings on sales of $2600.

6. At a rate of commission of $6\frac{1}{2}$%, how much does Jack earn on sales of $8000?

7. A $480 DVD player is on sale at 25% off. The sales tax is 3%. Find the total cost of the purchase.

8. A furniture store salesperson earns a monthly salary of $750 plus 5% commission on sales. How much does he earn in July if he sells $37,500 worth of furniture?

9. A telephone answering machine was reduced in price from $120 to $96. Find the rate of discount.

10. Draw a circle graph to show the cost of keeping a pet dog for one year.

food	$125	license	$2
vet visits	$75	dog toys	$2
boarding	$50		

11. Which is the better buy: a $60 watch at $\frac{1}{3}$ off c the same watch for $70 at 40% off?

12. The sales tax on a $48 item is $6. What percent is the sales tax?

13. Mr. Ali sold four used cars last week for $1400 $2140, $3300, and $1680. If his rate of commission was 5%, how much commission did he make on last week's sales?

Practice 13-1

Complete.

1a. 7.3 m = __?__ cm   **b.** 40 kg = __?__ g

2a. 27.4 L = __?__ kL   **b.** 73 dm = __?__ m

3a. 15 ft = __?__ yd   **b.** 14 pt = __?__ qt

4a. 3 mi = __?__ ft   **b.** 4T = __?__ lb

Compute.

5a. 7 ft 11 in.
     + 4 ft 9 in.

b.   9 qt
       − 5 qt 1 pt

6a. (2 yd 5 in.) × 3   **b.** (3 h 20 min) ÷ 4

Measure each line segment to the nearest $\frac{1}{8}$ in. and $\frac{1}{16}$ in.

7.

J   K

8.

W   X

Find the circumference and the area. Use 3.14 or $\frac{22}{7}$ for π.

9a. $d = 5.3$ m   **b.** $d = 2\frac{1}{3}$ yd   **c.** $r = 9$ m

Problem Solving

10. A dump truck hauling 2 T of topsoil unloaded 1200 lb of it at a building site. How much topsoil was left in the truck?

11. Jon's science book weighs 780 g. How much do 7 such books weigh?

12. Jill is 56 in. tall and Leslie is 4 ft 10 in. tall. Who is taller? How much taller?

13. Draw line segment *FG* that is exactly $3\frac{7}{8}$ in. long.

14. A circular swimming pool has a diameter that measures $23\frac{1}{2}$ ft. Find its circumference.

15. How many cups are in $7\frac{1}{4}$ gallons?

Practice 13-2

Use formulas to find the perimeter and area.

1a.

7 ft
7 ft

b. 3 cm

6 cm

c.
12 ft 15 ft
9 ft

2a.
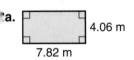
4.06 m
7.82 m

b.

3 in. 5 in.
5 in.

Find the surface area.

3a.
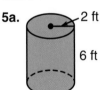
3 yd
9 yd 4 yd

b.
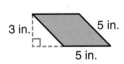
3.2 m
3.2 m 3.2 m

4a.
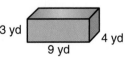
5 ft
3.5 ft
3.5 ft

b.
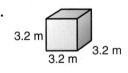
7 ft
10 ft
10 ft

Find the volume of each cylinder to the nearest tenth.

5a.
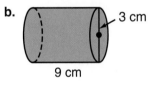
2 ft
6 ft

b.
3 cm
9 cm

Problem Solving

6. A storage bin measures 9 ft high, 6 ft wide, and 5 ft deep. Find its volume.

7. Li is painting the walls, floor, and ceiling of her closet. The closet is shaped like a rectangular prism that measures $8\frac{1}{2}$ ft high, $5\frac{1}{2}$ ft wide, and 4 ft deep. Find the surface area.

8. One can of paint will cover 144 ft². How many cans are needed to paint a wall that measures 26 ft by 15 ft?

9. The diameter of a half dollar is 30 mm. Find the area of one side of the coin in square centimeters.

REINFORCEMENT

CHAPTER 14

Practice 14-1

Solve and check.

1a. $5x - 10 = 35$ **b.** $4p + 9 = 33$

2a. $n + {}^-9 = {}^-30$ **b.** $^-8c = {}^+144$

3a. $\frac{y}{5} + 8 = 8$ **b.** $\frac{2x}{3} + 5 = 9$

Write an equation. Then solve.

4. A number decreased by 7 is 30. Find the number.

5. The sum of 7 and a number multiplied by 3 is 46. Find the number.

6. Graph each set of points in a coordinate grid.
 a. $A(^-3, {}^-3)$, $B(^+2, {}^-5)$, $C(^+2, {}^+4)$, $D(^-1, {}^+2)$
 b. $E(0, {}^-1)$, $F(^+1, {}^-2)$, $G(^-2, {}^+1)$, $H(^+3, {}^+1)$
 c. $I(^-1, {}^-1)$, $J(^+2, {}^-2)$, $K(^-3, {}^-2)$, $L(^-4, {}^-4)$

7. Name the points in exercise 6 that lie in each quadrant.
 a. quadrant I   **b.** quadrant II
 c. quadrant III   **d.** quadrant IV

8. Use the function rule to complete the function table.

Rule: $y = x + 6$		
x	y	(x, y)
$^-12$	?	?
$^-7$	?	?
0	?	?
$^+3$	?	?
$^+11$	?	?

9. Graph $A(0, 0)$, $B(^+4, 0)$, $C(^+4, {}^+4)$, $D(0, {}^+4)$ on a coordinate plane. On the same grid, graph each transformation and write the coordinates of its image figure.
 a. Reflect across the y-axis.
 b. Translate 3 units right and 5 units down.
 c. Rotate 180° counterclockwise about the origin.

10. The coordinates of the endpoints of $\overline{CD}$ are $C(^+4, {}^+1)$ and $D(^-3, {}^+2)$. Find the coordinates of its image after reflection across the x-axis.

Practice 14-2

Solve and check.

1a. $7.7 = 2.7 + 5x$ **b.** $75 = 11 + 16p$

2a. $n + {}^-15 = {}^-36$ **b.** $^-16c = {}^+144$

3a. $\frac{n}{4} + 4 = 10$ **b.** $17 = \frac{x}{2} - 13$

4. Find the next two terms of the sequence. Describe the pattern.
$$\frac{1}{2}, -\frac{1}{4}, \frac{1}{8}, -\frac{1}{16}, \ldots$$

5. Graph the reflection image of each point on a coordinate plane across the indicated axis.
 a. $(^+3, {}^+5)$, x-axis   **b.** $(^-2, {}^-3)$, y-axis
 c. $(^+7, {}^-1)$, x-axis   **d.** $(^+4, {}^+9)$, y-axis

6. Join the points $A(^+2, {}^+3)$, $B(^-2, {}^+3)$, $C(^-3, {}^-3)$, $D(^+1, {}^-3)$ in order on a grid. Translate the figure left 2 units. Give the coordinates of the vertices of the translation image.

7. Translate each point on a coordinate grid and give the coordinates of its image point.
 a. $A(^+3, {}^+9)$ left 4 units, up 3 units
 b. $B(^-5, {}^+4)$ right 3 units, down 2 units

8. Rotate each point counterclockwise about the origin on a coordinate grid.
 a. $A(^+5, {}^+7)$ **b.** $B(^-3, {}^-8)$ **c.** $C(^+5, {}^-13)$
      90°   180°   270°

9. Use the function rule to complete the function table.

Rule: $y = 3x - 5$		
x	y	(x, y)
$^-4$	?	?
$^-1$	?	?
0	?	?
$^+9$	?	?
$^+10$	?	?

10. If $2x + 3y = 12$ and $4x = 36$, then $y = $ ___ .

Brain Builders

SET 1

How many times greater is 2 in:

1a. 2 million than in 2 thousand?

1b. 7,025,100,000 than in 257,000?

Compare. Write <, =, or >.

2a. 6 billion _?_ 6 million, 20

b. 800 + 7 + 400,000 _?_ 500 thousand

3a. 48 + 63 _?_ 59 + 52

b. 107 − 59 _?_ 3072 − 2974

Write + or − to make each statement true.

4. 250 _?_ 78 _?_ 92 = 236

5. 688 _?_ 95 _?_ 86 = 679

6. 45,386
+23,492

7. 11,746
− 5,113

8. 50,000
−38,725

9. 629,735
+ 13,287

10. 70,006
−28,479

11. When 2 million is added to a number and the sum is subtracted from 5 million, the result is 500,000. Find the number.

12. Of 3 stadiums, one holds 89,549, another holds 89,594, and the third 89,459. Which stadium holds the most? the least?

13. One book costs $2.75, another is $3.45 more. Find the cost of both books.

14. A fish market sold 623 salmon, 755 tuna, and 389 monkfish. About how many fish were sold?

15. Frank gave away $\frac{1}{4}$ of his baseball cards. How many cards did he give away?

SET 2

1. What is 250 less than 5000?

2. From 1 million take 127 thousand.

3a. 46 × 10 × 100

b. 832 × 10 × 100

Find the value of n.

4a. 1700 + 30,000 = 30,000 + n

b. 120 − 120 + n = 40

5. 5100 + (200 + 3) = (5100 + n) + 3

6. 250 + (2600 + 750) = (2600 + 750) + n

Compare. Write <, =, or >.

7a. 382 × 36 _?_ 6 × 1735

b. 63 × 489 _?_ 72 × 382

8a. 839 ÷ 31 _?_ 738 ÷ 23

b. 18,057 ÷ 221 _?_ 39,653 ÷ 481

Write × or ÷ to make each statement true.

9a. 6 _?_ 213 = 1278

b. 2240 _?_ 64 = 35

10a. 4218 _?_ 3 = 1406

b. 81 _?_ 88 = 7128

11. At $1.06 a gallon, what is the cost of 250 gallons of gasoline?

12. There are chickens and cows on the farm with a total of 36 feet. There are more cows than chickens. How many of each are on the farm?

13. There are 8125 books to be shipped. Each carton can hold 16 books. How many books will be in the carton that is not filled?

14. A train takes 102 h to travel 7140 mi. A plane takes 17 h to go the same distance. How far does the plane travel in 1 h?

15. A baker uses 5 eggs for each cake he bakes. For 25 cakes, how many dozen eggs are used?

SET 3

1. What is the smallest nonzero number divisible by 2, 3, 5, and 9?

2a. 36)824

b. 4986 ÷ 48

3. 6 × 2 × 3 × 2 ÷ (16 ÷ 4) = _?_

In the number 5602.347891 there are how many:

4a. millionths? **b.** hundreds? **c.** thousandths?

Round to the nearest hundredth and thousandth.

5. 13.0736

6. 2.1087

Compare. Write <, =, or >.

7. 6.812 _?_ 6.81

8. 14.006 _?_ 14.060

9. From 16.065 take 0.283.

10. Take 0.10207 from 1.

11. A package of 100 tea bags sells for $20.15. What is the approximate cost per tea bag?

12. Kim can run 6 km in 26 min. Nel can run 4 km in 15.5 min. To the nearest tenth of a minute, how much faster can Nel run 1 kilometer?

13. Lee had 380 pictures. She put a dozen pictures on each page. How many more pictures does she need to complete the last page?

14. John is 57 in. tall. Jim is 46.25 in. tall. How much taller than Jim is John?

15. What number multiplied by 0.7 gives 4.48?

CHALLENGE

533

SET 4

1a. $8 + 0.7 - 0.53$ **b.** $2.6 - 0.3 + 1.9$
2a. 6.72×1.8 **b.** $7.856 \div 0.4$
3a. 2.06×17.04 **b.** $1.2\overline{)0.0672}$
4a. $0.4 \times (3.2 \times 1.7)$ **b.** $0.25 \div 0.005 - 50$

Order from least to greatest.
5. $627, 6.01 \times 10^3, 5.2 \times 10^2$
6. $3.9 \times 10^4, 4.1 \times 10^4, 39{,}500$

Evaluate each expression when $a = 6$, $b = 1.2$.
7. $2a + b$ **8.** $b \div a$
9. $a - 2b$ **10.** $a \times b - 7.14$

Write $+$ or $-$ to make each sentence true.
11a. $^-11 \underline{\ ?\ } \ ^-15 \underline{\ ?\ } \ ^+1 = \ ^+3$
b. $^-1 \underline{\ ?\ } \ ^+3 \underline{\ ?\ } \ ^-7 = \ ^-11$

12. Ted can swim the width of the pool in 15.24 s while it takes Tom triple this time. How much less time does it take Ted?

13. Dana earned $6.78 on Monday. Each day after, she earned a dime more. How much did she earn in 5 days?

14. How many even integers are between $^-30$ and $^+30$?

15. Mr. Wilson used 5.8 gallons of gasoline to go 92.8 miles. How far did he go on 1 gallon of gasoline?

16. Earl earns $25.92 a week selling newspapers. How many weeks will it take him to earn $181.44?

SET 5

Compare. Write $<$, $=$, or $>$.
1a. $2^2 \times 5 \underline{\ ?\ } 4^2$ **b.** $3^2 \cdot 2^2 \underline{\ ?\ } 2 \cdot 3^3$
2a. $\frac{2}{3} + \frac{4}{5} \underline{\ ?\ } 1\frac{1}{4}$ **b.** $11 - 8\frac{2}{3} \underline{\ ?\ } 3\frac{3}{4} - 2\frac{3}{8}$
3a. $\frac{2}{3} \underline{\ ?\ } 0.6$ **b.** $1.55 \underline{\ ?\ } \frac{13}{8}$

Complete.
4. The sum of $\frac{1}{8}$ and $\frac{3}{10}$ is close to $\underline{\ ?\ }$.
5. The sum of $\frac{7}{9}$ and $\frac{4}{15}$ is close to $\underline{\ ?\ }$.

What numbers between 20 and 28 have:
6. exactly 2 factors? **7.** exactly 4 factors?
8. Take 0.172 from 2.
9. What is 243.75 more than 51.9?
10. From 5280 take 79.32.
11. What is 316.001 more than 43.239?

12. Zach's boat can travel 1 mile in 3.2 min. How many hours will it take to go 67.5 mi?

13. Ms. Sims gave out cans of juice. The 16 5th graders each got 1. She got 5 more cans and gave 15 to the 6th graders. After 3 girls returned theirs, she had 4 cans left. How many cans did Ms. Sims have originally?

14. A theater used 48 lb of popcorn on Thursday. On each of the next 3 days, it used $1\frac{1}{4}$ the amount used the day before. How much was used on Sunday?

15. Use 3 of these fractions: $\frac{1}{2}, \frac{1}{3}, \frac{1}{4}$, and $\frac{3}{4}$, to make a true number sentence.
$\underline{\ ?\ } - \underline{\ ?\ } + \underline{\ ?\ } = \frac{7}{12}$

16. What mixed numbers complete this pattern?
$2\frac{3}{4}, 4\frac{1}{8}, 3\frac{5}{8}, 5, 4\frac{1}{2}, \underline{\ ?\ }, \underline{\ ?\ }$

SET 6

Compare. Write $<$, $=$, or $>$.
1a. $0.\overline{13} \underline{\ ?\ } 0.\overline{1}$ **b.** $\frac{5}{9} \underline{\ ?\ } 0.\overline{5}$
2a. $\frac{3}{4} + \frac{4}{5} \underline{\ ?\ } 1.55$ **b.** $4.5 - 3.8 \underline{\ ?\ } \frac{7}{9}$
3a. $2.\overline{01} \underline{\ ?\ } 2\frac{1}{100}$ **b.** $\frac{1}{2}$ of $8 \underline{\ ?\ } 10 \div 2$

Find the value of n.
4a. $2\frac{1}{6} \times n = 1$ **b.** $8 \times (\frac{3}{4} + \frac{1}{8}) = n$
5a. $\frac{7}{8}$ of $5.12 = n$ **b.** $\frac{3}{4}$ of $n = 15$

Complete. Write $+$ or $-$.
6. $\frac{4}{5} \underline{\ ?\ } \frac{1}{3} \underline{\ ?\ } \frac{1}{4} = \frac{13}{60}$ **7.** $6 \underline{\ ?\ } \frac{2}{3} \underline{\ ?\ } \frac{1}{2} = 5\frac{5}{6}$
8. $\frac{7}{8} \underline{\ ?\ } \frac{1}{5} \underline{\ ?\ } \frac{3}{20} = \frac{33}{40}$

9. From the sum of $3\frac{1}{2}$ and 0.75, subtract the sum of 3.25 and $\frac{3}{20}$.

10. Lynn bought 2 hams for a party. One ham weighed $10\frac{1}{8}$ lb; the other $12\frac{1}{4}$ lb. They ate $19\frac{1}{3}$ lb of ham. How many pounds are left?

11. Jan thought of a mixed number. She doubled it and subtracted $1\frac{3}{4}$. The result was $2\frac{11}{12}$. What was her original mixed number?

12. Of the 220 students who ate lunch, 145 ate salad, and 200 ate pizza. How many students ate both?

13. Jo, Tammy, and Drew run for president, vice president, and secretary. How many different ways might they be elected?

SET 7

1a. $2\frac{5}{8} \times 4\frac{3}{7} \div 7\frac{3}{4}$ **b.** $7\frac{3}{5} + 1\frac{1}{10} - 3\frac{3}{4}$

2a. From $\frac{1}{3}$ take $\frac{5}{18}$.   **b.** Take $5\frac{5}{7}$ from $7\frac{13}{14}$.

Find the value of n.

3a. $2\frac{5}{6} + n = 7\frac{1}{2}$ **b.** $n + 0.19 = 3$

4a. $n - \frac{4}{7} = 1\frac{1}{14}$ **b.** $n - 2.3 = 1.9$

5. Name 2 polygons that have 2 diagonals.

6. Name 2 straight angles.

7. Name 2 vertical angles.

ABXD is a square.

$\overline{AB} \parallel \overline{XD}$ so:

8. $\overline{AD}\ \underline{\ ?\ }\ \overline{DX}$ **9.** $\overline{BX}\ \underline{\ ?\ }\ \overline{XD}$

10. Draw a reflection, a translation, and a rotation for this figure.

11. Without looking, you pick a card from cards numbered 1–9, and flip a coin. Find P (even, H).

12. At $9.49 each, how much will it cost to buy 2 shirts each for 3 boys?

13. Fran scored 93, 87, 95, 95, and 88 points. By how many points does the mode exceed the mean?

14. Flo had 1 quarter, 1 dime, 1 nickel, and 1 penny. She gave 2 coins away. How many different amounts might she have given away?

15. Thirty students speak at least 2 languages. Nineteen speak Spanish and English, 12 speak French and English, and 3 speak all 3 languages. How many students speak Spanish and French?

SET 8

Complete each analogy.

1. A straight angle is to a right angle as $\underline{\ ?\ }$ is to 90°.

2. $\angle ABC$ is to $\overrightarrow{BA}$ as $\angle RPT$ is to $\underline{\ ?\ }$.

3. ⬠⬠ is to 60 cans as ⬠ is to $\underline{\ ?\ }$ cans.

4. Certainty is to 1 as impossibility is to $\underline{\ ?\ }$.

5. Prism is to rectangular face as $\underline{\ ?\ }$ is to triangular face.

6.   12 yd 1 ft 3 in.
  − 8 yd 2 ft 10 in.

7.   5 h 21 min 48 s
  +3 h 39 min 15 s

8. (2 yd 2 ft 8 in.) $\times$ 2

9. (4 gal 1 qt 1 pt) $\div$ 7

10a. $\frac{2}{5}$ of 1 km = $\underline{\ ?\ }$ m   **b.** $\frac{3}{4}$ of 2 ft = $\underline{\ ?\ }$ in.

11. When a store closed there were 6 newspapers left. If 42 people came in the store and every third person bought a newspaper, how many newspapers were there when the store opened?

12. On a circle graph, $\frac{1}{3}$ of Ed's day is spent sleeping, $\frac{1}{5}$ playing, $\frac{1}{10}$ eating, $\frac{1}{5}$ studying, and the rest reading. How many hours does Ed read?

13. In quadrilateral *EPRM* $\angle E = 140°$, $\angle R$ is half $\angle E$, and $\angle P$ is 20° less than $\angle R$. Find the measure of $\angle M$.

14. What is the probability of choosing a letter before N from a set of 26 alphabet cards?

15. How many ways can Leon draw 4 different quadrilaterals side by side on the board?

SET 9

1. $9\frac{1}{2} + 6\frac{3}{4} + 8\frac{1}{8}$ **2.** $6\frac{4}{7} - 2\frac{1}{3} + 1\frac{5}{7}$

Complete.

3a. $\frac{2}{3}$ of $\underline{\ ?\ }$ ft = 16 in.   **b.** $\frac{3}{4}$ of $\underline{\ ?\ }$ lb = 18 oz

4a. $0.14 \times 250 = \underline{\ ?\ }$ **b.** $0.2 \times 150 = \underline{\ ?\ }$

5. 50% is to 200% as $\frac{1}{2}$ is to $\underline{\ ?\ }$.

6. Radius is to diameter as 50% is to $\underline{\ ?\ }$.

7. 0.75 is to 75% as $\underline{\ ?\ }$ is to 4%.

8. 3 out of 5 is to 60% as 1 out of 8 is to $\underline{\ ?\ }$ %.

9. 25% is to 75% as 10% is to $\underline{\ ?\ }$ %.

10. 800% is to 5 + 3 as $\underline{\ ?\ }$ % is to $3 - 1\frac{1}{2}$.

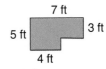

11. Find the perimeter.

12. Find the area.

13. How much less is the volume of a rectangular prism 8 m by 14 m by 8.5 m than a cube 10.2 m on each edge?

14. A rectangular field is 178 ft long and 145 ft wide. What is its perimeter in yards?

15. You put $1000 in a bank. Each year the bank adds $\frac{1}{10}$ of your total savings to the account. How many years will it take your account to be greater than $1500?

CHALLENGE

SET 10

1a. $(\frac{1}{5}$ of 30$) - (0.3$ of 20$)$ **b.** $\frac{2}{7}$ of $1.54

2a. Take 1.046 from 3.1.   **b.** From 1.5 take $\frac{1}{4}$.

3a. 40% of $2.00   **b.** $12\frac{1}{2}$% of $7.20

Find each missing dimension. Use $\pi \approx 3.14$.

4. $C \approx 15.7$ in., $d = \underline{\ ?\ }$

5. $A = 16$ cm^2, $\ell = 6.4$ cm, $w = \underline{\ ?\ }$

6. $V = 128$ m^3, $\ell = 8$ m, $w = 4$ m, $h = \underline{\ ?\ }$

Complete each analogy.

7. Circle is to πr^2 as triangle is to $\underline{\ ?\ }$.

8. Double is to 200% as triple is to $\underline{\ ?\ }$.

9. 60% of 30 is to 18 as $\underline{\ ?\ }$% of 20 is to 24.

10. 75% of 1 lb is to 12 oz as $\underline{\ ?\ }$% of 1 h is to 12 min.

11. $\frac{7}{8}$ of the distance between two towns is 147 m. What is the total distance?

12. What is the ratio of the area of a square 6 cm on each side to the area of a rectangle that is 8 cm by 5 cm?

13. Six pounds of coffee cost $19.74. How much will 4 lb cost?

14. A girl who weighed 97 lb lost 10% of her weight. How much did she weigh then?

15. What is the area of the shaded region of the rectangle?

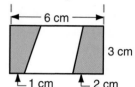

SET 11

Solve for n.

1a. $3 : n = 1.8 : 6$ **b.** $4 : 3.2 = n : 16$

2a. $n : 1\frac{1}{2} = 3 : \frac{1}{4}$ **b.** $2\frac{1}{4} : 9 = \frac{1}{2} : n$

3. $^-6 + (^-3 - ^-1) = n$

4. $^-12 - (^-8 + ^+4) = n$

5a. n% of 7 is 14   **b.** n% of 1.8 is 0.9

6a. $33\frac{1}{3}$% of n is 11   **b.** 600% of $n = 42$

7a. 15% of $0.2 = n$ **b.** 1% of $50 = n$

8a. n% of $\frac{3}{4} = \frac{1}{4}$ **b.** n% of $1.2 = 3$

Find the unit cost.

9a. $1\frac{1}{2}$ lb for $1.26   **b.** 2.5 L for $3.60

Find the tax.

10a. 6% tax on $17.35.

   b. 5.5% tax on $127.40.

11. A blazer listed at $44 was sold for 25% off. What was the selling price?

12. On a map the distance from City A to City B is 3.4 in. The scale is 1 in. = 25 mi. What is the actual distance?

13. The temperatures in 5 different cities for one day were 14°F, $^-$20°F, 31°F, 45°F, and $^-$5°F. Find the range. Find the mean.

14. The coordinates of the vertices of $\triangle FHM$ are (1,0), (2,5), and (6,0). Find the area of $\triangle FHM$.

15. A man sold a house for $150,000. If he received $7500 commission, what rate of commission did he receive?

SET 12

Solve for n.

1a. $n - 7 = 6 \div 2$ **b.** $n + 5 = 7 \times 3$

2a. $3n = 7 + 2$ **b.** $n \div 6 = 4 + 3$

3a. $^-20 + n = {}^+5$ **b.** $n - {}^-6 = {}^+10$

4a. $n + {}^-2 = {}^+8$ **b.** $^+3 - n = {}^-5$

Graph the points on a coordinate plane.

5. $C(^+1, {}^+8)$, $E(^+1, {}^+2)$, and $G(0, {}^+2)$
Find the coordinates of point H if $CEGH$ is a rectangle.

6. $A(^+8, {}^+1)$, $B(^+8, {}^+5)$
Find the coordinates of points C and D if $ABCD$ is a square.

7. Jim wrote down an integer. He doubled it and subtracted $^+11$. His answer was $^-5$. What integer did Jim write down?

8. If a and b represent integers between $^-2$ and $^+1$, how many equations can be written for $a - b = {}^-1$?

9. If point $(h, 1)$ is on the graph of $y = 5x - 4$, what is the value of h?

10. If $a - b = 9$ and $b = 6c$, and $3c = 7$, what is the value of a?

11. A translation moves $P(^+2, {}^+4)$ to $P'(0, 0)$. If $Q(^+4, {}^+2)$ is translated the same way as P, then what are the coordinates of its image Q'?

Mental Math

Listen to your teacher read the directions.
You do not need paper and pencil.

SET 1

1. Name the period.
   12,<u>452</u>; <u>321</u>,589; <u>6</u>,109,372; <u>710</u>,448; 626,<u>001</u>

2. Add 1 million to: 4,375,210; 508,119,042;
   62,137,429; 506,317,286,902

3. Give the value of the underlined digits:
   1,<u>6</u>24,<u>5</u>90,7<u>8</u>3

4. Add 2 to: 9, 6, 19, 16, 8, 28, 7, 17

5. Subtract 3 from: 10, 12, 25, 19, 32, 42

6. In the numeral 468, what is the value of 6?

7. From the sum of 9 + 6, take 3 + 4.

8. Mary had $3.50. She spent $1.30. How much
   did she have left?

9. Which is greater:
   36,101 or 30,000 + 6000 + 100 + 10 + 0?

10. What period is 25 in 25,607,384,590,012?

11. Of the numbers 36,803,251, 36,308,215, and
    36,803,215, which is the greatest?

12. Name the addition property used.
    $a + (b + c) = (a + b) + c$

13. The bookstore has 48 cat calendars and 61 dog
    calendars. Estimate the number of calendars.

14. What is the value of 8 in 30,820?

15. On Saturday, 478 people went to the show. If
    250 went to the A.M. show, about how many
    went to the P.M. show?

SET 2

1. Round to the nearest million. 3,733,415;
   2,165,899; 7,998,115; 31,236,709

2. Round to the place of the underlined digit.
   8<u>3</u>,724; 6<u>2</u>8,457; 3,<u>2</u>96,485

3. Find the missing number.
   16 + n = 16
   5 + 8 = n + 5
   (3 + 2) + 4 = 3 + (n + 4)

4. Estimate. 18 + 19 + 17   32 + 29 + 25
   48 + 11 + 13   56 + 12 + 25   65 + 12 + 21

5. Subtract 4 from: 9, 7, 16, 12, 23, 27

6. In the numeral 8,643,729,065 what is the value
   of 4?

7. Which 4 coins make $.75?

8. How much less than 9 + 8 is 7 + 3?

9. At a sale, the price of a rug was changed from
   $32 to $27. How much was it reduced?

10. Choose the operations:
    200 ? 75 ? 25 = 250

11. What is the difference in cents between
    8 dimes and 8 nickels?

12. The price of eggs was $1.08 a dozen. A week
    later, it was $1.23. How much had the price per
    dozen increased?

13. If the sum of 2 numbers is 13, and one addend
    is 4, what is the other?

14. Round 8325 to the nearest thousand.

15. Find n.
    10 + 4 + 3 − 6 + 9 − 11 − 3 = n

SET 3

1. 1 × __?__ = 11   13 × __?__ = 0
   36 × __?__ = 36   42 × __?__ = 0
   1 × __?__ = 25   50 × __?__ = 0

2. Add 4 to: 6, 7, 27, 8, 18, 9, 39, 16

3. Subtract 2 from: 8, 18, 13, 23, 17, 37

4. Name the first 4 non-zero multiples of:
   6, 10, 5, 4, 7, 9, 8

5. Multiply by 2, then add 3: 4, 8, 7, 9, 3, 10, 0, 5, 6

6. How much less than 2 times 8 is 2 times 7?

7. At 2 for $.35, what will 6 marbles cost?

8. How much greater than 3 × 0 is 3 × 6?

9. At $.20 each, find the cost of 30 stamps.

10. From the difference between 16 and 7 take 2 × 3.

11. At 40 miles per hour, how far will a ship go in
    8 hours?

12. Van's 50 cents in change contains
    1 quarter, 1 nickel, and d dimes. What is the
    value of d?

13. Dan packs 77 boxes per hour. At this rate, about
    how many boxes will he pack in 12 hours?

14. Evaluate 40 × 30 ÷ 40 × 300.

15. The nursery plants 240 trees in each of 20 rows.
    How many trees are planted?

MAINTENANCE

SET 4

1. Multiply by 8: 6, 4, 9, 2, 7, 3, 80, 60, 40, 90, 20, 70, 30, 50
2. Add 3 to: 9, 8, 17, 27, 16, 36, 47, 19
3. Give the standard numeral.
   10^3, 10^2, 10^5, 10^4, 10^6, 10^1
4. Give the exponent form: $3 \times 3 \times 3$;
   $5 \times 5 \times 5 \times 5$; 9×9; $7 \times 7 \times 7 \times 7 \times 7$
5. Multiply by 100: 6, 9, 10, 13, 19, 27, 32, 45, 63, 59, 83, 94, 50, 76
6. What is 10,000,000 as a power of ten?
7. Any number to the first power is __?__ .

8. If 4 bars of soap cost $1.00, how much will 12 cost?
9. Estimate the cost of 6 CDs at $9.95 each.
10. There are 30 children per class and 13 classes. How many children are there altogether?
11. At $4.05 an hour, how much will Bob earn in 9 hours?
12. What is the difference in cents between 9 dimes and 9 nickels?
13. Multiply 8 by 405.
14. At $.60 a meter, what will 8 meters of rope cost?
15. At $2 a yard, how many yards of drip-dry cotton can be bought for $18?

SET 5

1. $1\overline{)7}$ $10\overline{)0}$ $3\overline{)0}$ $67\overline{)67}$ $1\overline{)18}$
   $28\overline{)0}$ $1\overline{)136}$ $258\overline{)258}$
2. $5\overline{)25}$ $5\overline{)250}$ $5\overline{)2500}$ $5\overline{)25,000}$
   $3\overline{)210}$ $4\overline{)3200}$ $6\overline{)240}$ $2\overline{)2000}$
3. Divide by 4, then add 3 to:
   4, 12, 0, 20, 16, 28, 36, 32, 8, 24
4. Divide by 8: 9, 11, 13, 15, 17, 19, 21, 23
5. $2\overline{)412}$ $3\overline{)618}$ $4\overline{)328}$ $5\overline{)205}$
   $6\overline{)612}$ $7\overline{)147}$ $2\overline{)608}$ $3\overline{)312}$
6. What number divided by 2 will give 9 for the quotient and 1 for the remainder?
7. At $.92 for 4 pencils, find the cost of 2.
8. How much less than 3×1 is 2×0?

9. Rudy bought 8 meters of ribbon. If she paid $.96 for the ribbon, what was the cost of 1 meter of ribbon?
10. Divide 2432 by 4.
11. On Monday, 2076 students came to the zoo. On the average, each bus holds 49 students. About how many buses were needed?
12. At 50 mph, how long will it take to drive 300 miles?
13. Divide 3216 by 8, then subtract 2 from the quotient.
14. How much greater than 8×1 is $8 \div 1$?
15. Evaluate $6 \times 2 + 8 \div 4 - 3$.

SET 6

1. Which are divisible by 3? 41, 57, 68, 363, 245, 108, 417, 239, 512, 125
2. Which are divisible by 9? 167, 2514, 3620, 428, 396, 1539, 4335, 2007
3. Divide by 7: 16, 30, 8, 37, 24, 44
4. $20\overline{)640}$ $40\overline{)600}$ $30\overline{)750}$ $50\overline{)3100}$
5. Divide by 9: 10, 19, 28, 37, 11, 20, 29
6. At $.60 for a half dozen, find the cost of 3 pencils.
7. Divide 4963 by 7.
8. Which number is divisible by 2, 3, 5, 9, and 10? 109, 364, 575, 990

9. What number divided by 3 will give 8 for a quotient and 2 for a remainder?
10. A tank containing 28,200 gallons of fuel must be emptied into smaller tanks, each holding 300 gallons. How many smaller tanks are needed?
11. From 8×7 take $108 \div 9$.
12. The Scotts pay $2832 a year for insurance. How much is that per month?
13. In 9 hours a rocket covered 7200 km. What was its average speed per hour?
14. Ashlee paid $4.75 for a hat that had been reduced by $1.25. What was the original price of the hat?
15. How many inches are in 8 feet?

. Give the value of the underlined digit. 0.5<u>6</u>2,
   32.<u>4</u>, 1.43<u>79</u>, 0.00<u>4</u>, 35.178<u>3</u>, 8.0267<u>1</u>, 4<u>9</u>.7
. Read each decimal. 9.006, 21.35, 1.6285,
   724.6, 3.90, 4.00763, 6.000248
. Round to the nearest hundredth. 0.762, 2.8975,
   0.261, 0.538, 16.085, 0.1992
. Order from least to greatest. 0.4, 0.41, 4.0;
   3.7, 3.3, 3.9; 52, 5, 520; 7.13, 7.31, 7.11
. Compare. Use <, =, or >. 12.31 _?_ 1.23
   92.3 _?_ 92.33   0.54 _?_ 0.6
. In 3,178,242.377098, there are how many:
   millionths? ten thousandths?
. From 1 take 0.7.
. Add 0.3 and 0.7.

9. Estimate by rounding the total cost of a $59.95
   dress and a $17.98 skirt.
10. What is the sum: 6 + 0.67 + 16.13?
11. Kimo wants to run 12 km. He has already run
    7.8 km. How much farther does he have to run?
12. Place the decimal point to make the answer
    reasonable. Al's math score general average
    is 964.
13. Round 92.03729 to the nearest thousandth.
14. Which is greater: $316.25 or $361.25?
15. Fay spent $3.75 for lunch on Mon., Tues., and
    Wed. and $2.90 on Thurs. and Fri. Estimate by
    rounding how much money she had left from
    twenty dollars.

. 0.6 + 0.06   7.2 + 7.02   0.3 + 1.4
  0.5 + 2.1   1.30 + 0.04   0.12 + 0.07
. 0.9 − 0.09   5.5 − 2.3   1.08 − 0.8
  2.004 − 1.001   4.333 − 4.003
. Compare. Use <, =, or >. 3.07 − 1 _?_ 2;
  2.3 + 1.01 _?_ 3.4; 2.319 + 1.06 _?_ 3.379
. Multiply by 10. 0.12, 0.74, 0.3, 0.11, 0.04
. Multiply by 100. 0.2, 0.05, 0.89, 0.132
. What number is 3.75 greater than 6.25?
. The sum of 2.06 and another number is 9.37.
  Find the other number.
. The dress factory uses 2.4 yd of fabric to make
  each dress. Estimate how many yards are
  needed to make 285 dresses.

9. The original price of a jacket was $80. It was
   reduced $7. For how much was it sold?
10. Find $\frac{1}{9}$ of 54, and subtract the result from 20.
11. At $1.20 a dozen, find the cost of 5 dozen eggs.
12. Find the sum of 1.8, 2, and 0.2.
13. In the numeral 6.047, what is the value of 4?
14. Complete the pattern.
    0.524, 5.24, 52.4, _?_
15. At $.42 each, about how many folders can be
    bought with $19.95?

. Multiply by 1000. 0.1, 0.004, 0.178, 0.063, 0.5,
  0.35, 0.2436, 0.789201, 0.0891
. Multiply by 0.02. 0.3, 0.01, 0.5, 0.9, 0.08, 0.4,
  0.07, 0.11, 0.06
. Divide by 100. 300, 532, 483.1, 60.2, 8.2, 3.18,
  0.06, 0.4, 0.9, 0.15
. Divide by 10. 1.13, 24.8, 554.2, 47.6, 20, 0.3,
  0.28, 0.64, 0.004
. Divide by 1000. 6300, 700, 235.7, 4.88, 0.007,
  0.08, 0.1, 0.99, 8.72
. Van weighs $47\frac{1}{2}$ lb and Sam weighs
  $47\frac{7}{8}$ lb. What is the difference in
  their weights?

7. Express $\frac{625}{1000}$ as a decimal.
8. Each corsage uses 2.5 ft of ribbon for a bow. How
   many bows can be made from 62.5 ft of ribbon?
9. What number multiplied by 0.6 will give a product
   of 4.32?
10. A complete dictionary has a mass of 5.85 kg.
    A large telephone book has a mass of 5625 g.
    Which has greater mass?
11. At $4.50 a pound, what will 8 pounds of nuts
    cost?
12. Jim ran 2 km in 25 min. How far did he run in
    1 minute?
13. Which is greater: 6×10^8 or 6.2×10^7?
14. Write in scientific notation: 47,000,000.
15. Compute. $0.03 \times 2 + 0.03 \times 4$

MAINTENANCE

SET 10

1. Express each as closer to 0 or to 1.
$\frac{2}{13}, \frac{15}{16}, \frac{7}{8}, \frac{3}{20}, \frac{2}{25}, \frac{5}{6}, \frac{4}{15}, \frac{14}{17}$

2. $\frac{1}{3} = \frac{?}{9} = \frac{?}{15} = \frac{?}{12} = \frac{?}{6} = \frac{?}{18} = \frac{?}{27}$

3. Identify as prime or composite.
13, 15, 21, 11, 7, 31, 18, 26, 32, 41, 54

4. Name the factors of: 6, 14, 3, 8, 12, 9, 11, 18, 10, 17

5. Find the GCF.   8 and 14   36 and 48
9 and 30   28 and 35   6 and 18

6. Of the 20 animals in the pet shop, 9 are dogs. What fractional part are dogs?

7. Take 0.4 from 2.1.

8. Find the value of n. $\frac{34}{56} = \frac{68}{n}$

9. Choose the prime factorization for 60.
   a. 12×5 **b.** $2 \times 2 \times 3 \times 5$
   c. $2 \times 2 \times 2 \times 5$

10. Kim sleeps 8 h a day. What part of the day does Kim sleep?

11. If $\frac{3}{8}$ of a class are girls, what fractional part are boys?

12. Complete the pattern.
$\frac{1}{5}, \frac{3}{5}, \frac{2}{5}, \frac{4}{5}, \frac{3}{5}, 1, \frac{4}{5}, 1\frac{1}{5}, 1, 1\frac{2}{5}, \underline{\quad ?\quad}$

13. From the sum of $\frac{5}{8}$ and $\frac{7}{8}$ take 1.

14. Express 0.05 as a fraction in simplest form.

15. How many dozen eggs are in 42 eggs?

SET 11

1. Express in simplest form. $\frac{20}{28}, \frac{16}{32}, \frac{7}{21}, \frac{35}{45}$

2. Express as a mixed number. $\frac{9}{7}, \frac{13}{6}, \frac{19}{8}$

3. Find the LCM.   3 and 5   2 and 8
4 and 6   5 and 9   3 and 7   10 and 12

4. Give the equivalent fraction. $1\frac{1}{5}, 2\frac{7}{8}, 4\frac{3}{5},$
$1\frac{5}{6}, 3\frac{1}{2}, 2\frac{2}{3}, 3\frac{4}{9}, 4\frac{5}{7}$

5. Find the LCD. $\frac{5}{6}$ and $\frac{1}{12}$ $\frac{2}{3}$ and $\frac{5}{9}$
$\frac{1}{4}$ and $\frac{9}{16}$ $\frac{11}{14}$ and $\frac{1}{7}$ $\frac{4}{5}$ and $\frac{19}{20}$

6. In the gym $\frac{1}{5}$ of the people are swimming and $\frac{3}{10}$ of the people are jogging. Which sport has more people?

7. How many thirds are there in $3\frac{1}{3}$?

8. Order from least to greatest. $\frac{1}{2}, \frac{1}{6}, \frac{2}{3}$

9. Order from greatest to least. $1\frac{1}{4}, \frac{6}{4}, 1\frac{3}{4}$

10. Give the equivalent decimal for $\frac{9}{10}$.

11. Desiree has $\frac{3}{4}$ of a dollar. How much money does she have?

12. Give the equivalent decimal for $\frac{1}{4}$.

13. How much greater than $9\overline{)0.27}$ is $2\overline{)0.08}$?

14. Express 7.5 ft as a mixed number.

15. Express $\frac{2}{3}$ as a repeating decimal.

SET 12

1. Compare. Use <, =, or >. $\frac{1}{3} \; \underline{?} \; \frac{4}{12}$
$\frac{2}{5} \; \underline{?} \; \frac{7}{10}$ $\frac{1}{8} \; \underline{?} \; \frac{3}{16}$ $\frac{3}{4} \; \underline{?} \; \frac{1}{8}$

2. To 0.1 add: 0.4, 0.8, 0.03, 0.05, 0.25, 0.75

3. From 1 take: 0.6, 0.2, 0.8, 0.7, 0.1, 0.9

4. $\begin{array}{c}\frac{1}{3}\\[-2pt]+\frac{2}{3}\\ \hline \frac{3}{4}\\[-2pt]-\frac{1}{4}\end{array}$ $\begin{array}{c}\frac{3}{4}\\[-2pt]+\frac{1}{4}\\ \hline \frac{3}{3}\\[-2pt]-\frac{1}{3}\end{array}$ $\begin{array}{c}\frac{4}{5}\\[-2pt]+\frac{1}{5}\\ \hline \frac{5}{6}\\[-2pt]-\frac{2}{6}\end{array}$

5. $\begin{array}{c}\frac{3}{8}\\[-2pt]+\frac{1}{2}\\ \hline \frac{1}{5}\\[-2pt]+\frac{1}{10}\end{array}$ $\begin{array}{c}\frac{1}{4}\\[-2pt]+\frac{1}{12}\\ \hline \frac{1}{16}\\[-2pt]+\frac{1}{2}\end{array}$ $\begin{array}{c}\frac{1}{6}\\[-2pt]+\frac{1}{3}\\ \hline \frac{2}{3}\\[-2pt]+\frac{1}{9}\end{array}$

6. Simplify $\frac{12}{24}$ and add $1\frac{1}{4}$ to the result.

7. Julia has two ribbons. One is $1\frac{1}{9}$ yd, the other $1\frac{2}{3}$ yd. Which is closer to 1 yd?

8. Carol ran $1\frac{1}{2}$ mi, 1 mi, $2\frac{1}{2}$ mi, and $\frac{1}{2}$ mi. How many miles did she run in all?

9. To $\frac{1}{8}$ add $\frac{3}{4}$.

10. From 2 take $1\frac{3}{5}$.

11. How many $\frac{7}{8}$ are in $1\frac{3}{4}$?

12. Bruce walked $\frac{6}{7}$ mi on Monday. He walked $\frac{9}{14}$ mi less on Tuesday. How far did he walk on Tuesday?

13. One snake measures $12\frac{1}{2}$ ft. Another snake measures $3\frac{1}{3}$ ft longer. How long is the second snake?

14. Leon worked $4\frac{1}{2}$ h in the A.M. and $5\frac{1}{2}$ h in the P.M. Sam worked $6\frac{1}{4}$ h in the A.M. and $4\frac{1}{5}$ h in the P.M. Who worked longer?

15. How much greater than $\frac{33}{5}$ is $7\frac{1}{5}$?

SET 13

1. $(2\frac{1}{3} + 1\frac{1}{3}) - 1\frac{2}{3}$ $\quad$ $3\frac{1}{5} - (1\frac{4}{5} - \frac{3}{5})$
$(1\frac{1}{4} + 4\frac{3}{4}) + \frac{1}{4}$ $\quad$ $(5\frac{5}{6} - 3\frac{1}{6}) + 1\frac{1}{6}$

2. $\frac{1}{4} - \frac{1}{8}$ $\quad$ $\frac{1}{2} - \frac{1}{6}$ $\quad$ $\frac{1}{3} - \frac{1}{9}$
$\frac{1}{2} - \frac{1}{4}$ $\quad$ $\frac{1}{3} - \frac{1}{27}$ $\quad$ $\frac{1}{2} - \frac{1}{10}$

3. $18 \times \frac{1}{3}$ $\quad$ $12 \times \frac{1}{4}$ $\quad$ $21 \times \frac{1}{7}$ $\quad$ $30 \times \frac{1}{5}$
$7 \times \frac{5}{7}$ $\quad$ $10 \times \frac{3}{10}$ $\quad$ $6 \times \frac{5}{6}$ $\quad$ $4 \times \frac{3}{4}$

4. $\frac{2}{5} \times \frac{1}{4}$ $\quad$ $\frac{1}{3} \times \frac{1}{2}$ $\quad$ $\frac{5}{6} \times \frac{1}{4}$ $\quad$ $\frac{1}{6} \times \frac{1}{2}$
$\frac{3}{5} \times \frac{1}{3}$ $\quad$ $\frac{3}{10} \times \frac{1}{2}$ $\quad$ $\frac{3}{4} \times \frac{2}{3}$ $\quad$ $\frac{1}{4} \times \frac{2}{3}$

5. Give the reciprocal. $\frac{1}{7}$, 16, $\frac{2}{3}$, 9, $\frac{4}{5}$, 20

6. How much greater than $\frac{1}{9}$ of 63 is $\frac{1}{7}$ of 63?

7. How much less than $9\frac{1}{9}$ is $8\frac{6}{9}$?

8. Nan uses $1\frac{1}{5}$ skeins of red yarn, $1\frac{3}{5}$ skeins of blue, and $1\frac{4}{5}$ skeins of white to make an afghan. How many skeins is that?

9. How many pieces $\frac{3}{4}$ m long can be cut from 6 m of string?

10. Find the value of $\frac{3}{4} \times \frac{1}{3} \times 0$.

11. Solve. $35 \times \underline{\ ?\ } = 1$

12. On Monday, $4\frac{1}{2}$ gal of juice were served. On Tuesday, $1\frac{1}{4}$ times as much juice was served. How much juice was served on Tuesday?

Write what comes next in each pattern.

13. $\frac{1}{400}, \frac{1}{200}, \frac{1}{100}, \frac{1}{50}, \frac{1}{25}, \frac{2}{25}, \frac{4}{25}, \frac{8}{25}, \underline{\ ?\ }$

14. 32, 16, 8, 4, 2, $\frac{1}{2}$, $\frac{1}{4}$, $\frac{1}{8}$, $\underline{\ ?\ }$

15. 1.5, 1.6, 1.8, 1.9, 2.1, 2.2, 2.4, $\underline{\ ?\ }$

SET 14

1. $7 \div \frac{1}{4}$ $\quad$ $3 \div \frac{1}{2}$ $\quad$ $6 \div \frac{1}{4}$ $\quad$ $3 \div \frac{3}{5}$
$4 \div \frac{4}{7}$ $\quad$ $5 \div \frac{5}{9}$ $\quad$ $8 \div \frac{8}{15}$ $\quad$ $\frac{1}{2} \div \frac{1}{2}$

2. Find $\frac{1}{2}$ of: $\frac{2}{3}, \frac{2}{9}, \frac{4}{7}, \frac{4}{5}, \frac{6}{7}, \frac{6}{17}, \frac{8}{9}, \frac{8}{15}$

3. Multiply by 100. 0.25, 0.35, 0.42, 0.64

4. Divide by 4. 0.028, 0.004, 0.032, 0.020

5. $\frac{3}{4} + \frac{1}{4}$ $\quad$ $\frac{3}{5} + \frac{3}{5}$ $\quad$ $\frac{3}{5} \times \frac{3}{5}$ $\quad$ $\frac{3}{5} \div \frac{3}{5}$

6. $(\frac{5}{6} \div \frac{5}{6}) + 0.9 = \underline{\ ?\ }$

7. Regina has $2\frac{1}{2}$ yd of yarn. Into how many pieces $\frac{1}{2}$ yd long can the yarn be cut?

8. Don had $3\frac{1}{2}$ pizzas to share equally among 28 people. How much pizza did each person receive?

9. Zack had $7.25. He spent $\frac{1}{5}$ of his money. How much did he have left?

10. Find $\frac{1}{5}$ of 50 and subtract the result from 20.

11. From $1\frac{3}{4}$ take $1\frac{1}{2}$.

12. One twin weighed $5\frac{1}{4}$ lb at birth. The other twin weighed $1\frac{1}{3}$ times as much. How much did the second twin weigh?

13. How many sixths are there in $4\frac{5}{6}$?

14. Dorothy spent $\frac{1}{4}$ of the $33.56 she had saved. How much did she spend?

15. Add 0.6 to $\frac{1}{2}$ of 0.6.

SET 15

1. Decimal points must be moved how many places?
$0.2\overline{)4}$ $\quad$ $0.4\overline{)8.8}$ $\quad$ $0.03\overline{)6}$ $\quad$ $3\overline{)0.009}$

2. Multiply by 7. 0.2, 0.7, 0.9, 0.4, 0.8, 0.6, 0

3. Simplify. $\frac{5}{25}, \frac{5}{15}, \frac{5}{50}, \frac{5}{35}, \frac{5}{45}, \frac{5}{10}, \frac{5}{40}$

4. Express as a mixed number. $\frac{10}{9}, \frac{14}{9}, \frac{12}{9}$

5. Find $\frac{1}{3}$ of: 12, 21, 27, 3, 15, 24, 30, 6, 18

6. What is the difference in cents between 3 quarters and 7 nickels?

7. In the numeral 8.014 what is the value of 4?

On 5 different days, the class collected 24, 32, 28, 36, and 40 pledges.

8. Find the median.

9. Find the range.

10. Find the mode.

11. Key: Each ⬭ = 20 jars of honey. How many jars are there? ⬭⬭⬭⬭⬭⬭

12. What type of graph depends on the data adding up to 100%?

13. The probability of an event that is impossible is $\underline{\ ?\ }$.

14. The probability of an event that is certain is $\underline{\ ?\ }$.

15. In the last 3 ballgames, Emily scored 7, 11, and 15 points. What was the average number of points scored?

MAINTENANCE

SET 16

1. Express as a fraction. $7\frac{1}{8}, 5\frac{3}{8}, 2\frac{7}{8},$ $8\frac{5}{8}, 6\frac{7}{8}, 9\frac{3}{8}, 6\frac{5}{7}$

2. $\frac{1}{2} + \frac{1}{2}$ $\frac{1}{2} - \frac{1}{2}$ $\frac{1}{2} \times \frac{1}{2}$ $\frac{1}{2} \div \frac{1}{2}$

3. $0.2 + 0.1$ $0.03 + 0.01$ $0.08 + 0.01$
   $0.3 + 0.7$ $0.03 + 0.07$ $0.4 + 0.1$

4. To $\frac{1}{2}$ add: $\frac{3}{4}, \frac{1}{6}, \frac{3}{8}, \frac{2}{5}, \frac{1}{9}, \frac{2}{9}$

5. From 1 take: $\frac{1}{8}, \frac{1}{9}, \frac{1}{4}, \frac{1}{6}, \frac{3}{5}, \frac{5}{6}, \frac{3}{7}$

6. Read each decimal. 7.72 0.772 7.072

7. Divide 714 by 7 and add 8 to the quotient.

8. $(\frac{1}{4} + \frac{1}{4}) - (6 \times 0)$

In a box there are 4 red pencils, 5 blue pencils, and 3 yellow pencils. Find:

9. P (red)
10. P (blue or yellow)
11. P (pencil)
12. P (green)
13. What fractional part of a dozen is 10?
14. The amount $.48 is equal to q quarter, d dimes, and 3 pennies. Find the values of q and d.
15. At 3 for $.45, what will $1\frac{1}{2}$ dozen apples cost?

SET 17

1. Express as mixed numbers. $\frac{41}{8}, \frac{45}{8}, \frac{43}{8}, \frac{47}{8},$ $\frac{49}{8}, \frac{51}{8}, \frac{57}{8}, \frac{55}{8}, \frac{59}{8}, \frac{61}{8}$

2. Identify.

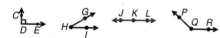

3. Identify.

4. Classify each angle.

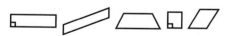

5. Tell how many congruent sides are in a square, rhombus, regular pentagon, isosceles triangle, scalene triangle.

6. What type of a polygon has: exactly 6 sides? exactly 8 sides?
7. What angle is formed by the hands of a clock set at 6:00?
8. In a triangle FGH, m$\angle F = 80°$ and m$\angle G = 60°$. What does $\angle H$ measure in degrees?
9. In quadrilateral $ABCD$, m$\angle A = 70°$, m$\angle B = 95°$, m$\angle C = 50°$. What does m$\angle D$ measure?
10. The playground circle has a radius of 7 ft. What is its diameter?
11. Which has the greater diameter, a saucer or a dinner plate?
12. Are these polygons congruent or similar?
13. How many lines of symmetry are in a regular hexagon?
14. Turning a card from one side to another is a translation, reflection, or rotation?
15. Does the letter G have a line of symmetry?

SET 18

1. Classify each triangle as *acute, obtuse,* or *right.*

2. Classify each quadrilateral.

3. Solve. $\frac{1}{4} + \frac{1}{4}, \frac{1}{4} - \frac{1}{4}, \frac{1}{4} \times \frac{1}{4}, \frac{1}{4} \div \frac{1}{4}$

4. Find $\frac{1}{2}$ of: 8, 12, 2, 16, 14, 20, 4, 18, 6

5. Find the value of each variable.
   $\frac{1}{3} = \frac{a}{12} = \frac{b}{24} = \frac{c}{72} = \frac{d}{144}$

6. In the numeral 6457.029, what is the value of 9?

7. Round 8325 to the nearest thousand.
8. Simplify $\frac{32}{56}$ and add 2 to the result.
9. Multiply 1.03 by 10.
10. Line segments or angles that have the same measure are ___?___ .
11. Jessie walks to school down Street A and crosses over Street B. So Street A and Street B must ___?___ .
12. A field is shaped like a rhombus. If one angle measures 150°, what are the measures of the other 3 angles?
13. The diameter of a solar disk is 11 m. What is the radius?
14. 12 is $\frac{3}{4}$ of what number?
15. How many days are 3 days less than 2 weeks?

MAINTENANCE

1. Complete. 7 km = _?_ m   5 km = _?_ mm
   3 m = _?_ mm   0.12 cm = _?_ dm
2. Compare. Use <, =, or >. 60 L _?_ 6 mL
   13 L _?_ 130 mL   5.3 L _?_ 53 cL
3. Name the best unit of measure, t, kg, or g.
   a feather   a car   3 raisins   a dog
   an elephant   a baby   a penny   a pencil
4. 15 ft = _?_ yd   84 in. = _?_ ft
   27 yd = _?_ ft   2 mi = _?_ yd
   7 ft = _?_ in.   2 mi = _?_ ft
5. 2 T = _?_ lb   8 pt = _?_ qt
   8 oz = _?_ lb   2 gal = _?_ pt
   3 c = _?_ fl oz   12 c = _?_ qt
6. From 2 gal 1 qt, take 3 qt.

7. Multiply 3 ft 6 in. by 2.
8. The mass of 2 bananas is 0.34 kg. How many grams is that?
9. A ribbon 3 m long was cut into pieces each 25 cm long. How many pieces were cut?
10. The fish tank contains 26 L of water. How many mL of water does it hold?
11. 3 dm^3 = _?_ L = _?_ kg
12. Divide 0.36 by 4.
13. How many grams are there in 3 kilograms?
14. Find the perimeter of a rectanglar rug 3 m by 4 m.
15. Dividing 20 by $\frac{1}{2}$ is the same as multiplying 20 by _?_ .

1. Simplify. $\frac{2}{4}, \frac{4}{8}, \frac{8}{16}, \frac{4}{12}, \frac{4}{24}, \frac{8}{32}, \frac{4}{22}, \frac{16}{32}, \frac{8}{24}$
2. Multiply by 4: 0.03, 0.02, 0.05, 0.06, 0.08
3. 0.2 − 0.1, 3 − 0.2, 0.4 − 0.1, 5 − 0.1, 4 − 0.6, 0.6 − 0.1, 0.8 − 0.3
4. Add $\frac{5}{7}$ to: $\frac{1}{7}, \frac{3}{7}, \frac{5}{7}, \frac{6}{7}, \frac{4}{7}, \frac{2}{7}, 1\frac{2}{7}, 1\frac{1}{7}$
5. Divide by $\frac{1}{2}$: 4, 7, 9, 2, 5, 6, 1, 10, 3
6. Find the perimeter of an equilateral triangle that is 8.9 cm on each side.
7. How many square meters of tile flooring are needed to cover a floor measuring 9 m by 12 m?
8. A square trampoline measures 8 yd on each side. How many square yards of material are needed to cover it?

9. Find the area of a triangular flag that has a base of 0.5 m and a height of 2 m.
10. Estimate the circumference of a circular tablecloth with diameter 5 ft. Use 3 for π.
11. A circle has a diameter of 12 in. Use 3 for π and estimate the circumference.
12. Find the volume of a closet that measures 2 ft long, 4 ft wide, and 7 ft high.
13. Find the volume of a cube that measures 6 cm on each side.
14. A train due at 8:20 A.M. is 30 minutes late. At what time will it arrive?
15. It is 6:55. What time will it be $1\frac{3}{4}$ h from now?

1. Simplify. $1\frac{60}{100}, 1\frac{5}{100}, 1\frac{4}{100}, 1\frac{2}{100}, 1\frac{75}{100}$
2. Divide by $\frac{1}{3}$: 3, 5, 8, 10, 1, 4, 7, 2, 6, 9
3. $\frac{1}{50} = \frac{?}{100}$ $\frac{3}{50} = \frac{?}{100}$ $\frac{7}{50} = \frac{?}{100}$ $\frac{9}{50} = \frac{?}{100}$
4. Add 0.4 to: 1.3, 1.5, 1.2, 1.4, 1.9, 1.8, 1.0, 1.1
5. Multiply by 10; by 100: 0.34, 0.04, 0.21, 0.16, 0.32, 0.27, 0.18, 0.03, 0.07
6. Give the simplest form of the ratio: 1 ounce to 1 pound; 1 yard to 1 inch.
7. At $1.44 a dozen, what will 4 rolls cost?
8. The ratio of baseball cards to basketball cards is 3 to 2, and the ratio of football cards to baseball cards is 1 to 2. If Ken has 36 baseball cards, how many basketball cards does he have?

9. To $3\frac{4}{7}$ add $2\frac{3}{7}$.

Complete each pattern.
10. 21, 18, 19, 16, 17, 14, 15, _?_ , _?_
11. $\frac{1}{16}, \frac{1}{8}, \frac{1}{4}, \frac{1}{2}$, 1, 2, _?_ , _?_
12. 0.2, 0.4, 0.6, 0.8, 1, _?_ , _?_
13. At the rate of 200 per hour, how many envelopes can be filled in $3\frac{1}{2}$ hours?
14. A poodle eats 6 cans of food every 4 days. A collie eats 18 cans every 6 days. Do the two dogs eat food at the same rate?
15. Multiply 0.004 by 10.

MAINTENANCE

SET 22

1. Express each ratio in simplest form. 6 to 10
   8 to 20   7 to 21   9 : 15   12 : 28

2. Find the value of n. $\dfrac{15}{20} = \dfrac{3}{n}$ $\dfrac{12}{6} = \dfrac{n}{1}$ $\dfrac{14}{18} = \dfrac{n}{9}$
   $\dfrac{32}{48} = \dfrac{n}{6}$ $\dfrac{27}{9} = \dfrac{3}{n}$ $\dfrac{15}{9} = \dfrac{n}{3}$ $\dfrac{8}{16} = \dfrac{n}{2}$

3. Are the ratios = or ≠? $\dfrac{6}{7}\ \underline{\ ?\ }\ \dfrac{18}{21}$
   $\dfrac{5}{8}\ \underline{\ ?\ }\ \dfrac{25}{30}$ $\dfrac{1}{2}\ \underline{\ ?\ }\ \dfrac{7}{21}$ $\dfrac{4}{1}\ \underline{\ ?\ }\ \dfrac{16}{1}$

4. Find the value of n. 1 : 3 = n : 15
   5 : n = 10 : 12 n : 1 = 4 : 4
   12 : 11 = 24 : n

5. Give each as a percent. $\dfrac{26}{100}, \dfrac{7}{100}, \dfrac{68}{100},$
   $\dfrac{57}{100}$, 0.41, 0.03, 0.75, 0.53, 0.39, 0.97

6. Of 100 tickets, 23 were given away free. What percent of the tickets were free?

7. On a scale drawing of a zoo, 1 in. = 12 ft. If the scale distance from the lion's den to the monkey house is 2.5 in., what is the actual distance?

8. Express 0.25 as a fraction in simplest form.

9. Write as a decimal: 75% of a class

10. Express $\dfrac{1}{3}$ as a percent.

11. How many seconds are there in 3 hours?

12. If golf balls sell 3 for $5.00, what is the cost of a dozen?

13. What percent expresses 10% less than 100%?

14. Two times a number is what percent of it?

15. The current value of a bike is $\dfrac{1}{2}$ of its value when it was purchased. Express this as a percent.

SET 23

1. Express as a fraction in simplest form. 25%, 50%, 75%, 20%, 40%, 60%, 10%

2. Express as a decimal. 25%, 16.2%, 3%, 82.36%, 45.9%, 6.24%, 33%, 19.8%

3. Express as a percent. 0.04, 0.02, 0.01, 0.09, 0.259, 0.17, 0.36, 0.438, 0.55, 0.623

4. Express as a percent. $\dfrac{1}{4}, \dfrac{1}{5}, \dfrac{1}{20}, \dfrac{1}{25}, \dfrac{1}{50}, \dfrac{2}{5}, \dfrac{1}{8},$
   $\dfrac{4}{5}, \dfrac{7}{50}, \dfrac{5}{50}$

5. Express as a percent. 1.06, 1.08, 1.09, 1.6, 1.72, 2.5, 1.24, 2.35, 3.64

6. In a basket containing 160 apples, 20% have stems. How many have stems?

7. Express 37.5% as a fraction.

8. To 50% of 18 add 10.

9. Sally spelled 70% of 30 spelling words correctly. How many words did she spell correctly?

10. What percent is equal to $\dfrac{3}{50}$?

11. Write 105% as a decimal.

12. (50% of 6) + (50% of 12) = $\underline{\ ?\ }$

13. Marc planted 25 flower plants and 20% of them died. How many plants lived?

14. (25% of 48) ÷ 3 = $\underline{\ ?\ }$

15. A DVD costs $250. How much is saved if it is on sale for 20% off?

SET 24

1. Express as a mixed number in simplest form. 120%, 250%, 320%, 110%, 480%

2. Find n. 5 = n% of 20   20 = n% of 80
   10 = n% of 25   2 = n% of 10
   40 = n% of 80   16 = n% of 100

3. Find 25% of: 24, 40, 56, 72, 48, 32, 64, 16

4. Express as a decimal. 10%, 20%, 30%, 15%, 25%, 5%, 4%, 2%, 1%, 8%

5. Find 40% of: 210, 320, 400, 300, 410, 220

6. Forty-two of 60 sixth-grade students ride the bus. What percent ride the bus?

7. A bicycle is on sale for $105. The sales tax rate is 6%. Find the sales tax.

8. Mr. Budd sold $15,000 worth of roses in one month. His rate of commission is 5%. What was his commission for the month?

9. If 10% of a number is 15, what is 30% of the number?

10. Of the 500 cars in the parking garage, 150 are on the first level. What percent of the cars are on the first level?

11. Divide 0.0081 by 0.0009.

12. Dresses were on sale for $10 off the original price of $60. What was the rate of discount?

13. Find the commission on sales of $2700 if the rate of commission is 3%.

14. Express $\dfrac{3}{5}$ as a decimal.

15. Find $\dfrac{8}{9}$ of 72.

. Name the opposite of: $^+11$, $^-8$, $^+15$, $^-3$, $^+24$, $^-1$, $^+5$, $^+17$, $^-13$, $^-20$, $^+6$, 0

. Compare. Use $<$, $=$, or $>$.
$^-3$? $^+2$ $\quad$ $^+6$? $^+11$ $\quad$ $^-5$? $^+1$
$^+8$? $^-8$ $\quad$ $^-4$? $^-2$

. Order from least to greatest. $^+5$, $^-4$, $^-1$; $^+10$, $^+7$, $^+4$; $^-2$, 0, $^-6$; $^+8$, $^+11$, $^-3$

. $^+3 + {}^+6$ $\quad$ $^+10 + {}^+8$ $\quad$ $^-7 + {}^-1$

. $^-7 + {}^+4$ $\quad$ $^+2 + {}^-9$ $\quad$ $^-12 + {}^-6$
$^+9 + {}^-9$ $\quad$ $^-5 + {}^+4$

. The temperature outside was $^-6°$. The wind made it feel $20°$ colder. What was the windchill temperature?

. Find the sum. $^-3 + ({}^+2 + {}^+5)$

8. A store's profits for the month were: 35% for furniture sales, 20% for home appliances, 10% for clothing, and 5% for shoes. The remainder of the profits came from toys. What percent are from toys?

9. In Jan. Matt lost 6 lb. He gained 2 lb in Feb. and lost 3 lb in Mar. What was his total weight gain or loss?

10. Express 65% as a fraction.

11. Multiply 0.724 by 1000.

12. Give 1492 as a Roman numeral.

13. Divide 1020 by 5, and take 4 from the result.

14. Express 75% as a fraction.

15. The temperature went from $^+11°C$ to $^-8°C$ during the day. How many degrees did the temperature drop?

. $^-7 - {}^-5$ $\quad$ $^+4 - {}^-9$ $\quad$ $^-6 - {}^-9$
$^+10 - {}^+12$ $\quad$ $^+3 - {}^-11$ $\quad$ $^-13 - {}^+4$
$^+17 - {}^+8$ $\quad$ $^-8 - {}^+4$

. Find 50% of: 8, 12, 2, 10, 16, 20, 4, 14, 24

. Express as a fraction. 20%, 25%, 50%, 75%, 80%, 15%, 10%, 5%, 60%, 35%

. $1\frac{1}{4} + \frac{3}{14}$ $\quad$ $2\frac{5}{6} + \frac{1}{6}$ $\quad$ $2\frac{1}{2} + \frac{1}{4}$

. Find $\frac{1}{6}$ of: 12, 30, 54, 42, 72, 48, 36, 18, 24

. A motorboat can go 7.8 mph. How far will it go in 5 hours?

. Write as a ratio:
3 quarters, 1 nickel to 3 dimes, 2 nickels.

8. Ella put $160 into savings. She withdrew $49. How much is left in savings?

9. In one game Ned won 9 points, lost 4 points, lost 2 points, won 7 points, and won 3 points. What was his final score?

10. 40% of 75 questions are essay. How many questions are essay questions?

11. 90 is $\frac{3}{4}$ of what number?

12. Evaluate $(\frac{3}{5} - \frac{3}{5}) + (\frac{3}{5} \div \frac{3}{5})$.

13. A batter has been at bat 27 times and has had 9 hits. What is his batting average?

14. Multiply 0.02 by 0.06.

15. How many pieces of wire $\frac{3}{4}$ yd long can be cut from 6 yards?

1. True or false if $x = 7$: $6 + x = 13$
$x - 6 = 13$ $\quad$ $3x = 27$ $\quad$ $56 \div x = 8$

2. True or false if $n = 8$: $n \div 4 = 4$
$\frac{n}{2} = 4$ $\quad$ $80 = 10n$ $\quad$ $\frac{1}{2}n = 16$

3. True or false if $n = 3$: $2n - 1 = 5$
$\frac{n}{2} - 1 = 5$ $\quad$ $1 + \frac{n}{2} = 5$ $\quad$ $1 + 2n = 7$

4. Choose the equations. $42 \div x$ $\quad$ $\frac{x}{4} = 3$
$2x - 6$ $\quad$ $\frac{x}{3} - 9 = 10$

5. $d = 6$ $\quad$ The value of $3 + 10d$ is ? .

6. 12 more than a number:
$12n$ or $\frac{n}{12}$ or $n + 12$

7. Product of a number and 20:
$p - 20$ or $\frac{p}{20}$ or $20p$

8. r divided by 6 is 5: $\frac{r}{6} = 5$ or $r - 6 = 5$ or $6r = 5$

9. 4 less than a number is 7: $x + 4 = 7$ or $4 - x = 7$ or $x - 4 = 7$

10. Letters a, x, n are ? .

11. An equation states that two expressions are ? .

12. Which operation solves $n + 33 = 96$?

13. Which operation solves $14n = 56$?

14. What is the value of x?
$x - 22 = 50$ $\quad$ $9 + x = 44$ $\quad$ $x + 17 = 39$

15. What is the value of n?
$\frac{n}{4} = 22$ $\quad$ $8 = \frac{n}{4}$ $\quad$ $9n = 54$

MAINTENANCE

(545)

Glossary
also on-line

A

absolute value The distance of a number from zero on the number line. (p. 150)

acute angle An angle that measures less than 90°. (p. 344)

acute triangle A triangle with three acute angles. (p. 344)

Addition Property of Equality If the same number is added to both sides of an equation, the sides remain equal. (p. 132)

additive inverse The opposite of a given number. (p. 150)

adjacent angles Two angles that are in the plane and share a common side and a common vertex, but have no interior points in common. (p. 334)

algebraic expression A mathematical expression that contains variables, numbers, and symbols of operations. (p. 52)

alternate exterior angles A pair of nonadjacent exterior angles on opposite sides of the transversal. (p. 336)

alternate interior angles A pair of nonadjacent interior angles on opposite sides of the transversal. (p. 337)

angle bisector A ray that divides an angle into two congruent angles. (p. 333)

arc A part of a circle, with all of its points on the circle. (p. 352)

area The number of square units needed to cover a flat surface. (p. 464)

arithmetic sequence A sequence generated by repeatedly adding or subtracting the same number. (p. 145)

Associative (grouping) Property Changing the grouping of the addends (or factors) does not change the sum (or product). (pp. 222, 254)

axis The horizontal or vertical number line of a graph or coordinate plane. (p. 308)

B

bar graph A graph that uses bars to show data. The bars may be of different lengths. (p. 325)

base One of the equal factors in a product; a selected side or face of a geometric figure. (pp. 38, 446)

benchmark An object of known measure used to estimate the measure of other objects.

biased sample A sample in which certain groups from the population are not represented. (p. 296)

bisect To divide a line segment or an angle into two congruent parts. (p. 333)

box-and-whisker plot A graph that includes a number line showing the extremes (greatest and least numbers), the median, and the quartile divisions of a data set. A *box* is drawn on top of the second and third quartiles. The *whiskers* are the part of the number line showing the first and fourth quartiles. (p. 304)

C

capacity The amount, usually of liquid, a container can hold. (pp. 450, 454)

Celsius (°C) scale The temperature scale in which 0°C is the freezing point of water and 100°C is the boiling point of water. (p. 166)

central angle An angle whose vertex is the center of a circle. (p. 352)

certain event The probability of an event that is certain is 1. (p. 274)

chord A line segment with both endpoints on a circle. (p. 352)

circle A set of points in a plane, all of which are the same distance from a point called the *center*. (p. 352)

circle graph A graph that uses the area of a circle to show the division of a total amount of data. (p. 318)

circumference The distance around a circle. (p. 470)

cluster The grouping of data. (p. 302)

combination A set of items in which order is *not* important. (p. 278)

commission Money earned equal to a percent of the selling price of items sold. (p. 432)

Commutative (order) Property Changing the order of the addends (or factors) does not change the sum (or product). (pp. 222, 254)

compass An instrument used to draw circles. (p. 338)

compatible numbers Numbers that are easy to compute with mentally. (p. 193)

complementary angles Two angles whose measures have a sum of 90°. Each angle is said to be the *complement* of the other. (p. 334)

complex fraction A fraction having one or more fractions in the numerator, denominator, or both. (p. 287)

composite number A whole number greater than 1 that has more than two factors. (p. 180)

compound event In probability, when one event follows another. (p. 276)

cone A solid, or space, figure with one circular base, one vertex, and a curved surface. (p. 362)

congruent figures Figures that have the same size and shape. (p. 354)

conjunction A compound statement formed by joining two statements with the connective *and*. (p. 491)

coordinate plane The plane formed by two perpendicular number lines. (p. 502)

corresponding angles A pair of nonadjacent angles, one interior and one exterior, that are both on the same side of the transversal. (p. 336)

corresponding parts Matching sides or angles of two figures. (p. 354)

cross products The products obtained by multiplying the numerator of one fraction by the denominator of a second fraction and the denominator of the first fraction by the numerator of the second fraction. (p. 382)

cross section A plane figure formed when a plane cuts through a solid figure. (p. 364)

cumulative frequency A running total of the number of data surveyed. (p. 298)

cumulative frequency table A summary of a data set in which each data value is paired with the sum of the frequencies of all values less than or equal to it. (p. 298)

customary system The measurement system that uses inch, foot, yard, and mile; fluid ounce, cup, pint, quart, and gallon; ounce, pound, and ton. (See *Table of Measures*, p. 564)

D

data Facts or information. (p. 298)

decagon A polygon with ten sides. (p. 342)

decimal A number with a decimal point separating the ones from the tenths place. (p. 34)

degree (°) A unit used to measure angles; a unit used to measure temperature on the Celsius (°C) or the Fahrenheit (°F) scale. (pp. 166, 330)

dependent events In probability, when the second event is affected by the first. (p. 277)

diagonal A line segment, other than a side, that joins two vertices of a polygon. (p. 342)

diameter A line segment that passes through the center of a circle and has both endpoints on the circle. (p. 352)

discount A reduction on the regular, or list, price of an item. (p. 426)

disjunction A compound statement formed by joining two statements with the connective *or*. (p. 491)

Distributive Property Multiplying a number by a sum is the same as multiplying the number by each addend of the sum and then adding the products. (p. 70)

divisible A number is divisible by another number if the remainder is 0 when the number is divided by the other number. (p. 178)

Division Property of Equality If both sides of an equation are divided by the same nonzero number, the sides remain equal. (p. 134)

divisor The number by which the dividend is divided. (p. 88)

double bar (line) graph A graph that uses pairs of bars (line segments) to compare two sets of data. (pp. 310, 312)

E

edge The line segment where two faces of a space figure meet. (p. 362)

endpoint The point at the end of a line segment or ray. (p. 338)

equally likely outcomes In probability, when the chance is the same of getting any one of the desired outcomes. (p. 274)

equation A statement that two mathematical expressions are equal. (p. 128)

equilateral triangle A triangle with three congruent sides and three congruent angles. (p. 344)

equivalent fractions Different fractions that name the same amount. (p. 184)

estimate   An approximate answer; to find an answer that is close to the exact answer. (p. 44)

evaluate   To find the value. (pp. 54, 126)

event   A set of one or more outcomes of a probability experiment. (p. 274)

expanded form   The written form of a number that shows the place value of each of its digits. (p. 36)

experimental probability   The ratio of the number of favorable outcomes that occur to the total number of trials, or times the activity is performed. (p. 275)

exponent   A number that tells how many times another number is to be used as a factor. (p. 382)

F

face   A flat surface of a solid figure. (p. 362)

factor   One of two or more numbers that are multiplied to form a product. (p. 66)

factor tree   A diagram used to find the prime factors of a number. (p. 182)

Fahrenheit (°F) scale   The temperature scale in which 32°F is the freezing point of water and 212°F is the boiling point of water. (p. 166)

formula   A rule that is expressed by using symbols. (p. 136)

fractal   A figure with repeating patterns containing shapes that are like the whole but of different sizes throughout. (p. 351)

fraction   A number that names a part of a whole, a region, or a set. (p. 184)

frequency table   A chart that shows how often each item appears in a set of data. (p. 298)

front-end estimation   A way of estimating by using the front, or greatest, digits to find an approximate answer. (p. 44)

function   A relationship between two quantities in which one quantity depends uniquely on the other. (p. 502)

Fundamental Counting Principle   If one event has m possible outcomes and a second event has n possible outcomes, then there are $m \times n$ total possible outcomes. (p. 278)

G

geometric construction   A drawing that is made using only an unmarked *straightedge* and a *compass*. (p. 338)

geometric sequence   A sequence generated by repeatedly multiplying or dividing by the same number. (p. 145)

greatest common factor (GCF)   The greatest number that is a factor of two or more numbers. (p. 186)

H

half-turn symmetry   The symmetry that occurs when a figure is turned halfway (180°) around its center point and the figure that results looks exactly the same. (p. 358)

height   The perpendicular distance between the bases of a geometric figure. In a triangle, the perpendicular distance from the opposite vertex to the line containing the base. (p. 466)

heptagon   A polygon with seven sides. (p. 342)

hexagon   A polygon with six sides. (p. 342)

hexagonal prism   A prism with two parallel hexagonal bases. (p. 362)

hexagonal pyramid   A pyramid with a hexagonal base. (p. 362)

histogram   A bar graph of a frequency distribution. The bars represent equal intervals of the data, and there is no space between the bars. (p. 316)

hypotenuse   In a right triangle, the longest side, which is also the side opposite to the right angle. (p. 409)

I

Identity Property   Adding 0 to a number or multiplying a number by 1 does not change the number's value. (pp. 222, 254)

impossible event   The probability of an event that is impossible is 0. (p. 274)

improper fraction   A fraction with its numerator equal to or greater than its denominator. (p. 190)

independent events   When the outcome of the first event does not affect the outcome of the second event. (p. 277)

inequality   A statement that two mathematical expressions are not equal. It uses an inequality symbol: $<$, $>$, or $\neq$. (p. 129)

integers   The whole numbers and their opposites. (p. 150)

interest   The amount paid by the borrower for the use of the principal for a stated period of time. (p. 434)

intersecting lines   Lines that meet or cross. (p. 332)

interval   The number of units between spaces on a graph. (p. 316)

inverse operations   Mathematical operations that *undo* each other, such as addition and subtraction or multiplication and division. (p. 222)

irrational number   A number whose decimal form is nonrepeating and nonterminating. (p. 472)

isosceles triangle   A triangle with two congruent sides. (p. 344)

iteration   A step in the process or repeating something over and over again. (p. 364)

L

lateral faces   The faces of a prism or pyramid that are not bases. (p. 362)

line graph   A graph that uses points on a grid connected by line segments to show data. (p. 308)

line of symmetry   A line that divides a figure into two congruent parts. (p. 358)

line segment   A part of a line that has two endpoints. (p. 338)

linear equation   An equation whose graph is a straight line. (p. 519)

linear measure   A measure of length. (pp. 448, 452)

lower extreme   The least number in a set of data. (p. 304)

lower quartile   The median of the lower half of a set of data. (p. 304)

M

mass   The measure of the amount of matter an object contains. (p. 450)

mathematical expression   A symbol or a combination of symbols that represents a number. (p. 52)

mean   The average of a set of numbers. (p. 300)

measures of central tendency   The *mean, median,* and *mode* of a set of data. (p. 300)

median   The middle number of a set of numbers arranged in order. If there is an even number of numbers, the median is the average of the two middle numbers. (p. 300)

metric system   The measurement system based on the meter, gram, and liter. (See *Table of Measures,* p. 564.)

midpoint   A point that divides a line segment into two congruent segments. (p. 333)

mixed number   A number that is made up of a whole number and a fraction. (p. 190)

mode   The number that appears most frequently in a set of numbers. (p. 300)

multiple   A number that is the product of a given number and any whole number. (p. 194)

Multiplication Property of Equality   If both sides of an equation are multiplied by the same nonzero number, the sides remain equal. (p. 134)

mutually exclusive events   Events that cannot occur at the same time. (p. 274)

N

negation   The denial of a given statement. (p. 245)

net   A flat pattern that folds into a solid figure. (p. 362)

n-gon   A polygon of *n* sides. (p. 350)

O

obtuse angle   An angle with a measure greater than 90° and less than 180°. (p. 344)

obtuse triangle   A triangle with one obtuse angle. (p. 344)

octagon   A polygon with eight sides. (p. 342)

odds   A comparison of favorable outcomes and unfavorable outcomes. (p. 281)

opposite integers   Two integers that have the same distance from 0 on the number line. (p. 150)

order of operations   The order in which operations must be performed when more than one operation is involved. (p. 122)

ordered pair   A pair of numbers used to locate a point in the coordinate plane. The first number is the *x*-coordinate and the second number is the *y*-coordinate. (p. 504)

origin   The point (0,0) in the coordinate plane where the *x*-axis and the *y*-axis intersect. (p. 502)

outcome   The result of a probability experiment. (p. 274)

P

parallel lines   Lines in a plane that never intersect. (p. 332)

parallelogram   A quadrilateral with two pairs of parallel sides. (p. 346)

pentagon   A polygon with five sides. (p. 342)

pentagonal prism   A prism with two parallel pentagonal bases. (p. 362)

pentagonal pyramid   A pyramid with a pentagonal base. (p. 363)

percent (%)   The ratio or comparison of a number to 100. (p. 394)

perfect square   A number whose square root is a whole number. (p. 83)

perimeter   The distance around a figure. (p. 462)

period   A set of three digits set off by a comma in a whole number. (p. 34)

permutation   A selection of different items in which the *order* is important. (p. 278)

perpendicular bisector   A line that is perpendicular to a line segment and divides the segment into two congruent parts. (p. 333)

perpendicular lines   Lines that intersect to form right angles. (p. 332)

pi (π)   The ratio of the circumference of a circle to its diameter. An approximate value of π is 3.14, or $\frac{22}{7}$. (p. 470)

place value   The value of a digit depending on its position, or place, in a number. (p. 38)

plane figure   A two-dimensional figure that has straight or curved sides. (p. 330)

polygon   A closed plane figure made up of line segments. (p. 342)

polyhedron   A solid, or space, figure whose faces are polygons. (p. 362)

population   In a statistical study, the set of all individuals, or objects, being studied. (p. 492)

power of a number   The result of using a number as a factor a given number of times. An exponent is used to express the power. $10^3 = 10 \times 10 \times 10$, or 1000. (p. 74)

prime factorization   Expressing a composite number as the product of prime numbers. (p. 182)

prime number   A whole number greater than 1 that has only two factors, itself and 1. (p. 180)

principal   The amount of money borrowed or saved. (p. 434)

prism   A solid figure with two faces called *base* bounded by polygons that are parallel and congruent. (p. 362)

probability   A branch of mathematics that analyzes the chance that a given outcome will occur. The probability of an event is expressed as the ratio of the number of desired outcomes to the total number of possible outcomes. (p. 274)

proportion   A number sentence that shows that two ratios are equal. (p. 382)

protractor   An instrument used to measure angles. (p. 330)

pyramid   A solid figure whose base is a polygon and whose faces are triangles with a common vertex. (p. 362)

Pythagorean Theorem   In a right triangle, the square of the longest side, called the hypotenuse c, is equal to the sum of the squares of the legs a and b. (p. 409)

Q

quadrant   A region of a coordinate plane. (p. 502)

quadrilateral   A polygon with four sides. (pp. 342, 346)

R

radius   A line segment from the center of a circle to a point on the circle. (p. 352)

random sample   A subgroup or part of a total group, each of which or whom has an equally likely chance of being chosen. (p. 292)

range   The difference between the greatest and least numbers in a set of numbers. (p. 300)

rate   A ratio that compares unlike quantities. (p. 380)

rate of commission   The percent of the total amount of goods or services sold that is earned by the seller. (p. 432)

rate of discount   The percent taken off the original, or list, price. (p. 426)

rate of interest   The percent paid to the depositor on the principal. (p. 434)

rate of sales tax   The percent of the list, or marked, price levied as tax. (p. 428)

ratio   A comparison of two numbers or quantities by division. (p. 376)

rational number Any number that can be expressed as the quotient of two *integers* in which the divisor is not zero. (p. 208)

ray A part of a line that has one endpoint and goes on forever in one direction. (p. 330)

reciprocals Two numbers whose product is 1. (p. 255)

rectangle A parallelogram with four right angles. (p. 346)

rectangular prism A prism with six rectangular faces. (p. 362)

rectangular pyramid A pyramid with a rectangular base. (p. 362)

reflection A transformation that moves a figure by flipping it along a line. (p. 356)

regular polygon A polygon with all sides and all angles congruent. (p. 342)

regular price The original price of an item before a discount has been given. (p. 426)

relative frequency The frequency of a category divided by the sum of the frequencies. (p. 298)

repeating decimal A decimal in which a digit or groups of digits repeats in an unending pattern. (p. 206)

rhombus A parallelogram with all sides congruent. (p. 346)

right angle An angle that measures 90°. (p. 344)

right triangle A triangle with one right angle. (p. 344)

Roman numerals Symbols for numbers used by the Romans. (p. 61)

rotation A transformation that moves a figure by turning it about a fixed point. (p. 356)

rotational symmetry A figure is rotated less than 360° around its center point and still looks exactly the same as the original figure. (p. 358)

rounding To approximate a number by replacing it with a number expressed in tens, hundreds, thousands, and so on. (p. 42)

S

sale price The difference between the list price and the discount. (p. 426)

sales tax The amount added to the marked price of an item and collected as tax. (p. 428)

sample A segment of a population selected for study to predict characteristics of the whole. (p. 292)

sample space A set of all possible *outcomes* of an experiment. (p. 274)

scale The ratio of a pictured measure to the actual measure; the tool used to measure weight; numbers along the side or bottom of a graph. (p. 308)

scale drawing A drawing of something accurate but different in size. (p. 392)

scalene triangle A triangle with no congruent sides. (p. 344)

scatter plot A graph with points plotted to show a relationship between two variables. (p. 313)

scientific notation The expression of a number as the product of a power of 10 and a number greater than or equal to 1 but less than 10. (p. 76)

sector A region of a circle bounded by two radii and their intercepted arc. (p. 352)

sequence A set of numbers given in a certain order. Each number is called a *term*. (p. 145)

similar figures Figures that have the same shape. They may or may not be the same size. (p. 388)

simple closed curve A path that begins and ends at the same point and does not intersect itself. (p. 342)

simple interest The amount obtained by multiplying the principal by the annual rate by the time (number of years). (p. 434)

simplest form The form of a fraction when the numerator and denominator have no common factor other than 1. (p. 188)

skew lines Lines that do not intersect, are not in the same plane, and are not parallel. (p. 332)

solution A value of a variable that makes an equation true. (p. 128)

sphere A curved solid figure in which all points are the same distance from a point called the *center*. (p. 362)

square pyramid A pyramid with a square base. (p. 362)

square root One of two equal factors of a number. (p. 83)

statistics The study of the collection, interpretation, and display of data. (p. 314)

stem-and-leaf plot   A graph that arranges numerical data in order of place value. The last digits of the numbers are the *leaves*. The digits to the left of the leaves are the *stems*. (p. 306)

straight angle   An angle that measures 180°. (p. 332)

Subtraction Property of Equality   If the same number is subtracted from both sides of an equation, the sides remain equal. (p. 130)

supplementary angles   Two angles the sum of whose measures is 180°. (p. 334)

surface area   The sum of the areas of all the faces of a solid figure. (p. 474)

survey   A way to collect data to answer a question. (p. 294)

symmetrical figure   A plane figure that can be folded on a line so that the two halves are congruent. (p. 358)

T

term   Each number in a sequence. (p. 145)

terminating decimal   A decimal in which digits do not show a repeating pattern. A terminating decimal results when the division of the numerator of a fraction by the denominator leaves a 0 remainder. (p. 206)

terms   The parts of an expression that are separated by an addition or subtraction sign. (p. 124)

terms of a proportion   The numbers that form the proportion. In $a : b = c : d$, a, b, c, and d are the terms. (p. 382)

tessellation   The pattern formed by fitting plane figures together without overlapping or leaving gaps. (p. 360)

translation   A transformation that moves a figure by sliding along a line without flipping or turning it. (p. 356)

transversal   A line that intersects two or more lines. (p. 336)

trapezoid   A quadrilateral with only one pair of parallel sides. (p. 346)

tree diagram   A diagram that shows all possible outcomes of an event or events. (p. 276)

triangular prism   A prism with two parallel triangular bases. (p. 362)

triangular pyramid   A pyramid with a triangular base. (p. 362)

U

unbiased sample   A sample is unbiased if every individual in the population has an equal chance of being selected. (p. 296)

unit fraction   A fraction with a numerator of 1. (p. 192)

unit price   The cost of one item. (p. 380)

upper extreme   The greatest number in a set of data. (p. 304)

upper quartile   (The median of the upper half of a set of data. (p. 304)

V

variable   A symbol, usually a letter, used to represent a number. (p. 124)

Venn diagram   A drawing that shows relationships among sets of numbers or objects. (p. 282)

vertex (plural: *vertices*)   The common endpoint of two rays in an angle, of two line segments in a polygon, or of three or more edges in a solid figure. (p. 330)

vertical angles   A pair of congruent opposite angles formed by two intersecting lines. (p. 334)

volume   The number of cubic units needed to fill a solid figure. (p. 478)

W

weight   The heaviness of an object. (p. 454)

whole number   Any of the numbers 0, 1, 2, 3, ... (p. 150)

X

x-axis   The horizontal number line on a coordinate grid. (p. 502)

x-coordinate   The first number in an ordered pair; it tells the distance to move right or left from (0,0). (p. 502)

Y

y-axis   The vertical number line on a coordinate grid. (p. 502)

y-coordinate   The second number in an ordered pair; it tells the distance to move up or down from (0,0). (p. 502)

Z

zero pair   A pair of algebra tiles, or counters, consisting of one positive and one negative. (p. 156)

zero property   Multiplying a number by 0 always results in a product of 0. (p. 150)

Index

Key: Italics = Enrichment/Challenge

Mathematical Symbols

=	is equal to	$^+4$	positive 4	ABC	plane ABC
≠	is not equal to	$^-4$	negative 4	$\triangle ABC$	triangle ABC
<	is less than	$|^-4|$	the absolute value	~	is similar to
>	is greater than		of negative 4	≅	is congruent to
≈	is approximately	10^2	ten squared	∥	is parallel to
	equal to	10^3	ten cubed	⊥	is perpendicular to
…	continues without	$\sqrt{\ }$	positive square root	π	pi
	end	$\overleftrightarrow{AB}$	line AB	cm^2	square centimeter
%	percent	$\overline{AB}$	segment AB	$in.^3$	cubic inch
.$\overline{3}$	0.333…(repeating	$\overrightarrow{AB}$	ray AB	°	degree
	decimals)	$\angle ABC$	angle ABC	2 : 3	two to three (ratio)
(3, 4)	ordered pair	$m\angle A$	measure of $\angle A$	$P(E)$	probablilty of an
	decimal point				event

Geometric Formulas

Perimeter
Rectangle: $P = 2(\ell + w)$
Regular Polygon: $P = ns$
Square: $P = 4s$

Circumference of Circle
$C = \pi d = 2\pi r$

Area
Circle: $A = \pi r^2$
Parallelogram: $A = bh$
Rectangle: $A = \ell w$
Square: $A = s^2$
Triangle: $A = \frac{1}{2}bh$
Trapezoid: $A = \frac{1}{2}(b_1 + b_2)h$

Surface Area
Cylinder: $S = 2\pi r^2 + 2\pi rh$
Cube: $S = 6e^2$
Rectangular Prism:
$S = 2(\ell w + \ell h + wh)$
Square Pyramid: $S = s^2 + 4(\frac{1}{2}bh)$

Volume
Cylinder: $V = (\pi r^2)h$
Cube: $V = e^3$
Prism (general formula): $V = Bh$
Pyramid (general formula): $V = \frac{1}{3}Bh$
Rectangular Prism: $V = (\ell w)h$
Triangular Prism: $V = (\frac{1}{2}bh)h$

Other Formulas

Celsius (°C) $C = \frac{5}{9}(F - 32)$ **Fahrenheit (°F)** $F = \frac{9}{5}C + 32$

Simple Interest = principal × rate × time: $I = prt$

Distance = Rate × Time: $d = rt$

Discount = List Price × Rate of Discount: $D = LP \times R$ of D

Sale Price = Regular Price − Discount: $SP = RP - D$

Sales Tax = Marked Price × Rate of Sales Tax: $T = MP \times R$ of T

Total Cost = Marked Price + Sales Tax: $TC = MP + T$

Commission = Total Sales × Rate of Commission: $C = TS \times R$ of C

Time

60 seconds (s)	= 1 minute (min)
60 minutes	= 1 hour (h)
24 hours	= 1 day (d)
7 days	= 1 week (wk)
12 months (mo)	= 1 year (y)

52 weeks	= 1 year
365 days	= 1 year
366 days	= 1 leap year
100 years	= 1 century (cent.)

Metric Units

Length

1000 millimeters (mm)	= 1 meter (m)
100 centimeters (cm)	= 1 meter
10 decimeters (dm)	= 1 meter
10 meters	= 1 dekameter (dam)
100 meters	= 1 hectometer (hm)
1000 meters	= 1 kilometer (km)

Capacity

1000 milliliters (mL)	= 1 liter (L)
100 centiliters (cL)	= 1 liter
10 deciliters (dL)	= 1 liter
10 liters	= 1 dekaliter (daL)
100 liters	= 1 hectoliter (hL)
1000 liters	= 1 kiloliter (kL)

Mass

1000 milligrams (mg)	= 1 gram (g)
100 centigrams (cg)	= 1 gram
10 decigrams (dg)	= 1 gram

10 grams	= 1 dekagram (dag)
100 grams	= 1 hectogram (hg)
1000 grams	= 1 kilogram (kg)

1000 kg = 1 metric ton (t)

Customary Units

Length

12 inches (in.)	= 1 foot (ft)
3 feet	= 1 yard (yd)
36 inches	= 1 yard
5280 feet	= 1 mile (mi)
1760 yards	= 1 mile

Capacity

8 fluid ounces (fl oz)	= 1 cup (c)
2 cups	= 1 pint (pt)
2 pints	= 1 quart (qt)
4 quarts	= 1 gallon (gal)

Weight

16 ounces (oz) = 1 pound (lb)   2000 pounds = 1 ton (T)

$1\% = \frac{1}{100} = 0.01$	$50\% = \frac{1}{2} = 0.5$	$12\frac{1}{2}\% = \frac{1}{8} = 0.125$	$87\frac{1}{2}\% = \frac{7}{8} = 0.875$
$10\% = \frac{1}{10} = 0.1$	$60\% = \frac{3}{5} = 0.6$	$25\% = \frac{1}{4} = 0.25$	$16\frac{2}{3}\% = \frac{1}{6} = 0.1\overline{6}$
$20\% = \frac{1}{5} = 0.2$	$70\% = \frac{7}{10} = 0.7$	$37\frac{1}{2}\% = \frac{3}{8} = 0.375$	$33\frac{1}{3}\% = \frac{1}{3} = 0.3\overline{3}$
$30\% = \frac{3}{10} = 0.3$	$80\% = \frac{4}{5} = 0.8$	$62\frac{1}{2}\% = \frac{5}{8} = 0.625$	$66\frac{2}{3}\% = \frac{2}{3} = 0.6\overline{6}$
$40\% = \frac{2}{5} = 0.4$	$90\% = \frac{9}{10} = 0.9$	$75\% = \frac{3}{4} = 0.75$	$83\frac{1}{3}\% = \frac{5}{6} = 0.83\overline{3}$